ROOSEVELT & HITLER

BY THE AUTHOR

WALDHEIM: THE MISSING YEARS (*Paragon House*)

THE WAR THAT HITLER WON: GOEBBELS AND THE
NAZI MEDIA CAMPAIGN (*Paragon House*)

WHEN NAZI DREAMS COME TRUE

THE NAZIS

WESTERN CIVILIZATION

ADOLF HITLER AND THE GERMAN TRAUMA

ROOSEVELT & HITLER

PRELUDE TO WAR

ROBERT EDWIN HERZSTEIN

PARAGON HOUSE

New York

Published in the United States by

Paragon House
90 Fifth Avenue
New York, NY 10011

Library of Congress Cataloging in Publication Data

Herzstein, Robert Edwin.
Roosevelt and Hitler : prelude to war / Robert Edwin Herzstein.
p.   cm.
Bibliography: p.
Includes index.
ISBN 1-55778-021-8 : $24.95
1. United States—Foreign relations—1933–1945.   2. Germany—
Foreign relations—1933–1945.   3. Fascism—United States—
History—20th century.   4. World War, 1939–1945—Diplomatic
history.   5. United States—Foreign relations—Germany.   6. Germany—
Foreign relations—United States.   7. Roosevelt, Franklin D.
(Franklin Delano), 1882–1945.   8. World War, 1939–1945—Causes.
I. Title.
E806.H48   1989
327.73043'09044—dc20   89-33922
                                                                     CIP

Manufactured in the United States of America

The paper used in this publication meets the minimum requirements of
American National Standard for Information Sciences—Permanence of Paper
for Printed Library Materials, ANSI Z39.48-1984

Second printing

For My Mother
Jean L. Herzstein

CONTENTS

PREFACE

ROOSEVELT AND HITLER
AFTER FIFTY YEARS

I N THE SPRING of 1945, I was a little boy, living in a red brick apartment building on New York's Lower East Side. One day, there was a knock at the door. A young Jewish woman, Mrs. Werner, entered the apartment and began to weep uncontrollably, for the radio had just announced that President Franklin D. Roosevelt had died in Warm Springs, Georgia. Other than poorly comprehended bits of war news, this scene became my first political memory.

Some blocks away, my grandfather, hearing the news of the president's death, asked plaintively, "Hoover?" The elderly gentleman had blocked out the truth, preferring to think that former president Herbert Hoover was the deceased individual. For me, with a father who was then active in Democratic party politics, "Roosevelt" clearly referred to some powerful source of strength and hope.

In the good years after the war, I went to school, and by the early 1960s I had graduated from college. I learned that Roosevelt had "cured" the Depression and defeated Hitler and the "Japs." FDR had been, as they used to say, "good for the Jews," though I now realized that many people did not like him. Right-wingers attacked Roosevelt for "selling out" to Stalin at the Yalta Conference. Professors argued that he had not saved the economy. Still, the country was prosperous, and I continued to believe in Roosevelt, as my family had before me. Then, in the late 1960s, disillusionment set in.

Now a young academic in Cambridge, Massachusetts, I strongly opposed the dispatch of American forces to Vietnam. Some claimed there was a direct tie between FDR's global "interventionism" during the Second World War and President Lyndon B. Johnson's "arrogance of power" in Vietnam. Newly troubled, I spotted another shadow darkening Roosevelt's image. Reviewing a new book, I published an angry article entitled "USA: Bystander to Genocide," which proved to be one of the earliest denunciations of Roosevelt's inaction on behalf of Jewish refugees from Hitler's Holocaust. Writing in a Jewish magazine, I attacked the Roosevelt administration for having done little or nothing to thwart Hitler's murder of European Jewry. In my essay, however, I managed to avoid all but a few direct references to Roosevelt himself. Some subconscious mechanism must have been at work in me, as I tried to preserve a vestige of respect for my fallen idol.

By the middle of the 1970s, left-wing writers, who opposed American "imperialism" and interventionism, and conservative neoisolationists seemed to agree on one point. Roosevelt's interventionism had been both wrongheaded and dangerous. FDR had, for a number of imperialistic and political motives, tricked the United States into entering the Second World War. Worse still, he had left a legacy that haunted the nation twenty years later, when another Roosevelt-loving interventionist, Lyndon Johnson, lying just like his mentor, deceived the nation into entering the Vietnam War in the aftermath of the Gulf of Tonkin incident.

In 1985, I attended a conference in Washington, D.C., on the historian and film. We were sitting in the Mary Pickford Auditorium at the Library of Congress, watching news film of one of Roosevelt's 1941 speeches, perhaps on the occasion of Navy Day. FDR, in good form, made some comments about aggressive German behavior on the high seas and then implied that, while the Nazis had fired the first shot, they would not be the ones to discharge the last round. I was stirred, but just then, a Jewish gentleman said in a loud voice, "Gulf of Tonkin!" In other words, the main point was not Roosevelt's opposition to Hitler, but his interventionist trickery.

If my colleague was right, why did the Jews cast almost all of their ballots for FDR in 1940 and 1944, during the Holocaust?

Was this really the Roosevelt story in foreign policy, one that led from interventionist deception to the Vietnam trauma, from appeasement at the time of Munich to the "relocation" of Japanese-Americans, from the abandonment of the Jews to the "sellout" to Stalin at Yalta?

I thought so when I began to do research for this book. I have discovered otherwise.

For many years, I had been interested in Roosevelt from a different perspective. As a scholar and writer concerned with Nazi Germany and the Holocaust, I knew about FDR's role in preparing this country for war. I had read enough to understand that American military power and economic strength had been instrumental in bringing about Hitler's defeat. I wanted to bring together my knowledge of Nazi Germany and my interest in Roosevelt and his America. I decided to go to the German archives and records and look at America through German eyes, and then undertake the corresponding task in the United States.

I first examined Hitler's view of America in the context of a widely disseminated German worldview, one extremely hostile to the United States. And I investigated the anti-German sentiments prevalent in young FDR's world after the turn of the century.

I began to see that the contest between Germany and the United States was a historical struggle for global hegemony. More importantly, both Hitler and Roosevelt understood this. The old European empires were in decline in the 1930s; the Soviet Union was going through turmoil engendered by purges and rapid industrialization, Italy was a second-rate power, and Japan was not yet an industrial giant. There remained Germany, technologically advanced and extremely disciplined, possessing a strong soldierly tradition—a Germany, one might add, led by an ambitious, nihilistic psychopath of unparalleled persuasive powers. And there waited another contestant, the United States. Though mired in economic depression, and equipped with a pitifully small army, Roosevelt's America had great potential. Once before, in 1918, it had stopped a German bid for hegemony in Europe. Could it do so again, for much higher stakes?

In Franklin D. Roosevelt, Hitler saw his nemesis, a man who would challenge Germany's new bid for global hegemony. Both leaders thought in broad, geopolitical terms, though Roosevelt's vision of an

"American Century" came to him a decade or more after Hitler had announced his plans for changing the map of Europe. Set apart by nation, ethics, ideology, and personality, Hitler and Roosevelt came to confront each other in a struggle for domination of much of the world.

Different challenges mandated contrasting strategies. Hitler had to subdue Europe by threats, then by force; Roosevelt needed to manipulate Americans, most of whom wanted to avoid war, by guile. Hitler and his propagandists worked to disabuse the German people of any remaining illusions about America. Lingering memories of its prosperity, generosity, and *unbegrenzte Möglichkeiten* (unlimited opportunities) needed to be rooted out of the corrupted German people.

Hitler's war against Jewry, which took the form of organized pogroms in the autumn of 1938, brought about revolutionary changes in Roosevelt's view of Germany and American foreign policy. In fact, FDR's German policies cannot be understood apart from their Jewish context. To Hitler, the essence of Americanism was Jewry. This fact justified his Americanophobia, but it also opened up pleasing prospects. If Nazi agents could play upon a combination of American resentment and anti-Semitism, U.S. foreign policy might be manipulated to the advantage of German interests. A hostile president, however, would present a formidable obstacle to such a plan.

The United States was a strongly anti-Semitic country in the autumn of 1938. Roosevelt knew this. He was cautious to avoid being tagged with the label "president of the Jews," as some called him. In a real sense, he *did* abandon many refugees, and in a shameful manner. There is no way of avoiding the restatement of this truth. Roosevelt's achievement, however, is slighted if one does not state a fact of equal importance. FDR effectively prevented the political mobilization of American anti-Semitism by isolating groups professing anti-Jewish sentiments. This ghettoization of the Jew-haters rendered them relatively harmless. Roosevelt worked in a subtle, even devious, manner. He used J. Edgar Hoover's Federal Bureau of Investigation (FBI) and, above all, the mass media, to convince Americans of two things: The Nazis abroad were dangerous to Americans at home, and anti-Semites, fascists, and even anti-interventionists were part of the "fifth column," a Trojan horse placed in the Americas by the Germans.

As war approached in the late 1930s, Hitler realized that he could neither intimidate nor destroy his hated American adversary. His fury erupted just before the war, when the German chancellor threatened to expose the president as a Jew or a tool of the Jews. "[T]he world," said Hitler, "would then be astounded."[1]

If Hitler was to be stopped, an activist American foreign policy would be essential. The struggle between Germany and the United States thus took place on several levels. It was a battle over the future of the American people. Would the interventionists prevail, or would "isolationists," the anti-interventionists of the left and right, triumph? I decided to examine the American public through the eyes of Nazi propagandists and White House manipulators. I found that Hitler had many friends in the United States; he could mobilize legions of patriotic, well-meaning Americans committed to "no more war" and nonintervention.

As Roosevelt became aware of the German threat to American democratic capitalism and its global ambitions, he needed to mold opinion while preparing for war. Looking at British, French, and Polish policy in 1939, I have concluded that the emergence of an anti-Nazi alliance owed much to Roosevelt, and to pressure and promises conveyed by two of his ambassadors. It was, however, a European alliance, not an American-led bloc. This first anti-Nazi coalition lasted until the late spring of 1940, when France suddenly collapsed. There followed a time of disorientation, then recovery, as the Roosevelt administration embarked on a new course.

In the center of this battle over intervention or neutrality stood the Jewish issue. As I read all the critics of Roosevelt, who have published a steady stream of denunciations since 1969, I was ultimately puzzled. Hitler seemed to have a different view of FDR. He saw him as his most implacable enemy, and denounced him in vicious terms as late as April 1945. Hitler hated FDR far more than he hated Stalin or even Churchill, but why? I found that Hitler, more than most historians who have written about him, understood that Roosevelt was hostile, pro-Jewish, and instrumental in forging the first anti-German military bloc, in 1939. FDR, the Führer sensed, could not conceive of coexisting with National Socialist Germany, or with a Europe under Hitler's control.

An analysis of Hitler's rhetoric shows that his two most vicious public attacks on a Western leader occurred on 28 April 1939 and 11 December 1941; both had Roosevelt as their target. But why did Hitler consider "warmonger Roosevelt" the prime instigator of the 1939 war, and the "greatest war criminal of all time" if FDR was, as we are often told, an opportunist who had "abandoned the Jews" and who entered the war only through the "back door" at Pearl Harbor? If FDR was the man portrayed by his recent critics, why did Hitler harbor such animosity toward the man he derisively called "Rosenfeld"? And why did Jews support FDR so solidly in 1940 and 1944? Could it be that FDR, rather than the deified Winston Churchill, was the most purposeful and consequential anti-Nazi leader of his time?

Roosevelt has too seldom been seen in the light of the world of his time. His image, clouded by the trauma of the Holocaust and then of Vietnam, has come to reflect the concerns of those looking at it through a lens warped by a later age.

This book is an appeal for perspective. Roosevelt's three great failures were indeed the refugee question, the incarceration of Japanese-Americans, and inconsistent dealings with Stalin on Eastern European issues.

There is, however, another, perhaps larger, truth. Between 1936 and 1939, FDR's view of the Nazi regime evolved, and by the winter of 1941 he was committed to a policy opposing peaceful coexistence with National Socialist Germany. Roosevelt did not seek entry into the war in 1941, but he hoped and worked for the destruction of Nazi Germany. This he kept secret from the American people, except for those who read between the lines of his speeches. If Roosevelt had his way, the United States would go to war only if the Allies failed to destroy the Hitler regime. And FDR, being unprepared militarily, did not want to enter the war before the spring of 1942, at the earliest.

But by the winter of 1941, Roosevelt was ready to commit the United States to a difficult war, rather than accept a compromise peace that would leave the German regime intact.

Roosevelt's entire European policy from the spring of 1939 was, I believe, predicated upon a commitment to destroying Hitler and all his works. There might have been no war in Europe in September 1939 had it not been for Roosevelt's pressure on London, Paris, and Warsaw. By the late summer of that year, FDR had secured an army in the field along the Rhine and the Vistula. If that army did not suffice, other armies would need to take the field, including an American one at some undetermined point. Because of his insights into the nature of National Socialism, and his manipulation of a confused and often hostile public opinion, Roosevelt emerges as the giant figure of his age.

In the name of defense of the Americas, Roosevelt was prepared to wage a war that could culminate in an era of unprecedented American hegemony. When in doubt about Roosevelt's intentions, it is edifying to return to German sources. Hitler, the Foreign Ministry, the Washington embassy, and secret German agents usually reported the same story, that FDR was an implacable anti-Nazi who was leading Europe, then perhaps the United States, to war against Hitler's Germany.

ACKNOWLEDGMENTS

I want to thank those who furthered my research on this subject. The late John Mendelsohn, of the National Archives, was, as always, most helpful. His colleagues, Robert Wolfe, George Wagner, Donald Spencer, and George Chalou of the National Archives (then at the Suitland branch), were extremely cooperative. Ms. Mary Komarnicki of the Daniel Yankelovich Group, Inc., shared important unpublished data on American anti-Semitism with me.

I would not have been able to write this book without gaining access to hitherto suppressed materials. I refer in particular to the German-American Bund records seized by the FBI after the Pearl Harbor attack. I owe thanks to Mr. John R. Franklin, chief of the Justice Department's Alien Property Unit and to Mr. Rex E. Lee, assistant attorney general and director of the Office of Alien Property.

I especially thank my senior senator, Strom Thurmond of South Carolina. Without Senator Thurmond's assistance, the government would not have permitted me to examine certain records so essential to this work.

Dr. Maria Keipert of the Auswärtiges Amt (Bonn) has once again kindly assisted me in my research. Several sections of the Bundesarchiv in Koblenz cooperated fully with me during my research time in their archives. I acknowledge in particular the important assistance provided by Dr. Josef Henke, Herr Raillard, Frau Marshall, and Herr Regel. Hermann Weiss of the Institut für Zeitgeschichte in Munich was most cooperative, as was Dr. Weidenhaupt of the Stadtarchiv in Düsseldorf.

Mr. Earle E. Coleman, university archivist, provided me with access to the Seeley G. Mudd Manuscript Library of Princeton University, which is custodian of the Princeton Listening Center records of short-wave radio broadcasts from Germany. I am grateful to that library's staff. The staffs of the Library of Congress Manuscript Division, as well as its Motion Picture Section, were most helpful. The same is true of the Museum of Modern Art's Motion Picture Archives. Charles Palm and Agnes F. Peterson of the Hoover Institution of War, Revolution, and Peace were attentive to my research needs. Dr. Harriet Jameson of the Rare Books Department of the University of Michigan made important pamphlet collections available to me.

Dr. Schumann, Archivrätin E. Giessler, and Archivinspektorin Bau-erschäfer of the Staatsarchiv Nürnberg provided me with valuable mi-crocopies of materials useful in writing this book. Mr. G. Knetsch of the Archiv der ehemaligen Reichsstudentenführung und des NSD-Studentenbundes at the Bayrische Julius-Maximilians-Universität in Würzburg made available to me materials on German-American stu-dent exchanges in the 1930s. In these microfilmed collections, I discov-ered important documentation concerning German press views of the United States.

Mr. Marek Web of the YIVO Institute in New York City was once again most helpful.

Ned Chase, a senior figure on the New York publishing scene, has inspired me, as always, with his interest and his suggestions, made over a period of many years.

My dean at the University of South Carolina, Dr. Carol M. Kay, and my chairman, Dr. Thomas L. Connelly, have consistently supported my research. The secretarial staff in the Department of History, and an assistant, Seann Gray, were helpful and pleasant. The American Philo-sophical Society generously assisted me in my work, and I am grateful to its officers. Mr. William Emerson of the FDR Library shared his insights into the Roosevelt era with me, and I thank him for them.

I also wish to acknowledge the assistance and contributions of my editors at Paragon House, Ken Stuart and PJ Dempsey, copy editor Nancy Carlton, as well as the support extended to me by my agent, Susan Ann Protter.

I am grateful to the staffs of the Archives du centre de documentation juive contemporaine (Paris); the Connecticut State Library (Hartford); the Staatsarchiv Hamburg; the Franklin D. Roosevelt Library (Hyde Park); the Haus-, Hof-, und Staatsarchiv (Vienna); and the Wiener Library (then in London).

Professor Walter Laqueur of the Wiener Library made helpful suggestions while I was doing my research. I am grateful to my colleagues Dr. Dean Kinzley, Dr. Marcia Synnott, and Dr. Kendrick Clements, as well as to Mr. Seymour Kurtz, for their suggestions.

Robert Edwin Herzstein
26 July 1989

PART ONE

HITLER'S AMERICA

CHAPTER
ONE

FROM PROMISED LAND
TO MORTAL ENEMY

BLINDED DURING A mustard gas attack on the western front, the twenty-nine-year-old enlisted man Adolf Hitler learned of the Armistice ending the Great War while recuperating in a field hospital. Devastated, the wounded soldier could not admit that his beloved Germania had lost the war. An evil force must have stabbed her in the back, just as cowardly villain Hagan had assassinated the hero Siegfried in Richard Wagner's epic tale. More than most of his comrades, Hitler, a unknown soldier of dubious social status, understood the role played by the United States in Germany's defeat.

Some months earlier, a thirty-six-year-old American politician had toured the western front. The scion of a wealthy and prestigious family, Assistant Secretary of the Navy Franklin Delano Roosevelt had been an amiable, upstate New York politician before the war, unremarkable except for his famous name. Roosevelt's experience during the war seemed to add depth to the man. He had begun to work harder, to think more deeply about the grave issues of war and peace. Now, inspecting the battlefields and meeting with Allied officers and politicians, President Wilson's political appointee saw what modern warfare meant. French soldiers and civilians regaled the fascinated young American with stories of atrocities committed by the *boches*. After observing the results of a German aerial bombardment of one French town, Roosevelt wrote that "about six houses on each side of the street were completely wrecked . . . and many people killed." "FDR" (as he styled himself in "chits" or memoranda), indignant about German excesses, now compared German prisoners unfavorably to French *poilus*. The French soldiers, he observed, had more "intelligence in their faces." Roosevelt later recalled, "I have seen children starving. I have seen the agony of mothers and wives. I hate war." Despite his famous phrase "I hate war," Roosevelt disliked war not in itself but for what it did to those whose virtue had led them to fight for righteousness.[1] He did not see what the war had done to Germany; reports about German suffering left Roosevelt cold. FDR departed ravaged Europe convinced more than ever of German savagery. Nothing would change his mind.[2]

Young Adolf Hitler, in contrast, liked war, and saw mass destruction as the natural result of a heroic struggle. An unhappy orphan, Hitler had left his Upper Austrian homeland in 1907, moving to the polyglot world of imperial Vienna. Lonely and poorly educated, Hitler lost himself in hate-filled fantasies about dark, frenzied Jewish monsters or stood enthralled at the opera, listening to Richard Wagner's epic music dramas. To young Hitler, the Viennese reality outside the State Opera contrasted badly with the ideal Germanic world of gods and heroes: Vienna had become a racially impure house, sheltering inferior Slavic and Jewish breeds. This cold city denied a young "Aryan" genius like Hitler his just due, twice rejecting his application for admission to the prestigious Academy of Fine Arts.

To Hitler, the nearby German Reich became the house of redemption, of purity and strength. The aimless young Austrian drifter, a would-be "architectural painter," fled to Germany before the war, one step ahead of the Austrian Army's draft board.

After settling in Munich, Hitler joined a Bavarian regiment when the European war erupted in 1914. In training camp and at the front, he gained a sense of identity, for Hitler gloried in being part of the mighty German Army. The enemies of Germany were *his* enemies, in a most personal way. In the trenches, Hitler reveled in the experience of shared sacrifice. He liked the sense of comradeship, which was less threatening than true friendship. The collapse of 1918, which led to Hitler's commitment to a political career, shattered the young man's world.

As a thirty-year-old politician in Munich, Hitler saw America as an upstart nation noteworthy for its treachery and crass materialism. In an early speech, Hitler put it this way: "Although this criminal Wilson was a big bum, one has to have respect for him nonetheless, since he managed to achieve great gains for his own nation."[3] He envied President Wilson's "success," noting that Prime Minister David Lloyd George of Britain and Premier Georges Clemenceau of France were mere bunglers in comparison. Wilson had softened Germany up, Hitler claimed, making her ripe for conquest by Jewish bolshevism and Jewish finance capitalism. He, Adolf Hitler, would restore German honor and foil Wilson's plan.[4]

Hitler's revulsion was not unique. Its roots lay in three decades of growing German hostility to the United States. The tragedy that made Franklin Roosevelt and Adolf Hitler adversaries in that autumn of 1918 could not have been predicted a generation earlier, when little Adolf played by the banks of the Danube and young Franklin roamed through the beautiful woods overlooking the Hudson River.

In the days of colonial America, however, those Germans who thought about Britain's North American colonies at all pictured them as parts of a vast, remote land of forests and Indians, containing a scattering of European settlers. The American Revolution changed Germans perceptions of the New World. Journalists, authors, and moralists praised the American uprising. In Frederick the Great's militarized Prussia, the *Berlin Monthly* exulted in the Americans' triumph:

Thou art free (proclaim it in the highest tones of victory, Enchanted song), free, America is now free
Exhausted, bowed, covered with shame
Thine enemy slinks away, and thou dost triumph.[5]

The radical Georg Förster praised America, "the freest government ever known to us in a great commonwealth. . . ."[6]

In the early nineteenth century, as Europe went through long cycles of revolution, war, and repression, America symbolized expansion, freedom, and life. Inspired by the explorations of Meriwether Lewis and William Clark, Johann Wolfgang von Goethe predicted that the United States would one day span the entire North American continent: "[I]t is absolutely indispensable for the United States to effect a passage from the Mexican Gulf to the Pacific Ocean; and I am certain that they will do it." The seventy-eight-year-old poet summed up the views of his countrymen, hundreds of thousands of whom would soon emigrate to the New World:

> *America, you have it better*
> *Than our continent, the old one,*
> *Have no decayed castles*
> *And no basalts;*
> *You are not thrown into inner turmoil*
> *In disturbed times*
> *By useless memories*
> *And vain quarrels.*[7]

Two generations later, after the creation of the German Reich as a result of three wars, and the preservation of the American union in the bloody Civil War, the two peoples seemed to have more in common. In both lands, unity had prevailed over federation or secession. Millions of families had relatives on the other side of the vast ocean. Both were new, rapidly industrializing, nations, and they shared some of the same problems: polluted air, cycles of boom and bust, rapidly growing cities. Americans respected German organization, social legislation, and higher education. Many Americans students studied in Heidelberg or Berlin. American families of means, including the Roosevelts of Hyde Park, New York, traveled to Germany and explored its famous spas, its medieval ruins, and the romantic Rhine.

In the long run, sadly, the contrasts between the two countries proved to be more important than the similarities. An authoritarian Prussian state had created the new Reich. Germany, with its permanent military establishment, steeped in aristocratic tradition, soon appeared in American caricatures as home to the jackboot and the monocle, to barbaric dueling scars and corpselike obedience unto death. Prussian hierarchy had triumphed over German liberalism, or so many Americans thought. In America, the standing peacetime army was tiny; suspicions of military establishments went back to colonial times.

Prince Otto von Bismarck watched American expansion in the Pacific with interest, but without undo alarm. During a conflict over the Samoan Islands in the South Pacific, he observed: "The commanders of our navy have strict orders to avoid every [possible] conflict with American warships." Samoa, Bismarck argued, was "not worth the evils which might result from a collision between the armed forces of Germany and the United States." Bismarck, tormented by his "nightmare" of an anti-German coalition, was more concerned with Europe than with America.[8]

After Bismarck's retirement in 1890, a drastic change in attitude and policies occurred. The young, ambitious, and unstable German emperor, Wilhelm II, wanted to turn the Reich into a *Weltmacht* (world power). This was the great age of imperialism, and, like many Europeans, Wilhelm believed in a national "mission." The Germans, he thought, were *Kulturträger,* or bearers of German culture to inferior breeds. Furthermore, the Germans needed raw materials and markets for their industrial goods. Germany was being excluded from the global plunder by the gluttonous British and hostile French. Wilhelm's attitudes, and those promoted by powerful lobbying groups like the *Flottenverein* (the Naval League) and the *Kolonialverein* (the Colonial League), mandated the creation of a modern, high seas navy.[9]

Wilhelm's vision of *Weltpolitik* (global policy) came to obsess the emperor at a time when the United States was becoming an imperial power in the western Pacific. German nationalists saw America's newly aggressive interpretation of the Monroe Doctrine as an arrogant justification of the domination of Latin American territories closed to European powers. Paranoia begat fantasy, an unstable base upon which to build a foreign policy. As if to put the Americans in their place, Wilhelm, encouraged by Admiral Tirpitz (who wanted a bigger navy), now dreamt of becoming the "Admiral of the Atlantic." The emperor mused about how a united Europe under his leadership would force the bumptious Yankees to apologize for their sins.[10]

As the new century dawned, German admiration for the United States diminished further, and visions of conflict replaced the ever fewer hymns of praise. As Britain and Germany plotted against each other with increasing dedication, London and Washington improved their relations, fortifying Wilhelm's sense of isolation and frustration. His bellicose words fed the flames of anti-German sentiment in America, much to the glee of Englishmen and their friends in the United States. A leading military figure argued, "[The United States] is still totally dependent intellectually upon [Europe], [yet] it desires to annihilate it economically; the final showdown will not be of a peaceful nature." Wilhelm himself responded to the American danger with this advice: "Therefore, quickly build a strong fleet. Then the rest will fall into place!"[11] As early as 1901, a German publisher brought out a book containing a blueprint for a confrontation with the United States. Baron Franz von Edelsheim's *Operations Upon the Sea: A Study* caused an uproar in the United States, and led to the further deterioration of the German image in America. Wilhelm's admiralty staff echoed Edelsheim: "There can be only *one* objective for Germany's war strategy: direct pressure on the American east coast and its most populous areas, especially New York. . . ."[12] Still, the prospect of war with the United States seemed farfetched.

In the summer of 1914, the German Reich went to war against Russia and France, and soon found itself locked in a life-or-death struggle with the British Empire. Now, with Europe at war and neutral America heavily pro-British, the thought of military conflict with the United States no longer seemed to be an abstract outlet for German frustration. Despite widespread knowledge of German-American loyalty to the United States, some German leaders and opinion makers fantasized about an armed alliance with a 500,000-man army, recruited by Irish-American and German-American volunteers. This "army," funded and armed by the German Reich, would invade Canada. The German foreign ministry studied this plan carefully, but ultimately rejected it.[13]

The imperial German elites and their publicists had an extraordinary inability to see themselves as Americans saw them.[14] Contemptuous and fearful of political democracy at home, they believed that it must weaken and corrupt those who embraced it abroad. The famed philosopher Max Scheler assured his countrymen, "The hatred against the Central Powers [Germany and Austria-Hungary] is a hatred of the peripheral areas against the center, of the extremities against the heart of Europe. . . ."[15] In denouncing their enemies, Germans often turned into the very "Hunnish" caricatures diligently depicted by British propaganda. The Germans could not seem to find a way to counteract powerful British propaganda about the "rape of Belgium" and other alleged atrocities.

Early on, the Germans lost patience with President Woodrow Wilson's so-called neutrality. British control of the high seas tended to guarantee that America's assertion of "neutral rights" would work in favor of the Allies. Germany's only effective weapons in the Atlantic war were the U-boats, whose deadly efficacy provoked protest from the American public. Wilson himself was convinced of the moral superiority of the Allies, though he harbored few illusions about their imperialistic war aims. Britain and France, however, were democracies; Germany-Prussia was autocratic and militaristic. The president feared Germany as an aggressive economic rival, liable to seize lucrative markets and valuable raw materials in Latin America and the Orient. At the same time, Wilson was horrified by the slaughter in Europe, and believed it might precipitate the collapse of Western civilization. He had become more aware of American power, and wished to help mediate an end to the great conflict. Wilson's efforts failed, while the neutral United States turned into the power whose exports kept Britain alive.

Like many of his countrymen, German seaman Richard Stumpf observed that all of Germany's enemies combined "have not harmed us nearly as much as the Americans." His bitterness increased as German losses mounted. "While the German lion is fighting for its life," said Stumpf, "America is trying to kick him in the pants."[16]

President Wilson's strong espousal of military preparedness in the election year 1916 reflected an appreciation of American politics, for he did not intend to be out-jingoed by former president (and presidential aspirant) Theodore Roosevelt.[17] When mediation efforts failed, the president became more committed to the Allied cause. The stories about German atrocities in Belgium and on the high seas affected Wilson mightily. As a great domestic reformer, however, he did not want war. Nevertheless, to German nationalists who craved a *Siegesfrieden*, or peace achieved through total victory, Wilson was a fake peacemaker, sanctimoniously attempting to cheat Germany out of just gains earned with the blood of more than one million men. America was now at the heart of the German *Feindbild*, a hostile image of one's adversaries.[18]

Sailor Stumpf bitterly derided Wilson's so-called peace note of 18 December 1916, noting that "gold is thicker than blood and also more valuable."[19] This venom poisoned German attempts to prevent America from entering the war, because it blinded the Germans to their own shortcomings. Even General Erich Ludendorff, the virtual dictator of Germany, did not understand that in modern war diplomacy and propaganda were as important as purely military factors.

Late in 1916, Ludendorff calculated that Germany's only hope was to starve Britain out, while bleeding France to death. Continued American aid would only prolong the war, leading to an inevitable German defeat. Ludendorff decided to gamble on a German victory in the near future, before a still unprepared America could send a large army to Europe. Despite the potential of the American economy, and its role in sustaining the Allies, the general told an industrialist, ". . . I look upon a declaration of war by the United States with indifference." He advocated a policy of unrestricted submarine warfare. Neutral shipping would be the major target.

The American declaration of war came on 6 April 1917. This event buoyed the spirits of war-weary British Tommies and French *poilus*. In the summer and autumn of 1918, brave (and sometimes foolhardy) American doughboys helped to crack the vaunted Hindenburg line, inflicting massive casualties. Ludendorff and his shaken kaiser faced nightmarish choices. Discontent at home could lead to socialist revolution, as had happened in Lenin's Russia. Almost as repugnant to the German imperial elites was the prospect of the emergence of a liberal democratic order in Germany. Ludendorff himself told the emperor that the war was lost. While surrender was out of the question, so was a new offensive. A decision had to made, and quickly, for the German high command believed that five million more American doughboys would face them in 1919. All one could do now, the government concluded, would be to hold out while seeking moderate peace terms. Ludendorff expected little quarter from the French or the British. Wilson, however, might react in a kinder manner, because he had repeatedly emphasized that he was not at war with the German people, just with aggressive militarism and Prussian thuggery. Reports about Wilson's democratic ideals helped to divide and weaken the German home front.

Wilson's promise of self-determination and a just peace was vague enough to leave Ludendorff and the German political leaders with some vestiges of hope. Unfortunately for the Germans, Britain and France did not hesitate to remind President Wilson that they had done all of the bleeding before the Americans belatedly entered the war. Wilson's idealistic Fourteen Points, a peace program drafted in January 1918, had not impressed that gnarled old French nationalist premier, Georges Clemenceau, who growled, "Even the good Lord had only ten!"

The German high command belatedly assented to the formation of a more liberal cabinet, under Prince Max von Baden. Calculated to sway the democrat Wilson, grudging liberalization failed to move the Allies. Whatever Wilson may have desired, the Allied supreme command would demand the de facto surrender of the German Army, followed by its almost total and permanent demobilization. The newly liberal German government put out desperate peace feelers to Wilson.[20]

Ludendorff now faced the prospect of an invasion of Germany. Naval mutinies and riots erupted amid widespread signs of war exhaustion and revolution; these events forced Ludendorff's hand. Wilson rejected the German peace feelers. Fearing for his safety, Wilhelm II fled to neutral Holland. Patriotic, moderate Social Democrats, committed to democracy, peace, and social reform, took over the Reich government for the first time. Ludendorff fled to Sweden, disguised as a businessman. The old era seemed to have passed, and in a most unheroic way.

A small but well-organized and armed group of radical "Spartacists," soon to call themselves communists, hoped to make a revolution in Germany. Demoralization, malnutrition, and fear now haunted the home front. The new German government, headed by provisional chief executive Friedrich Ebert and Chancellor Philipp Scheidemann, signed the Armistice on 11 November 1918. This "armistice" was, of course, a military surrender. The German Army had to withdraw from its positions in the west, making resumption of the conflict a virtual impossibility. In coming years, the provisional republic would be saddled with the blame for assenting to the "treacherous" document.

Still, Germans could hope that more goodwill would be shown by the Allies when they offered their peace terms. After all, Germany was now a republic, committed to the creation of a democratic constitution. Military leaders hoped that the Reich's new veneer of social democracy would preserve the control of Germany by military, industrial, and agrarian elites. Sailor Richard Stumpf concluded his diary with a plaintive question: "My Fatherland, My dear Fatherland, what will happen to you now?"[21]

Once more, America was the great hope. He might, said many a German, stand up to his own allies and force them to accept a just peace without annexations or indemnifications. Adolf Hitler, still in uniform, did not share this expectation.

CHAPTER TWO

AMERICA THE BETRAYER

FTER A TERRIBLE winter marked by hunger, revolts, and political violence came a spring filled with disappointment and accusations of betrayal. On 7 May 1919, the German delegation at the Versailles Peace Conference learned the terms of the imposed peace. Germany had little choice but to sign the so-called *Diktat*, which it did on 28 June. By its terms, the republic lost territory, was partially occupied, and agreed to pay reparations to the victors. Article 231 signified German acceptance of responsibility for the outbreak of the war, and for the suffering brought by the conflict upon the Allied nations. A further humiliation was the reduction of the German Army to 100,000 men. President Wilson himself had supposedly mused, "If I were a German, I think I should never sign it."[1]

Many German writers now added conspiracy to their charges against Wilson. The president, people said, had tricked the Germans into signing the Armistice by promising lenient peace terms. One scholarly observer concluded, "Among all those who shoveled at the grave of our people, none was more clever or more successful than Woodrow Wilson. That is the judgment one has to make now, and it will go down in history so."[2] One German critic called Wilson an "unctuous hypocrite." Wilson, some charged, had perpetrated the "greatest swindle in world history." He was one of the "fathers of our misery," and the "most dangerous enemy of our people."

Within two years of the Armistice, the "stab in the back" legend had become commonplace in republican Germany. If Woodrow Wilson, in league with German traitors, had betrayed the German Army, then Field Marshal Paul von Hindenburg and the German officer corps could escape blame for Germany's defeat. The German catastrophe would then be ascribed to the United States and its "Wall Street democracy."[3] This disillusionment with America enveloped both the right and the left. Liberals and socialists contrasted Wilsonian phrases like "lasting peace" and a "just peace" with the Treaty of Versailles and the heavy reparations payments mandated by the *Diktat*. German pacifists were particularly confused. In an open letter to Wilson, one wrote, "We sincerely admit our inability to understand your motivation; the contradiction between your words and the terms of this treaty draft is incomprehensible to us."[4] Nor were Germans alone in their view of Wilson. Prominent Austrians, such as Sigmund Freud, believed that Wilson had connived at destroying Austria-Hungary. In their view, Wilson had denied self-determination to six million Austrians, who wished to join the new German republic. In this sense, some later argued, Wilson could be held accountable for both the German defeat and the rise of Nazism, for both the Treaty of Versailles and the *Anschluss* (the seizure of Austria by Hitler in March 1938). This mistrust of America and hatred for Wilson undermined the fragile democratic ideology of the Weimar Republic and of the Austrian First Republic.

Fifteen years later, the American ambassador to Germany found the Nazis nurturing these old memories. Over and over again, Germans repeated, "Wilson defeated us, the treacherous Wilson."[5]

The historian cannot ignore Wilson's blindness to German perceptions and German problems. Had he acted differently, it is true, Germany might have won the war. It would then have created a great empire, run with military discipline. In the declining days of imperialism, in a nationalistic age, that empire would not have long endured. There might then have been no Hitler, no second German war, no Holocaust. Having defeated Germany, Wilson's America (despite the passionate urgings of its complex leader) abandoned a shattered Europe to misery and demagoguery. How ironic that this prophet of democracy should have contributed so mightily to the rise of antidemocratic ideologies and movements.

On the surface, the mutual hatred between Germany and the United States receded in the years after the war, at least outside German rightist and nationalist circles. American tourists returned to Germany. In the spring of 1923, the rector and student representatives of the University of Hamburg welcomed five hundred American students to their school. American warships visited German ports. By 1926 Germany seemed relatively stable and prosperous. Americans could admire the "new Germany," with its hardworking people and democratic constitution.[6]

In this atmosphere, a good number of liberal German thinkers attempted to revise the negative view of America embraced by so many of their countryfolk. The distinguished political economist Moritz Julius Bonn, a left-liberal and a democrat, was born into a German-Jewish banking family in 1873. A reparations expert at the Versailles negotiations, Bonn spent much time trying to disprove the "stab in the back" legend. He knew something about the United States, from firsthand experience and portrayed the United States in sympathetic colors.[7] Professor Friedrich Schönemann also warned against the German tendency to despise American culture. He pointed out that American prosperity had provided people with blocks of leisure time, giving them access to "more libraries and books than anywhere else in the world." Other German observers argued that American religion was a dynamic force for social reform, lessening tensions between the social classes. Germany could, they said, learn from this experience.[8] German writers praised American philanthropists for supporting charitable and cultural institutions, a phenomenon sadly missing in Germany.[9] A few bold German writers, including the prominent poet and critic Alfred Kerr, exposed and attacked the nationalists' parody of America. Kerr described these nationalistic *Amerika* experts as ignorant swindlers, viewing them as a threat to democracy. As one writer put it: "The opponents of what might be called 'social Americanism' are as a rule infected by the prejudices of the economically or socially privileged classes."[10]

Liberal writers were by no means uncritical admirers of the United States. Journalist Arthur Feiler, for example, observed: "No problem is as threatening [to the United States] as the Negro problem. This problem indicates how a wrong, once committed by a people, can go on poisoning them from generation to generation."[11]

Nor did all Germans believe that American democracy was necessarily an enemy of the *deutscher Geist* (German spirit). "The future of mankind," declared one commentator, "lies doubtless in binding together into a unity, European culture and European methodical thinking with the American love of freedom and justice, with the brilliant American intuition."[12]

The German right, by contrast, described the ideologies of Americanism and *Deutschtum* (Germandom) as two conflicting worldviews. In the right's demonology, democracy desecrated military honor; it sacrificed order to public license; it discouraged spiritual depth in its advocacy of a rampant materialism. German nationalists denounced Americanism for undermining racial purity by fostering the *Schmelztopf,* (ethnic melting pot). They argued that Germanic ideology must glorify soldierly heroism, a value locked in mortal combat with American (and Jewish) money worship. These powerful concepts supplied ideological ammunition to those seeking another war. And to anti-Semites, America represented Jewry, enthroned in a great nation-state.

German nationalists continued to be bitter about the German-Americans who had followed Wilson rather than the kaiser. German rightists described them as uprooted, uneducated, and lacking in leadership. Cultural and personal ties might bind some German-Americans to the old homeland, but they rejected dual loyalty, much less prime allegiance to Germany. One had to conclude that these people were "lost forever" to the fatherland. As one German-American told Arthur Feiler, "We are of German descent, but we are Americans." Assimilation had done its work, Feiler concluded.[13] He had more bad news: If England "were in distress tomorrow America would doubtless come to the rescue again, despite all the differences separating the two countries." A clever president, could, he said, overcome isolationist opinion in a short period of time. Feiler was a prophet without honor in his own country.[14]

No American impressed the Germans of the 1920s as much as Henry Ford. He symbolized the can-do spirit of Yankee ingenuity, applying techniques of mass production to the satisfaction of human needs. The Germans loved "America's great Prussian," not least for his opposition to wartime intervention against Germany. Ford's conservative, even reactionary, social views made him acceptable to the right, while the liberals saw him as a man who paid his workers well, stimulated mass demand, and raised the standard of living of all social classes. Germans purchased about 200,000 copies of Ford's autobiography after it appeared in 1923. German engineers and scientists flocked to the United States, and a visit to the Ford factories was high on their list of attractions. Liberal writers, ranging from the political thinker Friedrich Naumann to the great theologian Ernst Troeltsch, predicted that American capitalism would one day rule the world. Philosopher Hermann Keyserling hoped that Europe would be "saved in a timely manner from its own worst impulses by superior American power."[15]

In 1928, the famous American journalist Edgar Ansel Mowrer published his best-selling book *This American World*. (Translated into German, the title became *America: Model and Warning*, a change not without significance.) Mowrer, acknowledging that American power had led to widespread Americanization, did not paint a flattering portrait of American culture. To Mowrer, Americanism signified the triumph of the common man, who lived in a cramped world defined by Puritan repression, Prohibition, bizarre religious cults, and childish optimism. Imperialistic and intolerant, this American would one day brush aside the old European elites. Some Germans hailed Mowrer as a Jeremiah, warning of the triumph of Americanism. Other conservatives went further, and compared the soulless materialism of Mowrer's Americanized world to the hell created by the Bolsheviks in Russia.[16] They fortified their own social ideology by depicting America as "the country of the dollar." To people who agreed with such accusations, America was a "spiritual prairie."[17]

Lending his great prestige to this Americanophobia was the influential Oswald Spengler, the famous author of *The Decline of the West*. Spengler had finished much of this massive work before the war but published it only after the German collapse. The book touched the national mood, and became an instant sensation. Most impressed were conservative nationalists, who found in it an explanation for the German catastrophe. Suspicious of rising nationalism among Third World peoples and an ardent foe of democracy and liberal capitalism, Spengler came to equate the defeat of heroic Germany with the triumph of moneylenders and technological materialists—in a word, of Americans. During the late 1920s, when some Germans perceived good qualities in American life, Spengler seemed to agree with a friend's statement: "America is . . . chiefly responsible for our condition, with its intrinsic

mendacity and unctuous superiority; to me [it is] the most repugnant of
our enemies. . . ."

During the last years of his life, Spengler contributed other ideas to
the German nationalist view of the United States. America, he claimed,
could not absorb all its recent immigrants, and was hence on the verge of
disintegration. Corruption, alcoholism, and smuggling, with their "spiritual center in Chicago," sapped the strength of its ruling classes.
Spengler, however, overlooked his own contradictions. America, for
example, was supposedly corrupt and on the verge of spiritual collapse,
but it continued to pose a threat to the old cultures of Europe. Spengler
mused that perhaps only a modern Caesar could check the course of this
dangerous, rotten giant. To him, America was a warning, not a model,
and the old pessimist seemed to envisage a coming struggle for world
power.[18] Because of his prestige and his prejudices, Spengler's ideas
became part of the National Socialist view of the United States, with
ugly results.

During these last years of the Weimar Republic, the world economy
moved into a crisis phase. In the United States, the American economic
miracle gave way to breadlines, soup kitchens, Hoovervilles, and social
despair. Those Germans who had called for objectivity and empathy
toward America seemed to be discredited. Now the emphasis was on
lynchings in the South and poor Oakies looking for salvation in some
mythical California. Henry Ford's miracle yielded to pictures of poor
families living in broken-down automobiles, and Ford himself was on
the verge of bankruptcy. The country where money embodied a supreme value, some Germans gloated, could not even feed its own
people. Those who in better times had denounced America as the land
of free love, short skirts, and female emancipation now had the last
word. Corruption had resulted in social collapse. Some Germans
smugly cited Friedrich Schiller, arguing that history was indeed the
world's supreme court. Wilson's treachery, they said, along with American hypocrisy and the cult of money, had given the world the Great
Depression. Americans, one German psychiatrist wrote, were like children, "excitable, undiscriminating, not very profound, and in a remarkable degree uncontrolled by reason."

The Swiss analyst Carl Gustav Jung, who had a devoted German
following, now viewed the bizarre American character as the legacy of
racial pollution. "The characteristic walk with relatively relaxed joints,
or the swinging hips," wrote Jung, "which are seen so frequently on the

part of American women, stem from the Negro; the dance is Negro
dancing." Jung, famous for his profundity, concluded that "the American offers us a strange picture: a European with Negro manners and an
Indian soul."[19] To many German writers, jazz, a rage in Germany, was
the ultimate poison excreted by decadent Americanism. Jazz, a Negro
product, symbolized the American triumph. Bach and the choirs singing in the old cathedrals of Europe were being drowned out by a
primitive chorus, sung by the offspring of racial degradation. The Americans had become a white *Naturvolk*, children of nature, ready to over-
whelm the *Kulturvölker*, or civilized, ancient nations of Europe.

The eighteenth-century image of America as the land of forests and
freedom had yielded to the nineteenth-century image of America as the
land of "unlimited possibilities." The surly unease about Anglophile
America dominant in 1914 had given way to the sense of betrayal
prevalent in 1919. In the 1920s, rational German perceptions struggled
against stereotypes and prejudices, but the latter triumphed during the
Depression. By the winter of 1933, German anti-Americanism seemed
vindicated. It had become a crucial part of a new ideology with old
roots—National Socialism. Now it was Germany that was dynamic and
spiritually renewed, while America was decadent and mired in an
economic nightmare.

Adolf Hitler was a provincial man, but he thought in global, indeed
cosmic, terms. His tendency to personalize ideas gave Hitler's convic-
tions fanatical strength, but it also prevented him from modifying them
in the face of reality. Hitler had seen what American manpower and
economic strength could do to his German Reich. Largely landlocked
and outnumbered by the world empires of Britain, France, and the
United States, Germany's future as a great power was problematic
unless radical changes took place. Hitler became convinced that only a
united and racially cleansed Europe could prevent the Americanization
of the world. Hitler saw this contest as a struggle between rival imperialisms (he could never appreciate the appeal of democratic ideology). He
envied the totalitarian control imposed upon the people by Soviet
communism; he venerated Benito Mussolini, the duce of Italian fascism.

Hitler was fascinated by the Ku Klux Klan, and by the Jew-hater (not
the auto manufacturer) Henry Ford.[20] Hitler associated America with

pornographic exhibitionism, something which appealed to him. His friend Putzi Hanfstängl later recalled accompanying the future führer to a female "boxing match," an American import. The scantily clad ladies pretended to punch each other. Hitler became quite excited. Embarrassed about his reaction, he afterward explained that ". . . at least it was better than this duelling with sabres that goes on in Germany."[21] A prudish man, Hitler suppressed his fascination with pornography by transferring it to his list of American sins. Hitler's lifelong love for the novels of Karl May, set in a fantasy of the Wild West, confirmed Hitler's view that Americanism represented a corruption of nature, except in one sense. The Americans, hypocrites though they were, had conquered living space by exterminating natives. That achievement, he thought, was worth emulating. America offered proof that those who triumphed through Darwinian struggle could prevail, only to fall victim to racial and cultural pollution. America represented a warning and a challenge, but not a model.

Hitler, with his astounding faith in his own accession to power, knew that he would one day have to confront the United States. This most corrupt of all societies might, despite its internal problems, be on the verge of Western hegemony. A Europe shattered by war and communism was in danger of being overwhelmed by a society whose leading traits were materialism and degeneracy. The Americans would appear to have had all the advantages after Versailles, but that was misleading. Racially and perhaps socially disunited, Americans would soon face, according to Hitler, a powerful German Reich sustained by the labor and resources of an advanced continent.

To his dying day, Hitler was unable to accept the fact that the expansion of American influence might be due to factors such as internal social cohesion, shared democratic values, and a "can-do" spirit. Hitler preferred to blame Wilson, rather than the United States Army, for Germany's defeat. "The American," Hitler said, "is no soldier." On another occasion, he claimed, "The inferiority and decadence of this allegedly New World is evident in its military inefficiency." How an inefficient society could raise an army of millions and transport it thousands of miles across the sea sometimes escaped his notice.

Hitler, of course, *knew* better; his rhetoric often masked shrewd insights.

Hitler foresaw an expansionist America, stimulated by "the natural activist urge that is peculiar to young nations. . . ." The young Munich politician prophesied the coming war of the continents, which would pit a reinvigorated, German-led Europe "against the American Union." Lacking faith in American "isolationism," Hitler predicted in 1928 that economic factors would contribute to the new American expansionism. Whatever his views on American cultural decadence, Adolf Hitler did not underestimate the strength, ambitions, or ultimate hostility of the United States.

Nevertheless, Hitler preferred not to dwell upon American strengths. Fortified by the agreement of his courtiers, the Führer listened with approval to predictions that America "will never again be a danger to us." The United States, he had learned, consisted of a "medley of races," and "no other country has so many social and racial tensions. We shall be able to play on many strings there."[22] Hitler believed that a true landed aristocracy had met its doom in the American Civil War. The slave owners, he argued, gave way to upstart capitalists, who in turn inundated America with the scum of the Eastern European ghettos. The result was the polyglot urbanization of the kind Hitler had experienced (and hated) in Vienna two decades earlier. As American democracy degenerated, and the United States became a disunited, warring confederation of different ethnic tribes, the superior German element might become a unifying, cleansing factor. An American storm troop unit could be formed from German-American communities. During a time of social collapse, it could seize power. As late as 1930, Hitler fantasized that the Nordic element in the United States might prevail, and bring about an alliance with a new, third German Reich.[23]

Hitler contrasted the Nazi movement with the America depicted in John Steinbeck's *The Grapes of Wrath*. To him, the abduction and murder of the son of Charles A. Lindbergh, Jr., was a "typical product of American culture." Hitler ignored the universal condemnation of the act by American society. When President Franklin D. Roosevelt recognized the Soviet Union, Hitler could only declare: "[T]he Americans have teamed up with the Bolsheviks." He did not choose to admit that this "alliance" might have dire consequences for his geopolitical plans.

Hitler's view of the American nation did not prevent him from acting inconsistently when opportunism mandated concealment or mendacity. In 1928, he suppressed his "second book," in part because of its frank discussion of America's place in his vision of the world. And in the early 1920s Hitler gave a speech in which he speculated, "If Wilson hadn't been a swindler, he would not have become President of America." In a volume published in 1923, the phrase became: "If Wilson hadn't been a swindler, he would not have become president of a democracy." By this time, Hitler hoped (largely in vain) for assistance from friendly Americans, such as Henry Ford. In 1933, Hitler dropped the phrase about Wilson altogether.[24] He had become chancellor and needed to restore the German economy, in part through stimulating export industries once dependent upon the American market.

By the late 1930s, Hitler had convinced himself that that the United States contained only a small minority of racially valuable persons. He argued in 1940 that this America would not be a world power until 1970 or 1980, "at the earliest."[25] At the same time, Hitler believed, the growing racial and political corruption of the United States rendered her *more* dangerous in the immediate future. When thousands of Americans panicked upon hearing a radio drama about a Martian invasion, Hitler could only gloat that Americans were hysterical cowards.[26] He could not foresee that an American leader might manipulate this popular fear of the unknown by warning of a Nazi invasion of the Americas.

CHAPTER
THREE

HITLER'S AMERICA EXPERTS

L IKE MANY GERMANS, Hitler continued to be haunted by the "shame" of 1918. National Socialist circles shared his belief that Germany must learn to counter the enemy's propaganda, while undermining his will to fight. German propagandists, both military and civilian, thus paid careful attention to Ewald Banse's *Space and Nation in the World War: Thoughts on a National Military Doctrine*, which appeared just before the Nazi takeover.[1] Banse was a father of "psychological warfare." He viewed applied psychology as "a weapon of war . . . intended to influence the mental attitude of nations towards war. . . . It is essential to attack the enemy nation in its weak spots. . . ." Reflecting the rigid anti-American ideology prevalent among former German general staff officers, Banse's work became a guide to the United States.

Banse understood that the United States had raised an army of millions in a year and a half. He admitted that America was fabulously rich, and almost immune to outside attack. He argued that "without America we would not have surrendered in so pitiful a manner." Grudgingly admitting that American soldiers were not cowards, Banse nonetheless insisted on ascribing American victory to the Yankees' numerical superiority. Possessing a short attention span, and given to occasional bursts of short-lived enthusiasm, Banse's American was devoid of heroism. He was a greedy, big mouthed busybody, taking advantage of European troubles in order to augment his wealth. In Banse's case, as in that of many another "America expert," insight ultimately yielded to ideology. Yet how could Germany wage psychological warfare against a society it so badly misjudged?

B. G. von Rechenberg's book *Roosevelt's America: A Danger,* which appeared in the spring of 1937, so impressed Hitler that the Führer mandated its use by officials in various government ministries. Rechenberg, a onetime director of the Reich's foreign trade office in Hamburg, retired prematurely because of his involvement in a financial swindle. He quickly set sail for the United States. Once there, Rechenberg became the propaganda director of a Nazi cell in San Francisco. He proceeded to turn himself into a professional anti-Semite. With Hitler in power, it was safe for Rechenberg to go home to the fatherland.

In his book, Rechenberg argued that the Jews had taken over the United States. Roosevelt (himself a Jew, according to Rechenberg) was the American Aleksandr Kerensky, preparing the way for Jewish-bolshevik domination of the North American continent. The president was also dangerous in another way, because he was attempting to create a multiracial, global confederation. Many of Hitler's comments about the United States echoed Rechenberg's.[2]

Hitler's most famous "America expert" was Colin Ross, a world traveler and prolific author whose work received the German leader's personal attention and support. Born in Vienna in 1885 as the son of a Scottish father and an Austrian mother, Ross attended German schools. He later earned a doctorate of philosophy. A gifted journalist whose love of travel took him to the far corners of the globe, Ross lived in Chicago before and during the First World War. His enemies later charged him with being a spy and propagandist for imperial Germany. After the war, Ross appears to have dabbled in left-wing causes, while working diligently to establish his reputation as a travel writer. Abandoning political activism during the last years of the German republic, Ross resurfaced as an enthusiastic Nazi. He soon gained the backing of powerful publishers, including Brockhaus in Leipzig. After the Nazis "coordinated" the university community, the free-lance adventurer even won access to the *Journal for Geopolitics,* a prestigious publication. Ross's reputation,

augmented by his party credentials, guaranteed him a substantial reading public.[3]

Colin Ross argued that in earlier times an Anglo-Saxon ruling class
had dominated the ethnically mixed American masses. Economic
growth had ended in 1929, however, and the Depression was giving rise
to new demands by restive ethnic minorities. The grip of the old ruling
class, said Ross, was growing weaker by the day. One ethnic group alone
contained the racial potential needed to create a new ruling class. The
Germans might yet preside over a new, multiethnic federation. Ross
presented these ideas in 1936, in his famous book *Our America: The
German Role in the United States.*

German illusions about ethnic America had not died with the catastrophe of defeat in 1918. Once again, a writer tempted the politicians
by pointing to the political potential of a self-contained German-
American community, which was, Ross implied, waiting to be led by
Berlin. Nazi opinion makers and would-be power brokers swallowed the
bait. The prominent *National Socialist Monthly* urged that all party activists give the book "the most widespread attention."

Although the comparison was absurd, Nazi leaders believed that
German-Americans were not that different from Germans living as
"oppressed" *Volk* elements in Austria, Poland, or Czechoslovakia. Ross
understood the difference, but he made money by pandering to Nazi
fantasies, including Hitler's, so he slyly suggested that a revitalized
German element could help "resurrect" America. Ross concluded his
book with a glorious vision of an America in which the Germanic
element emerged as *Amerikaner,* not Americans.[4] American democracy
was dead, and in its place must come "Our America." The arrogant
phrase *unser Amerika* came to refer to a Germanic United States, allied
with the "New Germany." Ross chose as his symbol of things to come
the German-born U.S. senator Carl Schurz. He twisted the late Republican senator from Missouri into a sort of proto-Nazi. As in the works of
Banse and Rechenberg, here, too, one sees a corrupt America that could
only experience redemption by following the German path. Hitler
himself knew that this pleasant fantasy about "Our America" was not to
be. He admired Ross for his anti-Americanism, not for his optimism.

Condemnation replaced reverie in *America's Hour of Destiny: The United
States Between Democracy and Dictatorship,* published in 1937. Ross now
developed a popular Nazi theme, depicting President Roosevelt's re-
formist New Deal as "an attempt to prop up an obsolete economic and

social order by a system of makeshift measures, to alter the real nature of this order yet preserve its outward form." America was on the verge of dissolution, and only some form of fascism could solve its problems. A redemptive movement, Ross wildly conjectured, might emerge from the struggles of the trade unions against "economic despotism." These were strange words from a writer in whose country a "German Labor Front" had replaced free trade unions. They were, however, typical of Colin Ross. Facts (such as the rise of the Congress of Industrial Organizations, or CIO) could not be ignored, so they had to be twisted to fit a fascist worldview.

During these final prewar years, Ross continued to travel to the United States. He had a pleasant manner and spoke excellent English. Ross cultivated important people, and gathered information about his surroundings. He received speaking invitations from prestigious groups, such as the Foreign Policy Association. Colin Ross was actually a high-level agent of the Nazi party. He used the respected Dr. Martin Sprengling, professor of Semitic languages at the University of Chicago, as one of his many fronts. The German journalist was, according to Sprengling, merely trying to learn more about America's foreign policy and academic elites.

Speaking before pro-Nazi groups, Ross was less circumspect. He told one audience in New York City: "America is now controlled by a few wealthy men. In Germany the people are in control. . . . German-Americans should stand united behind the ideas of Germany and educate the American people to those ideals."

During his travels, Ross assembled collections of photographs in order to confirm the National Socialist concept of American society. These pictures depicted poor southern whites, oppressed Negroes, and downtrodden Indians. Ross intended to assemble a book of photographs that would document the final degradation of the American dream. A congressional committee indignantly called these illustrations "vile distortions." The charge was justified, though Ross's work did accurately portray the negative side of American society. The resultant uproar brought Ross's American travels to an end. Professor Sprengling energetically defended his friend, but to no avail. The State Department decided that Ross was a foreign propagandist and forced him to register as such.[5] Hitler's admiration for Ross increased, however, for in his eyes anyone who offended the Yankees must be a good man.

Returning to Germany, Ross was more pessimistic than ever. President Roosevelt, he believed, was leading America into a camp hostile to Germany. The German-American element could not be mobilized for Nazi purposes. Nor was American democracy (Ross called the Bill of Rights the "Bill of Jews") about to yield to a new form of fascism. In rage, he redoubled his attacks on President Roosevelt, or, as he called him, "Rosenfeld." Ross concluded that the Jews had persuaded the American people that Germany was one big concentration camp. The Jews would use America, he said, in their bid for world power. Ross hoped that the American people would overthrow this Hebrew hegemony, but he left the question open. Here, too, Ross struck a chord in Hitler's heart. More important than the verbiage was Ross's conclusion: Between 1939 and 1941, America did indeed move into the enemy camp.[6]

Hitler admired Ross, but other America experts had their doubts about him. Heinz Kloss of the German Foreign Institute believed that Ross's writings were misleading. Some of Ross's readers supposedly expected to see storm troop units greet them at the pier when they disembarked in the United States. In 1938, Kloss wrote an internal memorandum that documented the damage Ross was doing in the United States. Noted academics, such as Saul K. Padover and Robert Strausz-Hupé, as well as influential magazines like *Fortune*, were quoting Ross as a major Nazi authority on the United States. They used phrases like "Our America" to convince their countrymen that the Nazis were a menace.[7] What counted to Ross, however, was the opinion of Adolf Hitler, not that of Heinz Kloss.

The Third Reich's most prestigious "America expert" was Dr. Friedrich Schönemann, professor of German studies and literature at the University of Berlin. A man with wide-ranging academic contacts in the United States, Schönemann had a secure reputation in Germany by the time of Hitler's accession to power. The Nazis authorities decided that Professor Schönemann would be the best man to counteract hostile American propaganda about the "New Germany." At a time of outrage over Nazi treatment of the Jews, Professor Schönemann could explain the "truth" to audiences of students and professors.

Born in 1886 as the son of the house painter Hermann Schönemann, young Friedrich followed his father's wishes and became a skilled craftsman. Ambitious and highly intelligent, Friedrich defied Germany's rigid social norms by aspiring to a university education. He saved his money, and eventually enrolled in German studies (*Germanistik*) courses at the universities of Berlin and Marburg. A skilled writer, Schönemann financed his education by working as a journalist.[8] It is no wonder this upwardly mobile young man was fascinated by the "land of unlimited opportunities."

Schönemann was puzzled to learn that American studies or *Amerikanistik* had little status in German universities. He would evidently have to learn about the United States by going there. At the age of twenty-five, Schönemann embarked on his first voyage to his promised land. The young university graduate soon became an instructor at Wesleyan University and then at Harvard. He had arrived in 1911, and he stayed until the summer of 1920. During these years, Schönemann became a sad witness to the growth of anti-German sentiment. He sat in New England when American doughboys embarked upon their voyage to the killing fields of northern France. Dr. Schönemann saw what Americans could do to his *Vaterland*. He vowed to teach ignorant Germans more about the United States.

Once back home, Schönemann became a prolific author, an acknowledged expert on the United States. Active in the universities of Münster and Berlin, Schönemann tried to be objective. He did, however, pander to some of his public's distaste for the America of Woodrow Wilson. Schönemann quickly established a far-flung net of powerful contacts, ranging from the German Foreign Institute in Stuttgart to the German Academy in Munich.

Schönemann feared that the advent of the Hitler regime could lead to another war with the United States. He wanted to warn his countrymen about this danger, but in such a way as to enhance his own standing in Nazi eyes. Schönemann first embarked upon a highly publicized lecture tour in the United States. The breadth of American anti-Nazi sentiment shocked the professor. Returning to Germany, Schönemann was determined to speak and write about his experience. In a courageous address delivered before the Academy of Political Science, the professor warned his audience about the looming danger across the sea. Schönemann reported, for example, on a widely held American image of Hitler—that of a madman "surrounded by butchers." He had experienced the full measure of American revulsion against imported Nazi propaganda, and recommended its termination.

Schönemann's heretical ideas gained more publicity in 1934, when he published *America and National Socialism*. He ascribed some of the deterioration in bilateral commercial relations to the autarkic aims of

German economic planners. Schönemann admitted that the movement to boycott German imports was gaining broader public support and warned the Nazis that Americans from all social classes were hostile to the Third Reich. Schönemann told his readers that the anti-Nazi fervor of 1934 reminded him of the "anti-Hun" hysteria of 1918. Describing the United States as the "greatest and most powerful" country in the world, Schönemann told his readers that the German press's lurid emphasis upon kidnappings and scandals "over there" was misleading German readers. Contradicting illusions nurtured by Ross and Rechenberg, the professor warned his countrymen against expecting help from the German-American element. These people were, he said, as anti-Nazi as anyone else.

Schönemann was ambitious and opportunistic. In an advertisement for his own services, Schönemann advised the Nazis that only knowledgeable "America experts" should speak to the American public. The Nazi style would not do, for propaganda was a dirty word in the United States. Schönemann was depicting a hostile American public, whose views he, the professor, could change for the better.

In 1936, Schönemann returned to America, this time as a secret intelligence agent. Schönemann traveled to the Midwest, where Roosevelt was campaigning for reelection. Pretending to be a foreign journalist, Schönemann accompanied FDR on a campaign swing through Nebraska. Roosevelt, he reported, was capable of waging war in the name of peace and could easily become a second Wilson. America, Schönemann believed, "represents a danger of the first magnitude, threatening our security and our future." This was a rather extraordinary insight, for by 1936 President Roosevelt had said relatively little in public about Hitler's Germany. FDR hardly appeared to be Hitler's most dangerous enemy, especially since Congress had passed stringent neutrality legislation. Schönemann believed otherwise, for he saw Roosevelt as Nazi Germany's harbinger of doom.[9]

Schönemann was more alarmist than most of his colleagues. Professor Fritz Berber, an important consultant to the Foreign Ministry, argued that Roosevelt's America had surrendered some of Wilson's claims in defending of the rights of a neutral power. Even so, Berber was cautious about the long-term prospects for the new American neutrality. This was a volatile decade, and America was an explosive country. What Congress did, it could quickly undo. Furthermore, Berber warned, the president could apply the neutrality laws in ways not foreseen or intended by Congress. Conceived in the American interest, they could be discarded when they appeared to conflict with the welfare of the United States. Berber later became the leading Nazi expert on Roosevelt's violation of the neutrality concept.[10]

Schönemann, meanwhile, was careful to pander to the prejudices of Nazi ideologues. As much as he despised Colin Ross, he adopted some of his rhetoric. The professor, for example, now ascribed anti-Nazi sentiment in the United States to the machinations of American Jews, such as Secretary of the Treasury Henry Morgenthau, Jr., and Congressman Samuel Dickstein. He also used code words that were becoming popular among the Nazis, such as "Jew country" (*Judenland*) as a synonym for the United States. Despite these tributes to Nazi stereotypes, Schönemann convinced himself that he could modify German policy. Schönemann argued that the United States was moving in the direction of state socialism, just as Germany had done since March 1933. The American tradition of egalitarianism bore, he claimed, similarities to the Nazi *Volksgemeinschaft* (people's community).

In 1937, the professor journeyed once again to the United States, where he expressed his dismay about German hostility to the American way of life. Schönemann spent part of a semester as a visiting professor at the University of Nebraska, returning to the Reich in April. By May, he was warning a Berlin audience against disregarding the volatile nature of American public opinion. Isolation, Schönemann argued, could yield to war mobilization "within a few hours," so long as Americans perceived their cause to be a just one. Speaking to an audience that included Nazi officials, the professor denounced the German press. He covered himself by ascribing American anti-Nazism to the Jews, the communists, and the British, but Schönemann minced no words in concluding that ". . . it is rather foolish, and at the same time dangerous, for a certain section of the German press to indulge in wholesale criticism of the United States."

By 1939, Schönemann foresaw the looming catastrophe, and he tried to warn the regime about it. In *Democracy and Foreign Policy in the U.S.A.*, the professor told his readers that America was preparing for war against Germany. Schönemann clearly understood the manipulative powers and "personal magnetism" of President Roosevelt. The president was on a course that "threatens our security and our future." "What makes

President Roosevelt so dangerous today," he wrote, "is not Wall Street or the investment in armaments, important as they are, but rather the ideology of the American people."

Hitler ignored Schönemann's warnings, and with good reason. If the professor was right, only the destruction of the Nazi regime would satisfy the American president and much of his nation.

Schönemann returned to academic obscurity, writing occasional bits of journalism. Hitler probably never read his writings, though some of Schönemann's warnings reappeared in diplomatic dispatches to which the dictator had direct access.

In the winter of 1937, while Professor Schönemann mulled over his notes concerning his tour with Roosevelt, Ambassador Hans Luther sent an important cable to Berlin. He emphasized growing American interest in the affairs of Europe. This concern, said Luther, had nurtured the widespread conviction that "a European war or a second world war is now merely a question of time." Americans believed, he continued, that democracy and fascism were "two forces engaged in combat and in a struggle for supremacy." While isolationist sentiment still prevailed, and might preserve American neutrality in the event of war, Luther was troubled by an opposing tendency. The press, he implied, if manipulated by an interventionist leader, could undermine the isolationist consensus. "Although, as Germans," Luther concluded, "we know that the idea of a German aggressive war belongs to the realm of feverish fantasy, unfortunately we cannot count upon this being recognised in America."[11] Here, in broad brush strokes, Luther had depicted the pattern of events that would culminate in a great crisis.

Some months after the publication of Schönemann's book on foreign policy, Hitler summoned Colin Ross to a private audience. He had described this journalist as a "very clever man," and listened to him carefully. Ross favored the führer with his theories about a looming imperialist struggle between America and the British Empire. Ross asked Hitler for his government's assistance in preparing a propaganda map calculated to augment Anglo-American tensions through exploiting American anti-Semitism. He suggested that Germany strengthen its ties to the German-American element, and favored using American anti-Semitism against British interests in the Western Hemisphere. Ross assured Hitler that FDR's hostility resulted from his sense of inferiority to the great führer. This amalgam of fantasy and flattery pleased Hitler, who ordered his foreign ministry to cooperate in the production of the map.[12]

The writings of Banse, Ross, and Rechenberg were preparing National Socialists for a global struggle between two incompatible societies. Evidence that undermined this picture was brushed aside in National Socialist circles. The regime however, also needed to make sure that its *Feindbild* (image of the enemy) convinced the German people of American perfidy.

This time, no American siren song would lull the Reich into laying down its arms.

CHAPTER FOUR

AMERIKA: LAND OF JEWS AND JAZZ

CONCERNED ABOUT LINGERING popular sympathy for the United States, Nazi party leaders inaugurated a propaganda campaign calculated to inoculate the German masses against a false view of America. Drawing upon themes popular since the turn of the century, leaders such as Joseph Goebbels, Robert Ley, and Julius Streicher portrayed the United States as a corrupt society whose fate was a warning to spiritual and political opponents of Nazi Germany. The Nazis had access to more accurate sources of information, however.

In the spring of 1933, Hjalmar H.G. Schacht, the fifty-six-year-old president of the Reichsbank, reported to the new German government on his recent visit to the United States. Schacht, a brilliant financier whose arrogance masked a shameless opportunism, had spoken with President Roosevelt. He found the president to be animated and cordial, but there was no mistaking Roosevelt's warning about Hitler's policies. The persecution of the Jews was bound, he said, to strain relations between Germany and the United States. Roosevelt warned

Schacht that German talk about rearmament was making a negative impression in the United States. Upon returning to Germany, Schacht cautiously understated some of his conclusions, but his sense of foreboding was clear. Schacht's report was filed, then forgotten. No one in the Foreign Ministry paid it any heed.[1]

During the next few years, the German Foreign Ministry went through a period of inner conflict. Professional diplomats sought to maintain a certain objectivity in the face of growing Nazi pressures. Some of these men tried to convey the true situation to their new masters, usually by wrapping unpalatable facts in Nazi packages. Dispatches containing accurate reports on anti-Nazi sentiment in America might thus conclude by referring to "Jewish wire-pullers" as the source of anti-Nazi attitudes. The United States hosted, according to one report, the "strongest Jewish propaganda machine in the world."[2]

In Hamburg, the Foreign Ministry established a secret intelligence committee, or *Aufklärungsausschuss.* Its operatives obtained their data from persons who worked as shipping agents. They also culled through articles in the American press, wrote reports on U.S. business and industry, and analyzed American attitudes toward the new German regime. Agents working for the Hapag-Lloyd shipping line, for example, reported in 1934 that the anti-Nazi boycott, directed against German exports, was winning support among many non-Jews in the United States. The press and the radio media were also moving toward support of the boycott. Dr. Goebbels's belligerent statements were hurting the German cause. One informant enclosed a copy of an article entitled "Hitlerism Invades America," calculated to impress Hamburg with the extent of American anti-Nazi sentiment.[3]

The widely respected German Academic Exchange Service (DAAD) was a major source of intelligence about opinion in the United States. And DAAD's files were filled with alarming incidents. At the University of Cincinnati, the dean of the graduate school had warned DAAD that cooperation with its service would end if German students were required to swear an oath to the Hitler regime before leaving for the United States. The dean also tried to persuade German visitors not to give public speeches defending the Third Reich. DAAD's reports went to the National Socialist German Students' League, as well as to the foreign section of the German Student Office. Foreign Ministry officials had access to the material, but few officials made use of these potentially important files.

The Reich Students' League (RSL), for example, distributed press bulletins warning about "communist" agitation on American campuses, but usually ignored more realistic information provided by German exchange students. Reports describing American students as eager to learn and determined to succeed received scant attention. Nor did one hear much about their growing interest in global tensions. RSL accounts portrayed young Americans as childlike and shallow. Occasionally, the RSL's bulletin published dissenting articles, but these tended to disappear into musty files, for they violated the National Socialist consensus about *Amerika*.[4]

One of Dr. Paul Joseph Goebbels's great talents lay in his ability to share (to the point of mimicry) Hitler's enthusiasms and phobias. Reich minister for popular enlightenment and propaganda from March 1933, Goebbels became a major player in the hate-America campaign waged by the German media.[5] The German propaganda machine soon raised its decibel level. The barrage of hatred, in turn, reinforced Hitler's view of the United States. Goebbels, perceiving this, quickly launched even more strident attacks. American reaction, when reported to the German government, only confirmed Hitler's hostile views. It did not occur to leading Nazis that German policies and Nazi propaganda accounted for much of the grim news across the ocean. Goebbels's propagandists failed to grasp the lessons of the Great War. Illusion reigned, in the press and on the screen.

The dramatic film *Der Kaiser von Kalifornien* (The Emperor of California), starred the famous Luis Trenker. The story takes place during the California gold rush of the mid-nineteenth century. The hero, a hardy pioneer named John (Johann August) Sutter, has come to the United States from Germany. He migrates by covered wagon to the West, stoically enduring every hardship. Settling near Sacramento, he turns the arid land into a lush garden. Sutter marries, raises children, and is happy in every way. Then, the idyll abruptly comes to an end. Gold is discovered by a hired hand.

Sutter, foreseeing the tragedy that greed can bring, wants to keep the discovery secret. He fails to do so, and the county is overrun with hungry prospectors. Nobody works; everyone searches the streams for the precious metal. The land is raped by avaricious barbarians. Cheap bars and lawlessness defile the region. Sutter cannot find anyone who will do an honest day's work for him. The banks threaten to foreclose. Even his sons yield to the lust for filthy lucre, staking out claims on his property. They pay with their lives for this greed, for they are shot by a thug, who is not apprehended. Crippled by debts and harassed by his neighbors, Sutter is swindled out of his land. In despair, he goes off to serve in the United States Army, returning as a general. He intends to regain his land. A mob demands that Sutter give up his just claim, but he replies, "I insist on my rights!" He wins his lawsuit, thus regaining the property. A mob riots, burning down buildings on Sutter's property. Sutter kills his chief tormentor, but loses his best friend in the process.

The dramatic final scene shows Sutter in his army uniform, slowly walking up the steps of the Supreme Court building in Washington. He is old but not broken. Sutter's last vision is that of America dominated by great cities and smoke-belching factories, a world of pure materialism. He collapses on the steps. The promise of justice goes unfulfilled in the land of *unbegrenzte Möglichkeiten* (limitless possibilities). This scene represented a powerful warning to those Germans who rejected Nazi ideology.[6]

The German media played upon the public's fear of the colored peoples in their denunciations of America. In the 1930s, writers like Colin Ross and Johannes Stoye denounced American race mongrelization. Stoye, borrowing from Swiss psychoanalyst Carl Gustav Jung, mused, "The American provides the curious spectacle of a European with the manners of a Negro and the soul of an Indian." Nazi writers warned that America had produced a new threat to Western civilization, a mongrelized Negro who would soon outreproduce the white races. The film *Hans Westmar* (1933) was calculated to bring this fear home to German audiences. In one scene, set in a decadent Berlin nightclub in the late 1920s, black American swing musicians play a takeoff on the German patriotic hymn "The Watch on the Rhine." The indignant Nazi hero (modeled on the murdered Nazi "blood martyr" Horst Wessel) stops the band, crying out, "Not that song, not in a place like this!"[7]

Goebbels and Hitler wished to prepare the German people for ideological and perhaps military conflict with the United States. Obsession with American "treachery" in 1918 and 1919 provided Goebbels's men with much of their script. Sullen resentment, jealousy, and illusion took precedence over comprehension of the past.

The Nazi popular press presented America as "Dollarland," the home of plutocracy, pornography, race mongrelization, and Jewry. Having suppressed democracy at home, the Nazis needed to discredit it abroad.

A bulletin known as *Zeitschriften-Dienst* (Periodicals Service, or PS) provided the print media with approved information about the United States.[8] Publications were expected to work this subject matter into articles, though lazy (and cautious) editors and writers often published it verbatim. PS dispensed praise and criticism; one careless (or honest) writer found his piece listed on PS's "Please not this!" list, for he had praised Roosevelt as a charismatic and resourceful leader. PS favored themes such as "USA: Country Without a Social Policy," replete with details about strikes and unemployment. PS cautioned editors to avoid specific discussion of American wages, hours in the work week, or unemployment. It encouraged the discussion of child labor, migrant workers, infant mortality, and syphilis. Writers must be careful not to call American farmers "peasants," but they were free to blame Jewish capitalists for the plight of poor farmers. PS urged editors to commission articles blaming some of the Americans' problems on their irrational boycott of German goods.

By the late 1930s, the Nazi-controlled media had reached a consensus: The Jew, the source of all evil, dominated American society. A favorite quotation was ascribed to the economic historian Werner Sombart: "Americanism is nothing less . . . than the Jewish spirit distilled." The conclusion seemed inescapable that FDR disliked Hitler because he was a tool of the Jews, or a Jew himself. Much of the anti-Semitic material reached the press through a bulletin published regularly by the Institute for the Study of the Jewish Question, headquartered in Frankfurt. The influential *National Socialist Correspondence,* an important internal party bulletin, churned out similar material.

In Berlin, Dr. Eberhard Taubert of the Propaganda Ministry worked diligently through a "private" front organization, the General Association of German Anti-Communist Organizations. He assembled a huge number of newspaper clippings, book reviews, and translations from the foreign press (including Jewish publications). Typical of Taubert's work was the pamphlet "Jews Rule the Life of Non-Jews in the U.S.A." Two-thirds of the federal government's employees were Jews, it claimed, while other Jews controlled America's vice rackets, stock markets, and universities. According to Taubert's literature, the Jews even manipulated the Catholic Church.

As FDR evinced more hostility toward the Nazis, Taubert's propagandists gave a new twist to their anti-Semitism. The Jews, they averred, were pushing America into conflict with foreign powers. Jews in the fashion industry were militarizing dress styles, while "Jewish composers create military marches . . . made popular by the Jewish bandmasters."[9] Taubert made all of this material available to German editors. Much of the material distributed by Taubert could only mislead the media. Accuracy was irrelevant, however. The point was to confirm the National Socialist regime's worldview.

The leading Nazi daily, the *Völkischer Beobachter* soon informed its readers that ninety-seven percent of American newspaper publishers were Jews, as were seventy-six percent of the doctors and lawyers. The Jews even controlled eighty-seven percent of heavy industry. These absurd statistics stemmed from sources in Frankfurt, Berlin, and Nürnberg, and from anti-Semitic publications in the United States.[10] Dr. Robert Ley, Reich organization leader of the party, controlled the newspaper *Der Angriff* (The Attack). His paper concluded that American civilization consisted mainly of lynchings, gangsters, white slavery, unemployment, automobile mania, tap-dancing Negroes, and the third-degree police interrogation ("which usually ends in death"). *Der Angriff* declared, "This kind of civilization, by heaven, is not worth defending!"

Julius Streicher, the official *Gauleiter* or regional leader of Upper Franconia (Nürnberg), was an obsessive anti-Semite. His Jew-baiting often took the form of pornographic, sadistic rantings. Streicher's organ in his "work of enlightenment" was the newspaper *Der Stürmer* (The storm trooper). Many Nazi newspapers bemoaned the abduction and murder of Charles A. Lindbergh, Jr.'s son, describing it as a "typical American crime." Many people thought that Bruno Hauptmann, the German immigrant executed for the crime, had been the victim of a frame-up. *Der Stürmer,* however, came up with the theory that the crime was a Jewish plot—carried out for the purpose of obtaining the child's blood for a Purim ceremony. Streicher's clique concluded, "America is like an insane asylum—whoever makes the most noise wins."

Goebbels's ministry was obsessed with jazz. To Nazis, the bizarre rhythms and orgiastic seductiveness of jazz betokened a threat to civilization by Americanized African *Naturvölker* (peoples of nature). Jazz was banned from the German radio in 1935. Eugen Hadamovsky, director of broadcasting in the Reich, proclaimed, "Jazz is musical Bolshevism." Swing music was equally distasteful to Nazi prudes. For the next decade, alienated German youths shared their disenchantment with life in the Reich by dancing in secluded places to music recorded on forbidden gramophone platters. These young people liked to affect "British" styles of dress, ridicule the Hitler Youth, and engage in friendships (or worse) with foreign workers. Hamburg, with its "decadent" tradition of cosmopolitanism, was particularly vulnerable to the sounds of Duke Ellington and Benny Goodman. Admirers of jazz paid no heed to Nazi denunciations. This subversion angered high Nazi officials, including Goebbels; Reich leader of the SS, Heinrich Himmler; and Hitler's personal secretary, Martin Bormann.[11]

Nazi writers spent much of their time denouncing New York City, where German reporters charged the Jews with dominating rackets such as prostitution, usury, extortion, and drugs. In Heinz Halter's *The Polyp of New York*, the mafioso Lucky Luciano appears as a Jew enslaving Aryan girls on behalf of his lustful coreligionists.[12]

In Nazi propaganda, the enemy was one-dimensional; he was evil incarnate. In the late 1930s, Goebbels's associates made the mayor of New York City, Fiorello H. LaGuardia, their prime American target. LaGuardia relished the attacks, which did not hurt him politically in a city containing two million Jews. LaGuardia seemed to go out of his way to infuriate Goebbels's media hacks, treating the German regime as a kind of criminal mob, of the type that he was fighting in the gambling dens and on the streets of New York. He did untold damage to the image of the Third Reich in the United States.

During the winter of 1937, as officials were drafting their plans for the 1939 World's Fair in Flushing Meadows, LaGuardia suggested that the exposition contain a figure of Adolf Hitler "in a chamber of horrors." Referring to Hitler as a "brown-shirted fanatic," LaGuardia caused an international incident. The counselor of the German embassy, Dr. Hans Thomsen, protested to the State Department. Ambassador William E. Dodd countered by warning Foreign Minister Konstantin von Neurath of growing American unease over Nazi anti-Jewish policies. The foreign minister cut him off, as if this had nothing to do with the LaGuardia case. Secretary of State Cordell Hull, embarrassed by the incident, lamely pointed to his lack of authority in this situation.[13] LaGuardia easily won a second term in office.

The German News Agency then took to calling the mayor a "dirty Talmud Jew." Ley's *Der Angriff* fumed, "This shameless lout dared to doubt the Führer's love of peace. . . ." Referring to the mayor as a "Jewish apostle of hate," it described him as an accomplice of the Negroes. When LaGuardia compounded the injury by appearing at an anti-Nazi rally in Madison Square Garden, German headlines screamed, "AMERICAN JEW LEADERS INSULT THE GERMAN NATION."

Readers of the German press learned that "the scum of the city" had attended the meeting. LaGuardia now received the appellation "decomposed rot." Newspapers suggested that he was mentally ill and that he suffered from megalomania. The SS newspaper *Das schwarze Korps* (The Black Corps) published a cartoon depicting LaGuardia as King Kong. To much of the German press, LaGuardia was the symbol of Jewish-bolshevik control of the United States. The mayor became the "half-Jew" LaGuardia, a man whose mother, Irene Coen, was "a Sephardic Jew." LaGuardia soon declared that he would not call Hitler to account for these insults, for the Führer was not *satisfaktionsfähig*. (This meant that the German leader was of such low social status that a gentleman would not challenge him to a duel after being insulted by him.) After the predictable barrage of Nazi curses, LaGuardia announced that he was turning the German complaints over to his sewer commissioner.[14]

While outwardly outraged, astute German diplomats assumed a different tone when cabling their comments to Berlin. From New York City, Consul General Hans Borchers warned that press attacks on America, provoked by LaGuardia's behavior, had serious consequences. The United States, he reminded von Neurath, could conjure up huge armies from "nowhere." The attitude of the American people could, Borchers added, decide the "fate of the Third Reich." Ambassador Luther agreed, and warned that American opinion was turning against Germany. These insights made no discernible impact upon German press policy.[15]

Various Nazi writers now propounded unique interpretations of American history. One writer reminded his readers that Abraham Lincoln had told the Congress in 1789 (*sic*) that more Jews must be barred from entering the United States. Another Nazi wrote that the "foreign minister" of the Confederacy during the "Revolutionary War" (*sic*) was a Jew, Judah P. Benjamin. The *National Socialist Correspondence* specialized in denouncing Jewish exploitation in the Americas. Its writers argued that the Jews had profited most from the slave trade, in the process poisoning the blood of the Aryan peoples. After the Civil War, the Jews had bought up Southern plantations, then turned the poor former slaves into their permanent debtors. The Jews kept millions in poverty in order to enrich themselves. Jews were responsible for labor unrest. The American eagle had turned into a Jewish vulture.[16]

Baron Rechenberg, who contributed to Eberhard Taubert's antiSemitic front organizations, helped to build this party consensus. Reporting that West Coast longshore leader Harry Bridges was really named Izzy Heintz, Rechenberg accused him of conspiring with labor leader David Dubinski (*sic*) in a Red plot to destroy Christianity and gain world rule for the Jews. Taubert and Rechenberg liked to point to Yiddish newspapers in New York (such as the *Morgen Freiheit*) as their sources, for who was in a position to check them? Another America expert, Johannes Stoye, solemnly reported, "Italians take quickly, easily, to Anglo-Saxon customs and even become Methodists for the sake of assimilation." He did not reveal how many Italian Methodists he had met.[17]

Jews were indeed more prominent than ever before in American history. They worked for Roosevelt and his New Deal, made major advances in the professions and the arts, and often appeared as political radicals in various left-wing movements. Old barriers were falling, but the country was still troubled by economic political turmoil. In this setting, anti-Jewish sentiment thrived. The Nazis hoped to manipulate this situation for their own gain.

In the beginning of Roosevelt's first term, he had received a decent press in the young Third Reich. Writers sometimes compared his New Deal to the bold experiments undertaken by National Socialism. Between 1936 and 1939, however, Roosevelt changed from proto-fascist strongman to Jew-controlled troublemaker. Hitler was confident that American neutrality laws would shackle Roosevelt, but not forever. The German people must be disabused of any illusions about the president and his nation.

Nazi propagandists first turned to the president's entourage. Inspired by Goebbels's earlier attacks on German politicans, writers "unmasked" FDR's secretary of labor. "Behind the harmless name Frances Perkins," wrote one journalist, "really hides the Russian-born Matilda Rebecca Wutski." Treasury Secretary Henry Morgenthau was "a Jew with protruding, strongly short-sighted eyes behind thick pince-nez glasses." Supreme Court justice Felix Frankfurter appears as a "man of average height with strongly Jewish facial features . . ." a "trust-buster" who embraced monopoly capitalism once the Jews controlled it. The Jews, one writer believed, controlled Roosevelt through their "Brain Trust." "Wall Street pirate number one," financier and Roosevelt adviser Bernard Baruch, was guiding FDR toward another war of aggression against peaceful Germany. His goal was Jewish world power. [18]

Karl Goerdeler, the former mayor of Leipzig, watched these developments with growing concern. Goerdeler was convinced that a second, greater war was a strong possibility. He believed that the German people were becoming conditioned to thinking of America as an enemy. Goerdeler wanted to alter this mind-set. First, however, he had to change the views of the Nazi elite. During the winter of 1937–1938, Goerdeler journeyed to the United States. Upon his return to the Reich, the former mayor drafted a lengthy memorandum containing his observations. [19]

Goerdeler came home convinced that the entire Nazi consensus on America rested on false foundations. Far from being composed of a polyglot, fragmented series of ethnic groups, America was a nation with unique strengths and qualities. He described the quick assimilation process by which Germans turned into Americans. Goerdeler emphasized the economic might of a nation rich in coal, copper, iron ore, tin, gold, silver, and oil. The contrast with Hitler's vaunted efforts at "autarky" or self-sufficiency was clear. Goerdeler implied that American heavy industry could arm a powerful opponent.

Goerdeler demolished one Nazi argument after the other. Goebbels's ravings about exploitative American plutocracy held no water. Nor was American democracy on the verge of collapse. "This form of government," said Goerdeler, "is significantly stronger and more productive than Europeans imagine." The Americans, he continued, would master any challenge confronting them. Goerdeler warned his readers that Americans would not remain on the sidelines indefinitely in the event of a great European crisis. Two weeks after Goerdeler penned his memorandum, the German Wehrmacht crossed the Austrian border.

Goerdeler, frustrated by his inability to influence the Reich's rush toward catastrophe, became an anti-Hitler conspirator. He later played a prominent part in wartime efforts to overthrow the Hitler regime. Goedeler went into hiding after the 20 July 1944 attempt on the Führer's life. Hunted down by the Gestapo and captured, Karl Goerdeler was executed in February 1945.[20]

Nazi propaganda about the United States rested upon illusions, but its falsehoods vindicated a policy and an ideology that would change history. German propaganda about American disunion, decadence, and incipient fascism became more intense and widespread as crisis followed crisis. Coexisting with this public denunciation of America was Hitler's confused combination of respect and contempt for the one nation capable of crippling his bid for world hegemony.

PART
TWO

ROOSEVELT'S
GERMANY

CHAPTER
FIVE

COMING OF AGE IN AN
ANTI-GERMAN AMERICA

JAMES ROOSEVELT OF Hyde Park, New York, an aging country squire, Episcopal vestryman, and Wall Street investor, suffered from a heart ailment. He often traveled to Bad Nauheim in Germany, where he took the cure at the famous baths. On several occasions, James and his much younger wife, Sara Delano, brought their young son Franklin along on their trips to Germany. Sara, a domineering and imperious woman, believed in her precocious only child's special future. Like James, she had faith in the educational value of European travel. A young man of upper-class American stock must, they believed, acquire a veneer of sophistication. To James and Sara, this meant proficiency in foreign languages and exposure to the great European cultures. Thus, young Franklin D. Roosevelt came to know Germany and the Germans.

Franklin learned to read and speak some German. "I go to the public school . . . and we have German reading, German dictation, the history of Siegfried, and arithmetic," he wrote, "and I like it very much." Young Franklin thrilled to the Wagnerian music that surrounded him at the Bayreuth Festival. There was, however, a jarring note, for Franklin observed the Germans to be disciplined to the point of militarism. Franklin later had contradictory memories of his boyhood visits to the German Reich. He recalled, "I did not know Great Britain and France as a boy but I did know Germany. If anything, I looked upon the Germany that I knew with far more friendliness that I did on Great Britain or France."[1] At other times, FDR remembered having negative feelings about his days in Germany. His recollections, which were subject to the vagaries of politics, must be treated with caution.

Roosevelt's friendliness toward the Germans, if it ever existed at all, disappears from view during the decade before the First World War. A product of an Anglophile education at the Groton School and at Harvard University, Franklin quickly absorbed the growing Teutonophobia surrounding him. By the early years of this century, "old" American families like the Roosevelts viewed the arrogant Germany of Wilhelm II as an upstart nation, and a threatening one. To such people, the British Empire was a stabilizing force; Germany was revolutionary. From his Episcopalian faith, Franklin seems to have drawn a certain serenity of mood and an inner confidence. Such a man could hardly approve of the Teutonic bluster that so troubled the political landscape.[2] Franklin's cousin, President Theodore Roosevelt, fanned the young man's suspicions of German intentions. In the summer of 1905, after telling his mother about European admiration for Cousin Theodore, Franklin added a sour note. He wrote, "[T]he German tone seemed to hide a certain animosity and jealousy as usual."[3]

Domestic politics soon became the young man's main concern. Franklin won a seat in the state senate in Albany, where he made some powerful friends. During these last years of peace, Franklin D. Roosevelt was a fervent supporter of America's new naval power. His early travels and love of the sea made Franklin particularly susceptible to the writings of Alfred Thayer Mahan.

Born in 1840, Alfred Thayer Mahan graduated from the Naval Academy in 1859.[4] A pioneer of the new field of geopolitics as applied to the study of naval power, Mahan published *The Influence of Sea Power upon History, 1660–1783* in 1890, and soon thereafter *The Influence of Sea Power Upon the French Revolution and Empire* (2 volumes). These works influenced figures as diverse as Theodore Roosevelt and Wilhelm II of Germany. One thought would particularly interest Franklin D. Roosevelt. In a democracy, Mahan argued, leaders must see to it that the people are prepared for war. FDR would take to heart Mahan's demand that America be prepared to project sea power far from its shores. From his reading of Mahan, Roosevelt learned that a war, while called defensive, must conclude with the annihilation of the enemy, on or around his own sea approaches and territory.

In 1913, Woodrow Wilson took office. Franklin Roosevelt, a deserving Democrat with good connections and an even better name, was appointed assistant secretary of the navy. Two days after moving into his Washington office, Roosevelt welcomed a delegation of three French naval officers. They had come to the United States in order to establish trans-Atlantic telegraphic communications between France and North America. The symbolism of the visit is striking. Within a year and half, France would be looking to men like Franklin Roosevelt for a different kind of support. While a polarized Europe drifted toward crisis, the young politician favored closer cooperation with France's friend Great Britain. He believed, however, that the United States was safe, at least for the time being. Roosevelt embodied the self-confidence of a nation that had built the Panama Canal, one of the great engineering feats of the day. He never thought in defensive terms.

Roosevelt was always an "interventionist." In February, he observed, "Invasion is not what this country has to fear." "In time of war," Roosevelt stated, ". . . [o]ur national defense must extend all over the Western Hemisphere, must go out a thousand miles to sea. . . . We must create a navy not only to protect our shores and our possessions but our merchant ships in time of war, no matter where they may go."[5] This viewpoint can only be labeled American globalism. When FDR later spoke of "defense of the Western Hemisphere," and denounced involvement in "foreign wars," he usually did so for reasons of political expediency. As early as 1914, Roosevelt had come to fear Germany as the only viable competitor in the contest for ideological and economic hegemony.

When Franklin was a boy, he once declared, "I had a fight with a big boy of eleven because he cheated and I beat him." When the 1914 war erupted in Europe, Roosevelt saw the kaiser's Germany as the aggressor. Franklin's correspondence with Captain Mahan and Cousin Theodore reinforced Roosevelt's certainty. The more Roosevelt heard about the war, the more he recoiled at atrocities committed by the "Huns." Fear reinforced this revulsion. Deadly new German weapons, especially U-boats, now called into question America's age-old sense of oceanic security. Roosevelt returned to New York, where he lost a primary bid for a U.S. Senate seat. Coming back to Washington, he immersed himself in technical materials related to the navy.

Roosevelt's Germanophobia typified his generation, as well as his social class. When Franklin was a boy, German-Americans liked to quote Carl Schurz's reassuring thought: "[w]hile the Americans and the English are of kin in many important respects, and while they can and should do much in harmonious concurrence for the advancement of human civilization, their spheres of action are not the same." Prince Bismarck, a better political prophet, was warning his countrymen that linguistic ties between England and America could mightily affect the fate of the world in the twentieth century. Early in this century, the British Empire and the German Reich were becoming global adversaries. The United States, whose foreign policy was controlled by East Coast, upper-class leaders who greatly admired England, rapidly improved its relations with the British Empire.

German-American leaders, meanwhile, were complacent, and ignorant of what was happening around them. They knew that American children still read about the Revolution and the War of 1812, when England was the "bad guy." Thousands of Americans still recalled happy days at the German universities in Berlin, Heidelberg, and Halle. The industrial might and scientific achievements of Bismarck's Germany had gained much respect for the German Reich. Bismarck's restraint in the use of power caused the *New York Herald* to note, "One must go back to Charlemagne to find his equal." The *New York Times* gushed, "Bismarck is the greatest man in political history since the death of Napoleon."[6] Bismarck, however, left office in 1890. The next decade foreshadowed a drastic change in the American attitude.

The Americans had settled the West; some citizens now turned their gaze to lands across the seas. Many German industrialists, academics, and journalists favored an aggressive policy of imperial expansion. They lobbied for the acquisition of a great navy, colonies, coaling stations, and new markets for German industry. America was an industrial competitor. It, too, had its imperialist lobby; not content with a continent, some Yankees wanted to seize the Spanish Empire. When Ambassador Andrew D. White arrived in Berlin in 1897, he was surprised by the extent of anti-American sentiment.

The United States embarked upon its great imperial adventure just as Emperor Wilhelm II resolved to make Germany a *Weltmacht* (a world power). Herein lay the seeds of conflict.

Germans were slow to perceive the sea change in American attitudes toward Great Britain. After all, American politicians ranging from the conservative reformer Grover Cleveland to the prairie populist William Jennings Bryan won political points by "twisting the British lion's tail." American radicals accused the Bank of England of "crucifying" the American farmer on a "cross of gold." A large body of Irish Catholics held Britain accountable for sins committed against their forebears and brethren in Ireland.[7]

These feelings remained strong, but their ability to affect American foreign policy was in decline. The British Empire faced crises all around the world. Economic competition, imperialist conflicts, and the burden of global governance were sapping England's strength. The empire would have to retrench; it would need allies in order to safeguard its vital interests. As America gained strength relative to Britain, her political and economic elites looked more kindly upon the British Empire. Common interests and shared fears replaced an outmoded enmity.

There was now a good deal of talk about "racial solidarity." The Pittsburgh industrialist Andrew Carnegie, himself born a Scotsman, urged the "whole Anglo-Celtic race to get together." Brooks Adams, an American historian, wrote, "The support of the United States may . . . be said to be vital to England. . . ." He argued that "Great Britain may . . . be not inaptly described as a fortified outpost of the Anglo-Saxon race. . . ."[8] In Britain, the prestigious *Review of Reviews* endorsed the unification of the Anglo-Saxon world, as did well-known writers such as Conan Doyle and James Bryce. A British correspondent reported, "The most astonishing feature of the present time is the sudden transition in this country from Anglophobia to the most exuberant affection for England & 'Britishers' in general." Ideology and religion ratified thus choices imposed by political, economic, and military necessity.

The war between Spain and the United States represented a dramatic turning point in Anglo-American relations. The war was really a struggle for an overseas empire. British diplomacy undermined continental attempts to prevent the Americans from gaining control of the Spanish Empire, including Puerto Rico and the Philippines. Americans heard troubling (but unfounded) news about a threatening German naval force anchored off the Philippines.

Fearing that German and Russian ambition would jeopardize their economic interests, the Anglo-Saxon powers collaborated in developing the "Open Door" policy. Powerful British politicians like Joseph Chamberlain and Arthur Balfour strengthened their ties to the United States. On this side of the Atlantic, Senator Henry Cabot Lodge of Massachusetts declared, "If I had my way I should be glad to have the United States say to England that we would stand by her in her declaration that the ports of China must be opened to all nations equally or to none. . . ."

The British were not turning to Washington out of sentimentality. Unsteady in its course, giving out great clouds of bluster, the Reich frightened those who stood in its way. The kaiser was determined to build a modern navy, in order to bluff his way to territorial and political gains around the globe. He appeared to be an international troublemaker, determined to change the map of the world.[9] Wilhelm publicly gloated at Britain's discomfiture during its war with the Boers in southern Africa, and he attempted (with some fleeting success) to organize Europe against the British Empire. The American historian Henry Adams later recalled "the sudden appearance of Germany as the Grizzly terror which in twenty years effected what Adamses had tried for two hundred years in vain—frightened England into America's arms. . . ."[10]

The Boer War in southern Africa during the years 1899–1902 had exposed Britain's military vulnerability, and foreshadowed the end of its African hegemony. The British, having for a century experienced of imperial pride, understood America's new joy in overseas adventure. Britain surrendered her right to be America's partner in the construction and defense of a Central American canal linking the Atlantic and Pacific oceans.[11] By 1901, Britain had agreed to American construction, ownership, and fortification of the future canal.

The Americans were propounding a new interpretation of the Monroe Doctrine, one that antagonized various European foreign ministries. Originally intended to prevent Spain from retaking her former colonies, the doctrine was now used to justify American overlordship in the Americas, particularly around the Caribbean Basin. In 1902–1903, a consortium of European creditor powers decided to force repayment from their debtor, defaulting Venezuelan dictator Cipriano Castro. The Germans took the lead, dispatching a naval squadron to the Caribbean, where it sank several Venezuelan gunboats. This enraged President Theodore Roosevelt and the American public. The British, who were part of the creditor cartel, cleverly distanced themselves from the Germans. London asked young Franklin's cousin, President Theodore Roosevelt, to mediate the dispute. It eventually wound up before the International Court in the Hague. The clumsiness of the Germans and their lack of tact made them easy propaganda targets. The bellicose moves of Kaiser Wilhelm II and the ill-considered actions of his government brought England and America closer together.[12] The British, concerned about a German naval buildup, now had an alarmed friend in Washington.

Arthur James Balfour, prime minister of Great Britain from 1902 to 1905 told a cheering Liverpool audience, "We welcome any increase of the influence of the United States of America in the Western Hemisphere." He added, "[T]he Monroe Doctrine has no enemies in this country that I know of." In contrast, British writers asked, "Are people in Berlin crazy? Don't they know that they are inflaming public opinion more and more here?" After the Venezuelan affair, British diplomats reported, "[O]ne would be amazed at the language held in regard to her [Germany] by men in the highest positions in Washington." American politicians were describing the kaiser as "unstable, crazy . . . not to be trusted."[13]

British observers were a bit disingenuous, for, as an American reporter observed, "It was from a British news agency or through the English dispatches that we derived all our European news." Books published in Britain often appeared a year later in American editions. Americans, including the recent Harvard graduate Franklin D. Roosevelt, were looking at Germany through British eyes.

British reporters, authors, and diplomats were careful to provide their American cousins with harrowing examples of German intentions in the New World. Henry Cabot Lodge learned from unnamed sources, "[W]e may find ourselves called upon to protect Brazil or some other South American State from invasion [by Germany]." Lodge had heard that "three hundred thousand Germans" lived there. German imperialists railed against the Monroe Doctrine. "We cannot," said one blustering patriot, "and will not allow ourselves to be shut out from the only portion of the globe still left to us." The American ambassador noted with displeasure that the Berlin press had taken on a decided anti-American tone, subjecting American democracy to repeated ridicule.[14]

On the surface, relations between the United States and Germany remained correct. Kuno Francke, a distinguished professor of German

at young FDR's Harvard University, found many American readers for
his books emphasizing the humanistic aspects of German culture.
Prince Henry of Prussia was well received during his American tour. At
the end of 1903, President Theodore Roosevelt even told the kaiser, "I
doubt whether anywhere outside of your own country Your Majesty has
more sincere admirers than here in America." The president's private
sentiments were far more critical, however. And the kaiser sourly mut-
tered, "South America is of no concern to the Yankees." Referring to
the naval race he had unleashed, Wilhelm accused the Americans of
building a fleet "in the same manner that rich parvenues like to maintain a stable of race horses."[15] Wilhelm mused about uniting Latin
America against the Yankees: "If we were strong enough on the sea, we
would then find out what the possibilities were."

Franklin D. Roosevelt realized that his beloved New England coast-
line might at some point be vulnerable to foreign invasion or to bombardment. FDR recalled the fear that gripped New Yorkers back in
1898, during the Spanish-American War, when word spread about possible bombardment by enemy warships. Yet the Germans were far
stronger than the Spaniards, and apparently more aggressive, even
"crazy."

The East Coast elite, including men such as Elihu Root, Theodore
Roosevelt, Henry Cabot Lodge, and Princeton University president
Woodrow Wilson, reflected and promoted the new Anglo-American
solidarity, as did the establishment press. The newer, more sensational
popular newspapers tended to play upon the fears of their readers.
Germany became a tempting subject, with the kaiser supplying a lot of
material. By 1910, many Americans had become accustomed to thinking of Britain as a friend. Germany, however, was often viewed as an
unpredictable, perhaps dangerous, stranger, but one who did not yet
live in the immediate neighborhood.

By 1913, this had changed. Americans now reacted almost as negatively as Britons to militaristic books translated from German. The
works of General Friedrich von Bernhardi offer a case in point. *Britain
as Germany's Vassal, How Germany Wages War,* and *Germany and the Next
War* did not win friends for the kaiser's Reich.[16] Too many German
writers and speech makers appeared to view the world in apocalyptic
terms. *Weltmacht oder Untergang* (world power or collapse) seemed to be
their frightening watchword. As if in response to a German challenge,
Anglo-Saxon writers such as Charles Homer Lea preyed upon the pub-

lic's growing fear of the Reich's power. Lea's *The Day of the Saxon* bemoaned the decline of the British Empire. This best-selling book implied that only an Anglo-Saxon alliance could block Teutonic domination of the world. This was prophetic.[17]

Captain Mahan paid a good deal of attention to writers like General von Bernhardi. He believed that the United States could not ignore the fact that Germany was building some of the best battleships in the world. The *Army and Navy Register* wrote that the German fleet could one day render "European defiance of our tradition complete and effective." America had to be ready for a naval war with Germany, and by 1913 American military planners were preparing for such a contingency. Yet, aside from Captain Mahan and a few of his devotees (such as Franklin D. Roosevelt), Americans did not foresee the imminent conflict that would change their lives.

Price Collier's influential book *Germany and the Germans From an American Point of View*, which Roosevelt read, described Germans who viewed the British as "they would be were Germany in their place." Arrogant and brutal, Collier's Germans were tactless as well. Diplomat Herbert von Dirksen asked, "By what right does America attempt to check the strongest expansion policy of all other nations of the earth?" Collier told his American readers that the German press ridiculed "provincial Yankee intellects," people living in a land called "Dollarika."

Americans and Germans were engaged in creating two *Feindbilder*, two inverted images of an enemy.

Price Collier described the Germans as "lethargic about liberty," as a paranoid nation agitated by a saber-rattling kaiser. Collier left Germany with a longing for the Germany of the past, when culture and learning seemed more important than militarist bluster. He concluded with some wishful thinking about the kaiser: "Here's long life to your power, Sir, and to your possessions, and to you! And as an Anglo-Saxon, I thank God, that all your countrymen are not like you!"[18]

Young Franklin Roosevelt (who, despite his Dutch name, was of almost pure Anglo-Saxon descent) shared these sentiments. As he played politics in Albany, Manhattan, and Washington, and sailed in Long Island Sound and Chesapeake Bay, FDR's views about Germany and the role of the American navy were becoming more firmly fixed in his mind.

CHAPTER
SIX

FDR'S FIRST GERMAN WAR

T O MANY AMERICAN OBSERVERS, the "land of poets and thinkers" had transformed itself into a country of arrogant, strutting martinets. The German was now the bully. Most Americans did not equate the blustering kaiser with the local "Dutchmen" with whom they played sandlot baseball, but some Americans were beginning to worry about the role of "hyphenated" ethnics in the national life.

Since 1898, German-American leaders like Julius Goebel had opposed American imperialism, in part because it might enmesh the United States in a conflict with the ambitious German Reich. Leaders of the German-American Alliance had maintained friendly ties with the imperialist Pan-German League. Members of the alliance often expressed sympathy with the plight of an Irish population oppressed by British tyranny. England was the common enemy of both ethnic groups.[1] Who were these potential victims of Anglo-American entente, these millions of men and women known as "German-Americans"?

They had come by the thousands from across the sea, Swabian peasants, Saxon metalworkers, and Hanoverian religious dissidents, migrating to the shores of the New World from small towns and farming villages. Fleeing political and religious oppression, as well as wars and conscription, these Germans risked the hazardous, miserable journey across the North Atlantic hoping to find freedom and prosperity. Upon arriving in North America, they formed German-speaking islands in an English sea.

By the time of the American Revolution, almost one out of ten American colonists was of German origin. Half of these Germans in America lived in Pennsylvania. Their English-speaking neighbors saw them as pious, hardworking, and very frugal, though some of their "English" neighbors objected to the Germans' occasional fondness for taverns and smoking pipes.

The Germans' carefully tended farms dotted the lush southern Pennsylvania countryside. Community life centered around the churches, whose many different religious denominations and sects reflected the divisions of the old *Vaterland*. The Germans seemed to define liberty as the right to live and worship as they pleased, without pressure from the state. They had no intention of remaking the new land in the image of the old. The result was a rapid linguistic assimilation, especially after the Revolution. By the turn of the century, many of the German congregations were using the English language. One pastor in Lancaster sadly recalled, "I worked against the English as long as I could. . . ."[2]

Over the next three decades, Germans responded enthusiastically to books that glorified faraway America as a virgin paradise, a land of unlimited opportunity. Gottfried Duden's widely read book *Reports on a Journey to the Western States of North America and of a Several-Year Stay on the Missouri* told of the good life of the slave owner, and of the physical beauty of the New World.[3] The German mass migration to America was beginning; shipowners' agents scoured German towns and villages, looking for likely prospects. (They received a commission for each German leaving for America.)

Lutherans and Catholics, Pietists and Mennonites, freethinkers and radicals, they journeyed to America. Some emigrants were relatively well-off, possessing coins or valuables worth one hundred dollars in American money. Most were poor; they were often artisans displaced by the advent of new industrial machinery in the textile industry. Many were fleeing Prussian military conscription, or widespread agricultural depression. Adventurers and other black sheep joined their ranks. Sometimes, the entire village would make the decision about who should leave. It was common for families to depart together. At the appointed hour, a band would play; tearful embraces and farewells preceded the last parting.

Eighty thousand German emigrants arrived in the United States in 1846 alone. Having come to an East Coast port, or perhaps to New Orleans, the Germans usually thought first about settling down and farming. The gentle hills of Pennsylvania and, later, of Wisconsin would remind many new Americans of their German homeland.[4]

By this time, a debate had broken out among the Germans about their identity in the New World. A minority of the immigrants passionately advocated the ideal of total separation from the "English." In 1836, the German Society of Philadelphia urged "partial isolation" upon its members, so that they could "enjoy both the advantages of America and the pleasures of the Fatherland." Eleven years later, Franz Löher, a Bavarian architect, published his *History and Conditions of the Germans in America*. Löher had little sympathy for English-speaking Americans. He particularly disliked their puritanism and their slave-holding, not to speak of their antiforeignism. Löher feared that the Germans would be absorbed, losing their ethnic identity. He was dismayed by German *Vereinsmeierei*, the dispersal of German energies in thousands of clubs. He urged the Germans to build a powerful "New Germany" in America, one that would hold the balance of power while preserving German ways. A united Germany, Löher hoped, would soon proceed to help the Germans in America, while "New Germany" assisted the old *Vaterland*.[5]

The bustling, expansive America of President Andrew Jackson's day rendered such isolation impractical. Most of those committed to isolation eventually departed from their German utopias and wound up living among "English" in farm country along the Mississippi Valley, or someplace similar.[6] The lack of a common political background further undermined attempts to create a Germany-in-America. The great political theorist Francis Lieber spoke for a majority of Germans in America when he denounced the separatist fantasy. "[W]ithin less than fifty years," wrote this transplanted South Carolinian, "our colony would degenerate into an antiquated, ill-adapted element of our great national system, with which, sooner or later, it must assimilate. . . ."[7] Widespread talk about German voting power in the presidential election of 1844 strengthened the assimilationist thesis. The election of James K.

Polk supposedly showed that the Germans had emerged as a power in American national politics.

The revolutions of 1848 in Germany ignited much enthusiasm among Germans in the United States. More controversial was the radical rhetoric of some German revolutionaries. By 1849, Prussian arms had crushed the popular movement for unity and freedom. Many political refugees now fled to America, among them leaders like Karl Heinzen and Friedrich Hecker. Great crowds assembled to hear their impassioned appeals for a new Germany. As in 1848, however, most Germans in America responded with sympathy rather than with arms or money. Except for these newer political emigrés, the Germans in America intended to stay here. More and more, they reflected American values and argued about American problems. These second- and third-generation German-Americans attended Sunday *Gottesdienst*, drank German-style beer, and eagerly read three-month-old letters from the *Vaterland*, but they were becoming fixtures on the American scene. The new refugees either returned home, to further embitterment, or blended into the German communities in the United States.[8]

In the year 1854 alone, 215,000 German arrivals accounted for more than half the immigrants to the United States. Five million Germans emigrated to the New World during the last seven decades of the nineteenth century, over twenty-five percent of the total European immigration during that era.[9] Most would probably have agreed with Missouri political leader Carl Schurz, who told them, "It is only here that you realize how superfluous governments are in many affairs in which, in Europe, they are considered indispensable, and how the possibility of doing something inspires a desire to do it."

Antiforeign movements in the United States had been around for decades, often taking the form of attacks on Freemasonry and other "secret societies." In the 1850s, the Germans had to confront a new, powerful threat to their continued immigration and life-style. Economic upheavals, the bitter national debate about the extension of slavery, and an anti-Catholic, anti-immigrant frenzy gripped much of the country. "Native Americans" of English stock, grouped in the so-called "Know Nothing" party, railed against the Germans. They accused these "foreigners" of desecrating the Sabbath by sitting around drinking beer. One judge said that he even preferred Negroes to "emigrants from the land of Kraut." Nativist pressures compelled many German communities to fight back against puritanical blue laws. The antiforeign hysteria ended the German debate about isolation or assimilation. One could disprove the tenets of American fanatics only by displaying an overt loyalty to American values.

A new political party emerged at this time, in part as a successor to the failed Whigs. It welcomed the German element. The Republicans won the support of those who opposed the extension of slavery to the West. "Free soil and free labor" was an appealing concept to most of the Germans, particularly to those who had migrated westward over the course of the decades.[10] When the final crisis of the Civil War came, Germans flocked to the side of President Abraham Lincoln. The "Dutchmen," great in number and stalwart soldiers, caused Rebel generals no end of grief. The Union was saved, and the loyalty of the German element was no longer in doubt. People soon began to speak of "German-Americans."

A golden age had arrived. The foundation of the German Empire in less than a decade later further strengthened German pride. Two strong unions had come into being. Most Germans in the United States remained Republicans. They worked hard, attended their *Vereine* (clubs), drank in their beer gardens, and read one or more of the many thriving German-language newspapers. The Germans turned the celebration of the memory of General Friedrich Wilhelm von Steuben, who helped America become a free nation, into a glorious reminder of German contributions to American freedom. Sentimental Christmas gatherings impressed non-Germans, who soon adopted various German customs and songs. "O Christmas Tree" and "Silent Night" became as "native" as they once had been German.[11]

The federal census of 1900 indicated that almost 6.25 million persons were the offspring of German-born parents. More than 1.5 million people had a German-born father or mother. The next census showed that over 8.25 million Americans were of German birth, or were the children of at least one German parent. On the eve of the First World War, more than one-quarter of the Caucasian population had some German ancestral heritage. Now established as part of the nation, Germans no longer feared repression.

By the turn of the century, some members of the community were voicing concern about the loss of the German heritage. The distinguished historian A.B. Faust praised German-Americans for their "vigor, sturdiness, and vitality," but worried about the "equal distribution of the German population over the whole territory of the United States." Other critics, referring to the German-American community as a "melting iceberg," contrasted German political lassitude with the aggressive machine politics of Irish immigrants in Boston and New York. Pastors complained that young seminarians no longer received rigorous training in Lutheran theology.

Though American in spirit, German-language newspapers represented a living tie to the old *Vaterland*. Though there were 537 German-language newspapers in the United States in 1914, their great age of expansion was over. Journalists bemoaned the younger generation's ignorance of the German language. New German-language publications rarely appeared.[12] An alarm was sounded by Julius Goebel, a professor of German language and literature at Stanford University, and later at the University of Illinois. Goebel accused assimilationists like Carl Schurz of promoting a negative image of Germans as "beer-swilling musicians and clowns." The work of Prince Bismarck was a source of pride to all Germans. It should, Goebel believed, also inspire German-Americans. Goebel, like Faust, argued that the dispersal of the Germans among endless numbers of petty *Vereine* doomed attempts to preserve their great heritage. This situation must, he argued, be changed. The professor, however, rejected separatist fantasies, declaring, "What we have in mind is not a new Germany in America. . . ." Carl Ruemelin, a leader of Cincinnati's large German community, put it this way: "It is necessary for us to declare . . . that we have succeeded in remaining honorably German without at the same time being untrue to our new Fatherland."[13]

In 1901, the new German-American National Alliance began to work for the promotion of the German language in the public schools, opposition to puritanical blue laws, and amicable relations between the United States and the German Reich. Dr. Charles J. Hexamer, president of the alliance, advocated the "assimilation of the best German ideals with our American ideals." The alliance was soon active in forty states, and by 1914 claimed a membership of two million people. Hexamer and other alliance leaders hoped that young people, often the children or grandchildren of immigrants and secure in their Americanism, would embrace their German heritage. An optimistic Julius Goebel felt vindicated by the strength of the alliance. "An ethnic element," he wrote, "held together for two centuries by common ties of language, customs, and outlook, and that has, despite the loss of millions of people to an inferior civilization, preserved its unity within the body of the American nation, cannot disappear." (An unfortunate touch of arrogance often marred the statements of German-American leaders.) Deceived by the sun's brightness, Goebel, Faust, and Hexamer did not realize that it was setting.[14] German ethnic consciousness was growing stronger just as the image of Germany itself was becoming more threatening.

A struggle over American identity was taking place. Social scientists concerned with the ethnic question were divided into two main groups, the assimilationists and the cultural pluralists. Horace M. Kallen, writing for the *Nation* magazine, argued that American identity consisted of "a multiplicity in a unity, an orchestration of mankind." To Kallen, ethnic toleration, and patriotism represented Americanism at its best.[15] The assimilationists, however, followers of Richard Mayo-Smith, were winning the day. In 1890, Mayo-Smith had praised the German-Americans for their loyalty. Faced with a new wave of immigration from eastern and southern Europe, Mayo-Smith became apprehensive about ethnic pluralism. "[I]t is better," he commented, "that a man should have one country and not divide his allegiance. If we are to build up in this country one nationality we must insist upon one speech." Mayo-Smith disliked the new German-American leadership, with its insistence upon the preservation of the old language. He concluded, "[T]he great ethnic problem we have before us is to fuse these diverse [ethnic] elements into one common nationality, having one language, one political practice, one patriotism and one ideal of social development."[16] As Woodrow Wilson, then president of Princeton University, put it, "A man who thinks of himself as belonging to a particular national group in America has not yet become an American."[17]

In the summer of 1914, German-American leaders were nonetheless optimistic about the future. Germans, they argued, could be good Americans, while retaining their ethnic heritage. They were, as the phrase went, patriotic German-Americans.[18] Proud, even boastful about their love for both Germany and the United States, few German-American spokesmen realized that they would one day have to choose between two fatherlands.

A few frustrated German-American leaders had already realized that changes in world politics were undermining their efforts to preserve German consciousness in America. They could do little, it seemed, to alter the course of American foreign policy. The establishment was

Anglo-Saxon, and King Edward VII frightened Americans less than Kaiser Wilhelm II. Some German-Americans, distraught by the suspicions of their Anglo-Saxon neighbors, struck back in frustration. The young German-American journalist H.L. Mencken lashed out at Englishmen as "the least civilized of white men and the least capable of true civilization." His attacks on puritan hypocrisy only resulted in "Anglo-Saxon" counterattacks against the German-American brewery interests that backed the German-American Alliance. Neither Mencken nor his critics understood that Anglo-German rivalry was rapidly leading the world closer to war.

The recent waves of immigration were, many people now agreed, bad enough. The United States, the argument went, did not need a newly assertive, arrogant German-American element. The rise of German-American self-confidence seemed threatening to many "Anglo-Saxon" elites.[19] On the surface, everything appeared placid. A.B. Faust had argued in 1909, and still believed that "[t]he platform of the German-American Alliance is typical of the patriotic and progressive attitude taken by the German element in regard to the nation's best interests."[20] He was right, but Faust ignored the darkening clouds: Some of his countrymen were beginning to doubt his loyalty. Faust and other German-American leaders could not know how Americans would regard their work in the event of war between the United States and the German Reich. Indeed, German-Americans could not even bear to think of such a possibility.

In the middle of the summer, war erupted in Europe. The German Reich, Austria-Hungary, and their allies soon formed the "Central Powers." The Triple Entente—Russia, France, and Great Britain—formed the "Allied" camp. German-American leaders quickly rallied to the cause of the *Vaterland*. They accepted the Reich government's assertion that Germany was fighting a defensive war against an encircling coalition. Germany had supposedly declared war on France and invaded Belgium because it was fighting for its life against aggressors. Few German-Americans sensed the danger in the air. Hermann Ridder, the influential publisher of the *New Yorker Staats-Zeitung*, reaffirmed German-American loyalty. Why should there be any problem? America would merely have to observe an evenhanded neutrality. Charles Hexamer, speaking for the alliance, committed the organization to a defense of the German cause "against the hate and ignorance of a minority in this country."

Most people expected the war to end quickly. Articles in the German-language press recounted a stunning succession of German victories. The French defensive success at the first battle of the Marne dashed the hope for a rapid end to the conflict. British superiority in the North Atlantic, coupled with its blockade of Germany, decimated American trade with the Reich. The Allied need for food, munitions, and loans tempted American business and banking interests, and President Wilson refused to ban such commerce.

American neutrality became a code word for aid to the Allies, including munitions and other forms of contraband. German retaliation, in the form of U-boat attacks, infuriated the American public. The result was a darkening of the German image. Conversely, the defense of a one-sided American neutrality soon became a patriotic duty for many Americans. British propaganda dominated the American media, particularly in the East. The British could rest their case upon one basic truth: It was hard for the Germans to claim that Belgium had invaded Germany. The British distributed reams of material about German atrocities in Belgium and northern France, some of it lurid, much of its exaggerated or false.

It was easy for many Americans to picture the "Huns" of Wilhelm II committing mayhem in little Belgium. Stories abounded of German soldiers bayoneting Belgian babies, or filling trophy sacks with women's breasts. The French reminded American audiences of the heroine/martyr Joan of Arc. France was St. Joan, Germany was Attila the Hun. Idealistic Ivy League youths volunteered to serve as medics and ambulance drivers on the western front. For fifteen years, the United States and Britain had been de facto allies during various diplomatic and military crises. London was now reaping the benefits of both sentiment and power politics.

German troops were fighting on foreign soil, so it was difficult to describe them as innocent victims of an Allied encirclement conspiracy. The early successes of the Wehrmacht rendered Germany vulnerable to the charge that she was causing turmoil and revolution. When publisher Hermann Ridder flew the German imperial flag over his newspaper building, angry reaction caused him to remove the offensive symbol.[21] The Allied triumph in American public opinion and in the White House was a prelude to military triumph in Europe. Franklin Roosevelt, the

young assistant secretary of the navy, shared this excitement. He sometimes fantasized about serving at the front himself, and cheered each
Allied victory.

FDR worked for an indulgent and rather hesitant secretary of the
navy, Josephus Daniels. FDR thus became a leader in the Navy Department, not a mere functionary. The assistant secretary's moral fervor,
fostered by Germanophobia, had turned him into an unreserved adherent of the Allied cause. This created a dilemma, for Roosevelt, like
Admiral Bradley A. Fiske, believed, "The U.S. Navy is unprepared for
war." The energetic, almost frenetic Roosevelt soon ran a one-man
preparedness campaign. Fearing Allied defeat and German domination
of the Atlantic, young Roosevelt did not mince his words: "We've got to
get into this war." Secretary Daniels could only reply, "I hope not."
Roosevelt often went over his boss's head, sharing his concerns with
Colonel Edward M. House, Wilson's closest adviser, as well as with the
president himself. He continued to support Cousin Theodore's advocacy of more assistance to the beleaguered Allies. Young FDR began to
show his skill as a propagandist. He warned hushed audiences about
German designs in the Caribbean Sea.

FDR was coming to understand the relationship between foreign
policy and domestic emotion. It was clear that American nationalism,
even short of intervention, could be powerful and intolerant. If an ethnic
group was identified with an unpopular or threatening foreign power, its
own influence could be curtailed, even eliminated. Roosevelt was not
one to bait German-Americans, though he readily accepted the repres-
sive measures later adopted by the Wilson administration. FDR was
also learning deeper lessons. In attacking a foreign foe, one received
plaudits at home. The best propaganda, Roosevelt learned, consisted of
moral homilies, combined with appeals to fear. Roosevelt did not invent
the attacks on German-American loyalty, but the policies he espoused
prospered in an anti-German environment.

The Germans fought back, ineffectively. Hermann Ridder demanded that President Woodrow Wilson enforce American neutral
rights against high-handed British naval actions. The German government opened an information office in New York City. The German-
American propagandist George Sylvester Viereck used German money
for his purchase of the *New York Daily Mail*.[22]

Despite the odds against success, Dr. Hexamer worked to prevent
the export of capital and munitions to the hard-pressed Allies. He

discovered, for example, that the Colt Armory Company of Holyoke, Massachusetts, was producing machine guns for the Canadian government, a cobelligerent on the Allied side. Hexamer protested to President Wilson, but did not receive satisfaction. Four months later, with the German Army stalemated in the west, Hexamer again wrote to Wilson, telling him, "You cannot imagine, Mr. President, with what chagrin and bitterness it fills the Americans of German descent to see the resources of this great country . . . placed at the disposal of enemies who, with their overwhelming forces, have proclaimed it their avowed purpose to crush our ancestral home."

Alliance leaders organized petitions demanding an end to the arms trade with the Allies. One contained two million signatures. German-American organizations tried to intimidate banks, so as to prevent the sale of Allied war bonds in the United States. In Milwaukee, ten institutions, fearing the anger of German-American depositers, refused to float Allied bond issues. They thus provoked the more dangerous wrath of big, pro-Allied New York City financiers, such as J.P. Morgan. Few other banks followed the Milwaukee example. The Allies were winning more victories in the United States than on the western front. By the end of 1915, they had succeeded in financing and placing well over a billion dollars in weapons contracts in the United States.[23]

A German lack of tact played into the hands of British propagandists. One incident was particularly important. The Germans sank the British passenger liner *Lusitania* on 7 May 1915. American passengers had received a warning from the German authorities, informing them that the vessel would be sailing through a proclaimed war zone. We know now that the ship was carrying munitions for the Allies. After a German U-boat sank the *Lusitania,* with great loss of life, the Germans stupidly struck a medal honoring the submarine's commanding officer. This "Hunnish" behavior made good propaganda for Britain. Wilson soon became an advocate of military preparedness. Within a year, he would be marching down Pennsylvania Avenue with an American flag draped over his shoulder.

By 1916, America was nonbelligerent, but hardly neutral. Public opinion opposed entering the war, but supported the Allies. Thanks in part to Wilson, "freedom of the seas," neutrality, pro-Allied sentiment, and anti-Germanism were coming to be equated with good, old-fashioned American patriotism. Frustrated German-American leaders became more strident in their threats directed at those "waging war against the two Germanic nations under the cover of neutrality." There was talk of using "five million" votes to punish pro-Allied politicians.

Alliance leaders found that appeals for a return to true neutrality provoked hostile reactions. Former president Theodore Roosevelt questioned the integrity of these "hyphenated" Americans. The German image was indeed sinking to new lows. President Wilson seemed to equate military preparedness and patriotism with support for the Allies. He became intolerant of dissent. Wilson's attitude was, in the words of German-American leader Henry Weissmann, "quite an innovation and a mighty dangerous one." Wilson, goaded by Colonel House, was coming to see himself as the defender of virtue against Prussian boorishness. Those who disagreed, he thought, must be misguided, or even treacherous. [24]

Wilson had long been suspicious of German intentions. During the war, the president privately explained why he was pro-Allied. "No decent man," said Wilson, "knowing the situation in Germany, could be anything else." [25] Franklin Roosevelt, meanwhile, distributed volumes "authenticating" German atrocities and wrote articles advocating a more activist foreign policy. Long before Wilson came around to this view, Roosevelt favored the abandonment of neutrality.

Important wartime books rounded out President Wilson's view of German culture. In *German Philosophy and Politics*, noted philosopher John Dewey denounced the perverse alliance between German idealism and Teutonic technical efficiency. As he put it, "The more the Germans accomplish in the way of material conquest, the more they are conscious of fulfilling an ideal mission; every external conquest affords the greater warrant for dwelling in an inner region where mechanism does not intrude." [26] In other words, German idealism was merely a cloak for the exercise of brute force.

Another distinguished academician, George Santayana, argued in *Egotism in German Philosophy* that "Egotism—subjectivity in thought and wilfulness in morals"—dominated German thinking. The result was an unhealthy idealism, at once detatched and brutal: "The perversity of the Germans, the childishness and sophistry of their position, [which] lies only in glorifying what is an inevitable impediment [egotism], and in marking time on an earthly station from which the spirit of man—at least in spirit—is called to fly." [27] The anti-German campaign was winning the battle for American hearts and minds, on and off the campus.

By 1916, American newspapers were filled with stories about German sabotage and espionage in the Americas. Some of these accounts were true, some highly exaggerated, while others were completely false. Secret telegrams, thoughtfully supplied by British sources, "proved" that the Germans were enticing the Mexicans into an alliance whose aim was the dismemberment of the United States. William H. Skaggs's book *German Conspiracies in America* was a British product, preying upon American fears.[28] Americans were coming to believe that the stalwart French *poilus* and the heroic British Tommies were defending the United States and the entire Christian world against the Huns. The war was raging in American minds before America sent boys to fight on the western front.

Germany had suffered one million dead, and victory was not in sight. The German masses hungered for peace as the war of attrition dragged on. The last thing Germany needed was another major enemy in the field. The German people had to be reassured about American intentions. One thus read newspaper accounts predicting that six million or even ten million German-Americans would revolt against Wilson if he dared to enter the war. Such comments further inflamed American opinion.

The German-American leadership was unable to change public opinion, nor could it alter the administration's foreign policy. That policy created jobs for American workers; it made many people feel good; and it created vast profits for Eastern banks. Attempts to set up a German-American lobby in Washington met with howls of outrage. This was ironic, for Allied lobbyists had the run of the Congress, and were frequent guests in the White House. German-Americans were unprepared for the accusations that would soon be leveled against them. The *Wall Street Journal* commented that "citizens of German extraction could do with a little more extracting." The *Brooklyn Eagle* cracked, "When your true Hun leaves the Fatherland he doesn't emigrate; he hyphenates." Theodore Roosevelt, who saw entry into the war as a personal stepping-stone to a new term in the White House, loudly declared, "No good American, whatever his ancestry or creed, can have any feeling except scorn and detestation for those professional German-Americans who seek to make the American President in effect a viceroy of the German Emperor."[29] German-Americans were stunned.

By the summer of 1916, German-American leaders were in a state of despair, as cultural pluralism yielded to a new nativism. George Seibel tried to explain the German-American dilemma. In a widely reprinted address, delivered in Johnstown, Pennsylvania, he bemoaned the eclipse of the "hyphenate in American history," especially in its German-American form. Seibel denounced the uniformity of the American press.

Railing against British domination of American foreign policy, German-American despair yielded at times to wishful thinking: "Morgan may give John Bull our banks, and he may buy our newspapers, but Justice is mightier than Gold, and Truth defies the slanderous darts of Malice."[30] This was unlikely. Germany's decision to launch unrestricted submarine warfare against the British Isles threatened the island kingdom with strangulation, perhaps with starvation. Neutral shipping would suffer greatly. Wilson, along with a majority of his countrymen, did not feel threatened by the prospect of a British victory. A German triumph, by contrast, meant that a revolutionary new power would dominate the sea-lanes of the North Atlantic, as well as the continent of Europe. Markets might be closed to American exporters.[31] Democracy would supposedly suffer, even in places where it did not and had never prevailed.

No one cheered more than Franklin Roosevelt when Wilson sent his fateful war message to the Congress. On 6 April 1917 that body responded to Germany's desperate U-boat challenge with a declaration of war. German-Americans marched off to boot camp like everyone else, but their ethnic revival quickly became a casualty of the war hysteria. German-Americans found themselves victims of a new wave of ferocious anti-German feelings. German shepherds became "Alsatians," sauerkraut turned into "liberty cabbage," and hamburger quickly evolved into Salisbury steak. High schools banished the German language from their curricula.

Congress and the president adopted a series of security measures that affected persons of German origin. German subjects, even those who had taken out first naturalization papers, were "prohibited from living within or entering a one-half mile area around military zones or factories producing materials for war." German aliens were prohibited "from entering or living in the District of Columbia." By the spring of 1918, the government had expelled more than 1,500 such persons. They often had to leave their loved ones and their jobs on very short notice. In cases concerning the Navy, Franklin D. Roosevelt cooperated fully with the administration's security measures. He was not in the forefront, however, of those making demagogic attacks upon the German-American leadership.

German-Americans speaking German were sometimes threatened with violence. There were rumors of lynchings, most unfounded. Samuel Rea, president of the Pennsylvania Railroad, now demanded that Americanization must foster an "absolute forgetfulness of all obligations or connections with other countries because of descent or birth."[32] Congress placed the German-language press at the mercy of the local postmasters, a measure without precedent in U.S. history. Some newspapers lost their mailing privileges. In the summer of 1918, Congress repealed the charter of the German-American National Alliance. After the war, the same intolerance would be visited upon "radicals" and "foreigners." The search for a scapegoat continued to be a factor in American history.[33]

The worst anti-German excesses would pass soon after the signing of the Armistice on 11 November 1918. Pictures of starving German children touched the hearts of Americans, and the German language began to creep back into high school programs. The worst would be over, but the effects of the new nativism were permament.

America entered the war, and Franklin D. Roosevelt had his righteous battle. Young FDR wished to obtain an officer's commission, so he could play a personal role in defeating the "bully" Germany. This would also be good politics. The war ended too soon, however, and Roosevelt remained a civilian, although he did make a tour of the western battlefields. It left an indelible impression.

In July 1918, the restless assistant secretary arrived in Great Britain. He met with leading politicians, including Prime Minister David Lloyd George. At the end of the month, Roosevelt boarded a British destroyer at Dover and sailed to France. At Dunkirk and Calais, FDR saw the destruction wrought by German aerial and land bombardments. He then made his way to Paris, where the French government received the young statesman with appropriate consideration. FDR met with French military leaders, then embarked upon a hazardous but exciting tour of the western front. Appalled by the carnage, yet stimulated by the heroic and virtuous cause of the Allies, Roosevelt saw the Germans as savages.

Roosevelt was well served by his youthful charm, boyish enthusiasm for naval affairs, and adequate French. The Paris press lavished praise upon the young man "with the smiling and energetic face," who had shown himself to be worthy of his famous cousin. Roosevelt was just what his war-weary hosts needed. He looked to the future with sunny optimism, confident of an imminent Allied victory. He was the New World come to rescue tired, devastated Europe. FDR's reception by French naval circles was like a small dress rehearsal for the hopes placed in him twenty years later.[34]

FDR went on to inspect naval facilities at Brest and the Firth of Forth, then returned to London, and later to France. Denied his wish to obtain the commission of a naval officer, Roosevelt almost became a casualty after all. In France, he grew ill after contracting double pneumonia and influenza. FDR almost died during the trip home. He recovered quickly, however, and never forgot his wartime journey to Europe. Germany was, Roosevelt believed, a menace to civilization. An Anglo-American-French alliance must, he thought, restrain an expansionist German Reich.[35] Roosevelt viewed war against Germany as preferable to the domination of Europe by Germany. He felt this way in 1919 and again in 1939.

During his time at the Navy Department, the ambitious assistant secretary personally maintained voluminous scrapbooks documenting his rise to prominence. He carefully pasted news articles into them, generally three to a page. Important clippings for the year 1918 document FDR's trip to Europe and show that he was aware of the political dividends that might accrue thanks to that journey. Roosevelt mused about running for governor, but this was premature. He fantasized about resigning and joining the navy as a common seaman, and he made sure that the press printed the rumor.[36] Neither Wilson nor Daniels would have let him go at this point, and FDR knew it. There was, of course, a political side to Roosevelt's musings about military service. He knew what the Spanish-American War had done for Cousin Teddy's reputation. Years later, as president, Roosevelt clearly showed signs of embarrassment over his lack of military service. He was delighted when he saw his sons in uniform.

Franklin Roosevelt's Germanophobia reflected a powerful current in American life, one which influenced mightily power politics in our century.

By 1919, the young politician was a fervent interventionist and globalist. Yet Roosevelt's boundless self-confidence coexisted with a sense of permanent danger. In the next war, FDR believed, America might not have time for a long preparedness campaign. Roosevelt dismissed traditional American fears of a large, permanent military establishment. At a victory dinner in 1919, Roosevelt called for universal military service and the continuation of conscription into peacetime. The public, however, was disillusioned with European politics and European wars. The Wilson era was ending in failure, and the peace treaty was embroiled in political controversy. Roosevelt, too, trimmed his political sails. For a generation, his interventionism remained a credo, not a guide to action.

In 1920, FDR became a national figure. He received his party's nomination for the vice presidency. Young and handsome, with a famous name, Roosevelt worked hard in the fall campaign. The ticket, led by Governor James Cox of Ohio, went down to crushing defeat. Most Americans voted for Warren G. Harding and "normalcy," rejecting President Wilson's new globalism. The United States did not sign the Treaty of Versailles, nor would it enter the new League of Nations. Franklin Roosevelt, however, seemed to have a bright political future. Tragedy then struck, in the form of poliomyelitis. FDR fought back, exhibiting great will and courage. He returned to the political battlefields of New York State, winning the governorship in 1928. For the next four years, Roosevelt proved himself in a difficult office. Except for trade matters affecting New York State, however, FDR paid but marginal attention to foreign affairs during these years.

If there was a national consensus on foreign affairs in 1928, it seemed to reflect a desire to trade with all nations (except, some said, the Soviet Union), to avoid entangling alliances with any of them, and to remain outside world bodies such as the League of Nations. People favored the negotiation of arms control treaties, as well as antiwar covenants. "Isolationism" inaccurately describes this era; internationalism without military commitments or extrahemispheric interventionism was the order of the day. FDR himself was not immune to growing doubts about the wisdom and morality of Wilson's brand of interventionism.

"America expert" Colin Ross photographed by his son Ralph as he prepared to depart on a new global journey, 15 October 1938. (Credit: Bundesarchiv)

A Nazi view of Americanism: on the left, a flag-waving, peroxide blonde woman, accompanied by a black jazz player. These figures are contrasted with a symbol of European culture, a Gothic sculpture of the Virgin Mary. (Credit: Library of Congress)

The Nazis (and American racists) passed pictures like this one around. Here we see New York City Mayor LaGuardia (left) and Eleanor Roosevelt amidst an integrated group. (Credit: Wiener Library)

The Emperor of California portrayed American society as crude and racially polluted. John Sutter (Luis Trenker) goes from boom to bust. Cheated, he winds up vainly seeking justice from the U.S. Supreme Court. (Credit: MOMA Film Stills Division)

Two hate objects dear to Nazi propagandists: Mrs. Eleanor Roosevelt and Mayor Fiorello H. LaGuardia. (Credit: Library of Congress)

Assistant Secretary of the Navy Franklin D. Roosevelt campaigning for the vice presidency, 1920. (Credit: Library of Congress)

"Hurray for war!" Patriotic youths cheer the outbreak of the Great War. A scene from Carl Laemmle's *All Quiet on the Western Front*.
(Credit: MOMA Film Stills Division)

The reality of war is different from the heroism promised by the patriotic
schoolteacher. A battlefront scene from *All Quiet on the Western Front*.
(Credit: MOMA Film Stills Division)

In the last moments of *All Quiet
on the Western Front*, "Paul" (Lew
Ayres), marches toward heaven
with his dead comrades, looking
reproachfully at the living. To
audiences in 1930, he seemed to
be saying, "No more war! No
more intervention!" (Credit:
MOMA Film Stills Division)

Secretary of State Cordell Hull.
(Credit: FDR Library)

CHAPTER SEVEN

THE TRIUMPH OF NEUTRALITY

THE NEW ANTI-INTERVENTIONISM, in vogue at the time of FDR's governorship, owed much to the work of a prolific academician and popularizer named Harry Elmer Barnes. who had been anti-German during the war years. After the war, he quickly became disillusioned with the Allied cause. Barnes now saw the Treaty of Versailles as an unjust instrument of victors' vengeance. He believed that selfish interest groups, including American bankers, British propagandists, and munitions manufacturers or ("merchants of death"), had worked to deceive the American public about the true nature of the conflict.

By 1924, Barnes had come into contact with a number of German individuals and agencies committed to revising foreign attitudes toward the war and the treaty. Among these was the *Schuldreferat* (war-guilt office), a propaganda front working for the Foreign Ministry in Berlin. Barnes's arguments appealed to the Germans, while his academic prestige could serve their purposes. Though claiming to be opposed to nationalism among historians, Barnes came close to endorsing the xenophobic "manifesto" published by patriotic German professors during the war.[1]

A passionate man with infinite amounts of energy, Barnes seemed to look for controversy. His portrayal of Germany as an innocent victim aroused interest, and some support, in the United States. Visiting Germany on a lecture tour in 1926, Barnes found himself the toast of nationalist circles in Munich and Berlin. Not for the last time, a man who served German foreign policy goals refused to see any inconsistency between his stated devotion to "objectivity," and his American patriotism. Barnes became a professional "revisionist," blind to any viewpoint but his own.

The subsequent publication, by German archivists working for the Foreign Ministry, of the massive documentation entitled *Die grosse Politik der europäischen Kabinette* (The great power politics of the European cabinets) greatly influenced the debate over the outbreak of the war. Although it certainly contained documents detrimental to the German war-guilt thesis, the *Grosse Politik* was the product of selective editing, and it hardly allowed "the facts to speak for themselves," as Barnes claimed.

Two prestigious American diplomatic historians from Harvard, William L. Langer and Sidney Bradshaw Fay, now raised questions about the "Germany-is-guilty" theory.[2] Their timing was good. Americans were investing a good deal of money in Germany; tourists were flocking back to Munich and Cologne, to Berlin and the Black Forest. German theater, and above all, German films, enchanted many Americans interested in the arts. Few had heard of the National Socialist movement.

Most Americans had no idea about the degree of German bitterness and delusion. They knew nothing of the widespread "stab in the back" credo, which blamed the collapse of the Reich in 1918 on the Jews, pacifists, communists, and Wilsonians—on everyone, that is, except the German leadership and the German people. To many Americans who visited Europe, the Germans were preferable to the arrogant British and the contemptuous French. Germans were generally friendly and honest. Most had relatives and showed interest in the United States. Few Americans noticed a different strain in the culture, an antidemocratic ideology that owed much of its inspiration to Americanophobia. To Americans in Munich in 1929, Hitler was a local curiosity, not an aspiring national leader. One saw Nazis from time to time, but they controlled neither the Bavarian government nor the national Reichstag (parliament). Nobody was reading *Mein Kampf*, which was not available in English, even in abridged form, for several more years.

Germany seemed stable; the great inflation of 1923, while never forgotten, had been overcome. Men were building public works and laying out new urban parks. The Reich government was secure, a real democratic coalition, though a bit to the left of the American political mainstream. Favorable impressions of Germany made life easier for German-Americans at home.

The America that had rejected both the peace treaty and the League of Nations thus gave a respectful hearing to the revisionist viewpoint. At a time when the Allies called Uncle Sam "Uncle Shylock" (for demanding repayment of war loans), when the peace movement was strong and the armed forces weak, revisionism gained many adherents.[3] Homer T. Bone, Democrat of Washington, now declared that "the Great War . . . was utter social insanity, and was a crazy war, and we had no business in it at all."[4] And if that war "to make the world safe for democracy" and "a war to end all wars" was wrong, than perhaps *all* war was evil. This belief contributed to American support for the 1928 Kellogg-Briand Pact, which outlawed aggressive war.

Though relatively few Americans died of wounds incurred in battle during World War I (53,513, out of 4,743,826 who served in the armed forces), the mass slaughter inflicted upon human beings seemed to justify a revulsion against war itself. Weapons had become ever more destructive, but incomprehensible nationalisms continued to bedevil the European polity. If war was born of nationalism, and was in itself the enemy of humanity, then men must reject it altogether.

In this atmosphere, nobody wanted to be branded an "interventionist propagandist." The salesman and the huckster had come into their own, people said. One must beware of becoming a "sucker." The slick Europeans, having misled America once, might try it again. The cult of neutrality, girded in the words of President George Washington's Farewell Address, turned into an American chastity belt.

Neither the Great Depression nor the rise of the Nazis impeded the advance of revisionist attitudes toward the Great War. Barnes, now a respected newspaper commentator for Roy Howard's newspaper chain, continued to preach his gospel. Now, when problems at home were so severe, was no time to become involved in foreign entanglements, least of all on behalf of ungrateful former allies. This attitude, combined with economic nationalism in its most protectionist form, were not conducive to support for collective security against aggression.

Few documents captured this antipathy to war better than Hollywood producer Carl Laemmle's 1930 motion picture *All Quiet on the Western Front*. Telling the story of men "destroyed in the war," Laemmle created a sensation with this movie. Nazis rioted in the streets of Berlin and released snakes and white mice in theaters showing the film. The fact that Laemmle was a German-American emigré of Jewish origin particularly enraged these thugs. Although the film was approved by the German board of censors, the government forced the board to rescind its approval. The failure of the German republic to resist this Nazi pressure was a harbinger of its own destruction. Pacifist Oswald Garrison Villard, writing for the *Nation*, foresaw this in early 1931.[5]

Producer Laemmle and director Lewis Milestone destroyed all the romantic, nationalist shibboleths of an earlier generation. The movie's setting is the German home front, but at no point are the soldiers mere German caricatures. They could just as well be Frenchmen or Americans. The opening scene of this film shows a teacher whipping his students into a patriotic frenzy in 1914. Happy boys march off behind the teacher, anxious to sign up for the army. He, of course, returns to the classroom, where he lectures more young men on the virtues of death for the fatherland.

The boys go off to boot camp, festooned with flowers. The marching bands fade from memory, for basic training is harsh, dirty, and boring. And people seem to change when they wear a uniform. Dehumanization is the order of the day. Learn to kill; forget higher cultural aspirations. The boys are glad to leave the training camp. Now, at last, they will be soldiers, fighting for the sacred fatherland. Milestone graphically portrays the horrors of the trenches, where men fight rats for a few crumbs of bread.

The constant roar of artillery and machine guns causes some men to go mad. Here at the front no one speaks of "causes" or "fatherlands," but of survival and of home. There is indiscriminate slaughter, to no purpose (hence the ironic title of the film). No one really knows or cares who started the war. Some soldiers believe that the Kaiser or greedy manufacturers are responsible, but the men are not sure.

There are individual acts of humanity. Some are the gestures of Paul Baumer, a sensitive young man portrayed by actor Lew Ayres, himself a pacifist. Paul cares about his friend, the nineteen-year-old Franz, who lies dying in a field hospital. His love, however, is almost stupid, out of place in this brutal conflict. Later, Paul tries to comfort Duval, a dying French soldier whom he has stabbed. As if to mock such sentimentality,

Milestone shows us the home front. On leave, Paul has to listen to his father's armchair strategist friends, comfortable in their taverns, telling him how to win the war. Paul's teacher, still preaching patriotism and glory, shows him off to the class. Paul stammers something about what the front is really like. The boys are all shocked. "Coward!" yells one youth, though Paul is actually a decorated hero. A new generation is being readied for the slaughter.

In the end, the whole war effort seems meaningless. Paul reaches out beyond his sandbag barrier, hoping to capture a butterfly. A French sharpshooter kills him. In the final powerful scene, the dead and the living march off into eternity, against the backdrop of a huge military cemetery. Paul turns toward us, looking the living reproachfully in the eye. He seems to say, "Never again war!"

Reviewers were overwhelmed. The noncommunist left wing and the pacifist press loved the movie, while the mainstream *New York Times* described it as "vivid and graphic." *Liberty* reviewed the film in glowing terms, as did *Film Daily* and other trade publications. *All Quiet on the Western Front* strengthened pacifist sentiments in the United States. One could only contrast the stirring rhetoric of President Wilson with the carnage in northern France. Confused and disenchanted, Americans now saw that the great Wilsonian crusade had led to the rise of bolshevism and fascism. The Europeans and their endless wars, many Americans claimed, were to blame for the Depression engulfing the nation during the production of *All Quiet on the Western Front*.

The nation was in near despair when FDR gained his party's presidential nomination. He was inaugurated on 4 March 1933, five weeks after Hitler assumed the German chancellorship. Roosevelt struck the famous pundit Walter Lippmann as well-intentioned and charming, but lacking in intellectual depth or ideological commitment.

During his first administration, Roosevelt devoted most of his energy to the enactment of measures aimed at overcoming the economic and moral crisis that gripped the nation. Under his "New Deal," the federal government greatly expanded its powers. Roosevelt and his "Brain Trust," working with a heavily Democratic Congress, tackled a vast array of problems, ranging from unemployment to unionization, from agriculture to social security.

Foreign policy was secondary, but here, too, Roosevelt embraced an economic nationalism quite in keeping with his expansion of federal authority. The president exuded some vaguely internationalist sentiments from time to time, but he was careful to avoid being tagged a "Wilson II." The press, Secretary of State Cordell Hull observed, was of the "unanimous opinion that we must not allow ourselves to become involved in European political developments." Most Americans agreed. In this atmosphere, FDR was careful to maintain what he called a "more or less detached position," based on "impartiality." In 1933, the president supported the ill-fated Disarmament Conference and advocated close cooperation with Great Britain on arms issues. FDR believed that disarmament, along with economic cooperation and recovery, could overcome the "tyranny of fear" gripping Europe. It took Roosevelt and Hull some time to realize that a distant, largely disarmed nation, acting as a noncommittal mediator, could hardly convert Hitler and Mussolini to its liberal values.

Hull, a former Tennessee senator, had become secretary of state in 1933, at the age of sixty-one. He served for eleven years. Cordell Hull was a passionate believer in free trade, an adherent of the old liberal maxim that protectionism leads to war. A Wilsonian internationalist who had drawn certain lessons from the debacle of the league debate in 1919, Hull was cautious and hardworking. He was loyal to the president, though there was little warmth in the relationship. Roosevelt, outwardly respectful of Hull, often circumvented him. FDR contributed to the formulation and execution of policy.[6] His combination of nationalism and globalism contrasted with Hull's legalistic obsession with treaties and free trade. Hull was useful to Roosevelt for many years, precisely because he offered the president political cover.

Roosevelt needed this protection. Isolationists recalled his enthusiastic interventionism and his support for U.S. membership on the World Court. By the time FDR took office, opposition to Wilsonian internationalism had become a powerful factor in American political life. Those who resented American involvement in the last war and wished to avoid international commitments compromising American sovereignty were sometimes referred to as "isolationists."[7] These people believed that the United States could and should isolate itself from the crises looming in Europe and the Far East. They opposed American involvement in the League of Nations and even on the World Court. Led by powerful, senior members of the United States Senate, the congressional isolationists could make life difficult for an independent-

minded president. In the second year of FDR's term, Congress passed
the Johnson Act, which forbade extending loans to nations defaulting on
previous commitments. Britain and France might never pay up, but they
would never get another penny.

"Internationalists," in contrast, advocated an American role in collective security measures aimed at deterring aggression. They believed in
the utility of the league and favored U.S. membership on the World
Court. While Roosevelt's roots and intellect were internationalist, his
political instincts told him to pay heed to isolationist concerns. Polls
taken during Roosevelt's first term consistently indicated that ninety-
five percent of those questioned wanted the United States to avoid
becoming entangled in a new European war. In 1934, the Hearst
newspapers organized a petition drive opposing U.S. membership in
the World Court. Though the court was far less controversial than the
league, Hearst collected almost a million and a half signatures.

Senator Thomas D. Schall (Republican of Minnesota) captured the
isolationist mood when he said, "To hell with Europe and the rest of
those nations!" In 1934, the Nye Committee, named after Senator
Gerald P. Nye (Republican of North Dakota), began its famous investigation into the origins of American intervention in 1917. Some congressmen pointed their fingers at unpopular, but plausible culprits: In
Senator Nye's words, "[M]unitions sales, bankers' loans to the Allies,
and Americans sailing upon the vessels of nations at war, such as the
Lusitania, tended to bring us into a conflict which was in its inception of
no relation to us."[8] Money, rather than idealism, had motivated the
Wilson administration. The influential Kansas publisher William Allen
White summed up the feelings of the era. "The boys who died just
went out and died," he wrote. "And for what?" asked White, and
millions of others.[9]

Peace activists touched the lives of many Americans during this era.
Pacifists, who opposed the use of organized armed force in international
affairs, had many supporters. Rabbi Stephen Wise, as well as the
Reverend Harry Emerson Fosdick, pledged to refrain from using religion for the sanctification of war. In 1933, the year in which Hitler
became chancellor of Germany, Brown University's student newspaper
polled students attending sixty-five colleges. It discovered that about
forty percent of them claimed to be committed to absolute pacifism. In
the spring of 1935, sixty thousand American students sponsored antiwar
rallies and marches. Many of them took the "Oxford Oath," commit-

ting themselves to avoiding military service, even in the event of war.[10] The National Council for the Prevention of War, a Quaker group, helped to coordinate the work of thirty-one pacifist and peace-oriented organizations. Socialist Norman Thomas, an ordained minister, was active in the influential Fellowship of Reconciliation. Later, the famous A.J. Muste, an absolute pacifist, joined the group. (It was Muste who liked to say, "If I cannot love Hitler, I cannot love any man.")

In 1932, Roosevelt had dispatched an indirect emissary to Adolf Hitler, hoping to learn more about his intentions. Nothing important came of these tentative feelers. Hitler soon came to power, and Roosevelt decided, "I want an American liberal in Germany as a standing example." His choice for ambassador fell upon historian William Dodd of Virginia. Dodd, who became the annual president of the American Historical Association in 1934, had earned his doctorate at the University of Leipzig back in 1900.

Ambassador Dodd had few illusions about the Nazis, though in the beginning he did convince himself that "Germany can hardly fail to realize the importance of friendly cooperation with the 120,000,000 people of the United States. . . ." FDR hoped that the professor was right, though he himself feared a coming war between the victors and the vanquished of 1918.[11]

From the earliest days of his presidency, Roosevelt had insights into Hitler's nature and intentions. Writing in 1933 in his copy of the book *Mein Kampf,* Roosevelt noted, "This translation is so expurgated as to give a wholly false view of what Hitler really says—The German original would make a different story." Roosevelt was right. The abridged work gave no real sense of Hitler's Jewish obsession, nor of his frightening foreign policy goals. There was no complete English translation of the work until later in the decade. How did Roosevelt know about the difference? Perhaps from conversation, perhaps from looking at the German edition of *Mein Kampf.* Roosevelt had more pressing matters to deal with in 1933, and so did most Americans. Still, it is interesting to see that FDR had doubts from the start about the Nazis.

Despite these early concerns about Hitler, Roosevelt did not speak much about events in Germany. His comments about the Nazis were highly unflattering, but FDR devoted little time to a study of Hitler's policies. Ambassador Dodd had direct access to Roosevelt, and soon became the president's tutor. Nazi brutality, reflected in the bloody purge of 30 June 1934, shocked Dodd, and he conveyed his dismay to the president.[12]

Roosevelt, preoccupied with domestic questions and fearing political opposition to bold foreign policy initiatives, reacted cautiously in public to cries of alarm about the Nazi danger. He continued to exchange formal greetings with the Reich government. At times, both countries lodged notes of protest with one another, but there was no sense of imminent crisis. For his part, Ambassador Dodd did not at first fully grasp the extent of Hitler's ambitions, though he understood German resentment about the outcome of the last war. At the right moment, Dodd predicted, Hitler would wage war in order to restore the frontiers of 1918.[13] This appraisal proved to be too conservative by far. While Dodd fretted about German belligerence, the United States Congress decided to put severe constraints upon the president's powers in the domain of foreign affairs. Dodd realized that American isolationism could only foster the ambitions of this new generation of German leaders. So did Frank N. Belgrano, national commander of the American Legion. Perhaps looking ahead to unthinkable events such as the German domination of Europe, or a Japanese attack on the United States, Belgrano uttered prophetic words. "Those," he said, "who practice the theory of splendid isolation are smoking the opium of self-deception. They may have pleasant dreams for the moment, but some day they will awake to a nightmare of tragic reality." The American Legion repudiated its commander's comment.[14]

Reaction against the intervention in 1917, pacifism, and fear of unforeseen temptations and crises resulted in the Neutrality Act of 1935, as well as subsequent neutrality legislation. Roosevelt, having been burned by the World Court issue, overcame his misgivings and signed the act into law.

In the event of war, it read, the president "shall proclaim such fact, and it shall thereafter be unlawful to export arms, ammunition, or implements of war from any place in the United States, or possessions of the United States, to any port of such belligerent states, . . . or for the use of [a] belligerent country." Section 3 also prohibited American vessels from carrying implements of war to neutral ports, if these arms and munitions were destined for transshipment to a belligerent power. The legislation established strict governmental supervision over the armaments industry, which many Americans now blamed for U.S. intervention in the Great War. And mindful of the *Lusitania* tragedy of 1915, Congress authorized the president to warn American citizens sailing on belligerents' ships that they did so at their own risk. This legislation, if not rescinded or amended, doomed any effective American intervention on behalf of collective security against aggression. Politics was politics, however, and an election was coming up. Reports indicated that the looming war between Ethiopia and Italy might be a prelude to a broader European struggle.

Speaking of this Neutrality Act, former secretary of state Henry L. Stimson observed, "The President had done little or nothing to head off this legislative folly which would discourage the victims of aggression and not its perpetrators. . . ." Roosevelt, in signing the legislation, did wisely point out that "inflexible provisions might drag us into war instead of keeping us out."

Roosevelt's supporters in Congress wondered about the future course of American foreign policy. Would it take the form of adamant isolationism? Many British and French leaders believed that this legislation could only encourage hotheads in Berlin and Rome.[15] It was now clear to all that America was willing to surrender some of its rights as a neutral nation if it could thereby avoid becoming a belligerent power. The neutrality law was soon tested.

Mussolini's Italy attacked Ethiopia in early October 1935, and FDR promptly embargoed the export of arms and munitions to the warring parties. The League of Nations then voted to impose limited economic sanctions upon Italy. Secretary of State Cordell Hull, however, promptly informed the British that America would not feel bound by sanctions voted by the league.[16] Instead, Hull and the president called for a "moral embargo." This meant that American exporters were admonished to maintain the existing level of exports to Mussolini's Italy. In fact, American exporters made large profits by increasing exports of strategic metals and oil to fascist Italy. In his memoirs, Hull lamely argues that, absent the "moral embargo," the situation would have been even worse.[17]

In the name of freedom of the seas, neutrality, and profits, the American economy helped to prevent an Italian collapse. Roosevelt remained passive, as Mussolini demonstrated that aggression worked. The American public was not unduly upset. A Gallup poll showed that seventy percent of Americans opposed enforcing sanctions in cooperation with the league. Through all of this, Roosevelt could only promise,

"[T]he United States of America shall and must remain . . . unentangled and free."[18] While Marshal Pietro Badoglio prepared for his final victory drive in Ethiopia, and a week before Hitler sent German troops into the demilitarized Rhineland, Congress widened the neutrality legislation, though it now permitted the president to determine *when* "there exists a state of war between, or among two or more foreign states. . . ." Once the president had made this determination, however, the arms embargo would apply to any additional parties entering the conflict. This could only discourage collective security measures, for the amendment in question mandated an arms embargo applicable even to nations at war against an *aggressor.* And according to the new law, belligerents could receive no loans or credits. Roosevelt quickly applied the legislation to the war in eastern Africa, though this action did nothing to save Ethiopia, the victim of aggression. Later, Cordell Hull ruefully admitted, "If total sanctions had been applied, Mussolini might have been stopped dead in his tracks."[19]

"Total sanctions" would have required stronger measures by the league, and full support for them by its members, as well as by the United States. The failure of the league, whatever America's responsibility, hurt the interventionist cause. In the Midwest, where editorial opinion had been predominantly internationalist since 1917, isolationism took over as the dominant voice of the region.[20]

Roosevelt's growing hostility to the Nazis had not yet taken him past the way station labeled peaceful multilateralism. A collective antifascist alliance was out of the question, as was unilateral American action. Roosevelt mused about a peace conference, perhaps even a summit meeting with Hitler and Mussolini. FDR's program contained two basic elements: mutual reduction in armaments, and free access for all nations to international markets and raw materials. The problem was that the president did not yet realize that the acceptance of such principles was anathema to fascist states. If they agreed, they would cease to be fascist. Thus, far from being a kind of "appeasement," as some scholars have alleged, Roosevelt's idea was an impractical, idealistic concept predicated upon the return of Germany, Italy, and Japan to liberal political principles.

After the outbreak of General Francisco Franco's Spanish rebellion in the summer of 1936, the president invoked a "moral embargo" on arms sales to the insurgents and prevented the shipment of badly needed warplanes to the legitimate government of the Spanish Republic.[21] "Lift the embargo!" implored much of the American left, while pro-Franco activists in the Catholic community demanded, "Keep the embargo!" To rescind it, Roosevelt believed, "would mean the loss of every Catholic vote in the coming fall election. . . ."[22] After the election, when Congress passed another Neutrality Act, which prevented the export of arms, munitions, and implements of war to Spain, Ambassador Dodd sourly documented the elation of the German press.

It was clear that the Versailles peace structure was collapsing. Hitler had begun his massive arms buildup. France was politically unstable; Britain seemed to lack political will. Mussolini had taken Ethiopia, while the league had disintegrated as an effective body. FDR, concerned about the rise of dictatorships and the threat of war, ruminated about various approaches to the world crisis. Perhaps the president could persuade Hitler to outline his foreign policy goals for the next ten years. Maybe he could coax the Nazis into re-entering disarmament negotiations. He considered convening an international conference, but he hesitated to share this idea with a suspicious American people. On at least one occasion, FDR considered endorsing American participation in a multinational blockade of Germany, at least in a theoretical sense.[23] Yet it is hard to take these ideas too seriously, except as guides to FDR's increasing fear of Nazi aggression and barbarity. Presiding over an economically troubled nation separated from Europe and Asia by great oceans, Roosevelt commanded a paltry army of fewer than 200,000 men, and an unprepared, undermanned navy.

Concerned about American isolationism, Roosevelt found himself in a difficult position.[24] Most Americans disliked the Nazis, when they thought about them at all. Yet they detested the thought of another intervention in a European war even more. How could one change the worldview of an American majority? This was a great challenge; as the president put it in 1936, "A Government can be no better than the public opinion which sustains it."[25] Roosevelt's caution has led to much criticism. Some have seen his foreign policy during these years as that of a man unwilling "to make use of America's power and influence in international affairs." Ambassador Dodd was closer to the mark. He wrote that Roosevelt "fears violent opposition to any progressive move that he might make."

President Roosevelt's stunning reelection landslide in 1936 made him more amenable to interventionist suggestions. FDR's image, particularly in Europe, was becoming that of a world statesman. Roosevelt now believed that his great powers of persuasion might be brought to bear upon Hitler himself. Foreign reaction to Roosevelt's victory confirmed his own instinct about the American role in a world where evil forces, preying upon social misery, were planning new wars. As if to prove FDR correct, the Nazi press grew more hostile to him, while *Paris-Soir* exulted, "Henceforth democracy has its chief!" French political leader Paul Reynaud shared this view of FDR, as did Foreign Minister Yvon Delbos. The president would, they hoped, work to change public opinion, "to orient American policy in the direction of . . . the democratic countries and to [France] in particular."[26] That day would come, but not for at least two more years.

Democratic Europe, leaderless and demoralized, thus agreed with the ambassador to France, William Bullitt, who later told Roosevelt, "You are . . . beginning to occupy the miracle man position." The president heard from another admirer that "[o]nly the President of the United States, triumphantly re-elected by his entire nation, enjoys a prestige . . . which enables him to utter an appeal for peace which would have a chance of being heard."[27]

CHAPTER
EIGHT

TOWARD SELECTIVE
CONFRONTATION WITH GERMANY

DESPITE GROWING PUBLIC QUALMS about the goals of the dictators, FDR knew that dramatic presidential action might frighten and alienate the public. The neutrality mania was not the only problem. More than any other president in this century, FDR faced hatreds that were enduring and implacable. Many people from FDR's social class (or those who aspired to that status) viewed him as a "traitor to his class." To a large number of corporate executives, Roosevelt was a slave to distasteful ethnic and racial groups. Sitting in posh clubs in New York City or Chicago or relaxing in Westchester country club locker rooms after a golf game, these men cursed Roosevelt as a closet bolshevik. Eleanor's belief in racial equality filled these men with loathing. Many a Roosevelt-hater shook his head with disgust when discussing the famous "Nigger pictures," widely circulated photographs of Mrs. Roosevelt in conversation with Negro ROTC cadets from Howard University. Roosevelt may have boasted that he had saved capitalism; to his enemies, he had destroyed the good old order, and paved the way for "socialism," if not for dictatorship or even communism. Governor Alf M. Landon of Kansas, a progressive Republican, fell prey to some of this rhetoric during his ill-fated 1936 campaign. "Franklin D. Roosevelt," he told the electorate, "proposes to destroy the right to elect your own representatives."[1]

Others went further, charging that Roosevelt was the "real candidate—the unofficial candidate of the Comintern. . . ." Lieutenant Colonel Edwin M. Hadley voiced the thoughts of many a citizen: "What we have in Washington today is not a Republican administration. *Neither is it a Democratic administration.* It is a Socialistic-Communistic administration. . . ."

Roosevelt-haters included William Randolph Hearst, who had access to millions of people from all social classes through his control of twenty-eight newspapers and numerous radio stations, magazines, and assorted media outlets. Hearst's newspapers had a daily circulation of six million copies, perhaps one-seventh of the American readership. His contempt for the democracies, and his fear of the Soviet Union turned him into a major burden for Roosevelt. Hearst's hatred inspired various denunciations, one of them in verse:

> *A Red New Deal with a Soviet seal*
> *Endorsed by a Moscow hand,*
> *The strange result of an alien cult*
> *In a liberty-loving land*

Like Hearst, Chicago press lord Colonel Robert McCormick was a Roosevelt-hater, as well as a major spokesman for the isolationist consensus. McCormick's *Chicago Tribune* argued that the British Empire was hardly superior to Hitler's Germany, and warned that Roosevelt was bent upon establishing a dictatorship, with the help of communists and other New Deal proponents.[2] By 1935, McCormick, along with Hearst and two other Roosevelt-bashers, controlled about one-fifth of the daily national newspaper circulation, and over one-third of the Sunday readership.[3]

Of patrician background and manner, Roosevelt used his office on behalf of people despised by many members of his own social class. For this, they could not forgive him. "Old money" resented its loss of control, for the expansion of governmental power came on the heels of its own failure in the face of the Great Depression. A liberal with a great name had usurped its power.[4] Now, at the end of 1936, well-dressed ladies sometimes visited newsreel theaters, waiting for the moment when they could jeer the sight of FDR. Others refused to mention the name of "that man in the White House." Rumors circulated describing Roosevelt as a drunk, a syphilitic, a megalomaniac. At times the jibes were humorous, as in the cartoon in which God suffers from delusions of grandeur. "He thinks He's Franklin D. Roosevelt," read the caption. Upon occasion, an exasperated Roosevelt-hater was heard saying, "Well, let's hope somebody shoots him."

Many of the Roosevelt-haters rallied to the Liberty League, which claimed over 124,000 members in the summer of 1936. Its Washington offices were larger than those of the Republican National Committee. The league supported various reactionary groups, including the Southern Committee to Uphold the Constitution. This organization put out propaganda revealing that "President Roosevelt has . . . permitted Negroes to come to the White House Banquet Table and sleep in the White House beds. . . ." The league failed in its attempt to foil FDR's reelection. Indeed, it saddled the Republicans with an "economic royalist" and "fat cat" image that hurt candidate Alf M. Landon. Although its day had passed, the league left a legacy of opposition to Roosevelt that now assumed new forms.[5]

Wealthy Roosevelt-haters intended to sabotage foreign policy initiatives favored by the president. They much preferred fascism to communism, and they mistrusted Roosevelt's commitment to democracy. Nor were the right-wingers an isolated fringe. One poll found that Americans, when forced to choose between communism and fascism, chose the latter by a margin of twenty-two points.[6]

A strange "isolationist" alliance began to emerge, reaching its high point early in the next decade. Those supporting this foreign policy coalition included people who supported Roosevelt on New Deal issues. Among them were "Anglo-Saxon" Progressives, who recalled that war had brought about the demise of Wilsonian liberalism. They thus recoiled at the thought of renewed intervention in Europe. The isolationists also gained the support of many Italian-Americans. Proud of Mussolini's Italy, they resented FDR's growing coolness to the dictator. Aversion to America's onetime allies reinforced these isolationist tendencies. Roosevelt himself sometimes voiced fears about British attempts to inveigle the United States into actions intended to shore up the British Empire. Representative George H. Tinkham, Republican of Massachusetts, spoke for many when he claimed, "The President of the United States and the Department of State, his agent, are under the domination and control of the British Foreign Office." Reactionaries who hated Roosevelt saw his interest in the European crisis as the prelude to a new executive power play.[7]

So Roosevelt, unclear about his course and fearful of his critics, proceeded cautiously. In a widely heralded speech, he stated, "I have passed unnumbered hours, I shall pass unnumbered hours thinking and planning how war may be kept from this nation." As if to renounce Wilsonian messianism, FDR added, "I wish I could keep war from all nations, but that is beyond my power." At times, Roosevelt seemed to regret American entry into the Great War. He found some merit in the "merchants of death" argument. The great actor and supreme politician had not yet discovered his role as world statesman.[8]

Roosevelt's letters, conversations, and speeches reveal a man who was grappling with feelings of suspicion and unease. FDR would, over the next three years, become convinced that coexistence between the Western democratic community and Nazi Germany was unlikely. Roosevelt began to see himself as a kind of savior of the Western democracies. He foresaw the need for the creation of an anti-Nazi diplomatic coalition. The American ambassador to Berlin noted in his diary that "the real fear here . . . is that the President [Roosevelt] may organize all American peoples against Fascist Europe and even boycott any power that starts another war."[9] Dodd's comment proved to be prescient. By 1939, Hitler was telling his generals, "The attempt of certain circles in the U.S. to lead the continent in a direction hostile to Germany is certainly without success at the moment, yet in the future it could lead to the desired result. Here too time must be seen as working against Germany." Hitler's sense of urgency stemmed in part from his concern about the future of American policy. He needed to reorganize Europe in preparation for a global conflict that he both feared and desired.[10] Hitler's fear of America, expressed in his abortive 1928 book, was growing stronger.

If the United States eventually helped to destroy fascism, it would not do so in Spain. Americans influenced the ongoing civil war, but only because thousands of volunteers flocked to fight in the communist-dominated international brigades. Despite their heroism and the suffering of the Spanish Republicans, the government failed to crush General Franco's rebels, who were aided by German aircraft and military advisers, as well as by numerous Italian "legionaries." Roosevelt's sympathies were with the Republic, but he did nothing to terminate (or circumvent) the rigid arms embargo. The horrors inflicted by the Japanese Imperial Army upon Chinese civilians soon joined events in Spain as front-page news. Partially disarmed and committed to neutrality, the United States was not about to intervene militarily in Spain or China.

The United States could make its presence felt in other ways, however, and to the detriment of Germany. FDR seized this opportunity. German-American trade, which had been declining for years, deteriorated further. In 1929, the United States had produced 13.3 percent of Germany's imports, while absorbing 7.4 percent of her exports. By 1938, the figures were 3.4 percent and 3.4 percent, respectively. Secretary Hull, a passionate believer in free trade, strongly objected to Nazi trade policies. The secretary conveyed his anger to a sympathetic president. Hull argued, "The system upon which Germany conducts its international commercial relations . . . runs diametrically contrary to the principles upon which the commercial policy of the United States is based." The anti-Nazi boycott further undermined commerce between America and the Third Reich.

Roosevelt agreed in 1936 that certain German exporters would have to pay countervailing duties on goods exported to the United States. Despite qualms about German trade policies, Secretary Hull, more than the president, attempted to prevent a total breakdown in bilateral trade. Hull opposed the imposition of additional duties on imports, fearing their "deplorable repercussions on our foreign trade . . . with respect to Germany." FDR, in contrast, noted, "If it is a borderline case I feel so keenly about Germany that I would enforce the countervailing duties." Treasury Secretary Henry Morgenthau crusaded for these duties, and he usually prevailed. Hull seemed to miss the point entirely. He protested that the Treasury Department was not applying the duties to other nations "engaging in currency manipulation similar to Germany's."[11] Roosevelt, concerned about German rearmament and Hitler's foreign policy, was tending toward the view that there were few, if any, nations that could be called "similar to Germany." And that, of course, was the whole point. Germany now denounced the German-American trade agreement, in order to put pressure on Washington. The German-American Chamber of Commerce worked to reverse the Roosevelt-Morgenthau decision.[12] Both ploys failed.

Despite these problems, German-American trade did not cease. Complicated patent agreements between corporations doing business in both countries permitted the continued export of strategic products and materials to the Reich. Aircraft, petroleum, and chemical industries supplied Germany with important strategic materials, and some of this commerce flourished even after the outbreak of war in Europe. Americans promoting this trade subscribed to the philosophy of Alfred Sloan, Jr., head of General Motors. "[A]n international business operating throughout the world," wrote Sloan, "should conduct its operations in strictly business terms, without regard to the political beliefs of its management, or the political beliefs of the country in which it is operating."[13]

In December 1933, Standard Oil of New York deposited one million dollars in Germany for making "gasoline from soft coal for war emergencies." A few months later, United Aircraft negotiated the sale of numerous crankshafts, cylinder heads, and other items of military importance. These products enabled the German aircraft industry to produce about "100 airplanes per month." Sperry Gyroscope delivered automatic pilots, as well as the latest gyro compasses to the Germans, enough to equip "50 airplanes per month." It also sold some of its fire prevention systems, used on antiaircraft guns, to the Askania works in Germany. Bendix exported automatic pilot data to Siemens and Halsko. Such products were essential to the Luftwaffe, and the Germans paid in hard currency. In addition, American companies continued to sell patents to the Germans, who then exported some of their aviation technology to other aggressor states, such as fascist Italy. As early as 4 April 1934, Douglas Miller, acting commercial attaché in Berlin, warned the administration about American involvement in German rearmament. In his letter, Miller named names, showing how American firms were assisting in the construction of the German Luftwaffe.[14]

This lucrative and important strategic commerce proved to be the exception to the rule. German-American trade continued on its steep descent. Roosevelt had the authority to prevent the export of certain items, such as helium, and, at the urging of Interior Secretary Harold Ickes, he did so. The Germans would have liked to have imported large amounts of American cotton, selected foodstuffs, and steel, but were unable to place their orders. In some cases, American shareholders objected, as in the instance of steel exports. A more important factor was the ideological incompatibility between the two economic systems.[15] Morgenthau and Roosevelt had no intention of improving trade relations with an economy based upon autarky, export subsidies, and currency manipulation.

In Berlin, Ambassador Dodd grew more impatient. He warned Roosevelt that "pacifism will mean a great war and the subordination of all Europe to Germany if the pacifist peoples do not act courageously. . . ." Dodd informed the president that "Hitler and Mussolini intend to control all Europe." The ambassador believed that "Hitler is simply waiting for his best opportunity to seize what he wants." Roosevelt did not disagree, but relations remained outwardly "correct." The President, Goering, and Hitler exchanged condolences after a tragic explosion in New London, Texas. Roosevelt expressed formal regrets after the crash of the dirigible *Hindenburg* near Lakehurst, New Jersey.

The Spanish tragedy continued unabated. Hull and Roosevelt convinced themselves that the embargo on the export of arms to the Republic was the wisest course. Congress had made this policy mandatory, of course, but Roosevelt did nothing to change it.[16] The Americans claimed to be endorsing the European commitment to nonintervention in Spain, but the fact remains that Congress and the Roosevelt administration helped to seal the fate of the Republic. Had the Franco forces been crushed after their failure to take Madrid in late 1936, the Republic might well have prevailed. Roosevelt later regretted his own policy, but he believed in it at the time of its adoption. After all, as Hull recalled, "the United States was set in a concrete mold of isolation." Roosevelt refused to break that mold, except in cases related to bilateral trade and activities in the Western Hemisphere.[17]

During this first year of Roosevelt's second term, Congress modified the neutrality law. The Neutrality Act passed in 1937 maintained the mandatory arms embargo to belligerents. The law was more flexible in one sense, however. It contained a "cash and carry" clause, and this represented a victory for the president and for American exporters. Belligerents could buy American goods, including those of a strategic nature, so long as they exported the purchased goods to their homelands in ships other than those flying the flag of the United States. The purchasers would also have to pay cash in advance. This clause, scheduled to expire on 1 May 1939, could only favor Britain and France, because their naval power far exceeded that of Germany and Italy. Furthermore, the president had obtained discretionary authority in the application of the "cash and carry" measure. Another regulation flatly forbade American citizens from sailing on ships flying the flags of belligerent powers. The New York *Herald Tribune* called the law "An Act to Preserve the United States From Intervention in the War of 1917–1918."[18]

Roosevelt's concern about fascism was growing, but his policy of caution in regard to European commitments remained unimpaired. He moved more boldly, however, when confronting German influence closer to home.

Roosevelt's knowledge of geography convinced him that American security and prosperity depended upon a stable South American continent. Roosevelt and Secretary Hull were aware of the disturbing statistics. United States trade with Latin America had declined by about 75 percent between 1929 and 1933. In 1929, the U.S. had absorbed 34 percent of Latin America's exports; by 1934, the figure had dropped to 29.4 percent. In 1929, the Germans purchased 8.1 percent of Latin America's exports, and provided 10.8 percent of its imports. By the mid-1930s, the Germans absorbed 10.8 percent of these exports, and accounted for 16.2 percent of Latin America's imports.

In 1935, Germany provided Brazil with 20.7 percent of its imports, a figure comparable to that applicable to the United States. By 1936, Brazil was importing more automobiles from Germany than from Great Britain. In that year, it acquired 86,000 tons of coal from the Reich; a year later, the figure shot up to 200,000 tons. The Germans were making inroads into Chile and Mexico as well. Their share of these nations' imports rose dramatically. By 1937, the Germans accounted for 26 percent of Chile's imports and 17.7 percent of Mexico's. The Germans hoped to gain unlimited access to South American raw materials. They had a long tradition of trade with Latin America, and most of this commerce was nonstrategic in nature. And despite German gains, both Britain and the United States continued to maintain higher levels of capital investment in the region.[19]

Nevertheless, Hull and Roosevelt were greatly concerned, particularly after reading a report from Secretary of Agriculture Henry A. Wallace. This memorandum heightened FDR's fears of German and Japanese trade with Latin America. As early as December 1935, Roosevelt had thought about assisting Latin American countries with "supplies of one kind or another." Roosevelt, Hull, and Morgenthau had not, however, formulated a coherent policy for Latin America.[20] They were now beginning to do so. The administration was preparing the way for the first geopolitical conflict between the Third Reich and the United States. Here Roosevelt could operate in the realms of politics, economics, and ideology. Even isolationists supported the Monroe Doctrine.

The Germans usually paid for their Brazilian imports with blocked currency accounts that could only be used for the purchase of German exports, such as coal. The Reich government was subsidizing German exports, while preventing countries like Brazil from using German "currency" for the purchase of British or American products. Bilateral and exclusionary, the "Aski" system violated every principle of Hull's free trade ideology.[21] Worse still, countries like Argentina, Chile, and Brazil contained large Italian and German populations, and FDR was becoming more concerned about their rumored affinity for fascist or Nazi ideology.

Hans Stöckl, a German nationalist, had years before argued that a resurgent Germany could build bridges to *Auslanddeutschtum*, to the German communities in places like Chile. Now, with the Nazis in power, some nationalists believed that awakened German communities, working with their host nations, could contribute to the resistance against absorption by the Yankee behemoth.[22] The Nazis, moreover, were fully capable of denouncing the Monroe Doctrine, for their own rather transparent purposes. Roosevelt's State Department advisers knew that such siren sounds could tempt their restive Latin targets. In 1930, after all, a Mexican supreme court judge had announced that "[f]or Mexico the Monroe Doctrine does not exist," that it was merely "an infantile theory, to cloak the tutelage on the part of the United States over Latin America."[23] The president's advisers rushed to provide him with the requisite background information on his latest obsession, German influence in Latin America. It was clear to FDR that his global ideals of democracy, capitalist development, and free trade could never be achieved if Latin America became a pawn in the hands of hostile totalitarian powers.

The evolution of the "Good Neighbor" policy reflected FDR's worries about Axis subversion in Latin America. He wished to dominate Latin America's foreign trade, but with the approval of the republics there. This would be difficult, for, as Roosevelt knew, powerful nationalist currents affected the political cultures of countries like Argentina and Mexico. Diplomatic pressure, promises of credits and other investments, and sensitivity to differing viewpoints thus replaced gunboat diplomacy. There was a potentially dangerous trade-off, however, at least from Roosevelt's viewpoint. If America forswore armed intervention, might not other powers be tempted to establish bases in Latin America? The president was coming to equate American economic interests and strategic security with an anti-Nazi policy in Latin America.

Alarming reports continued to reach Roosevelt. Ambassador Dodd informed him that "a Chile man reported a Nazi Party in that country of 35,000 men, adding that the Chilean Government expects to be a German colony in a year or two. The Colombian Minister came to see me two days ago and said that the activity all over Latin America was so great that he wished me to report it."[24] Even Cordell Hull, who usually kept his emotions under tight control, expressed alarm. The Germans, he believed, were organizing their Latin American brethren into Nazi storm-troop units. Sumner Welles, a State Department expert on the Caribbean and Latin America, worked to strengthen the "Good Neighbor" policy. FDR came into closer contact with him, particularly after Welles's appointment as under secretary of state in May 1937.

Hull disliked Sumner Welles and feared that FDR was grooming the bright and scholarly under secretary as his successor. This appears not to have been the case. FDR needed Hull's contacts with his former colleagues in Congress, and he appreciated his loyalty. FDR would, however, use Welles when necessary. Roosevelt liked to keep the strings in his own hands. This meant working on the crucial issues of war, peace, and diplomacy with selected political appointees, among them Anthony Biddle, William Bullitt, and Sumner Welles. This talented team would serve Roosevelt well in the two years that lay ahead. These men challenged Roosevelt, helped him to formulate his ideas, and pushed him toward the achievement of goals that mattered to him.

CHAPTER
NINE

QUARANTINE OR
APPEASEMENT?

I N THE AUTUMN of 1937, President Roosevelt appeared to strike out
in a bold new direction. He gave public voice to some of his private
concerns about the direction of world affairs.[1] In a Chicago speech,
delivered on 5 October, Roosevelt denounced unnamed aggressors,
thanks to whom "civilians . . . are being ruthlessly murdered with
bombs from the air." For the first time, Roosevelt warned the people
that isolation and neutrality were no guarantees of American security.
He implied that aggressor nations, if not checked elsewhere, might one
day turn against the "Western Hemisphere," a vague phrase left unde-
fined. Roosevelt spoke of "positive endeavors to preserve peace," such
as imposing a quarantine on the aggressor.

The man who had signed the neutrality legislation, acquiesced in
continuing American military weakness, and embargoed arms shipments to the Spanish Republic was reacting uneasily to the emergence
of a new "Axis" stretching from Berlin to Rome. Japan, Germany, and
Italy were soon linked in a so-called "Anti-Comintern" pact, directed at
the Soviet Union. Roosevelt received more disturbing news from Secretary of State Hull, who informed FDR that Germany was "hell-bent on

war." Other incoming reports indicated that the Third Reich was in the hands of psychopaths.[2]

The "Quarantine Speech" received some support, both from newspaper editorialists and from concerned individuals. Clark M. Eichelberger, the national director of the League of Nations Association worked hard on behalf of the president's ideas. The Council on Foreign Relations, a body representing and serving the internationalist establishment, redoubled its efforts to inform the public about America's stake in collective security measures. The Carnegie Corporation soon provided it with fifty thousand dollars. The council was run by the kind of people who, like Roosevelt, sympathized with Wilsonian internationalism. Like Roosevelt, Hamilton Fish Armstrong, editor of the council's prestigious journal, *Foreign Affairs*, doubted that the United States could remain neutral in the event of a new war. Unlike the president, he soon said so publicly, because *his* constituency was sympathetic to this position.[3]

Despite these pockets of support, the loudest voices were raised in opposition to the president's speech.[4] Secretary of State Cordell Hull, taken aback by the furor, recalled, "The reaction against the quarantine idea was quick and violent." Hull saw the speech as a serious setback to the internationalists' "constant educational campaign." There were more substantial reasons for Hull's negative reaction. Despite his insights into Hitler's aims, the secretary had no use for Roosevelt's plan to convene an international conference dedicated to settling outstanding issues of trade, frontiers, and armaments. And Hull knew that polls showed that sixty-nine percent of the people favored *stricter* neutrality legislation. Even in the supposedly internationalist East, papers like the *Boston Herald* constantly warned against intervention in Europe. "Crusade if you must," it told FDR, "but for the sake of several millions of American mothers confine your expanding to the continental limits of America."[5] Only twenty-six percent of those polled wished to see the United States enter the League of Nations.

Soon after delivering the Chicago speech, the president told Endicott Peabody, his old headmaster at Groton School, "I am fighting against a public psychology of long standing—a psychology which comes very close to saying 'Peace at any price.'" The *Boston Herald* invoked bitter memories: "The mantle of Woodrow Wilson lay on the shoulders of Franklin Roosevelt when he spoke in Chicago." The *New York Daily News*, contradicting itself at every turn, praised Roosevelt for his initiative and advocated the provision of arms to China. In the same breath, however, the *News* urged Britain to share some of its colonies with Germany, and warned against American involvement overseas!

A nine-power conference, convened in Brussels to deal with Japanese aggression, accomplished nothing, thanks in part to American caution and Japanese contempt. Despite this setback, Roosevelt devoted more thought to the creation of an antiaggressor coalition. FDR still wanted to convene an international conference committed to furthering the causes of disarmament and open markets, though he was uncertain about its prospects. Ever convinced of his own powers of persuasion, Roosevelt continued to muse about a meeting with Hitler and Mussolini.

The Nye Committee, the World Court uproar, and the "Quarantine Speech" imbroglio proved once again that interventionism was a political mine field. Early in 1938, the House of Representatives barely defeated the notorious Ludlow Resolution. This legislation would have required a national plebiscite before the United States could go to war, except in the instance of a direct attack upon American territory. Roosevelt needed to puzzle out his course. He was not acting decisively or consistently in foreign affairs.[6] Neville Chamberlain, now British prime minister, welcomed Roosevelt's friendship, but counted "on nothing from the American but words."

The president received uncertain and divided counsel from the State Department. The chief of the division of European affairs, Pierrepont Moffat, described himself as preoccupied with preventing the "involvement of the United States in hostilities anywhere," and worked to "discourage any formation of a common front of the democratic powers." From his ambassadors, Roosevelt sometimes received the opposite advice. A political optimist, FDR did not doubt that strong executive leadership might change public attitudes. Polls, which fascinated him, seemed to bear this out. As early as the spring of 1936, forty-four percent of the polled public thought that the United States "will be drawn into the next European War." Within three years, that figure had risen to fifty-eight percent. If the public was fatalistic about war, it might be receptive to a message garbed in the rhetoric of "defense" and "preparedness."[7]

Some of the more articulate pacifists and peace activists were beginning to change their views, or at least their tactics. The rise of fascism was splitting the peace movement. Pacifist Reinhold Niebuhr, a distinguished theologian, had described all war as "worthless" in 1929. A few years later, he justified violence by oppressed classes and peoples, while advocating international intervention against fascist aggressors. Socialist Norman Thomas, while still favoring the use of nonviolent methods, now rejected pacifism as a response to fascist aggression. Meanwhile, the "Oxford Pledge," which required those who adopted it not to serve in their nation's armed forces or fight in its wars, was becoming less popular on college campuses. The communists, who had strongly supported the peace movements, now had second thoughts. When the Soviet Union entered the League of Nations (1934) and called for collective security measures, the Communist League Against War and Fascism transformed itself into the American League for Peace and Democracy.[8] The communists became less hostile to Roosevelt. Though small in number, the Communist party enjoyed the support of many trade unionists and intellectuals.

Certainly, the press would have to play its part in changing public perceptions of the American role in the world. Fifty million newspaper readers constituted the bulk of the potential electorate. The Hearst newspapers gave FDR much grief, as did Colonel McCormick and the *Chicago Tribune*. FDR went directly to the people with his "fireside chats" on the radio. And Roosevelt knew how to circumvent the prejudices and politics of powerful press moguls. He was a great manipulator of the print media. In the words of Washington bureau chief of the *New York Times*, Arthur Krock, FDR was the "greatest reader and critic of newspapers who had ever been in the president's office." Roosevelt tried to show reporters how to write a column, and he was not above conspiring to bring about the reassignment of a difficult newsperson.[9] Despite his complaint that "eighty-five percent" of the press was against him, the president often received fair, even favorable, treatment in the news columns. In fact, about seventy percent of the newspapers described themselves as Democratic or independent.

FDR held six times as many press conferences during his first term as had President Hoover.[10] FDR understood public opinion, and he learned a lot from the unprecedented flood of mail that arrived in the cluttered White House mail room (450,000 communications during his first week in office!). Roosevelt put this knowledge to good use. He played upon popular hopes and anxieties at his press conferences. With one hand, FDR gauged public opinion; with the other, he manipulated it.

Roosevelt diligently cultivated favored syndicated columnists, such

as Walter Winchell of Hearst's *New York Daily Mirror*. An early admirer of
Roosevelt, Winchell hated Hitler, calling pro-Nazis "swastinkas," and
"Hitlerrooters." Winchell was a power-hungry egotist, but he was also a
politically courageous man. Because he worked for Hearst, who now
despised Roosevelt with a vengeance, Winchell proved particularly
useful to FDR. His syndicated column was read throughout the nation,
and his famous radio broadcasts became standard fare for millions of
Americans. Hearst tried to censor Winchell, but failed. Winchell had
enough clout to write his own ticket. "He had power," recalled a former
co-worker at the *Mirror*.

Roosevelt captivated reporters with his humor, knowledge, self-
confidence, and accessibility. Hedley Donovan, a young journalist, still
remembered the famous charm more than forty years later. "I was
greatly flattered one day . . . ," Donovan writes, "to receive a large
wink from the President as he delivered some transparent piece of
humbug." Roosevelt was, he quickly adds, a "personality of deep
subtleties and complexity."[11] He knew how to pique interest by remaining silent until he was ready to show his hand. An observer described the result in these terms: "He won them [reporters] and he has
still a larger proportion of them personally sympathetic than any of his
recent predecessors." One correspondent spoke for many when he
rejoiced, "[W]e're not only welcome but we have the distinct feeling—
for the first time—that we belong here, that he's *our* President." They
laughed at his jokes, and if warned by the president about a foreign
menace, they would alert their readers without asking too many questions. Gathered around the president's desk while he smiled, chatted,
evaded, and manipulated, all the while scattering cigarette smoke and
ashes about him, reporters were mesmerized. Still, Roosevelt never let
the press forget who was president. He liked reporters when he could
use them, but he also knew when and how to avoid them.[12]

By the time of the "Quarantine Speech," Ambassador Dodd had ful-
filled his role. He had taught Roosevelt what he needed to know about
Hitler. Old, ill, and tired, Dodd retired. His outspoken anti-Nazism
had antagonized both Berlin and Washington. Powerful friends of Roosevelt, including William C. Bullitt and Sumner Welles, believed that a
moderate career diplomat might accomplish more in Berlin.[13] The

president acquiesced, by replacing Dodd with the more flexible Hugh R. Wilson. Roosevelt paid little attention to Wilson on policy matters.

As for Ambassador Dodd, he performed two more acts of selfless public service. Despite a debilitating illness, he embarked upon extensive lecture tours, warning complacent Americans of the Axis threat to democracy. Dodd then devoted much of his remaining time to preparing his diaries for publication. A scathing indictment of Nazi coarseness and brutality, they served to enlighten many American readers. Dodd had been one of the early prophets, warning of Hitler's ambitions. Roosevelt now turned more and more often to Anthony J.D. Biddle and William Bullitt, ambassadors to Warsaw and Paris. Biddle and Bullitt stimulated and cajoled the president, providing him with extra eyes and ears in Europe.[14]

Roosevelt needed to change public opinion; for the moment this objective was more important than the mechanics of collective security. He informed Biddle, "We cannot stop the spread of Fascism unless world opinion realizes its ultimate dangers." He hinted at an Anglo-American alliance directed against the dictators and militarists, stating, "[T]he United States and Great Britain have one great common concern—the preservation of peace throughout the world." Now, in this same year, the widely read columnist Walter Lippmann echoed FDR's words. "No matter what we wish now or now believe," he wrote, "though collaboration with Britain . . . is difficult and often irritating, we shall protect the connection because in no other way can we fulfill our destiny."[15]

Roosevelt was pleased when Ambassador Biddle reported that Polish reaction to the "Quarantine Speech" was highly favorable. The president hoped that the Poles, allies of the French, would reject any German demands that might be in the offing. Privately, FDR made some prophetic comments that give us a clue to his growth as a political manipulator and a global strategist. Speaking to his son Elliott, Roosevelt said, "Sooner or later there'll be a showdown in Europe." He then speculated on the unpleasant prospect of becoming embroiled in a two-ocean war. "Then," he commented, "you would have to be a bit shifty on your feet. You have to lick one of them first and then bring your military forces around and then lick the other."[16]

Ambassador William Bullitt forced Roosevelt to ponder some hard choices.[17] An erratic, brilliant man, Bullitt had accompanied Wilson to

the 1919 peace conference. He quickly became disillusioned with
Wilson at Versailles. Testifying against that president's foreign policy,
Bullitt earned the reputation as a disloyal and flighty young man. Bullitt
took his revenge by writing a scathing study of Wilson's personality
(Sigmund Freud contributed to the work), but political ambition caused
him to delay publishing the book for thirty-five years.

A staunch Democrat, Bullitt received another chance in 1933, when
FDR recognized the Soviet Union. Appointed the first U.S. ambassador to Moscow, Bullitt changed his views. Originally sympathetic to
the young Soviet state, Bullitt was now a fervent anticommunist, to the
exclusion of most other considerations. After he took up his duties in
Paris, he began to pay more heed to the menace across the Rhine River.
For at least a year, however, the ambassador judged the Nazi threat in
terms of the expansion of world communism. He feared that war would
lead to massive Soviet territorial gains, and would unleash revolutions
within the belligerent nations.[18]

Watching Hitler changed the ambassador's point of view. He became
as obsessed with the Nazis as he had been with the communists. Bullitt
now warned the president of the Nazi commitment to the preservation
of American isolation and neutrality. He foresaw an era of German
aggression. Over and over again, Bullitt spoke on behalf of those French
leaders who feared Nazi Germany. He stubbornly refused to acknowledge the need for a Franco-Russian military pact, because he still
hoped for a peaceful settlement of the European crisis. Germany, he
argued, would have to be the dominant power in the new European
order. Still, Bullitt was moving toward an antifascist position. The
ambassador worked to convince FDR of the crying need for dynamic
leadership. He voiced the hunger for a democratic leader of global
stature, because "Hitler has the ball and can run with it in any direction
he chooses."

FDR encouraged Bullitt and Biddle to deal with him through back
channels that led right into the Oval Office. Roosevelt listened carefully
to their reports, but his thoughts still raced ahead of his political
program. FDR stubbornly clung to his idea of an international conference; he also warned Biddle and Bullitt that they could make no
commitments on behalf of the American government.

Prime Minister Neville Chamberlain disliked Roosevelt's idea of a
multipower conference, in part because of the American refusal to make
prior commitments to collective security. Stubborn, self-righteous, and

unschooled in foreign affairs, Chamberlain intended to defend British interests by assuming center stage himself. Chamberlain did not understand the value of bringing the United States to a high-level international conference on trade and armaments issues. If he had, he might have assisted Roosevelt in moving American public opinion in a more interventionist direction.

Beginning no later than November 1937, when he sent Edward Halifax, Lord Privy Seal, to Berlin for high-level discussions, Chamberlain resolved to pacify Europe through bilateral discussions with Hitler. Roosevelt's ideological mutterings, devoid of any real threat to act, could only, Chamberlain believed, antagonize the dictators and render "appeasement" impossible. Foreign Secretary Anthony Eden thought differently, and feared Roosevelt's resentment. Chamberlain prevailed, and Eden was soon outside of the government.[19]

By the time the Nazis seized Austria on 11 March, FDR's conference proposal was outmoded. Chamberlain steadfastly continued his policy of appeasement. Appeasement required bilateral dealings with Hitler; the French, Italians, Czechs, Soviets, Americans, and other interested parties would be minor players, if invited at all. Above all, Chamberlain wanted to avoid being dragged into a war by Czech or Polish intransigence, or by French miscalculation. The prime minister was an anomaly, responsible for the British Empire, yet basically an isolationist. The French, however, appeared to be following Chamberlain's lead; they were delighted to avoid painful decision making. Bullitt was working hard to change this situation, but France's revival required time.

Chamberlain's policy rested upon the assumption that one could coexist with a strong (and perhaps stronger) Germany. Roosevelt was reaching the opposite conclusion, but public opinion needed to be monitored, as always. Roosevelt, reported British ambassador Sir Ronald Lindsay, "is strongly anti-German and is revolted at what the German Government are doing but . . . at the same time he fully appreciated limitations which public opinion places on his policies and actions."[20]

Between May and September, the European crisis grew more acute. Hitler prepared for an attack on democratic Czechoslovakia, whose "oppression" of its minority of three million Germans greatly aggrieved him. Many of these Germans lived in the border region known to the Germans as the Sudetenland. The Nazis seemed to be conjuring up the ghost of Woodrow Wilson: All the Germans wanted was "self-determination" for their oppressed brethren across the border. A war scare erupted in May, when there was talk about a German attack on Czechoslovakia.

Most Americans viewed the crisis as one more in a series of unending European quarrels. Even Bullitt seemed to blame the intransigent Czechs for the crisis. His reports to Roosevelt, however, did contain a new and crucial point. European states, said the ambassador, were convinced that if they resisted aggression, the United States would, at some point, be drawn into the new war. And Roosevelt knew that this conviction was worth mulling over.

FDR badly needed some new challenge. In 1937, he had suffered a major political defeat. He had attempted to strike back at a hostile Supreme Court by gaining the authority to expand it, under certain circumstances, to a maximum of fifteen members. Failing in this, the president in 1938 tried to "purge" some of the conservative Democrats who had deserted him. His candidates in the spring and summer primaries usually met with defeat. The polls predicted major gains for the Republicans in the fall elections.

Despite these domestic difficulties, FDR had preserved and expanded democracy at home. His vision now encompassed a similar victory abroad. A concept, however, was one thing; bringing it to fruition would be quite another, requiring both guile and brilliance.

In Berlin, U.S. ambassador Hugh R. Wilson sought consolation in the fact "that the relatively disinterested power of Great Britain is taking an active part in the [Czech] matter and [is] endeavoring to act as a sort of mediator between [Czech President Edvard] Beneš and Hitler." To Wilson, as to Chamberlain, appeasement had come to mean disinterested mediation between competing German and Czech claims. Wilson, like Chamberlain, would pay almost any price for the avoidance of war, for this was "the paramount consideration."

Roosevelt, in contrast, harbored growing doubts about Chamberlain's appeasement policy, though he kept them from the public. If Chamberlain succeeded in avoiding war, FDR believed, Hitler would be the stronger for it. In the meantime, however, a more powerful Hitler could only undermine appeasement and strengthen the president's own foreign policy hand. Roosevelt continued to exercise caution; he watched the public opinion polls and paid heed to the forthcoming congressional elections.[21]

Bullitt, meanwhile, was playing an interesting game, one which Roosevelt watched with approval. The ambassador held frequent conferences with French leaders. Bullitt was urging resistance to Hitler, without indicating how or with what means America would assist Germany's adversaries. The ambassador then took care to remind his interlocutors that they could *not* count upon American aid in the event of war. Bullitt thus protected both himself and Roosevelt against politically damaging leaks implicating the administration in meddling in the crisis "over there."

Despite his disclaimers, however, Bullitt did have confidence in Roosevelt's ability to maneuver around the Neutrality Act, short of going to war. He knew that the French were particularly frightened of German air power, for Colonel Charles A. Lindbergh, Jr., had told them about the "ten thousand warplanes" possessed by the Luftwaffe.[22] In addressing the president, the ambassador sometimes quoted foreign leaders who believed that the United States would ultimately intervene. He did so without comment.[23] Action belonged to the sphere of presidential decision making. Bringing about a massive shift in public opinion was Roosevelt's job.

The May war scare passed, but in August the Czech problem again became acute. Bullitt became more pressing in his messages to FDR, arguing that "[f]ear of the United States is unquestionably a large factor in Hitler's hesitation to start a war." He suggested that Roosevelt have a "quiet conversation" with German ambassador Dieckhoff. Roosevelt demurred. Such an encounter might remind Americans of President Wilson's talks with the German ambassador on the eve of American entry into the last war. Instead, in a related move, Roosevelt journeyed to Kingston, Ontario.

FDR delivered a powerful speech there, one that marked a turning point in his thinking. The talk was unilateralist and revolutionary in nature, though Roosevelt made it sound like a routine restatement of American foreign policy goals. In it, the president attacked brutal, undemocratic regimes, once again not naming them. Then, in a stunning statement, Roosevelt warned, "[T]he United States will not stand idly by if domination of Canadian soil is threatened by any other Empire." The press in Ontario was kinder to FDR after the Kingston speech than the American newspapers had been after the Chicago speech. His Kingston speech was complex, and not a little devious. FDR knew that Hitler could not yet threaten North America. If Chamberlain permitted continued Nazi expansion, however, this danger could one day become a reality. Since only Congress could declare war, Roosevelt was committing himself to a vast expansion of his authority as commander in chief. His vision of American democratic capitalism, at once hegemonic and altruistic, was taking shape.[24]

The growing Nazi threat led Roosevelt to move more quickly now. The president ordered the Joint Army and Navy Board to consider "various practicable courses of action . . . in the event of . . . violation of the Monroe Doctrine by one or more of the Fascist powers." Roosevelt defined this "violation" ever more broadly. Still, events in Europe preoccupied him for the rest of this dangerous summer.

Once back in the United States, the president was careful to reiterate his allegiance to the spirit of the neutrality law. In September, with Europe on the verge of war, he informed the French, "You may count on us for everything except troops and loans." Roosevelt hoped to strengthen Chamberlain's resistance to Hitler's demands.

Early in September, Hitler castigated Czech president Beneš and the Czechs in ferocious terms. While Bullitt pushed Roosevelt toward confrontation with Hitler, the president's ambassadors in London and Berlin urged him to support Chamberlain. Ambassador Joseph P. Kennedy admired the prime minister precisely because of his willingness to compromise with Hitler. In a proposal that reveals much about Kennedy and even more about British policy, the ambassador suggested that he be allowed to make a public statement disavowing American support for Britain in the event of war. Secretary of State Hull, with the concurrence of Roosevelt, refused to permit the issuance of the proposed statement. Kennedy, upset by this decision, moaned, "I can't for the life of me understand why anybody would want to go to war to save the Czechs."

Appointing a clever and magnetic Boston Irishman to be emissary to the court of St. James had been good politics but proved to be bad policy. Kennedy, a stock speculator, whiskey importer, and campaign financier (for Roosevelt in 1932) had served FDR as his first head of the new Securities and Exchange Commission. Roosevelt respected the charming, fifty-year-old Kennedy for both his business sense and his political connections. The problem was that FDR, dubious about appeasement from the beginning, was now moving to undermine Chamberlain's policy. Kennedy, on the other hand, had become a confidant of the prime minister and a fervent disciple of appeasement. "I have four boys," he once said, "and I don't want them to be killed in a foreign war." Ambassador Kennedy believed that Germany needed to expand to the east, and hoped that this development would be accepted by the democracies. Kennedy bemoaned the influence of Jews upon the American press and, by implication, upon Roosevelt.

FDR was unhappy with Kennedy, but he retained him in London for political reasons. While outwardly supporting Chamberlain's peace policy, Roosevelt spoke of it with contempt. The prime minister was, he said, working for "peace at any price if he could get away with it and save his face." When war finally came, Kennedy was in a state of despair, while Roosevelt seemed to feel particularly jaunty. This opposition of moods was reflected in Kennedy's decline in importance. Meanwhile, Ambassador Bullitt in Paris emerged to play a greater role. From Warsaw to London, he was soon coordinating American policy at FDR's behest.[25]

Englishman Oliver Harvey, private secretary to the foreign secretary, an antiappeaser, now observed, "Roosevelt is fully with us, and he authorised . . . Bullitt to make some strong remarks in a speech at a war memorial last week." The State Department, having seen the text in advance, wanted Bullitt to tone down his remarks. The ambassador appealed to the president, who did not appreciably weaken the text. Bullitt then went on to make the extraordinary statement that "[i]f war breaks out again in Europe, no one can say for sure if the United States would be dragged into such a war."[26] Roosevelt and Bullitt quickly corrected the impression given by the comment. Nevertheless, after duly noting the purely moral nature of Roosevelt's support, Harvey concluded that it was still "a very great deal more than we had in 1914."[27] Roosevelt diverted two U.S. cruisers to Great Britain, the *Nashville* and the *Honolulu*. The *Chicago Tribune* responded by a warning against repeating the mistakes of 1917.[28] In 1937, the *Tribune* had attacked FDR for what he said; now McCormick could lambaste the president for what he was doing.

Chamberlain and Daladier, however, were not satisfied by these gestures. Their countries, after all, were the ones that would have to go to war. They put even more pressure upon the Czechs, hoping that Prague would yield to the major German demands. Roosevelt was unhappy with this development, but proved unwilling to distance himself from the popular peace policy pursued by the Western powers. He also feared that war at this time would result in a quick Axis victory. In private conversation, however, FDR mused about a common blockade of (rather than a war against) Germany, a course of action that would enable him to evade the letter and spirit of the Neutrality Act. He confided to Sir Ronald Lindsay, the British ambassador, that "the United States might again find themselves involved in a European war," and that "an American army might be sent overseas." He could only conceive of such a course, the president quickly added, if Germany were on the verge of conquering Britain.

In remarkable detail, Roosevelt had sketched out his course of action over the next year. His global strategy was maturing, even as political caution caused him to give grudging support to Chamberlain's pursuit of peace. Privately, Roosevelt believed that there would be "an inevitable conflict within the next five years." German Ambassador Dieckhoff, intuiting Roosevelt's ultimate intention, urgently informed Berlin that if Germany used force, "the whole weight of the United States [would] be thrown into the scale on the side of Britain." Such an intervention would represent the culmination of what one keen observer of the president called his "slowly deepening and strengthening internationalism."[29]

Franklin Roosevelt, a deeply political man, could only be encouraged by the work of many makers of American public opinion. The image of Nazi Germany was changing, and rapidly. Time was of the essence, for FDR would be struggling against forces pledged to oppose him if he undertook to impose an interventionist policy upon a confused nation.

CHAPTER
TEN

THE GROWTH OF ANTI-NAZI SENTIMENT IN THE UNITED STATES

FOR SEVERAL YEARS, Edgar Prochnik, the shrewd Austrian minister to the United States, had closely monitored American attitudes toward Hitler's Third Reich. Prochnik knew how an interventionist American president could arouse the public, then lead it to war. Few Americans disliked Austria-Hungary in 1914; four years later, their government helped to destroy that empire. Now, in the mid-1930s, Prochnik hoped for a reversal of the process, a turnabout that might lend American support to his government's struggle for an independent Austria.

Prochnik's American sources were diplomats and politicians, as well as journalists. He described them as people concerned about the Nazi regime's irrationality. America's revulsion against Nazi persecutions, Prochnik knew, coexisted uneasily with a desire to avoid involvement in another European war. Americans would have to feel shocked, then threatened, before they would support a new interventionism. This transformation would require a massive public relations campaign, as well as brilliant political leadership.

*   *   *

On 27 March 1933, less than a week after Hitler consolidated his power, the American Jewish Congress, led by Honorary President Rabbi Stephen S. Wise, conducted a large, well-publicized anti-Nazi rally in Madison Square Garden. Politicians, clergy, and labor leaders addressed the gathering. As Rabbi Wise put it, "The time for caution and prudence is past. We must," he argued, "speak up like men." The rally heard from William Green, president of the American Federation of Labor (AFL), who told the cheering audience, "We will not remain passive and unconcerned when the relatives, families and brethren of the Jewish members of our great economic organization are being persecuted and oppressed."[1] Rabbi Wise and others, particularly Jews affiliated with the American Jewish Congress, now wanted to go further. They intended to hurt the Nazis by organizing a nationwide boycott of German exports. (Here the congress was following the lead of the Jewish War Veterans.)[2] Wise believed that the boycott would weaken Hitler by undermining his economy.

The fervor of the Madison Square Garden meeting masked severe divisions within the Jewish community. Wealthier, more established elements, often of German-Jewish origin, controlled B'nai B'rith and the American Jewish Committee. They favored cautious tactics, fearing for the safety of relatives and friends in Germany. In some cases, economic ties to the Reich influenced Jewish tactics. Judge Joseph M. Proskauer, a power on the American Jewish Committee, and Judge Irving Lehman, the older brother of New York governor Herbert Lehman, warned that a boycott of German imports could only hurt the German Jews themselves. "I implore you," begged Lehman, ". . . don't let anger pass a resolution which will [bring harm to] Jews in Germany." The Nazi anti-Jewish boycott of 1 April undermined the conservatives' position. On that day, storm troopers had picketed, defaced, and trashed Jewish retail shops, screaming, "Germans, defend yourselves! Don't buy from Jews!"

At this point, Samuel Untermeyer emerged as the most energetic leader of the boycott movement. A famous attorney and Zionist, Untermeyer had powerful political connections, both inside and outside the Jewish community in New York City. Untermeyer and other boycott leaders soon ran into opposition from some of the Jewish-owned department stores, such as R.H. Macy's. For many months, Percy S. Straus, Macy's president, resisted the boycott. His excuses included responsibility to shareholders and opposition to censorship. In January 1934, sign-bearing demonstrators surrounded Macy's. Among them marched the conscience of American pacifism and social reform, Norman Thomas. Straus decided that he would, after all, close down his German operations.[3]

Samuel Untermeyer realized that the boycott movement had to transcend its purely Jewish image. Its expansion resulted in the founding, in November 1934, of the Non-Sectarian Anti-Nazi Council (later, League) to Champion Human Rights. Untermeyer became its president. Hitler's boycott of the Jews, the Nazi harassment of Christian churches, the book burnings and violence, all contributed to the league's growth. Supported by William Green, head of the AFL, and John L. Lewis, longtime chief of the United Mine Workers, the league spearheaded the move to boycott German exports. The league also exposed the criminal backgrounds of many American fascists. Soon joined by left-wing groups such as the American League Against War and Fascism, the boycott movement distributed leaflets, put pressure on businesses advertising in pro-Nazi publications, and rendered militant anti-Nazi sentiments broadly acceptable to the public. The boycott did not greatly affect the policies of the Hitler government, but it indirectly helped to change American attitudes toward the German regime.

Watching these developments from Berlin, Professor Friedrich Schönemann grew concerned about the rising tide of American anti-Nazism. Drawing upon his many academic contacts, Schönemann came to America in the autumn of 1933. The professor lectured before a large, curious, and orderly audience in the chapel at Drew University in New Jersey. Schönemann came equipped with responses to some obvious questions. The concentration camps? Like "college dormitories," replied the professor. Schönemann even quoted a former socialist newspaper editor, who had allegedly "been happier in the concentration camp than when he had been [while] editing a newspaper." The answer reflected a kind of cynicism that was beyond the understanding of most Americans. Schönemann left Drew looking forward to his next assignment.

News about the professor's visit quickly spread to various campuses. Here, word had it, was a representative of Hitler's Germany, a professor from the land of book burnings. By the time Schönemann reached

Chicago, the antifascist hecklers and agitators were out in full force. The professor provoked one audience with gratuitous comments about the Jews in Germany. "Today," Schönemann declared, "there are many Jews in Berlin holding fine positions and [they] will continue to hold them." The professor had a ready explanation for the incineration of books by Jewish authors: They were pornographic in nature. "Einstein?" screamed a member of audience. Hitler, Schönemann implied, was opposed to the Jews only because left-wing leaders were "nearly always Jewish." Police in the auditorium prevented some nasty confrontations.

By the time Schönemann reached New England, in late November, he had become infamous. Ten thousand demonstrators awaited his entry into Ford Hall, near the Boston Common. Protected by mounted police, Schönemann entered the building, while arrests occurred around him. The professor looked puzzled, though the title of his talk, "Why I Believe in the Hitler Government," was rather provocative.

Addressing the issue of the concentration camps (Dachau was becoming a famous place), Schönemann described their inmates as criminals. Then, in a cynical phrase that reads like a ghastly prophecy, the professor righteously proclaimed, "I myself think it more humane to put people into these camps than to murder them." The audience was becoming more restive. Schönemann droned on, ascribing Hitler's victory to the democratic will of the German people. "Our Jews are happy and prosperous," Schönemann assured his American friends. A few moments later, with many listeners on the verge of revolt, a voice cried out, "You're a liar!" Sarcastic laughter, sprinkled with some loud curses and a thunderous burst of applause, filled the hall. Order was restored, for a moment.

Then, in this tense setting, a lady raised her hand, asking the speaker, "What was the reason for Professor Lessing's murder in Nüremberg the day I was there?" Schönemann seemed to freeze. He fumbled for an answer, but all that came out was a hapless, and incriminating, "I don't know." The jeering began all over again. It was time to end the agony. The host of the meeting was angry with the audience, and he praised the "courage and patriotism" of Dr. Schönemann. A shaken professor left Ford Hall. Things were worse over here than he had imagined.[4] Nazi propagandists clearly confronted a daunting challenge.

Politicians did not create the atmosphere that ruined Schönemann's tour, but they were quick to exploit it. In New York, Samuel Levy, borough president of Manhattan, refused to accept office furnishings provided by the city's department of purchase. The twenty-four spanking new cuspidors, he explained, were products of German industry. The leading New York political beneficiary of anti-Nazi activity was not Levy, however, but Mayor Fiorello H. LaGuardia. LaGuardia's constant fights with the Nazis fortified anti-Nazi sentiments in the United States. New Yorkers chuckled when the mayor ordered the protection of the German general consulate by Jewish policemen.[5] They laughed some more when he declared, "I have Jewish blood, but not enough to boast about." (Actually, he had more than enough, being one of a rare breed, an Italian Episcopalian of part-Jewish descent.)

The growth of anti-Nazi sentiment soon reached far beyond New York City. Denunciations of Nazi atrocities, even by congressmen from isolationist states with large German-American populations, became common.[6] Senator Harry S. Truman of Missouri and congressmen from Iowa, North Dakota, and Utah endorsed the massive anti-Nazi rally held in New York in 1937. That same spring, many great American universities refused to send representatives to the University of Göttingen's bicentennial celebrations. When Karl T. Compton, president of the Massachusetts Institute of Technology, accepted Göttingen's invitation, the student newspaper, *The Tech*, denounced him for condoning "political and racial bigotry."

A church going American Protestant informed Rolf Hoffmann, of the Nazi media apparatus, "[N]o propaganda can be effective with most Americans while [Pastor] Martin Niemöller is in a Concentration Camp." Charles S. Macfarland, a respected cleric, had opposed the boycott movement in 1934; he now endorsed it. Publisher and columnist Ernest Meyer of the *Washington Post* who opposed the boycott, glumly reported that "the boycott movement seems to be successful." How could it be otherwise, when conservative newspapers told of a husky German ship steward badly beating a short rabbi? People were outraged when the media described how a Nazi consul whipped a nineteen-year-old girl until "there wasn't a white spot on her back."[7] Meyer, however, remained opposed to the boycott movement. He feared unleashing hatreds that would "destroy not only Hitler and the Germans but us and half of the civilized world." Meyer, like the Nazis who denounced the "Jewish boycott agitation," dimly foresaw the time when a leader with a sense of mission would use anti-Nazi sentiment for his own ends.[8]

Distinguished refugees from Hitler's terror were having a great impact upon American opinion. Writers Heinrich and Thomas Mann and physicist Albert Einstein received wide press coverage when they expressed their views of the Hitler regime. (Heinrich and Mann reported, "My political passion began when I hated the Nazis.") Progressive and labor-oriented newspapers and magazines described the regimentation and exploitation of the German worker. Social Democratic refugee Wilhelm Sollmann warned American labor about the fate of its German counterpart. Only massive rearmament, Sollmann concluded, could save the world from Nazism. In New York, German-Jewish refugees founded the influential newspaper *Aufbau* (Reconstruction), which served as a bridge between pre-Hitler Germany and Roosevelt's America. Denounced as "Refu-Jews" by the Bund, these uprooted men and women were, according to *New York Herald Tribune* columnist Dorothy Thompson, the only good thing to emerge from Germany since Hitler had taken over.[9] Among those assisting the refugees in getting their message across was Mrs. Alfred A. Knopf, wife of the distinguished publisher.

The print media were instrumental in bringing about this change in public attitudes toward the Hitler regime. Mass circulation magazines became steadily less timid about venting their concerns. In the early 1930s, their editors seemed to believe that Americans were reluctant to read pieces on foreign policy questions unless a conflict or a war was imminent. Serious magazines, such as *Harper's Magazine* and the *Atlantic Monthly*, reflected an important change taking place in the public's mood, particularly after 1936. People were now hungry for information about the Nazis and other aspects of the global crisis. Frederick Lewis Allen, an associate editor of *Harper's*, recalled, "We tried a couple of years ago [in 1939], getting out an issue of *Harper's* with no public problems at all in it. . . . It was a flop." The views of the magazine's readers could indirectly influence the actions of the politicians and the media elites, for "the publisher was inclined to give his readers what he thought the majority wanted and agreed with."[10]

Harper's and the *Atlantic* soon enjoyed paid circulations of over

100,000. Well-educated, high-income opinion makers read these magazines. These largely upscale readers, however, were often hostile to President Roosevelt and his New Deal. A survey conducted early in 1939 indicated that Roosevelt's foreign policy had the support of only thirty percent of college-educated adults of high economic status, precisely the people who read the serious magazines. Gaining the backing of this group for a bolder foreign policy might assure President Roosevelt's political survival.

During the first years of the Nazi regime, the *Atlantic* tried to be "evenhanded." Articles covered topics such as Hitler's economic plans, written as if his was just one more normal, if slightly unpredictable, government. Other essays did mention Nazi landmarks such as the Dachau and Buchenwald concentration camps, but went out of their way to be "fair." The net effect was unfavorable to the Nazis, but only mildly so. Some writers found it possible to downplay Nazi pogroms and brutality, describing them as unpleasant growing pains, or ugly birthmarks.

After 1936, the *Atlantic*'s writers became more outspoken, thanks to growing unease over Hitler's foreign policy aims. By 1938, Joseph Barber, Jr., had concluded, "[T]he shadow of Hitler over Europe grows ever more ominous." While the *Atlantic* continued to publish pieces by apologists for the Nazis, such as Otto Jellinek, Fritz Berber, and Charles A. Lindbergh, Jr., their essays lacked the impact of more objective articles. "Dr. X.," for example, described a personal experience in a Nazi camp: "I received a violent blow . . . with a heavy stick."

German ambassador Dieckhoff reported in 1937 that few Americans held anything but negative views about Nazi Germany.[11] Anti-Nazism was becoming mainstream and respectable. Pollster George Gallup found that seventy percent of the American people supported the boycott movement. Even staunchly isolationist magazines, such as the *Saturday Evening Post* and *Reader's Digest*, published pieces exposing Nazi atrocities. This would not have happened without the deterioration of the international situation between 1935 and 1938. Could nation after nation be erased from the earth, while the United States remained untouched?

By February 1938, diplomat Edgar Prochnik could report a dramatic change in American attitudes.[12] He observed that Americans were "unusually upset" about the Nazi threat to his homeland. Five years of anti-Nazi propaganda, reinforced by Nazi aggression and barbarism, had altered the public mood—in certain ways. It was now clear that the attack upon the Jews, while unique in its ferocity, foreshadowed other violations. In the late winter of 1938, Edgar Prochnik's homeland disappeared from the map, becoming Hitler's *Ostmark*. Fewer people advocated "evenhandedness" in dealing with Hitler. A large majority of those polled believed that newspapers and magazines should be permitted to attack the Nazi regime.[13] The Nazi challenge was becoming a focal point of American interest. In 1937, Americans had not included a single European crisis (except for King Edward VIII's abdication) among the year's top ten news stories. A year later, the two "most interesting" news events were the Czech crisis and the Nazi persecutions.

Surveys indicated that anti-Nazi agitation had made the boycott a popular issue. In October 1938, fifty-six percent of those questioned supported the boycott movement. In November, sixty-one percent of polled respondents "would join [the boycott] of German goods." Six months later, the figure had gone up to sixty-five percent. Seventy-eight percent favored levying countervailing duties on German imports.[14] Thanks to popular pressure, Congress now required that imported products bear the name (in English) of the country of origin. This action could only hurt German exporters.

In 1935, Americans picked Germany as the country toward whom they felt most unfriendly. England won the "most friendly" contest. More revealing, however, was the fact that *half* the respondents still had no opinion. By the spring of 1937, after the fascist conquest of Ethiopia and the onset of civil war in Spain, the "no opinion" category dropped to less than ten percent. Pollster George Gallup's American Institute of Public Opinion found that two-thirds of those polled believed that Germany was the most untrustworthy nation in the world. By the winter of 1938, two-thirds of Gallup's respondents thought that "we should do everything possible to help England and France win, except go to war ourselves." A few months later, sixty-five percent of those polled hoped that Britain and France would win the next war, while only three percent favored Germany. After Hitler dismembered Czechoslovakia, ninety-two percent of the American public believed that the Führer harbored further territorial ambitions. Eighty-three percent of Americans opposed the return of any of Germany's former colonies to the Third Reich. Over the next year, polls indicated that between eighty-two and ninety-four percent of the people believed that Germany, or Germany and Italy together, would bring about another war.

A German agent reported in 1939, "The hatred for Hitler and National Socialism in this country is being fanned not only by the press and innumerable books, pamphlets, etc., and not only by the C.I.O. and the A.F.L. and other labor unions, but also by the American Legion; it is also being preached in the high schools and universities, and from the pulpits."[15] Polls vindicated the judgment of newspaper editors committed to anti-Nazism. In the summer of 1938, according to Roper, eight percent of those responding to a poll described the press as "too antagonistic" to Nazis and fascists. Only twenty percent believed that the press should *not* be allowed to "attack the Nazis in Germany."[16]

Americans now favored a substantial buildup of their armed forces. They were more hesitant about insisting upon the repayment of old war loans by Britain and France. Many powerful people were still loath to unlearn the "lessons of 1917," however. An important Senator, William E. Borah of Idaho, could say that the Nazi conquest of Austria was "not of the slightest moment" to the United States. The same people who thought the United States would be dragged into the next war opposed entering it, even if such intervention was vital to the achievement of goals they endorsed.[17]

Indignation, wishful thinking, and cost-free antifascism seemed to dominate the public mood. Seventy-two percent of those polled *opposed* allowing "a larger number of Jewish exiles from Germany into the U.S." In fact, fifty-two percent of respondents opposed providing government funds "to help Jewish and Catholic exiles from Germany settle in other lands."[18] Anti-Semitism, isolationism, and selfishness formed a powerful coalition. Aligned against this array of sentiments was a cautious liberal internationalism, antifascist but also hesitant about making sacrifices or taking bold actions. Only new shocks, accompanied by strong leadership, could change the mind of the American people.

The isolationists played a major role in sowing confusion among the American people. Their bromides permitted citizens to think that fascism in Europe and anti-Nazism at home could coexist indefinitely. When President Roosevelt pointed to the immorality and danger represented by aggression, Senator Nye suggested that we try "correcting our own ills . . . saving our own democracy rather than soliciting the trouble to come from any move to police and doctor the world." Senator

Hiram Johnson of California, an erstwhile "progressive," believed that "[Roosevelt] wants . . . to knock down two dictators in Europe, so that one may be firmly implanted in America."[19]

On Halloween Eve 1938, thousands of New Jerseyites fled their homes when Orson Welles and the Mercury Theater on the Air broadcast a dramatization of H. G. Wells's *War of the Worlds*. Those running in panic believed that Martians or other hostile creatures were invading the United States. Surveys of those who had fled from their homes often yielded phrases like "I felt the catastrophe was *an attack by the Germans*. . . ." Gloating Nazis asked, "How can a people which trembles before the attack of the Martians . . . solve world problems?"[20]

Other fears emerged from concerns closer to home. Writings predicting a fascist takeover in South America began to appear regularly. Carleton Beals's many books and articles informed Americans that "German colonization of the Americas has become more determined." Beals, writing in prestigious journals such as *Harper's* and *Foreign Affairs*, believed, "Efforts to plant Germans in strategic points are constantly made, often in conjunction with trade negotiations."[21]

These alarms affected public opinion. In the spring of 1937, 28.7 percent of Americans polled by *Fortune* favored the use of force in the defense of any Latin American country against an attack by a non-American power. By the summer of 1939, 54.17 percent of respondents were ready to defend Brazil. The percentage favoring the defense of Mexico was 76.5 percent. It was clear that an administration willing to use the rhetoric of the Monroe Doctrine could greatly influence public opinion. The danger, however, loomed not in Brazil, but along the Rhine.

In 1936, a minority (forty-four percent) of polled Americans believed that the United States would be drawn into a new European war. By 1939, that figure had risen to seventy-six percent. German chargé d'affaires Hans Thomsen concluded that "public opinion is being systematically reduced to a state of trance in which the proposition that it is inevitable that war will break out and that America will become involved is being given the force of an axiom."[22] This expectation, however, differed from a determination to *affect* events in Europe. Nations resigned to doing their duty, without enthusiasm, rarely win wars.

Opinion polls registered the changing attitude of Americans toward

Nazism, but they also exposed a crippling hesitancy about taking action to destroy Hitler. Public opinion needed to ascend to a higher level of consciousness. As Roosevelt understood, an unprepared nation going to war in a trancelike state was unlikely to frighten or defeat its enemies. Anti-Nazism and fear of Hitler were laudable emotions; they did not add up to a policy. Unless some leader in the West created an anti-Nazi front, Hitler might never be stopped.

Few Americans wished to face the consequences of the following, painful possibility: England and France might not be able to win a war against Germany *unless* we went "to war ourselves." Chargé Hans Thomsen reported from Washington that the "greater part of the press is advocating support of the democracies in Europe even more vigorously than before." He overlooked one vital fact, however. Americans did not look upon this "support" as a *prelude* to intervention (with its grim memories of 1917). Rather, people insisted on seeing it as a *substitute* for intervention.

At least two men had more prophetic insights. Edgar Prochnik believed that if the test finally came, the United States would not permit the defeat of the British Empire by Germany. And, in a remarkable article in the *Atlantic,* published in 1939, David L. Cohn painted a similar scenario.[23] Asking the grim question, "What will the United States do in the event of a world war?," Cohn warned that after a Nazi victory, "friendless and alone, we shall face the most powerful and ruthless dictator the world has ever known." Yet even Cohn offered no solution. Like most people, Cohn detested Nazi brutality, but he also wished to avoid confrontation with a European power.

The political implications of the polls were not lost upon the president. His own evolution on the Nazi problem was a complex affair. At first aloof from the boycott movement FDR came to see it as one weapon in democracy's struggle against totalitarianism. Yet he remained cautious. His concerns were mounting, but he kept his moistened finger to the wind. A strategy calculated to destroy National Socialism while isolating its domestic sympathizers, would take several years for him to develop. Whatever he did, Roosevelt would never publicly equate the destruction of Hitlerism with global intervention, war, and the foundation of a *pax americana.* To do so would have been poor politics.

*   *   *

Arrayed against Roosevelt and the growing anti-Nazism of the American media were the formidable resources of the German Reich, as well as numerous groups and individuals in the United States. Their number included persons who admired, took orders from, or agreed with Hitler on some fundamental points, including the need for permanent American neutrality. These people worked with great energy for Roosevelt's political demise. Other Roosevelt-haters conspired to rid American public life of alleged Jewish influences. A few of these people were Nazis, others were American fascists, while many were self-styled patriotic Americans whose success was in the interest of National Socialism. For three years, the Roosevelt administration would fight a two-front war against "Hitler's Americans" on the one hand, and the Third Reich on the other.

PART
THREE

HITLER'S
AMERICANS

CHAPTER
ELEVEN

AN AMERICAN CONSTITUENCY
FOR HITLER'S GERMANY

ROOSEVELT'S RHETORIC WAS still more forceful than his policy, but Hitler harbored few illusions regarding the president's ultimate aims. By the mid-1930s, Nazi propagandists had come to fear American intervention in a crisis provoked by German expansionism. They worked hard to counter the American media's growing anti-Nazi bias. One method employed was the cultivation of individual American citizens. Goebbels agreed, concluding, "[I]t will be necessary to obtain support of important people . . . and to use them in the service of our propaganda." Americans, according to Goebbels, must become convinced that "the United States should redeem the promise [of self-determination] made to Germany by President Wilson. . . ." All Germany wanted, after all, was "freedom and parity." The "atrocity" stories, Goebbels said, were untrue. The Nazis were merely protecting the German people against undue Jewish influence.[1]

The attempt to manipulate American opinion began early in Hitler's chancellorship. Important friends of the "New Germany," recruited, supported, or encouraged by Nazi organizations, were soon working to prevent FDR from veering away from isolation and neutrality.

Informed about the profascist proclivities of press lord William Randolph Hearst, Hitler granted a Hearst correspondent an exclusive. The widely read interview, conducted by Karl von Wiegand, offered Hitler an opportunity to scoff at charges leveled against the Nazis. Pleased with the publicity given to the interview, the *Völkischer Beobachter,* the official Nazi newspaper, happily described von Wiegand as "one of the outstanding figures in the American newspaper world." Hearst himself soon received an invitation to visit the New Germany. He arrived in Bad Nauheim right after the bloodbath known as the "Night of the Long Knives" (30 June–1 July 1934), when Hitler murdered a large number of political and personal enemies. The event did not unnerve Hearst. Top Nazis, such as Foreign Press Chief Ernst Hanfstängl and *Reichsleiter* Alfred Rosenberg, subsequently called upon the receptive press lord. In September, Hearst arrived in Berlin, where Hitler received him. The egocentric Hearst found Hitler to be an appealing fellow. He returned to the United States an advocate of a peacekeeping alliance between the U.S., Britain, and Germany. Hearst's antipathy toward Roosevelt grew.

Charles R. Crane, a well-connected if eccentric Park Avenue millionaire with connections that reached to the White House, could scarcely contain his enthusiasm when describing his own interview with Adolf Hitler. Hitler, Crane believed, was a sincere anticommunist, and what was wrong with that? As for the Jews, "Let Hitler have his way." Colonel House, now a Roosevelt adviser and a friend of Charles Crane, agreed. As he put it, "[T]he Jews should not be allowed to dominate economic or intellectual life in Berlin as they have done for a long time."

The damage to the German image because of Nazi persecutions could not be undone, but it could be mitigated. The publicity accorded to visits by prominent Americans helped to balance "atrocity" stories in the American press. In 1937, Dr. Hjalmar Schacht, minister of economics, honored a special American, Thomas J. Watson, president of International Business Machines, presenting him with the Order of Merit of the German Eagle. The decoration, "honoring foreign nationals who have made themselves deserving of the Third Reich," consisted of a ribbon supporting an eight-pointed, gold-framed cross with a swastika in each corner. It was bestowed upon Watson for being a leading businessman who continued to trade with the Third Reich. Watson's antiboycott line met with some success in a United States plagued by the Depression. A fully employed and dynamic Germany could not, some said, be ignored as a trading partner.

While Schacht praised Watson, an obscure priest named Father Biehl prepared to serve a four-year prison term for anti-Nazi activity. The Watson award received more publicity in the American press than did the conviction of Father Biehl.[2] The lesson was not lost upon the German leadership. Famous Americans could help to drive "atrocity lies" off the front pages of the American press. And Thomas Watson did not stand alone. A group of bankers visiting U.S. ambassador William Dodd railed against Jew-inspired boycotts of German goods: "There is going to be rioting in New York. [Boycott leader] Sam Untermeyer is apt to be attacked."

The Nazis wanted access to American hard currency, trade, industrial secrets, and military technology. If Roosevelt ever brought about a total break with the Reich, German military preparedness would suffer. Thanks to lobbying by Germany and its powerful American friends, however, it would prove difficult for the administration to break off economic relations with Germany, even if it wished to do so.

Rolf Hoffmann, Deputy Foreign Press Chief of the Nazi Party, also appreciated the contribution made by small businessmen to the Nazis' success. Hoffmann methodically filed the names of likely American propaganda targets. He obtained confidential information about them from banks and academic institutions in Germany. People as diverse as a Colorado dairy manager and an Oklahoma oilman soon began to receive the German propaganda publication "News From Germany." Both men thanked Hoffmann, and agreed that America was waking up to the truth about Germany and the Jews.[3] Such businessmen could be counted upon to put appropriate pressure upon local newspaper editors and politicians. Their views seemed to appeal to many Americans. The Nazi theme boiled down to this: The Jews were Christ-killers, bolsheviks, and troublemakers. Why let their machinations spoil trade relations between a Depression-locked America and a resurgent National Socialist Germany?

Given the growing fear of communism, and the large proportion of Jews in the Communist party in the United States, Hoffman could play upon American anti-Semitism. Politicians such as Representative Louis T. McFadden, Republican of Pennsylvania; Representative Thomas L. Banton, Democrat of Texas; Senator Josiah W. Bailey, Jr., Democrat of North Carolina; and former senator Arthur R. Robinson of Indiana already agreed with much of Rolf Hoffmann's analysis of the world. McFadden, talking on the floor of the House, denounced the Jews while praising the Nazis. He fervently believed in the existence of an international Jewish conspiracy. Banton regurgitated arguments supplied by Nazi propagandists. Bailey, attacking the Allies for defaulting on their war debts, announced that it did not matter if England fell prey to German domination. According to Ambassador Dodd, Bailey "talks like a National Socialist," and "advocate[s] German domination of all Europe." Senator Robinson mused about organizing German-Americans for the 1936 elections. All these men, and many of the lobbyists who flocked to them, protested against the Jewish-organized boycott of German exports.[4]

Hoffmann moved quickly to exploit the Jewish issue. In July 1936, Governor Alf M. Landon of Kansas, the Republican presidential candidate, responded to a query from the *Washington Post* regarding Nazi persecutions. In his rather restrained reply, Landon accused the Nazis of abandoning Christian principles. Maude S. De Land, a resident of Kansas City, Missouri, did not like what she read, and decided to provide Landon with some anti-Semitic arguments and information. Landon responded courteously, stating, "I am glad to have your views on the matter and I am sure that you know whereof you speak. Controversial matters of this kind always have several viewpoints. . . ." Encouraged by Landon's response, De Land provided the Landon campaign with more propaganda.[5] Landon lost the election in a Roosevelt landslide, but Hoffmann was not discouraged. American anti-Semitism was alive and well, and politicians were flexible creatures. One had to work hard, and endure setbacks with a patience born of a faith in victory.

Despite Nazi Germany's growing belligerence in Europe, Roosevelt continued to hesitate in a number of key areas. His timidity on bilateral trade issues, as well as his fear of being labeled "prorefugee," stemmed in some measure from the infiltration of pro-Nazi attitudes into American business and politics. Anti-Semitism was gaining respectability, and Roosevelt was daring only when he could rest secure in the support of a large majority of his fellow citizens. The Nazis could quote many respectable voices when they sought American support for their views on the Jewish question. These included Mr. Roosevelt's New York neighbor, the well-known writer Poultney Bigelow of Malden-on-

Hudson, who had allegedly declared, "I wish that we had a dozen Hitlers in the United States."[6]

Throughout the 1930s, the Nazis continued to cultivate important American visitors. The German authorities handled such celebrities with grace and discretion, showing their guests almost anything they wanted to see.[7] Selected tours and receptions gave the impression of a well-ordered, clean, and hardworking society. The Nazis provided their guests with literature and correspondence upon their return to the United States. A few examples are instructive. Professor M. McMeyer of Boston University, an expert on Protestant theology, returned from Germany convinced that the people loved Hitler. The famous actress Mary Pickford observed after visiting Germany, "Hitler seems to be a great fellow for the Germans. Things certainly are marvelous now in Germany."

Things never appeared more "marvelous" than in the summer of 1936. The Olympic games offered the Nazis an impressive opportunity. The German authorities were much interested in securing American participation in the controversial games, which they felt would constitute a moral recognition of the Third Reich. A presence would undermine attempts to destroy German-American trade, and deal a blow to "those Jews over there." The Reich government knew that the leaders of the Amateur Athletic Union (AAU) and the American Olympic Committee (AOC) were members of the American social elite. Proper cultivation of American athletic leaders might lead to long-term political gains for the New Germany.

The problem, as the Nazis saw it, was the Jews, meaning the boycott movement. Polls of news and of sports page editors demonstrated substantial support for the boycott position.[8] Those favoring the boycott had some strong arguments. Did it not, they asked, violate the tenets of amateur sport for the Olympics to be perverted into a backdrop for the Nazis?

The president of the AAU was a former star athlete and New York politician named Jeremiah T. Mahoney, who had succeeded Avery Brundage in December 1934. Two years earlier, the AAU had voted to boycott the Berlin Olympics because of Nazi discrimination against Jewish athletes. Calls went out in favor of transferring the games to another country. At the time of that vote, Brundage, now the president of the AOC, had assented to the boycott resolution. Hans von Tscham-

mer und Osten, president of the German Olympic Committee, worked
to change his American friend's mind. He asked Brundage to visit
Germany, and see for himself. Brundage, a crusty authoritarian enamored of order and anticommunism, was vulnerable to Tschammer's
message. To Brundage, the Jews were at best an annoyance, at worst
procommunist troublemakers.

Avery Brundage loved the dynamic sense of purpose and order that
surrounded him in the Reich. There were no workers' riots here, no sit-
ins at industrial plants, and apparently no crime. Tschammer easily
convinced Brundage that German Jews *were* permitted to participate in
tryouts for the games. Brundage informed his American colleagues that
German Jews were being treated fairly "from the sports point of view."
A skilled bureaucratic infighter, Brundage managed to dislodge boycott
supporter Mahoney as head of the AAU. By this time, it was too late to
change the venue of the games; America would send a team to Berlin, or
its athletes would stay home. Frustrated by continuing opposition,
Brundage accused his enemies of committing bribery, extortion, and
engaging in illegitimate forms of pressure.[9]

Brundage received the full support of retired Brigadier General
Charles H. Sherrill, member of the AOC and on the International
Olympic Committee. The general bragged a good deal, and the Nazis
soon learned of his anti-Semitism. An admirer of Mussolini, Sherrill also
believed that Hitler was "undeniably [a] great leader." He agreed to
visit the Reich, allegedly to make sure of "getting at least one Jew on
the German Olympic team. . . ." He felt uncomfortable about his mission, however, for it smacked of interference in another nation's internal
affairs. Indeed, Sherrill agreed with his AOC colleague F.W.B. Rubien,
who argued, "The Jews are eliminated because they are not good
enough as athletes." "Why there are not," he declared, "a dozen Jews
in the world of Olympic calibre." Sherrill blamed the Jews for Germany's troubles in the past, and warned that America might follow
the Nazi example. If the American Jews held the Olympic Games host-
age, Sherrill warned, Americans might retaliate against the perpetrators.[10]

Fully aware of Sherrill's views, Hitler invited him to visit his Munich
flat on 24 August. Sherrill spoke enthusiastically about American participation in the Berlin games and went away convinced that Hitler would
abandon the Olympics rather than permit the appearance of a Jew on

the German team. This put the general in a difficult position, but he refused to change his mind about the wisdom of sending an American team to Berlin.[11]

Sherrill informed President Roosevelt of his impressions, but also forwarded a copy of the report to the German embassy in Paris. Hitler, meanwhile, decided to invite the general to the forthcoming *Reichsparteitag* (Reich party rally) in Nürnberg as his personal guest. Overwhelmed by the spectacle of hundreds of thousands of young Germans smartly saluting their führer, Sherrill informed FDR's secretary, "France is safe, but God help the Communist Soviets when [Hitler's] army is ready!" By the time Sherrill arrived in Paris, he had tired of the "Olympic-Jew question." America must participate, he believed, and that was all there was to it. The Americans did indeed take part in the Olympics, but General Sherrill, who died in June, did not live to see them.[12] The games represented a great triumph for the Hitler regime. American athletes and guests rushed to shake Hitler's hand, and some bestowed the ultimate American encomium upon the Führer, calling him a "regular guy."

Avery Brundage returned from the Olympic games more enthusiastic than ever about Germany. In early October, he addressed a crowd of twenty thousand German-Americans assembled in Madison Square Garden. Denouncing the boycotters as a "vociferous minority," Brundage congratulated his hosts: "Thanks to the support of you people of German descent in America we were able to get our Olympic team abroad." The crowd repeated its shouts of "Sieg Heil!" as the hall became a sea of upraised right arms. Outside, six hundred police protected the rally against representatives of another "vociferous minority." Brundage later negotiated with the Germans in preparation for the 1940 winter Olympics, to be held at Garmisch-Partenkirchen. He did so in the name of a "sport friendship" that transcended issues such as racism and war.[13]

Soon after Hitler came to power, Goebbels's propagandists received information about the strengths and weaknesses of the American collective psyche from the Psychological Laboratory in Berlin. Select agents underwent training at the ministry's own Foreign Affairs Institute.[14] The most effective propaganda, they learned, must disguise its origins and conceal the goals of its inventors. The Nazis must never make the mistake of tipping their hand. Hitler, while keeping a straight face, promised a protesting American ambassador that "he would throw any German official into the North Sea if he sent propaganda to the United States. . . ."[15]

Goebbels began his campaign in the late summer of 1933. Concerned about "atrocity lies" spread by Jews in the United States, the Propaganda Ministry inaugurated a campaign aimed at teaching Americans about the "patrimony of National Socialist ideas" and the Führer's "most exalted thoughts." German agents received large amounts of propaganda materials, designed for distribution by front organizations or undercover agents.[16]

In the northeast, the German consulate general in New York City coordinated the dissemination of this propaganda. Baron Ulrich von Gienanth, a suave and sophisticated agent of the Propaganda Ministry, worked through a "Translation and Advisory Bureau," housed in the consulate general. T.S.J. Gaffney, former American consul general in Munich, assisted him, as did the prominent advertising agency Carl Byoir and Associates. Gienanth also retained the "clever big business propagandist" Ivy Lee as an agent. Byoir and Lee received tens of thousands of dollars for assisting in the distribution of Nazi propaganda.[17]

Those Americans doing the Germans' work were in danger of being compromised by their Nazi contacts, hence Gienanth devised an intricate money-laundering scheme. Helpful journalists were to receive checks from the German-American Chamber of Commerce, not from their real paymaster, the treasurer at the consulate general. Germans doing business in the United States were expected to support these efforts by donating funds to appropriate organizations. Ostensibly "independent," German correspondents then worked directly with friendly Americans, assisting them in the production of propaganda.

One friend of the Germans was George Sylvester Viereck, who often worked behind the scenes. Viereck despised the new "100-percent Americans" who dominated the German-American establishment after the 1917 war. He bemoaned the loss of *Deutschtum* (German ethnicity). Arrogant and aggressive, Viereck and his friends founded the small German-American Citizens League, or *Bürgerbund*. They intended to strike back at their persecutors and reward their friends. After supporting the successful candidacy of Warren G. Harding in 1920, Viereck and his associates demanded a political payoff. The new president was polite but noncommittal. He had won by a landslide, and hardly needed to contaminate his administration by listening to the discredited voices of chauvinistic Germans. A prominent Cincinnati editor attacked Viereck for "refusing to recognize the fact that we are not living in a German colony."[18]

Viereck surfaced again during the Depression, writing and lecturing in favor of German and American reconciliation. He saw Hitlerism as a useful tool in his campaign against the excessive Americanization of the Germans in the United States. Viereck knew how to take advantage of the situation, while advancing his own militant German cause. The Nazis soon embraced him.

Viereck used his access to the pages of the magazine *Liberty* as a platform for Herr Hitler, whom he presented as an intensely patriotic man out to right past wrongs. "Time and the recalcitrance of the French," wrote Viereck, "fight for Hitler." Viereck cleverly condemned Hitler's anti-Semitism, though in the mildest of terms. He asked Americans to accept Hitler's professions of goodwill: "[Hitler] desires friendly relations with the United States. He is puzzled by what he considers the persistent antagonism of the American government and a large part of the American press. . . ." Behind the scenes, Viereck received substantial German support.[19]

Americans saw through some of these words, though not all of them. Newspapers editorialized against Berlin's attempt "to colonize foreign lands with propagandists for Hitlerism. . . ."[20] Even publications less concerned about foreign propaganda were beginning to denounce Nazi atrocities. This rendered more difficult the task of German spokesmen, who more and more relied upon front organizations. They mobilized the resources of the Fichte League, which served "the cause of peace and understanding by giving free information about the New Germany, direct from the source. . . ." Bankrolled by the Foreign Ministry and staffed by Goebbels's protégés, the league printed over two million English-language copies of major Nazi speeches during the years 1933–1936. Ulrich von Gienanth, regularly alerted to the arrival of Fichte League materials, would contact sympathetic Americans, such as former consul Gaffney and Oscar Pfaus. Gaffney and Pfaus then saw to it that friendly American groups distributed the material.[21] In this way, "information," rather than propaganda, landed on the desks of prominent Americans.

Much of this material found its way into Heinz Beller's German Library of Information, which published bulletins, distributed books and phonograph records, answered queries, and provided groups with speakers. Rolf Hoffmann, who referred inquiries and requests from Americans to Beller, contributed to the library's imposing mailing list. In return, Beller supplied the Munich-based Hoffmann with the names of sympathetic congressmen. When the son of the governor of Massachusetts, Alvan T. Fuller, visited the Reich, Hoffmann urged the young man to contact Beller upon his return to the States. Young Fuller had, according to Hoffmann, come to understand the "goals of National Socialist Germany."[22]

Meanwhile, Ulrich von Gienanth was spending much of his time working with Matthias Schmitz, head of the German Railway (*Deutsche Reichsbahn*) Information Office in New York City. Schmitz ingratiated himself with out-of-town travel agents anxious to sample life in the big city. He invited them to his posh offices on West 57th Street: "If it's cocktail hour we might have a drink or two together, or I might even ask [them] home with me for dinner."[23] Schmitz saw American travelers as potential spokesmen for the New Germany. Equally important was their ability to provide Germany with badly needed hard currency. Schmitz thus encouraged the work of women like Alma Vödisch, a lecturer and travel agent who urged her audiences to visit the New Germany. Vödisch offered potential tourists free advice about youth hostels, health resorts, and sight-seeing attractions, such as the romantic castles overlooking the Rhine.[24]

Schmitz's glossy magazines presented his business clients with a sentimental view of Germany. His Reich consisted of the Black Forest, Kris Kringle, and the romantic Cologne festival. No Nazi police defiled this image, no concentration camp blocked one's view of the beautiful Bavarian Alps. Schmitz was anxious to demonstrate the value of increased German-American trade and so sold cheap advertising space to many prominent American corporations, including Greyhound, Inc., the bus company.

Rolf Hoffmann's academic contacts were both numerous and fruitful. Professor Karl F. Geiser of Oberlin College, a political scientist, received propaganda brochures from Hoffmann's Munich office. An admirer of the New Germany, Geiser signed his letter of thanks with the "German greeting" (Hitler salute). Copies of the correspondence found their way to Rudolf Hess's office, for Hoffmann wanted to impress his

CRUSADER WHITE SHIRTS
NATIONAL HEADQUARTERS
CHATTANOOGA, TENNESSEE

June 1,,1936

23432

Herr. H. Rolf Hoffmann,
Auslandspressabtlg.,
Reichsleitung der N.S.D.A.P.,
Braunes Haus,
München, Deutschland.

Dear Herr Hoffmann:

　　　　　　　I believe that you have had some communications
with my father, Dr. Ralph H. Major. As you know him slightly, I
wish to beg of you a favor.

　　　　　　　Since I have .... have been
commissioned as Mid-West Commander of the White Shirts, or American
Fascists, of which you have probably heard in Germany.

　　　　　　　As you are in a very high position in the German
administration, would it be possible for you to procure for me, a
portrait of Der Führer! The pictures shown of him in America are
very unattractive. I could never place them upon the walls in my room.

　　　　　　　Also, sir, as I class myself rather high in the
American Fascists, could you gain Herr Hitler's signature upon the
picture? If you could send me a picture of Herr Hitler with his
signature upon it, you would gain, sir, my everlasting gratitude.
Personal greetings and best wishes to you, sir, from,

　　　　　　　　　　　Sincerely yours,

　　　　　　　　　　　Ralph H. Major, Jr.
　　　　　　　　　　　Ralph H. Major, Jr.,
　　　　　　　　　　　COMMANDER MID-WEST DIVISION,
　　　　　　　　　　　CRUSADER WHITE SHIRTS,
　　　　　　　　　　　(AMERICAN   FASCISTS.)

Address me:
Ralph H. Major, Jr.,
6105 High Drive,
Kansas City,
Missouri,
U.S.A.

superiors. Hoffmann obtained information about the anti-Nazi press in
the United States from the son of Ralph H. Major, Sr., a professor of
internal medicine at the University of Kansas. Ralph H. Major, Jr., was
the midwestern commander of the Crusader White Shirts (American
Fascists).

*　　*　　*

The growing anti-Hitler bias of the American press enabled Hoffmann to pander to the American sense of fair play. As Professor O.M. Dickerson of Colorado State College put it, Hoffmann and his agents supplied "information of a kind that is impossible to secure through our public press." Professor Hauptmann, the chairman of the German Department at the New Jersey College for Women, certainly wanted to be evenhanded in his approach. Like many German departments in the 1930s, his contained both pro- and anti-Nazis. Hauptmann thus politely asked Hoffmann for information about "the new [Nazi] underlying philosophy in the field of education." Hoffmann was happy to assist the good professor.[25] Indeed, by the summer of 1939, Hoffmann was supplying "numerous professors and university libraries" with his propaganda sheet "News From Germany." Thousands of other Americans who "wished to be informed about events here on a regular basis" also received "News From Germany."[26] Ulrich von Gienanth assisted the Munich-based Hoffmann by replying to inquiries and requests that required quick answers.

Hoffmann paid special attention to high school teachers and college students. He supplied the Eldorado Township High School in Illinois with material on "the New Germany and especially the men who have made this great change possible." He agreed with a teacher from Hamden, Connecticut, who had observed that "we are both interested in promoting better relations between Germany and the United States." This gentleman quickly received useful materials. Hoffmann was careful to avoid soliciting potential clients. He responded to requests, but did not initiate them, thus spinning a web that created a network of sympathetic persons.[27]

Rolf Hoffmann was interested in American college students, especially those from elite schools and well-connected families. He encouraged visits to the New Germany, appealing to the American sense of "let me see for myself." Hoffmann worked with men like Dr. K.O. Bertling, head of the famous Amerika-Institut in Berlin, who put his cover to good use for the regime. A Harvard graduate himself, Bertling worked to "assist Americans coming to Germany in quest of learning or in the pursuit of other professional assignments." His prestigious list of sponsors included Professor Friedrich Schönemann.

No task was too mundane for Bertling. One of his correspondents informed Bertling that Allen Lee, the son of a prominent San Francisco businessman, would soon visit the Reich. Bertling learned that Lee was particularly interested in the "German solution of the labor question." By the time the young man arrived, Bertling had arranged for him to visit officials of the German Labor Front.[28] The Amerika-Institut, working with the Carl Schurz Foundation and the German Academic Exchange Service (DAAD), introduced the New Germany to students from dozens of elite American universities, including Harvard, U.C. Berkeley, Stanford, and Princeton. In the summer of 1934 a group of fifty-one students from twenty-six universities visited the Reich. The American Schurz Foundation made a film of the visit, which the powerful Universum-Film Aktiengesellschaft (UFA) film studio produced. Each student received a copy, which became available for projection on his or her campus. The film, "Germany of Today," attracted other students to the program. This propaganda helped to counteract what the Nazis called "Jewish atrocity propaganda."[29]

Some students rewarded their German contacts with more than naive propaganda about their kind treatment by the German regime. Hoffmann, for example, collected useful information from correspondents like Paul Hancock, a student at Princeton. Hancock, who had written a thesis on Nazi Germany, wanted to attend the September 1936 Nazi party rally in Nürnberg. Hoffmann was encouraged by the undergraduate's comment that "[s]ome of my best friends who were once rabid anti-Nazis, have finally become almost fanatic pro-Nazis in their opinions."

Hoffmann's files were crammed with similar letters. Hoffmann received a note written on behalf of three young attorneys, Oren Root, Jr., John Auchincloss, and Francis Shackelford. The young men, scions of prestigious families and the best universities, wished to attend the forthcoming Nürnberg rally. "We would like to choose the most beautiful and thrilling spectacles," their sponsor wrote, adding, "It would be fun to stay in a tent."

From his correspondents, Hoffmann learned that American "appreciation of folkic [racialist] movements is slowly increasing. . . ." Shackelford had already met Hoffmann, and was anxious to develop their friendship. Root's "folkic feeling" was especially intense.[30] As long as Americans did not view Germany as a threatening enemy nation, the Reich could nurture this group of admirers, and await their maturity with some optimism.

Hoffmann was not one to sit back and bide his time, however. Energetic and ambitious, Hoffmann worked hard to foster ties between the New Germany and American evangelical churches. Stories about incarcerated priests, and Protestant ministers such as Martin Niemöller, made it difficult to sell the Nazi regime to devout Christian Americans. Hoffmann, however, argued that Nazism was the defender of the Christian West against atheistic communism. Hoffmann made occasional breakthroughs, as when the German Evangelical Congregational Churches of America (claiming a membership of twenty-five thousand) used his propaganda materials in their publications.

The diligent Hoffmann was developing a potentially important following among influential individuals inclined to despise President Roosevelt. Miss E.M. Irre, a self-styled sociologist who did "enlightenment work in the U.S.A.," certainly did her best to expose the "lies" being spread about the New Germany. So did Mrs. Edward Sherwin, who lectured in Arizona on "Current Topics of International Importance." From German agent Ulrich von Gienanth, Mrs. Sherwin received materials on the "economic and social situation in Germany," as requested.[31] The concert harpist Mary Seiler was grateful to Hoffmann for sending "News From Germany" and other helpful materials. She believed, "[W]hen the American people get a clear picture of the New Germany, they will find much to admire and applaud in National Socialism." Hoffmann, ever the flatterer, thanked Seiler for working toward "a real understanding between the leading nations of the world." Seiler repaid the compliment by establishing a new network for the distribution of Nazi propaganda materials.

Hoffmann was particularly interested in developing contacts with American military personnel. America had a tiny army, and a few contacts could go a long way. Sympathetic officers might be able to head off any unpleasant surprise prepared by the president. To some Germans, a pro-Nazi American officer corps seemed within the realm of possibility. Authoritarianism, anticommunism, and hatred for Roosevelt were widespread among active, reserve, and retired U.S. Army officers, and Hoffmann knew it. Perhaps, thought Hoffmann, anti-Allied sentiment, anti-Semitism, and isolationism among officers would play into his hands. In General W.E. Easterwood, national vice commander of the American Legion, Hoffmann found a kindred soul. Easterwood denounced the atrocity stories and other "lies" about the New Germany. The Germans hoped that an Easterwood could counteract the influence of the antifascist American Legion leader Belgrano, who had publicly opposed the 1935 Neutrality Act. Ever the diplomat, Hoffmann was careful to avoid insulting the commander in chief, and always assured his correspondents of his undying respect for the U.S.A. This German agent insisted that one could be both patriotic and pro-Nazi.[32]

Of all universities, the one that most fascinated Hoffmann was the United States Military Academy at West Point, New York. Hoffmann had learned from German military attachés that some American officers stationed there were sympathetic to the Hitler regime. He cultivated his own contact at West Point, Lieutenant Colonel O.J. Gatchell, an expert in the latest types of ordnance. Hoffmann received an invitation to visit West Point.

The suave Hoffmann admired the beauty of the Hudson River Valley, and delighted his hosts at West Point. He was careful to avoid mention of the Jews. Instead, he emphasized the *positive* aspects of the New Germany: the *Autobahnen,* the full employment, the dynamism and self-confidence, the suppression of subversive trade unions, and above all, the destruction of Godless communism. Hoffmann talked a great deal about the restoration of military pride, but said nothing about German rearmament and plans for expansion.

Colonel Gatchell believed that in giving Hoffmann access to the academy he was promoting a "lasting friendship between nations." He soon provided Hoffmann with the names of officers who wished to receive materials on the New Germany.[33] The ever-courteous Hoffmann offered to assist any cadets who might visit the Third Reich. Hoffmann assured Gatchell that the young men would be well taken care of in Berlin, for the Carl Schurz Association (a Nazi front) would look after them. The colonel was very grateful.[34]

By 1939, Nazi agents had made valuable contacts in many sectors of American society. Most of these students, teachers, and lecturers were patriotic Americans, unaware of their work for the Nazi cause. Some were dupes, others deluded idealists. Their number included cranks and opportunists, powerful politicians and abject losers. In other words, these contacts included a cross section of modern society. Such people could help to prevent Roosevelt from meddling with Hitler's plans.

In order to mobilize a substantial body of Americans as allies in the struggle for neutrality, isolation, and friendship with Germany, Hoffmann and von Gienanth required a growth in anti-Semitism and fascism, a decline in FDR's political fortunes, and continued American economic distress.

CHAPTER
TWELVE

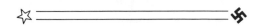

NAZIS IN AMERICA: THE
STRUGGLE AGAINST
ASSIMILATION

I N THE 1930s, an ethnic organization sympathetic to Hitler's Germany emerged in the United States. Popularly known as the "German-American Bund," this band of recent immigrants failed to win the allegiance of more than a handful of German-Americans. Even so, the Bund caused an enormous uproar in this country. Congressmen investigated it; federal and state agencies attacked it. Various German agencies observed the Bund's activities, some with dismay, others with hope.[1] The Bund itself, and the many Nazis who encouraged its rise, fatally misunderstood the history of the German-American community in the United States.

Why were Americans in the 1930s and 1940s so little concerned about the loyalty of their German-American fellow citizens, when hysteria and bigotry had prevailed in 1918? Hitler, after all, appeared to be a more evil figure than Kaiser Wilhelm II. Finally, did the Roosevelt administration use fears of the Bund for its own purposes? The Bund was a failure, but one crucial to an understanding of Roosevelt's eventual triumph.

The first American branch of the Nazi party emerged in the Bronx,

New York City, in 1922. Shortly thereafter, a group of Detroit auto-workers, mainly recent immigrants, formed the "Teutonia," a Nazi organization. Teutonia soon renamed itself the "National Socialist Union," and established branches in Chicago, Milwaukee, and Rochester. Nazis in New York City cultivated their ties to Dr. Hans Nieland, chief of the Foreign Department of the German party.

Kurt Lüdecke, an ambitious Nazi, came to the United States as a self-styled emissary from Adolf Hitler. He hoped to take over the American Nazi movement and replace Nieland when he returned to Germany. Lüdecke promptly accused Nieland of using German ships for the purpose of smuggling illegal alcoholic beverages into the United States. Lüdecke tried and failed to secure funds from the Imperial Wizard of the Ku Klux Klan, as well as from the Jew-baiter Henry Ford. Upon his return to the Reich, he sourly announced that German-Americans and American society were not ready for a true "folkic" movement.

Various National Socialists (at times Hitler among them) disagreed with Lüdecke's analysis. Why should the German-Americans be different from militant German minorities in the new states of Poland and Czechoslovakia? They had, after all, recently suffered from persecution; surely some among them would be receptive to the National Socialist message.

The Bund's story really begins earlier, at the end of the Great War, when shocked German-American communities in the United States began to assess the recent past, and their prospects for the future. The anti-German excesses passed soon after the signing of the Armistice on 11 November 1918. The worst was over, but the effects of the new nativism were permanent. German-Americans had served in the armed forces with distinction, and that was in their favor. They could retain some sentimental songs and memories, but they were now "Americans of German descent," not "German-Americans." In the words of Father Andrew Greeley, the Germans "understood that the best thing for a German ethnic group to do in the 1920s was to become invisible."[2]

Theaters that had produced German plays now showed American motion pictures, shipped by train from the West Coast. Parochial schools with a large German-American clientele lost pupils. The German-language press offered seventy percent fewer publications in

1930 than it had in 1910. This decline continued a pattern apparent before the war, but it proceeded at a much accelerated pace. Few dared to protest.

One national obsession particularly troubled many "Americans of German descent." A few years earlier, a German-American had protested that "the drink question is forced upon us by the same hypocritical Puritans as over there are endeavoring to exterminate the German nation." The Eighteenth Amendment and the Volstead Act closed down the old German beer gardens. In the eyes of the politician Andrew John Volstead and people like him, Prohibition was akin to patriotism: Those who opposed it were hyphenates or worse.[3] "Foreigners" were suspect. Raids against suspected anarchists, communists, and subversives led to deportations. Germans had to be cautious.

In the past, recent German immigrants had contributed mightily to the ethnic renewal of the German-American community. This, too, changed. The newer immigrants came from families that had fought *against* the United States; in some cases, they were former German soldiers themselves. Many of them were contemptuous of a German community that had done nothing to help the fatherland in its hour of need.

Patterns of German immigration were changing drastically, in part due to the Immigration Act of 1924. Quotas imposed severe limitations on the number of foreigners able to gain entry to this country. In 1924, over 75,000 Germans emigrated to the United States; nine years later, the figure was 1,919. The combined German and Austrian quotas for 1936 totaled but 27,370 persons. By this time, fewer than one-quarter of the German-Americans were German-born, and most of these people had been born before the war. In 1900, one-third of foreign-born Caucasians in the United States may have been of German origin. In 1930, the figure was one-sixth, and by 1950 it was less than one-seventh. In New York City in 1900, twenty-two percent of the population was of German extraction; by 1940, the figure was four percent.[4]

Many German-Americans now "Americanized" their names. English became the language in the home, except among some of the recent immigrants. The *Amerikanischer Turnerbund* turned into the American Gymnastic Union. Old-timers privately bemoaned the fact that "singing societies . . . had degenerated into English-speaking businessmen's clubs where German songs could sometimes be heard, but were sung by hired singers."

The Steuben Society of America, founded in the grim year of 1919, reflected the new reality. It called its members "American citizens of Germanic origin." The society worked for "the civic betterment of the United States. . . ."[7] Compared to the old alliance, the Steuben Society was a paltry operation, never attracting more than twenty thousand members. English was the society's official language. The leaders of the organization celebrated an annual "German Day," which consisted largely of picnics and parades, all calculated to impress Americans with the contributions of Germans to *American* society. Like the Carl Schurz Foundation of Philadelphia, the Steuben Society portrayed Germanism as a colorful addition to the American scene. The foundation published a *German-American Review,* and arranged academic and cultural exchange programs with the German republic. All of this was valuable and nonthreatening work, part of the society's successful efforts to dampen "anti-Kraut" hatred.[5] Its leaders did endorse the Progressive candidate, Senator Robert M. LaFollette, in the 1924 presidential race, and Governor Alfred E. Smith in the 1928 contest. Both men lost, however, and the society was more cautious after that.

We can follow the Americanization process in the city of New Haven, Connecticut. New Haven was home to about 5,500 German-Americans in the 1920s. Their community had organized thirty-seven clubs, choral groups, and lodges in the late nineteenth century; by the 1930s, only twenty-three still existed. The surviving organizations had fewer members than ever before. The major society had declined after 1917, because "it seemed the part of wisdom and good taste to partially withdraw." The advent of radio and the automobile, promising new diversions to old and young, accelerated the community's decline. By the late 1930s, membership in the *Singverein* was down to eight persons. The few remaining members were anxious to assure outsiders that "the society never celebrated any native German holidays."[6]

Members of German-American groups explained their decline as due to "lack of interest," or decreased immigration, but everyone knew that the real reason was the "effect of the World War." The pressure to Americanize, to conform, was enormous. The German Society's officers assured Americans that "the Society does not celebrate any national holidays as a lodge. . . . They do not observe any German holidays or customs. . . . Once in a while they sing German songs at their picnics."

In Cleveland, Dr. Herbert S. Reichle, protesting the loss of German ethnicity, declared that he was both an American patriot *and* a German-

American. Reichle's warning against the melting pot was ineffective.[8] Germans won a new acceptance, as loyal Americans, and few wished to upset their fellow citizens. The great social critic H.L. Mencken described the new German-American leaders as mediocre and materialistic. He missed the point; their characteristics were those of their time, and of their country. Their very mediocrity made them an accepted part of the American scene. This was, after all, the age of President Warren G. Harding. Why risk antagonizing one's fellow Americans?

The fickle American public had changed course once again. After helping to impose the treaty of Versailles upon the defeated Germans, the Americans rejected it. Many people believed that the British and French had been too harsh on the Germans. American tourists once again marveled at the sophistication of Berlin and the quaint baroque splendors of Munich. Now a democratic republic, with the "freest constitution in the world," Germany seemed stable, both politically and economically. Americans admired the hardworking Germans, who had allegedly restored their shattered economy. In 1928, American ambassador Jacob Schurman found himself "constantly and increasingly impressed with the similarity of the fundamental international ideas of the Governments and peoples of our two countries." Few Americans had heard of the Bavarian politician Hitler.[9] Nor did people pay any attention to the German malcontents in the United States.

Dr. Hans Nieland did not accept the concept of bourgeois, assimilated German-Americans, not with Hitler rising to power in the fatherland. He saw a chance to carve out his own Nazi fiefdom in the heart of America. In 1931, Nieland declared that the New York group would form the nucleus of a new "Gau [region] USA." The reorganized party soon expanded to other cities, where it put the remnants of the rival Teutonia out of business.[10] The "League [Bund] of the Friends of the New Germany" became the official Nazi organization in this country. The Bund was born.

The league divided the United States into three *Gaue*, East, Middle West, and West. Heinz Spanknöbel, a young German photoengraver, assumed the title *Bundesführer* or *Bundesleiter* (League Leader or League Director). Spanknöbel received financial assistance and advice from the Nazi party, as well as from German consular officials. Spanknöbel convinced Deputy Führer Rudolf Hess that thousands of German-

Americans were waiting for the new leadership that he offered them. Spanknöbel, a restless and ambitious man, believed in his American mission. He strove to bring the Nazi message to people of German blood.[11]

The assimilationists had won the day after the collapse of the old German-American leadership in 1914–1918. Spanknöbel now challenged them. His first order of business was to correct American perceptions of the young Third Reich. This was important, for the Jewish-led boycott movement was undermining Hitler's attempt to revive his export economy.

Spanknöbel was not a subtle man. He acted as a funnel for crude propaganda smuggled into the United States by officials working for Dr. Joseph Goebbels's Propaganda Ministry. Spanknöbel bullied German-American editors who rejected association with his league. Colonel Edwin Emerson, an admirer of the Nazis, soon complained that Spanknöbel was more trouble than he was worth. He was, said Emerson, making it impossible for the Friends of the New Germany to live up to its name.

Spanknöbel's conspiracies began to remind Americans of German espionage activity during the Great War. A congressional committee undertook an investigation of his subversive work. In the autumn of 1933, federal agents were prepared to arrest the Nazi organizer.[12] On the evening of 27 October, however, an agent of the Propaganda Ministry grabbed Spanknöbel at gunpoint, forcing him to board a German liner. The *Bundesführer* knew too much. If arrested, he could implicate other Nazis in unsavory activities. Once back in Germany, Spanknöbel told the press that he had fled the United States in order to avoid being framed by the Jews.

The German-American press breathed a collective sigh of relief. The *New Yorker Staats-Zeitung*, a victim of Spanknöbel's tactics, was more outspoken, exulting in the downfall of a man "who left his followers in the lurch and crawled away into a mouse hole." The German-language press tried to disassociate Spanknöbel from the Nazi regime, depicting him as an adventurer operating on his own.[13]

Some German-American newspapers and their readers were happy about Germany's renewed strength and self-confidence. Like many Italian-Americans who admired Mussolini, these people were not fascists.[14] At the same time, they had no intention of attacking the New Germany.[15] Prominent German-Americans now found themselves in an awkward position. Despite their pride in Germany, they continued to fear the crude pressure exerted by Nazi upstarts. They were afraid of the federal authorities and concerned about American attitudes toward them and their old fatherland.

The new leaders of the Bund, Walter Kappe and Joseph "Sepp" Schuster quickly gained notoriety by insisting that all German-Americans must vigorously combat the Jewish-led boycott movement. Kappe and Schuster tried to turn the antiboycott issue into an *American* one, arguing that declining trade with Germany was bad for a weak economy. One of their supporters declared, "We . . . oppose the boy-cott, which estranges peoples and destroys international good relations, especially since Germany has a passive trade balance with the United States."[16] The Bund established two antiboycott organizations, the DAWA (German-American Economic Alliance) and the DKV (German Business League). These groups promoted the sale of German goods. Members displayed the alliance logo on their stationery, on their adver-tisement brochures, and in shop windows. They organized fairs and exhibits.

Much of the antiboycott movement's propaganda was anti-Semitic. One organizer declared that the boycott had arisen because "Adolf Hitler and his 'Brown Shirts' have broken the influence and the power of the Jewish race in the political life of Germany." This race supposedly controlled "about 65 percent of the money of the world." The Bund worked to convince Americans that the boycott was a Jewish plot. By the end of the decade, the DKV had over a thousand members. Its agitation reinforced the administration's caution in trade matters, but German exports to the United States remained insignificant.[17]

The militant Nazism of Kappe and Schuster frightened or repelled most German-Americans. The Bund wished to convert all true Ameri-cans to the belief that Nazi Germany was a friendly power. This was difficult to do, for Americans read, saw, and heard about the persecution of the Jews, the suppression of the trade unions, the establishment of a one-party state, and Hitler's resumption of military conscription. Kappe and Schuster, ardent Nazis themselves, did little more than mimic the Nazi style, strutting about in ill-fitting uniforms as they showered contempt upon their enemies. Their recruits were mainly recent immi-grants, ill-educated, lower class people susceptible to the message of triumph and revenge coming from Berlin.

The Bund sponsored numerous political rallies, pale imitations of the

Hitler extravaganzas in Nürnberg or Berlin. Schuster and Kappe often addressed meetings celebrating Hitler's birthday and his accession to power, and they commemorated the 9 November 1923 Beer Hall Putsch, the holiest day on the Nazi calendar. These events took place in rented halls in Ridgewood, Brooklyn, Yorkville, or northern New Jersey. The air reeked of cigar smoke; one smelled kalbsbraten and other German standard fare. The atmosphere at these events was petit bourgeois and mock-heroic. Comrades who had fought in the trenches reminisced about the old days. Schuster would then address his audience on themes such as "A New Year of Struggle Begins." Bund locals became little ghettos, where the preachers spoke to the converted, in isolation from the broader American scene. In Detroit, for example, Bundists held a rally in honor of famed German aviatrix Elly Beinhorn, ending the occasion with a rousing, beer-fueled rendition of the *Horst Wessel Lied*.[18]

The Bund leaders did not neglect their "Americanism" theme, but it came across as forced and patronizing. The highlight of the George Washington birthday celebration, for example, consisted of a chorus singing the "Star-Spangled Banner" with thick Germanic intonation. Until about 1935, it was not uncommon for speakers to shout, *"Heil Roosevelt!"* Roosevelt was popular, and some participants praised him by comparing him to Hitler. Speakers usually attacked the Jews and communism as twin enemies of both Hitler's Germany and Roosevelt's *Amerika*.

In Brooklyn, the Bund decided to celebrate the reunion of the Saar district with Germany. Its band offered a concert of military music, and the boys from the Bund organized a torchlight parade, just like the Nazis. In Hoboken, New Jersey, where the Bund had actually gained control of Hudson County's German-American Society, a good-sized crowd of onlookers offered the Hitler salute to one hundred swastika-bearing Bundists. Bundists convinced themselves that they were engaged in a *Kampfzeit* (era of struggle) reminiscent of Hitler's rise to power in Germany. There, too, the Nazis were at first outnumbered and despised. When would America awaken?[19]

The Bund was mimicking the storm troopers (*Sturm-Abteilung*, or SA) who had conquered the German streets for Adolf Hitler. Sepp Schuster, who had served in the SA, established an *Ordnungsdienst* (Order Service, or OD). The *OD-Männer* (OD men) wore identical white shirts, black trousers, legionnaire-style caps, Sam Browne belts, and arm bands. They claimed to have between 1,200 and 5,000 people in their ranks. OD men spent a good deal of time drilling and marching. They guarded meetings, sang songs, drank a lot, and reminisced about the Great War, in which many of them had served—on the German side. Like other protofascist groups, the Bund made money by selling shirts and paramilitary paraphernalia. Its men had to buy uniforms for twenty-seven dollars, a lot of money in those days. Bundists told snooping congressmen and journalists that the OD men "were just ushers for our meetings."

The Bund also published a weekly newspaper modeled on the Nazi *Völkischer Beobachter.* Named the *Deutscher Weckruf* (German clarion), the Bund sold three or four thousand copies, and gave away perhaps twenty thousand more. The *Weckruf* "exposed" anti-Nazis, opposed the boycott, and crusaded against the Jews. It was particularly vicious in its attacks on German-American "traitors," men who rejected the Nazi message.

Bund leaders often excited their followers with inflammatory rhetoric. Speakers denounced boycott leaders Rabbi Stephen S. Wise and Samuel Untermeyer as "worse than swine." Bund sloganeers declared, "The Jewish sharks own already [*sic*] New York City," and "Most criminals, racketeers and shysters are Jews." "Hit the Jews wherever you can!" Bundists cried, "[w]e German-Americans must stick together in order to annihilate the Jews." New Jersey officials went to court in order to prevent the Bund from holding rallies, because these invariably resulted in the "the most vicious and violent attacks upon members of the Jewish faith."[20] Clashes with opponents were common. In Newark, 150 police arrived during a Bund rally and arrested twenty persons in the Schwabenhalle Hall. Walter Kauf, an unemployed mechanic and Bundist bodyguard, was sent to jail for carrying a concealed, lead-filled rubber hose. Several Jewish demonstrators wound up in jail with him. A group of New Jersey Bundists, on their way to a meeting in Irvington, were set upon by antifascists. Two persons were hospitalized, while thirty-five went to jail. The Bund was becoming notorious. In America street brawling was not considered a heroic, soldierly virtue. The Bund's extremist rhetoric repelled most German-Americans, as well as the public at large. There was, however, a sizeable audience for pro-Hitler hate rallies, and the Bund tapped it.

Alienated losers trapped in Roosevelt's America thronged to a Bund rally in Madison Square Garden in the spring of 1934, swelling the crowd to perhaps twenty thousand participants. George Sylvester Viereck was there, as was Schuster, dapper in his OD uniform. Viereck felt vindicated: German-America would be reborn. It was becoming common for police to protect Nazi meetings.[21] Hundreds of antifascists tried to mob the hall, ignoring police cordons.

Despite their Nazi trappings, Kappe and Schuster continued to insist upon the organization's "one hundred percent Americanism." The Bund even began to employ non-German propagandists in an attempt to broaden its appeal. Doug Brinkley, a "well known American radio commentator and world traveller," was a favorite speaker at Bund meetings. He addressed audiences in places like the Yorkville Casino, where he spoke about his life in the New Germany. Cited favorably in the German press, Brinkley repaid the favor by describing Adolf Hitler as "a simple man for the common man and a great idealist." He assured his audiences that Hitler treated the Jews well. True, they had lost some of their inordinate power, but, as "one influential Jew told me," the concentration camps were pleasant places. The German-American "historian" Frederick Franklin Schrader supported the Bund's claim that the German workers were happy. He also described Hitler as peace-loving; communism and the Jews represented the real threats to international harmony.[22]

Despite these concessions to "Americanism," the Bund was becoming a purely German organization. Its vindictive tactics, combined with the violence attendant upon the Bund's rallies, further isolated it. In earlier times, German-American newspapers and organizations had sometimes cosponsored Bund rallies, usually because of pressure exerted by Schuster and his friends. By the mid-1930s, many German-American groups were standing up to the Bund.[23]

For almost twenty years, German-Americans had been trying to recover from the anti-German hysteria of the Great War. Their leaders did not wish to provoke the wrath of their fellow Americans. They did not like to hear Bund speakers remind them that the "American German who has no loyalty to Germany is no man." Nor did Steuben Society stalwarts care for Schuster's view that ". . . our movement is not only not 'un-American,' it is the only real movement that German-America ever had." Kappe and his cronies despised German-American leaders as pipe-smoking, card-playing hacks, devoid of *Deutschtum* or any idealism. In their frustration, Kappe and Schuster gave vent to more openly Nazi sentiments. Kappe embraced the "National Socialist worldview," bragging, "We are the storm troop detachment of the German element in the U.S.A." Schuster and Kappe saw the hard-core Bundists as "America Germans," or as Germans with American passports. The Schuster clique intended to terrorize German-America into backing the Hitler cause.[24]

In his OD uniform, Schuster and his "ten thousand" comrades became German front fighters, avenging their fallen comrades by combating German-American betrayal. "A man," he screamed, referring to a Steuben Society leader who had refused to give the Hitler salute, "who does not hold high his right hand during the playing of the German national anthem and the Horst Wessel Song has, in our view, forfeited the right to be a leader of German people." This expression of outrage concealed a note of despair. Schuster was failing to enlarge the Bund's base.[25]

A change of course was in order. By the autumn of 1935, a new leader was emerging. His name was Fritz Kuhn, and he was an American citizen. A chemical engineer by profession, Kuhn had served in the German Army during the war. He later returned to school in Munich, where he fell upon hard times. Kuhn rifled overcoat pockets looking for money and ran afoul of the law. After Kuhn's release from prison, he came into contact with a Jewish friend. The Jew found work for Kuhn in his family's warehouse; Kuhn repaid the favor by stealing two thousand marks from him. He then fled to Mexico. Later relocating to Detroit, the young engineer found employment with the Ford Motor Company. Kuhn admired Ford's anti-Semitic ravings, and claimed to have been an early member of the Nazi party. He bragged that he had even marched behind Hitler during the ill-fated Putsch of 1923. This seems unlikely, but then Kuhn was given to exaggeration.[26]

Fritz Kuhn became leader of the Middle Western "Gau" of the Bund. He was as much a Nazi as were Kappe and Schuster, but he had broader goals. The United States, Kuhn thought, was fragmenting into various ethnic groups. He wanted his share of the pie for his German-Americans, a part of the plunder. In a sense, Kuhn wanted an affirmative action program for alienated German immigrants, in the name of Americanism. Kuhn was more politically savvy than Schuster. He intended to enter the political arena rather than indulge in endless storm trooper fantasies. He wanted to create an anticommunist group that would be a worthy ally for Irish, Italian, and patriotic American organizations. Instead of reacting to events the way the paranoids Kappe and

Schuster did, Kuhn intended to mold them. No longer the "League of the Friends of the New Germany," the Bund in 1936 became the *Amerikadeutscher Volksbund* (the People's League of Germans in America). Americanism, not the New Germany, must, Kuhn thought, be the dominant theme. Avid for publicity, Fritz Kuhn molded the public image of the new Bund. For many Americans, "King Kuhn" *was* the Bund.[27]

Fritz Kuhn was an intelligent man, though he had weaknesses as a political leader. His spoken English was inadequate, a serious hindrance to a man who wanted to make the Bund part of the American political scene. And Kuhn had an immense ego, fortified by frequent and egregious lies. His love of food and drink equaled his lust for women other than his wife, Elsie. In short, Kuhn did not cut the figure of a hero. Tall and impressive in his youth, he now walked or waddled with a ponderous gait, trying to hold in his sagging gut. Kuhn looked out at the world through narrow slits of eyes, blinking behind thick eyeglasses. His dark, thinning hair was combed straight back. Kuhn had a bulbous nose and smooth, almost feminine, facial skin. Humorless and vain, he sometimes sounded like one of the characters from the popular comic strip "Katzenjammer Kids."

When addressing Bund rallies, Kuhn parodied the style in favor among Nazi speakers. He strutted up to the podium and worked himself into a frenzy of anti-Jewish, "pro-American" and "anticommunist" ravings. Kuhn often mispronounced American terms, so the effect was sometimes comical: "De Choos [Jews], they are persecuting me again. Eleven times I have been to court and eleven times I have returned a free man. But I am glad to see that Amerika is vaking up. Ve shall have it yet—a Free Amerika!" ("Free America!" had replaced "Sieg Heil!" in deference to the Bund's Americanism program).[28] Breathing heavily and sweating profusely, the *Bundesführer* left the podium, got into a waiting automobile, and headed back to his Yorkville office. There, surrounded by beer-drinking cronies, Kuhn spat out mispronounced English obscenities, along with an occasional German curse.

Kuhn was getting a lot of publicity, but most of it was negative. He feared the "Jew-dominated" press, yet desperately craved its attention. The media could turn him into a major figure; German-Americans would never do so. There were setbacks, as when Kuhn was arrested in Massachusetts for "drunkenness and the use of profane language to a police officer," but the *Bundesführer* believed in his destiny. Hitler was remaking Germany and starting to change the map of Europe. Fritz Kuhn now decided to reach out to new allies. In May 1936, he outlined "The Program and Goals of the America-German People's League." Kuhn's next task was to convince all "Aryan" Americans that Nazi Germany was worthy of "honorable, loyal friendship." Applicants for membership in the Bund still needed to show they were of Aryan blood, but they no longer had to provide information about their *German* origins. Speaking to non-Germans, Kuhn posed a rhetorical question: "Do you know," he asked, "that many Americans of non-German descent are today in the ranks of the Bund?"[29]

Kuhn realized that anti-Semitism was widespread in the United States. It was waiting to be mobilized, the *Bundesführer* believed. In the words of one Gau leader, "You can be convinced that 95 percent of the Americans agree with us that the Jew is a filthy scoundrel. . . . The frame of mind of the Americans is against the Jews. We must cut into this notch." Kuhn's message was clear: Lenin was a Jew; J.P. Morgan (real name: "Morgenstern") had Jewish blood; the Jews controlled the Roosevelt government; and FDR's original name was Rosenfeld. Kuhn concluded that Americans wanted and deserved "a socially just, white, Gentile-ruled United States." Over the next three years, the *Bundesführer*, a relatively new immigrant, preyed upon another American fear, calling, in his thick foreign accent, for the "[i]mmediate cessation of the dumping of all political refugees on the shores of the United States."

Kuhn traveled to the Third Reich in the summer of 1936. Accompanied by Bund comrades, he attended the Berlin summer Olympics. It was on this occasion that the surprised Bundists received an invitation to meet with Hitler, who was curious about these Nazi Americans. Fritz Kuhn awkwardly presented the Führer with three thousand dollars, a gift for a Nazi relief fund. Hitler was not particularly impressed with this rag-tag group, but this did not bother Kuhn, if he realized it at all. Eager to trade on his new notoriety, Kuhn implied that he came home from Berlin bearing Hitler's blessing.

Kuhn had absorbed the anti-Roosevelt mood prevalent in Germany. He contemptuously observed, "I don't believe that I have to discuss Roosevelt and his policies." The days were gone when Bund rallies echoed to comingled cheers of "Heil Hitler!" and "Heil Roosevelt!" The *Bundesführer* issued Bund Command Number 2: "I recommend that in the name of the German-American Bund our members elect Governor [Alf M.] Landon, the Republican candidate [for President]."

The Bund's newspaper bragged, "Ten million united German-American votes will restore to us the respect that is our due!" Kuhn believed that a Landon victory would augment his own power. When Landon lost in a landslide, old Bundists like Kappe, who had opposed the endorsement, counterattacked. The moody Kuhn was defensive about the Bund's isolation, revealed to the whole world. He reacted sullenly, "We stand strongest on our own." Still, he needed to shore up his position.

Kuhn, trading on his alleged ties to Hitler, now prevailed in a bloodless purge. By the winter of 1937, he had taken over all Bund propaganda operations, including the *Weckruf* newspaper. Kuhn now established a News Service, through which he communicated his orders. While Kuhn preached the virtues of ethnic expansion, the Bund was becoming more Nazi, and less German-American, than ever before. At times, Kuhn seemed to welcome this development. If fascism in America was the wave of the future (and he believed it was), then the strongest, best organized force on the right would prevail. As Fritz Kuhn surveyed the American scene, he saw potential fascist allies emerging from North Carolina to Los Angeles. The Depression continued, and the Dust Bowl had destroyed entire counties. Perhaps, he thought, his hour would soon strike.

CHAPTER
THIRTEEN

THE RISE OF AMERICAN
FASCISMS

NATIONALLY SYNDICATED COLUMNIST Westbrook Pegler upset many of his readers when he told them about his latest insight into the American character. Pegler, who gained much of his reputation from fighting mobsters who were despoiling trade unions, was not one to pull his punches. Tough-talking, grouchy, and loudly patriotic, Pegler saw danger on the horizon. "[There] is," he wrote, "a good deal of native Fascism in the American makeup and a strong religious and chivalrous strain. . . . But bring [Americans] together under the spell of secrecy and the charm of a voice in the belief that they are morally better than the non-joiners and you have the nucleus of Fascism. . . ." Pegler warned against slick promoters touting the virtues of patriotism, the home, and the church.[1] His admonition made him part of a growing number of journalists and intellectuals worried about the possibility of a fascist movement in America. A Swiss observer, Walter Adolf Jöhr, feared that "*an American fascist movement is thoroughly within the realm of possibility.*"[2]

European in origin, fascist movements had emerged amid the despair engendered by the Great War. They rejected liberal democracy in favor of charismatic, authoritarian leadership, and attempted to build strong, mass-based organizations. The pioneering Italian *fascisti* used terror tactics against opposing groups, and then threatened to overthrow the state. Committed to militarism and intense nationalism, fascist movements were thriving in much of Europe during the troubled 1930s. Fascist parties often voiced "revisionist" demands for territorial expansion. They preached hatred for minorities and gave voice to widespread resentment of traditional social elites. Fascists appealed to lower middle-class elements threatened by social change and economic crisis. In many countries troubled by fascist movements (Germany, Rumania, Hungary), anti-Semitism was part of the political culture, not merely a personal prejudice.

Benito Mussolini, the duce of Italy, had built the corporative state, widely hailed as the successor to a failed liberal order. His *fascisti* had conquered Ethiopia. Austria abolished democracy and instituted a state on the Italian model, though with more Catholic overtones. In Rumania, the fascist Iron Guard Legion of the Archangel Michael threatened the monarchy. The Nazis had abolished unemployment and restored German pride. Hitler had remilitarized the Rhineland, while the democracies twiddled their thumbs. In Spain, General Francisco Franco, supported by fascists at home and abroad, was winning a bloody civil war. By September 1938, rightists from Rumania to Argentina hailed the emergence of the *Führerprinzip* (the principle of strong, perhaps divinely ordained, leaders).

Many Americans harbored what may be called fascist sympathies. These sentiments could not always be ascribed to the self-taught ignorance of the unwashed multitude. Richard W. Child, former ambassador to Rome, wrote, "It is absurd to say that Italy groans under discipline. Italy chortles with it! It is victor!" Child insisted, "Time has shown that [Mussolini] is both wise and humane." "[T]he Duce is now the greatest figure of this sphere and time," Child concluded. Press lord William Randolph Hearst wished that America had a Mussolini (perhaps Hearst himself). The editors of *Fortune* magazine saw in fascism "certain ancient virtues of the race, whether or not they happen to be momentarily fashionable in [one's] own country. Among these are Discipline, Duty, Courage, Glory, Sacrifice." Many a reader of *Fortune* contrasted President Roosevelt's "millions of shiftless welfare chisellers" with Mussolini's Italy, a no-nonsense country where the right people were in charge and the "trains ran on time." Capitalists did more than admire.

The House of Morgan found Italy a good place in which to invest 100,000,000 dollars, loaned to the Italian government in the late 1920s. Secretary of the Treasury Andrew Mellon renegotiated the Italian debt to the United States, on terms more favorable by far than those obtained by Britain, France, or Belgium.[3] To many people, fascism was good for business and law and order, and bad for communism.[4] Most American investors ignored or cared little about the decline of the ordinary Italian's standard of living.[5]

Mussolini had many admirers in the United States. Angelo Rossi, the mayor of San Francisco, agreed with Hearst that America needed a duce. He customarily gave the fascist salute when attending Italian-American functions. An informant for a congressional committee reported that Rossi's police department was riddled with fascist sympathizers. Governor Philip F. La Follette of Wisconsin kept an autographed photograph of the duce on his wall. He hoped to establish a "new party" and lead it to victory in 1938—or in the presidential election scheduled for 1940.[6]

"Technocracy" was much in vogue around 1937. It taught that the future belonged to the planners, not to the tired proponents of laissez-faire capitalism. President Nicholas Murray Butler of Columbia University, a prominent Republican, wrote, "A man with a plan, however much we dislike it, has a vast advantage over a group sauntering down the road of life complaining of the economic weather and wondering when the rain is going to stop." Historian Charles A. Beard, a progressive, also admired fascism's ability to plan ahead. Henry Morgenthau, secretary of the treasury, believed that Mussolini had restored Italy's economic health, and hoped that fascism would somehow give way to a restored liberal order. Roosevelt seemed to harbor similar sentiments; at times he referred to the duce as an "admirable Italian gentleman."

There were, of course, powerful impediments to the rise of fascism in the United States. Most Americans still believed in the special nature of their national experience. Resentments and prejudices, while essential ingredients of a fascist movement, could not create one unless faith in the existing political order collapsed. Democracy was stronger in America than in most of Europe. Americans mistrusted the state and questioned authority, at least to a greater extent than did most Germans. The United States had a continent at her disposal, and was separated from the nationalist hatreds of Europe by a wide ocean. A strong belief in social mobility, and a kind of ingrained optimism, had not died, not even during the Depression. Yet there were disturbing similarities to the European scene. Strikes, demonstrations, the shrill level of some of the rhetoric, and the growth of the Communist party brought European comparisons to the minds of many Americans.

Both Mussolini and Hitler had come to power by demagogic appeals to masses of disoriented people. They had received substantial support from big business. Through their contacts in the establishment, these aspiring dictators had neutralized the armed forces that could have crushed them. They had appealed in hard times to disgruntled war veterans, men who felt abandoned by the governments they had served. Americans had been debating the pros and cons of bonus marches for more than a decade. Many veterans believed that the government owed them something more for their military service in the Great War.

In the autumn of 1933, the public learned about a sensational plot. "General" Art J. Smith, a soldier of fortune who had fought in remote parts of the world, organized several dozen veterans into a group called the "Khaki Shirts." Smith controlled somewhere between thirty and one hundred followers. In July, some "Shirts" killed a heckler who disrupted a rally in New York City. As a result, several were convicted of perjury. As he gained notoriety, Smith's ambitions grew apace. He supposedly threatened to "kill all the Jews in the United States." Boasting that one and a half million men would follow him, the "general" intended to lead a march on Washington. It would be a prelude to the seizure of the state. Smith bragged, "The Khaki Shirts are going to kick every damn crook out of Washington." His idol was Mussolini, whose march on Rome had stunned the world eleven years earlier.

Unfortunately for Smith, the Philadelphia police received a tip about his arms cache. They raided the storage depot, and arrested twenty-seven Khaki Shirts on 12 October. Smith was finished; all he had left was a stock of unsold shirts.[7] After the raid, the press regaled an entranced nation with stories about plots to blow up power plants and shoot communists in the shadow of the Capitol. Hitler, too, had once been a ridiculous figure with few followers.[8]

In the 1930s, the United States was rife with sensational rumors about other conspiracies. In late 1934, U.S. Marine Corps (Ret.) General Smedley Butler testified before a congressional committee. He claimed that Wall Street brokers had offered him millions of dollars to be used in setting up a fascist-style army of 500,000 men. Butler testified that Gerald MacQuire of Grayson Murphy and Company had assured him that the whole thing would be legal. Roosevelt would remain as a figurehead president, while businessmen and generals ran the country. Both MacQuire and his boss, Colonel Grayson Murphy, described Butler's story as "absolutely ridiculous" and "a lie." Lie or not, the story received a lot of attention in the press, both at home and abroad.[9]

In Chicago, the American Vigilant Intelligence Foundation, founded in 1927 by admirers of Mussolini, hoped that an Italian-style revolution was about to happen here. The foundation was highly active by 1934, collecting large sums of money from businesses such as Sears, Roebuck Company, A.B. Dick, International Harvester, and First National Bank. The Chicago Police Department denounced the vigilantes as money skimmers, and destroyed them. Even so, the familiar prefascist ingredients troubled many American observers. These included militant anticommunism, support from the wealthy, and amoral methods.[10] On the other hand, the police were not yet plotting with the conspirators, as had happened in various European cities. This was small consolation to those alarmed by the rise of demagogues.

Much of this rampant speculation about American fascism centered about Huey P. Long of Louisiana. A man of enormous energy and charisma, Long combined demagogic social promises ("Every man a king!") with access to "the purses of the Big Businesses he attacked on the stump." Privately, he tried to convince business interests that he was "far less radical than Roosevelt." After seven years of his promises, Louisiana still lacked "minimum wage and child labor laws, unemployment insurance and old age pensions." Long was no race-baiter, nor did he indulge in the anti-Semitism typical of American fascists of the day. This disappointed Lawrence Dennis, a self-styled fascist thinker, who noted, "It takes a man like Long to lead the masses. I think Long's smarter than Hitler, but he needs a good brain trust. . . . He needs a Goebbels." (Dennis had himself in mind for this role.) Americans who feared that "it could happen here" breathed a sigh of relief when the assassinated Huey Long was buried in Baton Rouge on Sept. 10, 1935.[11]

The Depression seemed endless, and millions of Americans continued to bemoan the loss of an earlier, simpler social order. Followers of fascist leaders were often poor or newly poor. They generally came from small towns. Most were of Anglo-Saxon origin, with a small admixture of German-Americans. They had never been leaders in their communities, and tended to blame their failures upon political forces beyond their control. They were searching for scapegoats.

Many of these proto-fascist types denounced the New Deal because it was too radical; in their scenario, Roosevelt was an incompetent reformer who was preparing America for communism. Others, who saw fascism as a radical alternative to traditional capitalism, viewed the New Deal as a timid experiment. They wanted radical reforms, and sometimes demanded cheap money, the redistribution of wealth, guaranteed old age pensions, or the expulsion of "money changers from the Temple." Could a fascist leader organize a mass movement based upon this confused mix of resentments, hatreds, nostalgias, and crackpot nostrums? Fascist ideologue Lawrence Dennis thought so. "A fascist dictatorship," he wrote, "can be set up by a demagogue in the name of all the catchwords of the present system."

Gerald L.K. Smith, a preacher, offered additional counsel. "Religion and patriotism," he advised, "keep going on that. It's the only way you can get them really 'het up.'" Smith had emerged in rural Louisiana during the 1920s. He learned his trade by attending emotion-packed, fire-and-brimstone revival meetings. Smith understood something of the German experience, and bragged, "I'll teach 'em how to hate. The people are beginning to trust true leadership." Smith was an imposing figure, and he had no trouble seeing himself as the American Mussolini, especially when he practiced his histrionic gestures before a mirror. An admiring Huey Long described Smith as, "after me, the best rabble-rouser in the country." Smith became an effective organizer for Long's "Share the Wealth Clubs." His sweat-drenched orations attracted thousands of people to Long's program, which promised a five thousand dollar income to every American. Smith soon endorsed Dr. Francis Townsend's old age pension plan, considered extravagant at the time. After Long's assassination in 1935, Smith founded the Committee of One Million, dedicated to Americanism and the extirpation of communism. He appeared on platforms with Dr. Francis Townsend, inspired by the dream of seizing power for a new coalition in the 1936 elections.

While claiming to speak for the downtrodden, Smith was working to gain support from more respectable, right-wing circles. Much of Smith's program resembled the mainline conservatism in vogue among many

Republicans and Southern Democrats. The preacher promised a return to the rural values of his youth, to a lost America. Smith worked to combine lower class discontent with mainstream antiliberalism.

Wealthy Catholics, disturbed by New Deal liberalism, were among Smith's prime targets. Gerald L.K. Smith had avoided the anti-Catholic rhetoric used by many other fundamentalists. He had learned from Long about the importance of the Catholic vote in Louisiana. Smith now decided to prey upon Catholic anticommunists. Boasting of his ties to prominent Catholic spokesmen, whom he constantly praised, Smith courted potential contributors to his cause.

Smith was an avid follower of Henry Ford, whose anti-Semitism he admired. Thanks to Ford, the preacher read *The Protocols of the Elders of Zion*. He concluded that the Jews were conspiring against Christianity. Smith had not yet become the extreme, embittered anti-Semite of a later era, though he quickly learned how to manipulate crowds with a sardonic reference to Bernard Baruch. Smith refused to endorse Hitler's war against the Jews, though he perversely believed that German anti-Semitism had been good for the Jews. In fact, throughout history, Smith declared, the Jews had thrived on persecution. Smith bided his time.[12]

Despite its past failures and crackpot tendencies, one could not write off American fascism's future prospects. Antifascists continued to be alarmed, and some decided to warn their fellow citizens against this threat. Dorothy Thompson, a brilliant and controversial columnist for the *New York Herald Tribune,* had interviewed Hitler before he came to power. Repelled, Thompson soon became the first American correspondent expelled from the New Germany. Possessed of great integrity as well as a sharp wit, Thompson constantly insulted the Nazis. Her husband, Sinclair "Red" Lewis, a Nobel Prize laureate, was the most famous American novelist of his day. At times, Thompson's antifascist obsession grated on his nerves, but Lewis shared her basic concerns. Both Lewis and Thompson feared that successful American fascist leaders might emerge during the crisis of the 1930s. In their view, religion could contribute to the rise of such demagogues, furnishing them with a ready-made audience. Was not Smith a product of fundamentalist faith?

Hollywood was more cautious than Dorothy Thompson. The movie moguls did want controversy. During the Depression, people were flocking to the movies, especially to gala musicals and other forms of escapist entertainment. Even newsreels were sugarcoated. Feature films depicting fascism could only be depressing, and producers feared alienating large numbers of theatergoers, especially German-Americans and Italian-Americans. Jewish movie moguls were afraid that an endorsement of anti-Nazi films would ignite anti-Semitism. Still other Hollywood big shots saw "premature antifascism" as the product of left-wing circles, of communists and their fellow travelers. The result was, in the words of the popular *Literary Digest*, a "timid cinema, a junior art which has feinted with a couple of quick lefts and then run every time it has tangled with an anti-fascist theme. . . ."

An energetic clergyman helped to counter Hollywood's timidity. Few Americans could compete with the Reverend Leon Milton Birkhead's contempt for totalitarian regimes. This Unitarian minister from the American heartland had seen National Socialism at work in Germany, where Nazi Jew-baiting confirmed Birkhead's loathing for fascism. Convinced by late 1937 that it could happen here, Leon Birkhead founded the Friends of Democracy, Inc. A master publicist, the minister tirelessly denounced Nazi atrocities. He also warned Americans that hundreds of fascist groups (in 1938 he put their number at a rather high eight hundred) existed in the United States. Birkhead bore witness to the anti-Christian nature of Nazism, to good effect.[13] He worked to convince gentile Americans that fascism was more than a Jewish issue. Battle lines were being drawn, for by now Roosevelt himself was expressing more frequent concern about the anti-liberal and expansionist tendencies of the Italian and German regimes.[17]

In 1937, Robert S. Lynd and Helen Merrell Lynd published their pioneering work, *Middletown in Transition*. More than a decade had passed since the Lynds first studied "Middletown," a modest-sized, "typical" Midwestern town. Since 1925, a cycle of boom and bust had gripped Middletown. By 1933, nineteen percent fewer manufacturers were providing jobs for workers. The wholesale value of products turned out by their factories had dipped by thirty-one percent. The average number of wage earners had dropped by twenty percent, while total

wages plummeted by fifty-one percent. The economy improved somewhat after Roosevelt came into office, and Middletown gave FDR an
overwhelming mandate in 1936.[14]

On the surface, Middletown was still a friendly, all-American place.
The Lynds spotted some disturbing undercurrents, however. An almost
hysterical anticommunism gripped some of the town's residents. The
small Jewish population was nervous, for the Jewish issue was "ready for
kindling if and as Middletown wants a bonfire to burn a scapegoat."
Hard-pressed merchants sometimes denounced the "Jews and the chain
stores."[15] Demagogues such as Huey Long had substantial followings.
The Lynds sensed that people felt insecure. The Lynds feared that
Middletown would follow "a middle-class strong man." For the time
being, democratic traditions kept such impulses in check. Another
great Depression, however, and the dam could burst. The Lynds concluded their work on a pessimistic note, quoting poet Carl Sandburg:

> *In the darkness with a great bundle of grief*
> *the people march.*
> *In the night, and overhead a shovel of stars for*
> *keeps, the people march:*
>
> *"Where to? what next?"*[16]

Uprooted Okies and victims of the catastrophic dust bowl storms
were vulnerable to demagogic religious and political appeals. By 1937,
the New Deal recovery had yielded to recession. Urbanization, an
increase in federal power, and a government friendlier to minorities had
antagonized those who looked back to a better time. To traditional
elites threatened by Roosevelt's prolabor liberalism, communism was
the main beneficiary of the New Deal. To Catholics following the lead
of the conservative Irish hierarchy of the Church, communism, as in
Spain or Russia, was Enemy Number One. Many Americans were
obsessed with a fear of communism. Some of these citizens had already
given up on constitutional democracy, seeing it as a dying irrelevance.

Anti-Jewish prejudice had been present in the republic since its early
days, so the new anti-Semitism built upon a sturdy foundation. The
patrician historian Henry Adams hated the Jews, whom he described
early in this century as polluters of every grand ideal. An alien race,

Adams believed, was taking over Europe and the United States. "Westward the course of Jewry takes its way!" he wrote. Ignatius Donnelly's best-selling novel *Caesar's Column* (1890) depicted a world in which the Jews controlled gold, and everything else. The Jews were both the chief capitalists and the main revolutionaries, or so Donnelly seemed to think. By the 1920s, many Americans were reading *The Protocols of the Elders of Zion*, an anti-Jewish forgery claiming to reveal the existence of a Jewish world conspiracy. The *Protocols* caught the eye of Senator Henry Cabot Lodge, who described the book "as well worth having." Henry Ford, the publisher of the *Dearborn Independent*, believed that the "international Jew" was behind the troubles of the world. He insisted that his dealers read the book. Novelist Theodore Dreiser shared these views. Writing to journalist H.L. Mencken (another anti-Semite, though more defensive about it), Dreiser noted that New York is "a Kyke's dream of a Ghetto."[18]

Despite outbursts of nativist anti-Semitism and continued social exclusion from certain areas of life, the Jews were doing better in America than in Europe. Second-generation or older, they were moving up the ladder, attending better schools, and finding decent jobs. During the prosperous years of the 1920s, anti-Semitism appeared to be declining. In the last pre-Depression year, 1929, the editors of the *American Jewish Yearbook* noted that "the past year witnessed a practical cessation of all anti-Jewish propaganda." Classified advertisements containing phrases like "Gentiles only," had fallen to 4.8 per 1,000 lines in 1931. Despite the obstacles to further advancement, American Jews were succeeding as never before. They were breaking out of ghettos such as New York's Lower East Side. Many took college degrees; more were attending Ivy League schools.[19] Then came the mysterious stock market crash, the Great Depression, and Roosevelt's New Deal.

The prominent journalist Vincent Sheean, looking back on the old days from the vantage point of 1936, recalled a time when overt anti-Semitism was the norm in many quarters. Writing in his best-selling memoir *Personal History*, the thirty-six-year-old Sheean spoke of the University of Chicago during and right after the World War. It was, he said, considered wise not to associate with Jewish fraternities.[20] A "mixed" fraternity was quickly scorned as Jewish. Now, such bigotry was considered unfashionable. The rise of Hitler and the upsurge in American anti-Semitism occurred just as old barriers to advancement were falling. Contradiction, however, was the historic lot of the Jews.

The intense, irrational hatred for Roosevelt expressed by many Americans was sometimes an outlet for an anti-Semitism that could no longer be articulated in polite circles. In a strange way, Roosevelt's political fate and his place in history would be linked to those of the Jews, both here and in Europe.

To many Americans, the Depression and its social consequences were the symbol of a modernization gone wrong. Jews and Negroes, many argued, were the chief beneficiaries of the New Deal. Jewish refugees from Nazism were supposedly flooding into the United States, taking away the few jobs available to good Americans. "Jews not wanted" ads climbed to 9.4 per 1,000 lines by 1937.[21] Forty-seven percent of those surveyed by Gallup would not vote for a "well-qualified" Jew for president. Polls showed that a substantial minority of Americans believed that the Third Reich would be better off "in the long run" if it expelled all its Jews. One inquiry showed that "about one-third of all Americans thought Jews were less patriotic than other Americans; almost half of all Americans felt there was good reason for anti-Jewish feeling. . . ."[22] Fifty-three percent of those questioned by Gallup believed that anti-Jewish feeling was "staying the same" (twenty-four percent) or "increasing" (twenty-nine percent).

The Jews were becoming more visible, and apparently more successful, just at the moment when the broader society was enduring the shocks engendered by the Depression. Of course, Jews, too, suffered from bankruptcy and unemployment, but this fact remained hidden from many Americans. They saw pictures of Bernard Baruch advising FDR, or Henry Morgenthau working at the Treasury Department, or the Warner Brothers churning out profitable motion pictures in Hollywood. Grumbling that "[t]he Jews have it better," some Americans crossed the line dividing anti-Jewish stereotypes from anti-Semitic activity.

While German anti-Semitism dated back centuries, its recent manipulation by the Nazis was relevant to current problems in the United States. Hitler had come to power in part due to the Great Depression. The Jew was the perfect scapegoat in hard times, the "perpetual alien" who supposedly did well while others suffered. Many people wanted simple answers, and anti-Semitism could always be updated. Facts that did not fit could be dismissed or, better yet, twisted. Many American Jews, of course, were conservative and voted Republican, particularly those whose German-Jewish forebears had emigrated to this country generations before. Hollywood producers were, by and large, Republican (the Warners were an exception, for part of the time). It was the liberal or radical Jews, however, especially those close to "Rosenfeld," who became useful as scapegoats and hate objects. Professor Frankfurter, Secretary Morgenthau, Rabbi Wise, and others like them were favorite targets. Those who hated liberalism resented Jewish leaders, liberal, socialist, or communist. Anti-Semites hated Jews who embraced social change by freely criticizing the prejudices and xenophobic conservatism of the traditional order.[23] To anti-Semites, such criticism was incomprehensible, even heretical, for these haters were trying to escape from history, not comprehend it. Everywhere around them, anti-Semites saw Jews and more Jews. Hollywood, largely run by Jewish producers and their film studios, dominated the American entertainment scene. As barriers to Jewish advancement broke down, anti-Semites, many of them victims of social change, hated those who moved up past them on the social and economic ladder.

Jews, of course, still faced various forms of discrimination. Many changed their names in order to gain employment in professions, such as teaching and social work, formerly dominated by "natives." Banks and insurance companies were reluctant to hire Jews, alleging the plethora of Jewish holidays as one reason for their reticence. America was the secular promised land to the Jews, but many a Jew was on his guard. The mordant Jewish sense of humor, developed during centuries of exile and hardship, gave voice to a complex view of the American scene. In one joke that made the rounds, a Jew asks a friend, "Tell me, Irv, why [the Jewish baseball player] Hank Greenberg hit only fifty-eight home runs, when only three more would have broken Babe Ruth's all-time record?" Irv responds, "Because he didn't want to look pushy!" Stereotypes persisted; a poll of Princeton undergraduates, for example, reflected a view of Jews as "shrewd, mercenary, industrious, grasping."

The fear among Jews was that a fascist or ultra-rightist movement, mobilizing anti-Jewish sentiment, might one day win broad support from the American people. Perhaps Americans, looking at dynamic Nazi Germany, would then say, "Look what a country can do when it kicks out the Jews!" As usual, Jewish opinion was divided. Some leaders, such as Rabbi Wise, favored militant anti-Nazi activism. Other Jews, fearing antirefugee sentiment, urged caution. Jews with a sense of history knew that Jewish communities in other countries had prospered

(Spain, ca. 1450; Germany, ca. 1925), only to be expelled or destroyed during a time of crisis. Of course, America was different—or was it?

Prominent people continued to harbor, and even express, anti-Jewish sentiments. Milo Reno, leader of the Farmers' Holiday Association, believed, "The Jews invented usury . . . [and are] consequently responsible for the farmers' troubles." Novelist Theodore Dreiser argued that there were ninety percent too many Jewish lawyers, that the Jews would overrun America. He believed that "Hitler was right. . . . [T]he Jews . . . shouldn't live with others." H.L. Mencken, the most famous social critic of the day, thought that the proportion of Jews in certain professions was far too high. Novelists Sinclair Lewis and Thomas Wolfe placed Jewish caricatures in some of their books.[24]

No anti-Semite could compete with Henry Ford in fame and influence. Though Ford renounced some of his earlier views (perhaps for business reasons), anti-Semites still learned from him. Ford had criticized the Jews for corrupting gentiles with a whole series of evils, including syphilis, Hollywood, gambling, and jazz. In the 1930s, the *American Gentile* continued Ford's work. Describing itself as "a semi-monthly newspaper for the defense of the Gentile cause," the newspaper reprinted material received from the Nazi "World Service." The *American Gentile* republished the *Protocols* and disseminated Nazi works like "The Downfall of Russia—Bolshevism and Judaism." Like Ford, the fascist National Workers League, operating in the Detroit area, used selective, out-of-context, or fraudulent quotations. Thus, A. M. Rothschild had supposedly said, "Permit me to issue and control the money of a nation, and I care not who makes the laws." Benjamin Franklin had allegedly warned, "The Jews, Gentlemen, are an alien race. They threaten this country." Historian Charles A. Beard proved the fraudulent nature of the Franklin quotation, but few fascists listened to his disclaimer.[25]

The upsurge in anti-Jewish incidents troubled Jews and non-Jews alike. The following stories were typical of the 1930s; they are chosen from a survey of many similar incidents. At the University of Delaware, fraternity brothers, using silver nitrate, branded a swastika on the face of Joseph Holzman. The dean took action, and a hesitant student council voted to abolish the customary "baptism of fire for pledges." One autumn afternoon, two teenage boys were killing time in a park in Irvington, New Jersey. They decided that it might be fun to carve a "swastika on somebody's arm." Their prey came along, in the form of the nine-year-old Bernard Cohen. The youths grabbed the terrified child, drawing blood as they carved the symbol of hate on his little arm. Bernard's screams frightened off his tormenters, preventing them from going to work on his other arm. The police apprehended the perpetrators, who turned out to be of German and Italian extraction. In New York City, bartender Martin Tobin got into Sol Schiff's taxi. The driver turned on the meter, then asked his passenger "Where to?" Tobin replied with his own question, "Are you a Jew?" Schiff answered in the affirmative, whereupon Tobin left the cab in disgust. Schiff followed Tobin, who owed him twenty cents. The former passenger turned around and slugged the taxi driver, knocking him down. Tobin was arrested.[26]

Anti-Semitic groups numbering 121 arose during the 1930s. Many were small, fringe groups. Most did not last a long time, but some achieved notoriety. Each group reinforced the anti-Jewish feelings of dozens, hundreds, or thousands of followers. Typical were the "Paul Reveres," led by national president Lieutenant Colonel Edwin Marshall Hadley. "[T]he Red menace," warned Hadley, "is creeping like a thief in the night, toward the house it would rob." To Hadley, all radicals were suspect, including Jean-Jacques Rousseau, "a degenerate French Jew." Lenin was, according to Hadley, "the syphilitic conspirator who died a raving maniac," Before his gruesome end, said Hadley, Lenin had planted the "sinister, dirty, Red rag of Soviet anarchy." Most respectable people rejected words like these, but many gave credence to the thoughts they reflected. Wall Street brokers and Main Street bankers sometimes bemoaned the apparent appeal of communism to Jewish intellectuals. Hadley believed that his time would yet come. After all, Hitler had been unable to attract mainstream voters in any great numbers until 1930.

CHAPTER
FOURTEEN

CAN IT HAPPEN HERE?

S INCLAIR LEWIS PUBLISHED his book *It Can't Happen Here* in 1935.[1] Hurriedly written, almost as a warning, the novel depicted Lewis's vision of a fascist order: denunciation, torture, regimentation, envy, and hatred dominate society in the name of Americanism. The novel was melodramatic, the plot was improbable, and the characters were blatantly one-dimensional, but its very crudeness contributed to the book's success. Thanks to magazines and newspapers, people had become accustomed to reading the horror stories told by panic-stricken refugees. Now, Lewis said, a fascist America might emerge, unless liberals and people of goodwill worked against it.

Lewis put commonly heard phrases into the mouths of his vulnerable characters. "I don't altogether admire everything Germany and Italy have done," says one man, "but. . . ." Another good American denounces "the Jew Communists and Jew financiers. . . ." Some of Lewis's townspeople are upset with Roosevelt because of "all the lazy bums we got panhandling relief. . . ." Others fear "dirty sneaking Jew spies that pose as American Liberals!" Lewis was prophetic, for within a few years anti-Roosevelt isolationists would be denouncing the "Jew-controlled" motion picture industry, and sometimes the press. Lewis saw irony in America's transformation from the hope of humanity to fascist oppressor. "Albert Einstein," Lewis wrote, "who had been exiled from Germany for his guilty devotion to mathematics, world peace, and the violin, was now exiled from America for the same crimes." His prophetic hero, Doremus Jessup, begins to question the wisdom of the American break with England in 1776. Had we become free in order to turn into these kinds of human beings? Jessup's despair foreshadows the Anglo-American alliance against fascist expansion, which only became a reality half a decade later.[2]

It Can't Happen Here caused a sensation. Even the anti-Roosevelt press succumbed to its power. The *Chicago Tribune* declared, "It is too powerful a blow. . . . [T]he reader feels such a terrific impact that he doesn't stop to analyze what has hit him." The *Christian Science Monitor* believed that "if it helps to make Americans aware of the danger of Fascism at home, it will be useful." While these reviews were being written, Mussolini's forces attacked Ethiopia.

Some readers believed that Lewis's fictional demagogues were based on a real-life person, a man named William Dudley Pelley. Jews observing the fascist scene watched Pelley's Silver Shirts with profound concern. A great self-promoter, Pelley at one point succeeded in convincing a Nazi party official in Munich that his Silver Legion had a membership of three million men. These people were in revolt, he claimed, against the "highly successful Jewish Depression."[3]

William Dudley Pelley was the son of a poor, itinerant Methodist minister, "traveling from 'call' to 'call' in the northern Massachusetts back hills." His father later gave up the ministry and entered a more mundane line of work, establishing the Pelley Tissue Corporation, a toilet paper factory in Springfield. As his life unrolled, young Pelley proved to be a restless adventurer, smoldering with resentment against the establishment, especially mainstream religions. He became a prolific contributor to pulp magazines and tried his hand at producing motion pictures, but "most of them [were] flops, because I had a most uncanny facility for roiling the very persons whom I should have made my friends." Pelley was a failure, his life one of "struggle and disappointment," hounded by "bill collectors." He complained about "caustic critics," felt persecuted, and became an impossible colleague.[4]

Pelley became fascinated by the esoteric spiritualist sects that flourished in southern California. Turning his predilection for spiritualism to literary use, in 1929 Pelley told readers of *The American Magazine* about his "Seven Minutes in Eternity: An Amazing Experience That Made Me Over." Pelley described how, in April 1928, he had died and gone to heaven for seven minutes. He had emerged a new man, for his experience had caused him to renounce coffee, tea, tobacco, and alcohol.[5] He intended to stay on earth for a while and would not die a second time until 1962, or so Pelley predicted. His article caused a national sensation.

Pelley now sought fame and fortune as a religious teacher. He founded four enterprises in Asheville, North Carolina, in order to confer the blessings of spiritualism upon a gullible public. Pelley offered mail order courses on "social metaphysics" and "cosmic mathematics." He was exploiting spiritual hunger during a time of national prosperity. When the Depression struck, Pelley, like a good salesman, came up with a new product.

Pelley's pupils, like Pelley himself, were of "uncontaminated English stock," living out humdrum lives in a country changing too quickly for their tastes. Too many Jews and Mediterranean Catholics were in the news. The Depression and the New Deal had created a new kind of sucker, so Pelley decided to try his hand at politics. To raise money, he sold stock in his Galahad Press, mostly to elderly widows. The authorities caught up with him, however, fining him and imposing a one to two year sentence. While appealing, Pelley thought it wise to transfer some of his operations to Indiana. In late January 1933, Pelley saw a vision depicting a change of regime in Germany. A housepainter, said a prophetic voice, would became head of the German nation. He, Pelley, must establish a Christian militia in the United States. Lo and behold, Adolf Hitler became German chancellor. One day later, on 31 January, William Dudley Pelley founded his Silver Shirts, "the head and the flower of our Protestant Christian manhood."[6]

Pelley intended to mobilize the resentments tormenting his sad followers. Hitler's success showed him that anti-Semitic propaganda could lead to power and fame. Pelley believed that Hollywood Jews had ruined his movie career, that Jewish magazine editors had spurned his work. Why could he not become the American Hitler? The new "Chief" now declared, "I intend to lead the fight to rid our country of the Red Jewish menace."

Pelley's major propaganda organ was *Liberation,* a weekly magazine, which quickly attained a circulation of fifty thousand. Financial problems nearly destroyed the magazine, but it survived as a monthly, with perhaps fifteen to twenty thousand subscribers. Pelley also turned out "primers" exposing the Jewish world conspiracy. He distributed books like *Mein Kampf* and *The Protocols of the Elders of Zion*. Pelley claimed that he had a foolproof way of detecting hidden Jewish genes. If he suspected a Silver Shirt applicant of racial pollution, Pelley "burned a lock of his or her hair and studied the ash to detect Jewish genes."

Pelley hated Roosevelt from the beginning. His newspaper *Liberation* played to the prejudices of those small businessmen who feared the National Recovery Administration as a kind of bureaucratic oppression calculated to destroy enterprise by pandering to chiselers. *Liberation* contained the overblown prose of the hack mystic.[7] Combining praise for Hitler with denunciations of Jewish communism, Pelley's well-printed and designed paper reflected the views of what one might call Nazi fundamentalism. Pelley saw himself as an American Hitler, working to strengthen the United States, Japan, Germany, and other nations in anticipation of the ultimate crusade against bolshevism. Pelley also claimed to speak for the "Christ people," who, stemming from different classes, now worked in a selfless manner for the enlightenment of others dedicated to taking part in the "Upward Climb." Pelley's "Christ Democracy" promised the unemployed eighty-three dollars per month, so they, too, could join the crusade of the enlightened, engaged in struggle against the children of darkness. By the spring of 1933, Pelley's hatred for the Jews grew stronger. FDR's allies came in for particular scorn, especially "[a] nice little Jewish boy by the name of Walter Winchell." Roosevelt, said Pelley, was working in cahoots with Sam Untermeyer and Barney Baruch for a "world program."

In Germany, Julius Streicher's boycott of the Jews took place on 1–4 April 1933. That action provoked worldwide protests, and the German government was concerned about possible effects upon the Reich's exports. Pelley received Nazi propaganda and placed it in his newspaper. The Jews, said *Liberation*, should form their own army and invade Germany if they were so upset about the Hitler government! This was not our quarrel, he said. Hitler came in for lavish praise, as a mystic initiate who retreated to a mountaintop when in need of counsel from the Hierarchy of Presiding Dignitaries. "The Skies Are Crackling With Psychical Enlightenment," gushed a *Liberation* headline. When Germany left the League of Nations, *Liberation* promptly attacked the organization as part of the Jewish plot, just as the Nazis had been doing since 1926. Pelley, now forty-three years of age, was only a year younger than his idol, Hitler. He noted, "The Hitler Movement in Germany started from a sign painter making a speech from the top of a barrel. It is not too early to begin casting up our slates!" If a "sign painter" could move the masses, why not the brilliant son of a toilet-paper manufacturer? Could he too not wipe the slate clean by ascribing his failures in life to the Jews, and seize power during this greatest of all depressions?

Back in his Asheville headquarters, Chief Pelley cut a dapper figure. He strutted about, resplendent in his silver shirt, black trousers, Sam Browne belt, and riding boots. The Chief carried a whip, and sometimes wore a cape slung over his left arm. He was known as a "good talker," a man who could mesmerize his poorly educated followers. There was, however, a seedy and unkempt air about the man, something unsavory undermining his mock-heroic trappings. In and out of court over accusations of fraud and conspiracy in the sale of stock issued by his publishing house, Pelley managed to avoid prison, at least for the moment. A fanatic and a confidence man, Pelley fed his ego with the flattery of his courtiers. He fantasized about his political future and announced that he would contest the presidency in 1936 on the "Christian Party" ticket. Some might laugh, but others pointed out that only a few years before nightclub comedians in Berlin and Vienna had ridiculed little Hitler as *schöner Adolf,* (beautiful Adolf).

Pelley was trying to turn himself into the radical, Anglo-Saxon protector of threatened American values. He raved against "wild-haired little kikes [holding] important federal positions. . . ." Pelley and his followers recoiled in horror at the thought of the ethnic pluralism so fashionable in liberal and left-wing circles. The Jews must be behind all these hideous social changes, Pelley believed.[8] He charged that the Jews in America were taking their orders from Moscow, while Roosevelt (a "Dutch Jew, Franklin D. Rosenfelt") was working with Leon Trotsky. If the Jews, aided by Roosevelt's "Great Kosher Administration," had their way, the U.S.A. would turn into "the United States of Soviet America." Pelley railed against the labor movement, which he saw as both Soviet and Jewish.[9] "There is no such thing," Pelley claimed, "as any C.I.O. [Congress of Industrial Organizations] in the German steel industry. All that voracious Red nonsense has been squelched to stay squelched." Jews, added the Silver Shirt leader, controlled the Federal Reserve, and worked in cahoots with the "nefarious American Civil Liberties Union."

Pelley intended to lead the physical battle against "this plague of Jews." He lobbied against gun control legislation, because a cleansing bloodbath required the use of firearms. Pelley mused often about the coming slaughter of the "Jews and their allies." Through marches, leaflets, and the acquisition of guns and munitions, the Silver Shirts worked toward this bloody goal. They established "Aryan bookstores," which became centers for the distribution of anti-Jewish propaganda. At their peak, the Silver Legion had between ten and fifteen thousand active members; some estimates placed the figure as high as twenty-five thousand. Pelley later claimed to have attracted twenty-five thousand card-carrying members and seventy-five thousand fellow travelers. [10]

When federal authorities began to investigate his Silver Shirts, Pelley responded with pamphlets denouncing the FBI and the House Un-American Activities Committee. Federal pressure took its toll, however. Pelley's more cautious followers began to melt away. The chief responded by stepping up his attacks on the "Jews and their allies." It was clear to Pelley that the government was out to destroy him, but the chief was not about to surrender. "[Pelley]," a spokesman said, "doesn't give the kippered tail of a *gveltefische* what sort of wordy smokescreen the despoilers of America apply to their opponents!" Despite the bold rhetoric, the Silver Shirts had not broken out of the lunatic fringe. Pelley was not a great speaker, nor did this disreputable character attract competent followers. The Silver Shirts were important as a barometer of discontent among marginal types of people, not as a revolutionary vanguard movement. [11]

Pelley's problems led to "Christ Democracy's" rapid decline. Yet fascist attitudes would soon gain a new lease on life, as a major recession and the looming war in Europe contributed to a sharp rise in anti-Semitism. Pelley now began to exploit American fears about involvement in a second European war: "Shall the United States go to war at the finagling of a kosher president to make the world safe for Jewish bloodgut?" [12]

The endemic backbiting among would-be fascist leaders hurt Pelley, whose foibles became fair game for his rivals. Gerald L.K. Smith, who continued to run the late Huey Long's "Share the Wealth" clubs, was not complimentary when a reporter asked him about the famous Silver

Shirt Leader. "I saw him," Smith recalled, "when he was writing a piece for the *American Magazine* on 'seven minutes in heaven'—or was it hell?"

William Dudley Pelley also found himself competing with the Reverend Gerald B. Winrod of Kansas, head of the Defenders of the Christian Faith. Winrod had inherited a fervent fundamentalist belief from his father. The elder Winrod saw the light after the prohibitionist crusader Carry Nation smashed up his place of business—the Senate Bar. He became a traveling evangelist, preaching the gospel. His son claimed to receive messages directly from God, including a command in 1925 ordering "me to form this inner circle [of the Defenders]." Unlike Pelley, Winrod had a firm base in the evangelical mainstream. By 1936, Winrod's most important publication, *The Defender,* enjoyed a circulation of about 100,000 copies. Crusading tirelessly against atheism and "modernism," Winrod found himself attracted to Hitlerism: "Germany stands alone in her attempt to break Jewish control." Winrod decided to make a bid for political power. He contested the Republican nomination for the U.S. Senate in 1938. This, however, was just a first step. In the words of a supporter, "Dr. Winrod has no church of his own. The entire United States and Canada are his congregation."

Winrod's most influential pamphlet was called *The United States and Russia in Prophecy and the Red Horse of the Apolcalypse.* Reflecting and playing upon American fear and confusion, Winrod identified the fourth horse of the apocalypse as bolshevism, a theory later embraced by men so respectable as Herbert Hoover. Winrod argued, "This is a catastrophic period in the world's history," and concluded, "American Fascism is a new experiment." A Jewish financial conspiracy, he claimed, working in concert with liberalism, was bidding for global hegemony. The Jews already controlled Russia, whose Bolshevik regime owed its existence to a "certain large Jewish owned banking institution in the United States." Winrod's fascistic, patriotic fundamentalism seemed to have a political future in this country, unless, of course, people became fearful of its ties to a hostile foreign power.[13]

Gerald Winrod's pamphlets were part of a flood of anti-Roosevelt hate literature. The FDR Library in Hyde Park, New York, contains four grim boxes filled with this material, which continued to appear after the president's death in 1945. The Fellowship Press in Indianapolis published pamphlets like *New Dealers in Office*, which purported to show that these men and women were of Jewish ancestry. The Militant Christian Association of Charleston, South Carolina, depicted the Jews as grasping for world rule by the year 1941. FDR was part of their effort. In all of these paranoid ravings, one finds the combination of reactionary political views, hatred for FDR, and loathing of the Jews.[14]

Gerald Winrod was a pioneer in attacking the New Deal as early as 1933. Winrod's work had an impact upon Roosevelt-haters from New York City to southern California. Winrod traced Roosevelt's "radicalism" to his *Jewish genes*. FDR, according to Winrod, was descended from the "Rosenvelt" line. Publishing a fake genealogy, Winrod ascribed "Rosenvelt's" allegedly pro-Soviet, pro–international banker stance to his advocacy of "Jewry's world program."

Winrod quoted British economist Harold J. Laski, who allegedly said, "If the experiment for which Roosevelt is responsible, should in any serious degree *break down . . . there would be an outbreak of Anti-Semitism in the U.S. more profound than anything Anglo-Saxon Civilization has so far known.*" This proved to be prophetic, for by 1938 American anti-Semitism had reached alarming proportions. The fate of Jewry, and that of American fascists and anti-Semites, was indeed dependent upon the success of FDR's anti-Nazi, antifascist policies.

A spellbinding orator, Winrod described Roosevelt as a front for the Red Revolution, itself part of a Jewish plot aspiring to "gain control of all Gentile governments." Winrod's publication *The Revealer* warned against the high Negro birthrate, and linked Mrs. Eleanor Roosevelt to Negroes and hence to communism.

Winrod's combination of fascism and fundamentalism appealed to alienated and dispossessed folks who inhabited the small towns and farms of depressed rural Kansas. As he toured, Winrod did try to tone down his anti-Semitism, declaring, "I am not against the Jews as a race or religion." He added, "I only oppose the international Jew. . . ." Accused of being a Nazi agent, Winrod swore, "I don't get any money from Germany." This was misleading, however, for the Defenders of the Christian Faith received large amounts of propaganda materials from the offices of Nazi Jew-baiters Julius Streicher and Ulrich Fleischauer. In fact, Winrod's inflammatory anti-Semitism caused concerned observers to label him the "American Streicher."

During his Kansas senatorial campaign, Winrod distributed hundreds of thousands of pieces of literature. He hired twenty aides, and bought a lot of radio time. The Kansas Republican establishment, led by former governor and presidential candidate Alf M. Landon, began to fear a Winrod victory in a divided field. It belatedly closed ranks against him, though the "Jayhawk Nazi" still came in third, receiving almost thirty-five thousand votes. One in five Republican voters wanted him in the U.S. Senate. Winrod had failed, but he had also established a base. He continued his work throughout the United States, blasting the New Deal and Roosevelt's anti-Nazi statements. Winrod helped to keep anti-Semitism alive.[15]

Robert Edward Edmondson lacked Winrod's political ambitions, but not his fervent anti-Semitism. Edmondson, now in his sixties, discovered "sinister Jewish Leadership forces" while working for a publication "run by Jewish scandal-mongers." In 1923, he suffered a nervous breakdown, which he ascribed to "overwork." Apparently recovered, Edmondson devoted much of his time to exposing the Jewish menace. He soon revealed that "Talmudic Communism" was part of the "Rabbi Racket." He claimed that the Jews running Russia had erected a statue of Judas Iscariot in Szirsk (a town that no one could locate). Edmondson's Economic Service, active in New York City between 1934 and 1939, often accused the Jews of causing the Depression and subverting the nation's recovery. While denying that he opposed "industrious citizens of the Jewish Faith," Edmondson crusaded against "that class of . . . Asiatic revolutionary Communistic and Socialistic Jews who are destroying American Principles of Government."

Edmondson ran a lucrative business. He supplied antiboycott and anti-Semitic literature to groups such as the National Gentile League ("Vote Gentile! Buy Gentile!") and the American Nationalist Party. Edmondson received materials from Germany, and worked for principles espoused by the Nazi government. Only weeks before Hitler publicly threatened the Jews with extermination, Edmondson promised that he would "Make the World Jew-Conscious." Both Nazis and antifascists were beginning to take people like Edmondson more seriously.

Mayor Fiorello H. LaGuardia worked to have Edmondson indicted as a menace to public order. While his target sipped coffee across the street from General Session Court, LaGuardia's summons was filed with a magistrate. Accused of criminally libeling Labor Secretary Frances Perkins and the Jewish religion, the sixty-six-year-old Edmondson received help from the American Civil Liberties Union. Declaring, "We must suffer the demagogue and the charlatan," Judge J.G. Wallace threw out the indictment. LaGuardia's summons reflected his deep concern about rising anti-Semitism, which he feared could lead to public disorder. Nazi agents carefully filed materials prepared by Edmondson, believing that he had a future.[16]

The most notorious Jew-baiter of the day was James True, a former reporter and publisher working out of a small office in the National Press Building in Washington. True would bolt his door and cast furtive glances when discussing the Jewish problem. Believing that the Jews were out to get him, True intended to destroy them first. Accused of favoring their expulsion, True set the record straight. "We are," he said, "going to bury them right here!" In 1935, True received a U.S. patent for a new type of nightstick; True called it the "kike-killer." True would smile as he informed visitors, "My wife owns a Kike Killer, Lady's size, because the regular size might be too heavy. It can crack even a negro's skull wide open." James True was an American prophet of the Holocaust. After the defeat of Roosevelt, True predicted, a "Jew Shoot" or pogrom would take place. A group allied with True, the "Order of '76," printed cards containing the bizarre phrase "In case of pogrom, please pass the bearer through police lines." Senator Thomas D. Schall of Minnesota, an embittered Republican Roosevelt-hater, placed materials received from True in the *Congressional Record*. Nor was Schall the only congressman promoting True's program.[17]

Representative Louis T. McFadden, Republican of Pennsylvania, believed in an international Jewish conspiracy. Its aim, he said, was to leave the gentiles with paper, and the Jews with "the gold and lawful money." The Jews, according to McFadden, were not suffering persecution in Germany. Those who wanted to import 200,000 "communistic Jews" into the United States were, like Secretary of Labor Frances Perkins, part of the conspiracy engendered by a "Jewish-controlled administration." Perkins was a favorite target of these hate mongers. A longtime pioneer in social work, this woman of impeccable "native" credentials was, according to her enemies, a "Russian Jewess whose real name was Matilda Wutski." McFadden also believed in and circulated the *Protocols of the Elders of Zion*.[18] Defeated for reelection, he dropped dead of a heart attack in New York City, of all places. When McFadden lost his seat in the Congress, or Schall died, there were others to replace them.

Anti-Jewish leaders were competing for a limited constituency. Their base was expanding, but it could only support a finite number of uniforms, pamphlets, newspapers, and rallies. Pelley, Winrod, Edmondson, and True soon found themselves competing with George E. Deatherage, National Commander of the Knights of the White Camellia. Deatherage claimed a following of more than a million people, a considerable exaggeration. His magazine, *The White Knight*, was "devoted exclusively to the Jewish menace." Deatherage defined fascism as a "patriotic revolt . . . against Jewocracy (alias democracy)," and the "Jew Deal." Much of Deatherage's literature bore the swastika emblem, even though "Jewish propaganda . . . had done its best to cast odium on [it]." Deatherage had Napoleonic ambitions; he hoped to turn his American National Confederation (ANC) into a paramilitary army capable of seizing power. The commander dreamed of uniting American fascists and racists under his ANC leadership. Deatherage failed, because Pelley and the others had no intention of giving up their printing presses, private "armies," uniforms, and incomes.[19]

The Midwest provided fertile soil for anti-Semitic demagogues. Suspicion of "Eastern interests" (Wall Street and/or the Jews) was widespread, and it increased during the Depression. Michigan was home to the infamous Black Legion, a secret society advocating anti-Jewish, anti-Catholic, and anti-Negro action. Most legionnaires had small-town or rural roots. Many had learned their politics in the Ku Klux Klan, of which the legion was an offshoot. They had come north looking for better economic conditions, only to be overwhelmed by the Great Depression. Hostile to labor unions, legionnaires blamed the strikes and violence occurring in the Detroit auto factories upon communist conspiracies. The ethnic coalition formed by the New Deal repelled these Anglo-Saxon legionnaires. By 1934, they were looking back fondly to a simpler, better time. These men needed an explanation for their woes, perhaps a demon they could recognize and destroy. To many legionnaires, the *Jew* was the cause of the incomprehensible uncertainty that troubled their lives. Other activists were violently anti-Catholic. Some of these men may have attempted to burn down the Shrine of the Little Flower in Royal Oak, Michigan, made famous as the home parish of Father Charles E. Coughlin, the "radio priest." At its peak, the Black Legion contained forty thousand activists or supporters. Night riders, sadists, frightened men, murderers—the legionnaires were hardly in a position to overthrow the government. Law enforcement officials, however, began to wonder what these men would do next.

Some legionnaires reacted to the troubles of the 1930s by plotting acts of violence—arson, floggings, beatings and murder—that recalled the work of the Ku Klux Klan in an earlier time. Northern Klansman shared the legion's benevolent view of the Nazis.[20] "Hitler has appreciated the evil influences of the Jews and has realized that most of them are Communists," declared one northern Klan leader.

By the spring of 1936, the Black Legion was gaining national prominence. The *New York Times* ran a page one, column one, story about the flogging of one Harley Smith of Norvell.[21] He was, said the newspaper, abducted and beaten by a mob in Jackson County, in retaliation for Smith's decision to leave the legion. In Ohio, officials suspected legionnaires of threatening to kidnap the governor's daughter. Attorney General Homer Cummings did not move against the legion, for it had not, he said, violated federal laws.

The legion had frightened a lot of people, so much so that Hollywood momentarily forsook its habitual caution. In 1936, the Warner Brothers studio released the film *Black Legion*, starring a young actor named Humphrey Bogart. The movie premiered on 30 January, four years after Hitler had become German chancellor. *Black Legion* told the fictionalized story of an extremist fascist group operating in the Midwest. The film focused on bigotry, antiforeignism, lower middle-class frustration, and secret fascist conspiracies. The *New York Times* reviewer hoped "that its message reaches that type of mind to which the Michigan organization's aims appealed." That message certainly gained the attention of the Klan, which brought an unsuccessful suit against the Warner studio. This kind of publicity meant "controversy," which Warner and the other film moguls avoided like the plague. Despite its moderate success, *Black Legion* had no successor. Even as Hitler was becoming an international menace, producers did not wish to be accused of "warmongering" or (later), "interventionism."[22]

The legion's penchant for violence proved to be its undoing. A conscience-stricken legionnaire confessed to involvement in a plot to execute seventy-three "Detroit Jews with the aid of typhus bacilli." The authorities moved to crush the legion. In the winter and spring of 1937, a number of legionnaires were found guilty of arson and conspiracy to commit murder. They received jail sentences, a development which frightened some of their more fainthearted brethren. Each story about the sentencing of a legionnaire received less space in the newspapers than its predecessor.[23]

A troubling question continued to bother many people in the Detroit area, however. How many more legions could arise if the American economy remained mired in Depression?[24] And would they be so easily suppressed?

Promoting German tourism in New York City.
(Credit: National Archives)

The German government, anxious to obtain tourist dollars and American approval, promotes Germany as a quaint, traditional society: "Singing, Ringing, Laughing Cologne." (Credit: National Archives)

In its early days, the Bund made crude attempts to build up a patriotic, American image. (Credit: National Archives)

Sepp Schuster, in his study.
(Credit: Bundesarchiv)

Fritz Kuhn in a typical pose. Holding in his stomach
and grasping his belt, Kuhn proudly displays his Iron
Cross. (Credit: Hoover Institution Archives)

Bundists whooping it up during a Fourth of July celebration.
(Credit: National Archives)

California Bundists advertising the *Weckruf*, along with Julius Streicher's notorious Jew-baiting "newspaper," *Der Stürmer.* (Credit: Bundesarchiv)

Fritz Kuhn (second from left, looking toward the camera) some months after his attendance at the Berlin Olympics. He had become the unquestioned führer of the Bund. (Credit: Bundesarchiv)

Fritz Kuhn's fateful meeting
with Adolf Hitler.
(Credit: Hoover Institution)

Fritz Kuhn, capitalizing on notoriety gained by meeting Hitler, places an Olympic ribbon on a Nazi flag. (Credit: Bundesarchiv)

In the autumn of 1936, after returning from his meeting with Hitler, Kuhn vowed to defeat President Roosevelt's bid for reelection. (Credit: National Archives)

The Bund's violence-prone rhetoric led to
demonstrations and clashes with anti-Nazis. Here
thousands of Bundsmen demonstrate with their
friends in New York City. (Credit: Bundesarchiv)

"The Head Chef": Bundist anti-Jewish propaganda.
(Credit: National Archives)

DER "CHEFKOCH"

William Dudley Pelley, head of
the Silver Shirts.
(Credit: Wiener Library)

The "radio priest," Father
Charles E. Coughlin.
(Credit: Library of Congress)

One of the many versions of the *Protocols* circulating in the United States in the 1930s. (Credit: National Archives)

Humphrey Bogart being initiated into the *Black Legion*. (Credit: MOMA Film Stills Division)

Leaflet attacking Jews for making trouble for true Americans. (Credit: National Archives)

Poster promoting a Bund rally in the New York Hippodrome. Despite its "American" trappings, the Bund's Nazism was beginning to frighten and repel most German-Americans. (Credit: National Archives)

Fritz Kuhn at a rally in Camp Siegfried, accompanied by fascist leader Joseph Santi. (Credit: Bundesarchiv)

Bundists with families at an outing in the country, dressed in their Sunday best. (Credit: National Archives)

Severin Winterscheidt, "Bund Press Observer." (Credit: Bundesarchiv)

Fritz Kuhn in Yorkville.
(Credit: National Archives)

Fritz Kuhn in a typical oratorical pose.
(Credit: National Archives)

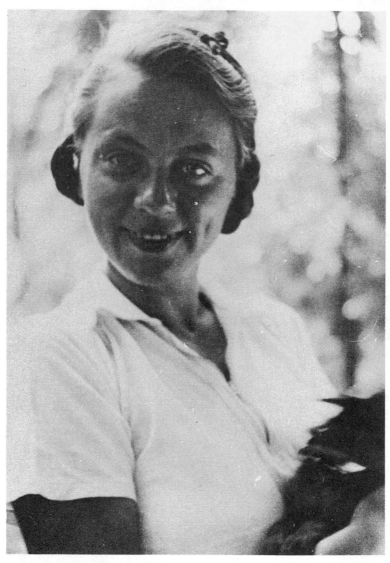

Erika Hagebusch, Leader of All Girls' Groups, February 1938.
Kuhn was particularly fond of her. (Credit: Bundesarchiv)

The Bund leadership, sensing the threats to the organization, hammered away at two themes, Americanism and anticommunism, both of which contained much anti-Semitism. It reached out for any allies willing to collaborate with it.
(Credit: National Archives)

Nazi propaganda poster, distributed by the Bund, shows that Germany has a population of 75,000,000, including 10,000 unemployed, while the U.S., with 130,000,000 citizens, has over 8,000,000 persons unemployed.
(Credit: National Archives)

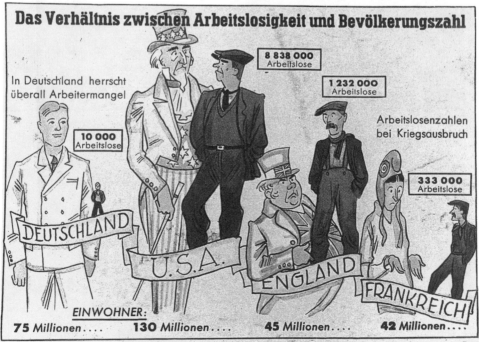

Despite his fears that the Bund would damage German-American relations, Ambassador Hans Dieckhoff sometimes found it expedient to greet Bundsmen and their affiliates. (Credit: Hoover Institution)

CHAPTER
FIFTEEN

"UNDER THE INFLUENCE
AND CONTROL OF
THE JEWS"

B Y 1937, THE United States was awash in a record quantity of anti-Jewish literature. Nothing obsessed the Jew-haters more than FDR's alleged favoritism toward Jews. In the words of the writer Franklin Thompson, "No administration in the history of the United States has been [so much] under the influence and control of the Jews as the present one."[1] Proponents of this thesis usually ascribed the rise of communism to the Jews. According to a diligent eccentric named Elizabeth Dilling, Roosevelt had "achieved more of the revolutionary Socialist program in a few months than all of the American Reds combined have in years. . . ." In a bizarre, privately published pastiche entitled *The Roosevelt Red Record and Its Background*, Mrs. Dilling accused Roosevelt of participating in a conspiracy to destroy the constitution.[2] A tightly printed compendium of out-of-context quotations accompanied by vitriolic commentaries, *The Roosevelt Red Record* circulated widely among rightists fearing a communist seizure of power. Combining slander, guilt by association, and hatred, Mrs. Dilling hammered away at the bolshevik plot.

Comparing the New Deal to the *Communist Manifesto*, Mrs. Dilling blasted Jewish communists while denying that she was anti-Jewish. She believed that "even if most of the Communists are Jews, it does not follow that most of the Jews are Communists." Among the Jewish radicals uncovered by Mrs. Dilling were Harvard professor Felix Frankfurter and Supreme Court Justice Louis D. Brandeis. Though written by a paranoid for true believers, *The Roosevelt Red Record* tapped a larger strain of discontent. Many thousands of small businesses had gone into bankruptcy, leaving embittered Americans in their wake. Businessmen unhappy with New Deal government sometimes passed copies of the book on to their friends. Conservatives from the Anglo-Saxon elite could read about the perfidy committed by Roosevelt, that "traitor to his class." Perhaps, as Mrs. Dilling suggested, he was also a traitor to his nation.

Dilling attributed the growing anti-Semitism to Roosevelt, "because he appoints so many radical Jews to key positions." Her admirer, William Dudley Pelley, argued, "[T]hese international [Felix] Frankfurters . . . have turned the Christian United States into a vast civic synagogue." The *Christian Free Press* of Los Angeles described Roosevelt adviser Samuel Rosenman as the evil genius behind FDR's "court-packing" scheme. Rosenman, working through the American Jewish Committee, supposedly ran the country according to principles first laid down in the *Protocols of the Elders of Zion*. Militant anti-Semites began to advance an even more daring theory: Was Roosevelt a Jew, as some Nazis, including Hitler, alleged?

During these years, a detailed genealogical chart made the rounds in right-wing circles. It purported to show that both Eleanor and Franklin Roosevelt were descended from Jews. According to garbled versions of a story advanced by Streicher and his associates in the New Germany, the Roosevelts were descended from Sephardic Jews who had fled Spain in 1492. After arriving in Holland, they changed their name from "Rossacampo" to "Roosevelt." Nazi writers began to speculate about Roosevelt's "Hebraic noises," and "Jewish features." Winrod was one of the first anti-Semites to use the name "Rosenfeld" for the president. Winrod observed, "Roosevelt inevitably draws upon his Semitic ancestry. It is, therefore, as natural for him to be a radical, as it is for others to be true Americans. . . . HE IS NOT ONE OF US!" This last phrase was taken from one of Adolf Hitler's 1934 speeches, when he declared that those Germans who rejected the tenets of Nazism "gehören nicht zu uns!" Edmondson claimed that New York Jews, elated over FDR's victory, had struck a medal with the president's image on one side and the Star of David on the other. He argued that B'nai B'rith ran the country. On another occasion, Edmondson claimed that six groups, each headed by a Jew, controlled the United States. Why six? Because of the Star of David. Jewish internationalists, bankers, and bolsheviks had taken over, breaking down traditional morality and handing the country over to foreigners and Reds. One of the agents was "Matilda Wutski," alias Frances Perkins, secretary of labor. "Rosenfeld," conspiring with Jewish conspirators, had placed "Wutski" in the government.

Roosevelt responded with contempt, laced with ridicule. On one occasion, the president laughed as he informed Senator Carter Glass of Virginia that, according to the Nazis, they were both "Jewish Freemasons."[3]

Anti-Semitism and fascism flourish during times of inexplicable crisis, when ideas advanced by lonely or even despised paranoids suddenly seem to make sense to normal people. A large number of anti-Semitic publications catered to the needs of a growing constituency. The *Beacon Light*, for example, published by a Mr. Kullgren of Atascadero, California, combined anti-Semitism with astrology. The *Constitution Legion Herald* argued that the pope (who had recently attacked Nazi racialism) was a Jew, his grandmother "having been a Dutch Jewess named Lippman." Edward James Smythe, a professional anticommunist, claimed that the convicted kidnapper of the Lindbergh baby was a Jew. Propagandist "Major" Frank Pease told the Jews to go back to the "camel dung and jackels of the desert. . . ." The *Highland* (New York) *Post* blamed the World War and bolshevism upon Supreme Court Justice Louis D. Brandeis, who supposedly asked a friend who was horrified by their vast number of victims, "What do you care, Charles; they were only Christians."

Anti-Semitic propaganda appealed to people anxious to counter the negative image of the Third Reich, an image disseminated by mainstream publications. A prominent Kansas printing company official put it this way: "[Y]ou Nazis are doing a good job and . . . the world will recognize the fact in a few years. Americans are becoming 'Jew conscious' and this might conceivably lead to the same solution you adopted." This gentleman had traveled to Nazi Germany and reported, "I had a very enjoyable visit to Dachau and was able to get a little story about true conditions there in the Kansas City Star." An anti-

Jewish, antiliberal undercurrent was spreading. One silent admirer of the Hitler movement, a New Yorker, had become tired of the scene that often took place on the street below him. Leaning out of his window, the observer had to listen to constant abuse of the Führer. He finally could take it no longer, and wrote to Hitler, complaining about the "big-mouthed Jews who hang around 88th Street and 2nd Avenue."

The man in his decrepit flat on Second Avenue was not alone. The problem for his would-be saviors was that these paranoids were too scattered, and they were being bilked by too many rival organizations. Personal defects aside, there was no *one* Hitler, as in Germany; there were dozens of them. "Captain" Eugene Chase, who headed Pelley's California operation, was frank in describing the different fascist movements. One party, he said, "plays for . . . what the Communists call proletarians. . . . Another . . . for the nuts—the kind that goes to fortune tellers and seances . . . our mainstay . . . there are more nuts in this part of the world than any place you can name outside of an asylum." It is worth remembering, however, that an observer had once compared the waiting room of Joseph Goebbels's Berlin office to an insane asylum. He made his observation when Hitler was still an obscure politician.[4]

Paranoid attitudes toward the Jews reinforced a widespread aversion to helping Jewish refugees attempting to flee Nazi Germany. Supposedly, the "Jewish Secret Super-Government within the United States," backed by a secret fund of fifty million dollars, was using the refugee question for a naked power grab: Nor was a combination of anti-Negro and anti-Jewish thinking uncommon among the followers of Pelley or the Black Legion:

> COLORED "FRENCH" REGIMENTS were let lose on
> WOMEN. . . .
>   I hear a FREEMASON boasting with his SECRET
>   KNOWLEDGE. . . .
> And the *DOCTOR* in INSANE HOSPITALS is being
> called
>   *CRAZY* by his own *Patients!* . . .
> *HAVE WE BECOME* that much *JUDAICED* so we would
> NOT
>   comprehend HONOR AND TRUTH?! . . .
>   YES! it is the ROTATIONS SYNAGOUGE wich
>   CREATES THE DESERT!!!

hardly anything is written in the paper if
a JEWESS SLAPES A GOYESS!

One protest against Roosevelt's attempt to expand the Supreme Court to fifteen members claimed that fifteen meant "Jehova" in Hebrew:

I read in "SALUTE THE JEW" page 38 what is

all

about
the prepared 15 SUPREME COURT JUDGES!

YES,
15 means JEHOVA IN HEBREW!
I look at the SYMBOLS OF JEWISM:
MYSTERY AND STARTS, YES, SIGNS OF NIGHT!

Like their German colleagues, many American Jew-haters saw Jewish demons all around them, causing them to fail, denying them their just social status. To such people, Roosevelt, with his Jewish friends, was the enemy, the "LAST American President, so complete has the control of our American institutions now progressed through organized Jewry."[5] The policies of such people had become law in the Third Reich. If the inmates could take over the asylum in one great country, why not here?

The fanatasies of demagogues and paranoids should not be dismissed as the exclusive ravings of isolated fringe groups. Many proper, prosperous mainstream Americans, particularly on the right, shared similar thoughts. The hatred for FDR and the New Deal common among Roosevelt's opponents took the form of a ditty that was much in vogue in the locker rooms of fashionable country clubs. Franklin is advising Eleanor:

You kiss the niggers, and I'll kiss the Jews
And we'll stay in the White House as long as we choose!

This widely recited couplet was not so different from a cartoon circulated by Julius Streicher. The picture depicted Eleanor and Franklin pulling the shades down. Then, garbed in weird Freemason outfits, replete with Stars of David, they engaged in some kind of strange Semitic cult dance. Back in the United States, people who would never have associated with Streicher, True, or Edmondson were often suspicious of Jewish radicals, called FDR "Rosenfeld," and chuckled at Westchester cocktail parties about Roosevelt's "syphilis." Many a stockbroker or insurance executive expressed shock at the famous "Nigger pictures," which showed Mrs. Roosevelt in the company of ROTC cadets at Howard University.

In Germany, the fringe types were the first to join Hitler; later, the respectable people came on board. A prolonged economic crisis and further social turmoil might lead to the political mobilization of anti-Jewish, antiliberal sentiments in the United States. The threat of fascism was worth taking seriously in the 1930s. Without understanding this, one cannot comprehend Roosevelt's brilliance in forging a political and international strategy during his second term in office.

Fortune magazine, owned by Time, Inc., served business interests opposed to Roosevelt's domestic policies. The recent upsurge in popular anti-Jewish sentiments was troubling, however, not least of all to the editors of the prestigious *Fortune*. The magazine reflected a certain ambiguity toward anti-Semitism. In a famous survey, conducted in 1935–1936, *Fortune* downplayed the strength of American anti-Semitism while pandering to some Jewish stereotypes. *Fortune* was happy that "only" 15,000 Americans spent most of their time agitating against the Jews. A further 500,000 persons, however, attended at least one anti-Semitic or fascist rally each year. The magazine's editors decided, "Anti-semitism in America, judged by its exponents, is a very sick donkey."

The conclusion may have been premature; indeed, the editors soon contradicted themselves. *Fortune,* having dismissed anti-Semitism, then argued, "The Jews are outlanders everywhere." The magazine went even further, acknowledging the "disproportionate Jewish participation in the economic life of the country." Yet *Fortune* also argued that "[the Jews] play little or no part in the great commercial houses." True, they had taken over some "subdivisions" of industry, particularly department stores and the clothing trades. True, one-third to one-half of the lawyers in New York City were Jewish, but that did not mean that the Jews possessed half of the "lawyer *power.*" True, Jews were highly visible in the Communist party, because "[t]he second-generation Jewish intellectual with his background of Talmudic dialectic is mentally predisposed to Marxism to a degree which he himself rarely appreciates." The magazine concluded on an ambiguous note, observing that "there is strong reason . . . for believing that Fascism can be defeated in this country."

The magazine's daring article revealed more than it intended about its own attitudes. The editors of *Fortune* had mobilized anti-Semitic clichés in order to fight anti-Semitism. An enlightened publication, with access to a highly educated readership, felt obliged to inform the world that the Jews did not run the American economy. Aware of its dilemma, *Fortune* lamely sought refuge in statistics reflecting a decline in the Jewish birthrate. The Jews, concluded *Fortune* would be well advised to be a bit less "aggressive and occasionally provocative." In other words, anti-Semitism was in decline, but it would weaken further if the Jews would be less successful and less pushy! Many individuals, including prominent Jews such as banker Felix Warburg, echoed this sentiment. And Colonel House, now advising President Roosevelt, thought that it might be good if the administration "[eased] off the Jewish boycott and reduce[d] the number of Jews in high positions in the United States." Congressman Owen Brewster of Maine accused the anti-Nazi Mayor Fiorello H. LaGuardia of "making a great race the pawn of the catspaw of politics." The far right, in collusion with the Bund, enjoyed the discreet support of many small businessmen in its campaign against the anti-Nazi boycott.[6]

American optimism, combined with a tradition of political decentralization, made life difficult for fascists like Pelley and Winrod. Fascists were divided and sectarian; they did not speak with a single voice. In Germany, the Nazis had a Führer, and they gained substantial business support in the winter of 1932. Men like Luce or William Randolph Hearst were not ready to back a Pelley or a Winrod, at least not yet. Luce and his readers disliked or even detested Roosevelt, and like their German counterparts, they feared the aggressive trade unions fighting under the leadership of the Congress of Industrial Organizations (CIO). Still, few business leaders were willing to back fascist revolution as an alternative to Roosevelt. Despite the New Deal, they owed allegiance to the democratic capitalist system. If the Depression grew worse and labor strife increased, their politics might change.

The appeal of Father Charles E. Coughlin troubled some American liberals, including many of those who listened to his radio broadcasts. The son of an Irish-American mother and an Irish-Canadian father,

Coughlin grew up in Ontario. Later moving to Michigan, he felt called to the priesthood and was assigned to the parish of the Shrine of the Little Flower in nearby Royal Oak. Passionately committed to a Catholic advocacy of social justice, Father Coughlin's mellifluous voice made him an ideal radio personality. He could take complex ideas and turn them into simple, obvious truths. His timing was perfect. By 1931, the nation was mired in its worst depression, and Coughlin had a large radio audience. By 1939, forty-seven stations carried Coughlin's broadcasts, bringing his message to ten to fifteen million listeners. Coughlin's followers were generally middle-class or lower middle-class people, conscious of their loss of status, fearful of "communism" and social change.[7] Often of German or Irish origin, most Coughlinites were Catholic. To the average Catholic, Coughlin was first and foremost a priest, and he did not discourage people from thinking that he spoke for the Church, at least on social issues. He offered hope, justice, and compassion in a world gone cold and black.

Father Coughlin fervently denounced the ills of an uncaring, selfish capitalist society. "The most dangerous Communist," the priest declared, "is the wolf in sheep's clothing of conservatism who is bent upon preserving the politics of greed." Communism, Coughlin charged, was infiltrating the newly powerful trade unions, especially the CIO. An early support of Roosevelt's New Deal, Coughlin later decided, "I will not support a New Deal which protects plutocrats and comforts Communists." He opposed Roosevelt on U.S. entry into the World Court, and sulked about his own lack of influence in FDR's White House. Coughlin's commitment to social justice was yielding to hate-filled demagoguery.[8]

By 1936, Father Coughlin's rhetoric reflected the priest's growing admiration for fascist ideology. He became more openly anti-Semitic, daring the Jews to explain why they rejected the Golden Rule. The tone was threatening, the arm waving more bellicose. Coughlin treated his audience like a collection of communicants, and they would sometimes pass before him in a long column, as if marching to the communion rail. American flags surrounding him, the Canadian-born priest would demand an "America for the Americans!" before moving on to attacking Jewish bankers and other enemies. Coughlin stood on platforms with the Reverend Gerald L.K. Smith, who praised him highly. No friend of the Jews, Coughlin believed that Professor Felix Frankfurter and labor leader David Dubinsky exercised undue influence on

FDR. He called them communists. Asked by a journalist for proof of the allegation, Coughlin punched a *Boston Globe* reporter in the face.

Coughlin claimed to have eight million followers, but his National Union for Social Justice was a decentralized organization with a spotty electoral record.[9] By 1936, Coughlin was engaged in a political struggle with Roosevelt. The priest pitched much of his appeal to Roman Catholics, a crucial component of FDR's historic coalition. Coughlin's presidential candidate, William Lemke of the Union Party, drew fewer than a million votes and carried no states. He received some scattered support, however, from rural Catholic voters of Irish and German origin. The Unionists promised that "our naval, air and military forces must not be used under any consideration in foreign fields or in foreign waters whether alone or in conjunction with any foreign power." The party's isolationism foreshadowed Coughlin's strident attacks on the foreign policy of the Roosevelt administration. After his victory, Roosevelt seemed to draw closer to the British Empire. Coughlin and his followers reacted with confused tirades against Roosevelt, the British, Eastern bankers, communism, and collective security. The priest quickly smelled the glue holding together these diverse forces—the Jew.

Many Catholics resented the prominence of Jews in the Roosevelt administration, particularly during the recession of 1937–1938. Roosevelt's Jewish advisers became targets of resentful people in places like New York City, "which used to be an Irish town." To many Coughlinites, Roosevelt and the Jews were preparing to fight a war at the behest of international Jewish bankers, on behalf of the British Empire and (Jewish) communism. Coughlin himself predicted that Washington would one day soon be renamed "Washingtonski." Jews began to turn off their radio sets when the priest came on the air. Coughlin's many enemies, abetted by friends in the Roosevelt administration, accused the priest of misleading the poor, while accepting money from the rich. Despite the growing controversy, the priest retained a vast following; the assets of his various corporate entities amounted to almost 500,000 dollars. Right-wing congressman, like Hamilton Fish of New York, rallied to Coughlin's defense.[10]

Coughlin's supporters usually came from small towns or farming communities. They were often Irish-American or German-American, generally Catholic or Lutheran, Anglophobe and isolationist. Not necessarily anti-FDR in domestic policy, Coughlinites tended to be poor, working class, or lower middle class in social origin and status.

Most lived in the heartland of the country, though some, usually Irish-Americans, inhabited big cities like Boston and New York. The Catholics among them resented liberal support for the Spanish "Red" Republic. Coughlin was helping to alienate these people from the Democratic Party, but not many were ready to vote Republican.[11]

Roosevelt's attempt to reorient American foreign policy faced many obstacles; Father Coughlin was one of them. If FDR moved toward intervention, Coughlin supported isolation; if the president challenged the Nazis, the priest attacked FDR. Coughlin's base of support, if expanded, could cost FDR his political future and abort any new, global role for the United States. Roosevelt was concerned, and struck back. He made sure, however, that no attacks on the radio priest could be traced to the White House.

Anti-Semitism was widespread, but its successful political mobilization continued to elude the leading Jew-baiters. There was no reason for Jews to be sanguine about the future, however. Surveys indicated that one-third of Americans objected to contact with Jews. Of those polled by Gallup, almost one-third with an opinion believed that the Jews themselves were to blame ("entirely" or "partly") for their own fate in Europe. At the same time, large majorities rejected the suggestion that a similar persecution could take place in the United States. Eighty-two percent would refuse to support a campaign against the Jews, if it did occur. Late in the decade, however, a large majority of those expressing an opinion to Gallup believed that "anti-Jewish feeling is increasing in this country."[12] Prolonged recession, and the perception that anti-Semitism was compatible with true Americanism, could transform anti-Semitism into a potent political current. Anti-Semitism would probably recede, however, if it appeared to be the tool of a foreign power hostile to the United States. American anti-Semitism had a political future, but not if its spokesmen were "agents, conscious or inadvertent, of Adolf Hitler."[13] And if the economy took a turn for the better, the Jews would be less threatened.

In the winter of 1938, the United States was at peace, but the land was troubled by labor strife and unemployment. Fashionable people sometimes commented that fascism was the irresistible wave of the future. It was too soon to write off American fascism and the emergence of more threatening forms of anti-Semitism. Roosevelt himself so feared these developments that he displayed extreme caution, even cowardice when faced with the problem of more visas for Jewish refugees from Nazism. By margins of two to one or better, Americans opposed bringing Jewish children from Germany to the United States. A majority opposed governmental assistance to refugees willing to settle in Africa or South America. And a good part of the minority supporting such aid did so in order to keep Jews out of the United States.[14]

CHAPTER SIXTEEN

IN BATTLE AGAINST
"ROSENFELD'S JEW REPUBLIC"

I N THE LATE 1930s, the German-American establishment stirred
from its lethargy and tried to resist the Bund's intimidation. In
Schenectady, New York, for example, Gerhard H. Seger spoke to an
audience at the Turnhalle. An anti-Nazi who had escaped from a concentration camp, Seger was editor of the *New Yorker Volkszeitung*. The
local Bund chapter tried to block his appearance, claiming that Seger
was a communist and a Jewish agent. Bundists denounced him as a liar.
The Bund could not destroy Seger, however, nor intimidate his sponsors. In New York, meanwhile, the Steuben Society now rejected
membership applications from known Bundists and Nazis. It finally
excluded the Bund from German Day celebrations. In 1938, the society
and its ally, the influential *Staats-Zeitung* newspaper, openly attacked
the Bund. Fears of deteriorating relations with the Jews played a role in
this decision.

Bund leaders became more defensive. They swore that the OD
(storm troop) was a harmless organization, that the Bund's relations with
German-American organizations were good. Still, the pattern in Schenectady was repeated elsewhere. In Cincinnati the *Freie Presse* declared
that the Bund, made up of irresponsible newcomers, was tarnishing

the hard-won image of German-Americans. In Texas, the *Freie Presse für Texas* attacked "foreign agitators," and called for an "America first" policy. The *Weckruf* responded with invective, but the Bund failed to close down the two newspapers, as threatened.[1]

Fritz Kuhn was losing his bid for control of the German-American electorate. He now turned to new "Aryan" allies. The Bund cosponsored rallies with White Russian fascists, Spanish nationalists, American Silver Shirts, and Italian *fascisti*. Kuhn paid particular attention to the Italians, for the world was talking about a new "Axis" about which Europe revolved: Berlin and Rome. Fascists, led by Dr. Salvatore Caridi, reciprocated by attending a joint rally at the Bund's Camp Nordland, in New Jersey. Kuhn was in good spirits, for the Irish-American state senator William A. Dolan delivered the welcoming speech. To Kuhn, Dolan's presence proved that the Bund was forging powerful new alliances. The senator assured the assembly, "[W]e appreciate all good German people." Signor Caridi and Kuhn exchanged fascist salutes before ten thousand admirers. The Italian embarrassed some of the Bundists by addressing them as "my Nazi friends," but the rally was a success. Kuhn could look back upon 1937 as "a successful year for the German-American Bund."[2]

Such optimism was misplaced. The Bund was reaching out, but to other pariah organizations. Nor had Kuhn attracted many new members. The Bund probably consisted of 6,500 activists in the summer of 1938, encouraged by 15,000 to 20,000 sympathizers. If one includes families and close friends, the Bund drew its audiences and contributors from a pool of 50,000 to 100,000 persons. This needs to be placed in ethnic context. About 1,500,000 German-born persons resided in the United States.[3]

Who were the Bundists? More than two-thirds of the organization's membership was male. Most Bundists resided in large cities in the East and Midwest. They were usually first- or second-generation Americans, but a large proportion of them were recent immigrants lacking citizenship papers. These people wanted to celebrate the achievements of the Third Reich without living there. Some had criminal records in Germany; others wished to avoid conscription into the Wehrmacht. Many older Bundists, like Kuhn, had fought in the German Army; others had served in right-wing paramilitary groups after the war. A few had been active in the Nazi movement in Germany. They came to the United States after the war, looking for work and opportunity.

Bund activists were of lower middle-class and working-class origin. Among these Bundists one found locksmiths, electricians, glass-blowers, toolmakers, barbers, delicatessen owners, hairdressers, shoe-makers, waiters, and cooks. When the Depression struck, many of these newly arrived Germans found themselves in dire straits. Unem-ployed or engaged in menial tasks like dishwashing, these disappointed people found solace in the Bund. They could leave their cramped cold-water flats, head for a local *Stube,* and sit around drinking beer. The conversation often turned to the Jews and to the misery of living in Roosevelt's America. Tens of thousands of such people attended Bund meetings and rallies. Better educated leaders, like Fritz Kuhn, found them easy to manipulate.[4]

Kuhn and his associate Gerhard Wilhelm Kunze made themselves the spokesmen for these alienated recent immigrants. Like Hitler, they hoped that the United States would fragment into an ethnic free-for-all. As one Bundist put it, "This will happen here. It is inevitable. When that day comes, and it is probably not far-off, we must be prepared to fight for the right kind of government. We must win the masses to our side."[5] When *der Tag* (the Day) arrived, the Bund had to be ready to grab its share of the loot.

Kuhn and Kunze headed an immigrant organization unique in Amer-ican history. The Bund worked *against* Americanization, on behalf of an anti-American foreign power. Kuhn needed a militant, Nazi-trained German element for the task that lay ahead. He expanded the Bund's *Jugendschaft* (Youth Organization) and the *Mädchenschaft* (Girls' League) in order to "check the shrinkage in the German population through the Americanization of its youth." By 1938, over two thousand children were participating in the youth group's activities. Camp Sutter, in Los Angeles, and Camp Siegfried, in Yaphank, Long Island, were nests of Bund activity.[6] The Bund taught German children that Ameri-canism and Nazism were compatible:

> *We are loyal and true to the Star-Spangled Banner*
> *But German blood remains German blood*

Three great patriots received respectful attention in the Bund's camps and training halls. They were Washington, Lincoln, and Horst Wessel, the Nazi "martyr" murdered in 1930.[7] All were supposedly "typical of their peoples." Perhaps this was true.[8]

Surviving autobiographies of Girls' League leaders in New York City reveal a high level of backbiting and paranoia. Hildegard K., for example, a Bronx *Mädchenschaft* leader, was born in Zwickau in 1921. Her father brought his family to America in 1922. He did not do well here. Hildegard heard about the Bund from another girl in her high school class. In 1936, this fifteen-year-old girl joined the *Mädchenschaft*. She traveled to Germany for Nazi indoctrination in 1939, returning to the Bronx in 1940. Hildegard was now a leader of her *Mädchenschaft*. She hated Franklin Roosevelt and worked to strengthen ties to Nazi Germany. Hildegard and her colleagues were envious of one another. They constantly spied on each other, an activity encouraged by the Bund.

In the writings of "Anna," we learn that "Ilse" had bad mannerisms. She would have to be removed, so that the girls did not imitate her habits. "Dippy" needed to purge her, along with "Agnes" and her whole clique. "Anna" was also spying on "Dippy," who was trying to land a position as governess for a Bund leader's child. "Anna" was concerned about an investigator who interrogated her about the Bund, "but he looked good, since he was not a Jew, and was otherwise a calm type of person."[9]

The Bund's youth camps flourished. In remote surroundings, far from the prying eyes of the press, Bund supporters could enjoy themselves among their own kind. Hundreds of people took train excursions from Pennsylvania Station to Camp Siegried, near Yaphank. Admission cost only ten cents. Brass bands and Hitler salutes (the "German greeting") welcomed visitors entering the camp compound. They heard the band play the Badenweiler March, and saw swastikas and American flags waving proudly in the wind. The guests and participants often polished off seventy-five kegs of beer in a single afternoon. They consumed enormous amounts of chicken, bratwurst, goulash, and beer. Rousing renditions of the *Horst Wessel Lied* echoed through the woods. Sometimes a Bundist would sing an original ditty:

> *Send them [the Jews] all to Jerusalem,*
> *Throw them out of here,*
> *But first cut off their legs,*
> *So they won't be coming back!*[10]

The revelers staggered back to the train station, and returned to their humdrum lives in the Bronx or Queens. For a few hours, they had been in Hitler's America, *unser Amerika* (our America). Forgotten for the moment were troubled digestive systems, unpaid rents, overdue bills, and unemployment.

The trip back to Roosevelt's United States was a journey to a failed paradise. Bund supporters, fearing the emergence of a powerful labor movement, attacked the "crazy Bolshevik Unemployment Insurance Law," that is "handicapping every line of business." Roosevelt was a prelude to communism, Kuhn screamed.

The international situation was becoming more tense in this winter of 1938. Hitler prepared for aggression against Austria. Events in Spain were giving wide currency to the term "fifth column," a kind of modern Trojan horse.[11] By the summer, Hitler's Nazi followers were working to destabilize Czechoslovakia from within.

The Bundists may appear comical to us today, but their critics took them seriously in 1938. Once, when Kuhn appeared in a Yorkville magistrate's court, a hundred Bundists rallied in the hallway outside in support of their *Bundesführer.* Anti-Nazi counterdemonstrators began booing and hissing. The court attendants, anxious to avoid trouble, ordered the Bundists to "Pass out, Pass out!" Suddenly, the Germans looked around in fear, whispering the words "Pass' auf! Pass' auf!" (Watch out! Watch out!) to one another. In their ignorance of English, the Bundists had misunderstood the guards' commands. Observers did not laugh, however. Rather, they asked themselves, What kind of Americanism was this?[12]

Under Kuhn's leadership, the Bund seemed intent upon playing a role cast by the American press. Fritz Kuhn had his Nazi followers and a few fascist allies, but not much else. By late 1938, correspondents portrayed the Bund as a violence-prone group of mobsters, led by a would-be Führer who was probably a traitor.

The Bund had been attracting a violent element for years. One of its followers put it this way, "Hitler is showing us how to take care of people who get in our way, and we can do the same thing here." Assault and battery charges followed Bund rallies the way beer follows bratwurst. A Bund meeting in Hans Jäger's Chicago restaurant resulted in twenty-seven damaged or destroyed chairs. In New York, Bundists disrupted a left-wing peace rally by throwing rotten cantaloupes at speakers' heads. Bundists seemed intent upon recreating the early Nazi era of the *Saalschlachten,* when Hitler's followers battled the enemy for control of Munich's beer halls.

New Yorkers read about the "Putsch on 22nd Street," where two Germans cursed an anti-Nazi Catholic priest. On another occasion, a thirty-eight-year-old machinist, Joseph Hasenstahe, stood on a New York sidewalk, obscenely denouncing anyone opposed to Hitler. A patrolman, William Murphy, tried to calm Hasenstahe down, where-upon the Nazi punched the officer in the eye. Similar incidents took place across the nation, though rarely in the South. [13]

Kuhn realized that the upswing in American anti-Semitism could be useful to him, at least in the short run. The *Bundesführer* and his colleagues declared that "Today, instead of a Hamilton or a Jefferson, we got a Barney Baruch and Felix Frankfurter, a Rosenfeldt [Roosevelt] and a Kosher LaGuardia!" "The whole Roosevelt administration is dominated by Jews," declared the Bund. Bund speakers, expressing themselves in German or heavily accented English, often told these Jews to "go back where you came from!" Men who had fired bullets at American soldiers from German trenches were telling Jews whose families had sometimes been here for generations to get out of America.

The *Bundesführer* claimed that boycott leader Samuel Untermeyer "went to Russia to get instructions on how to carry out his propaganda against the German people. . . . He is better liked in Moscow than in New York." Kuhn, in a public letter to anti-Nazi activist Rabbi Stephen S. Wise, raved that "all Jewry forms a compact army of schemers, propagandists, and parasites, animated by a common ambition to sap the sources of strength of the Gentile nations." Kuhn denounced "in-human" kosher slaughtering practices, as well as circumcision. He smugly informed the rabbi that "you have bitten off more than you can chew." [14]

Since Kuhn wanted to weaken the boycott movement and help the German export economy, he had to deny that Hitler was persecuting the Jews. The Nazis, he explained, were merely terminating Jewish domination of various professions and trades. Kuhn even claimed that German Jews had urged him to "tell the Jews in America to let us alone. We're all right." In 1938, Kuhn reported that the invasion of Austria was a "tremendous show." The Jews had not suffered. [15]

Kuhn had struck a responsive chord. The Bund received support from an increasing number of frustrated Jew-haters. One reader offered the *Weckruf* a forty-five thousand word manuscript exposing the "Inter-national Jewish Nation." A San Francisco trolley conductor, accused of spreading Nazi propaganda while on the job, blamed the Jews for his dismissal. A Los Angeles investor accused the Jews of ruining him twice, the first time in the film industry, more recently in the service station business. He now offered his services to the Nazis.

These Bundists had one thing in common, a paranoid fear of the Jews. The Jews did so much better in life; there must be a conspiracy against the German element. One anonymous Nazi, for example, wrote to the Bund as a man "on silent watch." The writer looked at the world around him, where "[t]he most dangerous enemy of the entire German people is the hundred per cent Jewified America." "On silent watch" believed that Jews were deflowering little Aryan girls. He drew obscene pictures of Jewish teachers copulating with terrified eight-year-old children.

The Bundists gloried in Hitler's triumphs over the Jews, Austrians, and Czechs. They wanted to act out their Nazi fantasies, but, as they did so, they confirmed American fears of a Nazi fifth column. The more Nazi the Bund became, the more it played into the hands of its enemies. Walter Kappe had proclaimed, "WE ARE AND REMAIN GERMANS. GERMANS IN AMERICA." The 1937 yearbook of the Bund admitted, "We stand here as heralds of the Third Reich, as preachers of the German world-view of National Socialism which has displayed before the eyes of the world the . . . miracle of National Socialism."

Acts of anti-Jewish violence by Bund types increased in number. A typical case occurred in Manhattan. Dozens of New York City subway riders looked on in dismay as two muscular young Germans (a welder and a mechanic) ridiculed an old Jew with a white beard yelling "Heil Hitler!" at him. The Jew was frightened, and he left his seat, shuffling down the aisle. His tormentors followed him. A jeweler, Solomon Shapiro, moved between the victim and his persecutors, demanding to know why the Nazis did not pick on a younger man? The Germans started beating the jeweler, inflicting contusions of the face, scalp, and back. The subway car was in an uproar as the train pulled into Grand Central Station. Police arrested the two thugs, who were later found guilty of assault.

The Bund's reputation for immorality of a different kind was also growing. The organization attracted a large number of people of the type commonly called sexual psychopaths. In Germany, this kind of person read the advertisements placed in Julius Streicher's anti-Jewish pornographic newspaper *Der Stürmer.* These sales pitches promised cures from everything from headaches to impotence to hemorrhoids (and sometimes all three at once). In America, several of these *Stürmer* types rose to prominence in the Bund.

Severin Winterscheidt, managing editor of the *Weckruf*, always insisted upon the Americanism of the Bund. This protegé of Julius Streicher lauded the "relentless fight of our movement against all enemies of Germany, who at the same time are adversaries of our new homeland. . . ." Like his mentor Streicher, Winterscheidt was a psychotic with paranoid tendencies. Early in 1938, he exposed himself before a young woman in New York City's jam-packed Pennsylvania Station. This led to his arrest and a sentence of thirty days in jail.

In April, feeling tense and overworked, the depressed Winterscheidt took the day off and went to the Empire Theater in Brooklyn. Winterscheidt decided to show a young girl his genitals, whereupon the victim ran screaming from the theater. The police again apprehended Winterscheidt, who appears to have wanted to be arrested. His Bundist friends tried to intimidate the little girl and the theater manager, but they pressed charges. This time, Winterscheidt received a six-month sentence, to be served in the New York County penitentiary. Fritz Kuhn declared, "[W]e cannot extol his virtues too highly," but he finally replaced Winterscheidt. Kuhn was concerned about the Bund's moral image.[16]

The *American Magazine*, which enjoyed a large circulation, had only recently published a long, lurid article by Joseph F. Dinneen. The journalist put the number of Nazis in America at 125,000. He claimed to have spoken with some of them, with sinister results. Dinneen then sought out Fritz Kuhn for an interview, whereupon the *Bundesführer* asked him, "Are you an Aryan?" A smiling Dinneen replied, "I presume so. My parents were Irish." "You look Jewish," Kuhn countered. To Dinneen, and to many of his readers, similar anecdotes proved the existence of a militant, paranoid Nazi underground, poised to strike.[17]

Captain Henry Landau's book *The Enemy Within* reinforced Dinneen's accusations. Claiming expertise in the field of countersabotage, Landau warned, "Twenty men willing to give their lives could probably put the Panama Canal out of action." Landau frightened his readers by alleging, "Foreign key agents for sabotage and espionage are already here in waiting. . . ."[18] Not to be outdone, the *Chicago Daily Times* claimed to have uncovered secret Nazi preparations for a takeover of the U.S. government on some undetermined "Day." Like the Red Scare of twenty years before, the fear of Nazi subversion provided a temptation

to those interested in gaining publicity, making money, or expressing
patriotic anxiety. The mounting concern did have a highly desirable
effect, however, for it increased concern about the real threat to humanity, National Socialist Germany. Hitler's words, as quoted (or fabricated)
by former Nazi Hermann Rauschning, seemed to confirm the threat
ascribed to Bundists and Nazi saboteurs. Rauschning's widely read
comments portrayed a Führer who believed, "It is a good idea to have at
least two German societies in every country. One of them can always call
attention to its loyalty to the country in question. . . . The other may be
radical and revolutionary."[19]

Kuhn provided an easy target for those concerned about the menace
posed by the Bund. His insatiable need for women and money resulted
in scandalous gossip. Bored by family life, Kuhn dated Miss Virginia
Cogswell, a fading Miss America (1924) enamored of money, nightlife,
and marriage (seven times). Old-timers interviewed in the 1970s recalled typical scenes. Fritz would pick Virginia up at her lower Fifth
Avenue apartment building, hail a cab, and head for some fashionable,
big-band club. "Fritzi" and Virginia would enter the Crillon Bar; the
headwaiter bowed smartly. Soon they had their intimate little table.
Reporters and other observers watched carefully. Kuhn usually had two
requests: drinks plus a rendition of "Flat Foot Floogie with the Floy-
Floy" (which he allegedly mispronounced in the most comical manner
as "flat fooot floogie mit der floy-floy"). Relaxing under the influence of
the liquor and the music, Kuhn started his act. Whispering, then
orating to Virginia, he bragged and threatened by turns, telling her that
he would take care of his many enemies. As for those Jews who accused
him of subversion, "Izzy" (anti-Nazi columnist Walter Winchell) and
"Dickschwein" (Congressman Samuel Dickstein), Kuhn had this to
say: "I vill hev them rubbed out!" Virginia egged him on, especially
when Fritz boasted that his men were everywhere, even in military
installations. By now Kuhn was raising his voice, attracting disapprov-
ing stares from neighboring tables. He didn't care. Fritz, a sadomaso-
chist, then bragged that he could slash his skin with a blade and ignore
the pain. Rumors made the rounds alleging that "darling Fritzi" asked
Virginia if he could carve a swastika (but just a little one) between her
breasts. Groggy but exhilarated, the couple left for lower Fifth Avenue.
On a typical evening out Kuhn spent fifty dollars or more, even though
he earned only three hundred a month as *Bundesführer.* Kuhn did not

realize that his phone was being tapped. Nor did he know that Miss Cogswell was working for federal undercover agents.

By 1938, Kuhn was working to prevent the United States from intervening in the European crisis. His speeches emphasized the virtues of isolationism, made feasible by America's "remarkably safe" geographical position. President George Washington's warnings against "entangling alliances," so dear to American politicians," became the Bund's new watchword. Meanwhile, Kuhn was trapping himself. While denying to the press that he was a Nazi agent, the *Bundesführer* wanted his gullible followers to believe in his special relationship with Adolf Hitler. By the autumn, alarmed federal, state, and local authorities were investigating the Bund's activities. Many Americans wondered if the Bund was a militarized agent of Nazi Germany. One thing was certain: It was hard to imagine Fritz Kuhn defending the United States against Nazi Germany.

A Gallup poll contained ominous news for the Bund. Asked, "Do you think that Nazis in the United States are a menace to the country?" fifty-eight percent responded, "Yes." Where the polls led, the politicians and courts were sure to follow.[20] Kuhn continued to play into the hands of enemies lurking all around him. Newspapers printed some of Kuhn's ravings, drawing more attention to Bund activities. Reporters depicted the Bund's summer camps as secret training bases for a Nazi fifth column.

Congressional committees were now alerting Americans to the nature of National Socialism, though their work was often self-serving. Starting as early as 1934, congressmen such as Dickstein of New York and Dies of Texas had been grabbing headlines by making farfetched accusations. Dickstein alleged that Kuhn had a twenty million dollar propaganda fund at his disposal. Dies, chairman of the House Committee on Un-American Activities (HUAC), denounced "well-organized, subversive, un-American spy systems." Dies heard testimony from sources who described the United States as host to "500,000" active pro-Nazis. The Bund, they further alleged, was training saboteurs, people who in the event of war would attack America from within. Kuhn's boasts about his relationship with Nazi leaders caught the eye of these ambitious, headline-seeking congressmen. Despite the headline mania, Representative John McCormack (Democrat from Massachusetts) was right to believe that the congressional spotlight "brought to the attention of the American public the damnable efforts that were being made in this country. It aroused public opinion." Federal Judge John O. Knox accused German agents of causing resentment against "the government of a great people"—their own.[21] Dies now wanted to hear from Kuhn himself. Kuhn reveled in the wave of publicity. He intended to rally isolationist forces against those Americans who spoke of the need to "quarantine" aggressor states.

Unfortunately for him, Kuhn had become the object of "attacks" by the FBI, whose prestige was higher than ever. Having gained great publicity for its assault on mobsters like John Dillinger, J. Edgar Hoover's organization was now paying a good deal of attention to totalitarian groups in the United States. Hoover kept the White House informed of his activities; indeed, he was working under a broad mandate conferred upon him by the president.

Hoover's activities proved most useful to Franklin D. Roosevelt, as FDR began his carefully orchestrated campaign against the "fifth column."

Fear of internal subversion fed off Nazi successes in Europe. Commentators spoke of a "Nazintern," of a conspiracy hatched by a "secret Nazi army prepared to overthrow our government, or at least to help overthrow it."[22] Editorials began to call for a prohibition on alleged paramilitary training camps, such as those maintained by the Bund. Before 1938, the FBI had been investigating about 35 alleged cases of espionage per year. The number of complaints rose to 250 in that year. The Bund suffered its worst publicity to date when the government, making use of an informant, successfully prosecuted Günther G. Rumrich, a deserter from the U.S. Army. The informant was Dr. Ignatz Theodor Griebl, a fanatic Nazi who had joined a spy ring created by the Security Service (SD) of the SS. The SD wanted information about U.S. coastal defenses and aircraft carrier construction. Griebl and his accomplices hatched some wild plots, including a plan to kidnap American military officers. The Americans foiled their plans, and Griebl, trying to save his own skin, began to inform on his former comrades. The government prosecuted several of them, including Günther G. Rumrich. This defendant, a confused man seeking money, prestige,

Attention — Important

PRO-AMERICAN RALLY

You are urged to attend a great
PRO-AMERICAN MASS MEETING
IN THE

ASSEMBLY HALL

NASSAU COUNTY POLICE HEADQUARTERS
MINEOLA, L. I.

Wed., November 16
1938

LOUIS ZAHNE on

"The Imminent Danger of Communism in the United States"

★

GEO. WILLIAM KUNZE on

"Are the Attacks Against the German American Bund Justified?"

★

SUED K. MUFARRIG on
"Arab Side of the Palestinian Question"

Meeting Sponsored by the German American Bund
P. O. Box 24, Hempstead, L. I.

★

EVERYONE WELCOME

Admission Free   8 P. M.

and adventure, had accepted an offer from German military counterintelligence, the *Abwehr*. He was caught while impersonating a State Department official in a failed attempt to obtain blank passports for use by Nazi spies. Griebl ultimately returned to Germany, but his notoriety hurt the Bund, for he had been active in that organization.[23] The FBI's files for 1939 contained information relating to 1,651 cases of alleged espionage. Many Americans now believed that the Bund was a nest of spies and saboteurs. This was hardly the case, but the perception hurt the organization.

In New York State, Senator John J. McNaboe was conducting hearings into Bund activities. Kuhn was called to testify as a witness before the McNaboe committee. Entering the Supreme Court building in New York City, the *Bundesführer* smirked at reporters and the assembled cameras. Kuhn proceeded to deny that the Bund was either Nazi or anti-Jewish. True, it did not admit Jews to membership. The Knights of Columbus, however, did not admit Protestants to membership, but that did not make it anti-Protestant! Smirking and self-confident, Kuhn parried questions of committee counsel. Asked if there were any good Jews, Kuhn replied, "If a mosquito is on your arm, you don't ask is it a good or a bad mosquito. You just brush it off."

The Bund's *Weckruf* celebrated Kuhn's triumph: "*The ghetto* had sent forth its tenants in force. . . . There were sweaty fat women and young girls and all species of humanity, representatives of the garment trade, stamped with dark Hebraic features, constituting an ideal *pants-pressers' club meeting*."[24] Convinced that he had won a big victory over the Jews, Kuhn rallied his forces, calling for "[a] tight inner organization of our entire movement."[25] Europe was heading toward war, and Kuhn was determined to prevent America from intervening.

The Bund had been a godsend to those authorities working to alert the American people to the Nazi threat. Politicians who favored intervention in the looming European crisis argued that if the Bund was subversive and an agent of Germany, then involving the United States in the European crisis on the side of the democracies made sense. Roosevelt could portray an interventionist foreign policy as *defensive* in nature. While combating subversion at home, one had to contain its sponsors abroad.

CHAPTER
SEVENTEEN

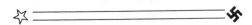

GERMAN AGENTS AND
AMERICAN FASCISTS

EPUTY FÜHRER RUDOLF HESS had received fair and timely warning. As early as the summer of 1933, right after Hitler came to power, Hess learned that Nazi activity in America was detrimental to German-American relations. Most German consular officials viewed Bundists as troublemakers who made life difficult for representatives of the Reich. Nazi activities there could only worsen relations between the two countries. There might, however, be less controversial ways of working for the German cause. Sources informed the deputy führer that Colonel Edwin Emerson's "Friends of the New Germany," which contained "real Americans" rather than immigrant Nazis, furthered the interests of Nazi Germany. Hess and the Nazi party organization heeded this advice, and forbade party members from engaging in political activity in the United States. Hess then went further, ordering the resignation of NSDAP (Nazi Party) members from the "League [Bund] of Friends."[1] From the beginning, however, Nazi policy toward the Bund was inconsistent. Hitler's attitude toward the organization was still uncertain. The strength of the Bund in New York City impressed Consul General Hans Borchers, for example, and he endorsed its continued support by German officials. Other consular officials, suspecting that the Bund might have a promising future, feared that a boycott of the organization would weaken ties between the Third Reich and German-American communities.[2]

The rhetoric of leading Nazis led many Americans to believe that the Bund was engaged in a dark, subversive conspiracy. Hermann Goering contributed to these fears when he shouted, "The German living abroad is either National-Socialist or nothing. . . . It is your duty to remain, in your host-land, a granite-block of Germandom." The influential *NS-Kurier* was even more explicit about the Bund's role in carrying out Nazi long-term aims. "We desire," it wrote, "to bring back Germans in the United States to the racial unity and common fate of all Germans. To this end the intellectual and spiritual reform of Americans of German extraction is necessary in accord with the model furnished by the old homeland."[3]

In accord with this goal (and despite Hess's strictures), German citizens and recent immigrants continued to form the backbone of the Bund. Bund leader Dr. Hubert Schnuch was nervous, however, for Roosevelt's administration was protesting their activities. Berlin had not yet made up its mind about the very popular president, and it soon moved to mollify prying congressmen and concerned immigration authorities. Word came from Berlin, ordering the Bund leader to obey new, stricter rules. Schnuch, knowing that the literal application of these rules would destroy the Bund, requested that "first paper" immigrants, at least, be permitted to remain in his organization. These were Germans who had declared their intention of becoming U.S. citizens—at some point. The State Department, as well as the German Foreign Ministry, saw through this maneuver. In October 1935, Berlin ordered Reich citizens and "first paper" immigrants out of the Bund by the end of the year. This order, if rigorously applied, would cost Schnuch at least sixty percent of his membership.

The twenty-one-year-old Schnuch had emigrated to the United States in 1913, but returned to serve his fatherland in the First World War. Returning to the United States, Schnuch was elected president of the Friends of the New Germany in 1934, Dr. Schnuch fell from power a year later. A respectable front for hard-core Nazis, Schnuch had neither the stamina nor the skills in infighting needed to keep his job.

Despite Berlin's order, only a few Reich citizens rushed to quit the Bund. The Bund's new leader, U.S. citizen Fritz Kuhn, survived by playing one Nazi agency off against another. To party officials obsessed with German-American "treason," Kuhn emphasized his re-Germanization efforts. When dealing with Reich agents who wished to enforce the expulsion order, Kuhn pleaded that he needed time in order to Americanize his organization. He offered proof of his good intentions. Kuhn had, after all, had even put the word "Amerika" into the Bund's official name. Kuhn broadly hinted that Hitler really supported the Bund, that perhaps the Führer was playing a double game. He strengthened this claim by alluding to his visit with Hitler in the summer of 1936. Kuhn smugly assured his allies that the Germans were not really serious about Reich citizens resigning from the Bund. German diplomats were enraged, then perplexed. Some now wondered if they should support the Bund, despite its terrible reputation among Americans. Few realized that Hitler's meeting with Kuhn was a spur-of-the-moment gesture, which he later regretted.[4]

The new ambassador to Washington, Hans Dieckhoff, was concerned about growing anti-Nazi sentiment in the United States. The ambassador was careful to lay the blame for American hostility at the doorstep of "Jewish and liberal" elements in the media. After tossing in this disclaimer, Dieckhoff pointed out in his cables that federal authorities feared the machinations of Nazi agents among "subversive" elements of the German-American community. Dieckhoff warned against illusions concerning Kuhn's group. The ambassador believed that the Bund's strident, pro-Nazi propaganda was hurting Germany's image in the United States. He ominously reminded the Foreign Ministry that America could quickly move from isolationism to interventionism.[5] Dieckhoff bluntly concluded, "[A]ny ties that still exist between agencies in Germany and the German-Americans must be broken off." He objected to participation by German consular officials in Bund rallies and picnics. The outraged Dieckhoff saw through Kuhn's game, and objected most strenuously to the Bund leader's statement that "[a]ll new consuls are National Socialist and under special instructions to give us the fullest cooperation in every way."[6]

Dieckhoff's response was to order the immediate withdrawal of all Reich German citizens from the organization. Persons with German passports participating in Bund activities must, he declared, surrender their travel documents. Dieckhoff indicated that he would permit contacts between confidential party agents and the Bund, so long as such liaisons were carried out under rules set by the German embassy and its consular officials. Actually, Dieckhoff would have liked to have rid himself of the Bund altogether. He mused about turning it into a bland cultural organization, perhaps to be renamed the "Immanuel Kant Society."[7]

Dieckhoff's pressure soon achieved results. The Foreign Ministry and some (though not all) party agencies supported his demand that Reich citizens resign from the Bund. Happy with his success, Ambassador Dieckhoff promptly informed Secretary of State Cordell Hull about Berlin's decision.[8] A furious Hans Dieckhoff soon learned that party agencies, among them SS Lieutenant General Werner Lorenz's *Volksdeutsche Mittelstelle* (Ethnic German Exchange Office) continued to provide the Bund with financial aid and propaganda materials. To his further dismay, the envoy discovered that Fritz Kuhn understood the Nazi system better than he did the American one. The Bund leader played one group off against another, knowing that party organizations competed for Hitler's favor. Their functions overlapped, and someone was always trying to increase his power. Kuhn did not always achieve his aims, but his constant maneuvering caused Dieckhoff no end of trouble.

Kuhn at one point met with the German consul in San Francisco, Fritz Wiedemann. Warning that the directives concerning German citizens would wreck the Bund, Kuhn pleaded for help. He hoped that dropping the names of Nazi leaders would impress the consul. Wiedemann, who was repelled by Kuhn, pressed his counterattack, alleging, "The German-American Bund has made relations between the German and American governments more difficult. . . ." Wiedemann warned that Kuhn must obey the laws of the United States. Kuhn went away empty-handed.

The Bund soon lost a good proportion of its membership, perhaps more than a third, as Reich Germans and party members finally began to leave the organization in large numbers. Kuhn was a good confidence man, however, and he confronted the Bund's convention as a triumphant friend of unnamed *Bonzen* (party leaders): "I tell you only this much, that had my [most recent trip to the Reich] been without success, or had I unfavorable reports to make, I would not be standing before you today, but would have withdrawn my constituency. . . . I need also not tell you with whom I have spoken. . . ."[9]

Kuhn was not just bluffing. Despite the new rules, he continued to maintain close ties to powerful Nazi organizations. He assiduously cultivated his relations with *Gauleiter* Ernst Bohle's *Auslands-Organisation der NSDAP* (Foreign Organization of the Nazi Party).

Bohle, later described by a prominent Nazi as "young, efficient, and fired with zeal to spread the concepts of the Nazi Party," hoped to infuse *Auslanddeutschtum* (German communities abroad) with the ideals of the Nazi revolution. By 1939, the *Auslands-Organisation* (or AO) had sixty-five thousand members and employed eight hundred persons.[10] Bohle's mission contradicted itself. The AO, according to Hitler, must preach obedience to the laws of host countries. At the same time, the AO official and all Germans abroad must "see in every German out there an ethnic comrade, a person of your blood, your nature, and your being." Bohle declared, "We look on Germans abroad not as Germans by accident, but as Germans through the will of God. Like our comrades in the Reich, they are chosen and obliged to cooperate in the work that Adolf Hitler began. . . ." Foreign Minister Konstantin von Neurath warned, "[W]e [will not] permit Germans living abroad to be singled out because of their Nazi convictions." Blood was indelible; state citizenship was mutable. Some AO directives were even blunter. The function of the AO was to make "Germandom abroad useful to the Reich." In certain situations, the AO station chief could assume the functions of the German state.[11] Despite this, the AO firmly denied that it was a center of "conspiratorial imperialism."

AO propaganda tended to encourage Fritz Kuhn, while it stoked fears among Americans of a Nazi "fifth column" in the Western Hemisphere. Journalists informed Americans that the AO was both hostile and conspiratorial. AO statements and slogans supported this contention: "If fight means unrest, then we admit that we created unrest." The AO and related organizations admitted, "Our aim will be achieved only then when every German abroad is so much imbued with the National Socialist *Weltanschauung* that he will never again forget his Germandom." Put another way, "We only know the concept of the complete German who as a citizen of his country is always and everywhere a German and nothing but a German, and this makes him a *National Socialist.*"[12]

Bohle lavished praise upon "the 10,000 Germans who came from all parts of the world [to] attend the [congress] held in Stuttgart in 1937. . . ." Why should such people not wish to become "as fervent National Socialists as the people in the Reich?" Bohle employed the rhetoric necessary for survival in the Nazi bureaucratic jungle. As war loomed on the horizon, the AO *Gauleiter* warned foreign nations against harming Reich Germans or innocent Nazis, whose only crime was loyalty to Hitler and National Socialism.[13]

It was in the AO's interest to boast about the growth of Nazi sentiments in foreign countries. In the case of the United States, that meant encouraging the Bund. Fritz Kuhn understood this well. So did the American ambassador in Berlin, who believed that Kuhn "represents Bohle of the Foreign Office [*sic*]." This overstated the case, for Kuhn was using Bohle, and vice versa. Bohle's heroic slogans provided a shield for Kuhn against German diplomats and rivals within the Bund. Kuhn was not a spy, but the fact is that the AO, using its foreign contacts, routinely passed on intelligence gained from American contacts to the SS, the Foreign Ministry, and Armed Forces Counter-Intelligence (*Abwehr*). Americans did not yet know this, but other, more public Nazi activities increased the public's fear of Nazi espionage in America.[14]

Bohle's Foreign Organization gleaned some of its information from the *Deutsches Ausland-Institut* (DAI), based in Stuttgart. Founded during the Great War, this German Foreign Institute worked to strengthen the bonds between Germans abroad and the Reich. The institute distributed information about German communities throughout the world; it offered advice and education to Germans living abroad; and it provided information about the Reich to Germans living in foreign lands. The institute's files contained sensitive information, such as names and addresses of Germans living abroad, the size of German communities, and the passport status of individuals. Some of these people worked as its agents.

The directors of the institute during these years were Dr. Karl Strölin, lord mayor of Stuttgart, and Dr. Richard Csaki, a German from Transylvania. Both were Nazis, though Strölin later became disenchanted with the regime. The institute worked closely with Bohle, and claimed Rudolf Hess as a patron.[15] Much of Bohle's information about German-America came from the institute's experts. As the *Gauleiter* later put it, "They had all data about everything."[16] Institute representatives abroad often became informers for the AO. Ostensibly private individuals, these men had good covers, and "[a]t times we can provide the party with confidential reports of kinds not available elsewhere."[17] The names of Germans abroad working for American corporations were of particular interest to the AO, and hence to the institute.[18] The institute also worked with the Propaganda Ministry and other agencies, setting up training sessions for German-American students. The opinions expressed by these friendly Americans were not, of course, typical of the majority of their countrymen. In fact, much of the institute's information was based upon distorted perceptions, shared by careerists engaged in wishful thinking. One institute expert admitted, "We always move in the wrong direction because we compare American Germandom with Germandom in other countries, and do not allow that this American Germandom remains a part of the American nation, as it is and as it wishes to be."[19]

The institute's leading "America experts" were Heinz Kloss and Karl Goetz. Their work vindicated Hitler's perception of America and justified continued links with organizations like the Bund. Kloss and Goetz depicted an America composed of an uneasy blend of potentially divisive ethnic groups. Assimilation, they said, was a threat to the Germans, but it could be reversed, for "[a] unified national America was an illusion."[20] By manipulating German-America, the Reich could accelerate the disintegration of the so-called "melting pot" and influence the course of American foreign policy. Nazis ascribing to this viewpoint concluded, "It is very necessary that these Germans be informed of the other sides of National Socialism such as the social and intellectual goals."[21] Heinz Kloss claimed that America was home to six million ethnically "folk-conscious" Germans, perhaps even ten million. He agreed with a colleague who said, "[T]he early German sects in Pennsylvania actually sought a 'Third Reich' in their new homeland. . . . Here we have for the first time a broad, and until now silent, base of German blood in America wishing to raise [its voice]." The distinguished historian of German-America, Professor Carl Wittke, publicly rebuked Kloss for his "wishful thinking." The professor noted that the Pennsylvania Germans "have less connection with modern Germany than New England has with England."

Kloss refused to change his line, however, for his job depended upon ideological purity, not factual accuracy. If National Socialism had failed to make inroads in America, then the Jews were to blame. Like other Nazis, Kloss was encouraged by the growth of American anti-Semitism. There was more good news, he wrote. The American custom of lynching, opined Kloss, offered proof of the continued existence of healthy, albeit animalistic, racist undercurrents in the United States.[22] American interest in Appalachian culture might lead its aficionados to that fount of National Socialist wisdom, *Blut und Boden* (blood and soil), the doctrine of racial renewal through a healthy, folk-conscious peasantry. And for those Germans abroad who, despite all, remained loyal to the Nazi homeland, there were words of consolation from Rudolf Hess. "We have not forgotten," declared the deputy führer, "what many of you have had to sacrifice merely because you are Germans. It is the hope of the homeland that she will one day be able to make up for what you have lost."[23]

Despite his forced public optimism, Heinz Kloss was in fact dubious about Nazi prospects in America.[24] He received discouraging reports from a leading Bundist; they showed that anti-Nazi agitation was reaching a new crescendo, frightening German-American "cowards" away from the Nazis. "No democracy," declared one informant, "has entered the fighting front of the enemies of the authoritarian states so definitively as have the United States."[25]

Like Kloss, Karl Goetz offered a mixture of optimism and pessimism, reconciled by Nazi rhetoric. Born in a poor Swabian village in 1903, the restless Goetz traveled widely. He worked as a laborer in the United States in the 1920s, then returned to teach public school in Germany. Goetz, ill at ease at home, became a school principal in Palestine, where he first became active in German ethnic work. A convinced Nazi, Goetz returned to Germany in 1933, later becoming a department head in the German Foreign Institute. Goetz then journeyed as an institute agent to the United States, where he came into contact with the Bund, a ray of light "in the middle of this bleak area."

Upon his arrival back in Germany, Goetz recommended that the institute step up its support for the Bund. Director Strölin himself then traveled to America in the autumn of 1936, where he followed Goetz's recommendation. On 6 October, Strölin participated in a noisy, enthusiastic German Day rally in Madison Square Garden, New York City. Most people in the audience were Bundists, or their friends and relatives. Strölin was impressed. In 1937, he invited about forty Bund members to the Congress of Germans Abroad in Stuttgart. Like other Nazis fighting for a part of the *Ausland* constituency, Strölin claimed, "A 'German Day' in . . . Chicago concerns us just as deeply as the struggle of our brethren near our frontiers."[26]

Karl Goetz's best-selling book *Brothers Beyond the Sea* could not disguise its author's growing disillusionment with *Deutschtum* in the United States. Roosevelt, he knew, seemed to be moving into the anti-German camp, especially after his resounding reelection in 1936. By the time

Goetz began work on *The German Accomplishment in America*, relations between the Third Reich and the Americans had reached a low point. Goetz bemoaned the lack of political leadership among German-Americans. He spied some sign of hope—the German-American Bund—but he was not optimistic.[27] Myths about the power of the Bund certainly died hard in institute offices, where DAI leaders wished to work "with some of the dependable and well-intentioned followers of Kuhn on a *personal* basis."[28]

Kuhn, for his part, worked hard to cultivate his ties to powerful Nazi figures. Rudolf Hess, a patron of the People's League for Germandom Abroad (*Volksbund für das Deutschtum im Ausland*), continued to follow developments among German communities overseas. Despite his own prior orders mandating the departure of Reich Germans and party members from the Bund, Hess did nothing to discourage contacts between the league and the Bund.[29] By the late 1930s, the league had fallen under the control of SS lieutenant general Lorenz. This ambitious SS bureaucrat was working to unite all German organizations under the central aegis of his Ethnic German Exchange Office.[30] Thanks to the SS, in 1938 the league was able to train thirty members of the Bund's youth group in a camp near Berlin.

While these young Bundists frolicked in their German camp, Rolf Hoffmann sat in a Munich office, building up voluminous files on their organization. He was a rising figure in the party media apparatus, having come to the attention of Ernst Hanfstängl, an old Hitler crony. Hanfstängl, a Harvard graduate, worked as the head of the Foreign Press Office of the NSDAP. He had a special interest in the United States. After Hitler came to power, Hanfstängl offered Rolf Hoffmann a position as his assistant. Married to an English woman and fluent in the English language, Hoffmann became responsible for gathering information about American (and other) press reaction to the Third Reich. Some of these exhibits wound up on the desks of Rudolf Hess and other Nazi personalities. Prodded by Hanfstängl, Hoffmann took a special interest in American attempts to combat "Jew lies" about the New Germany. The young editor closely monitored fascist American bodies "doing good work . . . in waking up the people to true conditions," groups such as the Bund and the Silver Shirts.[31]

Hoffmann obtained important intelligence from Americans as he built a small information empire. He kept records on boycott leader Samuel Untermeyer and on anti-Nazi columnists such as Dorothy Thompson. Hoffmann received his information from diverse sources, including Dr. Bertling, head of the America Institute in Berlin, and Oscar C. Pfaus, the Chicago publisher of a pro-Nazi German-language newspaper. A diligent bureaucrat who understood the value of manipulating a network of his own creation, Hoffmann established new ties between Nazi agencies. Pfaus helped to widen Hoffmann's impressive network into a kind of Nazi anti-Semitern. After Pfaus informed Hoffmann about the publication called the *The White Man's Viewpoint* (New York City), Munich provided that bulletin with propaganda on "world jewry and the communistic underground movement."

Hanfstängl, no administrator, let Hoffmann run his own shop. When Hanfstängl fled Germany under unpleasant circumstances, the wily, well-connected Hoffmann continued his meteoric rise within the party. He escaped from active military duty thanks to a back injury. Cultivating his ties to the SS, Hoffmann rose to the rank of *SS-Obersturmbannführer,* while taking over Hanfstängl's job as foreign press chief of the party.[32]

Within Nazi circles, Hoffmann was an effective advocate of the Bund. He received and distributed the organization's placards, photographs, pamphlets, and newspapers. From Kuhn's group, Hoffmann learned in advance about important anti-Nazi demonstrations, as well as impending visits to Germany by Nazi sympathizers. Hoffmann invited such people to come to see him in Munich, where he tried to make their stays in the Reich more interesting.[33]

Hoffmann worked to reinforce his contacts with American anti-Jewish organizations, especially after 1936. He made use of the World Service in order to discover the names of "national men" (fascists) in the United States. Ironically, *Fortune* magazine's piece on the "most important anti-semitic organizations in America" proved helpful.[34] Hoffmann was soon supplying Robert E. Edmondson with anti-Jewish materials, in return for which Edmondson mailed Hoffmann his own works on the Jewish conspiracy. Hoffmann replied, enclosing a secret mailing list, which contained the names of potential helpers. The people listed on the roster of names were either American citizens or Germans resident in the United States. Hoffmann had some power, as shown by the fact that a Nazi diplomat soon made it clear to Edmondson that he could count on German funding. Edmondson, however, drew the line here, declaring, "I won't take money from a foreigner."[35] He was, after all, a one hundred percent *American* Jew-hater.

Hoffmann's office provided other admiring Americans with frequent advice on the Jewish question. Robert Grainger, head of the Anti-Communist League, based in Boston's Back Bay, learned from Munich that "[in Germany] Jews were often found in connection with Communist plots and Communism generally." Grainger responded like a good pupil. "As in Germany," he noted, "Communists in this country are largely Jewish." Hoffmann received much admiring mail from fascists, including one Silver Shirt who claimed to be "one of a great movement to oust Jews from the control of our Photo-Play management." "Major" Frank Pease, Commander of the International Legion Against Communism, described his work in distributing "anti-Jew" material. From Ernest Elmhurst of New York, Hoffmann learned more about the Silver Shirts. This gentleman was impressed by William Dudley Pelley's reputation, too, opining that Pelley was the "greatest anti-Jew" in America.

Hoffmann was realistic, but also hopeful. Things might change for the worse in America, and anti-Semites must be ready to act. Hoffmann refused to be discouraged by the words of another American agent, who reported, "Individuals and small groups are struggling against almost overwhelming difficulties, not the least of which is the pathetic condition of the American people." Yet even if "the Day" did not arrive in the United States, Hoffmann would be a winner. Within the Byzantine labyrinths of the Nazi bureaucracy, he was carving out his own fiefdom. Indeed, some of Hoffmann's material wound up in speeches delivered by Goebbels and even by Hitler himself.[36] It was thus not in Hoffmann's interest to dismiss his informants as isolated cranks, though that is precisely what many of them were. Even if their material was misleading, it reinforced Hitler's view of American society, and Hoffmann was not one to quarrel with that.[37]

Hoffmann's men carefully filed every bit of encouraging news provided by sympathetic Americans. One pro-Nazi, Henry Fuller of New York City, informed "Adolph [*sic*] Hitler" that the Jews were behind all anti-Nazi movements. He hoped that the Führer would "be not disturbed . . . by these Jewish tactics. . . ." Gertrude Dunn, a widely traveled lady, informed Hoffmann that "with Adolf Hitler and the Germans today, human history emerges definitely, for the first time, from its ancient bounds onto a higher plane of responsibility than it has thus far known."[38] Hoffmann's staff thus acquired a huge and potentially useful list of pro-Nazi Americans. Their requests varied greatly, and some were comical.[39] One correspondent wanted to visit a concentration camp so he could refute anti-Nazi atrocity propaganda. Hoffmann regretted "to inform you that permits are no longer being issued for this purpose."[40] Despite this propensity for attracting eccentrics, Hoffmann and other Nazi agents were establishing valuable contacts in the United States. Time was of the essence, for more Americans, including the president, were coming to see the Bund and related fascist organizations as "fifth-column" harbingers of Nazi aggression. And an administration mired in economic and political stagnation might seek new adventures overseas, for political, ideological, and economic reasons.

Hoffmann and his colleagues saw no reason to despair, though the obstacles confronting them were formidable. Anti-Semitism was on the rise in the U.S., and economic conditions were uncertain. Roosevelt was losing political control, at least of domestic policy. Hoffmann's job was similar to that of the Washington embassy, which later received instructions mandating that it "continue to have [German] views spread . . . by prominent Americans in a manner which you consider suitable."[41] The activities of these friends—especially the dissemination of their isolationist foreign policy attitudes—would further the goals of the Hitler regime. This was of great importance by September, 1938, for Europe appeared to be on the verge of war. Hitler had threatened Czechoslovakia with destruction.

PART FOUR

FDR'S DECEPTIVE REVOLUTION IN FOREIGN POLICY

CHAPTER
EIGHTEEN

CONFRONTING THE APPEASERS
AT HOME AND ABROAD

URING THE CZECH crisis, President Roosevelt kept his distance
from British Prime Minister Chamberlain, except when it was
politically opportune to appear supportive of the British leader's
peace efforts. FDR had no intention of opening himself to the charge of
meddling in a foreign crisis. Even less did FDR intend to commend a
policy of capitulation to the British and French leaders. Roosevelt did
not agonize over the justice of German claims or the obstinacy of the
Czech government. The president was not cooperating in any meaning-
ful way. Chamberlain wished to address the American people on the
radio; Roosevelt prevented the broadcast from taking place, much to the
prime minister's dismay. For his part, Chamberlain continued to believe, "It is always best and safest to count on nothing from the Americans but words."[1]

Roosevelt's words, however, masked an ulterior motive. In advocating
negotiations "until a peaceful settlement is found," FDR hoped to
forestall a surprise attack on Czechoslovakia and her allies. It is inaccu-
rate to see his message as a form of "appeasement," for Roosevelt had
no way of foreseeing the outcome of such a settlement. Indeed, no one

could be sure that Hitler would even accept the idea of further negotiations.

The announcement of a four-power meeting in Munich came as a surprise. On the eve of the Bavarian summit, FDR cabled Chamberlain "Good man!" Fearing a war for which he felt unprepared, and echoing France's desperate desire to find a way out, the prime minister could only hope to achieve one goal—an orderly, legal transfer of territory from Czechoslovakia to Germany. Chamberlain fervently hoped to spare Europe the ravages of a new war. Winston Churchill, former first lord of the admiralty and current Tory backbencher, urged the government to threaten war in the event of German aggression against the Czech state. He viewed Chamberlain's appeasement policy as both shameful and stupid. It would not, Churchill added, lead to peace, but to humiliation *and* war. Before the Munich meeting, Churchill argued that the issue was not one of self-determination, "but . . . [murder] by a great state of a small one."

Hitler, who hated the Czechs, seemed to want war, but he was trapped by his own rhetoric about self-determination for the Sudeten German "persecuted minority" in Czechoslovakia. Either way, the destruction of Versailles-Czechoslovakia would be an act of revenge against Woodrow Wilson. At a conference run by Mussolini at the behest of Hitler and Goering, Chamberlain and French leader Edouard Daladier satisfied most of Hitler's demands.[2]

Daladier, much to his own surprise, found himself acclaimed as a hero by vast crowds, who had come to greet him at the airport upon his return to Paris. "The imbeciles," he commented, "if they only knew what they were acclaiming!" A few malcontents tried to spoil the celebrations, but most people were happy that Europe had avoided war. Chamberlain and his friends at the *Times* spoke of "[p]eace in our time," with the Führer "making no further territorial demands."

Winston Churchill did not join in the rejoicing. Repudiating his own prime minister, Churchill sadly observed that Czechoslovakia (and the Munich accords) would not long survive. "We are," Churchill continued, "in the presence of a disaster of the first magnitude. . . ."[3] President Roosevelt, despite his admiration for Churchill, appeared pleased with the Munich agreement. He even joked about his newly found affection for the Führer.

The Sudetenland fell under German control in early October. The vanquished state (soon restyled "Czecho-Slovakia"), stripped of its defenses, began to assume a more authoritarian caste, and aligned itself with Germany. Chamberlain, however, was at the height of his prestige. With the Czech question resolved, and the Spanish Civil War reaching its end, Europe, following the lead of the four powers in Munich, could presumably take off its gas mask and put away its guns. In Hitler's *Ostmark* (former Austria), Dr. Karl Renner, a retired socialist politician, argued in a manuscript that the new four-power alignment or "tetrarchy," if it maintained its unity, could undo the damage caused by the iniquitous 1919 treaties, and usher in an era of peace.[4]

President Roosevelt asked that any remaining problems be resolved through negotiation, though he refused to endorse Chamberlain's bilateral appeasement policy. Ambassador Hans Dieckhoff understood that the "Jewish situation" and unresolved trade questions imperiled German relations with the United States. The German government expressed its desire to improve relations with the United States, it was rebuffed. Secretary Hull, ever the free-trade dreamer, replied evasively to Dieckhoff's feelers. The secretary confined his reply to the pious but unlikely request that Hitler adopt a "liberal commercial policy."[5]

Though Roosevelt the politician claimed to be happy about the outcome of Munich, his actions and private comments belied the president's public pose. He seemed to regard the Anglo-French capitulation as acceptable, but only if it bought time for the democracies. One of Roosevelt's aims consisted of prying Mussolini loose from his friendship with Hitler. He thus let it be known in Rome that he was not unhappy about the Munich settlement, over which the duce had presided. That was meant for consumption in Italy. More important was FDR's observation that if Britain and France lost the next war, the United States might fall victim to a successful German attack.[6] The president became a strong advocate of conscription—in Britain. He believed that France needed to strengthen its air defenses. FDR now wanted to seek a 500,000,000 dollar supplemental appropriation for the armed forces. At no point did Roosevelt act as if he believed that Munich was an acceptable model for the restructuring of the international order. The president privately admitted that his failure to assist the Spanish Republic had been a mistake. The trend toward fascism and totalitarianism disturbed Roosevelt more than ever.

The post-Munich euphoria dissipated quickly. Even Ambassador Hugh Wilson, a believer in appeasement, was sending increasingly gloomy cables to Washington. Hitler, he reported, might denounce his

1935 naval agreement with Great Britain. Germany, according to the ambassador, would be ready for battle in the near future. Ambassador to France William Bullitt, who made long visits to Washington to consult with Roosevelt, urged that France rebuild her military aviation. Ambassador Anthony Biddle cabled from Warsaw that the small states were looking for leadership. Daladier and Chamberlain were unwilling to provide it, Biddle declared.[7] His conclusion, clear though left unstated, placed the burden of leadership on FDR's shoulders.

The French government signed a consultation pact with Germany in early December. Dismembered and threatened, Czecho-Slovakia moved to replace democracy with a form of fascism. Prime Minister Chamberlain, who had promised to support the remnants of the Czech state, now viewed them as an annoyance and an irrelevance. Early in the new year, Franco prepared for his final offensive against the Spanish Republic. Both Chamberlain and Hitler courted Mussolini; the Führer would win the bride, though the Italian leader was unhappy over the prospect of German hegemony in Central Europe. Despite all these signs, Chamberlain clung to his appeasement policy.

While Chamberlain disengaged from Central and Eastern Europe, Roosevelt intensified his work in the Americas. His great interest in naval strategy and geopolitics led him to ponder a number of diverse yet related issues. The president had concluded by the end of 1938 that "the United States must be prepared to resist attack on the western hemisphere from the North Pole to the South Pole, including all of North America and South America." FDR now talked about his fear of two thousand German planes, each with a range of 3,300 miles.

Roosevelt's interest in Latin America was economic and strategic (one might even say imperial) in nature, but in public he emphasized common defense against non-American aggressors. This was tactful, but it was clear that the United States would have to lead this military effort. The president, ever careful to appear respectful of Latin sensitivities, constantly harped upon the alleged Nazi menace. He revealed little of his own rather grandiose vision of the American destiny. Roosevelt's private words and public actions reveal a man who was coming to see himself as protector of the "Western Hemisphere," a term that was broad, yet hard to define. This combination of ambiguity and grandeur suited Roosevelt well. The vagueness offered FDR room for political and public relations maneuvering, while the magnitude of the problem appeared to his sense of greatness and righteousness. Chamberlain hoped to pacify Europe, and then muddle through. Daladier would probably follow Chamberlain, though he was becoming more interested in Roosevelt. Mussolini was more noise than power. Stalin was obsessed with safeguarding the Soviet state. Hitler thought in European and racial terms. Roosevelt alone was thinking in global terms, though his policy had not yet matured. In his favor was the stagnant American economy, which would only reach its full potential if harnessed to the demands of a defense-oriented state. Working against FDR was the mind-set of the American majority, suspicious of entanglements.

FDR and his advisers considered various solutions in planning for hemispheric defense. Throughout Latin America, Roosevelt's ambassadors, agents and emissaries preyed upon fears gripping local elites. Many of these concerns had to do with Nazi subversion, espionage, and sabotage.

Most people of German origin in Latin America were *not* Nazis, much less revolutionaries. Their problem was that local National Socialists often claimed to speak in their name. The Foreign Organization of the Nazi party encouraged public displays of loyalty to Hitler and his ideology, which frightened many influential Latins. Members of the traditional Anglophile and Francophile ruling classes sometimes questioned the loyalty of their German-speaking or German-descended minorities. Latin leaders all wished to avoid involvement in a new European war; in addition, most believed that the Reich would lose once again. War meant blockades and related problems, all of which were detrimental to economies dependent upon global commerce.

On 10 April, the Foreign Organization had coerced many Germans and former Austrians in Latin America into voting in Hitler's *Anschluss* plebiscite. They cast their ballots in embassies, legations, consulates, and on ships anchored beyond the three-mile territorial limit. The Czech crisis soon showed Latins that Berlin could use disaffected minorities on behalf of an aggressive foreign policy. The Argentine minister of education bluntly expressed his fears. "Argentine suspicions of the educational and racial activities of immigrants," he said, "are not directed towards those from Great Britain. It is other races and peoples which should command our attention."

Roosevelt helped to bridge the transition from fear to action. Some of his advisers pushed FDR in the direction he wished to go. If the United States did not act, wrote Treasury Secretary Morgenthau, Latin American nations would provide "a helpless field for political and economic exploitation by the aggressor states." Much remained to be done, but Roosevelt was moving decisively against the Germans in South America.[8]

The same Latin leaders who craved German coal and weapons now cracked down on Nazi and fascist organizations, as well as on ethnic German institutions. In Brazil, President Getulio Vargas, somewhat of a dictator himself, outlawed the fascistoid *Integralistas* after their *coup* attempt of 10 and 11 May. Suspecting collusion between the German embassy and these enemies on the right, Vargas drew closer to the United States. A happy British observer soon noted, "Brazil has proved herself to be the bulwark of Latin America against National Socialist penetration." Leftist Mexico, generally satisfied with Roosevelt's tactful handling of its oil nationalization crisis, moved in a similar direction.[9]

Who was behind this seemingly orchestrated program of national countersubversion? Well-informed German sources left no doubt as to the identity of the culprit: "Whereas last year, the United States carried on the fight against Germany principally in the economic and commercial spheres, it has now changed and extended the field of action, and . . . its opposition to Germany is [now] mainly political," stated Berlin's ambassador to Brazil. Meeting in emergency session, German diplomats from key Latin American capitals recommended that Berlin consider the repatriation of some ethnic Germans. As the German minister to Uruguay put it, "It cannot be denied that Roosevelt has achieved extraordinary results in South America generally." The president was fighting in the early stages of his own multifront war. While working to expunge German influence from the Americas, he would soon begin to undermine Chamberlain's appeasement policy in Europe.

The policy Roosevelt wished to replace still enjoyed widespread support. Appeasement had come to have miserable connotations of weakness, delusion, and surrender. Fifty years ago, however, a majority of Britons stood behind their prime minister and his commitment to negotiate with the dictators.

In moving toward a repudiation of appeasement, FDR was preparing to challenge a powerful intellectual and political current, one endorsed by articulate members of his own social class. In that winter and spring of 1939, many prominent Americans and Britons viewed Chamberlain's accommodation with the dictators as a form of *Realpolitik*. The distinguished (and far from reactionary) British historian Edward Hallett Carr was an influential member of this pro-Chamberlain intellectual lobby. Carr wrote, "The conception of a *pax Germanica* or *pax Japanica*, i.e., of a world order dominated by Germany or Japan, was *a priori* no more absurd and presumptuous than the conception of a *pax Britannica. . . .*" "Have-not" nations, such as Germany, were challenging the international order, but their demands were not necessarily unjust. Any sound world order, Carr believed, must be based upon a rational accommodation of differing national interests. The historian reached some stunning conclusions. Carr viewed Hitler, however repulsive he might be, as an agent of change. If denied justice, he would upset the international order; if satisfied, the German leader could become a pillar of a new system. The aim of British diplomacy, Carr argued, must be to channel "change" in a peaceful direction. Ignoring the nature of National Socialism, Carr convinced himself that the international community could coexist with Hitler's Germany.[10] In his view, Munich was a great triumph for peace, justice, and the new international order.

John Foster Dulles, a senior partner in the prestigious New York law firm of Sullivan and Cromwell, reached a similar conclusion, though by a more circuitous route. Dulles had served in the State Department in the days of President Wilson. Having attended the 1919 peace conference, he respected Wilson's struggle for a new international order based upon self-determination, disarmament, and a strong League of Nations. Dulles quickly realized that the failure to establish a just order among nations had sowed the seeds of another war. Dulles observed the early Nazi triumphs with a mixture of suspicion and aversion. Over the next few years, Dulles modified some of his views and tried to understand the German revolution. A frequent visitor to Germany, this leading Republican believed that one could do business with the new Reich, or at least, with the people who served it.

Dulles did not admire the Nazis, but he was a critic of the misplaced nationalism of the "satiated" powers, including the United States. Challenged by dynamic societies such as the new Germany, the West needed to display equivalent energy and intelligence in its quest for a viable world order. After all, Dulles believed, "no nation has a monopoly of the virtues or of the vices." If America was not absolutely good, Dulles thought, then Hitler could not be totally evil.[11] In his eyes, the Axis powers were trying to redress an awkward balance. Man was corrupt and might yield to the temptation of war, Dulles declared, but if he used his reason he would tame the beast and create a new, peaceful world order. John J. McCloy, a prominent attorney who disagreed with his good friend Foster, wrote that "[Dulles's] disposition to settle all disputes without resorting to violence rather influenced him in rationalizing this Hitler movement."

Dulles called his policy "peaceful change," the name bestowed upon a seminar he conducted in Paris in 1937. When the sessions turned into platforms for vituperative denunciations of fascists and Nazis, Dulles "felt people attending were not able to rise above their nationalistic self-interest and prejudices." Such pettiness only reinforced Dulles's self-righteous streak. Hitler's attacks on the Jews and his growing propensity for territorial expansion seem to have left Dulles unmoved. He disliked his sister Eleanor's criticisms of Nazi Germany as much for their emotionalism as for their content.

Sullivan and Cromwell had some lucrative operations in Germany, which a large majority of partners and staff wished to shut down. Twice a year, John Foster Dulles visited the Berlin office of the firm, located in the luxurious Esplanade Hotel. As if nothing had happened, he continued to work with representatives of I.G. Farben and other German companies. When Germany began to rearm, Dulles found excuses, such as "Germany . . . has now taken back her freedom of action." By late 1935, even Foster's brother Allen argued that the firm should give up its business in Nazi Germany.[12] Such a protest against Nazi crimes irritated Dulles, who only yielded when he found himself isolated in the firm's boardroom. When it came to making foreign policy, Dulles had more faith in Neville Chamberlain than in his partners.

If E.H. Carr was the prophet of Munich, then John Foster Dulles was its apostle. Early in 1939, the fifty-one-year-old lawyer published his influential book *War, Peace, and Change*, which defined appeasement as a rational accommodation to change. It was a realistic policy, he said, in the long run, a just one. The peace agreements of 1919, Dulles argued, had produced despotic regimes. Mussolini had intervened in Spain, Dulles claimed, only because the democracies failed to recognize the Italian conquest of Ethiopia in a timely manner. That invasion, in turn, had only occurred because of Italy's legitimate desire for some form of imperialist parity with her former allies, Britain and France. Hitler and Mussolini were thus morally equivalent to the men who had created the unjust peace structure of 1919. Woodrow Wilson's failure had ushered in an era in which vengeance and exploitation paraded as "peace."

The ideology of appeasement concealed a hidden agenda, disguising itself as dynamic when it was inherently reactionary. Carr, Dulles, and their followers, such as Charles and Anne Lindbergh, were anticommunist conservatives who feared Soviet Russia more than they loathed Nazi Germany. In fact, Carr and Dulles admired Chamberlain's work at Munich in part because it *excluded* the Soviets from this restructuring of the European order. Like Chamberlain, they understood that confrontation with Germany would require an alliance with Stalin, and they abhorred that idea. It would, however, do no good to oppose antifascism in the name of reactionary anticommunism. Best-sellers were being written about the twilight of capitalism, and if one did not wish to be left behind by history one had to appear progressive.

Carr and Dulles thus worked to change the language, turning those who opposed fascism into the real reactionaries. Fascism was young and dynamic, and it must be given its due. That would be the "progressive" approach. In the view of the advocates of appeasement, the unfortunate excesses of Nazism and fascism had stemmed from the failures of the old order. To Dulles, Munich proved that rational men could reach peaceful agreements with a revolutionary like Hitler.[13]

An energetic former president, deeply suspicious of Franklin Roosevelt's intentions, read *War, Peace, and Change* with sympathetic interest. Herbert Hoover, encouraged by recent Republican congressional gains, accepted Dulles's arguments as commonsense truths—and as good politics. The former president had seen the devastation wrought by war. As the "Great Humanitarian," Hoover had helped to feed starving millions, from Belgium to Russia. He was an intellectual of great integrity, but was also rigid and vain. Hoover became president in 1928 with a reputation as the "Great Engineer," the man who would preside over a country forever prosperous, a land in which human energy and Yankee ingenuity would overcome poverty. Instead, the stock market crashed, and Hoover became the hapless victim of the Great Depression. He was remembered by many as a cold man in an old-fashioned collar, dour and unfeeling. Hoover's name became synonymous with Democratic victory, social misery, and Republican eclipse.

Deeply hostile to Roosevelt since 1932, Hoover opposed the expansion of federal powers engendered by FDR. A "challenge to liberty" was the term the former president applied to the New Deal. Hoover viewed Roosevelt's experimentation as a dangerous form of collectivism. It could, he thought, one day rob Americans of their freedom, by replacing it with a presidential dictatorship. Hoover favored a confrontational attitude toward Roosevelt, and was disappointed in the Republican party's 1936 standard-bearer, Alf M. Landon. The candidate, after all, occasionally referred to himself as a "liberal."[14] A disappointed (rather than disillusioned) Wilsonian, Hoover now staked out a position as chief foreign policy spokesman for the Republicans. If he could not return to office (and obtain vindication) as an anti–New Dealer, Hoover would use anti-interventionism as his battering ram. (Hoover was an anti-interventionist rather than isolationist, for he fervently believed in an engaged foreign policy based upon international cooperation and assistance.) Speaking and writing with great frequency, Hoover lectured the nation on FDR's dangerous adventurism in foreign affairs. The president, he argued, needed something to divert the people from his failure to end the Depression.

His reading of Dulles's book convinced Herbert Hoover that American intervention in Europe would lead to involvement in another war. And, Hoover reasoned, "[a]ny major war means that our country must be mobilized into practically a Fascist government." War would lead to an expansion of communism. It would also be a boon to the devious, egomaniacal Roosevelt, who had ambitions to become a kind of dictator.

Hoover now expressed concern about FDR's rearmament proposals. He placed his own faith in the "fortress America" concept, pointing with confidence to the broad expanses of the Atlantic and the Pacific. Hoover warned that "a war to save liberty would probably destroy liberty," for "personal liberty and free economic life are not built for modern war." He turned out to be completely wrong, but many progressives agreed, for they had not forgotten the war of 1917–1919. That intervention had, they recalled, buried one progressive movement. Hoover now staked his political future and his credibility upon an alliance with antiliberal and isolationist factions within the Republican party, particularly in the West. This meant de facto support for Chamberlain's policy toward Hitler, precisely at the moment of Roosevelt's final rejection of appeasement.

At times, Hoover seemed to despise Roosevelt more than he did Hitler. And he certainly feared Stalin more than he did Japanese militarists or Italian fascists. Upset by Roosevelt's expressed interest in an antiaggressor coalition, Hoover argued on two grounds against intervention. The old Allies, he declared, could defend themselves in the event of war. There was, he believed, no clear and present danger. This was Hoover's view in March, after Hitler destroyed the Munich agreement by seizing Bohemia and Moravia. The great city of Prague was in German hands, and the skilled labor of the Czech people, and the Skoda armaments works, were now working for Germany's arms industry. The Greater German Reich sent troops into puppet Slovakia, thus enabling it to surround Poland on three sides. And Poland, of course, had within its borders a large German minority. The free city of Danzig, under a League of Nations high commissioner, might be Hitler's next conquest. Hoover remained unmoved; indeed, his position hardened.

In Herbert Hoover's view, even a triumphant Nazi Germany would not threaten the United States until at least 1964.[15] One would have thought that an engineer, even blinded by suspicion of Roosevelt, would be more cautious. Even if Hoover knew nothing about German experiments with rockets (which dated back nine years or so), or scientific talk about nuclear fission and uranium, how could he be so cavalier in dismissing the possibility of threats as yet dimly foreseen? Modern science in Hitler's hands should have given the Great Engineer pause for thought. True, Hoover, did acknowledge the need for some American rearmament, but he seemed to think that America could defend the hemisphere in isolation from other anti-Nazi or anti-Japanese powers. Stubborn, humorless, and self-righteous, Hoover sounded as if he wished to play the role of an American Chamberlain.

One can, however, sympathize to some extent with Herbert Hoover, for it is easy to share his humanitarian concern about intervention. A generation that had suffered in one war, and remained mired in a great Depression, wished to avoid further disaster. Hoover had seen mass starvation and malnutrition. He knew the human costs of war. He expressed genuine concern about the plight of the Jews.

Hoover now moved to organize a powerful anti-interventionist lobby. He quickly recognized that Colonel Charles A. Lindbergh, Jr., the famous aviator, would be a great catch for those opposing the abandonment of neutrality. Writing to him after Lindbergh had spoken out against war, the former president said he was "very glad that you spoke as you did." Hoover continued, "I do not agree with everything that you said, but I do agree with the result, and I feel that there is a grave danger that, under the influence of emotion, we will decide upon a national policy which is quite the reverse of what we had more or less agreed upon when we were thinking clearly."

Twelve years earlier, "Lucky Lindy," the "Lone Eagle," had become the authentic American hero. An all-American boy from small-town Minnesota, Lindbergh had made it across the Atlantic Ocean all by himself in 1927. An idealistic and talented inventor and aviator, the quiet, shy Lindy seemed to personify the daring and modesty of an earlier, more innocent United States.

Everything seemed to work in Lindbergh's favor, including his marriage to the talented writer Anne Morrow, daughter of the diplomat and Wall Street millionaire Dwight Morrow, a partner in the J.P. Morgan banking firm. Then, his world grew darker. Basically a withdrawn man, Lindbergh found himself hounded by the media and cheap publicity seekers. "How can democracy," he cried out, "hold its head high when there is no freedom for those who have once attracted the interest of its public and its press?" The tragedy of the kidnap and murder of his little child, a notorious trial, and more invasions of his privacy followed. Finally, Lindbergh escaped to Europe. As the years passed, Lindbergh embraced a sullen conservatism. His growing dislike of democracy reflected his anger at a society that could not even protect his infant son.

At first, Lindbergh's relations with Franklin D. Roosevelt were correct. In 1933, the president paid tribute to Lindbergh for his efforts on behalf of the American aviation industry. He dispatched a friendly telegram to the Lindberghs, congratulating them upon "the successful completion of this, another flight made by you in the interest and for the promotion of American aviation."[16] Listening to the conservative friends and relatives of his in-laws, however, Lindbergh soon began to detest and mistrust the president. America, he believed, was now the land of New Dealers, of chiselers on relief, and of Jews. Lindbergh's trips to Europe, especially to Germany, became more frequent and more prolonged. The Germans treated the Lindberghs royally but respected their privacy. No reporters from the *Völkischer Beobachter* hounded him. Here was a land of law and order, devoid of communists. Lindbergh was impressed by Germany's cleanliness, by its commitment to clean living among youth, by its devotion to good old values.

What Lindbergh saw seemed to confirm the theories of his friend, Nobel Prize laureate Dr. Alexis Carrel, a French surgeon employed by the Rockefeller Institute. Carrel, a racialist and elitist who greatly influenced Lindbergh, argued that "man is the hardiest of all animals, and the white races, builders of our civilization, the hardiest of all races. . . . The descendant of a great race, if he is not degenerate, is endowed [with a] natural immunity to fatigue and fear. . . ." The words seemed to apply to Charles Lindbergh.

Lindbergh had imbibed some health phobias from his mother, including aversions to smoking, cola, coffee, and tea. Women in Germany knew that they belonged in the home. The Nazis, Lindbergh was relieved to see, had not emulated the Soviets in obliterating "the God-made difference between men and women." German women did not drink or smoke in public, at least not around Lindbergh.

Charles Lindbergh had learned a lot from the German school of geopolitics, perhaps from Karl Haushofer of the University of Munich, a teacher and confidant of Rudolf Hess. Lindbergh, like Haushofer, had come to think of the world as divided into natural spheres of influence. Germany, he seemed to believe, had a right to primacy over much of Europe. Britain and the English, by contrast, disappointed and repelled Lindbergh. Like his father, a populist congressman who had served several terms, he disliked and mistrusted their sophisticated ways. Young Lindbergh noted that, "The more I see of modern England and the English people, the less confidence I have in them." Lindbergh began to see the British through German eyes. London, Lindbergh insisted, was more vulnerable to air attack than was Berlin. The aviator and his appeaser friends clucked about British pacifism, then denounced England's modest anti-Hitler moves as impulsive madness. Lindbergh began to worry about his own country, fearing that it might be taking the British road to ruin. "The decay of a country," he wrote, "is seldom recognized until some years after it starts."[17]

After observing extremist political activity in Britain, Lindbergh came up with an interesting comparison. A meeting of the British Union of Fascists, he said, "was of a much higher quality than that of the Communists. It always seems that the Fascist group is better than the Communist group." Convinced that war meant the triumph of the greater evil, communism, Lindbergh refused to question his dogmatic preference for Hitler over Stalin. Occasionally, Lindbergh harbored doubts about the rationality of the German leadership, but he shared them only with his wife, a few friends, or his diary. Lindbergh held fast to his own vision of despair: "If," he wrote, "England and Germany enter another major war on opposite sides, Western civilization may fall as a result." Lindbergh carefully said "on opposite sides." There were some in Britain and many in Germany (including Hitler) who hoped for joint action against Soviet Russia.

Lindbergh had heard about the "atrocity propaganda" concerning Nazi treatment of the Jews, but he came into contact with few, if any, Jews during his tours of the Reich. Lindbergh could not speak much German. He did not see the crudeness or brutality of the Nazis, when they assembled in their meeting halls, or when they beat up Jews. Reports of Nazi attacks on the Jews in 1938 bothered Lindbergh, but only because they eroded his treasured concept of German law and order. German atrocities put him on the defensive when talking to his British and American friends. More in sorrow than in anger, Lindbergh asked: "They [the Nazis] undoubtedly have a difficult Jewish problem, but why is it necessary to handle it so unreasonably?"

Lindbergh seemed to resent the Jews themselves for dividing the Western nations, when they should be uniting in the face of the bolshevik onslaught. The Jewish question was undermining appeasement, and, Lindbergh believed, "We should be working with the Germans and not constantly crossing swords. If we fight our countries will only lose their best men. . . . It must not happen." Lindbergh denounced "hysterical rearmament" in the United States. Like his hosts, he believed that the Jews had played a baneful role in German history. Lindbergh wrote movingly of the death of his beloved dog, Skean, but his long diary reflects not a word of personal sympathy for the plight of the Jewish people.

"In my experience," wrote the aviator, "it seems that Latin blood (and Asiatic) tends to suspicion, while Nordic blood tends away from it. Personally, I prefer to be with people who are not suspicious about everything in life."[18] "Asiatic blood," as the term was used in Nazi Germany, often served as a partial description of Jewish characteristics. Lindbergh, of course, now found Roosevelt to be inordinately devious and suspicious. Perhaps he believed him to be "Asiatic." If he did, Lindbergh had merely absorbed one more idea from his hosts, many of whom described FDR as "Jewish."

Lindbergh was interested primarily in aviation and privacy, both of which made him susceptible to Nazi blandishments. He rarely raised unpleasant questions for his gracious hosts. Lindbergh visited aircraft factories and air force bases with General Hermann Goering. Given freedom to see what he wished, he learned about some of the latest German production techniques and inspected new fighters and bombers. A straightforward man, Lindbergh did not fully grasp his host's motives. The Luftwaffe chief saw the air hero as a prestigious friend of the New Germany, a man who might influence other, equally important Americans. By emphasizing German might, Lindbergh became a front man for the Nazis' *Schrecklichkeit* doctrine, which implied that war would commence with the virtual destruction of cities like London and Paris. Lindbergh was indeed intolerant toward those who questioned German aerial superiority. Such people, he believed, were "irrational," just like the Germanophobes who berated him for having accepted the Service Cross of the Order of the German Eagle from Goering.[19]

Lindbergh, a staunch patriot, was bitter. Press accounts implied that he was too chummy with the Nazis. Yet Lindy had, after all, shared his Luftwaffe data with the War Department. In fact, he received the Distinguished Service Medal for providing the department with valuable information.

In 1936, Lindbergh had learned about the Messerschmidt 109, which became the Luftwaffe's basic fighter aircraft. He then prepared an estimate of German air power. A memorandum on the subject prepared for Ambassador Kennedy in London made its way to Roosevelt, as well as to the navy and army chiefs of staff. Lindbergh emphasized, perhaps overemphasized, German air superiority, but his estimates were valuable and proved to be prophetic. In his essay, Lindbergh wrote of the wonders of German aircraft production, concluding that "The German aviation development is without parallel."[20]

The problem for Lindbergh was that his estimates could be construed to emphasize Western incapacity and German invincibility. By 1940, military experts were routinely exaggerating German superiority over the West and the Soviet Union, sometimes by absurd amounts. Lindbergh's prestige lent credibility to estimates made by those who should have known better.

By the end of the decade, Lindbergh and the Roosevelt administration had reached a parting of the ways. Lindbergh deeply resented derogatory comments about him made by administration figures such as Secretary of the Interior Harold Ickes. Speaking to a meeting of the Cleveland Zionist Society, Ickes had asked, "How can any American calling himself a Christian accept decorations from the hands of a brutal dictator . . . ?" Lindbergh sometimes defended himself by saying things like this: I was a guest, the situation was awkward, what could I have done? At one point, the president said, "I would have known what to do with [the decoration] all right."[21]

Lindbergh, fearing FDR's tilt against the Axis powers, drew closer to anti-interventionist politicians. In June 1939, he went to the Capitol, where he conferred with Senator Harry F. Byrd of Virginia. Both men bemoaned the widespread influence of Jewish and British propaganda, and feared that "chaos" would result from American intervention in a new European war.

Though much unlike his father, Lindbergh shared the congressman's view of politics. Public service and advocacy, he believed, were virtuous so long as they served a righteous cause. Both men were anti-interventionists, for Lindbergh Sr. had opposed President Wilson's foreign policies, both in Mexico and in Europe. But Lindbergh's father was more of a pacifist than his son. When he spoke of war, it was with real passion: "War is paid for by the people. It is the slavery and drudgery that follows war that is more damaging than war itself."[22]

Abhorring the breast-beating mea culpas of Dulles and Carr, and the gloomy defeatism of Hoover and Lindbergh, President Roosevelt had reached an important turning point by the late winter of 1939. FDR's view of Hitler was rapidly evolving. He could no longer seem to conceive of a world within which Hitlerism and democratic capitalism coexisted. Now, in the first hours after news of Hitler's violation of the Munich accords reached the world's capitals, some illusions died, though not all. What view could one take now of Chamberlain who, two weeks before Munich, "had formed the opinion that Herr Hitler's objectives were strictly limited"?[23]

FDR now viewed poor Chamberlain with some disdain, though his dislike was mingled with a certain degree of sympathy. Roosevelt had concluded that the fashionable idea of appeasement was a dangerous failure. Chamberlain's first reactions to Hitler's dissolution of Czechoslovakia were more ambiguous. He felt betrayed by Hitler's move, and he feared that the occupation of Prague would undermine support for appeasement. Chamberlain would soon modify his foreign policy, but did not intend to abandon it. Roosevelt was moving closer to Churchill's harsh condemnation of appeasement, though, as a friendly head of state, he used more cautious rhetoric. FDR began to consider amending the Neutrality Act, whose "cash and carry" clause would soon expire.

Three days after Hitler marched into Prague, Samuel Flagg Bemis, a Yale professor of diplomatic history, addressed the Foreign Policy Association. Bemis was willing to consider amending the Neutrality Act so as to help Britain and France, but only on two conditions. First, outstanding questions of debt repayment must be settled. Second, the United States must *"secure from Great Britain . . . aerial and naval bases . . . in Bermuda, the islands of the Caribbean, British Guiana and British Honduras. . . ."* Bemis feared that Japan and Germany might gain ascendancy in the Pacific and the Atlantic. Though an anti-interventionist, he countenanced aid to the Allies, if this served America's continental and hemispheric defense interests. Bemis's argument did not help Roosevelt in 1939, but his bases-for-aid proposal became the foundation of FDR's policy in the late summer of 1940.[24]

FDR's future political plans were still unclear, but the identity of his successor, along with the foreign policy orientations of both parties, took on new interest. Perhaps the Republicans had found their issue. The thought that an isolationist might succeed him disturbed Roosevelt. With the economy floundering and the Democratic majority in the new session of Congress greatly diminished, FDR's political future was in doubt.

CHAPTER
NINETEEN

FDR, GERMANY, AND THE JEWS

PRIME MINISTER CHAMBERLAIN had preserved peace in Europe, but Munich brought no solace to Hitler's Jewish victims. During the night of 9–10 November 1938, Nazi arsonists, working at the instigation of Propaganda Minister Goebbels, launched a new campaign of terror against the Jews still living in Germany. The Gestapo, the Security Service, and the police arrested thousands of Jews, many of whom soon found themselves in concentration camps. Jewish property was seized, its former owners beaten, humiliated, and sometimes murdered. From Hamburg to Vienna, synagogues and Jewish meeting-houses went up in flames, forty-three in the former Austrian capital alone. The sidewalks were littered with broken glass, much of it valuable Belgian crystal, hence the name *Kristallnacht* (Crystal Night).

Hitler had made clear to the world that the Jews were his hostages. Anti-Nazi behavior abroad ("atrocity propaganda," boycotts), he threatened, would only hasten the demise of the Jewish communities trapped within the Greater German Reich. And, Hitler soon declared, if "international Jewry" started another war, the Jews would be destroyed. As Zionist leader Chaim Weizmann sadly observed, "The world is divided into two groups of nations, those which want to expel the Jews and those which do not want to receive them."

The pogrom disgusted Franklin Roosevelt. Nazi atrocities, inflicted upon helpless people, represented a frontal assault against humanity. Roosevelt wrote, "I myself could scarcely believe that such things could occur in a twentieth-century civilization."[1] His interior secretary, Harold L. Ickes, denounced "a brutal dictator who . . . is robbing and torturing thousands of fellow human beings." The German chargé protested, but Roosevelt's State Department refused to accept the note. The State Department (which contained its share of "social" anti-Semites) intervened strongly and with some success on behalf of American Jews who owned property in the Reich.

The president viewed the treatment of the Jews as a guide to the mental and moral health of a Western society. A regime that would victimize its Jews, he believed, would show no respect for international law. Coexistence with such a government no longer seemed possible. Roosevelt strongly denounced the pogrom at a 15 November press conference.

In a move that stunned (though it hardly deterred) the Hitler regime, the State Department recalled Ambassador Hugh Wilson for "consultation." He never returned to his post in Berlin. Surprised observers in Paris and London believed that Roosevelt's militancy might inaugurate a new strategy aimed at containing Nazism.[2] This possibility displeased the supporters of appeasement. The British ambassador expressed his concern to the president, explaining that "it would be very unfortunate if the United States Government could no longer converse with the German Government."[3] In Paris, Foreign Minister Georges Bonnet, pointing to the contrast between American sentiments and American action, supported appeasement. And, he added, the uproar over the recent pogroms reflected the special interest of the Jewish-controlled media.[4] More than ever, the weakness of the Anglo-French leadership seemed to indicate that the West had need of someone who could speak with a stronger voice than Bonnet or Chamberlain. Besides, from Roosevelt's viewpoint, selective anti-Nazism could also be good politics. Despite the many dissenters, one poll showed that more than seventy percent of respondents with an opinion approved of the "temporary withdrawal" of the American ambassador.[5]

Roosevelt seemed to take the recent pogroms as a personal affront, even as a threat to his own Jewish friends, of whom there were many.

His vigorous words and actions after 10 November could not be ascribed to political chicanery. The elections were over, and most Jews had already come to associate Roosevelt with opposition to Hitler. Roosevelt's timidity in regard to the refugee question had not deterred almost ninety percent of Jewish voters from casting their ballots for FDR in the 1936 election. Historians may properly condemn Roosevelt for his policy toward refugees, but most American Jews felt that FDR was the best man at the time, for them and for their country.

Roosevelt had learned much about Hitler's central obsession from Ambassador Dodd. Hitler, Dodd recalled, would sometimes repeat the phrase "Damn the Jews!" over and over again, even when the Jews had no apparent connection with the subject matter under discussion. Roosevelt, who was not immune to milder anti-Jewish stereotypes, would shake his head, and comment, "We must protect them, and whatever we can do to moderate the general persecution by unofficial and personal influence ought to be done." Nevertheless, governmental action was out of the question. "This is not," FDR said of the Jewish question, "a governmental affair." Roosevelt did, however, provide some assistance to refugees, and worked through private channels on behalf of Jewish victims of Nazism. By 1937, the United States had received thirty thousand such persons.

Roosevelt's Jewish friends, who often stemmed from older, wealthy German-Jewish families, were not among the militants who directed the anti-Nazi boycott. Cautious about pressing Jewish issues on the president, they nevertheless helped to sensitize him to the plight of their religious brethren. Sensitivity, however, did not always translate into action, especially when the tutors were cautious men themselves. FDR greatly enjoyed the advice, wit, and companionship of men like Samuel Rosenman, Felix Frankfurter, Bernard Baruch, and Henry Morgenthau, Jr. He saw these men as representative of a humane, intelligent people, the persecution of which offended his Episcopalian concept of Christian charity.

Domestic reaction to Roosevelt's protests against Crystal Night was generally, though not universally, encouraging. The American Legion endorsed his statements, as did the CIO. Prominent Hollywood stars, among them Fred Astaire, Claudette Colbert, and Bette Davis, suggested that the United States sever all economic ties to the Third Reich. By and large, the pogroms weakened American support for Chamberlain's policy of appeasement.[6] There were many discordant

Nazi Persecution of the Jews had
Low Saliency for Americans through WWII
as well as in the Pre-War Period

"Which news event interested you most in:"

1937*	Rank
Ohio Floods	1
Sino-Japanese War	2
Supreme Court Fight	3
Windsor Marriage	4
Amelia Earhart Lost	5
Present Business Slump	6
Texas School Explosion	7
Justice Black and the Klan	8
General Motors Strike	8
Supreme Court Decisions on the New Deal	10

1938*	Rank
Czech Crisis	1
Nazi Persecutions	2
Republican Gains	3
Corrigan's Flight	4
Wage and Hour Bill	5
New England Hurricane	6
Business Slump	6
World Series	6
Japan And China Conflict	9
C.I.O. and A.F.L. Troubles	9

1939**	Rank
England and France declare War on Germany	1
Congress Lifts Arms Embargo	2
Attempt on Hitler's Life in Munich Bombing	3
Scuttling of the Graf Spee	4
German "Blitzkreig" in Poland	5
Visit of English Monarchs	6
Russia Invades Finland	7
Germany Seizes Bohemia and Moravia	8
Roosevelt's Thanksgiving Proclamation	9
Russo-German Treaty of Friendship.	10

* Open-ended
* * Close-ended

Source: Gallup

Although They Disapproved of the Nazi Treatment of Jews, the Majority of Americans were Reluctant to Assist the Jews (or Other Nazi Victims) in Practical Ways.

EVIDENCE OF DISAPPROVAL
NOVEMBER 1938

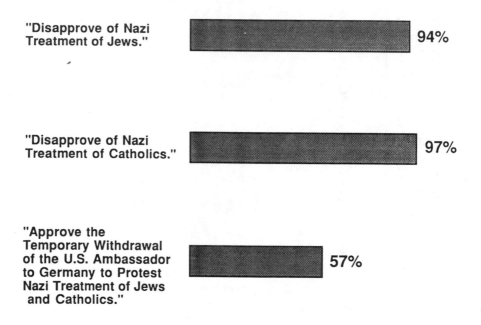

"Disapprove of Nazi Treatment of Jews."   **94%**

"Disapprove of Nazi Treatment of Catholics."   **97%**

"Approve the Temporary Withdrawal of the U.S. Ambassador to Germany to Protest Nazi Treatment of Jews and Catholics."   **57%**

Source: Gallup

notes, however. From Dublin, Ambassador John Cudahy informed his friend Roosevelt, "I am not in sympathy with our attitude towards Germany. . . . [F]rankly I cannot see the propriety of our action in protesting against the inhuman treatment by Germans of German Jews."[7] Robert B. Kirkman, president of the U.S. Tool and Machinery Company, spoke for many when he informed Roosevelt, "[Y]ou were elected President of the U.S.A. and not the entire world." He suggested that the president show more concern about "the victims of the economic policies of your administration."

In fact, Roosevelt did not do enough for the stricken Jews; his wife, Eleanor, wanted him to act more boldly. What he offered to the refugees, on the other hand, offended many American Jew-haters who sometimes recited the following ditty:

> *Oh Abie sails over the ocean;*
> *And Izzie sails over the sea*
> *So the shrine of each patriot's devotion*
> *Has to take in the damned refugee!*

Father Coughlin, who still had millions of listeners, denounced intervention in Germany's "internal affairs." "America for the Americans" continued to be the foreign-born priest's slogan. *Social Justice* was more anti-Semitic than ever.

Approval of the withdrawal of Ambassador Wilson did not mean that Americans wanted to receive a boatload of Jews with him. By better than three to one, Americans opposed allowing a larger number of refugees to come to the United States.[8] Sensitive to these polls, FDR worked with other nations through international conferences, which accomplished little or nothing. Roosevelt, expressing sympathy for Zionist aspirations, hoped that the British might solve much of the Jewish problem. They could do so, he believed, by admitting large numbers of Jews to Palestine and honoring their 1917 Balfour Declaration pledge to permit the establishment of a Jewish homeland in Palestine.[9] That would get him off the hook.

Expressing disapproval of the pogroms was good politics; helping their victims by bringing them to the U.S. was not. Roosevelt refused to defy Congress and public opinion by requesting changes in the immigration quotas. He refused to permit the steamship *St. Louis* to anchor at an American port, for fear that the refugees on board would seek asylum here. No excuse can be given for Roosevelt's calculated timidity. His policy toward the refugee question, however, must not be separated from a study of the president's increasingly bold antifascist policies at home and abroad. These courses of action would one day culminate in the isolation of the anti-Semitic right at home, and the destruction of the Nazi regime in Europe.

＊　　＊　　＊

While street sweepers cleaned up the mess left by Crystal Night, ambassador to Poland Tony Biddle finished drafting an urgent letter to the president. "The plight of the Jewish populations as a whole in Europe is steadily becoming . . . untenable," wrote Biddle. The ambassador concluded, "[I]t is steadily becoming clearer that you personally are the one to whom they all look more and more. . . ."[10]

Herschel Johnson of the Foreign Service, who worked at the U.S. embassy in London, received a horrifying report from the British Foreign Office. He forwarded it to the State Department, which passed it on to the White House. It detailed the treatment of Jews after their arrest on the night of 9–10 November. Describing how the SS and German police tormented, humiliated, and beat prisoners, FDR ordered the report placed in his secretary's file.[11] This "President's Secretary's File" consisted of important materials frequently consulted by FDR. At one point, a troubled FDR asked his speech-writer and friend Samuel I. Rosenman why some Jew did not kill Hitler? Why did the Jews take things lying down? Rosenman does not record his answer.

From Ambassador Biddle, Roosevelt learned about the misery of the impoverished Jewish masses of Poland. By this time, FDR had sent a strong message to Sumner Welles in the State Department. He wanted information about "places for Jewish colonization in any part of the world." Roosevelt's hopes regarding Jewish emigration to Palestine were crumbling due to imminent changes in British policy. By the middle of January, FDR's optimism had yielded to a darker insight. "Acute as the German [Jewish] problem is," he wrote, "it is, I fear, only a precursor of what may be expected if the larger problem is not met before it reaches an acute stage and indications are rapidly increasing that such a stage may be reached in the near future."

From Prague, the State Department received an urgent dispatch predicting the imminent seizure by the Germans of Bohemia and Moravia. This action would place 300,000 more Jews in jeopardy.[12] Roosevelt had become a sad prophet of the Holocaust, just as Hitler prepared to unleash his full fury.

Two weeks later, Sumner Welles sent the president a thick portfolio containing Nazi press reaction to FDR's protests. Vicious, almost pornographic in tone, it only fortified Roosevelt's sense of outrage. Historians would do well to examine this press, for it reveals a manic fear of the man in the White House, along with occasional (and astonishing) insights into FDR's intentions and tactics. The *Völkischer Beobachter,* for instance, described the Roosevelt clique as the product of "the criminal breeding place of American slums and East European ghettos." It predicted that FDR would create a war scare, so as to ensure his reelection in 1940. According to *Der Stürmer*, Julius Streicher's pornographic Jew-hating "newspaper," Roosevelt "fights for the interests of the Jews." *Der Angriff* called Roosevelt a warmonger, strongly hinting at a connection between the Jews, FDR's polio, and his foreign policy. Newspapers accused the president (a bit prematurely) of forging an anti-German alliance. He was thus the "Enemy of Peace Number One."[13]

In 1938, between seventy-one and eighty-five percent of the American public consistently opposed increasing national immigration quotas. Sixty-seven percent of those polls wanted refugees kept out of the United States, period. Early in 1939, sixty-six percent objected to one-time admission of ten thousand refugee children outside regular quotas. A bill to admit twenty thousand such children died in the Congress, and Roosevelt did not lift a finger on its behalf. It is hard for us to imagine that such attitudes once prevailed in the United States.

Bigotry and hard-heartedness had evolved into a national policy. These attitudes reflected anti-Semitism, fear of job loss through competition with new immigrants, concern about alien ideologies and spies sneaking in, and anxiety about padding the relief rolls and further taxing the citizenry. Shame over the failure to admit the Jews (and the subsequent Holocaust) would make possible the admission of Cubans, Vietnamese, and many other refugees in a later era.[14]

But throughout the winter of 1938–1939, many people denounced the "refu-jews," while Roosevelt did nothing to change the fundamental rules on immigration quotas. In the spring, in a move that confirmed Roosevelt's fears, the British Government chose to appease Arab opponents of Zionist immigration. Chamberlain's "White Paper" on the subject infuriated FDR, but he put other considerations before this one, and confined his protests to private correspondence.[15]

FDR had failed to end the Great Depression, for nine million people still lacked jobs. Roosevelt's grip on domestic politics was slipping. Now, Roosevelt had finally found a moral and intellectual challenge worthy of his gifts and his ego. Moved by Hitler's recent atrocities against Jews, and fearful of his hegemonic designs, Roosevelt was searching for a new, global role for a rearmed America. FDR consulted ever more frequently with two of his most useful ambassadors, Biddle in Warsaw and Bullitt in Paris.

Three weeks after the Munich Conference, President Roosevelt sat in his study in Hyde Park, carefully reading yet another alarming message from Ambassador Biddle. The envoy to Poland warned that more appeasement could drive the independent states of Eastern Europe into the German camp. Roosevelt passed the memorandum on to Secretary of State Hull, suggesting that he study it carefully.[16] A few days later, the president launched his first public attack on appeasement, for, he said, the idea of peace based upon fear "has no higher or more enduring quality than peace by the sword." Calling for national unity, the president declared that the United States "faced the possibility of an attack on the Atlantic side in both the Northern and Southern Hemisphere. . . ." This was hardly the case, but Roosevelt believed that the German bid for European hegemony mandated the use of scare tactics. Roosevelt now called for dramatic increases in airplane production, and predicted that the emergency defense needs would require a 300,000,000 dollar budget. Roosevelt had tried to calm fears in 1933; now he provoked them. Fear had helped to save the Union during the Civil War; Wilson had used the fear of German U-boats in his campaign for preparedness.[17] FDR well understood the value of national anxiety.

Early in December, FDR delivered an important message. Speaking at the University of North Carolina at Chapel Hill, Roosevelt began to outline his vision of what was in effect a *postwar* world. "What I am talking about," he said, "is that all of our young people in my section of the country and in every other section think that we are 'going places.' " "We are," Roosevelt declared, "not only the largest and most powerful democracy in the whole world, but many other democracies look to us for leadership in order that world democracy may survive." If survival was at stake, and America was the leader, and if survival meant winning a war, certain conclusions could be drawn. Roosevelt did not spell them out, and few saw through his verbiage. People were, however, beginning to rethink the old truths about intervention and isolation, and this reconsideration would help Roosevelt in his quest for a new policy for new times. Latin America was a good place to begin, because that was in "our backyard." Roosevelt moved warily in Europe, but more boldly in the Western hemisphere.

Roosevelt offered an example of his new interventionist leadership in Lima, Peru. At the Pan-American conference, the American republics almost concluded a collective security pact. Only the objections of Argentina prevented this from occurring. Despite this obstruction, the conferees unanimously passed a strong resolution committing them to resist foreign intervention, promote solidarity, and consult in the event of outside aggression against any American republic.[18] A few months later, Brazil received a credit of nineteen million dollars from the United States. This modest beginning inaugurated a time when strategic considerations and the promotion of American exports would take precedence over more mundane considerations. American bondholders were not happy, for Brazil was in default to them.[19]

In Britain, Oliver Harvey noted in his diary that a firmer British policy toward Hitler, if it evolved, would owe much to "the increasing interest and concern with which Roosevelt and U.S.A. are following world affairs . . ."[20] Harvey, counsellor and principal private secretary to the secretary of state for foreign affairs, was a man of some influence and a vehement antiappeaser. He now looked to FDR for the leadership he did not detect at 10 Downing Street. Roosevelt was carefully studying the increasingly agitated messages from Ambassador Bill Bullitt, with whom he had recently conferred. FDR learned from Ambassador Biddle that Chamberlain and Hitler "were at frequent intervals in touch with each other," hardly a comforting thought.[21]

The great Virginia historian Douglas Southall Freeman, referring to the coincidence that both Hitlerism and the Roosevelt administration had come to power at about the same time, made an important observation. Writing to Roosevelt's secretary, Marvin H. McIntyre, Freeman declared, "The future of the world may depend on the triumph of one force over the other."[22] The president received an encouraging message from British economist Harold J. Laski. "I do want you to know," he wrote, "that there are many, like myself, who though not American, look to you for that lead to the democratic peoples upon which, in these next years, the fate of civilization depends."[23] From Richmond to London, from Warsaw to Paris, important individuals of differing political views were beginning to see Roosevelt as a kind of democratic messiah, the one leader who could convince others to say to Hitler, "Thus far, but no farther."

In a message to Congress delivered on 4 January, the president offered some important clues to his thinking. "[I]t has become increasingly clear," he declared, "that peace is not assured.[24] Without naming the trouble-makers, Roosevelt offered a chilling vision to the legislators. He foresaw the day when "the new philosophies of force" might invade the North American continent."[25] Given the precarious state of the American armed forces (particularly of the army), FDR urged rearmament.

In Britain, Oliver Harvey described Roosevelt's message as "splendid," and the "best news we have yet had." He called the president "the real spokesman of democracy."[26] Franklin D. Roosevelt, whose personality contained messianic elements, could not fail to be pleased. Yet the strain would be great. Suffering from an enlarged heart, the fifty-seven-year-old president could only walk for a few feet at a time, supported by another man's arm, while leaning on a cane. He suffered from circulatory problems, hemorrhoids, and constant nasal infections, colds, and flus. Indeed, the president had a mild heart attack a year later. At times he had trouble sleeping, and would read a novel to calm his mind. By and large, however, Roosevelt remained vigorous for most of the time, until the spring of 1944. He looked fit and healthy until he reached the age of sixty-one.[27]

Despite his indomitable will, Roosevelt knew that he lacked one important thing: a great amount of time. Certainly, the genocidal fury of *Kristallnacht* and the threatening nature of the Hitler regime had convinced the president of the need to halt, then crush, the Nazi state. He hoped to help, while others carried out this task of annihilation. If Europeans wished to believe that America would become involved and opposed Hitler based on that belief, this did not unduly bother the president.

Roosevelt's increased anti-Nazi militancy encouraged some of his admirers to pen responses to the defeatism embraced by the likes of Dulles and Carr. An article of some importance (and great length) appeared in the January issue of the influential journal *Foreign Affairs*. Written by editor Hamilton Fish Armstrong, "Armistice at Munich" predicted that appeasement would fail, that there would be war.[28] The president was more cautious about fleshing out his vision. Though he believed that there would be war, he was not prepared to say so with certainty in public.[29] Even less was FDR willing to admit that the United States would enter that war.

Roosevelt wished to change public opinion, not become its latest victim. Thus, when a press report ascribed to him words such as "the

American frontier is on the Rhine," Roosevelt would describe the leak as a lie. Testing public opinion, and preparing it for a changing policy, Roosevelt refused to give his enemies more ammunition. When he met with Bullitt in January, for example, he assured reporters that the discussion was "[j]ust one of the continuous conferences."[30]

Roosevelt was inaugurating a new era in American foreign policy. Upon his return to Europe William Bullitt embarked upon a mission intended to bring about an anti-Hitler military alliance. This extraordinary commitment represented a total (as yet, private) rejection of Chamberlain's leadership, at a time when appeasement was still the order of the day.

CHAPTER
TWENTY

"GREAT VEHEMENCE AND STRONG HATRED": FDR'S BUDDING WAR PLANS

EVEN BEFORE THE end of 1938, Ambassador William Bullitt had spoken with "great vehemence and strong hatred" on the subject of Germany. He went so far as to declare that in the end only a war could halt the "insane expansion of Germany." Bullitt, going far beyond his mission as ambassador to France, predicted that the *United States*, France, and England would have to arm themselves to the teeth in order to confront Germany. Bullitt expressed these thoughts to Polish ambassador Count Jerzy Potocki in the afterglow of Munich, when relations between Poland and the Reich were still outwardly friendly.[1]

Bullitt went further. He promised Potocki that America would involve herself in the future conflict if and when Britain and France bestirred themselves to take action. Two months later, Potocki spoke again with Bullitt. Emphasizing America's "colossal" rearmament, Bullitt described Roosevelt as determined to end the policy of compromise with totalitarian regimes. America, he said, was abandoning isolation, and would align herself with England and France in the event of war.[2] A few weeks later, Jules Lukasiewicz, ambassador to Paris, spoke with Bullitt. The American diplomat again guaranteed U.S. intervention. "If a war should break out," said Bullitt, "we will certainly not take part in the beginning, but we will end it."[3] Of course, Bullitt added, American public opinion would not permit an active (i.e., armed) contribution to "a positive solution of European problems," but the United States would certainly try to prevent compromises (i.e., another Munich) on the part of Britain and France. Roosevelt and Bullitt were preparing the way for an anti-German coalition of encirclement.

And so it went throughout the year. An American ambassador, consulting frequently with Roosevelt, was working to establish a coalition that would wage war against Germany. Bullitt's "commitments" and predictions violated official American policy; their revelation would have caused severe problems for Roosevelt. Bullitt was making promises that he could not keep, but they changed the diplomatic mood in Europe.

Reports reaching Hitler indicated that Roosevelt was behind the firmer attitude of Germany's adversaries. This was true, but there was another side to FDR's activities. He understood that his interventionism, if not backed by a strong military, would fail to result in much of anything. Further, Roosevelt realized that the Neutrality Act, if not amended, could only encourage Hitler. Cautious about specifics, Roosevelt set about providing the nation with "defense" forces worthy of his bid for "leadership" of the democratic forces in the world. There was at the time no immediate threat to the United States from Germany, and Roosevelt knew this. In fact, FDR told some influential senators, "[W]e don't want to . . . frighten the American people at this time or any time," though that is precisely what he was doing. How else can one describe the president's view that Japan, Germany, and Italy were engaged in a "policy of world domination"? Of course, Roosevelt was an alarmist, but what else could he be? People needed to sense an *imminent* danger, for the public had a short span of attention, especially when it came to foreign affairs. Roosevelt was right about the threat in the long run, but he acted somewhat disingenuously about the short run. America, however, began to think about serious rearmament; public opinion began to change.

The fact is that Roosevelt wished to create a long-term threat *to* Germany, and that required a major military buildup. In order to obtain the rearmament appropriations he needed, Roosevelt conjured up a short-term threat from Germany. The French ambassador noted that Roosevelt's rearmament schemes had been "cleverly prepared by so-called secret alarmist declarations made by Messrs. Bullitt and

Kennedy. . . ." Certainly, the Nazi press reacted as if something important was afoot. Denouncing Roosevelt and other "hysterical internationalists," German newspapers called Roosevelt "another Professor Wilson," and "Wilson the Second."[4]

The president who did not discourage the "good man" Chamberlain from flying to Munich now decided that if America had rearmed "there would not have been any Munich." The man who eschewed "fear" tactics told a group of senators that Hitler contemplated a future attack on "Central and South America." "How far is it," the president then coyly asked, "from Yucatan to New Orleans or Houston?" If the source of all evil dominated Europe, one must wonder at FDR's conclusion, that "the last thing that this country should do is ever to send an army to Europe again."[5] This may not have been dishonest, however, in 1939.

Roosevelt was building his first coalition against Germany. The "Allies," if armed and supported by America, might crush Hitler in the event of war, or so Roosevelt thought. The British chiefs of staff were not so sure. The empire, they knew, was grossly unprepared for a major conflict. In a report to the cabinet, the chiefs argued, "The ultimate outcome of the conflict might well depend upon the intervention of other Powers, in particular of the United States of America." Even an appeaser like Foreign Secretary Lord Halifax looked more and more to Washington for clues to the future. The outbreak of war might well depend upon the attitude of Franklin D. Roosevelt.[6]

The Nazis now saw Roosevelt as the one man who could create an effective coalition against further German aggression. In late February, the German ambassador conversed with Lord Halifax, known to be sympathetic to German concerns in Central and Eastern Europe. He was extremely upset about Roosevelt's anti-German remarks, and concluded that "if France and Great Britain were involved in war, America would also join in . . ., not in two months, but in two days."[7]

Less than two months later, Roosevelt jolted the public by sending a message to Congress that contained a request for a supplemental defense appropriation of fifty million dollars. By April, he was speculating about an army of one million men, perhaps a sevenfold increase over the standing army in place at the time. Speaking off the record at a press conference, FDR tossed out a line calculated to change American thinking about war and peace. "I think," Roosevelt commented, "we want to keep out [of a new European war] but, on the other hand, I think we want to do everything we can to keep a survival of democracy."[8]

Bullitt's tone grew more alarmist. Writing from Paris, he predicted that Chamberlain might abandon France as he had Czechoslovakia. Playing upon FDR's Francophile sentiments and his disgust with Neville Chamberlain, Bullitt urged the president to put pressure upon the British prime minister. France, Bullitt promised, was now ready to fight, but it needed encouragement from Britain and the United States. Appealing to Roosevelt's imperial ambitions, Bullitt slyly hinted that aid to France might be linked to the establishment of American bases on French territory, in the Western Hemisphere. Premier Edouard Daladier, Bullitt continued, was enthusiastic about such a trade. Nothing came of this deal, for Roosevelt was uncertain about its political merit. A pattern had been set, however. A democracy in need of help would surrender some of its overseas territory to a wealthy friend anxious to expand—and to replace the decaying imperium with its own fiat. Daladier, uncertain about British support, clung to Bullitt (and, through him, to Roosevelt) like a drowning man.

Bill Bullitt was daring and cautious at the same time, a combination of qualities that appealed to FDR. Bullitt pressured Polish and French diplomats, urging them to resist German expansionism. He hinted at massive infusions of American aid and sometimes went even further. Bullitt would then issue a pious disclaimer, pointing to the limitations upon presidential power imposed by the Neutrality Act. He had no real sense of Roosevelt's broad designs, but the president himself had only begun to consider the implications of American resistance to the German bid for European hegemony.

Ambassador Lukasiewicz concluded in a dispatch to Warsaw, "President Roosevelt's policy will henceforth take the course of supporting France's resistance, checking German-Italian pressure, and weakening the British tendencies towards compromise." In Britain, Oliver Harvey felt that "the American attitude . . . in conjunction with our rearmament may be making their weight felt." The British, Polish, and French documents all confirm Roosevelt's vital role in the creation of an anti-Hitler front.

Roosevelt grew more impatient with British fecklessness. "What the British need today," he noted, "is a good stiff grog, inducing not only the desire to save civilization but the continued belief that they can do it."9 Ambassador Joseph P. Kennedy, by contrast, was "entirely in sympathy with, and a warm admirer of, everything the Prime Minister had done." German diplomats found Kennedy to be a congenial man, an appeaser who feared Soviet Russia and was apparently willing to give the German Reich a free hand in the East. Kennedy, however, was also an ambitious opportunist, anxious to save his diplomatic career. When pressure from Washington became intense, he was fully capable of reflecting the hard line pursued by Bullitt and Biddle. By March, Ambassador Kennedy was drawing Roosevelt's attention to the disastrous consequences for the United States of a British and French defeat.[10] He was preaching to the converted. More importantly, there was some sign that Chamberlain, thanks to Hitler's violation of the Munich accords, was paying more heed to Roosevelt's recent policy signals. On 17 March, in a speech delivered in Birmingham, the prime minister angrily denounced Hitler's violation of the Munich accords. Ambassador Bullitt gloated, "The invasion of Czechoslovakia ends definitely all possibility of diplomatic negotiations." The American diplomat George F. Kennan warned that Germany had plans for further expansion. In a personal note, he described Prague "as a wayside stop for the Germans on the way toward the east."[11]

Roosevelt, working closely with Bullitt, Biddle, and even Kennedy, was inspiring the creation of a new alliance system. After consulting with Under Secretary Sumner Welles, the president agreed to impose increased duties on German goods. The next day, Bullitt had a long talk with his Polish colleague. The Poles, fearing German aggression, received some consolation from the ambassador. He had just spoken with Daladier, Bullitt revealed, and "Poland could count on French military assistance if it was requested." Bullitt undertook the unusual step of meeting with the Polish foreign minister in Boulogne-sur-Mer.

The Polish ambassador believed that these firm American steps had affected Chamberlain. As the Manchester *Guardian* observed, "The United States is moving rapidly towards an affirmative foreign policy." What the *Guardian* did not know was that American ambassadors, guided by the president, were working to forge an anti-Hitler coalition. This would have been unthinkable a year earlier, and even now premature revelation would mightily upset many Americans.

Meanwhile, a sad British prime minister was offering assurances to a nervous Poland, emphasizing the importance Britain attached to "Polish independence." This guarantee did not, of course, preclude negotiations between the Poles and the Germans. The possibility of negotiations on the Munich model, which might lead to surrender, troubled Bullitt, Biddle, and Roosevelt. Chamberlain, who to his dying day believed in his appeasement policy, hoped to revive it by the guarantee to Poland, not bury it. The Poles, reassured by British support, would, the prime minister hoped, react favorably to any forthcoming German offer of bilateral negotiations.

Bullitt encouraged President Roosevelt in his public relations campaign. There was, the ambassador believed, a danger that a triumphant Nazi Germany would soon be ready to spring across the Atlantic. "You know this already," he told FDR, "and I apologize for repeating it. The important thing is that the people of the United States don't yet know it." Roosevelt began to move more quickly, as well as more deviously.[12] It was clear to the Poles and to the French that Roosevelt was attempting to forge some kind of anti-Hitler coalition, albeit without publicly committing himself to possible belligerency. He would not, indeed could not, save much of Central and Eastern Europe from temporary German domination, but he could, and belatedly did prepare the United States for a possible conflict with the Third Reich.

The president was positively jaunty as he prepared to leave Warm Springs after an Easter vacation. "I have had a fine holiday here with you," he remarked to his neighbors, adding, "I'll be back in the fall if we do not have a war."[13] Both Roosevelt and Bullitt now viewed war as preferable to further appeasement of Hitler. Bullitt reported with satisfaction that Daladier was "calm and determined" and that France's morale had risen. Kennedy, however, was straddling the issue. His motives were diverse. Jealous of Bullitt's access to Roosevelt, he also feared for his sons' lives in the event of war. In communications to the State Department, Kennedy appeared hopeful that the Poles, if threatened by Germany, would negotiate with Berlin. In his messages to FDR, however, Kennedy agreed that Chamberlain would have to resist German aggression.[14] FDR saw through Kennedy's double-dealing.

As if to confirm Roosevelt's prophetic comment about war, messages arrived from Berlin bearing grim news. The Germans, Secretary of State Hull learned, were confident that England would not guarantee the *existing frontiers* of Poland.[15] A high German officer bragged to the American military attaché that "the United States would [never] again . . . send troops to Europe because 8,000 out of every 10,000 would be lost."[16] Thanks to this kind of Nazi arrogance, Roosevelt was in a good political position. He was content to be seen as a man trying to deter aggression, not punish it. Hence he was delighted when the *Washington Post* published an editorial praising him for trying to prevent war. Yet Roosevelt's comments and actions during these months reveal a man who expected war, and *preferred* it to coexistence with a triumphant Greater German Reich.[17]

FDR continued to talk about lowering tariff barriers and opening all markets to trade and investment. Some have seen this as "appeasement" of Germany. There was no room, however, in Roosevelt's vision for "autarky," blocked currency accounts, and other devices used by the Reich. Because this system served the belligerent aims of the German leadership, its demise would have marked the end of Hitlerism. The Reich would never accept FDR's proposals. Perhaps that is why Roosevelt kept them alive into 1938. Now Roosevelt's language was becoming blunter, and more hostile.

On 14 April, FDR addressed a public note to Hitler and Mussolini, requesting that they pledge not to commit aggression against thirty-one specified countries. If the dictators behaved, so the note implied, negotiations dealing with access to markets, disarmament, frontier revision, and the expansion of trade might follow. Yet Roosevelt already knew that expansion was an essential part of the National Socialist program. Motives other than a desire to bring about conciliation drove him to send the insulting note. From Warsaw, Ambassador Tony Biddle had informed Secretary Hull that betrayal of the Poles would weaken the will to resist Germany among "other anti-aggression states."[18] FDR's message was not aimed at the dictators. He was really trying to encourage resistance to Hitler on the part of nations such as Poland. At the behest of Bullitt, Roosevelt again suggested to English contacts that his warning to the dictators would be taken more seriously if Britain reinstituted compulsory national military service.[19]

The stern note to the dictators encouraged antiappeasers in the British government. However reluctantly, Chamberlain endorsed FDR's message. At this point, Ambassador Kennedy sometimes sounded as if he represented Chamberlain rather than the United States government. In a move calculated to save the appeasement policy, Kennedy denounced "Polish intransigence." In a cable to Hull, he expressed the hope that the Poles would act "in a reasonable manner" in responding to German concerns regarding the free city of Danzig. Prime Minister Chamberlain, despite his friendly comments, continued to be skeptical about American intentions. As a man who had long scoffed at American rhetoric, Chamberlain viewed Roosevelt as a friend who urged him to act while sitting in a safe capital more than three thousand miles away. Until recently, Roosevelt had done little about the shameful state of the American army, which was nineteenth in size among the world's armed forces. Nor had this student of Admiral Mahan done much to create his vaunted "navy second to none."[20]

In the Reich chancellory in Berlin, however, Roosevelt's message had created a great disturbance. Germans over forty years of age held grim memories of American intervention in the last war. Hitler was reportedly planning a grand response to Roosevelt's challenge. That answer was aimed at the German people, and at the nations mentioned on Roosevelt's list.

For the first time since Woodrow Wilson had arrived in France, an American president was speaking for the West.

The president was in good form on the evening of 20 April. At a White House dinner for newspaper editors, presided over by his old Kansas friend William Allen White, FDR was charming and witty. He enjoyed a martini or two before dinner (though he preferred those he mixed himself), and puffed on cigarettes through his long, uptilted holder. The large, handsome head, often graced with a charming smile, the mellifluous voice, and the total self-confidence captivated the editors. Even hostile observers were taken with the man's commanding personality.

Eleanor Roosevelt understood that FDR's manipulative abilities rested upon his capacity for displaying different aspects of his persona. "[A] man like my husband," she wrote in *This I Remember* (1949), "who was particularly susceptible to people, took color from whomever he was with, giving to each one something different of himself. . . . [H]e made an effort to give each person who came in contact with him the feeling that he understood what his particular interest was." Mrs. Roosevelt left her story incomplete. What happened after "each person" had that feeling of being "understood"? There followed, of course, the point of the whole encounter: convincing the interlocutor that he must see the world through FDR's eyes. And so it was on that evening of 20 April.

At times, Roosevelt seemed to ramble, as he took his guests on a tour of world problems. Possessing a vast array of knowledge, both historical and geographical, Roosevelt shared a bit of his globalist thinking with his guests. He knew that many Americans asked, "What the hell difference does it [the global situation] make?" He bemoaned the fate of Ethiopia, a victim of fascist aggression. FDR wondered if one should apply the term "backward" to such nations, for Italy had certainly not acted in a civilized manner. After this criticism of European imperialism, the President referred obliquely to a German bid for world hegemony. He conjured up the nightmare of an attack on South America. FDR seemed to foresee a European war, but was careful to predict American nonintervention.

Mrs. Roosevelt's recollections throw light upon another FDR technique, the "off-the-record" bombshell. He would toss out shocking facts and viewpoints, knowing that they would appear in the print media. "There were times," Mrs. Roosevelt wrote, "when I felt that Franklin was indiscreet: he would recount things he had said to other people, or tell about something that had happened in a cabinet meeting perhaps; and he seemed to trust his guest never to repeat what they heard at his table. However, I came to realize that he had his own reasons for doing it—it was a way of testing people—that in any case he never told anything that could do real harm." Roosevelt's tour of world problems was not a way of testing people; it was a way of changing public opinion, by using the men and women of the press.

Roosevelt's off-the-record remarks were "background," of course, but the editors listened with mounting concern. Roosevelt's picture of totalitarian powers attacking the democracies, or even the Western Hemisphere, was not meant to reassure them.[21]

FDR's "peace note" enraged Hitler, who answered it with a display of public contempt on 28 April. Hitler's defiance was well-timed. The German embassy had reminded Berlin of the imminent expiration of the "cash and carry" clause in the 1937 Neutrality Act. After 1 May, unless Congress acted, friendly belligerent powers would not be able to buy raw materials, and other strategic products in the United States, even if they shipped them home in their own, or other non-American flagship vessels.[22] Roosevelt had done little to oppose or even modify the neutrality laws in 1935–1937; he now paid a price for his past policies. Americans were concerned about being dragged into another

European catastrophe, and Roosevelt had to be doubly careful, even as he created a more daring foreign policy.

Joseph Medill Patterson's New York *Daily News*, reminding FDR that he had not been elected "President of the World," deplored "the President's present foreign policy." Inconsistent and abrasive, the *News*'s editorialists lurched between support for Munich, criticism of British imperialism and German anti-Semitism, and praise for Roosevelt's peace messages. The *News* warned against intervention in European quarrels, and rejoiced that Hitler's caustic reply had brought the "debate" to an end.

Former President Hoover knew otherwise. He gravely warned, "The expressions of Ambassador Bullitt certainly warrant the European democracies in the belief that they may look to the United States for some sort of aid." He was right. Writing for the magazine *Liberty*, Hoover concluded soon after reading the Roosevelt challenge to the dictators, "These expressions are vague enough but at least indicate a radical departure from the categories of peaceful processes into the categories of force." Hoover sensed that the European democracies were coming to believe in the chimera of American aid. He was right here, too, for FDR, jarred by Crystal Night and Prague, had rejected the idea of coexistence with National Socialism. Roosevelt had finished with appeasement, but he would have to be careful before he openly abandoned all pretense of neutrality. [23]

Bullitt and Roosevelt continued to shore up Daladier's courage. On 4 May, the French government announced its firm commitment to the security of France. The language was strong and unyielding. [24] From Warsaw, however, Ambassador Biddle wired Washington that a Polish surrender to Germany would destroy the "antiaggression front." He was not so sanguine as Bullitt, though no less committed to anti-German diplomatic activity. [25]

The clever German chargé, Hans Thomsen, shared Herbert Hoover's concern about Roosevelt's designs. Like Hoover, he wished to prevent the president from intervening against the Axis powers. Earlier than most observers, Thomsen understood Roosevelt's short-term intentions. "[After] the outbreak of war," he predicted, "Roosevelt personally will endeavor to come to the aid of our opponents as quickly as possible with the full *moral* weight of the United States, by creating the conditions for, and by a skillful timing of, the entry into the war on their side." In an extraordinary prophecy, Thomsen foresaw that "Roosevelt will not neglect the possibility that as Supreme Commander of the Armed Forces he has the power to issue orders, which in the course of their execution might lead to the creation of a state of war. In the face of this, Congress is powerless." Roosevelt, he believed, had a "pathological hatred for the leaders of Germany and Italy." The chargé even predicted that Roosevelt, in order to further his foreign policy goals, might seek an unprecedented third term as president.[26]

For the thousands of Americans affiliated with groups on the far right, the situation was growing ominous. Roosevelt's more aggressive anti-Nazism, along with his ability to manipulate public opinion, threatened to place these anti-interventionists in an impossible situation. Roosevelt would try to paint extreme rightists and Bundists as traitors, beholden to a foreign power. Yet to some of these men, FDR's new interventionism represented an opportunity. They could now manipulate a popular issue, American neutrality in any future war. That issue could be used to forge new coalitions with mainstream anti-interventionist groups.

Could a combination of isolation, neutrality, anti-Semitism, Anglophobia, and Roosevelt-hatred derail the president's new direction in foreign policy?

As the international crisis grew, anti-Semites attacked the Jews for pushing America toward war. (Credit: National Archives)

America stopped and listened when Winchell, who hated the Bund, took to the airwaves: "Good evening, Mr. and Mrs. America, and all the ships at sea!" (Credit: MOMA Film Stills Archives)

Hermann Schwinn speaking at a California
rally, two days after the 1939 Madison Square
Garden event. (Credit: *Los Angeles Examiner*)

Publicity poster for the great "True Americanism" rally sponsored by the Bund. A heroic
figure, modeled on Nazi sculpture, grips an
American shield, ready to slay the bolshevik
(Jewish) dragon. (Credit: National Archives)

MASS-
DEMONSTRATION
FOR TRUE
AMERICANISM
FEB. 20TH 1939
MADISON SQUARE
GARDEN GERMAN AMERICAN BUND

Farewell to Fritz Kuhn. Convicted of grand larceny and forgery, the *bundesführer* prepares for Sing Sing Prison. (Credit: Wiener Library)

Junges Volk

Zeitschrift der Jugendschaft des Amerikadeutschen Volksbundes

Jahrgang 5, Folge 2.   Hornung (Februar) 1939.   Preis 10c.

German Blood Our Pride –

A Better America Our Goal!

ABRAHAM LINCOLN † 15. April 1865

HORST WESSEL † 23. Februar 1930

Beide starben für die Zukunft Ihres Volkes!

In its rush to Americanize the Bund's image, the group's leadership made some extraordinary comparisons. Here Horst Wessel, the murdered Nazi "martyr," is compared to Abraham Lincoln, because both men "died for the future of their nation!" (Credit: National Archives)

The scene outside Madison Square Garden on 20 February 1939. The police kept incidents like this one to a minimum. (Credit: Wiener Library)

An infamous scene at the rally. Bundists and their friends pledge allegiance to the United States in Madison Square Garden. (Credit: Bundesarchiv)

O.D.-Männer (Bundist defense
forces) maintain discipline at the
Washington Day rally.
(Credit: National Archives)

A camp of the German-American
Bund. Widely read reports
indicated that Bundists were
preparing for an armed uprising in
conjunction with a Nazi attack on
America. (Credit: Wiener
Library)

Edward G. Robinson and Dana Andrews in *Confessions of a Nazi Spy*. The script was based upon Leon G. Turrou's recent best-seller *Nazi Spies in America*. (Credit: MOMA Film Stills Division)

A "Bund" leader portrayed in *Confessions of a Nazi Spy* talks of how "we" will reclaim "unser Amerika" (our America). (Credit: MOMA Film Stills Division)

Roosevelt and the press. Harry Hopkins is on his right.
(Credit: Library of Congress)

Roosevelt meets King George VI at Union Station, Washington. They then proceeded to the White House. (Credit: FDR Library/Associated Press)

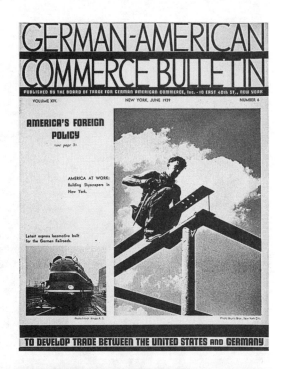

The *Bulletin* published the words of anti-interventionist American executives. It also obtained badly needed hard currency for the Reich by printing advertisements touting the wares of major U.S. corporations, such as Greyhound. (Credit: National Archives)

Joseph P. Kennedy and FDR after the Boston millionaire was sworn in as ambassador to Great Britain. (Credit: FDR Library)

Ambassador William Bullitt in France during the summer of 1938.
(Credit: FDR Library)

Ambassador to Poland Anthony J. Drexel Biddle, Jr. (center), watches the outbreak of World War II. The Germans are bombing Warsaw. (Credit: FDR Library)

CHAPTER
TWENTY-ONE

"KEEP AMERICA OUT OF THE
JEWISH WAR!"

O N 15 DECEMBER 1938, after the Munich "peace" and the Martian
"invasion," the largest circulation daily in the United States devoted fifteen columns to another big story. Doris Fleeson and John
O'Donnell, two top columnist/reporters of the New York *Daily News*,
told the public about a congressional investigation of anti-Semitism
under the headline "NEW DEAL PROBES ANTI-SEMITIC DRIVE
ON NEW CONGRESS."

In the first sentence of the article, readers learned that "New Deal
circles" were upset about a pamphlet uncovered by congressional investigators. The brochure, distributed by Pelley Publishers, was entitled
"Jews in Our Government." Then, in a move extraordinary even by the
standards of tabloid journalism, the newspaper proceeded to list every
one of the 275 "Jews" exposed by Pelley's research, although many of
the persons named were not even Jewish. The effect of the article was to
reinforce an impression common among many Americans—that the
New Deal was rife with Jews. If the Jews were to blame for the New
Deal, what charge would Roosevelt-haters hurl at them next?

On the very next day, the *News* editorialized that the Bill of Rights

255

"does *not* mean that Americans are forbidden to dislike other Americans
or religions or any other group. Plenty of people just now are exercising
their right to dislike the Jews." The Nazi press cited the *News* article,
gloating about the rise of American anti-Semitism. "Judah Rules America," declared the Nazis, for there were "62,000 Jews in the Administration of the United States."[1]

The polls were quite encouraging to Jew-haters. A survey undertaken
in March 1938, at the time of Hitler's conquest of Austria, showed that
forty-one percent of those responding believed the following statement:
"[T]he Jews have too much power in the United States." "Power" most
often meant financial and commercial control, in addition to domination
of the entertainment industry. One-quarter of those who believed this
felt that Jews should be kept out of "government and politics," while
one-fifth favored expelling Jews from the United States. Nineteen
percent of those fearing Jewish influence said they would support an
anti-Semitic campaign.[2]

In 1938, one-third of the American people believed that Jews were
more radical than other Americans, while almost twice as many polled
respondents found Jews undesirable in a number of ways. Unpleasant
qualities included greed, dishonesty, aggressiveness, clannishness, and
selfishness. Two years later, almost a third of those questioned favored
measures intended to "reduce" the power of the Jews. Nor were characteristics seen as "positive" devoid of anti-Jewish overtones. Two-thirds
of the respondents found admirable qualities in Jews, among them
business ability, ambition, intellect, and racial loyalty.[3]

Added to traditional Christian prejudices was a powerful accusation,
that of *warmongering*. A greater number of anti-Jewish organizations
sprang up in 1938 than in any other year in American history. Some were
fringe groups; others had substantial followings. Combined with the
aftershocks engendered by the recent recession, fears about a new war
created a jumpy, paranoid public mood. New kinds of weapons of mass
destruction, recently employed in Spain and China, contributed to the
sense of imminent catastrophe. Many Americans who were no better off
in 1939 than in 1932—and there were many—were heeding the words
of anti-Jewish rabble-rousers.[4] In their ranks were numbers of Irish-
Americans who listened to the radio addresses of Father Coughlin and
read *Social Justice*, which was beginning to sound like the Nazi *Der
Angriff.*

Roosevelt's hostile reaction to *Reichskristallnacht* troubled many Amer-

ANTI-JEWISH SENTIMENT IN THE 1930S

July 1939

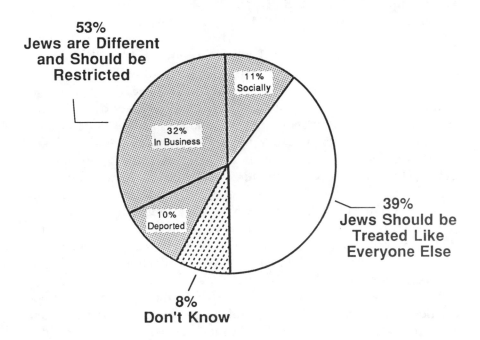

53%
Jews are Different
and Should be
Restricted

11%
Socially

32%
In Business

10%
Deported

39%
Jews Should be
Treated Like
Everyone Else

8%
Don't Know

Source: Roper

icans, as did his growing opposition to Hitler's expansionism. Mail to the White House and to the press reflected some of this ire. One "fed up American gentile" cabled a reminder to F.D.R.: "You seem to forget that genuine American gentiles . . . are completely unheard because we are unable to speak over our Jewish-controlled press, radio, and newsreel." The general manager of an Ohio manufacturing company, voicing the complaint of many small businessmen, asked why "aren't we just as good as the Jews?"[5]

The fascist right had a new cause: opposition to FDR's meddling in European affairs. The threat of intervention, cried anti-Semites, was the work of Roosevelt and his Jews. Robert E. Edmondson, publisher of the "Anti-Jewish Patriotic Bulletins," declared after Munich, "Hitler Wins the Peace, Red Jewry Loses the War." The respite was a temporary one, as new crises grabbed ever more shocking headlines. After having lambasted the "U.S. Jewish F.D.R. Brain Trust" for years, Edmondson now claimed, "World Jewry Plans Stock Exchange War."

Representative John E. Rankin of Mississippi, along with other anti-Semites among his congressional colleagues, grew bolder. "Wall Street and a little group of our international Jewish brethren," Rankin charged, planned to take the United States into the next European war. Commentator Walter Winchell had once called the lower body of Congress "the House of Reprehensibles." Rankin responded by describing the famous commentator and tabloid columnist as "a little slime-mongering kike." The congressman accused Winchell of hiding his real name, which he said was "Lipschitz." (His real name was Winchel.) Some years later, Harry Hopkins, Roosevelt's closest associate, paid tribute to Walter Winchell: "You really fought against Hitler when it was none too popular and I think you deserve all the credit in the world for it."[6] Roosevelt had cultivated Winchell for many years, and the courtship bore fruit. Few other journalists of Winchell's fame were willing to lock horns publicly with anti-Semites.

Among those who despised Winchell was the radio priest Father Charles E. Coughlin. This powerful orator sounded reasonable and even kindly, at least on the radio. At mass rallies, however, Coughlin waved his arms in histrionic gestures, and allowed his voice to rise and fall in dramatic fashion. Coughlin's attacks against the Jews cost him a small part of his radio audience, but millions (estimates varied) of other troubled Americans continued to heed his call. Surveys indicated that of the fifteen million people who sometimes listened to Coughlin's broadcasts, three and a half million were regular listeners. Polls showed that two-thirds of the loyalists and one-third of the "occasionals" approved of the radio priest's message. He continued to claim around nine million followers. The Jews, Coughlin inwardly believed, were Christ-killers and Christ-rejecters. Earlier, Father Coughlin had offered hope, social justice, and a voice for the "little guy." Now he peddled fear, conspiracy theories, and hatred. A large, imposing figure who could dominate a speaker's platform without opening his mouth, Coughlin spotted a new opportunity.

In the summer of 1938, Father Coughlin's newspaper *Social Justice* reprinted the *Protocols of the Elders of Zion*. The *Brooklyn Tablet*, an influential weekly published by the archdiocese and a Coughlin ally, linked Roosevelt to growing world tensions: "[In] the present crisis in Germany, the Jews in America have overreached themselves. They have corralled everyone from the President down to plead their case." The archdiocese was pandering to working-class and lower middle-class families disturbed by the rise to prominence of a better educated, Jewish middle-class. Tammany Hall was in decline; many jobs created by the New Deal were dispensed based on education and merit, rather than patronage. To the *Tablet*'s readers, the New Deal had mainly benefited the Jews.

Because of the Jews, many reasoned, FDR was spoiling for a fight with Germany on behalf of Britain, a nation which had starved millions of Irish to death during the great Potato Famine of the 1840s. *Social Justice* denounced the boycott of German goods, while attacking the Jews for their egotistical emphasis upon the persecution of their brethren. Coughlin viewed the persecutions as an "internal matter" for the Germans to solve. Many of Coughlin's devoted followers, often aging, disillusioned people uprooted by recent disasters, could not understand why people hated him so. He was not, some of them said, "anti-Semitic." Rather, he was "anti-Jewish," meaning that he opposed the "Jew bankers." And what was wrong with that?[7]

Father Coughlin found one Englishman to his liking. He described Prime Minister Chamberlain as "one of the most outstanding statesmen in the history of the British Empire." He was certainly preferable to FDR, for, as *Social Justice* announced, "PRESIDENT ROOSEVELT WANTS WAR FOR U.S.!" Soon, *Social Justice* demanded that Congress "Impeach Roosevelt!" Coughlin railed against talk of repealing the arms embargo, calling Roosevelt a "power-mad dictator who would place upon his own brow the crown of World Messiah." *Social Justice* described aid to England as a measure that would "substitute Karl Marx for George Washington."[8]

The Germans lavished great praise upon the radio priest. "Father Coughlin Does Not Remain Silent," declared the *Völkischer Beobachter.* The German press described Coughlin (who usually ignored anti-Catholic persecutions by the Nazis) as "America's most powerful radio commentator," and a man with "thirty million listeners." Leo T. Reardon, a confidant of Coughlin, visited Foreign Minister Joachim von Ribbentrop. As he prepared to leave, his host had a request for Reardon:

"Give my regards to Father Coughlin. I have a high regard for him."
Encouraged by incoming dispatches, Ribbentrop predicted that "there
would be anti-Semitic outbursts in America in the future. . . . " The
Nazis had found their favorite priest. "The American people," *Social
Justice* proclaimed, were being mesmerized by "British gold and Jewish
propaganda." Who were the real warmongers? *Social Justice* discovered
that "70 percent are from the Eastern states and 45 percent come from
New York City."[9]

Coughlin's followers tried to portray themselves as martyrs, fighting
for the true faith. One Coughlinite trick involved a cute, red-haired,
freckled little boy with bright blue eyes. There he stood, selling copies
of *Social Justice* on a city street corner. Suddenly, passersby would hear
him crying and screaming, his newspapers strewn on the sidewalk.
They would rush over to ask the little boy why he was in trouble.
Through his tears, he spat out the pitiful words, "A big Jew hit
me!" The concerned citizens would walk away, shaking their heads at
the cruel tactics of Roosevelt's friends. After they had departed, the
little boy would pick up his newspapers and choose another street
corner. A few minutes later, he would go through the same tragic
routine, as his supervisor watched in silent approval.[10]

Coughlin's appeal to anti-Semitism struck some of his listeners as
a call for righteous violence. Unemployed workers, drifters, and psy-
chotics were never in short supply, and an anti-Jewish message tended to
bring them into action. Some of those who answered the call joined the
Coughlin-sponsored Christian Front. Union members wary of Red subversion, Irish-Americans who hated the Jews, drifters and drunks looking for action—they filled the ranks of the new organization. These men
saw themselves as fighters in a holy war. By citing Coughlin, they could
justify violence while calling themselves good Catholics. Members of
the Christian Front entered training, looking forward to the day when a
Christian "Aryan" Army would take over the United States.

Like other fascist groups, the Christian Front found it hard to cooperate with rival organizations. One member expressed his view of Pelley
in this manner, "Pelley! That old goat ain't got a thing. We've got real
men—guys with guts." "Having guts" meant acquiring guns, bombs,
and plans for an armed uprising. Christian Fronters screamed for Jewish
blood, praised Hitler, and cheered speakers who asked, "Is this America? Who runs this country, the Americans or the internationalist Jews?"
Street fights with Jews and other antifascists became common. Rumors

surfaced alleging that four hundred New York City policemen were members of the front. The press, federal agents, and antifascist organizers paid closer attention to the organization. Hoodlums belonging to the front often appeared in court, and in the newspapers.

His encouragement of the front was costing the priest dearly, for local radio stations were receiving numerous protests from citizens and advertisers against the broadcast of Coughlin's programs. Coughlin began to equivocate, backing away from his unstinting support of these good Christian men. Fearing archdiocesan disapproval, Coughlin was less than forthright in avowing, "I am neither the organizer nor the sponsor of the Christian Front. . . ."

Given the growing fear of Germany, Coughlin's embrace of fascism played into Roosevelt's hands. FDR's drive for rearmament and diplomatic interventionism, though controversial, distracted people from the failures of the New Deal, including the recent recession. Administration sources, leaking stories about Coughlin's ties to Berlin, ascribed anti-interventionist propaganda to subversive motivation. This equation of anti-Semitic activism with near treason became one of President Roosevelt's staple tactics.

Articulate and dangerous cranks swelled the ranks of the anti-Jewish forces, as they had done in Germany. A group calling itself The "Mothers' and Children's Protective Union" accused FDR of causing the insanity of almost 742,000 syphilitic war veterans. Of course, the group explained, this was logical, for the president himself owed his paralysis "to his own misconduct." One Mrs. Schuyler, a Daughter of the American Revolution, revealed that Pope Pius XI was a Jew controlled by international bankers holding a fifteen million dollar mortgage on the Vatican. The same lady discovered that a letter published in the *New York Sun* contained an occult message intended for the Jews.

Paul Castorina, a New York fascist, became a major advocate of the anti-Jewish line. His newspaper, *The Blackshirt*, recounted stories making the rounds from coast to coast. Here is one of them:

> A man tries to board a crowded bus. The conductor, following regulations, politely requests that the passenger await the next bus.
> The irate commuter responds with the question, "Do you know who I am?"

To which the conductor replies, "No."
"I am the Chief Rabbi," says the angry man.
The conductor answers, "I don't care if you are the Chief Pop-Eye,
you're not boarding this bus."

The story ends with on a cautionary note, "The wheels work fast.
Now there is another conductor waiting to get his job back."[11]

The anti-Jewish message was usually a variation on the same old
themes. The Jews had it better. The Jews controlled Roosevelt and the
media. Working out of his enlarged Munich office, Rolf Hoffmann
quickly spotted propaganda potential for Germany's battle on behalf of
American isolationism. His contact E. J. Smythe, head of the Protestant
War Veterans of the United States, was working for the political demise
of "Roosevelt and his JEW Communistic advisors." Smythe provided
the Germans with material used in anti-Semitic propaganda: "Usary
[sic] here in New York City which is owned Lock, Stock, and barrell by
the jews is the order of the day. . . ."[12] Smythe was a crackpot, heading
a fringe group. Other sympathizers had contacts at the highest level of
American society.

German agents and Nazi propagandists kept careful files on General
George Van Horn Moseley, last seen campaigning fruitlessly for appointment as army chief of staff. Sixty-four-years-old and on the eve of
retirement, Moseley was more bitter and cranky than ever. He advocated the sterilization of refugees, so that "we can properly protect our
future." Moseley's future was an authoritarian version of America's past.
He, like his followers, longed for a lost world of small towns and thriving
farms that had been destroyed by a New Deal beholden to labor unions,
big city bosses, and Jews.

Late in 1938, the general retired and could now speak out more
frankly. In his farewell address, Moseley warned Americans against
moral decay, government spending, and communism. He omitted mention of the dangers represented by Hitler or the Japanese, and warned
the citizenry against an "un-American" dictatorship based upon New
Deal doctrines and presidential power. The speech would prove to be
moderate by Moseley's standards, a kind of swan song for the right-wing
ideology formerly preached by the Liberty League. Nevertheless, some

in the administration were appalled. Secretary of War Harry H. Wood-ring issued a statement blasting Moseley for being "flagrantly disloyal" out of disappointment over his failure to gain appointment as chief of staff.[13] Former President Herbert Hoover, whom Moseley had served in 1929–1933, soon placed the general in his pantheon of citizens working to save the republic from collectivism and worse. Moseley continued to believe that his service to Hoover had been held against him by the vindictive, Jew-controlled Roosevelt administration.

Consumed by political ambition, the general delivered a widely publicized address in Indianapolis. His audience cheered as Moseley denounced gun control and labor unions, while praising the Japanese for their work in controlling bolshevism in the Far East. The British, ac-cording to Moseley, would "ditch us at the first crossroad, if it served their selfish purpose to do so." The general was receiving a pension of six thousand dollars a year as an inactive officer, but this did not prevent him from advocating the protection of "our rights with force should it become necessary."[14] Though a rambling speaker, Moseley was in great demand among conservative groups. The general had some kind words for the Republicans, for he was thinking ahead to presidential politics in 1940. Moseley was coming to the attention of important, anti-Roosevelt organizations. The New York Board of Trade invited him to speak on 14 December.

While Moseley awaited the call to save his country, American fascists rallied to him. James True, the inventor of the "Kike-killer" club, saw Moseley as presidential timber. George Deatherage called the general "the most square-shooting patriotic American it has ever been my privilege to know. . . ." He vowed to unite eight hundred fascist groups in support of Moseley, who would become head of the new, "national Christian" organization.[15] Moseley was ambitious, however, and he stayed aloof from the fringe movements.

The general had attracted Deatherage's attention with his recent attacks on the Jews. Speaking before the Women's National Defense Committee of Philadelphia, which represented seventy patriotic groups, Moseley excoriated "Jews, Communists, and the White House," while praising American fascists and Nazis for working to "neutralize the effects of communism." Representative James E. Van Zandt had sent his "regrets," while several men in uniform left the hall as Moseley commenced his speech. The Pennsylvania American Legion commander called upon the groups involved to disavow Moseley. Nevertheless, congratulatory messages poured in to the general's suite in the Atlanta-Biltmore Hotel, his "office."[16]

The general filed everything written to or about himself. Lovingly, he pasted columns in thick scrapbooks, sometimes writing lengthy annotations in the margins. Moseley was convinced that his hour was about to strike. Those who viewed him as a bitter, aging crank would be in for a surprise, or so he thought.

Van Horn Moseley, after all, was saying what a lot of people on the respectable right were thinking. They knew that Eleanor was a "Nigger lover," and Franklin "Rosenfeld" was surrounded by "Kikes," but it was not smart to say so openly. A screaming headline in the Communist *Daily Worker* convinced Moseley that he had struck a nerve: "MOSELEY, TRAITOR GENERAL, NOMINATED BY FASCISTS TO BE THE AMERICAN HITLER."[17] The attention of the Reds proved to Moseley that he was on the right track. A know-it-all who believed in conspiracy theories, Moseley was a man of intense bigotry and racism who preyed upon American fears of the unknown, of foreigners, of Jews. That he could be taken seriously for so long is a commentary on the anxieties felt by many of his fellow citizens.

Chicago Tribune editorial writer Tiffany Blake, alarmed by Moseley's success, told the general that anti-Semitism was "hurtful to [the] American welfare." Moseley always had time for an ideological diatribe, and Blake received a long letter, a kind of condensed *Mein Kampf.* Bragging about his longtime study of the "problem of the Jew," Moseley predicted a "pogrom in the United States." He claimed to have Jewish acquaintances, who provided him with proof of Jewish internationalist treachery. Moseley claimed these Jews had documented their plot to establish a secret, Jewish government, supported by "Jewish money from New York City."

General Moseley had plenty of support when he denounced Senator Wagner (Democrat of New York) for proposing that ten thousand refugee children from Germany and Austria be issued special visas. President Roosevelt refused to support this unpopular measure, though he did not interfere with Eleanor's endorsement of the idea. Opponents of the Wagner bill included a large number of anti-Semites, like the Philadelphia man who accused the Jews of controlling the media, and making "millions" during the Depression. Other letter writers informed

EVIDENCE OF RELUCTANCE TO HELP

1938

"We should not allow a larger number of Jewish exiles from Germany into the U.S."

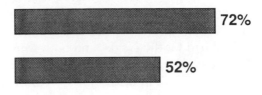 72%

"Our goverment should not contribute money to help Jewish and Catholic exiles from Germany settle in other lands."

52%

1939

"Oppose permitting 10,000 refugee children from Germany into the U.S."

 67%

"Oppose permitting 10,000 refugee children from Germany --mostly Jewish--into the U.S."

 61%

1946

"Oppose allowing more Jewish and other European refugees to live in the U.S."

72%

1947

"Oppose taking Poles, Jews and other displaced persons into the U.S."

59%

Compared to the Present:

1984

"Jews from the Soviet Union facing persecution should be admitted to the U.S.

 79%

Sources: Gallup with the exception of 1984 (Kane, Parsons and Associates).

Senator Borah of Idaho, an opponent of the bill, that the Jewish refugees were taking away their jobs, and that Hitler had a point about Jewish domination. The Jews, wrote Harold H. Duden to Senator Borah, "feed on the Christians." This correspondent was shrewd enough to conclude that FDR and Ambassador Bullitt were conspiring against Hitler. This was, of course, true, though Roosevelt hardly wanted to take the United States to war at the time of the Munich conference.

What emerges from letters denouncing the refugees is evidence of a common bond between anti-Semites in the United States and the Nazi regime. Both Hitler and Mr. Duden believed that FDR was good for the Jews and bad for the Nazis, and both were right, however much Roosevelt distanced himself from the issue of Jewish immigration. By refusing to be the "President of the Jews," Roosevelt was able to function as a president *for* the Jews and other anti-Nazis. This is why hatred for the president grew so much in 1938–1939, and why the Jews rallied to Roosevelt as never before.[18]

These Jews, according to Moseley (and many other distinguished Americans) were plotting to bring the United States into a new war. They were, he continued, utterly ruthless. Look, for example, at what the Jews did to that great non-Jew, Jesus Christ! Moseley's ideology proved to be a stale compendium of plagiarized material, taken from *The Protocols of the Elders of Zion*, the racialist theoretician Houston Stewart Chamberlain, General Erich Ludendorff, and the writings of thinkers like Pelley, True, Deatherage, and Father Coughlin.

Like other crypto-fascists, Moseley took Roosevelt's 1939 nomination of Professor Felix Frankfurter to the Supreme Court as a personal affront. Anti-interventionist senator William E. Borah (Republican of Idaho), a member of the Committee on the Judiciary, had supported the Frankfurter nomination. His advocacy of Frankfurter provoked a barrage of letters, postcards, and telegrams, filling four thick folders. Most of this mail was anti-Semitic. Frankfurter had long been a member of the ACLU's national committee, and his enemies were now equating that role with bolshevism or worse. An alarmed Arthur Garfield Hays, counsel to the American Civil Liberties Union, viewed these attacks on Frankfurter as a part of a broader assault against liberalism.[19]

The Senate confirmed the Frankfurter nomination, and the "Jew from Austria" served with distinction on the high court. Roosevelt's support for Frankfurter was thus courageous, and the justice was always grateful for it. Roosevelt could have retreated and named a less controversial figure, but he refused to do so. Nominating a man as well qualified as Felix Frankfurter could only discredit men like Moseley.

Moseley's followers certainly took the general seriously, as did the House Committee on Un-American Activities (HUAC). The general's friends did not help his cause. Paranoid and vituperative, Moseley's followers charged HUAC with being "Jew-controlled." "Christian Gentiles are being prosecuted," they charged. Moseley himself believed that occult conspirators were plotting to assassinate him. When testifying before HUAC, the general appeared to be nervous about the drinking water placed before him. "Is this water all right?," he asked. Assured that it was, he permitted the proceedings to continue.[20]

The committee displayed a letter in which the general had explained how his followers could benefit from his own murder. "If the Jews bump me off," wrote Moseley, "be sure to see that they get credit for it coast to coast. It will help our cause." Paranoid and egomaniacal, Moseley smugly testified to the connection between communism and "world Jewry."[21] Yet no one who had studied the rise of Hitler confused eccentricity or paranoia with political impotence.

The *New York Post* reported that a Jewish schoolteacher from Queens had interviewed the general in his suite at the Hotel Pennsylvania. Mrs. Rita Schenkman had come to defend her "race" against Moseley's fulminations. When Mrs. Schenkman asked him why he loathed Christian Scientists, the General blurted out, "Christian Jews, they are all the same." Moseley wanted the Jews to renounce world Jewry in favor of "Uncle Sam." More information surfaced, describing Moseley's fear of all dogs, including puppies. Moseley anticipated a conspiracy involving the kidnapping of his young child. The general appeared to be crossing the line between widely held views about the Jews and psychosis.[22]

Moseley was a classic modern anti-Semite. He blamed the Jews for his own problems, and for the social change that had ruined the America of his youth. Fortunately for his enemies, Moseley lacked charisma and was too insensitive to be an effective demagogue. Unlike Coughlin and Long, he had no rapport with the broad mass of the population.

Like Hitler, Moseley harbored obsessions about venereal disease and the collapse of society. The general solemnly informed his audience, "We have [in the United States] some 12,000,000 syphilitics," as well as four million criminals. Some of the general's best friends were Jews, he said; he only wished that their racial brethren would act to destroy communism. The Jews could eliminate communism in six months if they wished to do so through their control of the media. Like Hitler, Moseley was convinced that the Jews could *not* wish to do so. Their unpleasant characteristics, he thought, were genetic in nature. Anti-Semitism was thus a universal, healthy response to the Jews' evil traits.[23] Moseley had plenty of company. An unprecedented flood of

JEWS! JEWS!
Jews Everywhere!

The Roosevelt Administration is Loaded with Jews

12 Million White American Workers Jobless

OVER ¼ MILLION EUROPEAN JEWS ARE NOW COMING TO UNITED STATES
TO THROW WHITE AMERICAN WORKERS OUT OF JOBS

Benjamin Franklin Said:
"Jews are a menace to this country if permitted entrance And Should Be Excluded."

Samuel Roth Said:
"We Jews are a people of vultures, living on the labor of the rest of the world."

The Jewish Talmud Says:
"Jews are human beings, Gentiles are not human beings, but beasts." (Baba Mezia, 114, 6.)

Samuel Roth Says:
"WE JEWS, who come to the Nations, PRETENDING to escape PERSECUTION, are really the MOST DEADLY PERSECUTORS OF MEN."

Communism is Jewish

OUT WITH JEWS!!

LET WHITE PEOPLE RUN THIS COUNTRY AS THEY DID BEFORE THE JEWISH INVASION

Wake up!   **Wake** up!   **Wake** up!   **Wake** up!

Get in touch with your nearest Anti-Communist Organization

---

hate propaganda was being distributed. The leaflet reproduced here appeared in California, the Midwest, and elsewhere.

The general described fascism as a type of rule under which the "finest type of Americanism" could flourish. Moseley bragged about a conversation with the German ambassador, who offered a convincing justification for Hitler's demands in Central Europe. Moseley embraced the Bund as a great patriotic organization, while praising its struggle against communism. He lauded Fritz Kuhn as an upstanding anticommunist.

Moseley began to fear a communist revolution, and he urged that righteous citizens defend vital installations by forming guard units and vigilante committees. Moseley's America seemed possessed by a fascist blood lust: "Our domestic enemies should be warned . . . ," he declared, "not to excite the wrath of patriotic America, for once these patriots go into battle they will cure the disease definitely and make those massacres now recorded in history look like peaceful church parades." The general began to flirt with seditious ideas. George Sokolsky, a right-wing columnist for the Hearst press, denounced Moseley as a potential "military dictator surrounded by frightened screwballs who live in terror of their own shadows."[24]

Despite his growing eccentricity, Moseley continued to enjoy the respect of men like Herbert Hoover. Years later, he wrote to the former president, recommending that all Polish Jews be sterilized. Hoover responded politely, demurring because "I am rather too humane to stand for such drastic measures." He did find the general's letter "interesting," however.[25] While advocating this form of genocide, Moseley requested a favor of Bernard M. Baruch, whom he had earlier described as "a very dangerous Internationalist" and warmonger. Now, however, he needed something, so he wrote to Baruch care of the White House (where the financier presumably pulled the strings).[26]

The Nazi press blessed this growing alliance between American fascism and German foreign policy goals. The *Westdeutscher Beobachter* hailed the general's ideas about the sterilization of refugees. The Nazi press also gave much publicity to Moseley's attacks on FDR's rather modest military preparedness program. By portraying the American politico-military elite as divided on the issue of rearmament, the Nazi regime hoped to calm German fears about another war against a superior enemy coalition.

As Roosevelt moved closer to confrontation with the Nazis, Moseley embraced the German viewpoint. "The war now proposed," he declared, is for the purpose of establishing Jewish Hegemony throughout the world." Statements by the Nazi press, leaked to friendly American journalists by pro-Roosevelt figures, helped to persuade many Americans that Hitler had powerful allies in the United States.

Moseley's growing appeal to the Nazis made him appear to be a friend of a hostile foreign power. Roosevelt was succeeding in impugning the patriotism of men who embraced anti-Jewish views. The press was becoming aware of the general's strange views and alleged military shortcomings. Leaks from the White House, the FBI, and other agencies were destroying Moseley, though he himself contributed mightily to his own political demise.

Walter Winchell was Roosevelt's main agent in this anti-Moseley campaign. To the chagrin of the general, the most powerful columnist in America, a Jew himself, was treating him as a subversive crackpot. Strange to tell, Moseley's letters do not reveal any awareness of Winchell's Jewish origins, yet the columnist was the one Jew known to be determined to destroy the general.

Soon, the invitations to important Republican luncheons ceased coming. The phone rang with less frequency. The growing prointerventionist sentiment among veteran's organizations deprived the general of a major source of potential support. Moseley remained of public interest only to men like True and Deatherage. Moseley's phobias (from puppies to Christian Scientists), leaked to the media, were turning him into an object of public ridicule. Moseley was becoming a lonely, isolated crank, but only because FDR and his friends had worked for two years to *equate anti-Semitism with disloyalty.* In a pathetic letter, Moseley observed, "The enemy has completely silenced me. . . ." Roosevelt had won another battle. Others loomed.

It was becoming difficult to picture Moseley as the "American Hitler." Moseley disappeared from the public eye, and died twenty years later in obscurity. His rise and fall as a public figure showed both the extent and the limits of political anti-Semitism in America. One wonders what would have happened had Herbert Hoover rather than Franklin D. Roosevelt been president during these two years. No one was sadder about the general's fate than Hoover, Moseley's onetime patron and longtime friend.

CHAPTER
TWENTY-TWO

THE BUND'S STRUGGLE FOR
"TRUE AMERICANISM"

THE ANTI-NAZI DEMONSTRATORS began to flock toward Madison Square Garden early in the evening. These antifascists had ignored the advice offered by other, more timid voices: "The best way," cautioned the mayor's office, "to show your support for your democratic institutions is to shun this meeting of the German-American Bund as one would shun pestilence." Thirteen hundred New York City police guarded the arena and its approaches.

Fliers distributed by Fritz Kuhn's German-American Bund announced that a patriotic rally would take place this evening, 20 February 1939: "GEORGE WASHINGTON BIRTHDAY EXERCISES: Mass Demonstration for True Americanism." The next morning, thousands of leaflets, leftist and Nazi, littered the corners of Ninth Avenue and Fiftieth Street.

Kuhn was excited about the publicity that preceded the event. The press was present in great numbers; the mass circulation *Daily News* took a special interest in the rally; "24-HOUR POLICE GUARD ON NAZIS," screamed the headlines. Kuhn predicted that the rally would attract thirty thousand participants, including three thousand uniformed OD men. The event fell short of that, though it drew twenty-two thousand celebrants, a very large number.

By 8 P.M., thousands of people had taken their seats in the Garden. A muffled beat of drums announced that the OD men were entering the hall. They solemnly accompanied the honor guard toward the podium. Thousands of Kuhn's followers leaped to their feet, many with right arms outstretched in the "German greeting." Outside, large numbers of anti-Nazis screamed and cursed as the authorities kept them from pushing their way into the Garden. New York City's disciplined police maintained order, and violence remained at a tolerable level. There were arrests, however, including that of Peter Sanders, a thirty-four-year-old Negro.

Inside the hall, Bund leaders in OD uniforms strutted to the podium. National Secretary James Wheeler-Hill took the microphones, warning the audience that provocateurs would be dealt with by the OD men. Wheeler-Hill then launched his opening salvo, quoting George Washington's oft-cited lines about the avoidance of entangling alliances. He went on to portray a decadent America, weakened by radicals, class hatred, political abuses, and moral decay. Wheeler-Hill dismissed reports of racial persecutions in the Reich and then warned his audience against schemes hatched by "sons of Judah." Kuhn and his friends had solemnly assured the nervous managers of the Garden that the rally would not turn into a forum for heaping racial abuse upon any minorities. They had broken the Bund's word.

Patriotism and Americanism were the themes of the evening, and Wheeler-Hill soon called upon the audience to recite the Pledge of Allegiance to the American flag. Thousands of people, mainly middle-aged and older, saluted Old Glory in foreign-accented English. There was nothing unusual about this, because many immigrants did the same thing. What struck observers as bizarre was the Germanic intonation of the Pledge of "undivided" Allegiance by men and women whose right arms were raised in the Hitler salute. The cameras caught it all.

What kind of Americanism was this? The scene was too much for the anti-Nazi journalist Dorothy Thompson. She burst out in loud laughter, asserting "my constitutional right to laugh at ridiculous statements in a public hall." OD men quickly escorted her from the Garden. The next speaker, *gauleiter* of the East Rudolf Markmann, denounced politicians who persecuted German-Americans and failed to provide people with "work and bread" (another Nazi slogan).

Georg Froboese, *gauleiter* of the Middle West, approached the rostrum. He perked the crowd up with a violent anti-Jewish diatribe, attacking the "Jew Mordecai," whom most people call Karl Marx. Froboese denounced the boycott-Jews, the Jewish war conspiracy, and the Jew-controlled Federal Reserve System. He concluded with an appeal for a "Jew-free America!" Scattered responses of "Free America!" answered his plea. Froboese's rival in anti-Semitic propaganda was Gerhard Wilhelm Kunze, who read *Gauleiter* Hermann Schwinn's remarks. Denouncing kosher Hollywood movies and decadent Jewish culture, Kunze (Kuhn's heir apparent) complained that "Rosenfeld" had replaced Washington.[1] Alexander Hamilton had once been Secretary of the Treasury, but now the post was disgraced by Henry Morgenthau. The audience was coming alive. Every mention of Roosevelt's name brought forth jeers; the crowd cheered every reference to the American hero Colonel Lindbergh and applauded the mention of Father Coughlin's name. They booed the names of columnist Walter Lippmann and Labor Secretary Frances Perkins. Every allusion to Treasury Secretary Morgenthau or financier Bernard Baruch elicited catcalls of derision.

After Kunze came the main event. Fritz Kuhn pompously strutted to the podium, offered a calm "Free America!," and prepared to speak. Leaning forward over the podium, he struggled to hold in his bulging stomach, evidence of a prosperity unjustified by his meager salary. Kuhn was not at his best. He blamed the Jews for everything from Benedict Arnold's treason to intervention in 1917, to the "warmongering" of FDR. In effect, Kuhn read a boring lecture outlining the Bund's version of American history. Belittling those who attacked him, Kuhn informed his audience that he did not have "horns, a cloven hoof, and a long tail." This, said the *Bundesführer,* was the picture of him provided by the "Chooish-controlled press." The audience hardly reacted except when Kuhn mentioned Father Coughlin; then it cheered loudly.

The effect was almost comical, but not to Isidore Greenbaum, twenty-six, an unemployed plumber's helper from Brooklyn. He jumped onto the speakers' platform, crawled between two OD men, and headed toward Kuhn. The OD guards pushed Greenbaum to the floor, beating him up. In the struggle, Greenbaum lost his trousers. The police stopped the melee, then arrested Greenbaum for disorderly conduct.[2] The Nazi press cited the incident as proof of Jewish perfidy.

Kuhn was now in his element, for he was in complete control of himself. He had scarcely watched the struggle, displaying ice-cold disdain for his adversary. Greenbaum's actions seemed to vindicate Kuhn's argument on behalf of German-American cohesion. He completed his address. Perhaps, some Bundists now believed, 20 February, would be the American movement's 9 November. On the latter date in 1923, sixteen Nazis fell during Hitler's abortive "Beer Hall Putsch." They became "blood martyrs," spiritual guarantors of the movement's final triumph. The analogy was ludicrous, though the desperate Bundists clung to it as to a lifeboat.

Exiting from the hall, many of Kuhn's followers returned to Yorkville after the rally. They wanted to drink and celebrate all night. They had "beaten the Jews," obtained enormous publicity, and taken in a good deal of money. Perhaps now people would understand their patriotism, and respect it. Far from being an alien fifth column, the Bundists had shown themselves to be patriots who understood the real meaning of George Washington's rejection of entangling alliances. In his bulletins, Fritz Kuhn gloated for months about the rally. "All America is speaking of the Bund," he claimed. In a sense, Kuhn was right. Many people *were* talking about his organization, among them FBI agents.

As early as 1934, President Roosevelt had expressed an interest in gathering intelligence on fascist groups. The FBI's ambitious director, J. Edgar Hoover, moved to expand his investigations. He could thereby play to public concerns regarding foreign subversion. Hoover knew that his investigations would convince the Congress of the bureau's need for increased manpower. Hoover had good relations with Roosevelt, and FDR praised the bureau in the presence of cooperative reporters. Walter Winchell, working at FDR's behest, built up Hoover's latest image, that of anti-fascist and Nazi basher. All three men were happy with the result.

At Roosevelt's suggestion, Hoover's FBI investigated the alleged training of "Nazi storm troopers" in the United States. The bureau looked into possible ties between the Bund and foreign governments. Despite intensive investigations, the FBI found no evidence of a conspiracy to overthrow the government. Hoover reported his findings to Attorney General Homer Cummings.[3] Nevertheless, by 1938, leaks to the media were stoking public concern about our "Nazis." Winchell was hard at work, in his column and on the air. He was in frequent communication with both Hoover and FDR.

America expert Arthur Feiler had written some prophetic words a decade earlier: "Anyone [in the U.S.A.] suspected of wanting to endanger the present order by force is forcefully removed from the political arena. . . ." In an editorial published two days after the Washington Day rally, the *New York Times* predicted, "If any groups attempt to overcome those limits [on proper political activity], ample and legal force exists to put them down. . . ."[4] Ambitious politicians reminded people of German sabotage efforts during the Great War. The Roosevelt administration, working with the Congress, veterans' groups, and the media, moved to crush the Bund. Fritz Kuhn's behavior helped them greatly.

Kuhn's real fatherland seemed to show more appreciation of his *Heldentum* (heroic gesture). The German Weekly Newsreel, seen by millions of people, showed film of the "Jewish Greenbaum," a "Jewish individual," attempting to assault the innocent patriot Fritz Kuhn. Inspired by that event, the German Foreign Institute produced an exhibition, "America-Germandom in Battle." Consisting of photographs and exhibits glorifying groups like the Bund, the exhibition traveled to a number of German cities. The Bund, German visitors learned, was "the most influential" German-American organization. Those German-Americans of value were people who "know that Germany is encircled, and their hearts go out to German heroism and their pride in Germandom is strengthened."

Not every German official shared Kuhn's euphoria about the Washington Day rally. Consul General Hans Borchers reported from New York that "in spite of the unquestionably well-meaning intentions of its promoters, [the event] had done no service to the German cause in the United States." The embassy tried to distance itself from Kuhn. Wilhelm Kunze, acting under chargé Thomsen's pressure, released a letter stating that "neither German authorities . . . nor the German Embassy . . . have maintained any relations with the German-American Bund or its officials." In San Francisco, Consul Fritz Wiedemann informed his superiors, "I don't like the Bund. . . . With their stupid speeches they can give us only trouble." Rolf Hoffmann assured his American contact Douglas Chandler that "There is no question of the Bund attempting to import National Socialism in [*sic*] the U.S. . . ." Privately, however, various German officials remained in contact with the Bund.[5]

Correspondence received from Germans in America reflected the growing crisis engulfing the Bund. One Bundist griped, "Those who have not found their way to the Bund by now can't be helped. Anyway, they are not worth much." Kuhn faced personal problems, and the Bund had entered its last phase. Germans reading their newspapers, however, learned nothing from the Nazis about the Bund's irreversible decline.[6]

The Bund moved to cash in on the enthusiasm and publicity engendered by the Washington Day rally, but it stumbled on its old nemesis, the question of identity. Was the Bund, people asked, a Nazi front, or was it a legitimate German-American anticommunist organization? G. Wilhelm Kunze, for example, reiterated the group's opposition to President Roosevelt, who "should look for the first hole and put himself into it." He then contrasted FDR with Adolf Hitler, who "was the greatest talker and thinker that Europe has ever produced. . . ."[7] Such statements usually provoked cries of "Hang Roosevelt!" from the audience. This type of scene was too extreme for most isolationist groups. Kuhn's intention of broadening the organization's base was long on energy, but short on results.

The Bund's contradictory rhetoric reflected its difficult situation in the year 1939. Bundists more than ever before rallied to the Nazi cause. At a meeting in the Hippodrome in New York, the participants, according to one observer, were "extraordinarily aggressive in an entirely unfit manner . . . something like a beer club." Such behavior was hardly in Germany's interest. Kuhn understood that the Bund must become part of an effective anti-FDR coalition or face extinction. It was, he thought, fine to give Nazi speeches at the Bund's Camp Nordland; coalition politics required different tactics.[8] In his desperation, Kuhn became involved with characters even more unsavory than his usual associates.

Kuhn resolved to form an alliance with the Ku Klux Klan, and Kunze pursued this course. "Doc" Young, who had obtained his degree from the school of divinity of the Pillar of Fire sect, accepted the offer. The New Jersey Klan leaders hoped that pro-Nazi German-Americans would flock to an organization that was both racist and anti-Semitic. Professional anticommunist Edward J. Smythe brought his followers into the coalition, too. Consummation of this alliance was to take place 18 August, at Camp Nordland. Kuhn, Smythe, and Young hoped for fifty thousand participants. Three thousand people actually showed up, but the new allies put on a good performance. Speakers cursed the Jews and Roosevelt. The Klan burned a cross, while jeering hecklers shouted from the distance, "Put Hitler on the cross!" The media, as well as federal and state authorities, pursued the two pariah organizations with renewed vigor. Congressman Dickstein perceived a menace to the nation in the alliance.[9]

Kuhn decided to work with Joe McWilliams, a renegade Coughlinite who headed a New York fringe group called the Christian Mobilizers (CM). At a mass meeting in the Bronx, eighteen hundred people heard Kuhn promise support for "der Christian Mobilizers." He also averred, "Der Cherman Amerikan Boont duss not try to throw down Amerikan government. Dat's Chewish propaganda" (phonetic version). Joe McWilliams listened intently to Kuhn's words. John Olivo, head of the Christian Mobilizers' storm detachment, dipped the colors while the Bund choir intoned the strains of "Carry On," an Americanized version of *O Deutschland, Hoch in Ehren*. Kuhn had dismissed rumors about Olivo's past, information disseminated by the Reverend Birklend's anti-Nazi organization. On 11 October, 1934 New York police had arrested the future fascist for rape and theft. After attacking his victim, he allegedly made off with her pocketbook.

Not to be outdone by Kuhn, Wilhelm Kunze formed an alliance with Anastasi A. Vosniatsky, the wealthy chief of the All-Russian Fascist Organization. Violently anti-Bolshevik, the ARFO represented a clique of exiled White Russians. In 1922, young Vosniatsky married a rich forty-five-year-old widow, taking up residence on her huge estate near Thompson, Connecticut. A visionary and egomaniac, Vosniatsky strutted about his estate dressed in storm-troop garb, dreaming of his triumphant entry into Moscow. He erected a large statue of himself, clad in a czarist army officer's uniform. Vosniatsky, a fervent Nazi, even painted swastikas on the turtles inhabiting the picturesque ponds that dotted the estate. Kunze became his good friend, pledging to assist Vosniatsky in destroying "the Red Godless scourge which has held the peoples of your homeland enslaved for a quarter of a century." Both men shared a fervent faith in the "liberating might of the Germany of Adolf Hitler."[10]

The Bund was still attracting a goodly number of deranged persons. Rotting away in seedy apartment buildings and boarding houses, such people were sad reminders of the failure of American society. They were haters and cranks, prepared to offer money and advice to any fringe movement or racket that could alleviate their loneliness and their suffering. An elderly resident of New York's Upper West Side, for example, claimed to be the author of thirty-four "small books." Sadly, the "Jew-controlled Publishing Companies" were boycotting her books, "no matter how well they may be written." She now offered the manuscripts to the Bund, in return for one-third of the proceeds. The woman had written numerous articles on the "Jew question." Like many a crank on the far right, this woman was a self-deluded mystic; she was also peddling a scheme for the attainment of eternal youth. She claimed to have "passed through all the Initiation on the Road to Immortality and can take others through." The immortalist slyly offered the Bund a book concession at the forthcoming World's Fair, "where I will be an exhibit to prove that the rebuilding of the body is a fact and no fake."[11] Who was conning whom?

The Bund leadership grew more egomaniacal, even as the organization declined. Bundists dismissed the craven German-American leaders. "We," they declared, "have assumed 'America,' the German element is our own." Kuhn attacked FDR's anglophile policies: "The German Element in these United States is," he roared, "as American as ANY OTHER and is not taking a back seat; *this our Country will not be again made an appendage of the British Empire while we can help it!*"

Some of Kuhn's statements had once seemed funny, but no longer. The *Bundesführer* pledged, "We will fight like our forefathers for this country!" Yet he had no American forefathers, and had fought in the German Army against the United States. Would he do so again? After reading about the rally in Madison Square Garden, more Americans were asking, "Can it happen here?" Walter Winchell, in his column in the *New York Daily Mirror,* attacked the "Bundits" as subversives. At one point, two Bund members apparently attacked and beat Winchell. Friendly detectives "took care" of the thugs. In San Francisco, the American Legion and over fifty other organizations planned to alert the public to the menace of the Bund. Two thousand demonstrators took part in the rally. Around the time of the Washington Day meeting, State Senator John J. McNaboe of New York introduced a bill intended to curb the Bund's secret activities. He was making a career out of investigating the organization.[12]

Obscene letters and postcards poured into the Bund's New York offices. Typical messages contained denunciations of "Shitler," as well as unsolicited counsel: "You all ought to get the hell out of U.S.A. and go to Hitler." An irate recipient of Bund literature complained about "having had a copy of your newspaper dropped in my car by some citizen, who, no doubt, could not find a sewer." "Hey you Louse," wrote one correspondent, "Don't get your bowels in an uproar—

because I am *not* a Jew—but if I were—I would spit in your face personally." Blasphemy against the person of the Führer became common: "How in this damn era occurs such a crime to permit," asked one correspondent, "one lousy, dick—crazy—abominated dirty painter to become the head of a 'German' nation? This son of a filthy bitch, this prostituted murderer. . . ."[13] Many former supporters wrote to the Bund, requesting that it cease mailing propaganda to them. These fainthearted people were wary of the postal authorities, or their neighbors, or their employers, or the FBI. Journalists began to write exposés of the Bund's recreational facilities, such as Camp Siegfried on Long Island. Raymond Moley, a former Roosevelt adviser who had spent five years warning people about the Bund, claimed that armed Nazis were training for "the Day."

Harassment of the Bund caused further disruption within the organization. The Disabled War Veterans of America accused the Bund of violating the Civil Rights Act of 1923. It had allegedly failed to provide the secretary of state with a complete roster of its summer camp participants. This was a technical violation, but six Bund leaders found themselves under arrest. Later released, they became victims of a media campaign of harassment by the authorities.

An eager reading public turned Leon G. Turrou's *The Nazi Spy Conspiracy in America* (originally a series of articles) into a best-seller. Turrou, a former FBI agent, accused the Bund of being "the hand of the Nazi arm reaching into America." He put the number of Bund activists at seventy-five thousand men, an absurdly inflated figure. Turrou discovered a few pro-Nazis of Russian origin in the New York National Guard, and made much of the fact. The comical arrogance and ignorance of Kuhn's "beer-German clowns" became, in Turrou's book, a warning to the American people. Dr. Albert Parry's magazine *The Hour* undertook the laudable task of alerting Americans to the Nazi menace. Like Turrou, however, Parry engaged in hyperbole, warning about everything from Nazi plots in Mexico to a fascist penetration of the American armaments industry. Men like Turrou and Perry could justify their lurid prose by pointing to American complacency in the face of danger.[14]

The changing public mood affected one Hollywood studio's boardroom. In the winter of 1938–1939, the Warner studio (premature antifascists at the time of the *Black Legion*) concluded that the public was ready for an exposé of the "Nazi spy conspiracy" outlined by Turrou and others. This decision was not an easy one; Jack Warner often said, "If I want to send a message, I'll use Western Union." Hollywood producers, sensitive about their Jewish background, avoided controversy. Fearful of protests and even physical violence, Warner shot the film under conditions of unusual secrecy. Actor Edward G. Robinson badly wanted to play a role in the film. *"I want to do that for my people,"* he wrote to Hal Wallis of the Warner studio.[15] The FBI appeared on the screen as the first line of defense against Hitlerite subversion.

A dramatic, well-acted movie, *Confessions of a Nazi Spy* played upon widespread American fears. The "Bund" leader in the movie speaks about "our America" (Colin Ross's phrase) and a "German destiny of America," and demands equality for German-Americans. He sounded like Fritz Kuhn, who had become a notorious figure. *Confessions* depicted an America subverted and surrounded by Nazi spies. It was a filmic tribute to five years of work and agitation by men like Dickstein, Turrou, Landau, Parry, and Dies and represented an alliance between the Warner Studio and the Roosevelt administration.

Warner feared boycotts and even attempts to suppress the film entirely. Major studios wanted their stars to avoid the Hollywood premiere. Metro-Goldwyn-Mayer tried to insure compliance by inviting its stable of players to a party in honor of the celebrated actor Lionel Barrymore. The reception was scheduled so as to conflict with the opening of *Confessions*. Other studios informed their actors that it would be wise for them to absent themselves from the Warner reception. Warner survived this challenge by its Hollywood competitors, as well as a lawsuit for five million dollars by the outraged *Bundesführer* Fritz Kuhn.

Released in New York on 6 May, *Confessions of a Nazi Spy* received rave reviews. The public and the media were clearly hungry for this kind of film. "Hard-hitting," wrote *Newsweek*, while the New York *Herald Tribune* described *Confessions* as a "compelling indictment of Nazi espionage." *Stage* saw the film as "daring, fearless, provocative, [and] gripping." There were dissenting voices, reflecting the divisions in American public opinion. Frank S. Nugent of the *New York Times* described the movie as an oversimplified exposition of important themes, while Otis Ferguson called it a "hate-breeder if there ever was one."

The picture earned almost two million dollars, an enormous sum, equivalent to perhaps twenty million dollars in 1989 purchasing power. *Confessions* proved that Americans would pay hard-earned Depression money in order to see a film about a Nazi conspiracy aimed at the United States. Yet the movie had no immediate successor, and for this Kuhn was grateful. Studios still feared this type of controversy, and Warner itself had no desire to repeat its experience.[16] Hollywood reflected America more than it affected it.

Fear of a German fifth column now increased in direct ratio to the growth of international tensions. The House Un-American Activities Committee (HUAC) charged that the Bund commanded 480,000 (!) followers. Congressman Dies (Democrat of Texas) investigated Bund propaganda, while his colleague Representative Dickstein (Democrat of New York) probed the Bund's alleged infiltration of National Guard units. Congressional leaders decided that Dickstein, a Jew, would suffer from a credibility problem, so Dies soon emerged as the key inquisitor. The Texan was hungry for headlines. His committee's energetic investigator, Richard Rollins, worked to uncover evidence of treasonable and immoral Bund activities. He hoped that his efforts might result in another best-selling book about subversion in America.

Dies subpoenaed an unrepentant Fritz Kuhn. The *Bundesführer* welcomed the challenge. He bragged to friends and dates that he would easily finish off the likes of Dies. On a hot August day in 1939, Kuhn briskly strode into a hearing room on Capitol Hill. The camera bulbs flashed, and reporters readied their notebooks. Arrogant and smirking, Kuhn's interrogation went badly for him from the very beginning. Committee counsel Rhea Whitley asked, "Have you ever been arrested in the United States?" Kuhn responded, "Yes." "On what occasion," inquired Whitley, "and for what?" "Different occasions," replied Kuhn. "The charge," he continued, "was drunkenness and profanity, and grand larceny."

Responding to questions about his income, Kuhn denied even having a checking account. He claimed to live off three hundred dollars a month. And he was no Jew-hater, said Kuhn, for "[a]ll we want is for the Jews to let us alone." An interrogator asked Kuhn, "Is not Mr. Hitler anti-Semitic?" Kuhn, taken with his own cleverness, responded with a question: "Aren't you anti-Semitic?" "I am asking you the question . . . ," came the reply. Kuhn, ever the wise guy, then smirked, "What do I have to do with Mr. Hitler? Subpoena Mr. Hitler here." A year after Austria and the Sudetenland, the witness assured Congress that National Socialism was not for export.

Kuhn exploded when one HUAC member accused him of racketeering. "Do you call us a racket,?" he asked. "You will have to go to the United States Court of Appeals before you call us a racket."

Convinced of his political triumph, Kuhn briskly strode out of the hearing room. He relished his fan mail, such as this missive: "Congratulations. Keep up your fine work. Put the Jews where they belong." Privately, Kuhn acted like a man under siege. "They are out to get me," he would repeat. The 20 February rally seemed to be an isolated event, in some mythical, happy past.

Kuhn had reason for concern.[17] A few days after he testified, a nineteen-year-old girl named Helen Vooros responded to the committee's questions. A veteran of the Bund's youth movement, Miss Vooros described these "German-American" Nazis as subversive, well-funded fanatics. Then, speaking in her soft voice, Miss Vooros told stories that sent reporters scurrying to the telephones. Miss Vooros described the Bund camps as dens of moral iniquity, where camp leaders did not prevent "the boys and girls there together, doing what they should not be doing." She quit the movement, Miss Vooros said, because "They made several attempts to attack me." The witness shyly recalled that Dr. Goebbels had once made sexual overtures to her. Banner headlines turned the Vooros story into the greatest moral blow to the Bund since Severin Winterscheidt had exposed his genitals in a Brooklyn cinema.[18]

In September, Dies decided to seek perjury (and possibly contempt) charges against Fritz Kuhn. Recalled as a witness the next month, Kuhn permitted himself to be baited by counsel. The interrogations produced little that was new, but the headlines continued to appear. Given Hitler's policies in Europe, people were willing to believe a great deal that otherwise sounded exaggerated or even absurd. The chairman alleged that in the event of American entry into the war, the Bund, along with other Nazi agents, intended to paralyze the West Coast through acts of sabotage. The organization, Dies concluded, "was always and everywhere a Nazi agency working for disruption, espionage, sabotage, and treason." Wildly exaggerated though it was, Dies's charge represented a broadly held viewpoint.[19]

Municipal, county, and state officials now came up with ingenious regulations. They withdrew the Bund's liquor permits and stripped the Bund of its uniforms, "in the interest of public order." One reporter described the defrocked OD men as a group of "coatless, gray-shirted and disconsolate-looking individuals. . . ." Unhappy but sober OD men, dressed in their best (though inexpensive) Sunday suits, stared at the ground, muttering curses.

No schnapps, no uniforms: New York and New Jersey were attempting to destroy the Bund. Members now found themselves spending much of their time in court, fending off charges that ranged from slander to disorderly conduct. Cases dragged on for months, or even years, costing great amounts of money. Attorney Wilbur V. Keegan, an admirer of the Bund, defended many of these actions. At times, he received assistance from the American Civil Liberties Union. A typical offense had occurred in Sussex County, New Jersey, where a Bund speaker had pledged, "We will get rid of Rosenfelt and his crew of Jew friends. . . . Rosenfelt and his Jew visitors have these dreams of invasion by peaceful Germany."

A year earlier, a Bund-hater gleefully had sent this prophetic message to Kuhn: "Just what are you going to do now—it seems that everything is going against you in N.Y. State—you poor misunderstood bastard." Kuhn's personal life was in a shambles, and the law was indeed "out to get me." Harassment by state and federal authorities, encouraged by the White House and the FBI, were leading to the Bund's downfall.[20]

Two generations later, critics would point to Roosevelt's "imperial presidency" as the source of postwar arrogance and mindless interventionism. Roosevelt, however, was using questionable methods as tools in his struggle against fascism and anti-Semitism at home and Nazism abroad. His cause was a worthy one, and it did not merely justify his means; it sanctified them.

Fritz Kuhn's troubles in New York went back to a chance meeting during a cruise to Germany in 1938. While on board, the *Bundesführer* spotted an attractive, blond divorcée. Mrs. Florence Camp (promptly dubbed "Mein Camp" by the tabloids) agreed to see Kuhn in New York when he returned from the Reich. He took the Los Angeles woman to dinner at the Biltmore and began to court her. Kuhn promised marriage, showed off his Bund camps, and did a lot of his usual bragging. The idyll ended for the moment, when Mrs. Camp returned to Los Angeles. This meant that her "Fritzi" would have to spend a lot of money on phone calls. He would require even more money when Mrs. Camp decided to move to New York. Kuhn managed to spend over seven hundred dollars on phone calls, and several hundred dollars more on "Mein Camp's" moving expenses.

Thomas E. Dewey, the ambitious district attorney in New York County, was not amused or touched. The intense young Republican had recently come close to unseating Governor Herbert Lehman, a popular incumbent. He was now thinking ahead to the presidency.[21] Like FDR, Dewey knew that it was good politics to take on Fritz Kuhn. Dewey proceeded to accuse Kuhn of embezzling proceeds from the Washington Day rally. Even more shocking was the allegation that Kuhn had made off with monies intended for the legal defense of persecuted Bundists. Accused of immorality, theft, and betrayal of his trust, the *Bundesführer* counterattacked. Dewey, he said, was gunning for votes; the D.A. was part of a Jewish conspiracy. The beleaguered Kuhn began to sound pathetic. The Bundists, confused and in an uproar, finally rallied around their leader, but their doubts were growing. Kuhn's attorney did not believe that his client would receive a fair trial, for public opinion was against him. The American Civil Liberties Union protested the use of criminal statutes for political purposes. These objections were made to no avail.

On 29 November, a jury found Kuhn guilty of five counts of grand larceny and forgery. "Another racketeer," Dewey's office reported, "had been disposed of by a New York County jury." The would-be leader of German-America was just another crook. The feared subversive was now an object of derision. Newspapers, in a parody of the German phrase "*Drang nach Osten*" (Drive to the East, referring to Hitler's foreign policy goals), spoke of Kuhn's "Drang nach Ossining." Sing Sing Prison was located in Ossining, New York.[22]

The *Bundesführer* was undone by his own vices: greed, lust, egomania, and stupidity. The Bund continued to merit headlines, though not so often as during Kuhn's heyday. The well-orchestrated media campaign, directed by the White House in rare collusion with the Dies Committee, now resulted in the further isolation of the Bund.

Roosevelt and J. Edgar Hoover, through persistent comments, innuendos, and leaks to journalists, were working hard to equate militant anti-Semitism and neutrality with disloyal fascist sentiments. Americans now tended to view the Bund as Nazi and treasonous. Martin Dies, a publicity-hungry congressman, and J. Edgar Hoover, a power-crazy bureaucrat, were useful to Roosevelt in his campaign to destroy the far right. In assisting him in this endeavor, they served their country well.

CHAPTER
TWENTY-THREE

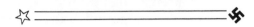

THE FIRST ANTI-NAZI
COALITION

ROM BERLIN, THE American chargé wired an ominous message to Washington. Hitler, he said, guided by his faith in Western inaction, might suddenly attack Poland.[1] A new factor, which FDR was among the first to perceive, made revision of the Neutrality Act an urgent priority. Stalin, like Roosevelt, had reached new conclusions in the six months after Munich. The dictator had no intention of fighting Germany while Britain and France stood aside. Stalin now showed interest in renewing trade negotiations with Nazi Germany. Foreign Minister Maxim Litvinov, who was both Jewish and a longtime proponent of collective security, departed. On 3 May, Stalin named a replacement, Vyacheslav M. Molotov, known for his tenacity in carrying out orders.

Hitler quickly realized that he might be able to safeguard his eastern flank during a war in the west. With France and Britain acting more hostile, and Poland intransigent, Hitler paid close attention to reports arriving from Moscow and Rome. Cables arriving from Rome were encouraging, for Mussolini, preparing to align himself with Nazi Germany, was mouthing Hitler's phrases. He asked the American ambassador, "Why should you interfere?" The duce, like the Führer, answered his own question. The United States, he said, was "largely controlled by Jews. . . ."[2]

The United States was indeed beginning to "interfere." Nowhere was this intervention more apparent than in distant Warsaw. The forty-one-year-old Anthony Joseph Drexel Biddle, Jr., ambassador to Poland since May 1937, had close ties to Roosevelt and his administration. The scion of a prominent Philadelphia family, Biddle had no training as a diplomat. He was, however, anti-Nazi and loyal to FDR, and these qualities rendered Biddle useful to the president after Munich. Biddle had no doubt about Hitler's destructive aims. First, the German leader wanted Danzig and extraterritorial rail and road links through the Polish corridor. Then he cast his gaze upon Upper Silesia and Posen and pled the case of the poor, oppressed ethnic Germans. Throughout this year of 1939, Biddle worked to strengthen Poland's ties to the West. He spoke to the White House about the "antiaggression" front, which Bullitt was helping to create from Paris. Biddle worked to undermine attempts at mediation between Poland and Germany, fearing another Munich. He pursued FDR's encirclement policy, which Hitler feared, and the Poles belatedly embraced. While his Polish contacts assured Biddle of their comprehension of American neutrality, they had reason to be encouraged by Roosevelt's policy. Polish diplomats often assured Biddle that they would remain part of the antiaggression front.[3] Roosevelt encouraged this course. He constantly reminded Biddle of "the weaknesses of our British friends," and even informed his ambassador of Axis military mobilizations that had not taken place.[4] Roosevelt was doubtless exaggerating, in order to convey something to Biddle and his Polish friends: Do not yield.

By late spring, Adolf A. Berle, Jr., the astute and cautious assistant secretary of state, noticed a change taking place around him. There was, he believed, a "war party" at work, striving to remake American foreign policy. Though FDR, he believed, was not overtly part of this clique, Berle did not understand the extent to which FDR was manipulating its spokesmen, such as Interior Secretary Harold Ickes. This outspoken anti-Nazi, who was working to change public opinion, would not have written a belligerent, controversial article on foreign policy for *Look* magazine without a tacit clearance from the White House.[5]

The situation was becoming graver, in FDR's view. A militant

German-Italian alliance might soon confront two unprepared democracies, Britain and France, while Soviet Russia stood aside. FDR
was now intent upon gutting part or all of the Neutrality Act. Roosevelt
believed that the threat of massive American aid to the democracies
might deter and contain Hitler. Ambassador Bullitt sent Secretary Hull
an urgent message, which confirmed Roosevelt's belief. Ribbentrop, he
declared, was convinced that in the event of war Britain and France
would receive "no military supplies or airplanes" from the United
States.[6] Roosevelt, energized by his desire to check German expansion,
began to speak about national unity in the event of war, while expressing the pious hope that America would never feel compelled to use its
armed forces.[7] Public demonstrations of his pro-British orientation occurred in tandem with statements denouncing totalitarianism.

A long-awaited state visit by the British royal family was a success.[8]
The Americans greeted King George VI and Queen Elizabeth with
great enthusiasm, from the moment the royal couple crossed over from
Canada at Niagara Falls late in the evening of 9 June. After visits to
Washington, the World's Fair, and other places of interest, the king and
queen motored ninety miles from New York City to the Roosevelt home
in Hyde Park. Church bells rang, and flowers were cast before the royal
couple's motor car. The drive took two hours longer than expected, for
the crowds along the route were enormous. One observer noted, "No
American ever received such an ovation from his countrymen." Whatever the polls might say, it was clear that a carefully contoured Anglophile foreign policy would attract the support of many Americans,
particularly in the East.

Awaiting the king and queen in his library, the president offered
cocktails to the tired but happy couple. "My mother," said the president, "thinks you should have a cup of tea; she doesn't approve of
cocktails." The king replied, "Neither does my mother," as he grate-
fully sipped his drink.[9]

Charmed by the rustic beauty of the place and warmed by FDR's
relaxed manner, the reticent king quickly felt at home. The monarch
later commented, "[The president] is so easy to get to know, and never
makes one feel shy." The conversation went on until 1:30 A.M., whereupon the host informed his guest, "Young man, it's time for you to go to
bed."

The rest of the visit proved to be more substantial. In a long conversation, the president revealed his developing strategic concepts to the

monarch, ideas that he had never shared with Prime Minister Neville Chamberlain. Public exposure of this conversation would have led to demands for FDR's impeachment. Both heads of state knew that war was near. Abandoning his public commitment to neutrality, Roosevelt sounded like a potential (though nonbelligerent) ally of Great Britain. FDR even predicted American entry into the war in the event of Nazi attacks upon London.

It was clear that FDR's protection of British interests would have as its price their ultimate displacement by American ones. Long before the famous destroyer-for-bases deal of 1940, Roosevelt expressed an interest in acquiring American access to British bases in the Caribbean. The president's comments foreshadowed an alliance that was yet to come, one in which the United States would be the senior partner. These remarkable and highly confidential conversations could only heighten the king's doubts about Chamberlain. Suddenly, the issues that had long vexed relations between the two democracies—tariffs, imperial preference, trade agreements—seemed remote and minor.[10] The king realized the importance of Roosevelt's comments. Throughout the war, he kept his notes of the conversation near him, safely stored in a special briefcase.

FDR now returned to the task at hand, which was the revival of the expired "cash and carry" legislation. In addition, Roosevelt wanted to amend the Neutrality Act of 1937 by lifting the arms embargo. Belligerent powers would then be able to purchase arms in the United States, so long as they transported them in their own or other (neutral) ships, and at their own risk. Roosevelt worked for the legislation with great energy, sensing, in a friend's words, that "the nations are now more than ever looking to America to point the way."[11] In late June, however, Bullitt's Paris embassy warned of an impending "second Munich."[12]

A recalcitrant Congress dug in its heels. Roosevelt, frustrated and exhausted, charged ahead. At one point, Vice President John Nance Garner, an anti-New Dealer who hoped to succeed FDR, smugly informed his "Captain" that "we may as well face the facts. You haven't got the votes, and that's all there is to it." (Roosevelt's doubts about Garner's presidential capacities grew.) On 11 July, the president's proposal died in committee. Privately, he was furious, suggesting that "we ought to introduce a bill for statues of . . . [Senators] Vandenberg,

Lodge and Taft . . . to be erected in Berlin and put the swastika on them."

While Congress delivered this blow to Britain and France, Hitler worked to isolate Poland. He bemoaned the fate of Danzig, a city cut off from the Reich by the unjust Versailles *Diktat*. The city's population was about ninety-eight percent German-speaking. The case for self-determination was at least as powerful as that put forth on behalf of the Sudeten Germans at Munich. Ambassador Biddle glumly predicted that "hopes for a reasonable and just settlement of the Danzig question seem remote."[13]

FDR saw a bit of silver lining in this cloud. If war erupted, some of his friends could blame Congress for failure to deter Hitler, and Roosevelt could then press for lifting the arms embargo. Polls showed that two-thirds of the public favored selling arms to the Allies in the event of war.[14]

Roosevelt paid little heed to the need for Soviet participation in an anti-Nazi alliance system. Like many of his contemporaries, FDR underestimated Russia's strategic importance and overestimated her military weakness. FDR avoided the issue of a Soviet alliance in most of his discussions with Biddle and Bullitt. His chargé now reported that proappeasers in France cited the West's failure to secure a Soviet alliance as a justification for Western inaction in the face of German pressure on Poland. Biddle and Joseph E. Davies, ambassador to Belgium, warned that failure to include the Soviets in an anti-German alliance system could lead to a German-Russian *rapprochement.*

In July, hoping to prevent Stalin from making a deal with the Nazis, Roosevelt admonished the Soviet ambassador that "as soon as Hitler had conquered France, he would turn on Russia. . . ."[15] In early August, Roosevelt sought to bring about an alliance between Russia and the West, but his moves were halfhearted and inconsistent. His prophecy would prove accurate, but his statecraft was ineffective. For his part, Chamberlain continued to oscillate between firmness and appeasement, as he had since the end of March.[16] The West had no common policy. From Paris, Bill Bullitt wired Washington that rumors were circulating to the effect that "at the last moment Chamberlain will let down Poland."[17]

Hitler, already demanding the return of the German free city of Danzig to the Reich, as well as extraterritorial rail and road links cutting through the "Polish corridor," now appeared to covet more territory.

In the Late 1930s, the American Public Knew about Nazi Expansionism in Europe, and Disapproved.

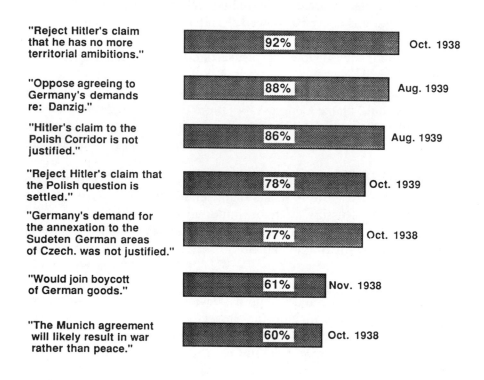

"Reject Hitler's claim that he has no more territorial amibitions." **92%** Oct. 1938

"Oppose agreeing to Germany's demands re: Danzig." **88%** Aug. 1939

"Hitler's claim to the Polish Corridor is not justified." **86%** Aug. 1939

"Reject Hitler's claim that the Polish question is settled." **78%** Oct. 1939

"Germany's demand for the annexation to the Sudeten German areas of Czech. was not justified." **77%** Oct. 1938

"Would join boycott of German goods." **61%** Nov. 1938

"The Munich agreement will likely result in war rather than peace." **60%** Oct. 1938

Source: Gallup

Hitler raved about Polish mistreatment of *Volksdeutsche* (ethnic Germans). Poland, he believed, was an abomination created by Versailles. He demanded plebiscites in disputed territory, but it was not clear how much territory he wanted. Hitler wanted to reduce Poland in size, perhaps turning her into a German satellite. But did he want war, one which might mean a struggle against a global alliance system, including the Soviet Union?

Influential isolationists, fresh from another victory over the hated Roosevelt, remained glib, even insouciant about the threat of war. Senator Borah of Idaho predicted, "[w]e are not going to have a war. Germany isn't ready for it." Publisher J.M. Patterson of the *New York Daily News* assured the public that peace would prevail. "I have just returned from ten days in Germany," he wrote. "I think the chances are more than ten to one against general European war before September, and four or five to one against war this year."[18]

Polish Foreign Minister Josef Beck assured Ambassador Biddle of the incompatibility "between the two doctrines of Naziism and Communism." The Soviets and the Germans," said Beck, could never reach "complete agreement."

Hitler, speaking to a high League of Nations official, now demanded Danzig, plus the right to control an extraterritorial passageway through Polish Pomerania. Other German officials were talking about the cession to the Reich of the entire Polish corridor, as well as Upper Silesia.[19] Hitler, who did not expect resistance from the British and French *Arschlöcher* who had surrendered at Munich, was belligerent and vague at the same time. He was pushing Chamberlain into a corner. Bullitt and Roosevelt feared that the prime minister would find a way to capitulate, while saving face for himself, and perhaps for Poland. Ambassador Kennedy worked to save appeasement.

The prospect of war did not alarm FDR nearly so much as the prospect of more appeasement and surrender. Of course, with one eye on American public opinion, FDR wanted the Germans to fire the first shot.[20] This was equally true two years later.

And what would Britain and France do? Bullitt worked without respite on behalf of his antiaggressor coalition.[21] Western negotiations with the Soviet Union dragged on into August, without result. Problems that should have been worked out in 1935 or 1936 haunted the desultory negotiations between Stalin and the West. The British army was too small, and the French were wedded to a static policy of defense. Poland and Rumania were vehemently anti-Soviet, and had no desire to see Soviet air and land forces traverse their air space and territory, even in pursuit of a German aggressor. Daladier warned Bullitt that if the Poles sabotaged a Soviet alliance, he "would not send a single French peasant to fight in the defense of Poland." The ambassador indicated that he did not take this statement "too seriously although [Daladier] repeated it three times." Stalin, meanwhile, cynically awaited a Franco-British offer, while casting strong hints to Berlin that he was interested in further trade negotiations with the Reich.

By encouraging resistance to Hitler, American ambassadors helped to prevent another Munich. They did not, however, have any answer to one key question. If the United States did not go to war, and if Stalin stood aside, or joined Hitler, what would happen then? Bullitt took lingering proappeasement sentiments quite seriously, as did Roosevelt. From its London embassy, the State Department learned of a putative "joint move" by Rome and London.[22] Appeasement, though in its death throes, still twitched and gasped.

Three months earlier, the Greater German Reich had celebrated Adolf Hitler's fiftieth birthday; 20 April 1939 marked a great occasion. Hitler, this "unknown soldier of the Great War" had destroyed the Versailles system erected by Wilson and the Allies in 1919; he had created Greater Germany, *das grossdeutsche Reich*, without firing a shot. Anti-Nazi foreigners estimated that eighty percent of the German people approved of his rule. Hitler, however, viewed the recent past as a mere prelude to a colossal future. Germany now dominated Central Europe. The Führer had earlier bragged, "I will go down in history as the greatest German of all time." He now hoped to reduce Poland to the status of a satellite, and wished to obliterate France as a great power. Controlling much of Europe and enjoying the friendship of fascist Italy and imperial Japan, Hitler one day intended to strike eastward. There he would destroy "Jewish-Bolshevik Russia" and carve out *Lebensraum*, living space for the German people.

Hitler continued to seek a modus vivendi with Great Britain, but his recent violation of the Munich Agreement had provoked Prime Minister Chamberlain. More to the point, Hitler feared Franklin Roosevelt and the growing military potential of the United States. The German dictator needed to act before his greatest enemy created a coalition formed for the sole purpose of destroying the New Germany. Hitler needed a neutral America in order to create his New Order in Europe.

The mere mention of Roosevelt's name now drove Hitler into a frenzy. Luftwaffe chief Hermann Goering, voicing his Führer's rage, dreamt about a plane that could bomb New York: "I would be very happy," Goering declared, "about such a bomber, in order to shut up those arrogant people over there." A week after his birthday, Hitler ridiculed the American president, putting him in the class of "international warmongers" who provoked "a nervous hysteria."[23] Roosevelt seemed to be an implacable meddler. Hitler correctly assessed FDR's global ambitions. Roosevelt's democratic and capitalist ideology had always been expansive in nature, though phrased in terms of a broadly defined (or ill-defined) "Western Hemisphere." To his dying day, Adolf Hitler hated Roosevelt more than all his other political enemies put together. He would have the satisfaction of outliving him by eighteen days.

Roosevelt had become more of a menace over the past year and a half. He had spoken of a "quarantine" against aggressor states; he demanded assurances of Hitler's peaceful intentions. The president protested against Nazi treatment of the Jews; he withdrew his ambassador from Berlin; and now he was scheming to undo the Neutrality Act. Working through his agents in Paris and Warsaw, Roosevelt undermined the policy of appeasement conducted by Britain and France. Hitler believed that Roosevelt was a Jew-manipulated Wilson, attempting to push other nations into a belligerent alliance against Germany. Roosevelt represented everything Hitler hated: a pampered child of the upper classes, a friend of the Jews, a liberal, an interventionist, an antifascist.

The German leadership sensed that the international situation was changing. Despite Hitler's great foreign policy successes in the preceding four years, a new enemy coalition seemed to be emerging. A hostile alliance, consisting of Britain, France, Poland, and the Soviet Union could encircle and contain the expansionist Greater German Reich. Why had Neville Chamberlain altered his attitude toward Germany? Only a few months earlier, he had foreseen "peace in our time." The Führer himself believed that Roosevelt was behind the malevolent change.

At the end of April, as Hitler prepared to show his contempt for the president's recent meddling in European affairs, a press campaign was in order. FDR must be unmasked.

Nazi propaganda now attacked Roosevelt as a Jewish Freemason. FDR was indeed a proud member of the Holland Lodge Number 8, where he was initiated on 10 October 1911. (He became a thirty-second degree mason on 28 February 1929.) FDR took his membership very seriously and at least two of his sons followed him into that lodge.[24] One may summarize the more virulent Nazi press notices as follows. Roosevelt was a capitalistic speculator, a Jewish Freemason who, along with his Negro-loving wife Eleanor, was unleashing race mongrelization and bolshevism upon the God-fearing, peaceful peoples of the West. To the list of accusations was added the term *warmonger,* which, within a few years, would become *war criminal.*

A few days before the chancellor's speech responding to Roosevelt's latest "peace note," so-called "American expert" Adolf Halfeld published his shocking discovery that FDR was a Jew, descended from Sephardim named Rossacampo. Hitler knew better than his propagandists what all this meant. If the Jew Roosevelt provoked another war, his racial brethren would pay the price. At the same time, Hitler did not intend to play into FDR's hands by offering him a pretext for an alliance with England, or for war. [25]

Hitler was relying upon more than his vaunted intuition. Aside from Hitler and Roosevelt himself, few persons had any sense of FDR's ambitious foreign policy goals, though there were exceptions. Hans Dieckhoff, the German ambassador, was noted for accurate and objective reporting. He repeatedly predicted that "in the next war, it will not be two and half years until the United States enters; it will be much shorter, much less." Dieckhoff later pointed to the Munich Agreement as a turning point, when "stopping Hitler" became henceforth the chief aim of American foreign policy. [26]

An informed diplomat, reporting from Washington in late March, cabled Berlin, "Roosevelt is inwardly convinced that Germany is the enemy who must be crushed, because she has so upset the balance of power and the *status quo,* that America also will feel the consequences should she fail to get in first." Fritz Wiedemann, Hitler's former adjutant and later a German consul in San Francisco, passed a similar report on to Berlin. He quoted Hearst journalist Karl von Wiegand (no crusader against Nazi Germany) to the effect that "President Roosevelt fights for his democratic aims with the same fanatic idealism as does the Führer for National Socialism." [27]

Chargé d'affaires Hans Thomsen offered his masters in Berlin some rare glimpses into FDR's goals and tactics. As Roosevelt took more daring steps, Thomsen looked ahead to apocalyptic events that lay two years in the future. Roosevelt's policy, Thomsen wrote, represented a "bid for leadership in matters of world politics [that is] aimed at annihilating National Socialist Germany with all means available. . . ." More brilliant prophecies have seldom been voiced. Roosevelt did not want his nation to live in a world that contained Nazi Germany. Today, this seems to be a moral, even logical proposition; in the summer of 1939, it was breathtaking, and politically dangerous.[28]

In his hostility to Roosevelt, Hitler resembled many of the president's American detractors. Unlike them, he was willing to appease FDR until a united Europe under German leadership stood ready for confrontation. Early in the year, Hitler hinted at his interim policy when he assured the Polish ambassador that "Germany desires peace and friendship with America also."[29] It was painful for Hitler to practice this restraint with regard to America. Like Goering, Hitler often mused about bombing the United States into submission once he conquered Europe. He bravely predicted that "before the Americans begin to rearm a second time we will be so far ahead they never will be able to catch up." The Führer dismissed the threat of American intervention, for "[t]hese Jewish Democrats never have shown any determination and will not sacrifice their mammon." Hitler did not really believe any of this, though the hatred and contempt that inspired his words were real enough. Though Hitler knew that "the United States was not ready to wage war," he feared Roosevelt's hostile machinations.[30]

Like many Americans, Hitler believed that Great Britain, if in trouble, would attempt to drag the United States into the conflict. Winston Churchill, whom the Nazis variously described as a drunk, a syphilitic, a bed wetter, and a warmonger, had uttered a dire prophecy two years earlier. According to German ambassador Joachim von Ribbentrop, Churchill warned that "once things come to a direction where things don't run well, you know we are pretty good at getting people into war [on our side]. . . ."[31]

By the summer, Hitler was blaming FDR for undermining his demands concerning the Polish corridor and the free city of Danzig. Roosevelt, Hitler informed the Polish ambassador, was now his number one enemy: "He also blamed the United States for opposing economic negotiations between the Reich and the states of South America."[32] Roosevelt, the Foreign Ministry alleged, was working with these warmongers in order to undermine the Neutrality Act. Hans Dieckhoff, studying diplomatic dispatches from 1939, later concluded that Roosevelt "bears a great, if not a decisive, part of the responsibility for the outbreak of the war and prolongation of the war." Describing the president as "a peculiarly dominating personality," he portrayed Roosevelt as fighting for American hegemony in the Western hemisphere. Dieckhoff was privy to a good part of the truth.[33]

Two days later, Soviet foreign minister V.M. Molotov signed a historic pact with German foreign minister von Ribbentrop. The "Hitler-Stalin Pact" of nonaggression looked ahead to the division of Eastern Europe into two spheres of influence, German and Soviet. Poland might cease to exist, for even with limited British and French assistance, it could not long resist an armed attack by Germany and Russia. It was, however, possible that Warsaw would yield to increased German pressure and revive the sinking stock of appeasement. At the very least, the work of Biddle, Bullitt and Roosevelt would soon be tested. Would the Western democracies resist German aggression against Poland, even at the cost of a war for which they were grossly unprepared?

Appeasers were hard at work. Chamberlain fatuously continued to believe that "there is nothing in the questions arising between Germany and Poland which could not be resolved without the use of force if only confidence could be restored." The prime minister held fast to this belief, despite evidence that secret clauses in the Nazi-Soviet pact envisaged the forceful partition of Poland: Ambassador Kennedy met with Chamberlain, who bemoaned the "futility of it all. . . ." "After all," he continued, "[we] cannot save the Poles; they can merely carry on a war of revenge that will mean the destruction of the whole of Europe." Foreign Secretary Lord Halifax told Kennedy that "My reason shows me no way out but war, but my instincts still give me hope." In Paris, Foreign Minister Georges Bonnet, a wily appeaser, turned to Ambassador Bullitt for help. He hoped that the president would find a way to prevent war and save Europe from destruction, and from the "sacrifice of 30,000,000 soldiers."[34]

For a time, however, Bullitt seemed confused, admitting for once that "he is now at a loss what advice to telephone to the President. . . ." The ambassador was beginning to show signs of strain, though his spirits revived after speaking to FDR. He worked to strengthen military ties between Britain and France, while urging the Allies to conduct a vigorous propaganda campaign against Germany. Bullitt, acting at Roosevelt's behest, was helping to create an overtly anti-German alliance, hardly the act of a neutral ambassador.[35]

Roosevelt, concerned about the new constellation of forces, continued to mistrust Chamberlain. Information coming to him revealed a British desire to put pressure on the Poles, perhaps through American intermediaries. Chamberlain viewed his guarantee to Poland, issued at the end of March, as a kind of safety net for the Poles. A reasonable Poland would, he hoped, avoid testing Britain's commitment. In Berlin, British ambassador Nevile Henderson worked to bring about a meeting between the Poles and the Germans.[36]

Roosevelt did not cooperate with Chamberlain. Instead, he moved to take the Polish-German dispute out of the prime minister's hands by appealing to Poland and Germany. Back in Paris, Ambassador Bullitt advised Roosevelt on how to make propaganda at Germany's expense. It was essential, he believed, that the Germans fire the first shots, and bomb civilian populations.[37] FDR agreed, for he had already turned to Hitler on 24 August, calling on him to forswear "military conquest and domination." He referred the Führer back to his own, rather insulting message of 14 April, hardly a pleasant memory in the mind of the German leader. Roosevelt now requested that Hitler abjure the use of force, while the parties searched for a resolution of their problems.

The president offered Hitler three alternatives: direct negotiation with Poland, arbitration, or conciliation through the good offices of a neutral moderator. Roosevelt was trying to maneuver Hitler into refraining from attacking a vulnerable neighbor, while the Western powers and Poland formed an anti-German front. If Hitler insisted upon war, his rejection of the Roosevelt plan would make Germany the obvious aggressor.[38] The president of Poland accepted FDR's proposal immediately, and FDR so informed Hitler the next day.[39] The Poles were more than ever looking to Roosevelt and to Ambassador Biddle.

Ambassador Bullitt assured the president that Britain and France stood by Poland.[40] Nevertheless, he remained nervous about possible British constraints on the Poles. Despite Chamberlain's assurance, London might force the Poles to yield to inflated German demands. FDR and Bullitt worked to stay Chamberlain's hand, and they succeeded.

In the bitter words of Joseph P. Kennedy, uttered at a later time, "neither the French nor the British would have made Poland a cause of war if it had not been for the constant needling from Washington." On another occasion, Kennedy blamed Bullitt for the outbreak of hostilities. Polish and French documents bear out much of Kennedy's charge.[41]

FDR now called in the British ambassador. He indicated that he "would be anxious to cheat in favor of His Majesty's Government." Roosevelt intended to delay signing a neutrality proclamation for five days, during which time the British could remove "all possible arms and ammunition" purchased in the United States. The ambassador described FDR's "impish glee" as the president described his plan to delay the departure of German merchant ships, while expediting the exit of British vessels.[42] Roosevelt had sworn to insure that the laws were faithfully executed, and the Neutrality Act was one of them. He clearly believed that harming Hitler was more important than observing the letter of his presidential oath.

While Roosevelt, Bullitt, and Biddle worked to shore up resistance to Hitler, Kennedy wired Hull that Chamberlain and Halifax still favored negotiations. One must, argued Kennedy, leave Hitler an escape hatch. He warned that Polish intransigence would further the goals of German warmongers while placing "the onus of a breakdown on Poland." Chamberlain, said Kennedy, was worried about Polish stubbornness, for he still hoped to resolve the Danzig situation, then move on to a general European economic settlement. These crocodile tears left Roosevelt unmoved, for he was moving in an opposite direction.

From Warsaw, Hull and Roosevelt received better news. Biddle reported that the Poles would never yield to Hitler's "gangster extortion."[43]

FDR met with the new British ambassador, Lord Lothian. The envoy came away with the view that "[t]here is certainly nothing neutral about the President's personal attitude towards the conflict . . ."[44] Roosevelt had begun to pursue various schemes, all intended to support the British war economy and take pressure off the Royal Navy.[45] Yet war had not yet broken out. Roosevelt was careful to keep his innermost thoughts from all except a few close advisers and friends. Among them was Harry Hopkins.

Hopkins's relationship with Roosevelt was an extraordinary one. Now fifty-one years old, Harry Lloyd Hopkins had come to then governor Roosevelt's attention through his outstanding work as an administrator of various social and medical welfare agencies. Appointed FDR's chief of the Temporary Relief Administration, Hopkins owed his drive to a complex mix, which included the social gospel, pacifism, and raw ambition. A man of great courage, Hopkins lost two-thirds of his stomach to cancer before World War II. He lived to serve Roosevelt, and this proximity to power gratified the former social worker. Hopkins then served for two years as secretary of commerce, but he was far more important as an advisor and an emissary. A discreet man with many contacts, he was at the president's beck and call. By 1939, Harry Hopkins saw the world much as FDR did, and this made him a perfect go-between. The world, these men now believed, was engrossed in a great struggle between Hitler's New Order and democracy.

In the midst of this last interwar crisis, FDR received a telegram of symbolic, and perhaps political, importance. Two days before World War II began, a cable from John W. Boehme, Jr., an isolationist congressman from Indiana, informed the president of his conversion to the "neutrality program offered by [the] administration." "I will support," Boehme added, "the administration program because I am convinced of the correctness of your position as regards our foreign policy."[46] Aside from public spiritedness, Boehme's message reflected his reading of the latest polling data. By August, fifty percent (up from thirty-one percent) of those queried in a public opinion survey approved of American arms sales to Britain and France. Most Americans, however, wanted to "stay out" of the war: Only one-sixth of those polled could conceive of a situation in which it would be advisable for the United States to enter the war without being directly attacked.

During the last hours of August, Ambassador Bullitt informed Washington that "Hitler will attack Poland in the near future." France and Britain, he continued, "will fulfill their obligations and fight to assist Poland."[47] On 1 September, German troops crossed the Polish frontier. Two days later, Britain and France declared war on Germany. This decision on the part of the democracies was a great triumph for Roosevelt. Though his army was weak, and his nation anxious to avoid involvement in a foreign war, the president had helped to forge a coalition that would ultimately grow into a mighty alliance pledged to the destruction of the Hitler regime.

Roosevelt's comments to family members and intimates, as well as his actions, indicate that he longed for a world in which Nazism would be nonexistent, in a century dominated by Christian values, a responsible capitalism, and democratic ideology. Publicly, however, FDR spoke only of the German threat and America's *defensive* response. People, disillusioned with a crusade against the kaiser, were in no mood for one against Hitler.

During this tense time, French premier Edouard Daladier, fearing the catastrophe facing his nation, became even more dependent upon the American ambassador. Indeed, the premier ascribed France's "recovery" to Bullitt's interventions. "In consequence," the ambassador continued, "he asks my judgment about nearly everything of great importance not only in the field of foreign affairs but also in the field of domestic policy, and what's more, he is apt to do what I advise." Concerned about the democracies delay in declaring war on Germany, Bullitt found comfort in the premier's determination "to fulfill to the full the obligations of France to Poland. . . ."[48] France and Britain commenced hostilities on the next day, 3 September. During the early months of the war, the premier was sometimes overcome with emotion in Bullitt's presence. He hoped that America would once again save his homeland from the *boches*, though, sadly, he knew better. Daladier arranged for Foreign Ministry appointments suggested by the American ambassador. He wanted to purchase a house next to Bullitt's.[49]

The president's secretary was responsible for filing, preserving, and making accessible important and confidential papers of continuing interest to FDR. Among these files one finds three large black books, containing telegrams from Ambassador Bullitt and his staff from the time of Munich to the outbreak of war. These materials, relayed by the State Department, were of particular interest to President Roosevelt. Sensitive in nature, they clearly document the success of his interventionist, anti-German foreign policy in 1938–1939. While providing proof of his (and Bullitt's) moral concerns and diplomatic cleverness, the "Bullitt books" were political dynamite. Premature revelation could severely embarrass Roosevelt, and undermine his foreign policy.[50]

War had displaced appeasement, and this pleased FDR. His friend Henry Morgenthau recalled that Roosevelt liked to have things going on around him every minute. There was now plenty of action. Even better, the course pursued by the president reflected his renewed sense of moral purpose. This commitment gave FDR a new source of energy. He was still the great actor, however, and did not often share his innermost views with the nation. As always, Roosevelt gathered the reporters around his desk. Affecting a grave demeanor, he "sincerely hoped" that we would stay out of the war. Though he foresaw the possibility of American belligerency, and had told his son Elliott so as early as 1938, it was important that the people believe that Roosevelt's intention was to keep America out of war. His thoughts were running along quite different lines. If Germany could be defeated without American intervention, fine. If not, other courses of action would be necessary.

PART
FIVE

PRELUDE
TO WAR

CHAPTER
TWENTY-FOUR

HITLER APPEASES ROOSEVELT

PRESIDENT ROOSEVELT MOVED quickly to take advantage of the global crisis. Impressed by Ambassador Bullitt's fear of an Anglo-French defeat, Roosevelt intended to push for revision of the Neutrality Act.[1] The looming defeat of heroic Poland rendered his task easier. Though a German invasion of the Americas appeared to be a remote possibility, Bullitt did not shrink from conjuring up this specter in his cables to the president, and FDR made cunning use of the nightmare.[2] FDR's agents worked to shore up Allied morale, while dashing hopes for a negotiated peace. In a strongly worded message to Ambassador Kennedy, Secretary Hull rejected any peace move that would "make possible a survival of a regime of force and of aggression."[3] The secretary's words were meant to warn the ambassador against reviving the discredited policy of appeasement. FDR's disenchantment with the Boston millionaire was growing. Kennedy was, the president would conclude, an appeaser who was doing more harm than good.

Hull's statement was extraordinary. A *neutral* power appeared to be calling for the destruction of the Nazi regime, with which it had diplomatic relations. Hull's message was doubly appropriate, for several weeks later Hitler did make a "peace offer" to France and Britain.[4] Roosevelt wanted no part of it, and the Allies rejected Hitler's overture. FDR was clearly pursuing a kind of neutrality far different from that which had prevailed in 1914. His success would hinge upon remolding American public opinion, and changing minds in Congress.

Roosevelt was a more subtle thinker and more of a strategist than his friend Bill Bullitt. While the Soviet incursion into eastern Poland on 16 September greatly annoyed the professional anticommunist Bullitt, FDR seemed little concerned about this action. He refused to break off relations with the Soviets, despite Bullitt's urging. In the United States, however, appeasers and isolationists were denouncing the "Commu-nazi" pact as something that "ought to teach us once more that we have no business in Europe" (*Daily News*). Roosevelt rejected the newly fashionable argument that Hitler and Stalin were equal threats to the world. Russia, which Roosevelt did not know well, was poor and relatively isolated. Germany was strong and centrally located. There was, to FDR, no comparison between the two powers.

Roosevelt now regretted having signed the 1935 Neutrality Act, and bemoaned his own refusal to help Republican Spain. On 21 September the president proposed repeal of the arms export embargo.[5] Under his plan, the Allies would be able to buy arms and munitions here, then export them to Europe on their own ships.[6] The president had his work cut out for him. One survey indicated that 65.6 percent of the public opposed aid to *any* belligerent power during the European war.[7]

Given British control of the North Atlantic sea-lanes, repeal of the arms embargo, accompanied by a restoration of cash and carry, meant assisting Britain and its allies at the expense of Germany. Britain would, of course, have to pay cash before taking delivery of munitions and other contraband, and transport it in non–U.S. flagged ships. Roosevelt and his followers in Congress steadfastly maintained that repeal of the embargo would help to *prevent* the United States from going to war.

Roosevelt confided to his friend, Kansas editor William Allen White, that "my problem is to get the American people to think of conceivable consequences without scaring the American people into thinking that they are going to be dragged into war." The "problem" was, that "people" might sense that aid to Britain foreshadowed, rather than precluded, American belligerency. Roosevelt needed to move in an extremely subtle manner. He did not fear, or even dislike, the idea of *eventual* intervention. His countrymen, however, were more recalcitrant.

Secretary Hull, with FDR's full approval, worked to gain public support for the president's plan. For the time being, Roosevelt cloaked his moves in the garb of nonintervention. The British and French, he seemed to be saying, would defend the Americas by fighting to the end on European soil and on the high seas.[8] Early editorials were encouraging. FDR's scare tactics even impressed some of the isolationists. The *New York Daily News* quickly rallied to support the repeal of the arms embargo, largely due to its poll of reader sentiment. Calling for stronger American defenses, the *News* took seriously the threat of a Nazi invasion of North America.[9]

Nevertheless, the fight for repeal would not be an easy one. In addition to the usual anti-Wilson crowd, powerful business executives, in some cases encouraged by German representatives, worked against Roosevelt. James D. Mooney, a General Motors vice president and good friend of the German-American Board of Trade, strongly believed that America should trade with Hitler's Europe. A decorated veteran, as well as lieutenant commander in the Naval Reserves, Mooney was the recipient of the Order of Merit of the German Eagle. Important German interests hoped that Mooney and his friends would intensify their efforts against Roosevelt's interventionist policy.

The German-American Board of Trade, founded in 1924, was a front for German interests in the United States. Subsidized by Nazi sources to the amount of 2,500 dollars per month, the board enabled the Germans to cultivate important American businessmen. The I.G. Farben concern, assisted by the propagandist George Sylvester Viereck, was particularly active in disseminating useful statements by Americans. The Board's slick *Bulletin* contained insights such as those offered by Graeme K. Howard, general manager of General Motors Overseas Operations. "We cannot blame Hitler," according to Howard, "for seeking to regain for his people the things they lost." Stay out of European conflicts, Howard argued, and trade with *all* nations. The *German-American Commerce Bulletin* reprinted Howard's remarks as a lead article.[10] Major American corporations, including Rockefeller Center, RCA, and Greyhound, were happy to advertise in that magazine. After all, America was at peace, and business was business. The Germans claimed to desire better commercial relations with the United States, so the *Bulletin* published long lists of visiting German businessmen. Some of them were acquainted with Colonel Charles A. Lindbergh, who was making a dramatic return to the public arena.

In a macabre phrase that reflected deep personal turmoil and profound commitment to reconciliation with Germany, Anne Morrow Lindbergh greeted the outbreak of war this way: "The child is dead. The child is dead in Europe."

By the autumn of 1939, with the encouragement of Herbert Hoover, Lindbergh made a fateful decision. The man who valued privacy above all else would go public. Flattered if a bit bemused, Lindy smiled at Senator Borah's comment about a Lindbergh presidential candidacy in 1940. FDR, however, was not amused. Lindbergh's plunge into controversy concerned his wife, who believed that he was "criminally misunderstood, misquoted, and misused."

Lindbergh reached the public through the *Reader's Digest*. He seemed to call for a peaceful division of the world by the Allied and Axis powers, in order to preserve the white race and combat bolshevism. Lindbergh consistently called for a virile, well-armed America, yet he voiced no enthusiasm for Roosevelt's rearmament programs, denouncing them as either too late, or excessive. Lindbergh mistrusted Roosevelt and feared the consequences of providing him with modern armed forces.[11]

Roosevelt's supporters needed to respond to men like Lindbergh. The president himself, according to Secretary of the Interior Ickes, said, "[T]here was a pretty wide suspicion that Lindbergh was a fascist." This was vintage FDR. Note that *he* was not accusing Lindbergh of fascism. Unidentified sources were doing so. Ickes was particularly close to Dorothy Thompson of the *Herald Tribune*. In late September, Lindbergh made a broadcast in which he denounced Roosevelt's pending revision of the Neutrality Act. While the War Department stripped Lindbergh of his active status in the army, Thompson slashed Lindy in a scathing article accusing the air ace of being pro-Nazi, cruel, and the recipient of a German medal. Someone in the government, probably Secretary Ickes, had clearly assisted Thompson. Administration leaks to friendly media persons such as Thompson and Walter Winchell were essential elements of Roosevelt's unfolding campaign against Hitler and his American paladins.[12]

In fighting against right-wing and left-wing resistance to intervention, Roosevelt leaned heavily upon a core of Eastern internationalists and Midwestern liberals. Roosevelt was, for example, in frequent contact with Clark M. Eichelberger, national director of the League of

Nations Association. An idealist whose worldview rested upon the concept of global interdependence, Eichelberger had served in France during the last war. Appalled by the carnage, the Illinois native had returned to America a fervent advocate of the league. FDR, who had been ignoring the league in his public statements, now encouraged Eichelberger's consultations with other pro-Allied Americans. Foremost among them was the progressive Republican editor William Allen White, with whom Eichelberger conferred in Emporia, Kansas. Five days after the president made his repeal proposal, the Non-Partisan Committee for Peace through Revision of the Neutrality Act came into being, headed by Eichelberger and White.

Editor of the famous *Emporia Gazette*, William Allen White enjoyed the reputation of being a philosopher, a liberal Republican, and a patriot.[13] Convinced that American neutrality had helped Hitler to alter the map of Europe, White and his colleagues worked to lift the arms embargo. As a midwesterner and a Republican, White helped to counter the image of interventionists as a small clique of Eastern "establishmentarians."

Prominent figures began to flock to the committee, including Chicago publisher Colonel Frank Knox, the 1936 Republican vice presidential candidate; Mrs. Dwight Morrow, Anne Lindbergh's mother and acting president of Smith College; and actor Edward G. Robinson. Robinson, of Rumanian-Jewish origin, showed great courage in joining, for in so doing he defied a still-timid Hollywood establishment.[14] The committee attracted broad bipartisan support. Its backers ranged from former secretary of war (and state) Henry L. Stimson to University of Chicago economics professor Paul H. Douglas, actors Helen Hayes and Melvyn Douglas, labor leader David Dubinsky, New York City mayor Fiorello H. LaGuardia, cultural historian Lewis Mumford, Harvard political scientist Carl J. Friedrich, theologian Reinhold Niebuhr. Young, highly articulate Democrats such as Adlai E. Stevenson of Illinois and J. William Fulbright of Arkansas worked with the "White committee."

Though at times elitist and "East Coast," the White group at least had some kind of social and ideological coherence. Its enemies, by contrast, consisted of a strange mélange of the far left, hard-core pacifists, hidebound isolationists, right-wing Republicans, outright reactionaries, and embittered, aging progressives. In the Senate, the crusty old William E. Borah led the battle against repeal. Seventy-four years of age, Borah was in failing health. He had helped to prevent American entry into the League of Nations. Now, with that institution in ruins, thanks in part to Borah's victory over Woodrow Wilson, the Idaho senator became the last great hope of the anti-interventionists. Borah received enormous amounts of mail, much of it anti-Semitic. One writer claimed that only the Jews and the money changers wanted to alter the Neutrality Act. Borah, who was not particularly anti-Semitic or pro-Nazi, used the communist phrase "imperialistic war" in denouncing the Allied cause, yet he received support from Archbishop Beckman of Dubuque, Iowa. Francis F. J. Beckman, an admirer of Father Coughlin, accused the Soviets of fomenting and perpetuating the conflict. This crazy theory, articulated at a time when Stalin was *allied with Hitler*, made Beckman a tactical ally of the American Communist Party. Not all of Senator Borah's mail was friendly. One telegram made an interesting point. If England fell thanks to a lack of U.S. support, said this writer, Borah would be responsible for American entry into the war.

Harold Ickes, Secretary of the Interior, grumbled in his diary, "In our own country, not only Coughlin, but the little Fascists everywhere . . ., have been . . . building up a defense against Communism by shielding Naziism." Ickes lumped Joseph P. Kennedy together with Coughlin, accusing him of having sabotaged a Russo-British treaty against Hitler. [15]

The moral inferiority of the anti-interventionist position was reflected in the alliances it engendered. Those who favored Communism were coming to oppose repeal, while those who most feared Communism also opposed repeal. This maelstrom contained a dialectical impossibility, and upon this contradiction the isolationist cause ultimately foundered. Worse still, the anti-interventionists would have to oppose Roosevelt while avoiding the appearance of helping Hitler. FDR was doing his best to make this impossible.

William Allen White honestly believed that aid to the Allies could keep the United States out of the war. "We have no reason," he wrote, "to fear the effects upon us of a French-British victory. We have a whole lot to fear in the case of a Hitler victory." [16] Roosevelt's goals, however, went beyond the avoidance of war. Buried in one of FDR's letters to the Kansan was an interesting revelation. "I do not want this country," declared Roosevelt, "to take part in a patched up temporizing peace which would blow up in our faces in a year or two." [17]

The great editor was a bit naive about Roosevelt's intentions, but that made him a better propagandist for the president. White faced a whole array of anti-Roosevelt activists, some of whom had been allies of the president during earlier battles. The traditional isolationists, like senators Borah, Nye, and Wheeler, could be counted upon to oppose FDR on repeal, but there was another side to the public opinion battle. Roosevelt's interventionism and Stalin's pact with Hitler turned the embargo issue into a kind of civil war on the left.

White's committee worked to counter the propaganda of groups like the Keep America Out of War Congress, a pacifist and socialist group whose chief spokesman was Norman Thomas. Thomas was concerned about the infiltration of his peace committee by another anti-interventionist group, the Communist Party.[18] After September, the communists, who viewed the war as a contest between rival imperialisms, worked to sabotage Roosevelt's interventionist foreign policy. They came up with a catchy bit of doggerel, that went like this:

> *Let the bugler keep on blowing,*
> *Let the drummer beat his drum;*
> *They are in for disappointment*
> *For the Yanks will never come.*

No one argued the noninterventionist case better than Vito Marcantonio, the left-leaning New York City congressman. Marcantonio's renewed commitment to pacifism became apparent only after Stalin entered into his famous agreement with Hitler. "[W]hen you prepare for war you are bound to have war," Marcantonio declared. Like many Americans, he reinforced his case by referring to the last intervention, in 1917. "America had no business in the last war," according to "Marc." Though not a communist, Marcantonio followed Moscow's line in foreign policy. "The Yanks are not coming," he thundered. Like Stalin, he branded the current conflict an "imperialistic war."[19]

The communist *Daily Worker* called for lifting the arms embargo, then changed its line. After the fall of Poland, when Hitler made his 6 October "peace offer" to the West, the *Daily Worker* ascribed the Führer's new pacifism to the "universal will of the peoples for peace. . . ." Stalin, who wanted an end to the fighting, now blamed the imperialist democracies for the continuation of the war. The *Worker* compared Nazi atrocities to British crimes in India, and urged resistance to any measures calculated to involve the United States in the "imperialist war." The communists, though small in numbers, exercized great influence among intellectuals, as well as in certain labor unions. Their opposition to Roosevelt's actions increased the possibility of strikes and sabotage in the burgeoning defense industry.[20]

After the initial flurry of bipartisan support for President Roosevelt, signs pointed to a divisive partisan debate. Publisher J. M. Patterson, who ran the *New York Daily News*, soon regretted his support for repeal of the arms embargo. For the next two years, his newspaper supported "a philosophy of keeping our noses out of other people's affairs, especially out of Europe's wars. . . ." Ironically, the *Worker* used some of the same arguments made by the right-wing *Daily News*. In the autumn of 1939, the *News* devoted an entire editorial to Dalton Trumbo's novel *Johnny Got his Gun*. The leftist author had told the story of a young, patriotic idealist who does his duty for his country. Horribly mangled in combat, Johnny is reduced to the status of a thinking vegetable. A powerful work, *Johnny Got his Gun* bolstered the pacifist cause. After reading the book, *any* war seemed to be a great folly, to be avoided at all costs.

It is ironic that the rightist *Daily News* should have seized upon a work by a left-wing (some said communist) author. In fact, writers like Dalton Trumbo later made the Hollywood blacklist in part due to Red-baiting by papers like the *News*.[21] In late 1939, however, at the end of an ugly decade, both the *News* and the *Worker* shared a common bias against involvement in events or ideologies "over there."

In the event of a short war, Germany had little reason to be concerned about the United States. As Hitler put it, "America is as yet no danger to us, because of her neutrality laws. Strengthening of the enemy by America is still insignificant." Hitler predicted that two or three years would pass before the Americans could send an army to Europe.[22] A German naval officer expanded upon the Führer's views. "Even if we are convinced," he wrote, "that, should the war be of long duration, the U.S.A. will enter it in any case . . . it must be our object to delay this event so long that American help would come too late." According to State Secretary Ernst von Weizsäcker of the Foreign Ministry, Germany policy aimed at "preventing the United States from throwing in their full weight on the side of our enemies." Because of the American threat, Hitler emphasized the "further need for the utmost speed in driving apart the enemies in Europe and beating them to their knees."[23]

General Friedrich von Bötticher, Germany's army attaché in Washington, provided the Foreign Ministry, the Supreme Command of the Armed Forces, and the High Command of the Army with vital information about Roosevelt's rearmament program. For the time being, he said, the United States could not even provide adequate supplies for its own, small armed forces. Within a year, however, American industry would be turning out large amounts of military equipment. And by 1942, according to von Bötticher, the United States would be capable of producing more armaments than any other nation.

Though sometimes coated with Nazi prejudices, von Bötticher's information confirmed the potential strength of Roosevelt's America. His reports tended to augment Hitler's concern about American intervention. From Hans Thomsen, Berlin learned, "Roosevelt is determined to go to war against Germany, even in the face of resistance in his own country." A global conflict meant a war of attrition, production, and blockade. Germany could not win such a conflict, and Hitler did everything he could to avoid one.

Hitler was caught in a paradox. As he saw it, Roosevelt could turn the European war into a world war. Hitler thus needed to avoid provoking him, at least until Germany won the war in Europe. Hitler, recalling Foreign Minister Ribbentrop, promulgated "a very strict order even in the articles of the leading correspondents, to be very careful not to do anything or say anything against the United States of America." The Periodicals Service, which provided ideological guidance to German magazines, gave appropriate orders. "Let us," it advised, "avoid everything which might strengthen the United States in its fears that its importance could be weakened through German victories."[24]

The hateful tone with regard to Roosevelt and America, so prominent a year earlier, all but disappeared from the press. Respectful comments about FDR's leadership ability appeared in newspapers. Readers, however, were cautioned against undue optimism. America, after all, was rearming, and the United States might change her policy one day, especially if Roosevelt won reelection in 1940.[25] Despite this caution, for a time Nazi leaders such as Hermann Goering and Alfred Rosenberg convinced themselves that Roosevelt might play the role assigned to him by Berlin. In October, after the fall of Poland, Rosenberg noted that FDR would probably try to mediate the conflict, then run for reelection as the "angel of peace."[26]

Hitler's American policy mandated caution, even appeasement. There was a danger for him in pursuing this policy, however. Hitler assumed that Roosevelt might well wish to enter the war, but would probably not do so while he was unprepared to fight. If the war ended quickly, the United States might not enter it at all. In avoiding war with the Americans, however, Hitler was giving Roosevelt time, precisely what he needed. FDR could use this respite for his own purposes, such as building up his armed forces, aiding the Allies, and warning the public about an alleged Nazi menace to the Americas.

The German government proclaimed a blockade around the British Isles, so its navy (mainly U-boats) could attack neutral vessels carrying contraband into this small area. Britain, however, could not survive without its imports, including those from the Western Hemisphere. If Hitler was to "bring Britain to its senses," he had to destroy *all* merchant ships and tankers bound for the home islands. Many of these vessels simply unloaded their cargoes in British-controlled or Canadian ports, whereupon English ships, accompanied by Royal Navy destroyers, escorted them home. Unless the Germans enforced a stricter blockade, and challenged British domination of the great sea-lanes of the North Atlantic, they could not bring the island kingdom to its knees. In late October, Admiral Raeder, commander in chief of the navy, called for a broader policy, one aimed at stopping "entirely all commercial traffic of neutrals or allies with Britain and France." The war against England, he believed, might be won or lost in an "extended war zone" in the Atlantic Ocean.

The American states, however, working at Roosevelt's behest, had in late September decided to create a Pan-American Neutrality Zone. This three hundred mile wide belt around the Americas was designed to prevent belligerent ships from venturing anywhere near international waters abutting the coasts of the Americas. The measure, of course, would keep German warships out of a crucial area. Britain, which had an ally in Canada and bases in the Caribbean, at first opposed the neutral zone. The zone, however, hurt Germany more than it impeded the activities of the Royal Navy, so Britain eventually accepted it.

What would Hitler do about the "Pan-American Safety Zone"? The basic problem, complained Raeder, went back to restrictions placed upon German naval warfare. German U-boats and surface raiders were not permitted to attack neutral merchant ships, "sailing alone or in neutral convoys." In addition, "all neutral ships sailing alone to enemy ports which are not carrying contraband and are behaving correctly" were permitted to proceed to enemy ports (i.e., to English docks).[27] Raeder, speaking for his colleagues, wanted to sink "without warning all neutral ships proved to have contraband for England on board." This, Hitler realized, might provoke a war with the United States. From the German leader's viewpoint, such a conflict would be most unfortunate.

Germany, Hitler knew, possessed only 57 submarines. By March 1942, however, she planned to have 253 of these deadly vessels ready for action. At that point, Germany would be in a better position to isolate Britain from its American suppliers. For the moment, Hitler hoped to end the war with Britain on some kind of compromise basis, while the United States remained neutral. A frustrated Admiral Raeder had to wage war with one hand tied behind his back, for Hitler turned down his request for authority to move aggressively against neutral shipping. His orders were clear, and they prevailed for the next two years. "U.S. ships," Hitler said, "are not to be stopped, captured, or sunk." Raeder reluctantly followed Hitler's command. He informed his top commanders that "all difficulties which might result from a trade [i.e., naval] war between the United States and Germany be avoided. . . ." Raeder noted in January that the "careful treatment of America will also have to be maintained with every additional intensification of warfare against merchant shipping . . . for political reasons." "American crews," Raeder reported, "are treated with the greatest consideration."

Politics and propaganda had forced the German Navy into a difficult position. Britain had to be isolated and choked to death. This meant offending the Americans, who might then enter the war. Yet Germany did not expect to have an adequate number of U-boats until the spring of 1942.[28] The Germans were sacrificing their rights as a naval belligerent in order to appease the hated Roosevelt. Hermann Goering, who had so recently mused about bombing the Empire State building, now purred at the United States. The Americans, he claimed, had nothing to fear from a triumphant Germany. "Even if you don't like us," Goering declared, "give us some credit for common sense and reason."

The Foreign Ministry received orders compelling it to tone down protests against pro-Allied measures undertaken by the president.[29] This was particularly galling, because that same ministry had obtained Polish documents "proving" that Roosevelt conspired to unleash war in 1939. The documents certainly indicated that William Bullitt, Roosevelt's agent, had urged the Allies to wage war, in the expectation of American belligerency. Though used for propaganda purposes by isolationists in the United States, these documents had no effect upon Hitler's policy. He had no intention of waging preventive war against the United States.

The William Allen White committee established branches in thirty states and organized an effective lobbying campaign. It enjoyed the support of media magnate Henry Luce of Time Inc., whose publications supported revision of the Neutrality Act.[30] In October, only 24.7 percent of respondents to one poll had argued against aiding either side.[31] The polls soon showed that a majority of respondents favored repeal of the arms embargo (by 58 percent to 34 percent), in the full knowledge that it would benefit Britain and France at the expense of Germany.[32] Roosevelt prevailed in November. The Allies could now purchase arms on a "cash and carry" basis, though other provisions of the Neutrality Act of 1937 were retained. What Congress had denied to Roosevelt and the Allies in July, it granted in November, after the fall of Poland.

The war in the west continued in a desultory manner. The Germans sat behind their "Siegfried line," while the French grew bored and frustrated in the impressive fortresses known as the "Maginot line." Unlike the *Blitzkrieg* (Lightning War) against Poland, the war in the west seemed to be a *Sitzkrieg* (Sitting War). The war at sea went more favorably for the Allies, but it was hardly decisive. There was no sign that Germany would collapse as a result of the much advertised Allied blockade. The German blockade of Britain was equally indecisive.

The lack of action at the front encouraged those in the business community who hoped to preserve American neutrality, perhaps until a compromise peace could insure the continuation of global trade. *Business Week* received its readers' support after editorializing against American involvement. The National Association of Manufacturers believed that "we must be . . . determined to refrain from any act that might lead us into [the war]."[33]

In January, Roosevelt launched a new propaganda offensive against this kind of thinking. Warning that the world would be a "shabby and dangerous place to live in . . . if it is ruled by force in the hands of a few," he again planned to increase expenditures for armaments. To Roosevelt, the very existence of the Nazi regime meant permanent danger. The momentary lull gave him no reason to stop planning for its destruction. At this point, that meant assisting the Allies. Though Poland had fallen quickly, and the Allies had done little to harm Germany, Roosevelt still hoped that Hitler could be defeated by the first anti-Nazi coalition without American military intervention.

Secretary of the Treasury Morgenthau worked closely with Allied purchasing agents. American industry was soon capable of turning out 19,280 aircraft engines per year, whereas a few months earlier the figure had been a mere 7,290. The British and French projected a need in 1940 for 20,000 engines and half as many planes. Army Air Corps officers who did not like the new policies sometimes found themselves threatened with "exile" to the base on Guam.[34]

Roosevelt foresaw the political impact of massive arms production. It would, he predicted to a group of congressmen, "mean prosperity for this country and we can't elect the Democratic Party unless we get prosperity. . . . Let's be perfectly frank."[35] He promised prosperity without war, but this was a commitment based upon the premise of an Allied victory.

A strange pattern had begun to emerge. Adolf Hitler was working to preserve American neutrality, as mandated by congressional legislation in the years 1935–1939. Franklin Roosevelt, in contrast, was doing everything in his power to change the concept of neutrality, in order to help a belligerent nations whose survival was essential to his long-term plans. FDR's remarks betrayed increasing concern about the Allied war effort. He now worked to prevent Germany from attacking in the west, and to keep Italy out of the war in the Mediterranean.

CHAPTER
TWENTY-FIVE

☆ ══════════════════════ ⤨

THE NEAR DEMISE OF THE
FIRST ANTI-NAZI COALITION

RESIDENT ROOSEVELT DID not share the public's confidence in the invulnerability of the Allied armies in France. He decided to send Under Secretary of State Sumner Welles to the capitals of the belligerent powers, and also to Italy, ostensibly on a fact-finding mission. Welles' report, and related documents, tell a different story. Once again Roosevelt's goals were clear, his methods deceptive.

Under Secretary since 1937, Welles, like Roosevelt, enjoyed a background of wealth and privilege. Outwardly formal and in control of himself and his environment, Welles was in reality a tormented man. The forty-eight-year-old diplomat was a homosexual. Upon rare occasions, he would become intoxicated, and once, in a Pullman car, he made advances to a porter. The incident, though reported by the porter, was hushed up for the time being, and did not lead to Welles's downfall for another three years.

In his conversations with Mussolini and Hitler, the under secretary expressed American interest in the construction of a liberal postwar order within a "stable, just and lasting peace." According to Welles, all nations would gain access to markets and raw materials; prosperous and interdependent, they could then disarm. Of course, this kind of liberal

318

international order could only be created after the destruction of fascist autarky and aggression.

The idea that Roosevelt sent Welles to Hitler, in the middle of a war, in order to gain Germany's assistance in restoring a liberal world order is preposterous. In fact, the president feared a compromise peace that would leave the Nazis in power. Roosevelt had, after all, helped to sabotage Hitler's so-called peace offer of 6 October, 1939.

FDR, concerned about Allied vulnerability, sent Welles to Europe because his military instincts told him that Hitler would launch a spring offensive against a vulnerable France and that Italy might enter the war, thus forcing a two-front war on a troubled French Army. In Italy, Welles was shocked to meet a prematurely aged Mussolini ("very heavy for his height, and his face in repose falls into rolls of flesh. . . . under some tremendous strain. . . ."). In a bitchy aside, Welles noted that Mussolini might be fatigued because he had recently procured a "new and young Italian mistress." He urged the duce to stick to his policy of "nonbelligerency." Foreign Minister Count Galeazzo Ciano promised to work in this direction.

Resuming his journey, Welles arrived in Berlin on 1 March. He warned State Secretary Ernst von Weizsäcker against expanded military activity. Such an adventure would, Welles argued, risk the danger "that everything which made life worth living would be destroyed." "The U.S.A.," he continued, "could not remain unconcerned in face of this possibility." Foreign Minister Ribbentrop, and Luftwaffe chief Hermann Goering countered by assuring their American visitor that Germany had no intention of attacking the Western Hemisphere.

Later, to Welles's dismay, Mussolini reported that "Germany would undertake an immediate offensive. . . ." Ciano accurately predicted the bombing of London and other cities. The Welles mission failed or, put more accurately, Roosevelt had engaged in a failed bluff. There was no chance that Hitler would agree to restore Germany's old frontiers or acknowledge Anglo-French supremacy in Europe. He was indeed preparing his spring offensive. FDR intended to use this respite on behalf of the Allies, by strengthening their naval and air forces.[1] The president received a small public relations bonus. The Welles mission reinforced Roosevelt's image as a cautious protector of American interests and a man pledged to peace. Intended to deter Hitler and Mussolini in the spring, while Britain and France armed to the teeth, Welles was an instrument not of peace but of war. The Allies were still FDR's only

frontline combatants in the struggle against Hitlerism, and he sent
Welles to Berlin and Rome in order to help them.[2] Hitler and Ribbentrop seemed to sense this.

While Welles journeyed to Europe, Roosevelt had to counter growing
suspicions about his role in the outbreak of the war. The Germans,
having captured Polish Foreign Ministry records, published a "White
Book." Though selectively, even tendentiously, edited, the enclosed
documents were indeed genuine. Purporting to expose Bullitt's belligerent stance in 1939, the German volume threatened to expose Roosevelt's efforts at establishing an antiaggressor front. Such a revelation
could only hurt him at home, at a delicate time. At a press conference,
the president dodged reporters' questions about Bullitt's activities.
Bullitt came to Roosevelt's rescue, by persuading Daladier to write a
letter of exoneration. "I feel," said the French leader, "I should tell you
that during the past two years when I was Prime Minister, Ambassador
Bullitt always said to me that in the case of a European conflict, France
should make her decisions knowing that . . . the United States of
America would not enter the war." This half-truth appeased Roosevelt,
who cabled Bullitt that he was "very much pleased with Daladier's letter
of April 4." A press uproar over the president's past diplomatic moves
was thereby averted.[3] Roosevelt had had a close call, but even the most
vehement mainstream anti-interventionists were afraid of being labeled
"pro-Nazi" if they used the German book of documents against FDR.

There was little else to cheer Roosevelt. Within a week of Daladier's
statement, German forces had taken Denmark and were overrunning
Norway. Rumors circulating in Rome pointing to an imminent entry of
Italy into the conflict. Roosevelt warned Mussolini that Italian belligerency might lead to a dangerous situation. Unidentified neutrals, he
declared, "might yet find it imperative in their own defense to enter the
war." On 10 May, the Germans invaded Holland, Belgium, Luxem-
bourg, and France; within two weeks, they had won a strategic victory.

On that same dark day, Britain's first lord of the admiralty, Winston
Churchill, replaced Chamberlain as prime minister. Publicly, Churchill
was defiant, offering nothing less than "blood, toil, tears, and sweat."
Privately, he soon complained that the United States had "given us
practically no help in the war." A frustrated Lord Lothian, ambassador
to Washington, cried out that the U.S. was "dominated by fear of war—
which is exactly what Hitler wants. Oh for Theodore Roosevelt!!"[4]
From Paris, Bullitt, in a state of shock, informed Roosevelt that "unless

God grants a miracle . . . , the French army will be crushed utterly."[5]

By the end of the month, most of the British Expeditionary Force had evacuated the continent at Dunkirk. Churchill promised that this retreat was no prelude to surrender or defeat. "We shall go on to the end," he declared, ". . . we shall defend our Island, whatever the cost may be, we shall fight on the beaches, we shall fight on the landing grounds. . . ."[6]

A German offensive along the Somme River inaugurated the final phase of the Battle of France. From the channel to the Maginot line, the "greatest army in the world" soon lay prostrate. The half-American Churchill wistfully longed for the day when "the New World, with all its power and might, steps forth to the rescue and the liberation of the Old."[7] The French premier, Paul Reynaud, addressed passionate appeals to the president. He wanted "waves of planes" and a declaration of war. Bullitt reinforced Reynaud's plea with images of German atrocities: "Two aeroplanes came down and machine gunned [a group of children] and the road was filled with little bodies."

Mussolini declared war on 10 June, thereby, in Roosevelt's words, stabbing his fallen neighbor in the back. The magnitude of the catastrophe left even Roosevelt disoriented and feeling helpless. The public, much less the Congress, was not ready for war. Besides, the United States possessed only 160 pursuit planes, and 52 heavy bombers.[8] Premier Reynaud desperately appealed to Roosevelt, urging him to promise a declaration of war "within a short space of time." France, he said, was about to go under like a drowning man. Churchill confirmed the urgency of the situation. FDR had long admired his fellow naval enthusiast Churchill, but he felt compelled to advise him that American belligerency would not be forthcoming.[9] A desperate Churchill advised Roosevelt of his fear of strangulation by the combined German and Italian submarine fleets. He pleaded with the president for "thirty or forty old destroyers you have already had reconditioned. . . . The next six months are vital." The Battle of Britain, Churchill believed, was about to begin.[10]

Roosevelt was dubious about Congress and public opinion. Already, skeptics, isolationists, neutralists, and appeasers were muttering against giving Britain more aid. Might its fleet not fall into Nazi hands? Did the United States not require all of its war production for defense needs? Speaking privately to a group of businessmen, Roosevelt described the French Army and the Royal Navy as essential to American

security. That army was now out of the picture. If the British capitu-
lated, he continued, "the American system would be directly and
immediately menaced by a Nazi-dominated Europe."[11] FDR needed
to use such words in order to create a sense of *imminent* danger. He was
beginning to recover from the shock of the bad news about France.
FDR now saw how that nightmare could be of use to him.

Stunned Americans soon watched newsreels of the arrogant Germans
marching through the *arc de triomphe* in Paris. Stories circulated about
fifth-column Nazi agents who had assisted the Germans during the
French campaign. The *New York Times* reported a disturbing story from
London. Tyler G. Kent, a young cryptology clerk at the American
embassy, had stolen about 1,500 cables exchanged with the State
Department. Anti-Semitic and apparently pro-German, Kent seemed
to be all too typical of the gilded, profascist youth of the era. Kent
denied any imputation of treason or espionage.[12]

Recent events seemed to confirm Hitler's words, as allegedly recorded by his former confidant Hermann Rauschning in his best-selling
book *The Voice of Destruction*. Here Americans read of Hitler's uncanny
prophecy regarding the fall of France—delivered in 1934. Roosevelt
had often expressed his concern about German ambitions in Latin
America. According to Rauschning, Hitler had declared, "We shall
create a new Germany [in Brazil]." The German leader believed that
"Only the most capable and industrious people in the world, namely,
the Germans, would be able to make something of [Mexico]." "You
could get this Mexico," declared the Führer, for a couple of hundred
million."[13] Fifth columnists, traitors, spies—American fears were
widespread.

How long could England survive? French military experts like General Maxime Weygand and Admiral Jean Darlan, who had failed to
defend their own nation, now swore that Britain could not resist Hitler's
Wehrmacht. An American magazine publisher tried to commission an
"eyewitness account of the upcoming German entry into London."[14]
Would the Italians take the Suez Canal, thereby strangling the British
empire? Churchill, concerned about the western approaches to the
home isles, pleaded again with FDR for naval assistance.[15]

In Washington, the Joint Board of the armed forces recommended the
adoption of an updated "Rainbow Four" plan. In this scenario, the
Americans fought alone, concentrating all of their strength upon a
buildup of forces in the Western Hemisphere. Respected military men,

such as Army Chief of Staff General George C. Marshall and Chief of Naval Operations Harold Stark, argued against sending war material to Britain, a power on the verge of possible defeat. Roosevelt disliked the new plan, which assumed the imminent defeat of England. The president prevailed, and a revised plan was predicated upon the survival of, and aid to, Great Britain. Roosevelt had decided that his advisers were wrong about the value of aiding Britain.

Roosevelt now moved energetically on both the propaganda and policy fronts. William Allen White offered support. Writing to playwright Robert Sherwood, White advocated the delivery to Britain of "our aged and obsolescent destroyers." "If the President really wants to do it," said White, "it can be done."[16] White and his associates from the embargo repeal campaign now headed the Committee to Defend America by Aiding the Allies. Endorsed by a wide array of interventionists, the committee soon established hundreds of local affiliates. Reinhold Niebuhr, once a pacifist, joined the committee. Frank Knox, publisher of the Chicago *Daily News,* worked with the committee, as did Morgan banker Thomas W. Lamont, and many other distinguished Republicans. Father Coughlin promptly denounced it as a "dangerous fifth column" headed by a "sanctimonious stuffed shirt named William Allen White."[17]

While White still favored staying out of hostilities if possible, other prominent Americans demanded an immediate declaration of war on Germany. The informal "Century Club group," (named after the prestigious men's club in New York City) consisted largely of northeastern and midwestern lawyers and businessmen with international connections. While overlapping with the White committee, the Century Club men were more overtly interventionist; some wanted war with Germany now. The United States had to *defeat* Germany, they believed, then preside over a new world order. This confident belief in the American destiny coincided with Roosevelt's own views in 1920 and later, though he was more cautious about articulating them in public.

Confidence was a quality exuded by the dapper Dean Acheson, an eloquent, arrogant, and highly gifted attorney. "Nothing seems to be more foolish," wrote Acheson, "than a policy designed to assure that if we must fight, the fighting shall be done on our own territory." Joining Acheson, a Democrat, were interventionist Republicans of high caliber, among them President James Bryant Conant of Harvard University, and President Ernest H. Hopkins of Dartmouth College.

In "A Summons to Speak Out," issued on 10 June, thirty prominent interventionists urged that Roosevelt move more quickly. Yet the president was not ready to request a declaration of war, because the public was not prepared for so drastic a step.[18] Congress would not have cooperated, nor was the country armed for global conflict. Despite these important reservations, Roosevelt shared one of the Century Club's major assumptions. A decent world could not coexist with a National Socialist Europe. Unless the American people believed in an imminent danger, however, the nation would not support the interventionist position.

Roosevelt finally began to take some important initiatives. He warned the new French government of Marshall Henri-Philippe Pétain not to surrender its fleet to the Germans. The president returned to his theme of a German threat to the Western Hemisphere. During the coming, uncertain summer, British antisubmarine escorts could only patrol the North Atlantic to a point two hundred miles west of Ireland. What might the Germans do, since their submarine construction program was increasing production dramatically? Encouraged by Churchill's vow to fight on until victory, Roosevelt decided to move forcefully on the rearmament issue.

In a message to Congress, FDR called for the production of "at least 50,000 planes a year," a stunning, some said preposterous, figure. New monies were forthcoming. Roosevelt was using the sense of national emergency for his own complex purposes. Having helped to bring about the anti-German alliance in 1939, he now moved to secure its survival. The question of whether the Allies could defeat Germany without American participation was, for the moment, a theoretical one. The first order of business was the survival of Britain.[19]

The concentric circle around Germany, consisting of Britain, France, and Poland, had cracked. Roosevelt now entered into his second anti-Nazi arrangement, what one might call the war of the revised coalition. Britain and its empire, assisted by the United States, would fight on until victory came. The United States would not seek war, but would do all in its power to help those at war with Germany. This coalition was later expanded to include allies such as Yugoslavia, Greece, and Soviet Russia. If that did not suffice, there would be a new coalition, with the United States as a prime belligerent.

Roosevelt now maneuvered his interventionist allies like pawns on a chessboard. Behind the scenes, he encouraged playwright Robert E.

Sherwood, who became his foremost propagandist. A towering (six-foot, seven inches) man, Sherwood was vehement in the advocacy of his beliefs. In the Great War, he had fought as a volunteer in a Scottish-Canadian regiment. Sherwood still looked the part, for he was mustachioed and handsome in a dark, brooding way. A film critic and journalist, Sherwood became an important speech writer for FDR. As a crusader for world peace, Sherwood saw Roosevelt's foreign policy as a vindication of Woodrow Wilson's worldview. The forty-four-year-old Sherwood believed that "if the Allies should be defeated, the next war will follow quickly and it will be fought in this hemisphere." Roosevelt liked his agents to believe in their work, even when their views were ahead of, or behind, his own. White urged people to help Britain, because Roosevelt told him that this was the way to avoid war. Sherwood stoked fears of a Nazi fifth column in America, because he believed what Roosevelt was saying about this problem. Fear was good for preparedness, and the playwright's eloquence caught the public ear.

Sherwood sometimes wrote Roosevelt's lines, but he lacked the president's sense of timing. Like Sherwood, Roosevelt, too, viewed full intervention as a possibility, but later rather than sooner. Like Sherwood, Roosevelt too favored full intervention as a possibility, but later rather than sooner. FDR controlled Sherwood by means of the more careful William Allen White.[20] White had his own problems. Referring to the "Century Club crowd" and to people like Sherwood, White spoke to Eichelberger of impatient young men whose boldness caused him grief. For many months, tension built up between White and the New York interventionists. The easterners had money and clout on their side. Henry Luce, the media mogul, was a big contributor to the committee, while New York State accounted for about forty-eight percent of its cash income. The Century Club group wanted more action, perhaps the escort of British convoys by American warships or even a declaration of war on Germany. White took Roosevelt at his word and opposed these stirrings. FDR encouraged both factions.[21]

Spiritually secure, and possessed of boundless self-confidence, Roosevelt manipulated his friends without hesitation or qualm. They served his purposes, even when the president's goals were unclear to them. The Whites and the Sherwoods did not have to worry about public opinion as a whole, for they were assigned specific tasks. Roosevelt's own tasks were broader.

CHAPTER
TWENTY-SIX

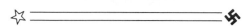

AMERICA UNDER SIEGE:
FDR'S FEAR TACTICS

FRANKLIN ROOSEVELT WAS not at all unhappy about growing American anxieties about imminent German aggression in the Western Hemisphere. Since 1938, after all, the president himself had been warning the public about a possible attack on the Panama Canal. He now claimed to fear German domination of South America, and a not-so-distant air attack on the United States from bases in Mexico or Costa Rica. Like a steady drumbeat, these fears accompanied (and usually preceded) FDR's appeals for aid to Great Britain or for new military appropriations.

Roosevelt would gather the reporters around his desk. There was less banter than in the old days; indeed, one could hear a pin drop. The president, displaying his knowledge of geography, strategy, and economics, proceeded to paint a frightening picture of an Axis victory. FDR's concerns often reflected alarmist information received from his naval aide, Captain D.J. Callaghan. Another sometime confidant of the president, ambassador to Chile Claude Bowers, provided his chief with even more alarming news. Writing from Chile, Bowers told FDR, "[T]he Germans, who are numerous, are thoroughly organized with the view of a coup d'état." Soon, articles appeared reflecting the president's latest fears. Roosevelt was arousing the nation. Few reporters dared to press Roosevelt regarding his sources. In that age, few journalists saw themselves as investigative adversaries of the White House. When an intrepid reporter did press in too hard, Roosevelt dismissed the question with a joke, changed the subject, or flicked his cigarette and continued the lecture. FDR and his advocates at times crossed the line separating public concern from mass hysteria. Given the widespread apathy about the consequences of a German-dominated Europe, such transgressions were excusable.

A series of articles in the *New York Times* exposed the "subversive" effects of Nazi propaganda in Brazil, Argentina, and Bolivia. Appearing in a newspaper noted for its caution and accuracy, the articles were broadly influential. They drew some of their inspiration from comments made by the president over the past year.[1] The same was true of the writings of respected author Howell M. Henry, who convinced himself that "25,000 trained German soldiers held as extralegal storm troops" had already landed in Brazil. Speaking of these and similar allegations, Foreign Minister Ribbentrop later told Allied interrogators, "I can assure you that [they] always struck us as so ridiculous that we never even thought of it."[2]

Roosevelt's supporters became conduits for the "Trojan horse" message. In late July, Cornelius Vanderbilt, Jr. supplied William Allen White with a shocking confirmation of FDR's fears. The millionaire recalled a 1939 meeting with Dr. Joseph Goebbels, during which the propaganda minister threatened America. "[W]hen we get good and ready," Goebbels had declared, "we expect to take your impertinent nation from within." Mr. Burton Stevenson, a librarian in Chillicothe, Ohio, did not for a moment believe this kind of thing. He informed White of his belief that "the British have never fought for any interests but their own, and never will. . . . [We] should . . . say 'To hell with all of you.' " Stevenson's view was receiving less support with each report of a new German threat. White, a powerful propagandist himself, believed Vanderbilt. Roosevelt was gradually achieving one of his aims, the equation of anti-interventionism with fifth-column activity, or the type seen recently on the Western front.

The collapse of the Allied effort in France and Belgium was, according to Charles A. Lindbergh, Jr., Britain's concern, not ours. America was, said Lindbergh, immune to a German attack, and should therefore refrain from meddling in purely "European" conflicts. To some of his supporters, however, such as Secretary Ickes, Roosevelt was not acting quickly enough. An enraged Ickes believed that Lindbergh and his friends on the right were Nazis, hence anti-American. The administration helped to arrange a rebuttal to Lindbergh's address. Delivered by Senator James F. Byrnes of South Carolina, the radio speech placed Lindbergh in the position of opposing his government at a time of emergency.

Hardly mollified, the aroused Ickes turned to his own intelligence sources. Unbeknownst to the public, Ickes coordinated a private investigative group, dedicated to exposing Nazi propaganda efforts in the United States. Directed by T.H. Tetens, the three-man task force presented Ickes with startling information. The Germans, according to Tetens, were spending money on behalf of far-right groups like the Christian Mobilizers, the Silver Shirts, Father Coughlin, "and others." Ickes promptly turned this material over to the attorney general, and during the next year bad things happened to the subjects of the investigations. Roosevelt knew what Ickes was up to, at least in outline. So long as the secretary's timing did not disrupt FDR's plans, the president permitted selective leaks to the media, and encouraged appropriate action by J. Edgar Hoover of the FBI.[3]

If Britain fell, or lost control of the seas, what would the Germans be able to do in a few years? Roosevelt projected a future danger onto the present in order to arouse public opinion. In so doing, he was honoring his obligation to "preserve, protect, and defend the Constitution of the United States."[4] Strategy aside, as an ethical and religious man Franklin Roosevelt no longer considered viable the option of temporary peaceful coexistence with the Greater German Reich. Such a "peace," he knew, was a contradiction, besides being morally unacceptable and strategically foolhardy, if not treasonous.

If the long-term danger was extreme, then dramatic countermeasures were in order. Toward the end of this troubled spring, Roosevelt surprised the nation with two unusual cabinet appointments. The War Department had suddenly become the most important cabinet office, and Roosevelt, who had long since tired of his ineffectual, pro–Neutrality Act war secretary, Harry Woodring, offered Henry L. Stimson the position on 19 June.[5] Confronted by the greatest challenge of his life, the seventy-two-year-old Stimson was alert and vigorous. Roosevelt also nominated Frank Knox, Republican vice presidential candidate in 1936, as secretary of the navy. Confirmed several weeks later, Knox and Stimson were ardent advocates of rearmament and aid to Britain.

Henry Lewis Stimson had long been a power within the Republican establishment and had served under several presidents. A fervent believer in international law as laid down in multilateral agreements, Stimson viewed infringements upon it as immoral acts conducive to anarchy. He authored the famous "Stimson Doctrine," by which the United States refused to recognize the Japanese conquest of Manchuria. Troubled by the collapse of French resistance in May and June 1940, Stimson spoke out in favor of universal military training, repeal of the Neutrality Act, and American escorts (if needed) for ships convoying war supplies to beleaguered Britain.

Roosevelt invited Stimson to the White House, seeking his counsel and support during this tense time. Stimson had no choice but to serve, for to him patriotism, integrity, and service were synonymous. His appointment shocked isolationist Republicans, some of whom called Stimson a traitor to his party.

As always, FDR operated on two levels. To some, the Stimson appointment offered proof of his patriotic bipartisanship in a time of national danger. To others, Roosevelt had once again put politics first. By appointing a distinguished Republican, he was splitting the opposition and positioning himself to run for an unprecedented third term. Both supporters and critics were right. Stimson proved to be a brilliant choice. He worked well with the army chief of staff, General George C. Marshall, who shared Stimson's patriotic commitment to the concept of duty through sacrifice. And the effect of the Stimson and Knox appointments was to undercut the Republican's isolationist wing, at least at the presidential level. FDR had, in effect, created a coalition government, the better to carry out his own aims.[6]

Roosevelt kept even close friends guessing about his intentions, but he seems to have had no doubt about his indispensability to the nation. Ever since the end of 1938, FDR had been working to form a coalition that could check, then strangle, fascist aggressors. Now, with France fallen and Britain fighting for its life, it was no time to quit.

The "White Committee" launched a major propaganda campaign on behalf of aid to Britain. Taking out full-page newspaper advertisements, the committee demanded, "STOP HITLER NOW." Roosevelt encouraged the committee, but eschewed the strong language used by Robert Sherwood: "Anyone who argues that the Nazis will considerately wait until we are ready is either an imbecile or a traitor." White, while more cautious, warned Roosevelt, "You will not be able to lead the American people unless you catch up with them. They are going fast." By midsummer, 67.5 percent of respondents polled by Henry Luce's *Fortune* magazine favored granting aid to Britain.[7] Roosevelt still received divided counsel on the wisdom of aiding Britain. Once it was clear, however, that Churchill would never surrender (either his nation or his fleet), FDR's mind was decided.

Hitler seemed to offer "peace" at a victory rally at the Reichstag on 19 July. His Majesty's government rejected Hitler's offer three days later. In the United States, admiration was growing for Churchill's commitment to continued struggle.

The Havana Pan-American conference, held in July, convened against the backdrop of France's collapse. The participants warned that aggression against one of them would be considered "an act of aggression against the States which sign this Declaration." The American states agreed to prevent any transfer of territories from one European power to another, thereby blocking possible German incursions into territories held by defeated powers, such as Holland and France.[8] Hailed as a great success by the American press and a tribute to the skills of Secretary Hull, the conference marked one more step towards Roosevelt's protectorate over the Western Hemisphere. Various elements of FDR's strategy were coming together, and even the precarious situation of the Allies worked in his favor.

Anti-interventionist internationalists like Herbert Hoover came up with new arguments against the president's policy. In May, the former president spoke with real compassion about the fate of Belgium, once again overrun by German armies. When France collapsed, Hoover endorsed aid to Britain, but he did so without enthusiasm and attached many conditions to his support.[9] The former president repeated his view that "[T]he 3,000 miles of ocean is still a protection."

Establishment internationalists, by contrast, worked to alert public opinion to the German menace. These people, connected by ties of birth, education, wealth, and profession, were, if anything, greater Anglophiles than Roosevelt. On 25 July, many of the originators of the "Summons to Speak Out" met again in the Century Club in New York

City. The group discussed how America might prevent Germany from winning the war.[10] Out of these discussions would come policy formulations that influenced both the White House and public opinion. It was an exciting, dangerous time.

Roosevelt had only begun to reformulate American priorities. U.S. industry had not yet geared up for total war; public opinion needed to be molded along the proper lines. Roosevelt believed that a Republican victory would enable Hitler to solidify his control of Europe and perhaps win the war. He encouraged a number of possible Democratic nominees but kept his own plans secret. Roosevelt saw no one of his own stature on the Democratic horizon. When James A. Farley, a Roman Catholic and the incarnation of the wily New York "pol," informed Roosevelt of his own presidential ambitions, the president threw back his head and laughed heartily. Vice President Garner was too old and too conservative. No New Dealer had the time to make a national name for himself. There remained FDR.

The Republican candidate, Wendell Willkie, was a lawyer and businessman known for his opposition to much of the New Deal. He had never held elective or appointive office. Willkie was an ally of, and in part the creation of, the eastern internationalist wing of the Republican Party, including publisher Henry Luce. An article, "We the People," published in *Fortune*, had helped to make Willkie a presidential prospect.[11] Willkie appealed to big business because he was an outspoken proponent of privately controlled utilities. He had fought against the establishment of the Tennessee Valley Authority. A nominal Democrat before 1940, Willkie was attractive to independent and swing voters. His foreign policy views, if he held any, were largely unknown. Wilkie's nomination, though carefully planned by his supporters, disturbed most party regulars. The candidate was a new face to most of the public. He now headed a party filled with anti-interventionist activists, appeasers, and assorted obstructionists like Taft and Vandenburg. Willkie was, however, a strong, even charismatic personality. What would happen to Roosevelt's adamant commitment to intervention against Hitlerism should the Republicans win back the White House?

FDR, through his communications with Churchill, was in these very weeks laying the groundwork for an Anglo-American alliance, with the Americans as the senior partner. He seemed to exude an almost religious sense of mission. In his political dealings, Roosevelt worked with his old dexterity, mixing charm, ambiguity, and guile in equal amounts.

After keeping possible alternative candidates off balance (and off center stage), he engineered his own "draft" by a relieved, if confused and frustrated, convention.

Roosevelt released his delegates, leaving the decision up to the party, assembled in Chicago in the middle of July for its national convention. Uncertainty and confusion prevailed on the floor, though there was no longer much doubt about the outcome of the deliberations. At a key point, the roar "We want Roosevelt!" engulfed the hall. (The cry had started with the misnamed "voice from the sewer," belonging to a party regular from Chicago, acting on his organization's instructions.)

Hymie Shorenstein, a Brooklyn politician, gave a poignant example of FDR's importance to party stalwarts. Speaking to a local politician, who was troubled about his own election prospects in the light of Republican gains in 1938, Hymie told his friend not to worry. Roosevelt, he explained, was like a large tugboat, hauling a garbage barge out to sea. "It takes all the crap," said Hymie, "and the chewing gum wrappers, and bottles, and dumps them where they belong; then returns safely to port. Don't worry, you'll win—Roosevelt is the tugboat and you are the barge!"

At 12:25 A.M., FDR broadcast his dramatic acceptance speech to the convention. The hall was hushed as FDR pledged to arm the nation as a defense against the worst tyranny of all time. Warning against turning the country over to "untried hands," the president lashed out at "appeaser fifth columnists who charged me with hysteria and warmongering." The tone of the speech suggested that FDR alone could lead the nation to safer times, without war. It is doubtful if he believed this. He was planning for war, though he hoped to avoid entry into the conflict. Britain, perhaps, could win on its own.

Roosevelt and his associates used the "appeaser fifth columnist" scare to whip up their own form of "hysteria," for the president's own purposes. All in all, he delivered a brilliant speech.[12] Roosevelt played to widespread fears, then appealed for calm and confidence, under his leadership.

German chargé Thomsen reported (with some exaggeration) that anti-German hysteria had reached 1917 levels. He shrewdly noticed how proadministration spokesmen effectively juxtaposed terms like "isolationist" with pejorative expressions such as "fifth column." The Department of Justice now appeared to regard every Nazi party member resident in the United States as an actual or potential fifth columnist. Party members were required to register with the federal authorities. Thomsen, reporting to Berlin, observed that to American opinion, "Germany is America's enemy, ideologically, politically, and economically." Americans, he said, saw the defeat of Britain as a prelude to a war with Germany.

Thomsen emphasized the need for strict control of all German intelligence activities in the United States. As he had urgently informed the Foreign Ministry, subversive activity here could cause "irreparable damage . . . for the German conduct of the war." Thomsen received reports depicting American fears of German propaganda agents in places like Texas. He lamely recommended that Germany respond by blaming this hysteria upon the machinations of British agents.[13]

In April (and again in June), Hitler had warned Admiral Wilhelm Canaris, chief of the *Abwehr* (military counterintelligence), against the commission of sabotage by agents stationed in the United States. The avoidance of American belligerency was Thomsen's main assignment, and *Abwehr* appeared to be subverting his work. In late May, however, Thomsen learned that one "Bergmann," reporting to the New York consulate general, claimed to have sunk a steamer of the Red Star line as it lay docked in Baltimore Harbor. Bergmann identified himself as an agent of Major Hans Oster of the *Abwehr.*

The *Abwehr* replied by denying the whole thing. "No official office," it stated, "has ever assigned missions to *carry out* acts of sabotage in the U.S.A." The Wehrmacht, according to the foreign ministry, pleaded innocent of all knowledge of "Bergmann," who was probably a "provocateur." Thomsen rejected the argument, believing that at the very least the *Abwehr* employed incompetent agents, who damaged relations with the United States. *Abwehr* chief Canaris was also bitter, but for a different reason. The Wehrmacht, he argued, needed certain kinds of information, but "the (*Abwehr*) agents working in the U.S.A. were compelled to carry out their work without any support from the German embassy and the German consulates as long as they were in the U.S.A." Not all German diplomats shared Thomsen's suspicions. Consul General Hans Borchers firmly believed that the acts of "sabotage" were industrial accidents ascribed to the Nazis by Roosevelt.[14] Actually, sabotage and related "fifth-column" activities were not, despite FDR's comments to the press, urgent problems.

Espionage was a different matter, but, even here, legal methods garnered most of the information obtained by the German armed forces.

Abwehr agents provided von Bötticher with valuable material clipped from American newspapers. Admiral Leopold Bürckner later commented, "[A]ll the military information . . . needed was easily obtainable from magazines and government publications." For ten cents, the Germans obtained a copy of the Industrial Mobilization Plan.[15] *Abwehr* personnel acquired significant data, by observing activities in ports and around munitions plants. Canaris smugly concluded, "The success of the secret military intelligence service . . . sufficiently proves that the structure of the intelligence network or the selection of agents in and for U.S.A. have been necessary and correct."

Agent S-3097, for example, radioed the following information to *Abwehr* Auxiliary Branch in Bremen:

> **November 30, 1939**—A French freighter was taking on war material at a pier on West 48th Street, New York City.
>
> **August 22, 1940**—The U.S. government had ordered that 4,200 war planes, mostly bombers, be flown to England.[16]

Abwehr agents collected impressive inventories documenting American aid to Britain. These reports contained information about the storage of materiel in army and naval arsenals, the export of copper, and manifests and inventories of freighters bound for Allied ports. One *Abwehr* operative later concluded, "In the year 1940, America saved England." This was an exaggeration, but it well described Roosevelt's current priority. First save England, then destroy Nazi Germany.

The German intelligence services had access to other, higher level sources of information. Foreign Minister Ribbentrop knew as early as May that FDR was mulling over a plan to dispatch fifty over-age destroyers to Great Britain. It appears that Hans Thomsen may have had an informant in either the White House or the State Department. Certainly, the Germans intercepted top secret messages relayed to President Roosevelt by Ambassador Joseph P. Kennedy in London. Their Washington embassy was well aware of Kennedy's doubts about aid to Britain.[17] *Abwehr* espionage thus had its occasional successes, though it did little damage to the Allied cause. The Roosevelt administration leaked some information about German espionage to the media.

While the popular press, prodded by FDR, spoke of coming invasions of the Americas, Hitler continued his policy of naval restraint. America, he ordered, was "to be spared as much as possible." Hitler still hoped to secure the friendship of Britain, through a compromise peace settlement. He wished to preserve American neutrality, while Germany worked to end the war in the west and on the high seas.

Hitler reluctantly ordered military preparations for "Operation Sea Lion," mandating an invasion of England. But how could a country that could not even isolate the British Isles from world commerce invade England? The German blockade inflicted tactical damage upon the British war economy, but it failed to secure the Reich's strategic goal, which was "the destruction or disruption of enemy shipping and the blockade of important bases and harbors."

Hitler faced an insoluble dilemma. If he took the measures necessary for a true blockade of Britain, he would antagonize the American public. Germany would, for example, need to occupy various Atlantic islands belonging to neutral Spain and Portugal, as well as Gibraltar, and launch all-out attacks on neutral shipping in the North Atlantic. Such measures would play into FDR's hands, for they would lend credence to his warnings about German aggression in the Western Hemisphere.

Perhaps, Hitler concluded, there was a way out. If the Luftwaffe could destroy the Royal Air Force and bomb Britain effectively, London might make peace. An invasion was unlikely, or even impossible. Aerial warfare might cause Churchill to change his mind, while Roosevelt remained neutral. Intensified Luftwaffe activity, combined with continued moderation on the high seas, represented a compromise, though an illogical one. Naval restraint meant that Britain's war economy could receive *more* help from the United States. Because an invasion was a long shot in any event, one could only conclude that everything depended upon a change in British policy. But if Britain survived the coming assault, it would be stronger, not weaker. Hitler risked losing the war by not taking bolder action in the North Atlantic and the Mediterranean during this summer of 1940.

While frightening the Americans (thanks in some measure to FDR's media manipulation), Hitler was giving them time to arm. At this point, he may well have lost the war. The United States was unready, and a true naval blockade in an extended war zone might have crushed the British war effort. Giving Roosevelt time represented a fatal mistake, as did Hitler's naval strategy (or lack of it) against Britain. Roosevelt now realized that he could become "nonbelligerent" rather than neutral with impunity. His decision to increase American military aid to Britain did not merely rest upon his view that England could survive. In fact, he was not so sure. Roosevelt's decision was based not upon British strength but upon German weakness and indecision. Hitler might lose the war because respect for neutrals' rights led him to conduct a phony blockade of the British Isles.

Hitler was greatly upset by new reports coming from the United States. By September, he knew that Roosevelt's fifth-column scare campaign had achieved important results. The führer decided to go directly to the American people. In the course of an interview with Hearst journalist Karl von Wiegand, Hitler vigorously denied that he was subverting the United States. It was clear that, to Hitler, Roosevelt was the culprit who had provoked war in 1939. Now, as the Battle of Britain raged, FDR was the man whose promises helped to sustain the British war effort.

The outbreak of war in Europe greatly increased J. Edgar Hoover's power at home and elsewhere. The president, through an order issued to his attorney general, instructed the FBI to take charge of all investigative work in matters related to espionage, sabotage, and violations of the neutrality regulations. An unstated premise undergirded FDR's order. The FBI would not merely combat terrorism or espionage; it would contribute to Roosevelt's public relations campaign, and to the successful implementation of his foreign policy.

Hoover's mandate thus included inquiries into "fifth-column" activities, as well as domestic political surveillance. Hoover, though himself more antagonistic to communism than to fascism, gave the White House what it wanted. Writing personal notes to General Edwin "Pa" Watson, FDR's military aide, Hoover provided Roosevelt with detailed intelligence, some of significance, some based on unsubstantiated rumor and testimony. The FBI director wrote to the White House almost daily, providing information about German military affairs, anti-sabotage efforts in American industrial plants, "peace rallies" (especially communist and communist-front ones), and labor strife. Hoover was a skilled bureaucratic infighter; his work was his life. He used Roosevelt's concerns about Nazi infiltration of the Americas in ways calculated to increase the FBI's power.

Hoover placed agents throughout Latin America, especially in Mexico, where they gathered intelligence about Axis propaganda, espionage, and subversion. Most of the evidence accumulated by Hoover was pretty tame stuff, but it tended to substantiate Roosevelt's charges.[18] Leaked to the press, allegations that Nazi agents were planning to seize Mexico frightened many Americans. People would support military preparedness and Roosevelt's foreign policy if they felt threatened. The *New York Times* helped when it printed headlines like "Nazi Agents Found Busy in Mexico; Viewed as Threat to U.S. Defense."[19] Based on "reliable information," the *Times* had received a tip from the FBI, which Hoover had gathered for General Watson and President Roosevelt.

Hoover knew that FDR, who enjoyed scurrilous, useful gossip, was not above reading raw files on his isolationist enemies. The director dutifully provided derogatory material on men like Senator Nye, though he carefully noted that the reports were unsubstantiated. True or false, the material wound up in the president's official file, where it could one day be of use to him. The director also managed to provide the White House with anticommunist material, presented in a disguised manner. This was the era of the Hitler-Stalin Pact, and the communists were loudly proclaiming their support for peace and isolation. Hoover told the White House that he was concerned about communist sabotage in the defense industry, and about communist-front manipulation of the peace movement and other isolationist enemies of the administration.[20] Communism was not a Roosevelt preoccupation, however.

J. Edgar Hoover clearly stated his belief that the Germans were anxious to avoid provoking the United States. Citing a British source, Hoover insisted, "The enemy today relies far more on propaganda than on espionage and uses the mails and cables little for the latter purpose."[21] Hoover's cautious analysis did not comport well with FDR's preparedness campaign, as the president continued to warn the public about the Nazi fifth-column threat to the Americas. Hoover quickly changed his tone. Now he took German propaganda more seriously, at least in his memos to the White House. He gravely reported on the seizure of phonograph records containing German speeches, one of which foresaw the end of the British Empire. This material could be used to buttress administration claims regarding German ambitions in the Western Hemisphere. Some months later, an important German source complained that the United States was "taking a leaf out of the German propaganda school when it says that the United States is being encircled by Axis powers." More seriously, Colin Ross warned the German government that "if the U.S.A. is once in the war it will fight with the same tenacity and the same unceasing utilization of all her mighty strength, just as in the War of Independence or the War of Secession. . . ."[22]

Roosevelt's comments about the fifth-column menace, along with lurid stories in the media, had indeed convinced most people that sabotage, riding a Trojan horse, threatened American security. Voices opposed to the reception of refugees argued ever more loudly that Nazi agents had infiltrated their ranks. Roosevelt himself, prodded by Bullitt's horror stories about Jewish refugee spies in France, believed in this threat.

Roosevelt sometimes made sweeping charges that were patently exaggerated, or even absurd. At one point, he declared to stunned reporters that pro-Germans had infiltrated the ranks of "the Army and the Navy." Another time, the president spoke gravely about attempted sabotage in "forty or fifty factories in this country." One reporter stood his ground, and seemed to chastise FDR. "But [such comments]," he said, "[add] fuel to the fire—the war hysteria."[23] Stories about treason or sabotage in Europe made headlines; Roosevelt would comment on (undocumented) American cases of the same thing, and new headlines would appear.

At times, concern about fifth columnists did lead to hysteria. Authorities arrested an old man in Nashville, Tennessee, after discovering that he was walking around with a map of Memphis in his pocket. After learning the man's mental history, the police released him. In other cities, newspapers hounded theater owners who played even innocent German films. In New York City, the police arrested a drifter and sometime housepainter, the thirty-eight-year-old Caesar Kroeger. The former merchant seaman had a fondness for *Mein Kampf*, revolvers, and the Bund. The police and the pliant press turned Kroeger into a conspirator ready to take on the world, for he had in his possession a map, which contained a big circle around the Americas! The New York *World-Telegram* claimed that at least 100,000 Nazi fifth columnists were at large in this country. Even so seasoned a reporter as the brilliant William L. Shirer believed that war would trigger "sabotage by thousands of Nazi agents from coast to coast. . . ." *Liberty* magazine published an article equating pacifism with treason.

There was no doubt that public opinion was changing, and quickly. The staid Republican *Oregonian* denounced the "Spawn of the Trojan Horse." In a chilling editorial, carefully filed by a grateful White House, the paper referred to "termites" boring from within, while Americans acted like ostriches. As France's armies crumbled along the Meuse, northwestern lumberjacks discussed local fifth-column suspects in their taverns and forests.[24] If democracies like France and Belgium could, as alleged, be destroyed from within, why could it not happen here?

Most important of all was a paradoxical fact relating to the anti-interventionist, anti-Roosevelt press. Newspapers that opposed Roosevelt printed the same lurid stories, thus undercutting their own editorial positions. Publishers like McCormick and Patterson, who hated Roosevelt, ran headlines that helped him, like ones about German spies and fifth-column traitors.

The success of the fifth-column scare brought new challenges in its wake. Politicians wanted to be part of the action. The White House maintained thick and ever growing folders on the fifth column, particularly after the fall of France. Governor Burnet R. Maybank of South Carolina, for example, put his state at Roosevelt's disposal in the struggle against "espionage and Fifth Columnists." Liberal congressman, such as Emmanuel Celler of New York, worked with the Justice Department in abolishing certain restrictions on the use of wiretaps. Citizens flooded the White House with letters, suggestions, and denunciations. Some wanted to join the FBI. Missives containing twenty or thirty names of suspicious persons came to the attention of the White House staff.

Roosevelt would work in his own way. Martin Dies, chairman of the House Un-American Activities Committee, wanted to turn the fifth-column near hysteria to his own use. FDR, however, informed Dies of his opposition to legislation outlawing the Bund, the Communist party, and fascist organizations. Dies suspected the Roosevelt administration of communist tendencies. By linking the Nazis to the Reds (the Hitler-Stalin Pact), Dies could embarrass the White House, gain power and headlines for himself, and bash the communists. Roosevelt, who had helped to create the fifth-column fear, had no intention of losing this centerpiece of public opinion to the Texas congressman. An intricate game of open letters and secret maneuvers now ensued. Far rightists like Joseph P. Kamp, head of the Constitutional Educational League, Inc., tried to turn the countersubversion thesis against Roosevelt by attacking "the Fifth Column in Washington." This subversion, said Kamp, consisted of Reds and procommunists in the Roosevelt administration. Kamp's arguments, though calculated to help the likes of Martin Dies, boomeranged.

Dies, an anti–New Deal demagogue with presidential ambitions, asked Roosevelt to share some FBI agents with his investigative committee. FDR had no intention of complying with this request. Dies's power grab failed, though his actions helped to prepare the way for a later generation of McCarthyism. Roosevelt was building up an antifascist national security apparatus, while Dies stoked the fires of anticommunism. The newly strengthened state, with its penchant for internal investigations of fifth columnists, would later be put at the service of Dies's ideology.

For the moment, Roosevelt's victory resulted in a new assignment for Secretary Ickes. FDR ordered him to set up machinery for combating subversive propaganda. Ickes assembled an able committee of helpers, including the redoubtable Dorothy Thompson, pollster George Gallup, Henry Luce, and theologian Reinhold Niebuhr. Over the next year, he helped to undermine what he called profascist or Nazi subversion and propaganda. Dies was being outflanked. Meanwhile, Roosevelt's minions went to work attacking profascist and isolationist forces. Had they not received timely assistance from media magnate Henry Luce, their work would have born more meager fruit.

Henry Luce controlled the Time, Inc. empire. The son of missionaries, Luce promoted American democracy and capitalism with an almost religious zeal. As far as he was concerned, America was already at war. While an early admirer of Willkie and a staunch Republican, Luce was coming to support Roosevelt on foreign policy questions. Time's influential newsfilm series *The March of Time* became a virtual mouthpiece for Roosevelt's interventionist policy. Advocating both preparedness and neutrality, the production subtly contributed to changing public perceptions of American intervention in the First World War. One segment, filmed late in 1939, warned against quick analogies drawn from past experience. The *March of Time,* which appeared every four weeks in thousands of movie houses, was powerful propaganda, slickly produced. Produced by Louis de Rochement, the series had a great following in the 1930s and 1940s. Presenting one theme or a mix of interrelated stories, the *March of Time* pioneered a new form of cinematic journalism. In late 1938, responding to the European crisis, the *March of Time* staff had decided to embark upon an ambitious project.

The new film would, like *Time*, inform and proseletyze at the same time. Americans must learn of their own destiny in the event of a German victory. And they could see into this grim future, thanks to film footage of occupied Europe. War was beginning to permeate the national consciousness. To some, it was no longer a question of avoiding war, but of averting invasion. This was an ideal state of mind, from Roosevelt's viewpoint. And Luce's contribution was vital.

Film could be a natural interventionist medium, as both Henry Luce and FDR realized. Everything depended upon direction, editing, and narration. Scenes of battle carnage could augment isolationist sentiments, so one had to use them only in certain contexts, and with caution. But if Americans saw one side as the victim and the other as the aggressor, sympathy would accrue to the attacked party, in this case, the Allies. Roosevelt outlined the threat, and Henry Luce and other media giants brought it home to the American people. Germany must be defeated, but what, asked Luce, if England could not do it alone?

Henry Luce's great contribution to psychological prewarfare, released at the end of August 1940, was called *The Ramparts We Watch*. Screened throughout the nation, *Ramparts* filled a gap left by Hollywood's timidity. Luce was not particularly afraid of controversy. He knew that the same studios that avoided political filmmaking would distribute a work of propaganda called by the critics "newsfilm" or "documentary."

By depicting the impact of the First World War upon Main Street Americans, who played themselves in New London, Connecticut, *Ramparts* avoided the appearance of omniscience, "preachiness," or bias. Smoothly produced and brilliantly edited, *Ramparts* combined staged reenactments with newsfilm footage. *Ramparts* rejected bigotry against German-Americans, and it placed pacifists and isolationists in a sympathetic light. These people, film seemed to say, are our neighbors, and they mean well.

Bit by bit, *Ramparts* vindicates prowar, patriotic fervor. As seen through Time's camera lens, America, possessing a tiny army and riddled with internal dissension, is vulnerable to German outrages. Yet the United States, under a strong and good president (Wilson then, Roosevelt now?), manages to pull itself together. A vast citizens' army goes to Europe, defeating the forces of evil.

Ramparts was brilliant in manipulating the past in order to affect the present. The audience sees a 1918 photograph of Republican standard-bearer Wendell Willkie as a second lieutenant in the United States Army. And there on the screen, in the same year, we see another interventionist, Franklin D. Roosevelt, visiting the front as assistant secretary of the navy. Like all good propagandists, the Time writers were clever in their omissions. They deleted all mention of the Treaty of Versailles, of the League of Nations, of the Wilson tragedy.

By the time the film delivers its final message, the audience is predisposed to accept it, for it has reached the same conclusion. In case anyone missed the point, *Ramparts* added an appendix, which dealt with the Nazi threat to American security. German terror, it declared, was part of the Nazi arsenal. Quoting *Mein Kampf,* the film concluded with scenes taken from a Nazi propaganda documentary, called *Baptism of Fire,* which had been seized by the British and turned over to Luce.

A fifth column, the script implied, was undermining America, but strong men like Willkie and Roosevelt, now shown in scenes taken from 1940 newsreels, were once again uniting in support of liberty—and Britain. Ending with the national anthem, the last frames depict Plymouth Rock, a symbol of survival in liberty, despite the ravages of a storm-tossed sea.[25]

Opening at the Radio City Music Hall in New York City, *Ramparts* was a commercial and critical success. A typical reaction came from the liberal *New York Post,* which described *Ramparts* as an old tune that "sounds better, more convincing, than during the skeptical years."[26] Hitler and Roosevelt had changed American attitudes toward intervention, neutrality, and history. Like Roosevelt, Luce and his producers studied the Roper and Gallup polls. The film was a great propaganda success, not least of all because of its subtle distinctions. Those who opposed intervention in 1917, *Ramparts* implied, were honorable people, however misguided. Today, however, given our hindsight, how could anyone justify isolationism?

Henry Luce's people retained the services of the distinguished poet and playwright Archibald MacLeish, who proceeded to become a highly visible advocate for *Ramparts.* MacLeish, who produced advertisements and statements endorsing the film, faced angry foes. Among them was Otis Ferguson, film critic for the influential *New Republic*, which was itself veering away from Ferguson's isolationist views. Ferguson described the film as a "stinking little tent show," "smooth as oil," using "high and noble emotions" to sell a discredited product—intervention.[27] The anti-interventionist *New York World-Telegram* denounced the film's "emotional hysteria," and "flagrant pleas for our entry into World War II."[28]

Isolationists like Senator Wheeler despised and feared this production. So did historian Charles A. Beard, who attacked the film's admirers, such as MacLeish, for ignoring its historical inaccuracies. Dredging up all the old criticisms of Wilsonianism, Beard portrayed *Ramparts* as a propagandistic travesty of the truth. Beard's parting salvo would come back to haunt him. The historian asked if MacLeish could foresee the state of a postwar America, nine years hence.[29] Actually, the world and the United States were much more secure in 1950 than they were in 1941. Much of the credit must go to "warmonger" Roosevelt and those in the media who, for whatever pecuniary and idealistic motives, assisted him in his interventionist work.

Controversy swirled around *Ramparts* in the late summer and early autumn of 1940. The Pennsylvania Board of Censors banned most of the film's last reel, which contained the scenes taken from the Nazi propaganda film *Baptism of Fire*. Fearing the movie's "terrifying effect on the masses," the board was unmoved by producer de Rochement's denunciation of appeasement. "The thing you are doing," he told the board, "is promoting appeasement—surrendering to fear—the most dangerous thing facing America today." The board reiterated its view that the last scenes of the film were not in agreement with "the moral and customs here and the American way of life." That, of course, was the point: to show that American values could not long endure in a world remade by Nazi actions.

Common Pleas Court Number 3 upheld the board's decision. The uproar provided Luce with great publicity. In Reading, a group of National Guardsmen marched in support of *Ramparts*. Meanwhile, German authorities attempted to suppress the film. The embassy denounced Time for using "pirated" footage from *Baptism of Fire*. This cloak-and-dagger episode made audiences even more anxious to see *Ramparts*. The Bund threatened to disrupt showings of the movie. Ulrich von Gienanth snarled, "Germany is not a small country and she will not permit such things to be done to her." He threatened a lawsuit but soon dropped the whole matter, probably because this adept propagandist understood that his statements were grist for MacLeish's propaganda mill.[30]

While the Pennsylvania Board of Censors fretted about the effect of German terror footage on innocent Americans, Hitler's Luftwaffe began its attempt to smash England.

General of Artillery Friedrich von Bötticher (left), and former chargé Dr. Hans Thomsen being decorated on 29 May 1942 by Hitler for their work in the United States. (Credit: Bundesarchiv)

FDR signs the repeal of the arms embargo, 4 November 1939. (Credit: FDR Library)

The Roosevelt administration made much of the alleged German threat in Latin America. *Beware! Fifth Column in U.S.A.* helped to alert people to this "danger." (Credit: Wiener Library)

President Roosevelt signs the Burke-Wadsworth Conscription Act, 16 September 1940. Among those looking on are Senator Key Pittman (on left), Representative Sol Bloom (second from left), and Secretary of State Cordell Hull (fourth from left). (Credit: FDR Library)

Secretary of Commerce and key Roosevelt confidant Harry Hopkins. (Credit: FDR Library)

Wilhelm Kunze strikes back at the Bund's tormentors, who were attempting to expose, then suppress, the group's allegedly "subversive" summer camps. (Credit: National Archives)

The Bund's leading propaganda artist, Egon Scheibe, responds to those who charged the Bund with incipient treason. (Credit: National Archives)

Charles A. Lindbergh visits Germany. (Credit: FDR Library)

Was there a New Order in the American future? A scene from *I Married a Nazi*. (Credit: MOMA Film Stills Archives)

Little children sometimes became frightened by scare propaganda telling them that Hitler would invade the United States. (Credit: Wiener Library)

Roosevelt's alarms about a "fifth column" began to influence the popular media in the summer of 1940. (Credit: Wiener Library)

By 1941, the anti-Nazi propaganda had become a popular and profitable activity among publishers of popular magazines and comic books. (Credit: National Archives)

Roosevelt's unrelenting emphasis upon American vulnerability had borne fruit. For some, the question was not whether, but *when*, Hitler would attack America. (Credit: National Archives)

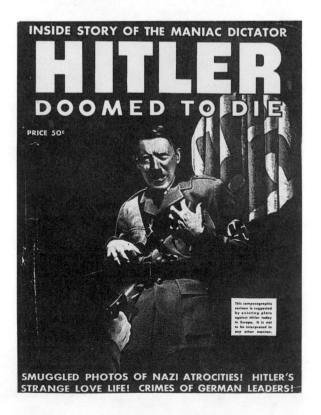

Anti-Semitism joined forces with Rooseveltphobia during the struggle against the lend-lease legislation. Here Jewish villains (Morgenthau, Baruch, etc.) work with FDR and Republican interventionist Wendell Willkie on behalf of the "gold hoard." America is crucified upon a cross marked "H.R. 1776."
(Credit: National Archives)

During the debate over lend-lease, many Americans sensed that the nation was at a crossroads. By this time, the American Legion had abandoned its anti-interventionist stance.
(Credit: Library of Congress)

CHAPTER
TWENTY-SEVEN

ON THE EVE OF
THE AMERICAN CENTURY

A S WINSTON CHURCHILL had predicted and as Roosevelt had feared, the fall of France foreshadowed the Battle of Britain. Starting on 13 August, the Luftwaffe launched massive attacks on British fighter bases, radar installations, and port facilities. The Royal Air Force did not lose control of the skies over Britain, though it was indeed a close call. Then, Luftwaffe chief Hermann Goering changed his tactics, and from 7 September London and other British towns became the targets of fierce Luftwaffe raids. Still, Britain resisted. Here, thought many Americans, was a nation worth helping. At the same time, many people, having heard the president's speeches, wondered if bombs like those falling on London would one day come crashing down on New York or Boston. In neat suburbs of big cities, particularly near the Atlantic coast, wealthy families were reported to be keeping a second automobile, filled with gas. One could then move inland in the event of a Nazi invasion.

During these two months, Americans became accustomed to hearing the eyewitness reports of CBS broadcaster Edward R. Murrow. In his smooth, baritone voice, the thirty-two-year-old North Carolinian brought home to Americans the sacrifices, heroism, and humor of the British people. Describing the aftermath of a Luftwaffe "blitz," Murrow spoke of "the little people who live in those little houses, who have no uniforms and get no decoration for bravery." He often reported within eyeshot of bombed-out buildings and flaming wreckage. Murrow's background music was the sound of air-raid sirens, of people walking quickly but calmly into the shelters. One of his great broadcasts came on 7 September, when 625 bombers blasted London.[1]

Unflappable himself, Murrow sadly reported, "A thousand years of history and civilization are being smashed." Yet out of the flames hope emerged. "England can take it," Murrow seemed to say; to which many Americans replied, "What can we do to help?" There was no Murrow reporting from bombed German towns. Instead, CBS and the other networks were conveying a sense of German *Schrecklichkeit* (terror tactics) that shocked the average American. This misuse of air power gave credibility to Roosevelt's clever ruminations about German intentions.[2] The president paid tribute to Murrow, describing the "debt owed him by millions of Americans."[3] No one owed more to Murrow than did Franklin D. Roosevelt, the public opinion manipulator.

Collier's Magazine produced an effective documentary called *London Can Take It,* narrated by Murrow's good friend Quentin Reynolds. His understated tone, combined with the images of steadfast heroism, impressed American moviegoers. "Civilians make good soldiers," intoned Reynolds, offering a thought appropriate for an America on the verge of conscription.

FDR's knowledge of the media served him well. Hollywood, in part responding to presidential encouragement, was growing less reticent about making antifascist films. Affected by events in Europe and prodded by the activist patriotism embraced by Roosevelt and his administration, the movie moguls finally took sides. Moviegoers could find new reasons for voting for Roosevelt.

The Man I Married, "an indictment of Hitler and Nazism, more outspoken than any of its akin predecessors," shocked audiences. The movie told the story of an American woman married to a man born in Germany. The couple decides to take a nostalgic trip to the fatherland, whereupon "Eric" becomes a fervent admirer of the Nazi system. He deserts his good wife for a fervent young "BDM" (League of German Maidens) leader. At the end of the film, however, Eric learns from his father of his mother's Jewish origins. His new girlfriend recoils in horror.

"Gasps and short screams were heard at the denouement," wrote a critic. Despite the Jewish theme, Hollywood was still shy about depicting Jews as the prime victims of Nazi sadism. A scene of degradation makes a man of Czech origin the prime casualty.[4] Nevertheless, the film reinforced anti-Nazi sentiment.

The release of Alfred Hitchcock's *Foreign Correspondent* coincided with the onset of the Battle of Britain. It told the story of Johnny Jones, an American reporter covering Europe, who, when informed that he is to cover the European crisis, naively asks, "What crisis?" Once in Europe, Johnny Jones witnesses political assassinations and conspiracies perpetrated by an unnamed force—clearly, the Nazis. At the end of the film, Jones sends a stirring broadcast to the States. Against the noise of screaming sirens, the movie ends as Jones cries out, "The lights are going out in Europe. . . . Ring yourself around with steel, America!"[5] Jones had become symbolic of public opinion: He was ready for defense but not for intervention. The concluding image of the film, however, was that of a nation surrounded by a world in flames. In this kind of situation, a forward strategy of pushing Germany out of the North Atlantic altogether might soon appear to be *defensive* in nature.

The Republican nominee, Wendell Willkie, relentlessly attacked the "third-term candidate," though he, too, favored aid to Britain. It was still unclear what form that assistance would take, for Roosevelt was negotiating with Churchill and had made no public announcement. Information was soon forthcoming, and the anti-interventionists did not like what they heard.

FDR, for several weeks hesitant about the political and constitutional aspects of the aid, had finally acted. Under the National Defense Act, nonessential naval equipment (so certified by the Chief of Naval Operations) could be sold or transferred abroad. While senators Taft and Vandenberg grumbled, Willkie voiced no *substantive* objections when Roosevelt concluded his destroyers-for-bases deal on 3 September. The destroyers, if refurbished by the British in six or seven weeks, would assist America's de facto ally in protecting sea-lanes essential to the importation of food, raw materials, and arms from the New World.[6]

The destroyer "deal" further extended American power in the Western Hemisphere. Along with a recent joint defense agreement with Canada, Roosevelt would, over the next few months, make the armed forces the eastern bastion of defense against the Old World. From Newfoundland to Bermuda and Trinidad, the American flag soon flew over guns and planes preparing to confront National Socialist Germany.[7] Eight bases, extending over four thousand miles of the Atlantic coast, now ringed the Americas. If Britain contained Germany, these bases and forces could be the vanguard of an offensive that would destroy Hitler. If Britain fell, the bases would become the symbols of American hemispheric hegemony, and would form the outer ring of bicontinental defense.

Anti-Nazism and the augmentation of the American imperium were clearly linked in FDR's mind. He was helping England not in order to save its empire but to keep it out of Germany's hands. Roosevelt had come to see Britain as a strategic asset in his struggle against Hitlerism. His hard bargaining with Churchill over the destroyers, and his demand for a no-surrender commitment in regard to the British fleet, were devoid of all "Anglo-American" sentimentality. Beneath FDR's charm lurked the suspicious, ambitious Yankee, fearful of being victimized by clever Brits.

The United States was well on its way to replacing the British Empire and the Royal Navy in the Western Hemisphere. Of this, FDR said nothing. Nor did Roosevelt allude to the fact that some of the bases could one day be of assistance to patrols and convoys sailing through a U-boat infested North Atlantic. "Convoy," a forbidden word, conjured up sour memories of the 1917 war.[8]

Given the pressures of the campaign, Willkie sometimes lapsed into demagoguery, denouncing the *form* of the destroyer agreement as "dictatorial." While the British public greatly preferred Roosevelt, it took some comfort in Wendell Willkie's aid-to-Britain rhetoric. This was probably a mistake. Whatever his intentions, Willkie the president would have been beholden to the isolationists in his own party. Even if he did not cave in to them, he lacked FDR's ability to manipulate Democratic congressmen, not to mention editors and public opinion.

Two weeks later, the president signed into law the first American peacetime conscription act. Opponent Willkie approved of the law. It would be in effect for one year, and provided for the training of 1,200,000 soldiers, as well as 800,000 reservists. The draftees could not be sent outside the Western Hemisphere. Sixteen million men registered, and the first drawing, by lottery, was due to begin in the autumn. Cynics predicted that FDR would defer the first drawing until after the election. It took place on 29 October. Roosevelt was getting people accustomed to thinking of a Nazi attack upon the Americas; he was vague about geography and constantly expanded the "Western Hemisphere." In this context, one could conceive of our "boys" being sent not to a "foreign war" but to a defensive struggle set somewhere in the ever more broadly defined "Western Hemisphere."

Roosevelt was molding a new national consensus. He sold aid to Britain and the U.S. military buildup as deterrence, when they could well be seen as *preludes* to intervention. It was no wonder that German chargé Hans Thomsen was discouraged. "[T]he great mass of people," he cabled Berlin, reflected Roosevelt's hatred for Germany. The consensus among knowledgeable Germans was clear: Roosevelt's victory meant war, sooner or later.

Roosevelt had changed the parameters of the debate to such an extent that Willkie at times accused Roosevelt of having left the United States defenseless, of having assisted the appeasers at Munich. Willkie was proving to be an adept and exciting campaigner, and FDR was concerned about the outcome. Though Willkie had lost most of his voice and was a poor campaign organizer, Democratic politicians were nervous. Roosevelt, they said, would have to change his tactics and make more promises.

In late September, FDR conferred with a delegation from William Allen White's committee, thus firing up his aid-to-Britain, interventionist followers. The president hoped to shelter himself against political fallout from White's endorsement of Willkie. As White later recalled, "I never did anything the President didn't ask for, and I always conferred with him on our program."[9] The result was that White's endorsement carried little weight, except to hurt Willkie among isolationist voters. On the same day, FDR received a group of British diplomats. In Berlin, the Axis powers and Japan had only hours before signed the Tripartite Pact.

Hitler had continued a policy of appeasing Roosevelt, even after he had learned in late August of FDR's intent to commit "an openly hostile act [the destroyers-for-Britain deal] against Germany." Again and again, his supreme naval commander asked for a change in policy. Raeder's naval chiefs pleaded for the right to attack shipping in the Pan-American Safety Zone, for "this safety zone benefits British interests alone." In addition, Britain had colonial possessions within the zone, and under international law these were legitimate objects of enemy attack. Hitler refused to budge. "At present *the Führer* does not wish to take up the matter with the U.S.A. . . ." There were to be no German attacks on shipping in the "neutral" zone. Hitler offered his navy a highly speculative concession. The navy could draw up plans for the occupation of the Atlantic islands, off the coasts of Iberia and Africa. Bases there might be used during a war against the United States, possibly in the autumn of 1941.[10]

Attaché von Bötticher provided little consolation to his military colleagues in Germany. He reported from Washington, "In the course of 1941 and by the summer of 1942 *at the latest* an army of 1,200,000 men, excellently equipped and trained, and with the highest morale, as well as a constantly growing Air Force of the first order must be counted on."[11] Hitler refused to act militarily; in the place of naval action, he engaged in a diplomatic bluff.

The Tripartite Pact represented a vague blueprint for cooperation in the creation of a new world order, organized by the three Axis powers. To Hitler it had a more important aspect. The published treaty pledged the signatory powers to mutual assistance if one or more of them became the victim of an attack by a power not presently at war with them. To Hitler, this meant the United States. Hitler hoped that the prospect of Japanese belligerency would prevent FDR from rushing headlong toward war in the North Atlantic. And coming only about six weeks before the American elections, the pact might frighten the American electorate into rejecting Roosevelt's bid for a third term.

Attaché von Bötticher seemed to confirm the wisdom of Hitler's latest stroke of genius. He portrayed the American economy as export driven, and hence vulnerable to Japanese attacks. Von Bötticher described American embargoes as "ineffective" and downplayed American naval power in the Pacific. The military attaché presented a different picture to the Luftwaffe and the Army High Command. Von Bötticher had learned that the Americans had stockpiled a one- to two-year collection of strategic war materials. The United States was thus less vulnerable than before to a Japanese attack.[12]

The pact had no appreciable effect upon Roosevelt's policies in the Atlantic. And it threatened to drag Hitler into war with the United States at a time chosen by the Japanese.[13] Hitler lamely argued in October that the Battle of Britain, which would soon end in a Luftwaffe victory, vindicated his policy of appeasing the United States. Britain would come to its senses, for America could not save it.

Privately, Roosevelt took this and related dangers seriously. Japan might move against Southeast Asia, and threaten the American position in the Pacific. He was sending a message to the Germans and the Japanese that he was not intimidated. Despite his confidence, no one in late September could predict the effect of the pact upon a concerned American electorate. Roosevelt had proven to be right about England's survival. His warnings about the global ambitions of the Axis were now confirmed. The average voter might think twice about replacing this president.

In the military sphere, FDR consulted ever more closely with Admiral Harold ("Betty") Stark, the chief of naval operations, and Admiral Ernest J. King, commander of the Atlantic Fleet. The president's vast knowledge of seafaring and naval history served him well, though the fact that he "did not have enough navy to go around" frustrated him. The disturbing prospect of German control of the sea-lanes of the North Atlantic had concerned FDR since his days as a student of Mahan. Now he mulled over strategies calculated to frustrate a revolution in the maritime situation.

Edward R. Murrow's broadcasts, fortified by the latest antifascist films, provided an apocalyptic setting for the election campaign. Roosevelt was now the defender of the nation, in the midst of a world gone mad. FDR's supporters produced an outpouring of emotion unlike any he had ever seen. His critics attacked Roosevelt's "messiah complex," but many a voter regarded FDR as a kind of savior. "I hope and pray each night," one supporter wrote, "that the Almighty God above will keep you well and fit to carry on." "I don't know how anyone can fail to see," wrote another, "that you are one of the greatest Presidents we ever had and no doubt in years to come your name will go down in history as the greatest American of modern times when the others are forgotten." You are a *God sent* man and I pray for you every night . . . and I voice millions when I say we wish you could be our leader always." A woman wrote to the president, telling him, "You are the most wonderful President America has ever had and I'm sure of you being our President for the next four years. . . . I am just a colored woman 58 years old . . . if you Pardon me Sir For saying so I love you. . . ."[14]

Inspired by his own perception of Roosevelt's historic mission, Time Inc. continued to turn out film footage devoted to the Roosevelt cause.

The *March of Time* glorified Edward R. Murrow, reporting from beleaguered London. It quoted polls showing that sixty percent of respondents favored aid to Britain, even at the risk of American involvement in
the war. Shots of J. Edgar Hoover denouncing "Bundsmen" and other
unsavory types seemed to equate anti-interventionism with treason.
Luce, moreover, did not permit his films to be marred by undue
reference to the Jews. Interventionism was American and patriotic, not
an adjunct to what the fascists called the "Jewish war." Anti-Semitism
was as strong as ever. There were signs, however, that fewer people were
willing to work openly on its behalf.

Roosevelt's foreign policy approval rating was steadily climbing.
Those favoring aid to Britain, even at the risk of war, now represented a
majority of respondents. A large majority of Americans polled feared the
adverse affects of a Nazi victory over England. Forty-three percent of
those responding to a *Fortune* poll feared that a Germany triumphant
over Britain would wage war against the United States. Huge majorities
of respondents favored the expansion of the armed forces. Congress
quickly passed a major naval construction bill, authorizing the launch-
ing of 250 warships, including 19 aircraft carriers and 140 submarines.

The campaign became quite nasty in its last weeks. William Randolph
Hearst predicted that a reelected FDR would take the nation into the
war that "he has been busily fomenting for the last three years."[15] The
president responded, promising that he would never send our armed
forces "to fight in foreign lands outside of the Americas, except in case
of attack." Roosevelt said nothing about his desire to help Britain
survive in order to destroy all vestiges of Hitlerism. In October, a
politically concerned president promised a Boston audience that he
would not send the boys to fight in foreign wars unless America was
attacked. This was a reckless, dishonest pledge, except for one important fact. To the average listener, FDR knew, a war against Germany
represented entry into a "foreign war." To Roosevelt, it meant entry
into a struggle on behalf of civilization, American power, and democratic ideology. And to him, these were hardly foreign values.

Roosevelt had acquired a supporter and a bitter opponent at the same
time. As if to balance his interventionist views, Willkie indulged in a
brass-knuckles campaign, accusing Roosevelt of everything from warmongering to dictatorial aspirations. Willkie's surrogates were even

more vitriolic. John L. Lewis accused FDR of being a "traitor to labor." Willkie later ascribed these excesses to "campaign oratory."[16]

On election night, the early returns showed Willkie running a strong race, and FDR grew despondent. He wanted to be alone, perhaps to contemplate the implications of defeat. Ultimately, Roosevelt prevailed quite easily, winning 449 electoral votes to Willkie's 82. Substantial numbers of Irish-American and German-Americans voters had defected to the Republicans, in an arc stretching from New England to the Upper Plains states. If one removes the solid South from the tally, the election was much closer than the popular vote indicated. Still, victory was victory. Republican Henry L. Stimson, who kept the world guessing about his vote, noted that "the election will be very salutary to the cause of stopping Hitler."

The gruff old man had come to appreciate the president, whose combination of evasion, heartiness, and caution could frustrate the bold secretary of war. Speaking with Roosevelt, Stimson once said, was "like chasing a vagrant beam of sunshine around a vacant room."[17] Nevertheless, he voted for Roosevelt. After the election, Stimson prepared to name two brilliant special assistants, John J. McCloy and Robert A. Lovett. Their work would prove to be crucial in the year ahead, particularly in connection with aid to Britain and war mobilization.

In England, Harold Nicolson, a junior member of the Churchill government, could scarcely contain his joy over FDR's reelection. "It is," he confided to his diary, "the best thing that has happened to us since the outbreak of war. I thank God!"[18]

The polls now indicated that seventy percent of the population believed in one or both of the following propositions: (1) Roosevelt's reelection was "the best thing that has happened to the country," or (2) "we will probably get along all right with Roosevelt." Two-thirds of the people believed that England would win the war, while ninety-one percent foresaw a German defeat. The fatalism quotient (the percentage of Americans believing that we would ultimately go to war) consistently passed sixty percent. The American Legion, reflecting the new consensus, reversed itself and called for massive assistance to Britain.

The president had made clear that he would refuse to accept a world in which Hitler reigned supreme. Privately, FDR held a more extreme view, one that would have upset a majority of his fellow citizens. Roosevelt could not conceive of existing in a world that also contained Adolf Hitler. Even after the United States had been at war for over a year, the State Department continued to insist that Roosevelt had really feared a German attack upon the United States.[19] True, in the longer term, such an attack was a possibility, but certainly not during the next few years. This was not Roosevelt's major concern, however. He feared a faraway war that Hitler might win, or a peace agreement that let the Nazis survive.

In a letter written at the end of December, Roosevelt told a friend a truth that he was not willing to share with the people. "For practical purposes," wrote FDR, "there is going on a world conflict, in which there are aligned on one side Japan, Germany, and Italy, and on the other side China, Great Britain and the United States."[20]

Roosevelt knew that Germany and the United States would play the leading roles. It was for this reason that Hull and Roosevelt wished to avoid war with Japan, for such a conflict would detract from American support for the "British war against Germany."[21]

Hitler did not want war with the U.S.A. at least not until the spring of 1942, if at all. This reticence gave Roosevelt enormous amounts of time, for 1942 seemed far off. Roosevelt was determined to be ready for war, while helping Britain defeat Germany. Both men were gambling against enormous odds. Hitler hoped that timidity, combined with bombing, would achieve his goals in the west. Roosevelt hoped to defeat Germany while staying out of the war. There was always the chance that Britain would fall, in which case FDR's strategy would lie in ruins. If Britain survived, however, and grew stronger, Hitler would face a de facto alliance of enormous potential. He would only be able to respond with all-out U-boat attacks, because the Germans lacked aircraft carriers and cruisers with flight decks.

There was another possibility, however, though it was an unlikely one. German U-boat production might so increase that by the spring of 1942 an all-out assault in the North Atlantic could isolate and starve Britain. If Hitler could resist his impulse to destroy "Bolshevik Russia," he could concentrate upon his western, northern, and southern fronts. If he did so, the United States could be in grave peril at some point in 1942. Occupation of the Azores Islands would, according to Hitler, open the possibility of bombing the Americas with Messerschmidt aircraft possessing a range of about eight thousand miles. The United

States, distracted on another front, might not be able to respond with its full might.

But Hitler was already talking about invading Russia; he continued to respect Spanish (and American) neutrality, to his own strategic detriment. He waged a halfhearted war on the seas, while bluffing about an invasion of England. Hitler appeased Roosevelt while America was weak, at the same time preparing for a possible war ("in 1942, if at all") against a much stronger United States. He did not understand that one did not invade England; one starved it into submission or compromise. Bombing was calculated to increase American respect for the British war effort, thus playing into FDR's hands.

Britain had shown that it could survive, but at the risk of financial collapse. Nor could the United States bail Britain out, even if Congress wished to do so. The Johnson Act forbade loans to nations in default on prior war debts. True, the Americans had agreed to devote half of their weapons production to British and Canadian forces, but how, Churchill plaintively asked, "was all this to be paid for?" Britain had already paid out 4,500,000,000 dollars in cash and had sold off 335,000,000 dollars worth of American stocks and bonds, requisitioned from private individuals in England. Shipping losses were mounting, and the tonnage would have to be replaced. If "cash and carry" remained the policy, Britain would soon be unable to finance its purchases of American war supplies.

Winston Churchill made an emotional, personal appeal to President Roosevelt. He also threw in a politically cunning observation: Unemployment in America would rise if her factories ceased to produce goods for Britain. FDR himself came up with a novel idea. It would involve "leasing" arms munitions to Britain, which would return them or compensate the United States for them after the war. The president talked the plan over with an appreciative Stimson on 18 December, and then decided to launch a major public initiative at the end of December. Roosevelt's clever lend-lease proposal, carefully refined by advisers like Felix Frankfurter and Henry Morgenthau, would not require the amendment or repeal of the Neutrality Act, though it appeared to differ from it in letter and spirit, and would even supersede parts of that law. [22]

The time was propitious. Business, as well as strategy and ideology, mandated the increase of aid to Britain. Lend-lease could be sold as highly profitable to the United States and its economy. British assets, including gold, would continue to fall into the hands of Americans, for at least a few more months. (Churchill later grumbled, "The President sent a warship to Capetown to carry away all the gold we had gathered there.")[23] New factories were to be built, and industry was to turn out more war matériel than ever before. Workers would be hired by the millions. And Americans, though undergoing military training, would not fight in "foreign wars." The president spoke to the nation in a "fireside chat," delivered on 29 December, urging that the United States become "the great arsenal of democracy." Referring to the British financial crisis as "an emergency as serious as war itself," FDR explained, "The people of Europe who are defending themselves do not ask us to do their fighting." "They ask us," he continued, "for the implements of war . . . which will enable them to fight for their and for our security." Roosevelt's lend-lease law would transfer war matériel on a "temporary" basis to antifascist powers.[24]

Roosevelt had recently used the analogy of a fire in the neighborhood. In such a case, one did not dicker with the owner of the burning home, one granted him the temporary use of one's garden hose. Roosevelt himself would have the authority to determine if lend-lease for a friendly nation was in the American national interest. This represented a great expansion of executive authority, but the legislative branch would have to appropriate the requisite funds. Public opinion polls soon reflected a highly favorable response (eighty percent) to Roosevelt's proposal.

Churchill later described the lend-lease measure as "the most unsordid act in the history of any nation." It was not sordid, but it reflected more than a commitment to friendship for Britain. The conversion of industry to rearmament, supported by billions of government dollars, could bring about a boom. States like Connecticut were special beneficiaries of this transformation. By 1940, the state's economy was about thirteen percent stronger than in 1929, while expenditure for poor relief and welfare was steadily dropping. Many people of German and Italian descent were unhappy with the president's foreign policy, but their lunch pails were full. Detroit was selling cars (3,717,385 vehicles) at a brisk clip, enjoying the best year since the onset of the Depression. Firms like Packard, Continental Motors, and Murray were receiving lucrative aircraft contracts. Despite bottlenecks and inefficiencies, Stimson could report real progress. By late summer, 6,832 planes were under contract, and plans were underway for the construction of almost

12,000 more aircraft. Unemployed Pennsylvania miners and poor mountain people from Appalachia and the upper South, began to trek toward factories in Ohio, Indiana, and Michigan. The conversion to defense would cause shortages of materials and new outbreaks of unemployment as well as troublesome strikes and racial violence, but the outlook for the economy was suddenly bright.[25] This could only affect the national mood in the president's favor.

In his State of the Union speech, the president reiterated his lend-lease proposal. He depicted America as a kind of non-belligerent ally of countries like Britain, China, and Greece, struggling to secure freedom for humanity.

Roosevelt sold lend-lease to the people as an insurance policy, intended "to keep war away from our country and our people." "[Any] talk about sending armies to Europe," Roosevelt continued, was "deliberate untruth." It is doubtful if FDR believed this himself. The president was offering this prelude to war as a substitute for intervention. In fact, Roosevelt probably shared the view embraced by his chief military advisers. In the words of Secretary Stimson, they "agreed that this emergency could hardly be passed over without this country being drawn into the war eventually."[26] Britain had survived the blitz, though London and other cities were still suffering from raids by the Luftwaffe. Most frightening of all, new German "wolf packs," consisting of teams of U-boats, were beginning to decimate merchant vessel convoys plying the dangerous sea-lanes between the United States, Canada, Iceland, Ireland, and Great Britain.

Roosevelt's major concern in late 1940 was thus a valid one. How long would Britain fight on alone, *without compromise?* Churchill, after all, was an old, mortal man. Stalin might join the Tripartite powers. Only American participation could *guarantee* the defeat of Germany on terms mandating the unconditional surrender of the Nazi regime.

Toward the end of the year, Hitler's naval high command had warned Hitler that American supply shipments were "developing favorably for Britain." Hitler's naval commanders found this disturbing, for "Britain's ability to maintain her supply line is definitely the decisive factor for the outcome of the war." The Americans were now relieving the Royal Navy of some of its patrol and escort duties in North American waters. This freed British ships for the task of defending sea-lanes in the North

Atlantic and around the home islands. Hitler responded with more bluff: "In what do they [the British] place their hopes? In America? I can only say: we have taken every possibility into consideration in making our calculations!" General Franz Halder, chief of the Army General Staff, made a laconic note in his diary. Hitler predicted "[war with] America not before 1942—if at all."[27] By 1942, according to the war plans of men like Roosevelt and General Marshall, the United States would have a large, powerful army and untold thousands of fighter and bomber aircraft. By 1942, Germany expected to deploy over two hundred submarines.

During this same winter of 1941, Henry Robinson Luce published an essay entitled "The American Century." The Republican media magnate had spent years attacking most New Deal measures. He remained convinced that "Roosevelt has continually reached for more and more power, and he owes his continuation in office today largely to the coming of the war." Like Roosevelt, whose vision he now articulated, Luce understood that British imperial decline invited, even demanded, American global primacy. As he put it, "[T]he complete opportunity of leadership is ours." Luce shared Roosevelt's boyish enthusiasm for global power, moral leadership, and unheard of industrial productivity. Luce lacked Roosevelt's public charisma and he enjoyed but a fraction of the president's global fame, but by the winter of 1941, his impact upon American public opinion may have been second only to that of the president himself. Through Time, Inc., Luce reached millions of Americans, including a goodly proportion of America's one million college graduates.[28]

Luce still criticized the New Deal, but in muted tones. "Our job," Luce believed, "is to help in every way we can . . . to ensure that Franklin Roosevelt shall be justly hailed as American's greatest President." Tired of the negativism, isolationism and defeatism of so many Republicans, Luce cared only that "Roosevelt must succeed where Wilson failed." In Dorothy Thompson's words, "This will either be an American century or it will be the beginning of the decline and fall of the American dream."

Henry Luce came down on Roosevelt's side, but it may have been a close call. Former ambassador John Cudahy, who favored doing business with Hitler, was about to tour Europe on behalf of the Luce publications. He would doubtless share his views with both Roosevelt and Luce. And Malcolm Lovell, executive secretary of the Quaker

Service Council based in New York City, who favored a compromise peace, had helped to arrange a meeting between Luce and a source close to the German embassy. The German agent's goal was to convince Luce of Roosevelt's folly in indicting the Nazis for threatening the Americas. The agent went away thinking he had made an impact upon the publishing magnate. He was wrong, but J. Edgar Hoover did not take any chances. Informed of the discussion, the FBI chief sent a memo to the White House detailing the contents of the talk. He also gave advance warning of the Cudahy mission. General Watson forwarded the FBI report, dated 17 January, 1941, to Roosevelt himself. A change of mind by Luce would have been a disaster for Roosevelt, and he knew it. FDR saw nothing wrong in having Hoover keep tabs on his sometime allies.[29]

Other powerful figures, including men and women associated with the opposition party, were moved by Roosevelt's leadership, and came to aid him in this troubled time. Thompson, Luce, Robert Sherwood, William Allen White, and many others who thought of themselves as leaders were following FDR with enthusiasm, sometimes with too much of it to suit the president.

White's work was nearing its end. His committee had taken in nearly a quarter of a million dollars, and was spending it effectively. It had become a nationwide propaganda organization. The committee played to win. It leaked material derogatory to isolationists, making sure that friendly columnists like Walter Winchell received these items. The White committee worked with congressional staff investigators, hoping to assist them in investigations into isolationist or "fifth-column" groups. These inquiries met with the approval and received the assistance of cabinet secretaries convinced that Roosevelt had secret information about internal subversion. Secretaries Stimson and Ickes were particularly concerned about this "threat."[30] The White committee promoted attacks on isolationist companies by stockholders, and friendly columnists and shareholders, in turn, served as intelligence conduits to the committee.

William Allen White served his country well. He had mightily affected public opinion, but the editor was losing control of his own troops. The eastern wing of the White committee was bridling at its chairman's caution. Many members favored abrogation of the Neutrality

Act, along with American escorts for British convoys. In a letter to isolationist publisher Roy Howard, White reiterated his stand against these proposals. Worse still, from the viewpoint of many interventionist colleagues, the sage of Emporia, by his choice of words, seemed to seek common ground with the isolationists. Declaring that he had formed the committee in order "to keep this country out of war," White firmly opposed carrying "contraband of war into the war zone."[31]

Events were moving too fast for the old man, and the president's encouragement seriously misled William A. White. He refused to endorse measures not advocated by Roosevelt. That FDR might be preparing the way for drastic, new policies, while advocating the old ones, did not occur to the straightforward White. His adversaries attacked him as a turncoat, and White soon resigned as chairman of the committee. Though remaining as honorary head, his day had passed.

Clark Eichelberger replaced White. Deprived of the old sage's patience, the committee soon embraced interventionist measures that Roosevelt was not ready to endorse. White broke with the committee over its advocacy of escorts and further neutrality revision. Privately, he bemoaned the steps advocated by the "warmongers." As late as the following summer, White praised Roosevelt for keeping the U.S. out of war and defending the Americas from attack, two highly questionable propositions. Still, he remained consistent, comparing Republican obstructionism to measures supported by Adolf Hitler.[32]

A new generation was preparing to come forward. As the cautious White passed from the scene, his young colleague Dean Acheson, an acerbic, brilliant, and ardently interventionist lawyer, prepared to reenter the government as assistant secretary of state. He had little affection for FDR, but Acheson believed that the president had "a sense of direction in which he constantly advanced." Like many others, Acheson hoped to increase the "rate of that advance."[33] The new assistant secretary was soon a key player in crucial areas of modern warfare: gaining passage of lend-lease, outlining an economic program for the postwar world, and using the freezing of foreign assets as a weapon. Roosevelt had an uncanny ability to attract energetic men of commitment. They brought with them access to equally talented and well-connected friends and acquaintances. The administration needed the strength provided by these men, as well as the wisdom and devotion to duty offered by Hull, Stimson, Morgenthau, Marshall, and Stark.

Incoming reports indicated that in 1941 Germany would try to invade England, and perhaps conquer the Soviet Union.[34] The intelligence was at times contradictory and murky, but its deeper import was clear to Roosevelt. Hitler could not achieve total victory in a long war of attrition, so he would probably act in some dramatic way, calculating that a bold gamble offered his only hope for achieving victory. Meanwhile, Hitler's American allies had fallen on hard times.

CHAPTER
TWENTY-EIGHT

THE COLLAPSE OF
HITLER'S AMERICA

A MONTH BEFORE PRESIDENT Roosevelt announced his lend-lease
plan, William Allen White wrote a letter to longtime FBI chief
J. Edgar Hoover. He expressed his view that "you have done in
the last year a tremendous, necessary job in a competent way. . . ."[1]
The far right, allegedly subversive, was in terrible condition, thanks in
part to harassment by the FBI and state authorities. Roosevelt, through
his use of the media, had helped to change the image of militant anti-
Semites and fascists. In the 1930s, when they were actually stronger,
the president had largely ignored them in his public comments. Now,
since 1939, he had turned them into dangerous subversives whose work
was akin to treason. At the same time, FDR distanced himself from the
plight of the Jews in Europe and handled the refugee issue with great
care. Roosevelt thus bought support for his anti-Nazi policies among
people ill disposed toward the Jews. Many rightists and anti-Semitic
conservatives, some of them Roosevelt-haters, were coming to see
"fifth-column" fascists and "Nazi" Bundists as more dangerous than
the Jews. By Christmas 1940, FDR and his agents had convinced most
Americans that profascist and pro-Nazi sentiments were akin to treason.

These rightist groups were in disarray, even as they made their last stand against "Rosenfeld" and intervention.

To General Moseley, Fritz Kuhn, Father Coughlin, and William Dudley Pelley, Roosevelt was still a "warmonger" controlled by Jews. The war issue seemed to breathe new life into the radical right. Now it could appeal to a combination of anti-Semitism and xenophobic nationalism, in theory a potent brew. Yet the right's vituperation masked real weaknesses, even fatal ones.

Part of the far right's problem lay in its apparent admiration for Hitler. Whatever Americans thought of the Jews, most citizens blamed the new war on the Nazis. In other words, the German example—anti-Semitism linked to war—was broadly unappealing to most Americans. And far right paranoia repelled many people. Even Hearst's Roosevelt-hating columnist George Sokolsky preferred the president to "mob rule led by a military dictator surrounded by frightened screwballs [e.g., Moseley] who live in terror of their own shadows."

The eccentric and brilliant Ezra Pound, a leading poet of the century, now captured the true spirit of far-right Rooseveltphobia. He called him "Franklin Rosenfeld, the supreme swine and betrayer, who infected the whole State Department with his moral leprosy." The poet concluded, "If Americans had the sense to abandon Rosenfeld and his Jews, there would never have been a war. . . . What I exposed was *usurocracy* and the economic frauds perpetrated by the Morgenthau-Rosenfeld treasury." Pound did not spare Winston Churchill, either, referring to him as "Weinstein Kirschberg." Many years later, after bouts with treason and alleged insanity, poor old Pound moaned, "At seventy I realized that instead of being a lunatic, I was a moron."[2]

The White House, the FBI, the Dies committee, and an ambitious politician named Thomas E. Dewey were isolating the Bund. Wilhelm Kunze took over the shattered group. Kunze quickly expelled Kuhn from the organization. He saw himself as a kind of Goebbels, a propagandist who would derail Roosevelt's interventionist policy and thereby save the German Reich. In a dramatic and personal appeal to FDR, Kunze urged the president to "avoid involving this country in another European war. . . ."

The Bund mandated some changes in its propaganda apparatus. The *Weckruf* newspaper became the *Free American,* with more space devoted to English-language articles. Any American who wanted a copy of the *Free American* could now obtain the newspaper free of charge.[3] The paper crusaded against selective service (the draft), "the international brotherhood" (Jews and communists), and FDR's bid for a third term. The Bund's Americanism was still suspect, however. While advocating strict neutrality, the Bund's publication *Junges Volk* (Young nation) read like a German government press communiqué.

The Bund, caught between its Nazism and its "patriotism," seemed perplexed at its own isolation. A few German-language newspapers worked in tandem with Kuhn and Kunze, but their number was fast dwindling. Frustrated Bundists asked why pro-Nazi sentiment in a German-American was reprehensible, while "native Americans" could freely express their admiration for Churchill and his countrymen. "Americans," declared an angry Bund propagandist, "look in the Wrong Direction for the Dangers that Menace our Institutions. . . ." Roosevelt and the FBI disagreed.[4]

The respected analyst Edmund Taylor informed his readers that "the final tactics of terror and treason . . . enabled the German army to forestall the Allies . . . [in southern Norway]." He spoke about the "propaganda of moral sabotage," about the defeatism, pacifism, and neutralism that had undermined the will of Hitler's latest victims. It all sounded like a cautionary tale to more and more Americans: Those who spoke most loudly against rearmament and interventionism were likely to become the biggest traitors. The Roosevelt administration encouraged this concern, warning against "The Trojan horse" and "the Fifth Column that betrays a nation unprepared for treachery. Spies, saboteurs and traitors are the actors in this new strategy. . . ." The only thing Americans had to fear, Roosevelt seemed to say, was a lack of fear in the face of Nazi triumphs. The master manipulator, working toward a hidden design, knew his nation.[5]

Harassment and fear were destroying the *Amerikadeutscher Volksbund.* The Bund's finances took a turn for the worse. Paid advertising copy in its newspaper dropped off enormously. Fewer copies of the *Free American* came off the printing press. One can observe the Bund's decline in Los Angeles, where the Aryan Book Store produced some revenue. In addition to selling literature, it distributed pamphlets for a small fee. Many people who might once have attended Bund fundraisers, however, now stayed away. They feared persecution by the authorities.

The Bund's image continued to suffer from self-inflicted wounds. An open-air concert in Hindenburg Park turned into a fiasco. The event itself went off without a problem. After its conclusion, however, the edified Bundists staggered off, no doubt in search of a little schnapps and beer. They forgot about the piano, which suffered damage during a subsequent rainstorm. The proprietor demanded, and received, compensation.

Some of the Bund's operations required substantial amounts of money. WHIP in Chicago, and KRKD in Los Angeles, as well as WHBI in Newark offered "German Hours," during which the Bund attacked "warmongers" and engaged in membership drives. Advocating American neutrality in the face of German victory, Bund broadcasters made use of propaganda supplied by German officials. Station managers, however, were becoming nervous. Subjected to pressure by advertisers and fearing federal intervention, they distanced themselves from the Bund. WHBI informed the group that "all announcements are to be made in English and . . . this program shall carry no propaganda. . . ." The Bund dropped its programming on WHBI, pleading a shortage of funds.[6]

By June of 1940, eighty-seven percent of the people polled for *Fortune* hoped that the authorities would adopt one or more of the following measures in regard to Nazi sympathizers: Put them in jail, track them, prevent them from agitating, or keep track of them *and* prevent them from agitating. Polls reflected influence upon an alarmed public. Speaking to the press off the record, he wanted the media to know that "there are a lot of people who are not members of the Bund . . . who are doing just as much for the objectives of the Bund as if they were. I don't think I need to elucidate on that at the present time." Having discredited and broken the Bund (with its own assistance), FDR began to use his antisedition language more broadly.

How did the Bund survive? It appears that it received secret subsidies from operatives of Goebbels's Propaganda Ministry, and other Nazi organizations. There is no evidence, however, that the Bund engaged in espionage or sabotage.

Prodded by Roosevelt, the attorney general ordered another investigation of the Bund. He wanted to know if it had circumvented the immigration laws in attempting to maintain, or increase its membership. The Treasury Department looked into financial ties between German consulates and the Bund. Members were now in danger of denaturalization and deportation. The federal government froze all assets of the Bund, on the pretext that the group was an appendage of the German Reich. New Jersey shut down Camp Nordland, calling it a "Nazi agency." The Bund's chief attorney reported that "every German American is obsessed with fear." Facing arrest, Wilhelm Kunze himself fled to Mexico for a time. The Bund was finished as a viable organization.

Catholics were an important part of the New Deal coalition, and millions of them still listened to Coughlin. Roosevelt needed their support for his bold foreign policy plans. He had no intention of forfeiting Irish and other ethnic supporters to the likes of Father Coughlin. At the same time, FDR had for years refused to attack Coughlin publicly while the radio priest regularly blasted the administration on issues ranging from the Spanish Civil War to the monetization of silver. The administration's new campaign began in the autumn of 1939.

Privately, Roosevelt coyly observed that Coughlin rarely, if ever, criticized Hitler. FDR's pugnacious Interior Secretary, Harold L. Ickes, picking up the hint, noted in his diary, "Father Coughlin and his fascist associates and allies are particularly vigorous in their onslaughts against the [embargo] legislation.[7] Coughlin was currently losing access to radio station after station, thanks to actions undertaken by the administration's friends, such as the owner of WMCA in New York City. The priest's power was eroding. Internal dissension had already caused him to shut down his National Union for Social Justice. Coughlin's overt anti-Semitism and his apparent toleration of the Nazis made him fair game.

Federal agents infiltrated the Christian Front, and early in 1940 the FBI arrested seventeen members of a Front "sports club" in Brooklyn. The federal agents uncovered a cache of guns, ammunition, and bomb accessories in the homes of the alleged conspirators. J. Edgar Hoover claimed that the fronters had planned to murder many Jews, communists, and "about a dozen congressmen" as part of an armed uprising in

New York City. The government put fourteen of the men on trial for sedition.

"Recognizing that opposition to Communism is on trial," a hesitant Father Coughlin professed his solidarity with the accused. He was exultant when the jury acquitted the men on 24 June. "The result of it all," said Coughlin, "will be that the Christian Front movement will emerge more victorious and potent than ever."[8] This was not to be. Thanks to the propaganda skills of the administration, the profession or advocacy of fascist views came to be equated with sedition or even treason. Coughlin, despite his brave words, moved to distance himself from radical groups operating in his name. Coughlin opposed any alliance with the Bund, which too many committees described as a German Trojan horse. He himself called it "un-American," though at times Coughlin himself parroted Berlin's propaganda.

The Reverend Maurice S. Sheehey supplied his friend Ickes with allegations that Coughlin was receiving "his ammunition from Germany and . . . Germany is also financing him." Ickes had no proof, but he leaked this and related information to sympathetic reporters.[9] Soon, Coughlin was damaged goods. In the presidential election of 1940, Coughlin seemed to back Wendell Wilkie, but the candidate repudiated the support of any group "opposed to certain people because of their race or religion." The bad publicity and the ire of the administration would soon lead to Coughlin's political demise. The Church silenced him, with the help of federal postal authorities, and the "radio priest" died an obscure parish priest many years later.

Other fascist groups, such as the Christian Mobilizers, had also fallen on hard times. Their leader Joe McWilliams had disassociated himself from the Christian Front, which he found to be too timid. Despite his name, which he used to political advantage, McWilliams was part Native American. Born on an Indian reservation in Oklahoma, McWilliams had a murky past as a restless drifter and gifted confidence man. Winrod and Pelley had come to politics by way of religion. They had once offered heaven; now they offered fascism, or a combination of hatred and salvation. The future "Joe McNazi" was more eccentric, but he too was the product of the era of the failed salesman.

Handsome and vain, with dark good looks, McWilliams's carefully coiffed hair (some said he had it waved and bobbed) gave him the appearance of a movie actor in "Grade B" pictures. At times, when he appeared unshaven in public, the big talk and endless bragadoccio revealed something unsavory about the man. McWilliams had a lot to hide. Jews had helped him in the 1920s, when he was a struggling inventor. Ray Halpern remembered that "he was closer to the Jews than any Christian I have ever known." Complimented in those days for his tolerance, McWilliams would reply, "Sure, that is the way it is for me." In the early 1930s, McWilliams attended Marxist meetings; he may have dabbled in Zionism. His past concealed arrests for burglary, rape, and disorderly conduct. In the late 1930s, McWilliams saw great potential in the anti-Jewish sentiment so evident around him. He quickly obtained celebrity status among local fascists.

An outspoken admirer of the Nazis ("Adolf Hitler is the greatest leader in the history of the world"), McWilliams promoted himself as the savior of America. "In a few years," he declared, "we will need a leader who will be like a knight of old. A man in shining armor. . . . That's what we'll need to bring together our forces for a nationalist America." In the spring of 1939, taking some of the tougher Christian Front punks with him, McWilliams formed the Christian Mobilizers. He created an alliance with the Bund, Castorina's Blackshirts, and the Ku Klux Klan. McWilliams's violent rhetoric and charismatic appeal gained him widespread notoriety. He claimed a membership of twenty thousand for the Mobilizers, a greatly inflated figure.

Father Coughlin viewed McWilliams as a seducer of well-intentioned schismatics. Yet the radio priest feared McWilliams and hoped to regain the allegiance of his followers. Coughlin thus took care to condemn McWilliams in rather cautious language. "We know," said the priest, "that at least 90 percent of those who belong to the Christian Mobilizers are good people and friends of social justice. Unfortunately, the followers have been led by Mr. McWilliams into an alliance with the Bund, which no one can gainsay is an un-American organization."

As he drew closer to the Bund and the Klan, McWilliams's attacks on the Jews became more venemous. He needed to stand out from the crowd, and he did. By 1940, McWilliams had become the most notorious Jew-baiter in New York. McWilliams acquired a hard-core following of six hundred toughs. "Keep America out of the Jewish war!" he urged, while booming General Moseley for the presidency. As for the Jews, McWilliams promised, "I would ship [them] to some such place as Madagascar."

"Joe McNazi's" fame was spreading through the anti-Jewish grapevine. McWilliams himself decided to contest the Eighteenth Congressional District, on Manhattan's Upper East Side. He planned to run in the Republican primary, which much upset Republican leaders. If he failed, McWilliams decided, he would run on his own party ticket in the fall. McWilliams founded the American Destiny Party (ADP). His ambitions were now national in scope, and the party planned to field congressional candidates in Oregon and California. The ADP's platform was simple: "Stay out of the war, kill the Jews, buy Christian."

The mobilizer chief was at home in the district, a stronghold of the Bund. James True, a patron saint to anti-Semites, and the Bund itself helped McWilliams during the campaign. Some Bundists saw Mc-Williams as a substitute for the incarcerated Fritz Kuhn. McWilliams refused to moderate his message: "Let's make this country the paradise that Hitler has made Germany. . . ." If elected, he promised there would be no "Jew war for the U.S."

For a year, Walter Winchell had been keeping Roosevelt personally informed about the Christian Mobilizers. Using sources whose identity he refused to reveal (even to the White House), Winchell supplied detailed information about their meetings, purposes, and personnel. Winchell was a veritable intelligence service for the White House during these years. He had started as early as 1934, when Winchell contacted Democratic National Chairman James A. Farley about the Silver Shirts, *Liberation* magazine, and William Dudley Pelley. Farley forwarded the correspondence to the White House. Now, during the war, Winchell exposed the financial backers of the Keep America Out of War Committee, one of whom, William R. Davis, was allegedly a pro-German oilman. Winchell did his best to provide information linking Charles A. Lindbergh, Jr., to pro-Nazi individuals. Winchell was of great use to FDR, especially because he operated in the heart of the enemy empire, the press conglomerate controlled by the profascist William Randolph Hearst. By portraying fascist groups as threats to the nation, Winchell helped to legitimize moves against them by the White House, the Department of Justice, and local courts and law enforcement agencies. The pressure was put on the mobilizers; it became good politics for local authorities to go after them.[10]

Back on the streets, McWilliams had to be more careful not to violate city ordinances against inciting to riot. He could no longer call for pogroms against the Jews. Though humorless, the candidate now drew laughs with his vehement denunciations of the "Eskimos" (meaning the Jews). At times, McWilliams got carried away, publicly denouncing the Jews instead of the Eskimos. At one point a Democratic magistrate booked him for "inciting to riot" on the corner of 85th Street and First Avenue. Offered the choice of a fifty dollar fine or thirty days in jail, McWilliams announced that he would appeal. In fact, he declared, he was merely "in that court putting on a show and to obtain publicity . . . from the prostituted, lying, filthy press."

The district, though containing many Bundists, was not particularly anti-Roosevelt. Polls indicated that a majority of its voters favored a third term for FDR. Republicans leaders breathed a sigh of relief when McWilliams went down to crushing defeat. More trouble for Mc-Williams began on 7 August. City officials decided that the mobilizer chief, speaking on behalf of his candidacy, had incited to riot once again. Some days later, a process server attempted to approach Mc-Williams with a summons to court and was attacked by mobilizer William Fox. On 3 September, Magistrate Edgar Bromberger commit-ted Fox to Bellevue Hospital for psychiatric observation.

To McWilliams, this was a Jew trick. He ranted and raved, then smirked and showed "disdain" when the magistrate lectured him. McWilliams's attorney, Frank J. Walsh, seemed to imply that his client was disturbed. Perhaps he hoped that Bromberger would let him off with a suspended sentence. Unconvinced, the magistrate still insisted that McWilliams be sent to Bellevue for observation. Walsh, whining, "Everybody is peculiar in some respects," charged that this commit-ment represented an attempt "to destroy Joe McWilliams' reputation as far as the general public goes." He was right.

City, state, and federal officials, encouraged in various ways by Roo-sevelt, the attorney general, the FBI, and certain congressional commit-tees, were engaged in an all-out assault against Hitler's Americans. Nazi observers perceived the danger to their friends. Foreign Minister Rib-bentrop later acknowledged the imminent triumph of "Jewish warmon-gers." He lamely grasped at straws, predicting that these devils would suffer a terrible fate *after* American entry into the war. "The result will be that one day all the Jews in America will be killed."[11]

That event, if it ever took place, would fail to save Joe McWilliams. Notoriety attracted inquisitive reporters. Journalists began finding juicy tidbits in McWilliams's past. They uncovered various criminal convic-tions, as well as a bizarre ideological pilgrimage. While McWilliams sat in Bellevue, the press finished him off. For several weeks, Bromberger refused to release McWilliams from the hospital. Then, after clinical reports showed him to be sane, McWilliams returned to the campaign trail, only to lose in November. A shadow of his old self, McWilliams continued to address dwindling crowds of mobilizers and Bundists. The law, plus a carefully orchestrated campaign of ridicule, had destroyed him. The only notoriety awaiting him now was a wartime indictment for sedition.[12]

The fascists had many leaders, but no one leader. Their organizations were usually decentralized, often consisting of local chapters filled with corrupt or psychopathic people. Kuhn, Coughlin, and Pelley lived in a country where nationalism had not gone berserk. The United States had not lost a war, nor had it been victimized by a "lost peace." Militarism was not an ingrained tradition. Kuhn was in prison; Pelley in deep legal trouble; and Coughlin's voice was growing fainter, his audiences smaller.

The polls spoke eloquently of the turnabout in public attitudes. Stereotypical images of the Jews persisted. People as a whole were no more tolerant in late 1940 than they had been at the time of the 1939 Senate controversy over the admission of German-Jewish children. More important, however, was the growing awareness of anti-Semitic agitation as an unwelcome or *subversive* activity. The Bund and the Silver Shirts had become well known for their anti-Jewish demagoguery. Fritz Kuhn was known to seventy percent of the public, General Moseley to forty-one percent. It was clear from the polls that any anti-interventionist group or persons accused of anti-Semitic agitation would suffer in the public opinion polls. By 1940, poll respondents, answering a question about a hypothetical anti-Semitic candidate for Congress, indicated by forty-five percent to fourteen percent that his "being against the Jews" would negatively influence their judgment of said candidate.[13] In 1938, nineteen percent of respondents responded favorably to the idea of a campaign against the Jews. Two years and one month later, the figure had declined to twelve percent.

The United States remained a strongly anti-Semitic country, which makes these figures particularly striking. So long as anti-Semitism was considered to be a legitimate "nativist" attitude, it was dangerous, because it could be mobilized by political movements. Once it became associated with a hostile foreign power, it lost its political momentum. Indeed, it became less fashionable in all social circles, at least in public.

It was part of Roosevelt's genius that he placed nativist movements in a Nazi ghetto, successfully associating them with Germany, Trojan horses, and fifth columns. He did so in part by dissociating himself from most of the controversy surrounding immigration quotas and refugee issues, except for the blandest humanitarian statements. FDR and his agents could point to anti-Semitic statements by a Pelley or a Coughlin, and turn these men into virtual Nazis. Extrapolating further, it was not difficult, given the fears engendered by the war, to place anti-interventionists in the same boat, if they stooped to overt anti-Semitism.

The decline of the Christian Front, the collapse of the Christian Mobilizers, and the near demise of the Bund bore witness to the success of the Roosevelt administration's strategy. And the Constitution did not crumble into dust, despite the warning of mainstream conservatives and far-right agitators.

As he planned to announce the lend-lease legislation, Roosevelt had gained several advantages. War production had revived the economy. Unemployment had dropped from nine million to under five million. America was a huge country, where people could still believe that they were, as Roosevelt put it, "going places." Still, there were grave challenges to Roosevelt's interventionist foreign policy. The United States had reached an historical crossroads. The far right, though discredited, had helped to sour the public mood, and it remained vocal. Far more serious, from the viewpoint of Roosevelt, Stimson, and their colleagues, was a broad coalition of anti-interventionists. Represented by a national hero, and appealing to a combination of pacifism, nostalgia, defeatism, and Roosevelt-bashing, the isolationist coalition would not easily surrender its banner. A looming threat in the Far East could play into the hands of these people, who argued against confrontation with Hitler's Germany.

CHAPTER
TWENTY-NINE

THE JAPANESE DISTRACTION

WHILE ROOSEVELT PREPARED for the battle over lend-lease, disturbing events were taking place elsewhere. The uneasy mix of militarism, political cliques, emperor worship, and feudal tradition in Japan lacked the psychotic element spawned by National Socialism. Nevertheless, hostile actions on Japan's part could prove an unwelcome distraction. The Japanese Navy frightened Roosevelt less than German U-boats. Tokyo might wish to rule East Asia, but Hitler, Roosevelt believed, had ambitions that were global in nature. A modus vivendi, valid for a time, might be worked out with Japan, but never with the Nazis.

By the winter of 1941, powerful elements in the Japanese Army preferred war with America to a withdrawal from China and the surrender of hegemony in East Asia. If forced to fight the Americans in a long war of attrition, Japan could not hope to win, but it might prevent the Americans from interfering in Asia. Admiral Yamamoto Isoroku, commander in chief of the combined fleet, had designed a plan for the destruction of the American Pacific Fleet.[1] Perhaps the execution of that attack would lead to a favorable outcome for Japan.

* * *

For years, Washington's policy toward Japanese expansionism had been contradictory. In 1931, when Japan attacked Chinese Manchuria, then secretary of state Henry L. Stimson was shocked. This blatant violation of treaties could, he believed, undermine all respect for international law and destroy the collective security of nations. Such aggression violated the Washington Treaty of 1922 as well as the Kellogg-Briand Peace Pact of 1928, and other agreements. The liberal international order could not weather many more actions of this kind. The United States, Stimson announced, could not "admit the legality of any situation *de facto* nor does it intend to recognize any treaty or agreement entered into between those governments" detrimental to American rights, or to the territorial integrity of China. A further blow fell when the League of Nations endorsed the "Stimson Doctrine," at which time Japan left the League. The Roosevelt administration continued the nonrecognition policy, further antagonizing Tokyo. From this time, pulp writers in Japan began to sell more books and stories depicting a future war between Japan and the wicked United States.[2]

While opposed to Japanese aggression, the United States refused to make firm commitments to the British regarding a combined military strategy against Japanese expansion. Prime Minister Stanley Baldwin had been sarcastic about the possibility of joint action. "You will get nothing out of Washington," he complained, "but words. Big words, but only words." The Japanese had absorbed Manchuria; now they threatened much of China. The European crisis could only encourage Japanese expansionists. Besides distracting the colonial powers, Britain, France, and Holland, it made Tokyo wonder about Western intentions. Would powers that abandoned a nearby democracy, Czechoslovakia, rally to the defense of their own interests ten thousand or more miles around the globe?

While Roosevelt mulled over the failure of Munich, British military leaders had concluded that an alliance with the United States was necessary and hence possible. Unlike the military chiefs, British diplomats were divided on the wisdom of waiting for the American alliance. Foreign Secretary Lord Halifax was nervous about entrusting British Far Eastern interests to the goodwill of the Americans, particularly since FDR was so enigmatic. Perhaps Britain, with her fabled diplomatic gifts, could work something out with the Japanese. Though the Anglo-American treaty failed to emerge, Roosevelt and Hull were taking stronger measures in the Far East. Roosevelt was still reluctant to develop a joint strategy, however, much less offer guarantees. He did offer some modest economic assistance to beleaguered China, and imposed a "moral embargo" upon the export of aircraft and aviation equipment to Japan.

In a laconic sentence penned for his diary, Assistant Secretary of State Adolf Berle noted the following on 27 June: "[We] reached a tentative decision to push the fleet into Pearl Harbor. . . ." A few weeks later, this astute intellectual made another interesting observation. The American public, he noted with some disgust, hated the thought of intervention in Europe, while it was prepared to rush headlong into confrontation with Japan.[3] In July, the Americans notified Tokyo of their intention of abrogating (within six months) the 1911 trade treaty between the two nations.

While relations between the United States and Japan deteriorated, the Soviets defeated Japan in some impressive border battles in 1939. Taken aback by Nazi Germany's pact with the ideological enemy, Japan grudgingly adjusted to it. Substantial segments of her army still dreamt of the "strike north," into the Soviet Far East, but for the moment their hopes were dashed. The following summer, the Japanese Army commanders watched with undisguised glee as the German armies overran the Low Countries, then France. The German entry into Paris inspired the Japanese.

Many militarists in the army looked forward to the day when the Rising Sun would fly over the restive colonies of the decadent, alien European empires. Desperate to secure sufficient foodstuffs, oil, tin, and rubber, Japanese industrialists and economic managers longed for the riches of the Dutch East Indies, perhaps of Indochina and of independent, neutral Thailand. It seemed to many in Tokyo that the day of the White Man had come and gone; only the British and the Americans remained in the field. Even Churchill appeared to appease Japan, closing the Burma Road, a supply line to besieged China, for three months. To the consternation of Japan's leadership, the United States was acting in a *less* accommodating way. Roosevelt had earlier sent the fleet from its West Coast base to Hawaii for maneuvers, but now he kept it there.

To the Japanese, America was attractive and repulsive at the same time. They admired America's economic modernity, but despised its racism and harsh immigration laws.[4] Once before, some Japanese argued, an American president, Wilson, had robbed Japan of her just deserts in China. Now, the Americans were doing the same thing. Polls showed Americans favoring the Chinese cause by seventy-six percent to two percent over the Japanese side.[5] No wonder the Chinese continued to resist. If Washington and London yielded to pressure, or were defeated in battle, surely the Chinese would accept their place in Japan's Greater East Asia Co-Prosperity Sphere.[6] Many Japanese were thinking along these lines, while Roosevelt was promising not to send American boys to fight in a foreign war.

To some Japanese military thinkers, only the Western strongpoints in Singapore, the Philippines, Guam, and Pearl Harbor stood in the way of Japan's New Order. "Asia for the Asians" would be Japan's response to insulting Western blather about international law and the "Yellow Peril." (Goebbels had banned the use of the term in Germany). While the Germans kept the Russians friendly to the Axis camp, the Japanese might expand to Burma and India, ultimately dominating China, Southeast Asia, and the entire western Pacific.

The Axis victories in Europe changed Japan's mind about the wisdom of a military and diplomatic alliance with Germany and Italy. Indeed, Germany's good relations with the Soviets had become attractive bait to Tokyo. If Japan moved into Southeast Asia, it would require the acquiescence of three powers, Russia, the United States, and Britain. A pact with Germany, so some said, would insure Russia's continued neutrality, while the new German-Japanese-Italian combination would intimidate America and Britain in the Far East. Fighting for his life in the Battle of Britain, Churchill was hardly in a position to prevent the reordering of East Asia. America, desperate to assist Britain, and unprepared for war, would also stand aside, according to thoughts voiced by leading Japanese diplomats.

From the summer of 1940, American military and diplomatic leaders, including the president, were well informed regarding Japan's ambitions. Military intelligence had broken a Japanese diplomatic code. Dispatches filed by the embassy in Washington and cables directed to it by the Foreign Ministry in Tokyo contained disturbing information.[7] By allying itself with Nazi Germany, Japan could threaten the United States with a two-ocean war. Foreign Minister Matsuoka Yosuke favored such a pact. An admirer of the German Reich, Matsuoka wished to turn

Japan into the center of a New Order in Asia. He, along with the premier, Prince Konoye Fumimaro, called this imperium the "Greater East Asia Co-Prosperity Sphere."[8] Intimidation might be appropriate, Matsuoka now believed, for Roosevelt had been acting more hostile. Working around the more cautious but equally ambitious Konoye, Matsuoka, backed by strong pro-German factions in the army, reoriented Japanese policy toward the Axis powers. So long as Germany laid no claim to Western colonies in Southeast Asia, Matsuoka could pursue his pro-Axis course.

The president had authority to license (or embargo) the export of a long list of strategic items, including oil, scrap metal, munitions, and machine tools. These exports were vital to the Japanese war economy. For the time being, Roosevelt embargoed only the export of fuel for aircraft, lubricants, and certain kinds of processed metals. The embargo, however, frightened and enraged the imperial authorities.[9] A pact with victorious Germany might bring the Anglo-Americans to their senses. Trade would then resume as in former times, and presumably Singapore, India, the Philippines, and Guam would remain unscathed by war. Matsuoka went so far as to propose that "Japan should push boldly forward, hand in hand with Germany," even to the point of a "double suicide," if it came to that.

The result of this thinking was the Tripartite Pact, signed in Berlin on 27 September 1940. The key provision read as follows: "They [Japan, Germany, and Italy] further undertake to assist one another with all political, economic, and military means when one of the three contracting Parties is attacked by a power at present not involved in the European war or in the Sino-Japanese conflict." Prodded by skeptics within the armed forces (especially the navy), Matsuoka insisted upon an escape clause. He did not want to be dragged into a war with the democracies over a clash between America and Germany in the North Atlantic. Secret correspondence indicates that the Germans accepted the escape clause. In other words, the three parties would have to agree that an "attack" had taken place. There would be no automatic declaration of war. To Americans, however, the pact appeared to be aggressive and even threatening.[10]

The Japanese appeared poised to strike south. Roosevelt did not want war with Japan, at least not for the foreseeable future. On one point, however, FDR was adamant. Japanese domination of the Dutch

East Indies, and adjacent strong points was unacceptable, because Tokyo was an ally of Germany. Its regional hegemony would gravely weaken the Allies in East Asia and threaten Burma and India.

The Japanese miscalculated, on two levels. They hoped to intimidate Roosevelt by concluding the pact with Germany. This they failed to do, and they also misconstrued FDR's patience as a long-term commitment to appeasement. Roosevelt's caution sprang from daily concerns about the battle of the North Atlantic sea-lanes. More importantly, Tokyo did not understand that the alliance with Germany meant that, in due time, Roosevelt would react to every move by Japan as part of an Axis plan for global hegemony. Any concession to Tokyo might strengthen the New Order. Japan, Roosevelt argued, must not be allowed to strengthen itself at the expense of beleaguered Britain. Against this, FDR weighed the consequences of a war in Southeast Asia, which could only distract Americans from the real task at hand. Only as a crisis became imminent did the White House concentrate more upon the Far East.

Roosevelt was playing for time. He was a bit unkind to himself when, in a rare moment of self-doubt, he told his son Elliott that "We are, in essence and in fact appeasing Japan."[11] Concerned about Britain's survival, FDR paid little attention to incoming diplomatic reports purporting to document Japan's plan to attack the Dutch East Indies and Singapore. Secretary Hull was equally cautious.[12]

Roosevelt tended to underestimate Japan's daring, as well as its military potential. He believed, as he had in 1923, that economic pressure (and inducements) could curb Japan short of war. FDR appeared little concerned at this point about the fate of China, despite his affection for the Chinese people. He wished to deter Japan, not provoke it.[13] At some point, however, firmness might strike Tokyo as intolerable pressure. Roosevelt took care not to cross that line, at least not for the first half of 1941. He did not appreciate that Japan was an unstable element, oscillating between desires for conquest and fear of widening the war.

The United States needed more time. The American and Filipino forces stationed in the Philippines were pitifully weak. The Asiatic Fleet was not much stronger, and modern aircraft were in short supply. Why would Japan feel threatened, or, more to the point, why would it widen the war in Asia? A fatal weakness now appeared in the considerations dominating the Far Eastern strategy of the Roosevelt administration. A contradictory tendency to belittle Japanese capabilities yet to see Japan's fears as a smoke screen for a program of unambiguous aggression along the lines of *Mein Kampf,* dominated Washington's thinking. Japan was a primitive little boy who had drifted into bad habits by keeping unsavory company. If Japan acted aggressively, it was, so Washington thought, because it was copying Hitler. Economic pressure and some small military buildups would deter such ill-considered action. That embargoes could lead to a sense of impending strangulation and doom among a broad spectrum of Japanese leaders escaped Roosevelt and his closest advisers. American diplomats in Tokyo, who better understood Japanese thinking, were more prescient in their analyses.

Even fantastic rumors and well-presented intelligence briefings could not convince American authorities that the Japanese were capable of carrying out a sudden attack against *American* forces. On 27 January, the embassy in Tokyo informed the State Department of a disturbing report. The Peruvian ambassador had heard of a plan by which the Japanese would launch "a surprise mass attack on Pearl Harbor," home base of the Pacific Fleet. No one investigated the rumor, and it quickly faded.[14] At about the same time, secretaries Knox and Stimson received detailed warnings about the possibility of a bombing or aerial torpedo attack on the Pacific Fleet, while it lay at rest in Pearl Harbor.[15] Some weeks later, an intelligence report indicated that Japan might launch "a surprise attack on Oahu including ships and installations at Pearl Harbor." The American forces in the Pacific theater had the responsibility for the security of the fleet and installations in Hawaii. Despite the warnings, neither Washington nor U.S. commanders in the Pacific really understood the implications of their own intelligence.[16]

One can sympathize with the navy officers. Even as they learned of possible threats to their fleet, the president seemed preoccupied with the Atlantic battle. FDR did not wish to provoke Japan, nor did he wish to enrage isolationists by appearing to defend the discredited colonial empires of Asia. Roosevelt was trying to impress Japan without unduly alarming it, a goal that would elude him. The Pacific Fleet's mission as a deterrent was thus unclear. It seemed destined to project American *counteroffensive* power, rather than to act as a deterrent. Yet it could not venture too far afield, since it lacked the necessary tankers and transports. Because its ships usually had to refuel in port, they would often be lined up at Pearl Harbor within a single, narrow channel. In the long run, the fleet could become a dire threat to Japan; in the short run, it was vulnerable to a strike by the Imperial Navy.

Americans did not expect to be attacked, while Japanese officials had difficulty understanding American policy. A highly knowledgeable American diplomat shocked a Japanese official by intimating that an attack on Singapore could well result in war with the United States. Actually, this was by no means certain, and Eugene Dooman was speaking for himself, not for Hull or Roosevelt.[17]

From Tokyo, American Ambassador Joseph C. Grew warned Washington that major diplomatic moves were in the making. Embargoes on certain strategic exports, such as scrap metal, were causing great concern among Japanese leaders. Japan, Grew advised Washington, might try to resolve its differences with Soviet Russia, thereby weakening Chinese resistance and clearing the way for a move southeastward into the rich colonial possessions of Holland and Britain.[18]

As seen from the White House, a great Axis now ran from Vichy French Africa, through German and Italian-occupied Europe, to the Soviet Far East and Japanese-dominated mainland Asia. Some rumors reported that Stalin was negotiating entry into the Tripartite Pact. He had recognized the Japanese puppet state of Manchukuo (Manchuria), and would probably decrease assistance to the hard-pressed Chinese. The toll taken by U-boats in the Atlantic was reaching dangerous levels.

Japan's northern flank adjacent to Russia appeared to be secure for the moment, though both countries kept large numbers of troops in the region. Encouraged by Britain's problems in Greece, North Africa, and the North Atlantic, Matsuoka and some of his military colleagues looked longingly to the rich natural resources of Southeast Asia. Reports reached Washington indicating that Japan was removing forces from some fronts in China in order to send them south or southeast. In Washington, Secretary Hull readied himself for new negotiations with Japan. While the United States exercised pressure by placing an embargo upon many strategic exports, Hull took a firmer line with Japan.

The United States also desired a renunciation of the Tripartite Pact by Japan. Tokyo, for its part, hoped to achieve a number of things, including a compromise on Indochina and China (though not to the point of total military withdrawal), and resumption of normal trade relations. It was not unreasonable for Japanese diplomats to assume that some kind of settlement might take place. In attempting to divide

America from Britain, Japanese policymakers sadly miscalculated Roosevelt's purposes. On the surface, why should the United States care about the fate of Hong Kong? Unfortunately for the Japanese, FDR viewed a viable British Empire as crucial to his strategy for destroying Nazi Germany. Ironically, Roosevelt's informal alliance with Britain was stronger than Japan's pseudoalliance with Hitler. The Germans could do little for Japan, but thanks to their pact the Japanese strengthened Roosevelt's conviction that the Japanese were his enemies.

Roosevelt, however, needed more time for his buildup, both in the North Atlantic and in the Far East. The worst nightmare would be for an unprepared America to be at war in the Far East, while Germany remained "neutral." Churchill's worst-case scenario, by contrast, foresaw Britain at war with Japan, while the United States remained a nonbelligerent. It was the prime minister who hoped that America would find a "back door" into the war, if it did not declare war on Germany. ·

Roosevelt thus stuck to his "Germany first" strategy. If Japan struck, Germany would be the first to pay a very heavy price. Most American experts expected that Japan might at some point attack the Dutch East Indies, and perhaps Britain's possessions, such as Hong Kong. No one in Washington seemed to expect any imminent attack by Japan on American territories, though the security of the Philippines was crucial. Secretary Stimson, former High Commissioner of the Philippines, took a personal interest in assuring the safety of the island chain. The author of the "Stimson Doctrine" had also been the honorary chairman of the American Committee for Non-Participation in Japanese Aggression. This did not bode well for Japan.

Piecemeal but overly ambitious American measures symbolized Washington's arrogant underestimation of Japan's military capabilities.[19] The War Department seemed to lack a sense of urgency in regard to the Far East. An inability to see the interrelatedness between trade policy and military considerations was also endemic in the State Department. Japan was, according to its leading expert on the Far East, Stanley Hornbeck, lacking in "military capacity sufficient to warrant an attack by her on the United States." Japan would *not*, he later added, go to war out of sheer desperation.[20] To the contrary, Japan *would* only go to war against the Western powers out of "sheer desperation."

Roosevelt had no sympathy for Japan's predicament, and Tokyo mistrusted the West's intentions. Once Japan had made itself an appendage of Hitler's global designs, to the president's way of thinking, it had forfeited any right to be treated as a sovereign state with legitimate interests worthy of consideration.

For the moment, however, a settling of accounts in the Far East would have to await more urgent problems. In January, Roosevelt, resolved to render major assistance to Britain, began working to secure the passage of his lend-lease legislation. It was soon apparent from the Anglo-American staff talks that 1941 would see major new American initiatives in the North Atlantic. These anti-German measures took precedence over the Japanese threat to Southeast Asia. In fact, Roosevelt and Hull intended to stall the Japanese, even to the point of tantalizing Tokyo with the prospect of a reasonable, negotiated settlement.

CHAPTER
THIRTY

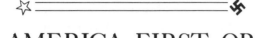

AMERICA FIRST OR
AMERICAN CENTURY?

O N THURSDAY, 23 JANUARY, Colonel Charles A. Lindbergh strode
briskly into the Capitol hearing room. He was the star of the
hearings. Tall, blond, with all-American looks, Lindbergh acted
as if his natural modesty and shyness had yielded to the call of patriotic
duty. Surrounded by a phalanx of reporters, photographers, and ap-
plauding bystanders, he prepared to deliver a major statement on H.R.
1776 (the lend-lease bill).[1] Troubled by recent polls reflecting support
for FDR, Lindbergh hoped to change the direction of public opinion.[2]
He was again at the center of the very media which he so despised.[3]

Lindbergh's frustration surfaced during the fall of France. "Here, at
this moment," Lindbergh moaned, "I feel in contact neither with the
world of men nor with the world of God. . . . What can be done to bring
this country back? What has happened to America?" Lindbergh
seemed concerned not about the fall of France but about the prospects
for American intervention. He hoped that the French would make peace
quickly. The defeat of a major democracy seemed to confirm his views
on decadence.[4] Chargé Thomsen reported in the summer of 1940 that
Lindbergh believed in the imminent collapse of Great Britain. He
attacked FDR for pushing Britain and France into war.

The German embassy was now paying a great deal of attention to Lindbergh, who was emerging as a leader of the anti-interventionist forces. A high Foreign Ministry official later recalled, "Lindbergh enjoyed a very high regard not only among the German officials, but also with the German people generally. Ribbentrop said to me on several occasions that it would be very desirable from a German point of view if Lindbergh could become President of the United States." Military attaché von Bötticher predicted that "the Jews," meaning the Roosevelt administration, would try to discredit Lindbergh. They needed to do so, argued von Bötticher, because "[t]he circle about Lindbergh . . . now tries at least to impede the fatal control of American politics by the Jews."[5]

Thomsen claimed that he had good access to Lindbergh, though one must not discount the diplomat's desire to impress his superiors in Berlin. "His commanding spirit," cabled the attaché, "takes the lead in circles which can become decisive for America's future attitude toward us and in combating the fight of international Jewry against Germany." Lindbergh's success was considered crucial to Hitler's strategy, which demanded the isolation of America from the European war.[6]

Intellectual certitude and fear of Roosevelt blinded Lindbergh to certain realities. He showed no understanding of General Charles de Gaulle's resistance movement. The heroism of the Royal Air Force and the stirring speeches of Churchill failed to inspire the American hero. Lindbergh refused to consider the implications of an Axis victory. Not willing to acknowledge his lack of faith in America, Lindbergh attacked Roosevelt. At times, he seemed to argue that a lack of defeatism undermined the American future. "We are in danger of war today," he wrote, "not because Europeans attempted to interfere in our internal affairs, but because Americans attempted to interfere in the internal affairs of Europe." Lindbergh used the term "Europe" as if it were a free, distant entity, worthy of respect, rather than an occupied war zone. "Our dangers are internal," Lindbergh argued. "We need not fear invasion," he continued, "unless Americans bring it through their own quarreling and meddling with affairs abroad." Lindbergh had little to offer but safety based on despair. Lindbergh was becoming an accomplished speaker, however; the earnest voice, the well-turned phrases, and the low-key warnings soon became familiar throughout the land. Anne helped him with the texts of his speeches, and she was a superb stylist.

Lindbergh played an equally important role behind the scenes. Soon after the fall of France, Colonel Lindbergh conferred with R. Douglas Stuart, Jr., the young heir to the Quaker Oats fortune. Stuart, a law student at Yale University, had in the fall of 1939 organized a group called Defend America First. He quickly recruited other students, including Sargent Shriver and Kingman Brewster, Jr. Lindbergh put Stuart in touch with General Robert E. Wood, chairman of the board of Sears, Roebuck and Company. The general, who had a good military record, had at one time advised the president on the 1935 public works bill, and had attended a 1937 presidential conference on economic recovery. Wood subsequently broke with FDR over issues of foreign policy.

Now a wealthy contributor to right-wing causes, General Wood despised Britain. During the fall of France, he wrote to Colonel Frank Knox, "We are weakening our defense by trying to bolster up a decadent system and nation. Nature's law is survival, and if a race is not strong enough to survive unaided, it will perish." An admirer of the fascist theoretician Lawrence Dennis, Wood argued that intervention would spell "the end of capitalism all over the world."[7] Stuart dropped Lindbergh's name when contacting William R. Castle, a wealthy former academic and diplomat popular with the Nazis and their favored American propagandists. Castle was close to the Lindberghs, having brought Charles into contact with the Anglophobe broadcaster Fulton Lewis. Thanks to Lewis, Lindbergh had begun to make frequent speeches on the radio. Castle, an adviser to prominent Republicans, believed that Germany would win the war. Stuart knit together this circle of Roosevelt-haters, Anglophobes, and anti-interventionists.

The result of these and other consultations was the America First Committee, formally proclaimed on 4 September. The committee had headquarters in Chicago, with Wood as national chairman and Stuart as executive director. It worked with the financial backing of men like Jay. C. Hormel, the meat-packing giant, along with other powerful Republican businessmen from the Midwest. America First's leadership was held together by a shared belief in Roosevelt's evil designs and a common lack of faith in American strength.

The program of America First consisted of several major premises, each controversial in itself. There was, said the committee, no imminent danger to the United States from Germany, even if it won the war in Europe. A restoration of diplomatic and commercial ties between the

United States and Germany was possible and desirable. War, according to the committee, would be an economic disaster for the United States, meaning a lower standard of living, mass hardship, and a loss of social gains made in the 1930s. A strong America should look to its own continent and to Latin America, while refusing to become entangled in alliances with devious powers like Britain.

The committee received help from the slick publicity operations of Quaker Oats and Sears, Roebuck. Hormel obtained additional assistance from the large advertising firm of Batton, Barton, Durstine and Osborn, while the gifted publicists working for Benton and Bowles helped the committee in the East. William Benton, a former partner in this firm, was vice president of the University of Chicago. Like its president, Robert Maynard Hutchins (a wunderkind who was appointed at the age of thirty), Benton favored isolation. "Don't forget it," he once said, "smart money in this country is on our side." Chester Bowles of Connecticut volunteered his services to Stuart, who quickly accepted the offer. Though a political liberal skeptical of appeasement, Bowles favored isolation from the global struggle. Robert Bliss, onetime partner in the J. Walter Thompson agency, took over the committee's promotion account. Some of these publicists worked for the committee at the behest of commercial clients who backed America First.

In other cases, professionals promoting America First feared for their reputations and their client lists, and labored for the committee on a purely personal, voluntary basis. John Foster Dulles, last seen as a legal and moral apologist for appeasement, helped to set up the America First organization. He worked behind the scenes, claiming to be laboring on behalf of Edwin S. Webster, Jr., a partner in the powerful Kidder, Peabody brokerage firm. On at least one occasion, Dulles's wife Janet helped to defray the costs of a Lindbergh rally.[8] Controversial from the beginning, America First mounted a major challenge to Roosevelt's foreign policy.

Rejected by the communists as imperialist and retrogressive, many liberals, socialists and pacifists endorsed the committee. One of these liberal reformers was John T. Flynn, author of the best-selling campaign book *Country Squire in the White House.* Flynn had been a commentator on financial and economic matters for the liberal *New Republic.* Deeply disillusioned by the chauvinism and reaction that resulted from intervention in the last war, the publication was wary of entry into any new European conflict. By 1940, however, the magazine was lining up with

FDR on foreign policy issues, and it parted ways with John Flynn. Convinced that intervention meant war, and then hysteria, repression, and reaction, Flynn insisted it was Roosevelt who had betrayed the promise of the New Deal. Flynn helped to found America First, becoming the director of its New York City chapter, as well as a member of the national executive.[9] Flynn was possessed of boundless energy, generated in part by his rather irrational hatred for Franklin Roosevelt.

Some pacifists now joined America First. Oswald Garrison Villard, a pacifist who had broken with the progressive magazine *The Nation* on the question of intervention, joined Flynn in America First. Villard, chairman of the Keep America Out of War Congress, denounced the conflict as imperialist. He agreed with the late Senator Borah that "[P]ermitting ourselves to be involved in a foreign war would be definitely calculated to establish a totalitarian government in this country. . . ." Though appearing at America First rallies, the old socialist Norman Thomas always looked askance at the committee's commitment to "excessive" rearmament. Other Protestant pacifists, such as Yale historian Roland Bainton, theologian Harry Emerson Fosdick, and Harlem clergyman Adam Clayton Powell, Sr., rallied to the committee. Dorothy Detzer, head of the influential Women's International League for Peace, supported America First, though she was a committed pacifist. While most pacifists refused to participate in the work of the committee, those who did often possessed great prestige on university campuses. Soon, thousands of college students were marching and demonstrating against both aid to Britain and American rearmament.[10] They protested the resumption of conscription.

Thanks in part to clever promotion, America First grew quickly, ultimately claiming a membership of some 800,000. America First was strongest in the heartland of the Midwest, in the counties and states around Chicago.[11] It had little appeal in the South, where support for Roosevelt's foreign policy was solid.

John Flynn was particularly delighted when historian Charles A. Beard agreed to work with America First. A progressive with a wide readership, Beard had great prestige. His presence at America First seemed to belie charges made by the committee's detractors, who denigrated it as a collection of fat cats, pro-Nazis, and reactionaries. A man of high principle, Beard had resigned his professorship at Columbia University during the First World War over the dismissal of instructor Leon Fraser. The young man had voiced objections to President

Wilson's preparedness policies. The United States, Beard believed, had not gone to war in an idealistic crusade against German militarism. British propaganda, Eastern banking interests, munitions manufacturers, and Wilsonian guile (and naiveté) had involved the United States in that sorry war. The conflict fostered bloodshed abroad and reaction at home, Beard concluded.

Beard was an early admirer of the New Deal. He sent autographed copies of his books to President Roosevelt, who responded by appointing Beard to the U.S. Constitution Sesquicentennial Commission. Upon right-wing protest, the historian withdrew his name from consideration. It was just as well, for Beard was becoming disillusioned with Franklin D. Roosevelt. Convinced that the Depression would not end soon, Beard feared that the president might provoke a war with Japan in order to overcome the economic crisis. Beard agreed with Barnes about the result: "The moment we join the war the New Deal and all its promises of a 'more abundant life' will fold up, as did the New Freedom of Woodrow Wilson in 1917."

In 1938, Beard argued against Roosevelt's plan for increased naval expenditures, fearing that the battleships would find service in "aggressive warfare in the Far Pacific or Far Atlantic."[12] Roosevelt, he argued, would take the road that led through collective security to war. In his next book, *A Foreign Policy for America*, Beard called for adequate defenses combined with isolation from foreign war. Beard testified against lend-lease, for he agreed with Senator D. Worth Clark's assertion that H.R. 1776 was "substantially an act of war." Using his congressional privileges, Clark distributed ten thousand copies of *A Foreign Policy for America*.

Beard sensed that men with more impure motives were infiltrating America First, which he had not joined. He refused to appear on the same platform with fascists and extremists. Acknowledging Roosevelt's success in molding public opinion, Beard sadly observed, "All the people I have always liked seem to be on the other side."[13] Nevertheless, he supported the anti-interventionist work of the committee, and defended Colonel Lindbergh against harsh attacks. Beard soon became convinced of Roosevelt's malevolent motive, which was to drag the United States into an unconstitutional war. He had come to hate "that son of a bitch."[14]

Charles C. Tansill held even stronger views. An early admirer of Hitler and the Nazi regime, he defended the German government as a bulwark against bolshevism. The professor of history lauded Hitler for the "evident charm of the man." The chancellor, said Tansill, had "a smile that dissolves doubt." After bearing witness to Germany's peaceful intentions, the Roosevelt-hating professor credited the new regime with reviving the German economy. Like other anti-interventionists, Tansill believed that Roosevelt was another Wilson, lying his way into war.[15] Tansill backed America First and denounced H.R. 1776.

This crusade against lend-lease was America First's great challenge. If that legislation passed, then Roosevelt would be in a powerful position to advance his interventionist goals "short of war." In Illinois, America First collected anti–lend-lease petitions containing half a million names. John T. Flynn won applause for demanding the enactment of the Ludlow Amendment, which would in most cases require a foreign invasion followed by a referendum before war could be declared.[16] Senator Nye called for the cessation of aid to Britain, warning that a naval clash with the Germans could give Roosevelt a pretext for going to war. University of Chicago president Robert M. Hutchins went further. "I believe," he declared, "that the American people are about to commit suicide."

Hutchins had gained one extraordinary insight, however. "The conclusion is inescapable," he wrote, "that the President is reconciled to active military intervention if such intervention is needed to defeat the Axis in this war. . . ." This was right on the mark.

Charles A. Lindbergh, Jr., rarely criticized the Nazis, and continued to believe in the superiority of the Luftwaffe over the RAF. Lindbergh continued to insist that even Britain and America combined could not defeat Germany. When the Nazis failed to subdue Britain, Lindbergh put this setback into his arsenal of defeatist arguments. The German failure over Britain proved that Hitler was no threat to the Americas, he said. Lindbergh now called for the production of thousands of aircraft, but refused to speculate about their target. How could he, when Lindbergh declined to name Nazi Germany as a possible threat to the Western Hemisphere?

The world Lindbergh desired to see would contain a powerful America, a strong Germany, and a reasonable Britain, all working in harmony for the prevention of bolshevik revolution. At the same time, the United States would hold Japan at bay, without intervening in the Far East.

On 13 October, in a radio speech, Lindbergh again blamed the president for America's lack of preparedness (a valid point), then ridiculed Roosevelt's call for drastically higher rates of aircraft production. "We do not," Lindbergh declared, "need untold thousands of military aircraft unless we intend to wage war abroad." Of course, Roosevelt was preparing to wage war abroad, if necessary. Unlike Lindbergh, it was hard for FDR to picture a world in which Hitler ruled Europe and much of Africa, while America went about its democratic business unmolested.

William Allen White responded to Lindbergh with a blistering editorial, published four days later. Referring to "Lindbergh, The Appeaser," White asked why the colonel blamed "Europe" for arming, when everyone knew that *German* rearmament, not that of the Allies, masked aggressive intent. White exposed one motive behind Lindbergh's hostility to FDR. "It is," said the editor, "because Mr. Roosevelt blazed the trail of public opinion in 1937, that all appeasers today hate him most bitterly."[17] Lindbergh, declared White, "utters folly and people shake their heads and walk away."[18] It was not that simple.

The organizer of the newly formed America First Committee hesitated before recruiting the eager Colonel Lindbergh. By this time, the "appeaser" label had begun to stick.[19] Still, Lindbergh was a tremendous drawing card, and he claimed to endorse the idea of a strong America, isolated from foreign wars. In October, Lindbergh addressed more than three thousand students in Woolsey Hall on the campus of Yale University. Lindbergh talked for almost two hours, drawing frequent cheers and applause. He advocated coming to terms with the "new powers in Europe." Kingman Brewster, editor of the *Yale News*, became a convert, as did many others. These privileged young people had no desire to fight in "FDR's war," or in any war, for that matter. Some were pacifists or socialists, but, given that Lindbergh was neither, it seems clear that the students had come to hear an attack on Roosevelt's foreign policy. The faculty was more pro-Roosevelt.

Lindbergh was becoming a nonstop campaigner. He refused to be discouraged by Roosevelt's third-term victory. He was pleased when Henry Ford, the union-busting labor tycoon, joined the America First campaign. Ford's speeches sounded like Lindbergh's, as he argued, "We are not now in the position where we can adopt that 'big brother' attitude toward anybody, we should NOT meddle in the affairs of other people." Wood and Stuart were more nervous about the emergence of

Ford as a key player. They feared that his anti-Semitism and controversial labor record could hurt the cause. Lindbergh seemed oblivious to the danger.[20]

Working closely with Roy Howard of the Scripps-Howard newspaper chain, Lindbergh found ideal outlets for his statements and speeches. "I chose Howard and the [United Press]," Lindbergh noted, because I know him well, and he is taking a decided stand with his papers against American intervention." Howard assisted Lindbergh in distributing huge amounts of carefully targeted America First propaganda, almost three million pieces of literature within nine months. Roosevelt was depicted as a budding dictator, who, working with sinister international interests, had sold the country out to British propagandists and New Deal bureaucrats.

During these hectic months, poet Anne Morrow Lindbergh enjoyed the fame bestowed by the public upon best-selling authors. She had recently published *The Wave of the Future: A Confession of Faith*. There were sixty-seven thousand copies in print within a few weeks of publication. In simple, lyrical language, Mrs. Lindbergh expressed thoughts first articulated by men like E.H. Carr, John Foster Dulles, Herbert Hoover, and Charles A. Lindbergh, Jr. The world crisis, she wrote, was the outcome of a struggle between the "have" and the "have-not" nations. The revolutions that had taken place in Russia, Italy, and Germany might not be attractive, but they were like childbirth, preparing the way for a new world. In a memorable phrase, she referred to totalitarian unpleasantries as "scum on the wave of the future." Privately, Mrs. Lindbergh expressed shock at Nazi thuggery, but she ascribed it to the nature of war.[21] Five years after the Nazis had published their Nürnberg racial laws, Mrs. Lindbergh could still describe the Hitler revolution as riding on the "wave of the future."[22] Nevertheless, the wife showed more compassion for the victims of Hitlerism than did her better known husband.

Including Soviet Russia (which she hated) was clever, for it endowed Mrs. Lindbergh's book with a certain detached, objective air. On one side stood change; on the other, the wicked interventionists, who wished to prevent the world from fulfilling its destiny. *The Wave of the Future* was defeatist in tone. America, said Mrs. Lindbergh, could not affect the course of history in Europe and Asia. Calling for a regeneration of the American spirit, she clearly blamed Roosevelt for its decline. A few months later, Charles put it this way: "These same leaders who have failed to solve even our peacetime problems, who have a consistent record of promise followed by failure, now ask us to put ourselves in their hands again as they lead us steadily toward that climax of all political failure—war."[23] Mrs. Lindbergh concurred, observing, "The good part of America does not seem to find any expression. . . . I want to find the America I dream of when abroad."[24] The expatriates had come home in search of a lost nation, or one which had never existed.

Philosopher Irwin Edman reacted in this way: "Mrs. Lindbergh," he said, "writes better than her husband but her soothing words are still the language of appeasement." Richard Scandrett, a prominent New York City attorney, and a cousin and dear friend of Mrs. Lindbergh, rejected her arguments. Scandrett ridiculed a mind-set that could accept the German domination of Europe, including England. He sensed that the Lindbergh clique misused progressive concepts, such as coming to grips with a changing world. To the contrary, Scandrett believed, these people were conservatives deeply fearful of social change, an anxiety which explained their willingness to coexist with fascism. Scandrett called for full cooperation with Britain in support of a new internationalism, one which could usher in a less gloomy future.[25]

Like Scandrett, we may wonder at the alternative offered by Mrs. Lindbergh. She admired Quakers as well as fascist theoretician Lawrence Dennis; presumably they were all resisting intervention. What kind of a worldview could reconcile such opposites? Mrs. Lindbergh's own roots were eastern, internationalist and interventionist. Under Charles's influence, she described her family as secure, rich, and "brought up in a hedged world so far from realities."[26] Mrs. Lindbergh insisted upon portraying Charles as the logician and the realist. Undermining the portrait was his acceptance of a world in which Hitler achieved many, if not all, of his goals. Despite her loyalty, Mrs. Lindbergh was troubled when she looked at some of Charles's admirers. And the situation was worse than she realized.

Nazi agents were manipulating Colonel Lindbergh as part of their subversion of American foreign policy. In the winter of 1941, George Eggleston, a propagandist with high connections in the German embassy, founded a mass circulation magazine, *Scribner's Commentator.* Secretly subsidized by the embassy, Eggleston had access to laundered American money. The funds came from the fortune of Charles S. Payson, a millionaire admirer of Colonel Lindbergh. Adopting the format popularized by *The Reader's Digest*, Eggleston offered a "mixture of political, economic, and general topics. . . ." Each issue contained about one hundred pages; printings of 100,000 issues were common. This effective propaganda sheet had but one aim, "to explain that an actual military participation in the war by the United States would be detrimental to the United States." Lindbergh was the real hero of the magazine, so much so that fascist Lawrence Dennis described it as "Lindbergh's organ." Lindbergh himself found Eggleston to be a bit eccentric, but did nothing to discourage him.

Ensconced in his headquarters in Lake Geneva, New York, safe (he thought) from prying eyes, Eggleston pondered his next move. The success of *Scribner's* led to the creation of a second publication, *The Herald*. More blatantly pro-Nazi than its sister publication, *The Herald* depended upon money from Nazi agents. Eggleston received instructions from Germany via shortwave, and *The Herald* smacked of Goebbels-like propaganda. Impressed by the publication, chargé Thomsen worked to place *The Herald* in the hands of American servicemen.[27]

Another German favorite was Burton K. Wheeler, the fifty-eight-year-old senator from Montana, who had turned into a passionate opponent of Franklin Roosevelt. A Democrat who had run for vice president in 1924 on a ticket headed by Progressive Robert La Follette, Wheeler broke with FDR over the president's "court reform" plan. Convinced that FDR intended to "purge" him at the first opportunity, the senator worked hard to undermine FDR's foreign policy by preserving the remnants of the Neutrality Act. An embittered isolationist, Wheeler had hoped to replace Roosevelt as his party's presidential nominee in 1940. Aid to Britain, Wheeler believed, was the president's pretext for creating an incident that would drag America into the war.

Senator Wheeler crisscrossed the nation, speaking to tens of thousands of enthusiastic isolationists in every region. He reveled in the national publicity. An anti-interventionist, bipartisan ticket of Wheeler and Lindbergh in 1944 might not, some of his friends believed, be beyond the realm of possibility. If America First formed a third party for the 1942 elections, the two men would certainly be major players in its inception and destiny. Wheeler and his associates caught the eye of Germany's Washington embassy, which reported to Berlin about their work.

German chargé d'affaires Hans Thomsen ordered his diplomats to help the committee. Of course, they had to operate in a subtle manner, so as not to awaken doubts about the organization's Americanism. As diplomat Ulrich von Gienanth said to the pro-Nazi aviatrix Laura Ingalls, "The best thing you can do for our cause is to continue to promote the America First Committee." Frau von Lewinski, wife of a German diplomat, followed Thomsen's orders by cultivating her friendship with Mrs. Wheeler. Lewinski made sure that the Wheelers and their many friends received the latest information about Hitler's "peace plans." Whatever the source of his information, Wheeler claimed to believe that the Nazi leadership was sincere when it used the slogan, "America to the Americans, Europe to the Europeans!"[28]

Like the Nazis, President Roosevelt watched Senator Wheeler closely. FDR had his own sources of intelligence about Wheeler and America First. He received important information from the White committee, which informed interested parties (such as the White House) about persons engaged in America First activity. It learned from Walter Winchell, for example, that Thomas E. Dewey, frequently mentioned as a Republican presidential candidate, was negotiating to take over the America First committee. America First, moreover, was vulnerable to the kinds of attacks and FBI inquiries orchestrated by the White House and its friends, and the ambitious Dewey backed off.

The lend-lease legislation was Roosevelt's great, postelection political challenge. Frustrated, and convinced that Roosevelt was bent upon war, furious anti-interventionists counterattacked. Former president Hoover opened the debate by complaining that H.R. 1776 would give the president too much power. Under its provision, the president could, he claimed, wage war at his own discretion. Aid to Britain, Hoover added, must be furnished on the case-by-case decisions of the Congress. Hoover and his friends also argued that Britain's survival offered proof of America's invulnerability. If Hitler could not defeat the nearby island, how could he threaten a rearmed United States? In other words, this nation could prosper and survive in coexistence with German-dominated Europe. Hoover bemoaned the "war psychosis" erupting in the country, and he ascribed the lend-lease bill to that mood.

In Chicago, Colonel Robert McCormick was blunter. Roosevelt, his *Tribune* believed, was trying to establish a dictatorship. Lend-lease, introduced in both houses of the Congress on 10 January, was, McCormick thought, a "bill for the destruction of the American Republic." The colonel, who had been more upset by the Soviet attack on Finland than by the Nazi assault on Poland, intended to testify against lend-lease.[29]

During the campaign Wendell Willkie had remained in touch with the White House through William Allen White, at the request of Roosevelt and Stimson. At first, Willkie had been cautious, but the courtship had been successful. Willkie became a confirmed proponent of aid to Britain.[30] He now found himself attracted to the charming, manipulative man in the White House. Willkie began to serve the president in a number of capacities. He agreed to work for the passage of lend-lease, though he expressed reservations about aspects of H.R. 1776.

Former Ambassador Joseph P. Kennedy was unhappy about FDR. The Boston millionaire had returned home before the election. Roosevelt wanted his support, and he received Kennedy's endorsement. Privately, however, the president made no secret of his contempt for the "appeaser." To the Lindberghs, Kennedy expressed contempt for Englishmen, diplomats, and William Bullitt, whom he blamed for "pushing war here and there." Brash and self-confident, Kennedy was certain that England was through.[31] While FDR struggled to help Britain and engage the public in the world crisis, Kennedy urged a defense buildup at home, while describing Britain as a lost cause. At one point, the president exploded, saying, "I never want to see that son of a bitch again as long as I live. Take his resignation and get him out of here."[32]

Now, as he prepared to testify on H.R. 1776, Kennedy claimed to favor aid to Britain, but not at the expense of the constitutional prerogatives of Congress. While at odds with Roosevelt, Kennedy had no intention of destroying his own ties to the Democratic party. Kennedy was prepared to support Roosevelt on aid to Britain if H.R. 1776 passed.[33] Kennedy's ambiguous opposition to aspects of the bill, though a boon to the isolationists, did not equal in importance Wendell Willkie's support for H.R. 1776. He had, after all, only recently been the Republican standard-bearer.

Inspired by his own perception of Roosevelt's historic mission, Henry R. Luce continued to turn out reams of copy and much film footage devoted to the Roosevelt cause. Isolationists received little exposure in these Luce newsfilms, and when they did it was unflattering. In one *March of Time* issue, the procommunist Vito Marcantonio was allowed to appear, but only in order to discredit the isolationists. Audiences watching *The March of Time* in Omaha or Los Angeles looked at pictures of a once fractious organized labor movement uniting in support of defense preparedness. Instead of the labor-baiting and anti-CIO ("anticommunist") reports typical of earlier issues of *Time*, *The March of Time* portrayed labor as sensible and patriotic. The "American Century," these films seemed to say, would be one in which labor, capital, and the administration worked together.

Roosevelt was inspiring a broad array of powerful people. In some cases, fear played its role. For years, Jewish producers in Hollywood had feared an anti-Semitic backlash (as well as empty theaters) if they produced "war movies" or anti-Nazi films. Now, motivated by patriotism, anti-Nazism, and admiration for FDR, they worked to mobilize public opinion in support of the president. Hollywood was praising itself for marching in time with the government. By the end of 1940, it was clear to all that the Roosevelt government would be in power until the winter of 1945. Poolside in Beverly Hills or in Hollywood studio boardrooms or downtown nightclubs, producers discussed plans for "war movies," for films that would appeal to audiences sympathetic to the government's policies. Jack Warner was in the forefront of these producers. Roosevelt's voice had long dominated the airwaves; now his desperate enemies felt they were losing another media battle. On all fronts, the debate was turning nastier and the FBI became busier.[34]

As far as Senator Robert A. Taft of Ohio was concerned, the blame for all the warmongering rested with "the business community of the cities . . ., the radio and movie commentators, the Communists, and the university intelligentsia."[35] Every defeat rendered Taft more bitter, and more determined, but the lowest blow was struck by Senator Burton K. Wheeler of Montana. He described H.R. 1776 as a bill to "plough under every fourth American boy."[36] Wheeler was later ashamed of that statement.

Political intelligence played a crucial role in Roosevelt's White House. FDR had a great sense of timing, and he knew when to strike. A comment to Ickes could result in a barrage of publicity, catching the isolationists off guard. Thanks to J. Edgar Hoover, the White House received detailed political intelligence on figures such as Joseph M. Patterson, publisher of the New York *Daily News*. Patterson was employing a reporter who freely denounced the president as a warmonger, reported Hoover. The correspondent in question also opposed FDR's policies in Europe and Latin America, and attacked the FBI for engaging in a witch-hunt. "I thought," said the helpful Hoover, "the President and you [Watson] would be interested in receiving these data." Encouraged by the White House's reaction, he stepped up his surveillance of America First and other groups.

Nazi propagandists, American extremists, mainstream isolationists, and various pessimists were all working to brand FDR a warmonger, taking the country into the war. Lend-lease exposed the country to a vitriolic battle over intervention. It also demonstrated the extent to which the president had defanged the far-right opposition, while outmaneuvering more mainstream isolationists. While Congress awaited hearings on the lend-lease authorization, the anti-interventionists stepped up their attack. Roosevelt was the target of this abuse—though a moving one.

The fundamental question facing the nation at the end of the winter of 1941 might be phrased this way: Did people want an "American Century" and the defeat of Nazi Germany, at the risk of possible war? Or did they desire the world of America First, in which a "strong" America coexisted with Germany for at least a few years, while the United States devoted most of its attention to South America and Asia? Roosevelt, judging by his policies and private comments, had answered these questions; most Americans had not even considered them.

If America First was to prevent FDR from moving closer to forms of cobelligerency, its lead actor would have to be the charismatic hero Lindbergh. Lindbergh's vast and passionate following placed much hope in his testimony against lend-lease. Lindbergh agreed with Congresswoman Frances Bolton, that "we are being trained into the thought habit of the inevitability of getting into the war." This, of course, was true, but Lindbergh seemed incapable of accepting the argument that a victorious war might be preferable to "peace" in Hitler's company.

People, Lindbergh believed, needed to understand that lend-lease was a prelude to war and dictatorship. The colonel had taken great care in preparing his comments. Perhaps this was the last chance to stop Roosevelt, a devious man whom Lindbergh suspected of megalomania.

Chairman Sol Bloom of the House Foreign Affairs Committee, a Roosevelt ally and apologist, treated the great airman with deference. Lindbergh called for an American air corps of ten thousand planes, as well as the establishment of air bases throughout the Western Hemisphere. Such measures, he argued, would guarantee the safety of the Americas. When pressed, however, he ruled out bases in Greenland and Iceland, perhaps because of rumors that FDR wanted to obtain them. When all was said and done, Lindbergh refused to believe in a clear and present danger to American interests. To the contrary, he argued, "If England is able to live at all with bases of the German air force less than an hour's flight away, the United States is not in great danger across the Atlantic Ocean."

The aviator had amazing blind spots. Lindbergh failed to point out that Britain continued to engage German U-boats, aircraft, and manpower, thus protecting American interests in various parts of the world. Nor did he seem to understand that the reality and expectation of American assistance helped to insure the survival of Britain. Lindbergh refused to consider other possibilities, such as the consequences of a British collapse. Nor did he, despite his scientific and military background, consider the implications of fissionable materials, rockets, or intercontinental missiles in German hands. Perhaps he did not wish to think about such disturbing matters.

Rigid and self-righteous, Lindbergh valued consistency above all else. When pushed, he did not flinch. Stubborn and courageous, the onetime hero responded to questions courteously and effectively. He denounced FDR for having encouraged Allied resistance in 1939, while neglecting the defenses of the United States. The colonel seemed a bit uncomfortable when Congressman Laurence F. Arnold asked him to recall the days (not so long ago, either) when people who urged America to rearm were cursed as warmongers.

The colonel made clear his preference for a negotiated peace. No, he did not think that a British defeat would endanger the United States, nor did he prefer a British victory to a compromise peace settlement. In fact, Lindbergh seemed to be positively annoyed that the British had decided to fight on, rather than negotiate with the Nazis. He thought that Britain's position would deteriorate unless it parlayed with Berlin. Lindbergh did not believe that Britain and America, if they fought as allies, could defeat Hitler.

Here Lindbergh showed less concern than an anonymous *Abwehr* agent, who predicted that lend-lease would enable the United States to increase its shipments to Britain of war-related materials by twenty to forty percent. Another German agent predicted that "as soon as the Lend-Lease bill is passed, the American fleet will secure American trade routes to the Far East and Africa." These insights did not jibe with Lindbergh's vaunted expertise.[37]

Lindbergh even refused to acknowledge that Germany had lost the Battle of Britain, insisting upon the continued superiority, on average, of German military aircraft. Here too, he was wrong. Not surprisingly, Lindbergh concluded that Americans must be prepared to do business with Hitler's New Order in Europe. Lindbergh often referred not to occupied Europe or Nazi-ruled Europe but just to "Europe."[38] This term paralleled fascist propaganda, which depicted the "New Europe" as a reordering of the continent on behalf of a just social order. The term "Europe" implied acceptance of a kind of German and Italian Monroe Doctrine, with which we should come to terms. Congressman W.O. Burgin, however, landed a blow for H.R. 1776 when he asked Lindbergh whether Hitler "has . . . made any generous concessions to his so-called enemies . . . ?" The witness could only reply, "Not so far as I know, sir."

Lindbergh seemed unaware of Hitler's concern about American intervention. He underestimated his own country's potential and failed to recall the American impact upon the final decision in 1918. Lindbergh went so far as to opine that full American belligerency would not "alter the outcome of the war to any great degree." The colonel seemed not to have heard Edward R. Murrow's broadcasts from London. If he had, Lindbergh did not understand his fellow citizens' admiration for the plucky little island kingdom. At best, Lindbergh sounded neutral in the struggle between Hitler and Churchill. Certainly, he seemed to fear Roosevelt more than Hitler, warning that H.R. 1776 would put too much power in one man's hands, depriving Congress of its constitutional prerogatives.

The flattery lavished upon him by isolationist congressmen allowed Lindbergh to dig himself into a deeper hole. Speaking with a straight face, he explained his failure to publicly condemn Hitler. He wished, Lindbergh said, to "maintain as far as possible a position of complete neutrality."

Lindbergh bemoaned the influence of British propaganda upon Americans. He did not, indeed could not, consider the possibility that Roosevelt was using British resistance to Hitler on behalf of purely American interests. Churchill was forced to sacrifice certain British imperial interests in his pursuit of England's salvation. Already, he adopted the tone of a junior partner when addressing FDR. Lindbergh

LESSENING OF ANTI-JEWISH SENTIMENT

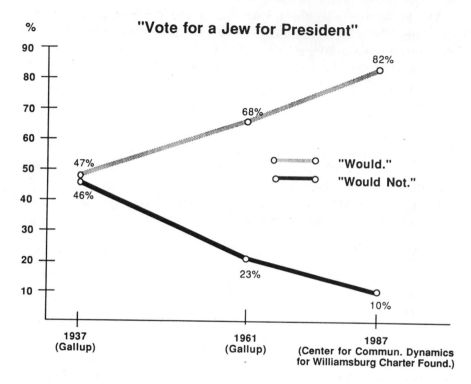

seemed unable to face the prospect of American global hegemony. He preferred neutrality and peace, even coexistence with Germany to the triumph of FDR. Lindbergh detested Roosevelt, who reciprocated his contempt.

FDR was devious to the point of dishonesty, but also expansive, confident, and imperial; Lindbergh was consistent, defeatist, and reactionary. The colonel was walking blindly into a trap set by Roosevelt and his co-workers. The president's tactics turned Lindbergh's strengths into fatal weaknesses. Self-assurance became arrogance, and conviction turned into bigotry, thanks in large measure to constant goading by Roosevelt and his associates.

Though the lend-lease bill passed in March with surprising ease, the struggle had welded America First into a viable political pressure group, ready to return to the battle another day. Indeed, the rhetoric of the committee and its friends grew more heated in defeat. Historian

Charles C. Tansill argued, was "distinctly bent on war," while Hitler, it seemed, really wanted peace. "It is very clear," he wrote, "that Chancellor Hitler has won the confidence of the German people and is creating a 'New Germany' that looks confidently into the future." The coming of war confirmed Tansill's fears. He now made the rounds of numerous faculty clubs and college auditoriums, telling attentive audiences about the grim lessons of 1917. Listening to Tansill, it sounded to many as if Roosevelt, not Hitler, was the real menace to peace.[39] Ambassador Hans Dieckhoff admired Tansill's book *America Goes to War*. Thanks to him, a large number of copies reached the Amerika Institut in Berlin, where Director Bertling arranged for their distribution to important personalities, like Hermann Goering. Inscribed "To the German People with the High Esteem of the Author," the books provided the German propaganda authorities with useful ammunition.[40]

Despite their defeat on lend-lease, the anti-interventionists remained a determined group of people. Roosevelt's German strategy, which required the containment, then the quarantine, of divisive domestic elements, had not yet run its course. The stakes were high, and the tactics were ugly.

Mrs. Lindbergh was at first saddened by the break with her interventionist friends; then she came to see them as idealists groping for belief in a materialistic age; finally, and most discouraging of all, this brilliant and sensitive woman came to view her new political allies as second-rate, if not worse. Anne Morrow Lindbergh's diary notes give us a sense of the moral crisis that FDR's victory engendered among the very best of his opponents.

The notoriety that would engulf Anne's beloved Charles was not long in coming. Lindbergh was drawing larger and larger crowds. The White House and its friends were not prepared to let this man's political career advance much further. In December, a cranky Secretary Stimson had noted in regard to Wood and Lindbergh, "Tell F.D.R. time to get busy." Stimson believed that these men had "no morals on international affairs."[41] He believed that the president should attack them frontally, though this was not Roosevelt's preferred technique. In the words of a critic, FDR liked to lead with someone else's jaw.

The Roosevelt White House carefully filed all correspondence concerning Colonel Lindbergh, especially after 1937. In some cases, Press Secretary Steve Early and Roosevelt himself read the correspondence. There is evidence that they encouraged anti-Lindbergh letter and petition campaigns, especially by organized labor.[42]

Ickes and Roosevelt began to make good use of intelligence purporting to link the colonel and his associates to the Nazi cause. Nazi newspapers and radio broadcasts, in translation, proved devastating to Lindbergh and his patriotic image.[43] Roosevelt selectively leaked this material to the press. Pro-Roosevelt cartoonists began to have a field day. The aviator remained confident and oblivious to all danger. When baited, he became more extreme.

The strident debate over aid to Britain was affecting everybody. Nerves were frayed. National discourse was being cheapened by the attacks on the administration. Lindbergh sincerely believed that FDR was trying to take the United States to war. He never understood that Roosevelt was working to destroy Hitler, which was not necessarily the same thing.

CONCLUSION

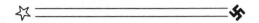

ROOSEVELT AND HITLER IN
THE WINTER OF 1941

T HE AMERICAN CENTURY is over, we are sometimes told. If so, then it should be possible to step back and examine its origins more objectively. Thanks in large measure to Roosevelt's policies, the United States became involved in a faraway quarrel, among nations viewed with suspicion by a large majority of the citizenry. Roosevelt's mix of economic, ideological, ethical, and political motives led him to pursue a policy representing a violent break with recent American attitudes, including his own.

Roosevelt believed that active intervention by the White House on behalf of Jewish refugees and victims of Hitler would endanger his strategy. By isolating and politically castrating the Jew-haters, through means both fair and foul, Roosevelt helped to take the United States in an anti-Nazi direction in foreign policy. To explain, however, is not always to excuse. Let Roosevelt be condemned for his timidity or even cowardice on the refugee question. In the interest of historical truth, let FDR also be judged on the basis of his successful antifascism at home, and anti-Nazism abroad.

Roosevelt showed real sympathy for the plight of Polish Jews, for example, and the barbarities of the Nazis repelled him. Still, the president refused to support changes in the immigrant quota system so as to provide sanctuary for Austrian and German Jewish refugees. He feared congressional reaction, as well as a domestic anti-Semitic backlash. Roosevelt viewed a battle with Congress over the refugee question as a diversion, one that would only give respectability to fringe groups and assorted anti-Semites.

FDR's strategy, which encompassed the establishment of an anti-Nazi diplomatic front, and, if necessary in the longer term, a shooting war against Germany, had dramatic ramifications for the domestic front. It resulted in the isolation of anti-Semitic groups; Judaeophobia of the Nazi type would, in the event of an international crisis, be seen as a traitorous Trojan horse. At the same time, Roosevelt's perception of political reality in a highly charged, anti-Semitic atmosphere led him to resisted being classified as a front for Jewish interests. Roosevelt was thus too cautious when dealing with the refugee question, and at times betrayed a lack of humanitarian compassion. In making such assertions, his critics have been right. Nevertheless, the prime interest of the Jews, and of all humanity, was to rid the world of Hitlerism. Roosevelt's policy toward the immigration issue must be put in the broader context of his revolutionary foreign policy. This interventionist initiative, developed when the country was economically troubled, isolationist, and at peace, is our best guide to Roosevelt's intentions, and to his greatness or failure. Jewish refugees were tragic pawns, for FDR sacrificed them to a strategy calculated to ensure American global hegemony in a world free of the Nazis.

FDR knew his public. He constantly told the people that his measures were intended to assist Britain, and keep the war away from American shores. The truth, as he saw it, was that aid to Churchill was but one measure in an evolving strategy calculated to destroy Hitlerism. Military considerations, and the state of public opinion, would dictate the nature and timing of Roosevelt's moves after March, 1941. Woodrow Wilson, by effecting the defeat of imperial Germany, had created Hitler the politician. It took a young Wilson appointee, Roosevelt, to destroy Hitler and thus bring to an end the second German bid for hegemony in the West.

Roosevelt had seized the initiative from those who used American entry into World War I as a reason for refusing to assist Britain in World War II. With the help of his allies, FDR had isolated and destroyed the more menacing movements on the far right. He had helped to bring about a drastic rise in anti-Nazi attitudes, particularly since June 1940. Nevertheless, the anti-interventionists remained powerful. Any major blunders by Roosevelt, and they might regain the power that had slipped out of their grasp in November 1939. FDR also needed relative quiet in the Far East at least during the crucial months that lay ahead. Much rested on chance. If Hitler abandoned his appeasement policy in the Atlantic, or if Japan attacked British or even American possessions, the results could be catastrophic. The United States was unprepared for war, and much of what it produced was earmarked for Britain. Roosevelt badly needed a neutral Japan and a Germany uninterested in abandoning its defensive policy in the Atlantic. Incoming intelligence reports, plus the growing British tendency to share information with the Americans, boded well for a more aggressive American strategy in the North Atlantic. Rumors about a German attack on Russia, by contrast, were most disturbing. Still, Roosevelt welcomed the future, with all its challenges. The period following the winter of 1941 promised to offer "something going on every minute."

To a pessimist, England and the Americas, not the totalitarian and militarist states, were now surrounded and largely isolated. In the world of the winter of 1941, expansionist totalitarian or militaristic states dominated Europe, threatened England and North Africa, and were poised to strike into Southeast Asia and perhaps beyond. Roosevelt's strategy in 1941 would be a kind of counteroffensive, an optimistic reaction to danger and confusion. It would at least buy time, until something developed. FDR had faith that something would turn up.

Roosevelt's foreign policy ushered in the "American Century." Some say that this "century" lasted but twenty-five years, ending in the jungles of Vietnam, on the loading docks of Japanese harbors, and in the phone booths and motel rooms of the Watergate conspirators. Looking back on the past fifty years, we have to ask ourselves about the rewards and the costs of global preeminence. With all our mistakes, arrogance, and blunders, the world created by "Roosevelt's warmongering" is better than any imaginable alternative. FDR's single-minded pursuit of his goal, the destruction of the Nazi regime, did achieve its great aim. This quest represented the only real justification of his presidency after 1938. In achieving his goal, the elimination of the greatest evil ever to befall humanity, Roosevelt sometimes used questionable methods. In his hands, however, and in this cause, the end did not justify the means; it invested them with an aura of moral probity.

Franklin Roosevelt was a very complex man—a man of vast charm, yet hard to know and easy to hate. He could justify his maddening deviousness and political caution as dictated by the greater goals of the statesman. These traits could also serve the momentary interests of the politician.

Had Roosevelt not discredited the far-right and anti-Semitic movements between 1938 and 1941, would the United States have been willing to accept his forward policy in the North Atlantic after March, 1941? If Roosevelt had not helped to secure an anti-Nazi alliance and begun to prepare the United States for war in 1940 and 1941, would any Jews have been alive west of Moscow in 1945? If Roosevelt had taken the easy way out, there would have been no Grand Alliance, no extermination of Hitler. The most likely outcome would have been a German victory, or a strategic stalemate in Europe.

The Americans friendly to Germany, so assiduously cultivated by men like Rolf Hoffmann, would have gained in influence, and a new generation of young Americans would have grown up accepting a mighty German Reich as a viable trading partner and fact of life. American mobilizers of renewed anti-Semitism, fed by continued economic depression due to low industrial output, would no doubt have emulated the German example. Their political mobilization, which Roosevelt prevented by associating anti-Semitism with fifth-column subversion, might have been successful had the president pursued a truly neutral foreign policy. Instead, FDR and his associates destroyed the far right as a viable entity, while working to encircle, undermine, and then defeat Germany. Had Roosevelt acted otherwise, anti-interventionist sentiment would have secured an isolationist victory at the polls. Who, after all, needed Roosevelt in 1940, if he intended to honor the Neutrality Act in the fashion recommended by Herbert Hoover? Would England have held out in such an environment?

A common fear and loathing brought Churchill and Roosevelt together, but they had arrived at this point from different places. Had they remained in power after the war their different destinations would have become apparent. For the moment, during this dramatic winter of 1941, their paths ran parallel. Churchill wanted the United States in the war and, failing that, hoped for massive economic, military, and financial assistance. Churchill was groping for ways to save England, while Roosevelt planned to destroy the Nazi system, then replace German hegemony with a democratic capitalist order along American lines. Churchill saw the United States as, he hoped, a long-term ally, one that would enable Britain to survive with her empire intact. Roosevelt saw England as a weapon against Germany, and he would later view Greece, Yugoslavia, and the Soviet Union in the same manner. To FDR, antifascist belligerents were eligible to become supporting players in the *pax Americana,* after the victory came to the West and its allies in the ideological and moral struggle against the New Order.

In the Far East, the Anglo-American powers were moving towards a de facto military alliance. For the moment, Roosevelt was committed to the survival of European power in Southeast Asia, but only because its demise would, he thought, help Germany in her European struggle against Britain.

Roosevelt did not take this country to war in 1941, but he put it in a position where war was highly possible, even probable. He did not want to be attacked, but was willing to risk attack. A forward strategy against Germany and her allies entailed this risk. By the late winter of 1941, Roosevelt had come to see the world as divided into two camps, that of the Germans and that of Hitler's enemies. This sometimes led him to misjudge certain situations, but to FDR, a nation or a policy was either a strategic asset in the anti-Nazi struggle or it was helpful to Hitler. The British Empire was acceptable, for the moment, because it was vital to England in its primary role, that of an aircraft carrier for future attacks on Hitler's Europe. Japan was becoming increasingly unacceptable, not so much because of its alliance with Germany, but due to the growing threat it represented to Western interests engaged in a struggle against Nazi Germany. On this issue, Roosevelt proved to be implacable. He lacked subtlety in his appreciation of Japanese policy, and of the constraints imposed by militaristic circles upon Tokyo's policymakers. He saw Japan through anti-German eyes.

Given his negative view of British, Dutch, French, and Japanese imperialism, it appears that FDR did indeed harbor ambitions in Asia, perhaps a kind of *pax Rooseveltiana,* where the United States would protect hapless China and bring democracy and progress to Southeast Asia. These plans were scarcely applicable to the world around Roosevelt in the winter of 1941, but they would be useful to him later. Democrat and imperialist, dedicated anti-Nazi, visionary, and shameless political opportunist, Roosevelt was complex, devious, and wrong on many major issues. He badly miscalculated in the Soviet case. Even as he aged and grew ill, Roosevelt remained confident that his persuasive powers were intact. It proved to be tragic when he applied them to J. V. Stalin.

By January 1941, Hitler realized that only a major U-boat campaign in the North Atlantic could isolate the British Isles and perhaps cause Churchill's downfall. Once again, however, the Roosevelt nemesis undermined Hitler's prospects for success. The Italians were losing in the Balkans and in North Africa; the Soviet Union was an uneasy ally, soon to be a target. In this situation, Hitler knew, the British government looked upon possible Soviet military involvement, along with lend-lease, as its salvation. Japan was an uncertain ally, reluctant to expand its war against China to American, British, and Dutch possessions in the East. If Hitler followed Admiral's Raeder's advice, he would wage all-out war against the Anglo-American lifeline in the North Atlantic, but at the price of American intervention. If he did not do so, Germany could gain no more than a strategic stalemate.

How ironic that Hitler should be losing the war because of his ill-considered respect for the neutrality of three nations—Spain, Portugal, and the United States! Had Hitler moved quickly on Gibraltar and closed the Mediterranean to British shipping in 1940, while securing bases in the Atlantic islands, the war might have ended differently.

There was, Hitler believed, another way out, but it trapped him in a fatal miscalculation. Hitler knew that the United States would not be ready for European intervention before 1942, at the earliest. If the Soviet Union collapsed under the Wehrmacht's hammer blows while Japan engaged Anglo-American forces in the Far East, Britain might come to terms before the Americans could gear up for real war. How could Hitler induce Japan to step up its pressure on the Anglo-Americans? This was one of the great riddles confronting him during the winter of 1941. There was only one answer, and German diplomats, from Ribbentrop on down, began to hint at it, then say it: Germany would declare war if Japan became involved in a conflict with the United States. The Germans would engage part of the American fleet in the Atlantic. Japan should now feel free to act aggressively in the Pacific.

And here we perceive another irony: Roosevelt enabled Hitler to keep his promise. During the winter of 1941, he and his top naval and army advisers decided to adopt a forward strategy in the North Atlantic, step by step. Their aim would be to secure the lifeline from the Western Hemisphere to Britain, and this meant ultimately pushing the Germans out of the North Atlantic before they could isolate Britain from her suppliers. The Canadians and especially the Americans would begin to relieve the Royal Navy of some of its burdens in the western Atlantic Ocean. The naval diversion of American forces from the Pacific to the Atlantic had not yet taken place, but Roosevelt was beginning to mull over the possibilities inherent in such a move. From Mahan, he had learned never to "divide the fleet," but this was a special case. Once the Japanese warlords saw this diversion taking place, they could place some faith in a German promise to declare war on the United States.

Hitler's fear was that he might soon be pushed into war by Roosevelt, while Japan remained neutral. This would enable the Americans to concentrate their forces against him, and he knew from the last war what that meant. Despite his cultural, racial, and personal hatred for the Americans, especially Roosevelt, Hitler's appeasement of the United States reflected an understanding of American power.

Roosevelt's nightmare was the reverse side of Hitler's hope. The thought of becoming embroiled with Japan, while Germany remained neutral and continued to pound England, was most troubling. With Americans fighting in the Pacific, would public opinion and military judgment accept the idea of going to war in the Atlantic, even as England continued to survive on her own? Hardly.

Roosevelt did not necessarily want war, certainly not before 1942 or 1943, when his armies would be ready to invade Europe, should that be necessary. He would, however, not accept a stalemate or a British defeat. A deal with Hitler was unthinkable, much as a truce with the Confederacy would have been unacceptable to Lincoln. To Roosevelt, World War II was a civil war within Western culture. The values dear to him were warring against forces of darkness erupting within a sick, but curable, society.

If Roosevelt could protect Western interests against the Axis in Asia, while pursuing a forward strategy in the North Atlantic, he would do so. Roosevelt's aim was to destroy Hitler and "all his works"; this did not mean that he was plotting to go to war. Yet there is another side to this concept. Far from deterring FDR, knowledge that Germany would go to war against America in the event of a Japanese attack on the U.S.A. almost *guaranteed* that he would pursue a more aggressive strategy in the North Atlantic. Hitler, for his part, would try to maintain American nonbelligerency for at least another year, while building up his U-boat fleet to a capacity of over 250 ships. Then, if assured of Japanese belligerency, he might well strike. Viewed in this light, Hitler's declaration of war on the United States clearly does not appear to have been an irrational act of pique. It resulted from strategic and production considerations that dated back almost a year.

In this winter of 1941, Italy was losing the war, Japan could not even conquer China, and Germany could not subdue little England. All the talk about the New Order in Asia and Europe appeared to some to be hot air, pompous diplomatic footage for German newsfilm. Who would believe that the new year would see an extension of the conflict by Axis powers to Moscow and East Asia? Roosevelt had reason to believe that an expansion of the war might well take place. With striking insight, he also saw Allied opportunities for expansion, counterattacks, and counterpressure.

Almost a year before Pearl Harbor, the White House received a startling communication from FBI director J. Edgar Hoover. The administration learned that Germany would allegedly honor the Tripartite Pact and declare war on the United States, but only "if Japan would begin war with the United States." The precise date was 4 February 1941, when Hoover informed the president via General Watson of intelligence gleaned from a "special correspondent" named Hallett Abend.[1] While the White House, the War Department, and the Army Chief of Staff could not be sure of the report's accuracy, it did give one pause for thought. This was especially true of the president, whose officers were engaged in sensitive and secret discussions with their British counterparts.

Hoover's news, if accurate, meant that no matter how far the American "neutral power" pushed the Germans in the Atlantic, Hitler would *not* declare war. And if Hitler would *only* declare war on the United States in the event of Japanese belligerency, he might be even more patient if the war turned against him in North Africa, or on untested fronts. Roosevelt could thus test Japanese patience, but only up to a point. The new intelligence mandated caution in the Pacific, and possibly bold new measures in the North Atlantic. How hard Roosevelt pushed would depend upon other strategic factors, particularly the course of the war on the continent of Europe. Hoover's report, if credible, dictated the avoidance of a showdown in the Pacific, while Roosevelt and Churchill took care of the Germans in the North Atlantic.

Roosevelt thus had every reason to avoid conflict with Japan. During the first half of 1941, Roosevelt and Hull seemed willing to deal with Japan on the basis of a compromise over China and Indochina.

Roosevelt, Stimson, and Marshall busily planned for the contingency of all-out war, thinking ahead to the year (1943 or 1944) when the United States would have a trained, well-equipped army of many millions of men. Should Hitler still be in the field at that point, he could expect one of his prophecies of 1928 to come true. Having subdued and "organized" much of Europe, a war between the continents would ensue. History would determine whether autarkic, racially cleansed National Socialist Germany would prevail, or whether decadent but materially gifted *Amerika* would achieve global hegemony. The struggle for Europe, foreseen by both Roosevelt and Hitler a quarter of a century earlier, would then decide who would dominate the West—for a thousand years or perhaps for only half a century.

Roosevelt's prospects were, during this grim winter, better than Hitler's or Churchill's. Despite the territorial extent of Axis dominion, the Germans had not yet subdued Britain. Even if Britain defeated the Reich without full American belligerency, she would emerge from the titanic struggle bankrupt and in danger of losing her imperium. If the defeat of the Nazis required the dispatch of Marshall's armies to Europe, then the United States would speak for the West.

The historical dialectic has played peculiar tricks on the United States. Success contained within it the germs of subsequent anguish. It was not possible to work effectively for the elimination of National Socialism without achieving "superpower" status. Given the manner in which the Allies destroyed the Nazi regime, however, one seeks in vain for an alternative as of 1945.

One must acknowledge a major lacuna in Roosevelt's thought at this point. He knew of reports predicting a German assault on Soviet Russia, but gave little thought to Stalin's role in the post-German world. Unimpressed by communism, he refused to take it seriously. Roosevelt thought in Western hegemonic terms, going back to his reading of Mahan; to FDR, winning the succession to the British imperium guaranteed a stable postwar order. Any problems could be managed by American power, a winsome personality and apparent goodwill. Tragically, FDR still believed this in 1945. He was right about Hitler, but wrong about Stalin. The world survived Stalin, could it have survived Hitler?

In one important respect, Churchill's task was far easier. He came to power during a losing struggle, while the enemy held a knife at the throat of his people. Few Englishmen could picture much of an alternative to fighting on, though Churchill deserves great credit for inspiring his people. Roosevelt, by contrast, had to convince an indecisive and presently *secure* nation that it must intervene in a faraway struggle. Instead of deceiving people (who wanted to be tricked) by promising an avoidance of "foreign wars," FDR could have sincerely pledged himself to staying out of the war, period. Of course, with Hitler surviving, the long-term threat might have been most unpleasant, particularly if a successor Nazi regime turned its interest to fissionable materials and intercontinental rockets. So, if FDR had been the opportunist he is often accused of being, he would have acted much differently than he did. Morally Roosevelt had little choice. The most consequential and consistent anti-Nazi statesman of his time, FDR made possible a world without National Socialism. One of those men most useful to Roosevelt, the playwright and speechwriter Robert E. Sherwood, later paid tribute to the "goals he had fought for, so gallantly and with such great vision, against such terrible opposition, at home and abroad."

Even some of Roosevelt's enemies unwillingly gave him credit for his achievement. Adolf Hitler, with understanding born of hatred, laid the blame for Polish resistance in 1939 at Roosevelt's door. "From November, 1938," he declared, "[Roosevelt] methodically and consciously begins to sabotage any possibility of a European appeasement policy." Nor did Hitler fail to note that "In January 1939 this man begins to intensify his campaign of agitation and before Congress threatens to move against the authoritarian states with all means short of war." Hitler declared that Roosevelt was "mentally ill," just like Woodrow Wilson. Hitler appears to have believed that Roosevelt was the best thing for the Jews in the world as it stood in early 1941. This, too, was accurate. FDR may have hated the Nazis more than he loved the Jews, but his insight into Hitlerism owed a great deal to the pogroms of 9–10 November 1938. Hitler understood this, and correctly perceived the tie between the interventionist foreign policy and revulsion against Nazi pogroms.

Winston Churchill was a great patriot, and he did indeed prove to be the salvation of his nation. True, he had no use for the guttersnipe Hitler, but mainly because the Nazis threatened England. Roosevelt's loathing for the whole National Socialist *regime*, in evidence by 1933, cannot be found in Churchill's writings until 1940. Roosevelt saw that modern Western society faced four choices in the twentieth century: imperialism, fascism, communism, and capitalist/social democracy. He rejected the first three, selected the fourth, and believed in the possibility of coexisting with the third possibility, communism. Churchill, by contrast, argued that imperialism had a future, even as he "sold" parts of the empire in order to gain support for England's battle.

The difference in views between Roosevelt and Churchill was apparent to observers as early as 1935. Churchill admired the way communism had been obliterated in Germany. He wrote of Adolf Hitler, "If our country were defeated, I hope we should find a champion as indomitable to restore our courage and lead back to our place among the nations."[2] Roosevelt's increasing anti-Nazism was indeed more principled than that of his great British ally. His nation was not threatened by the Luftwaffe in 1938 (or in 1941, for that matter), when the president began to undermine Britain's appeasement policy. In 1935, when Churchill uttered his words about Hitler, the great German novelist Thomas Mann visited President Roosevelt. He recalled, "When I left the White House after my first visit [on 30 June, 1935], I knew Hitler was lost."[3] The imagination of the novelist saw more deeply than the observers who accused Roosevelt of timidity or lack of direction. Mann later avowed, "I passionately longed for war against Hitler and 'agitated' for it; and I shall be eternally grateful to Roosevelt, the born and conscious enemy of l'Infame [the infamous one, i.e., Hitler], for having manoevered his all-important country into it with consummate skill." A "born and conscious enemy"—this is what Hitler saw, and why he hated FDR so.

Another observer, who had reason to revile Roosevelt for his inaction during the Holocaust, says something of even greater significance. No one spent more time trying to tell the world about the Holocaust than the Polish resistance courier Jan Karski. He had been inside a Nazi camp and had seen the Warsaw Ghetto. Forty years later, he was still haunted by his inability to awaken the West to the full horror of his story. This Jan Karski visited Roosevelt on 28 July 1943, and spoke with him for eighty minutes. FDR asked a lot of questions about the Jews, "but he didn't tell me anything." Surely Karski would be bitter about this man, who viewed the military destruction of the Reich as the great aim of the Allied cause? No. Karski still views FDR as the embodiment of "[g]reatness. Power. I saw in him the height of humanity. Everyone did—all the people of Europe. Roosevelt was a legend. So much so that when I left his office, I walked out backwards." Karski does not accept nor does he condemn the military explanation for Allied failure to save the Jews. He concludes in sorrow more than anger: Yes, "[s]ix million Jews perished. Six million totally helpless, abandoned by all." But Karski adds, "What do I know about strategy. They won the war, didn't they? They crushed Germany. If it were not for this victory, all of Europe would be enslaved today. That I know."[4]

For the moment, while British and American officers prepared to confer a few blocks away, President Roosevelt returned to the political matter at hand, passage of the lend-lease legislation.

FDR's enemy Charles Lindbergh, while preparing his testimony against FDR's "warmongering bill" deserves the last word. Early in 1941 he made an interesting and prophetic notation in his diary. "If Roosevelt took this country into war and won," said the aviator, "he might be one of the great figures of all history."[5]

ABBREVIATIONS

AA	Auswärtiges Amt (German Foreign Ministry)
AHR	*American Historical Review*
BA	Bundesarchiv (Federal Archives, West Germany)
CEH	*Central European History*
CSL	Connecticut State Library
CT	*Chicago Tribune*
DBFP	*Documents on British Foreign Policy, 1919–1939* (Third Series)
DDF	*Documents Diplomatiques Français, 1932–1939*
DGFP	*Documents on German Foreign Policy 1918–1945* (Series C and Series D, published by the U.S. Department of State)
DH	*Diplomatic History*
DW	*Daily Worker*
FDRFA	*Franklin D. Roosevelt and Foreign Affairs* (edited at the Franklin D. Roosevelt Library, Hyde Park, New York, in sixteen volumes)
FDRL	Franklin D. Roosevelt Library
FDRPC	*Franklin D. Roosevelt, Complete Presidential Press Conferences*
FNC	*Führer Conferences on Naval Affairs*
FPO	Foreign Press Office (of the Nazi Party)
FRUS	*Foreign Relations of the United States*
FZ	*Frankfurter Zeitung*
GCD	German Captured Documents (Library of Congress microcopies)
G.O.	Gallup Organization
GVDAKV	Gesamtverband deutscher antikommunistischen Vereinigungen (General Organization of German Anti-Communist Associations)

415

HI	Hoover Institution
IMT	International Military Tribunal
JCH	*Journal of Contemporary History*
LOCMD	Library of Congress, Manuscript Division
MG	*The Guardian* (Manchester)
MVHR	*Mississippi Valley Historical Review*
NA	National Archives
NAM	National Archives Microcopy, followed by T-
NAS	National Archives, Suitland, Md.
NYDN	*New York Daily News*
NYHT	*New York Herald Tribune*
NYP	*New York Post*
NYSZ	*New Yorker Staats-Zeitung*
NYT	*New York Times*
NYWT	*New York World-Telegram*
PPAFDR	*The Public Papers and Addresses of Franklin D. Roosevelt* (volumes indicated by year covered)
RCS	Roper Commercial Study
RG	Record Group (referring to the National Archives)
RLZ	*Rheinische Landeszeitung*
SJ	*Social Justice*
VB	*Völkischer Beobachter*
VJHfZ	*Vierteljahreshefte für Zeitgeschichte*
WB	*Westdeutscher Beobachter*
ZD	*Zeitschriften-Dienst*

NOTES

CHAPTER ONE

1. Frank Freidel, *Franklin D. Roosevelt: The Apprenticeship* (Boston: Little, Brown & Co. 1952), 335–70; Elliott Roosevelt, ed., *F.D.R.: His Personal Letters*, vol. 2, *1905–1928* (New York: Duell, Sloan and Pearce, 1947), 399–419.
2. Freidel, *Roosevelt*, 240–47, 267, 333. Relevant material may be consulted in RG 10/137/192 (FDRL, assistant secretary of the navy).
3. On Hitler's view of Wilson's United States, see D. Dedake, "Das Dritte Reich und die Vereinigten Staaten von Amerika 1933–1937" (Ph.D. diss., Hamburg, 1969), 309 n. 10. On Hitler's views of the United States, see Gerhard L. Weinberg, "Hitler's Image of the United States," *American Historical Review* 69, no. 4 (July 1964): 1006–21.
4. These comments are based upon an outline for a speech delivered by Hitler early in his career. See Werner Maser, ed., *Hitler's Letters and Notes* (New York: Harper & Row, 1974), 333–39.
5. See Horst Dippel, *Germany and the American Revolution 1770–1800: A Sociohistorical Investigation of Late Eighteenth Century Political Thinking* (Chapel Hill, N.C.: UNC Press, 1977), 3, 8, 105; and Paul C. Weber, *America in Imaginative German Literature in the First Half of the Nineteenth Century* (New York: Columbia University Press, 1926), 4, 8, 9.
6. Dippel, *Germany*, 289, 297, 332; Fritz T. Epstein, "Germany and the United States," in G.L. Anderson, ed., *Issues and Conflicts* (Lawrence, Kans.: Univ. of Kan. Press, 1959), 296; and Weber, *America*, 19.
7. Dippel, *Germany*, 239; Weber, *America*, 84–85, 270–71; and *Conversations of Goethe With Eckermann* (London: G. Bell & Sons, 1930), 173–74.
8. See Otto zu Stolberg-Wernigerode, *Germany and the United States During the Era of Bismarck* (Reading, Pa.: Henry Janssen Foundation under auspices of Cary Schurz Memorial Foundation, Inc., 1937).
9. Particularly useful in the Anglo-American context is Jonathan Steinberg,

Yesterday's Deterrent: Tirpitz and the Birth of the German Battle Fleet (New York: Macmillan, 1965), chaps. 1, 4.

10. Holger H. Herwig, *Politics of Frustration: The United States in German Naval Planning, 1889–1941* (Boston: Little, Brown, 1976), 16–18, 22, 150.

11. Ibid., 30, 61, 86; Dexter Perkins, *Hands Off: A History of the Monroe Doctrine* (Boston: Little, Brown & Co., 1941), 222–24.

12. Herwig, *Politics of Frustration*, 44, 62, 85.

13. For an account of ethnic politics in its international context, see Louis L. Gerson, *The Hyphenate in Recent American Politics and Diplomacy* (Lawrence, Kans.: Univ. of Kan Press 1964), especially 50 and passim. See also Herwig, *Politics of Frustration*, 125, 153.

14. Herwig, *Politics of Frustration*, 125, 153.

15. Max Scheler, *Die Ursachen des Deutschenhasses* (The Causes of the Hatred for Germans) (Leipzig: K. Wolff Verlag, 1917).

16. Daniel Horn, ed., *War, Mutiny and Revolution in the German Navy: The World War I Diary of Seaman Richard Stumpf* (New Brunswick, N.J.: Rutgers University Press, 1967), 187–88.

17. See the essays by Arthur S. Link, Eric F. Goldman, and William L. Langer in Arthur P. Dudden, ed., *Woodrow Wilson and the World of Today* (Philadelphia: Univ. of Penn Press, 1957); and John M. Blum, *Woodrow Wilson and the Politics of Morality* (Boston: Little, Brown & Co. 1956), which presents a balanced view of Wilson's character.

18. See the comments of Ernst Fraenkel in Arthur S. Link et al., *Wilson's Diplomacy: An International Symposium* (Cambridge, Mass.: Schenkman Pub. Co., 1973), 45–48, 60–61. Since the 1960s, German scholars have arrived at more evenhanded evaluation of Wilson's European diplomacy.

19. Horn, *War, Mutiny and Revolution*, 283.

20. John L. Snell, "Wilson's Peace Program and German Socialism, January–March 1918," MVHR, no. 9, vol. 38, No. 2.

21. Horn, *War, Mutiny and Revolution*, 409, 433.

CHAPTER TWO

1. Peter Berg, *Deutschland und Amerika* (Lübeck: Mattheisen 1963), 15–24; and Herbert Hoover, *The Ordeal of Woodrow Wilson* (New York: McGraw-Hill, 1958). Hoover, who favored Senate ratification of the treaty (with amendments unacceptable to the president) views Wilson as a tragic, heroic figure.

2. For an analysis of these and similar attitudes, see Ernst Fraenkel's comments in *Wilson's Diplomacy*, 64–65, 68, 72. The words quoted in the text are those of the medievalist, Professor Dietrich Schäfer. The more charitable, American view of Wilson as stubborn, idealistic, and tragic finds

expression in Arthur Link, *Wilson the Diplomatist: A Look at His Major Foreign Policies* (Baltimore: The Johns Hopkins Press, 1957).

3. See Fraenkel, in *Wilson's Diplomacy*, 58–59, 75; and Berg, *Deutschland*, 33–43.

4. Berg, *Deutschland*, 27; and Fraenkel, in *Wilson's Diplomacy*, 54.

5. William E. Dodd, Jr., and Martha Dodd, eds., *Ambassador Dodd's Diary* (New York: Harcourt, Brace and Co., 1941), 219, 283.

6. Clippings in file SH/SPI/CII 1, and ibid., Akten (Hamburg), for the years 1923–1924 and 1932.

7. Wolfgang Benz and Hermann Graml, *Biographisches Lexikon zur Weimarer Republic* (München: C. H. Beck, 1988), 34–35. Bonn lost his position and fled to Great Britain after Hitler came to power.

8. Berg, *Deutschland*, 99–107, 130–35; and Earl R. Beck, *Germany Rediscovers America* (Tallahassee, Fla.: Fla. State Univ. Press, 1968), 187, 220. The latter work is of great importance to researchers studying German views of the United States.

9. M. J. Bonn, *The American Experiment* (London: G. Allen & Unwin Ltd. 1933), 288–300.

10. See Beck, *Germany*, 20, 246; Bonn, *American Experiment*, 294; and Berg, *Deutschland*, 143–44.

11. Arthur Feiler, *America Seen Through German Eyes* [1930] (New York: Arno Press, 1974), 135–44, 203–9.

12. On these issues, see Beck, *Germany*, 247; and Bonn, *American Experiment*, 284–85.

13. Beck, *Germany*, 63–68; Bonn, *American Experiment*, 58–64; and Feiler, *America*, 214 and passim.

14. Feiler, *America*, 218ff.; and Beck, *Germany*, 135.

15. Berg, *Deutschland*, 54, 98.

16. Edgar A. Mowrer, *Amerika: Vorbild und Warnung* (Berlin: E. Rowohlt Verlag 1928), 132 and passim; Beck, *Germany*, 247; and Bonn, *American Experiment*, 284–85.

17. SH/SP II/Akten (Hamburg), includes the Tostmann/Kehl folder, with contains the American consul general's protest against press attacks on American society. See also Mowrer, *Amerika*, 132–33; Beck, *Germany*, 20, 246; Bonn, *American Experiment*, 294; and Berg, *Deutschland*, 143–44.

18. Oswald Spengler, *The Spengler Letters 1913–1936* (London: Allen & Unwin, 1966), 28, 233; Spengler, *Der Untergang des Abendlandes*, 2 vols. (Munich: C. H. Beck, 1923), vol. 2, 197, 595–96, 633; and Spengler, *Jahre der Entscheidung* (Munich: C. H. Beck 1933), 79–86.

19. Peter von Zahn in Franz M. Joseph, ed., *As Others See Us* (Princeton: Princeton Univ Press, 1959), 95–96; and Beck, *Germany*, 83–84, 137–38, 155–63, 234–43.

20. Ernst Hanfstängl, *Zwischen Weissem und Braunem Haus* (Munich: R. Pieper, 1970), 46–47; Hanfstängl, *Hitler: The Missing Years* (London: Eyre & Spottiswoode, 1957), 51; "Conversations With Ribbentrop," 25 July 1945, and the interrogations of Joachim von Ribbentrop in Nürnberg, 31 August and 5 October 1945, RG 238 (NA).

21. Hanfstängl, *Hitler,* 61.

22. Ernst Jäckh, *Amerika und Wir: 1926–1951 Amerikanisch-Deutsches Ideen-Bündnis* (Stuttgart: Deutsche Verlags & Anstalt 1951), 128–29.

23. Günter Moltmann, "Weltherrschaftsideen Hitlers," in *Europa und Übersee,* ed. Brunner and Gerhard (Hamburg: Verlag Hans Bredow-Institut, 1961), 204–5.

24. Konrad Heiden, *Der Führer: Hitler's Rise to Power* (Boston: Houghton Mifflin, 1944), 138–39. The early version of the speech had appeared in the *Völkischer Beobachter;* it then surfaced in a book entitled *Adolf Hitler, sein Leben und seine Reden* (München: E. Boepple, 1923), and in a later edition of the same volume (1933).

25. Weinberg, "Hitler's Image," 1012; Saul Friedländer, *Prelude to Downfall: Hitler and the United States 1939–1941,* 161 and passim; and Max Domarus, comp., *Hitler Reden und Proklamationen 1932–1945: Von einem deutschen Zeitgenossen Kommentiert* (Wiesbaden: 1973), vol. 2, 1612.

26. Hanfstängl, *Hitler,* 188, 223, and *Zwischen Weissem und Braunem Haus,* 251; and Weinberg, "Hitler's Image," 1010.

CHAPTER THREE

1. Ewald Banse, *Raum und Volk im Weltkriege* (Oldenburg: O. G. Stalling 1932), 337–49.

2. Dedake, "Das Dritte Reich," 338–45.

3. Robert Strausz-Hupé, *Axis America: Hitler Plans Our Future* (New York: G. P. Putnam's Sons, 1941), 38.

4. Colin Ross, "Die Neuverteilung der Erde," *Zeitschrift für Geopolitik* 13:582ff., and *Unser Amerika* (Leipzig: F. H. Brockhaus 1936); and Strausz-Hupé, *Axis America,* 65–67. This fantasy owed much to Goethe's *Faust,* where a blind visionary pictures a happy community building dams against the raging North Sea. This image rested upon an illusion, and proved to be a phantasmagoria.

5. Hoffmann's aide to Ross, 5 January 1939, NS 22/Vol. 11, and Hoffmann to K. Kranzle, 26 June 1939, NS 42/14 (BA); consulate general in Chicago, Abschrift Pol IX 302, 24 January 1940, NAM T-120/393/304291 (NA).

6. Colin Ross, "Das jüdische Phänomen in den Vereinigten Staaten von Amerika," *Wille und Macht,* 15 July 1941.

7. Heinz Kloss, "Über Colin Ross," T-81/351/508005-010. Extremely useful

is Arthur L. Smith, Jr., *The Deutschtum of Nazi Germany and the United States* (The Hague: M. Nijhoff 1965), 52–53.

8. Erwin Hölzle, "Friedrich Schönemann," *Jahrbuch für Amerikastudien* 2.

9. Friedrich Schönemann, *Amerika und der Nationalsozialismus* (Berlin: Junker und Dünnhaupt Verlag, 1934); and *Demokratie und Aussenpolitik der USA* (Berlin: Junker und Dünnhaupt, 1939), especially 57–63. Schönemann himself contributed to the anti-Roosevelt campaign. See his articles "Präsident Wilson der Zweite," *Schlesische Zeitung*, 22 November 1938, and "Gegen wen rüsten die USA?," *Stuttgarter NS-Kurier*, 8 May 1939. See also Ernst Fraenkel, *Amerika im Spiegel des deutschen politischen Denkens* (Köln: Westdeutscher Verlag, 1959), 311–13.

10. American neutrality inspired a vast amount of important German literature, both before and after 1939. See Fritz Berber, "Die Rolle der Neutralen in einem künftigen Kriege," *Hanseatische Rechts- und Gerichtszeitschrift* (Abhandlungen) 19, no. 7: 242ff.; "Das Ende der Neutralität?," *Hamburger Monatshefte für Auswärtige Politik* (1936), 35–39; Aufzeichnung of VLR Freytag, Serial 57/38905ff., German Foreign Ministry; and F. Berber, *Die amerikanische Neutralität im Kriege* (Essen: Essener Verlagsanstalt 1943). The noted scholar Walter Simons concurred. See his "Über die Freiheit der Meere," *Zeitschrift für ausländisches öffentliches Recht und Völkerrecht* 6, L,: 30ff. The work of Kurt Keppler, an expert on international law, is relevant here, especially "Die neue Embargopolitik der Vereinigten Staaten von Amerika und das Neutralitätsrecht," *Zeitschrift für Völkerrecht* 21: 173–206. See also Ulrich Schleuner, "Die Neutralitätspolitik der Vereinigten Staaten seit Beginn des Krieges," *Auswärtige Politik* 8 (2/41): 83–93.

11. Luther to AA, 15 February 1937, DGFP, C, vol.6, 438–45.

12. Domarus, *Hitler*, vol. 2, 1482–83; O. John Rogge, *The Official German Report* (New York: T. Yoseloff, 1961), 104–5; and James V. Compton, *The Swastika and the Eagle* (Boston: Houghton Mifflin, 1967), 12–13.

CHAPTER FOUR

1. Schacht to Foreign Ministry, DGFP, C, vol. 1, 390–93, 423–24. (May 6 and May 15, 1933).

2. Memorandum by an official of Dept. III, December 20, 1937, Ibid., C, vol. 2, 252–55; Ambassador Hans Luther to Foreign Minister, 22 March 1934, ibid., 653–54.

3. See the reports dated 10 April 1934 in Schumacher/420 (BA).

4. Relevant correspondence may be consulted in file I*o1 g 42 (Würzburg).

5. See Robert E. Herzstein, *The War That Hitler Won: Goebbels and the Nazi Media Campaign* (New York: Paragon House, 1987), chapter two.

6. I viewed the film *Der Kaiser von Kalifornien* in the Bundesarchiv Film

Collections in Ehrenbreitstein Castle, near Koblenz, Federal Republic of Germany. See the comments by David Stewart Hull, *Film in the Third Reich: A Study of the German Cinema 1933–1945* (Berkeley, Calif.: Univ of Calif Press, 1969), 105–6.

7. A print of *Hans Westmar* can be viewed in the Motion Picture Section of the Library of Congress. See also Herzstein, *The War That Hitler Won*, 181, 262–63, 344. I deal with this film and related issues in "No Second Revolution: Joseph Goebbels and the Roehm Crisis, 1933–1934, The Cinematic Evidence," in *The Proceedings of the South Carolina Historical Association, 1984*, 53–66.

8. I am grateful to Dr. Agnes F. Peterson of the HI for calling the important *Zeitschriften-Dienst* collection to my attention. Its editorial guidelines (particularly the *"Bitte nicht so!"* warnings) are extremely important.

9. GVDAKV/128 (HI).

10. Strausz-Hupé, *Axis America*, 107–13; GVDAKV/123; NG-2166; and VB, 19 May 1936.

11. NAM T-81/675/5484196-208; Zsg 116/17 (BA); relevant clippings from the *Hessische Landeszeitung* and the *Stuttgarter NS-Kurier* from 1935 may be consulted in NS 15 (BA). See also Strausz-Hupé, *Axis America*, 101–5. On the Third Reich's musical tastes and aversions, see Michael Meyer, "The Nazi Musicologist as Myth Maker in the Third Reich," JCH 10, no. 4 (October 1975); and by the same author, "Musicology in the Third Reich: A Gap in Historical Studies," *European Studies Review* 8, no. 3 (July 1978). Of relevance here is the interesting article by Michael H. Kater, "Forbidden Fruit? Jazz in the Third Reich," AHR 94, no. 1 (February 1989), 11ff.

12. H. Halter, *Der Polyp von New York* (Dresden: F. Müller 1942); see also Paul Scheffer et al., *USA 1940: Roosevelt-Amerika im Entscheidungsjahr* (Berlin: Im Deutschen Verlag 1940), 49, 125–27, 167–68.

13. Memorandum by the foreign minister, 12 March 1937, DGFP, C, vol. 6, 542; and Luther to AA, 17 March 1937, ibid., 564–65. See also David M. Esposito and Jackie R. Esposito, "LaGuardia and the Nazis, 1933–1938," *American Jewish History* 78, no. 1 (September 1988): 38–53. Though limited by its failure to consult German sources, this article correctly credits LaGuardia a devotion to human rights.

14. NYP, 4, 16, 17, and 31 March 1937; NYT, 4–7 March, and 21 May 1937; NYWT, 13 March 1937; clippings in GVDAKV/127; *Fränkische Tageszeitung*, 14 January 1939; W. Arntz, *Zwanzig Profile Scharf Geschnitten* (Berlin: Schützen-Verlag 1942), 247–58; and Strausz-Hupé, *Axis America*, 76.

15. Borchers to Dieckhoff, 13 March 1937, DGFP, C, vol. 6, 543–47; and Luther to AA, 17 March 1937, ibid., 565.

16. Hans Hummel, "New York . . . ," in *Mitteilungen über die Judenfrage*,

vol. 2, 1.; Karlheinz Rüdiger, "Die Enkel der Sklavenhändler," *Nationalsozialistische Korrespondenz*, Folge 303 (28 December 1938); WB, 15 August 1938; GVDAKV/127/129; *Der Angriff*, 7 March 1937; *Der Stürmer*, 26 June 1936; *Junge Garde*, 22 May 1937; and VB, 30 December 1934.

17. *B'nai B'rith Messenger*, 18 September 1936; GVDAKV/123/127/128/129/130; *Deutsche Zeitung*, 20 June 1934; *Fränkische Tageszeitung*, 23 July 1934; Scheffer et al., *USA 1940*, 134; "*Studenten-Pressedienst*," Folge 17, Blatt 7 (30 April 1938), in file I*90 phi 600 (Würzburg); and *Die Bewegung*, 25 October 1938.

18. Beck, *Germany*, 126; Daniel S. Day, "American Opinion of German National Socialism, 1933–1937," (Ph.D. diss., University of California at Los Angeles, 1958), 69; Strausz-Hupé, *Axis America*, 78, 155–57; and Arntz, *Zwanzig*, 175–98.

19. Karl Goerdeler, "U.S.A.," 2 January 1938 (Goerdeler file, HI).

20. Fabian von Schlabrendorff, *The Secret War Against Hitler* (London: Hodder & Stoughton, 1966), 319.

CHAPTER FIVE

1. Elliott Roosevelt, ed., *F.D.R. His Personal Letters* (New York: Duell, Sloan and Pearce, 1947), 19–20; Frank Freidel, *Franklin D. Roosevelt: The Apprenticeship* (Boston: Little, Brown & Co., 1952), 33–34; Geoffrey C. Ward, *Before the Trumpet: Young Franklin Roosevelt 1882–1905* (New York: Harper & Row 1985), 148–53; and Nathan Miller, *F.D.R.: An Intimate History* (Garden City, N.Y.: Doubleday 1983), 6–24.

2. On Roosevelt's faith, see Ward, *Before the Trumpet*, 156–58.

3. Robert Dallek, *Franklin D. Roosevelt and American Foreign Policy 1932–1945* (New York: Oxford Univ Press, 1979), 6.

4. See "Mahan" in Edward M. Earle, ed. (with Gordon A. Craig and Felix Gilbert), *Makers of Modern Strategy* (Princeton: Princeton Univ Press 1943), 416ff.

5. Cited by John T. Flynn, *Country Squire in the White House* (New York: Doubleday, 1940), 18–19, from the *Scientific American*, 28 February 1914.

6. Carl Diehl, *Americans and German Scholarship 1770–1870* (New Haven: Yale Univ Press, 1978), 1–5, 155; Stolberg-Wernigerode, *Germany and the United States*, 89–124, 272.

7. Charles S. Campbell, Jr., *Anglo-American Understanding 1898–1903* (Baltimore: Johns Hopkins Press 1957), 1.

8. Ibid., 10–24.

9. See Ludwig Dehio, "Gedanken über die deutsche Sendung 1900–1918," in *Deutschland und die Weltpolitik im 20. Jahrhundert* (Frankfurt: Fischer Verlag, 1961); and Fritz Fischer, *Germany's Aims in the First World War* (New York: W. W. Norton, 1967), 3–49.

10. Campbell, *Anglo-American Understanding*, 22; and Henry Adams, *The Education of Henry Adams* (New York: The Modern Library, 1931), 362.
11. Campbell, *Anglo-American Understanding*, 26–49, 353–56.
12. Ibid., 53, 281–87.
13. Ibid., 290–99; Perkins, *Hands Off*, 221, 224; and Herwig, *Politics of Frustration*, 94.
14. Alfred Vagts, *Deutschland und die Vereinigten Staaten in der Weltpolitik* (2 vols, New York: Macmillan, 1935), vol. 2, 1634, 1763, 2008–11.
15. Stolberg-Wernigerode, *Germany and the United States*, 273; Thomas A. Bailey, *The Man in the Street* (New York: Macmillan Co., 1948), 217; Perkins, *Hands Off*, 211; and Herwig, *Politics of Frustration*, 68–80.
16. Friedrich von Bernhardi, *Germany and the Next War* (New York: Longmans, 1911), 37, 74, 95–97, 117, 144, 153, 287.
17. Charles Homer Lea, *The Day of the Saxon* [1912] (New York: Harper & Brothers, 1942), 30–36.
18. Price Collier, *Germany and the Germans from an American Point of View* (New York: C. Scribner's Sons, 1913) 105–55, 470–71, 543–52, 590–602.

CHAPTER SIX

1. Richard O'Connor, *The German-Americans* (Boston: Little, Brown & Co., 1968), 379–84.
2. Ibid., 35; J. O. Knauss, *Social Conditions Among the Pennsylvania Germans in the Eighteenth Century* (Lancaster, Pa.: New Era Print Co., 1922), 119–67; and Marcus L. Hansen, *The Atlantic Migration* (New York: Harper, 1961), 74–76. According to Hans Gatzke, *Germany and the United States: A "Special Relationship?"* (Cambridge, Mass.: Harvard Univ Press, 1980), 28, eight or nine percent of the American population was of German origin at the time of the Revolution. Gatzke's work provides a useful overview of the German-American relationship, from its origins to the postwar period.
3. O'Connor, *German-Americans*, 68–70; Hansen, *Migration*, 123, 149.
4. Ibid., 188, 229; O'Connor, *German-Americans*, 103–9; W. H. Cartwright and R. L. Watson, Jr., eds., *The Reinterpretation of American History and Culture* (Washington, D.C.: National Council for the Social Studies, 1973), 81–87; and Oscar Handlin, ed., *Immigration as a Factor in American History* (Englewood Cliffs, N.J.: Prentice-Hall, 1959), 24–25.
5. Franz Löher, *Geschichte und Zustände der Deutschen in Amerika* (Cincinnati, Ohio: Eggers und Wulkop 1847); O'Connor, *German-Americans*, 77, 113; and Timothy L. Smith, "Religion and Ethnicity in America," *American Historical Review* 83, no. 5 (December 1978): 1170.
6. Hansen, *Migration*, 123–25, and his *The Immigrant in American History* (Cambridge, Mass.: Harvard Univ Press, 1940), 133; and O'Connor, *The*

German-Americans, 73. For a valuable account of German emigration in the nineteenth century, see Leonard Dinnerstein and David M. Reimers, *Ethnic Americans: A History of Immigration and Assimilation* (New York: Dodd, Mead, 1975), 14–25.

7. O'Connor, *German-Americans*, 78; Stolberg-Wernigerode, *Germany and the United States*, 25.

8. Robert E. Herzstein, "New York City Views the German Revolution, 1848," *Proceedings of the Consortium on Revolutionary Europe, 1976;* and Hansen, *Migration*, 167–68.

9. K. Wust and N. Muehlen, "Span 200: The Story of German-American Involvement in the Founding and Development of America" (Philadelphia: "Published in Behalf of Institut für Auslandsbeziehungen, Stuttgart," 1976).

10. Handlin, *Immigration as a Factor,* 109–11.

11. O'Connor, *German-Americans*, 121–28, 288–91; Albert B. Faust, *The German Element in the United States* (Boston: Houghton Mifflin Co., 1909), 7, 23–24, 126–29; Hansen, *Immigrant*, 139–40; T. Huebener, *The Germans in America* (Philadelphia: Chilton Co., Book Division, 1962), 144.

12. Faust, *The German Element*, 475; Carl Wittke, *The German-Language Press in America* (Lexington, Ky.: Univ of Kentucky Press, 1957), 6–8, 222; J. A. Hawgood, *The Tragedy of German-America* (New York: G. P. Putnam's Sons, 1940), 290; O'Connor, *German-Americans*, 360; Clifton J. Child, *The German-Americans in Politics 1914–1917* (Madison, Wis.: Univ of Wisconsin Press, 1939), 179.

13. Julius Goebel, "Zur deutschen Frage in Amerika," *Das Deutschtum in den Vereinigten Staaten von Nord-Amerika* (München: J. F. Lehmann, 1904), 36ff.; Hawgood, *Tragedy of German America*, 274.

14. Goebel, "Zur deutschen Frage," 1–7, 39–41, 75–84; and his *Gedanken Uber die Zukunft des Deutschtums in Amerika* (probably written ca. 1910), and *Der Kampf um Deutsche Kultur* (Leipzig: Dürr, 1914).

15. Handlin, *Immigration as a Factor,* 153–57, reprints some of Kallen's work.

16. Mayo-Smith in ibid., 158–63.

17. Milton M. Gordon, *Assimilation in American Life* (New York: Oxford Univ. Press, 1964), 100–101.

18. Wittke, *German-Language Press*, 243–45.

19. See Maldwyn Allen Jones, *American Immigration* (Chicago: Univ of Chicago Press, 1960), 238–77.

20. Campbell, *Anglo-American Understanding*, 46–47 n. 60; O'Connor, *German-Americans*, 347–53; and Faust, *German Element in the United States*, 200.

21. Huebner, *Germans in America*, 147; and Wittke, *German-Language Press*, 243–47, 260.

22. Huebner, *Germans in America*, 146; and Wittke, *German-Language Press*, 238.

23. Child, *German-Americans*, 25, and "German-American Attempts to Prevent the Exportation of Munitions of War, 1914–1915," MVHR 25, no. 3 (December 1938); and Hawgood, *Tragedy of German-America*, 292.

24. See the interesting analysis by Alexander and Juliette George, *Woodrow Wilson and Colonel House: A Personality Study* (New York: Day, 1956). Richard Hofstadter, *The American Political Tradition* (New York: Alfred A. Knopf 1948), in "Woodrow Wilson: The Conservative as Liberal," places a similar emphasis upon House's role in warning Wilson of the dangers presented by the German military. On Roosevelt's changing attitudes toward England and Germany, see Henry F. Pringle, *Theodore Roosevelt: A Biography* (New York: Harcourt, Brace, 1931), especially the chapters entitled "Lord of the Navy," and "Hemisphere Diplomacy".

25. Child, *German-Americans* 107; Huebner, *Germans*, 146; O'Connor, *German-Americans*, 389; and Wittke, *German-Language Press*, 256.

26. John Dewey, *German Philosophy and Politics* (New York: H. Holt & Company, 1915).

27. George Santayana, *Egotism in German Philosophy* (London: JM Dent & Sons Ltd., 1916). An enterprising British publisher reprinted this book in 1940.

28. Child, *German-Americans*, 41, 178, and "German-American Attempts," 359; O'Connor, *German-Americans*, 392.

29. Bailey, *The Man in the Street*, 18; Gerson, *The Hyphenate in Recent American Politics and Diplomacy* (Lawrence, Kans.: Univ of Kansas Press, 1964), 66. For a case study of a German-American community during this time, see David W. Detjen, *The Germans in Missouri, 1900–1918: Prohibition, Neutrality, and Assimilation* (Columbia, Mo.: Univ of Missouri Press, 1985).

30. George Seibel, "The Hyphen in American History" (Pittsburgh, Pa.: Neeb-Hirsch Publishing Co., 1916), RG 131/121 (NA).

31. For useful accounts of Wilson's strategic, legal, and geopolitical considerations, see Edward H. Buehring, *Woodrow Wilson and the Balance of Power* (Bloomington: Indiana University Press, 1955), and Kendrick A. Clements, *Woodrow Wilson: World Statesman* (Boston: Twayne, 1987), 159–66.

32. Howard B. Furer, comp., *The Germans in America 1607–1970: A Chronology and Fact Book* (Dobbs Ferry, N.Y.: Oceana Publications, 1973), 133; Wittke, *German-Language Press*, 268; Child, *German-Americans*, 173; and R. L. Mawson, "War Against Freedom: Civil Liberties in Washington, D.C. During the First World War," paper presented as part of an exhibit at the Wilson House, Washington, D.C., 1977–1978.

33. Wittke, *German-American Press*, 262–65; and Robert K. Murray, *Red Scare: A Study in National Hysteria, 1919–1920*. (New York: McGraw-Hill,

1964) Murray attributes some of the postwar hysteria to the government's attack upon civil rights during the war.

34. " 'Style Roosevelt,' " *Victoire,* 22 August 1918; "Declaration de Franklin Roosevelt," *La Justice,* 23 August 1918; and "Le Haut de la Côte est atteint, dit M. Franklin Roosevelt," *L'Homme Libre,* 22 August 1918.

35. See Kenneth S. Davis, *FDR: The Beckoning of Destiny 1882–1928* (New York: Putnam, 1972), 520–29.

36. *The Evening World* (New York City), 1 November 1918.

CHAPTER SEVEN

1. Harry Elmer Barnes, *A History of Historical Writing* (New York: Dover Publications, 1963), 277–78.

2. See William L. Langer, "The United States as a World Power," in Carl E. Schorske and Elizabeth Schorske, eds. *Explorations in Crisis: Papers on International History* (Cambridge, Mass.: Belknap Press of Harvard Univ Press, 1969).

3. Herman J. Wittgens, "German Revisionist Propaganda in the United States," German Studies Association, Twelfth Annual Conference, Philadelphia, Pa., 9 October 1988 (section no. 60, paper no. 1).

4. John E. Wiltz, *From Isolation to War, 1931–1941* (New York: Crowell, 1968), 7.

5. Oswald G. Villard, "On the German Front," *The Nation,* 14 January 1931, 38. See also articles by John Elliott in the NYHT, 11 December 1930; NYT, 11 December 1930; *The World,* 7 January 1930; and *Variety,* 25 February 1931.

6. Roosevelt to Norman H. Davis, 30 August 1933, Norman H. Davis Papers, Box 51 (LOCMD). See also Donald F. Drummond, "Cordell Hull," in Norman A. Graebner, ed., *An Uncertain Tradition: American Secretaries of State in the Twentieth Century* (New York: McGraw-Hill, 1961), 184ff.; and Thomas H. Greer, *What Roosevelt Thought: The Social and Political Ideas of Franklin D. Roosevelt* (East Lansing, Mich.: Michigan State Univ Press, 1958), 162–63. Greer concludes that FDR supported cooperation with the league when it served American interests, so long as the United States reserved to itself all rights of independent decision making.

7. Warren F. Kuehl, "Midwestern Newspapers and Isolationist Sentiment," DH 3, no. 3:286.

8. Nye, cited by Norman A. Graebner, *America as a World Power: A Realist Appraisal From Wilson to Reagan* (Wilmington, Del.: Scholarly Resources, 1984), 26.

9. Lawrence S. Wittner, *The Rebels Against War: The American Peace Movement, 1933–1983* (Philadelphia: Temple University Press, 1984), 2–3.

10. Wittner, *Rebels Against War,* 6–7.

11. Klaus Schwabe, "Die Regierung Roosevelt und die Expansionspolitik Hitlers vor dem Zweiten Weltkrieg: Appeasement als Folge eines 'Primats der Innenpolitik'?," in Karl Rohe, ed., *Die Westmächte und das dritte Reich 1933–1939: Klassische Grossmachtrivalität oder Kampf zwischen Demokratie und Diktatur?* (Paderborn: 1982), 105.

12. Hanfstängl, *Missing Years,* 188; Martha and William E. Dodd, Jr., eds. *Ambassador Dodd's Diary 1933–1938* (New York: Harcourt, Brace, and Co., 1941), 3; and Franklin L. Ford, "Three Observers in Berlin: Rumbold, Dodd, and Francois-Poncet," in Gordon Craig and Felix Gilbert, eds., *The Diplomats* (New York: Atheneum, 1963), vol. 2, 449.

13. Francis L. Loewenheim, "The Diffidence of Power—Some Notes and Reflections on the American Road to Munich," *Rice University Studies* [*Studies in History*] 58, no. 4 (Fall 1972): 19.

14. Roscoe Baker, *The American Legion and American Foreign Policy* (New York: Bookman Associates, 1954), 156.

15. Graebner, *America as a World Power,* 36; and Robert D. Schulzinger, *The Wise Men of Foreign Affairs: The History of the Council on Foreign Relations* (New York: Columbia Univ Press, 1984), 53–54. Stimson is cited by Loewenheim in "Diffidence of Power," 23.

16. David F. Schmitz, *The United States and Fascist Italy, 1922–1940* (Chapel Hill, N.C.: U. of N.C. Press 1988), 160–61.

17. Cordell Hull, *The Memoirs of Cordell Hull* (New York: Macmillan Co., 1948), vol. 1, 460–61.

18. See FDRFA, First series, vol. 4, 136–38, 406; Alexander DeConde, ed., *Isolation and Security* (Durham, N.C.: Duke University Press, 1957), 11; and A. J. Barker, *The Civilizing Mission: A History of the Italo-Ethiopian War of 1935–1936* (New York: Dial Press 1968), 139–41, 202.

19. Hull, *Memoirs,* vol. 1, 471.

20. Kuehl, "Midwestern Newspapers," 303–6.

21. Dodd, *Diary,* 307, 378; Roosevelt, *Personal Letters,* vol. 1, 626n; Dodd to Roosevelt, 7 December 1936, in FDRFA, first series, vol. 3, 526–28; and Dallek, *Franklin D. Roosevelt,* 143.

22. Cited by Loewenheim, "Diffidence of Power," 44.

23. William E. Kinsella, Jr., "The Prescience of a Statesman: FDR's Assessment of Adolf Hitler Before the World War, 1933–1941," in Herbert D. Rosenbaum and Elizabeth Bartelme, *Franklin D. Roosevelt: The Man, the Myth, the Era, 1882–1945* (Westport, Conn.: Greenwood Press, 1987), 75. It is my view that FDR hoped to liberalize the fascist regimes, convert them to the virtues of enhanced commercial cooperation, and then bring his famed charm to bear upon their leaders. This combination of naiveté and arrogance, however, cannot be labeled "appeasement." It was in

1936, in this context, that FDR was interested in persuading Hitler to outline his foreign policy goals for the next decade. The chancellor, Roosevelt hoped, would then agree to a renewal of disarmament negotiations. See Gordon Craig, "Roosevelt and Hitler: The Problem of Perception," in Klaus Hildebrand and Reiner Pommerin, eds., *Deutsche Frage and Europäisches Gleichgewicht: Festschrift für Andreas Hillgruber zum 60. Geburtstag* (Cologne: 1985), 181.

24. Dallek, *Franklin D. Roosevelt*, 102–3; Gerhard L. Weinberg, *The Foreign Policy of Hitler's Germany* (Chicago: Univ of Chicago Press, 1970), 156; and Dodd to Roosevelt, 7 December 1936, in FDRFA, first series, vol. 3, 526–28.

25. Cited by Loewenheim, "Diffidence of Power," 20.

26. Howard C. Payne, "French Security and American Policy in the 1930's: A Triangular Drama," in Payne et al., *As the Storm Clouds Gathered: European Perceptions of American Foreign Policy in the 1930s* (Durham, N.C.: Duke U. Press, 1979), 32–37.

27. Schlesinger, *Politics of Upheaval*, 656; Dallek, *Franklin D. Roosevelt*, 135; and Paul Claudel to Roosevelt, 9 January 1937, in FDRFA, second series, vol. 4, 13.

CHAPTER EIGHT

1. Frederick L. Allen, *Since Yesterday: The Nineteen-Thirties in America* (New York: London, Harper & Brothers, 1940), 232–34; E. Digby Baltzell, *The Protestant Establishment* (New York: Vintage Books 1966), 248–49; Robert Bendiner, *Just Around the Corner: A Highly Selective History of the Thirties* (New York: Harper & Row, 1967), 170; and James M. Burns, *Roosevelt: The Soldier of Freedom* (New York: Harcourt Brace Jovanovich, 1970), 442.

2. R. Carlisle, "The Foreign Policy Views of an Isolationist Press Lord," JCH 9, no. 3; and Raymond Gram Swing, *Forerunners of American Fascism* (New York: J. Messner, Inc., 1935) 134ff.

3. Michael W. Miles, *The Odyssey of the American Right* (New York: Oxford Univ Press, 1980), 31.

4. Nelson W. Aldrich, Jr., *Old Money: The Mythology of America's Upper Class* (New York: Alfred A. Knopf, 1988), 238–41.

5. George Wolfskill, *The Revolt of the Conservatives* (Boston: Houghton Mifflin, 1962), 152, and 177; Seymour M. Lipset and Earl Raab, *The Politics of Unreason: Right-Wing Extremism in America, 1790–1970* (New York: Harper & Row 1970), 201; and Baltzell, *Protestant*, 244–45.

6. Manfred Jonas, *Isolationism in America, 1935–1941* (Ithaca, N.Y.: Cornell Univ Press 1966), 1; Bendiner, *Just Around the Corner,* 216; Norman, "Influence," 213; Warren I. Cohen, *The American Revisionists* (Chicago: Univ of Chicago Press 1967), 189; and John P. Diggins, *Mussolini and*

Fascism: The View from America (Princeton: Princeton Univ Press, 1972), 333–34.

7. Wolfskill, *Revolt of the Conservatives*, 100–101; NAM T-81/25/22216; E. M. Hadley, "The Rape of the Republic," RG 131/106 (NA); and B.D. Rhodes, "Anglophobia in Chicago," *Illinois Quarterly* 39, no. 4.

8. Bailey, *Man in the Street*, 118, 184; Dallek, *Franklin D. Roosevelt*, 108. Roosevelt cited by Graebner, *America as a World Power*, 27. See also Loewenheim, "Diffidence of Power," 64.

9. William E. Dodd, *Diary*, 363.

10. Weinberg, "Hitler's Image," 1014 n. 28; Ribbentrop statement, Nürnberg interrogation of 31 August 1945, 1430 hrs., pp. 1–9, RG 238 (NA).

11. Hull, *Memoirs*, vol. 1, 472–73.

12. Dallek, *Franklin D. Roosevelt*, 125; Dodd, *Diary*, 196; Gerhard L. Weinberg, *The Foreign Policy of Hitler's Germany: Diplomatic Revolution in Europe 1933–36* (Chicago: Univ of Chicago Press, 1970), 152–55; Hull to H.A. Johnson, 12 November 1938, RG 131/218 (NA).

13. Gabriel Kolko, "American Business and Germany, 1930–1941," *Western Political Quarterly* 15, no. 4; Franklin D. Roosevelt, *The Public Papers and Addresses of Franklin D. Roosevelt, 1938 Volume* (New York: Random House 1940), 335; Arnold A. Offner, *American Appeasement*, Cambridge, Mass. Harvard Univ Press, 1969, 239–44; and Dodd, *Diary*, 254, 283, 358.

14. Miller to Willard L. Thorp, 4 April 1934, PSF/Diplomatic File/Germany 1933–1938/Box 44 (FDRL).

15. Gerhard L. Weinberg, *The Foreign Policy of Hitler's Germany: Starting World War II, 1937–1939* (Chicago: Univ of Chicago Press, 1980), 251.

16. Dodd, *Diary*, 307, 378; Roosevelt, *Personal Letters*, vol. 1, 626n; Dodd to Roosevelt, 7 December 1936, in FDRFA, vol. 3, 526–528; and Dallek, *Franklin D. Roosevelt*, 143. Also useful on the neutrality policy is Harry Dahlheimer, "The United States, Germany and the Quest for Neutrality, 1933–1937" (Ph.D. diss., University of Iowa, 1976), chapter four and appendix D.

17. Hull, *Memoirs*, vol. 1, 493.

18. See the relevant comments of Selig Adler, *The Isolationist Impulse* (London: Abelard-Schuman, 1957), 262–65.

19. Allen F. Repko, "The Failure of Reciprocal Trade," *Mid-America* 60, no. 1:3ff.; and Fred Rippy, "German Investments in Latin America," *The Journal of Business* 21, no. 2:63ff.

20. Dallek, *Franklin D. Roosevelt*, 118, 176; and Wallace to Roosevelt, 5 June 1936, FDRFA, first series, vol. 3, 315–16.

21. John D. Wirth, "A German View of Brazilian Trade and Development, 1935," *The Hispanic-American Historical Review* 47, no. 2:225ff.

22. Hans Stöckl, "Hat das Deutschtum in Chile eine Zukunft?," *Deutsche Arbeit* 30, no. 11:286ff.
23. See Strausz-Hupé, *Axis America*, 189–92; and O. John Rogge, *Official German Report: Nazi Penetration, 1924–1942; Pan-Arabism, 1939-Today* (New York: T. Yoseloff, 1961), 235.
24. N. P. Macdonald, *Hitler Over Latin America* (London: Jarrolds Ltd., 1940), 32–57; and Dodd, *Diary*, 362–63.

CHAPTER NINE

1. Roosevelt to the editorial board of the *Christian Science Monitor*, 10 April 1937, in FDRFA, second series, vol. 5, 35; Roosevelt to Biddle, 10 November 1937, in *F.D.R.: Personal Letters 1928–1945*, vol. 1, 725; Roosevelt to Sumner Welles, 12 November 1937, ibid., 726; and Bullitt to Roosevelt, 23 November 1937 in Oliver H. Bullitt, ed., *For the President, Personal and Secret* (Boston: Houghton Mifflin, 1972), 237. Mark M. Lowenthal offers a useful overview of this period in his article "Roosevelt and the Coming of the War: The Search for United States Policy 1937–'42," JCH, vol. 16 (1981), 413–40.
2. David Brinkley, *Washington Goes to War* (New York: Alfred A. Knopf, 1988), 15.
3. Schulzinger, *Wise Men*, 56–57; see also Leonard Silk and Mark Silk, *The American Establishment* (New York: Basic Books, 1981), 197.
4. Nancy H. Hooker, ed., *The Moffat Papers: Selections From the Diplomatic Journals of Jay Pierrepont Moffat 1919–1943* (Cambridge, Mass.: Harvard Univ Press, 1956), 153–55.
5. Cited by Michael Leigh, *Mobilizing Consent: Public Opinion and American Foreign Policy, 1937–1947* (Westport, Conn.: Greenwood Press 1976), 34–36. See also Robert D. Accinelli, "Militant Internationalists: The League of Nations Association, the Peace Movement, and U.S. Foreign Policy, 1934–38," DH vol. 5, no. 1:19ff., and, Drummond, "Cordell Hull," in Graebner, *An Uncertain Tradition*, 200.
6. Hooker, *The Moffat Papers*, 162–86. Japan ignored the Nine-Power Conference, declaring that the "China Incident" did not come within its purview. Chamberlain is cited by Graebner, *America as a World Power*, 40. For a sympathetic view of the opposition to interventionism, then and later, see the works of Wayne S. Cole, *Senator Gerald P. Nye and American Foreign Relations* (Minneapolis: Univ of Minnesota Press, 1962); *Roosevelt and the Isolationists, 1932–1945* (Lincoln, Nebr.: Univ of Nebraska Press, 1983); *America First: The Battle Against Intervention, 1940–1941* (Madison, Wis.: Univ of Wisconsin Press, 1953); and Tom D. Crouch, ed., *Charles A. Lindbergh: An American Life* (Washington, D.C.: National Air and Space

Museum, Smithsonian Institution; distributed by Smithsonian Institution Press, 1977).

7. Leigh, *Mobilizing Consent*, 42.

8. Wittner, *Rebels*, 14 et passim.

9. Arthur Krock, *Memoirs: Sixty Years on the Firing Line* (New York: Funk & Wagnalls, 1968), 182.

10. Leila A. Sussmann, *Dear FDR: A Study of Political Letter-Writing* (Totowa, N.J.: Bedminster Press, 1963), 9. The *Washington Post*'s distinguished columnist David S. Broder, writing more than four decades after Roosevelt's death, still marveled at the number of FDR's press conferences. See *Behind the Front Page* (New York: Simon and Schuster, 1988), 151.

11. Hedley Donovan, *Roosevelt to Reagan: A Reporter's Encounters With Nine Presidents* (New York: Harper & Row 1987), 19. On Roosevelt and the media, see Richard W. Steele, *Propaganda in an Open Society: The Roosevelt Administration and the Media, 1933–1941* (Westport, Conn.: Greenwood Press, 1985), pp. 33–66.

12. Roosevelt to Dodd, August 5, 1936 in *F.D.R.'s Personal Letters, 1928–1945*, 605–6; Daniel J. Boorstin, "Selling the President to the People," *Commentary* (November 1955): 421ff.; Krock quoted by Deborah E. Lipstadt, *Beyond Belief: The American Press and the Coming of the Holocaust 1933–1945* (New York: Free Press, 1986), 4; Graham J. White, *FDR and the Press* (Chicago: Univ of Chicago Press, 1979), 6–12, 69–73; and R. L. Strout's review of White's book, *Columbia Journalism Review* (July–August 1979). See also FDRPC 14-342 and 15:455–457.

13. Loewenheim, "Diffidence of Power," 20.

14. FZ, 6 October 1937; *The Public Papers and Addresses of Franklin D. Roosevelt, 1937* (New York: Random House, 1941), 406ff.; Michael Leigh, *Mobilizing Consent*, 34; Dallek, *Franklin D. Roosevelt*, 68, 151; *Literary Digest* 123, no. 12:12 (30 October 1937); and *F.D.R.'s Personal Letters*, vol. 1, 716–17.

15. Schulzinger, *Wise Men*, 56.

16. Elliott Roosevelt, *As He Saw It* (New York: Duell, Sloan and Pearce, 1946), 4–5.

17. On Bullitt, see Ronald Steel, "The Strange Case of William Bullitt," in *The New York Review of Books*, 29 September 1988, 15ff.

18. Will Brownell and Richard N. Billings, *So Close to Greatness: A Biography of William C. Bullitt* (New York: Macmillan, 1988), 195–204.

19. Graebner, *America as a World Power,* 44.

20. See Wayne Cole, *Roosevelt and the Isolationists 1932–45*, 277.

21. See the Wilson dispatches of 14 May (no. 246), and 18 May 1938 (no. 156), PSF/26 (Germany, Communications) [FDRL].

22. Brownell and Billings, *So Close to Greatness*, 221.

23. See the Lukasiewicz dispatch of 27 May 1938, in Waclaw Jedrzejewicz, ed., *Diplomat in Paris 1936–1939: Papers and Memoirs of Juliusz Lukasiewicz, Ambassador of Poland* (New York: Columbia Univ Press, 1970), 91–99. The Polish ambassador to French Foreign Minister Bonnet's reference to American support. This type of comment reached Roosevelt through diplomatic "back channels." ("M. Bonnet said that France had the support not only of England but also of the United States. . . .") Lukasiewicz then downplayed Bonnet's comment, though he later echoed his French colleague's optimistic evaluation of American policy. Of interest here is John M. Muresianu, *War of Ideas: American Intellectuals and the World Crisis 1938–1945* (New York & London: Garland Publishing Co., 1988), Chapter 1.

24. Roosevelt, *Public Papers, 1938 Volume* (New York: Random House, 1940), 491 ff.; and Joseph Lash, *Roosevelt & Churchill, 1939–1941: The Partnership that Saved the West* (New York: Norton, 1976), 27.

25. Cole, *Roosevelt*, 283; Jane K. Vieth, "Joseph P. Kennedy and British Appeasement: The Diplomacy of a Boston Irishman," in Kenneth P. Jones, ed., *U.S. Diplomats in Europe, 1919–1941* (Santa Barbara, Cal.: ABC-Clio, 1981), 169ff.

26. Francois-Poncet to Bonnet, 5 September 1938, DDF, vol. 2, 11, 12. On Roosevelt's correction of this remark, see Truelle to Bonnet, 10 September 1938, ibid., doc. 76, 3d par.; and Hooker, *Moffat Papers*, 197.

27. John Harvey, ed., *The Diplomatic Diaries of Oliver Harvey, 1937–1940* (London: Collins, 1970), 170. (6 June 1938).

28. Harvey, 176; and Hooker, *Moffat Papers*, 204–5.

29. Lindsay to Halifax, 20 September and 21 September 1938, DBFP, vol. 7, 627–30. Of particular importance here is David Reynolds, *The Creation of the Anglo-American Alliance 1937–1941: A Study in Competitive Cooperation* (Chapel Hill, N.C.: UNC Press, 1982), 20–46. See also Kinsella, "The Prescience of a Statesman," in Rosenbaum and Bartelme, 78. Saint-Quentin to Bonnet, 28 September 1938, DDF, vol. 2, 11, 639–40. Roosevelt to Ambassador William Phillips, cited by Cole, *Roosevelt*, 284. Dieckhoff's cable was dispatched on 27 September 1938, and is cited by William L. Shirer, *The Collapse of the Third Republic: An Inquiry into the Fall of France in 1940* (New York: Simon & Schuster, 1969), 382–83. Raymond Moley, cited by Frank P. Mintz, *Revisionism and the Origins of Pearl Harbor* (Lanham, Md.: University Press of America, 1985), 84.

CHAPTER TEN

1. Gottlieb, *American Anti-Nazi Resistance*, 28–34.
2. Ibid., 46–47.
3. Ibid., 131–34.

4. NYT, 25 October 1933; Fritz T. Epstein, "Germany and the United States," in George L. Anderson, ed., *Issues and Conflicts*, 303; and CT, 15 November 1933.

5. NYP, 11, 12, and 17 March 1937; NYT, 7 March 1937; NYWT, 8 March 1937; and NYHT, 13 March 1937.

6. See the relevant materials in RG 131/121 and 122 (NA); NYT, 1 February 1937; *The Congress Bulletin*, 5 and 27 March 1937; *Jewish Examiner* (Brooklyn), 7 May 1937; and Ralph B. Levering, *The Public and American Foreign Policy 1918–1978* (New York: Published for the Foreign Policy Association by Morrow, 1978), 61–62.

7. NYHT, 28 July 1934; *Jewish Examiner*, 6 August 1937.

8. NYT, 6 June 1934, and 28 September 1935; NYP, 18 March, 1, 3, 5, 8, and 10 May, 9 June, and 2 September 1937; Ronald H. Bayor, *Neighbors in Conflict: The Irish, Germans, Jews, and Italians in New York City, 1929–1941* (Baltimore, Md.: Johns Hopkins University, 1978), 68; *Volksparole*, 27 March 1933; and *Pforzheimer Anzeiger*, 31 August 1935.

9. NYT, 14 July 1936; NYP, 26 December 1936; *The New Leader*, 23 and 30 January and 27 February 1937; NYT, 7 January 1978; Ada and F. McCormick to Hoffmann, 31 March 1938, NS 42/10; and J. Radkau, *Die deutsche Emigration in den USA: Ihr Einfluss auf die amerikanische Europapolitik 1933–1945* (Düsseldorf: Bertelsmann Universitätsverlag, 1971), 67.

10. Frederick L. Allen, "American Magazines," 1741–1941," *Bulletin of the New York Public Library* 45, no. 6; and the Association of National Advertisers, "Magazine Circulation and Rate Trends, 1940–1969" (New York: Association of National Advertisers, 1970), 30.

11. These observations are based upon an analysis of the *The Atlantic Monthly* vols. 152–165.

12. Wien 565/103–104 contain Prochnik's reports for the years 1933–1938.

13. RCS .0016.020 (8/38).

14. Gottlieb, *American Anti-Nazi Resistance*, 262–63.

15. Gabas to Hoffmann, 6 August 1939, NS 42/13 (BA).

16. RCS .0016.015 (8/38); and RCS .0016.020 (8/38).

17. Levering, *The Public and American Foreign Policy*, 55; Leigh *Mobilizing Consent*, 21; Bailey, *Man in the Street*, 183–224; Allen, *Since Yesterday*, 326; and Bendiner, *Just Around the Corner*, 217.

18. See, the relevant charts in Daniel Yankelovich and Mary Komarnicki, "American Public Opinion of Holocaust Events: 1933–1945," prepared for "The Holocaust and the Media," a conference held at the Harvard Divinity School, Cambridge, Mass., May 1988.

19. John P. Diggins, *Mussolini and Fascism*, 316–27; John Norman, "The Influence of Pro-Fascist Propaganda on American Neutrality, 1935–1936," in D. E. Lee and G. E. McReynolds, eds., *Essays in History and*

International Relations (Port Washington, N.Y.: Kennikat Press 1949), 195ff.; Dallek, *Franklin D. Roosevelt*, 95–101, 187; Wayne S. Cole, *Senator Gerald P. Nye and American Foreign Relations* (Minneapolis: Univ of Minnesota Press 1962), 158–60; and Bendiner, *Just Around the Corner*, 218.

20. Hadley Cantril, *The Invasion From Mars* (New York: Harper & Row 1966); and Strausz-Hupé, *Axis America*, 144.
21. Wilbur Burton, "South American Grab-Bag," *Current History* (November 1937): 54ff.; and Carleton Beals, *The Coming Struggle for Latin America* (Philadelphia: J.B. Lippencott Co. 1938), 39.
22. Thomsen to AA, 17 May 1939, DGFP, D, vol. 6, 526–533.
23. See David L. Cohn, "Neutrality or Bust," *The Atlantic Monthly*, June 1939.

CHAPTER ELEVEN

1. See Ernst Kris, "German Propaganda Instructions of 1933," *Social Research* 9, no. 1 (February 1942).
2. NYT, 2 and 3 July 1937.
3. NS 42/10 and 14 (BA); and NAM T-81/26/22659.
4. Dodd, *Diary*, 10–11, 42, 212; and Kris, "German Propaganda Instructions," 68.
5. *Kansas City Star*, 23 July 1936; and Landon to De Land, 27 July 1936, NAM T-81/36/32438.
6. Schumacher/420 (BA), contains a relevant letter dated 15 September 1933, as well as other choice quotations.
7. Dodd, *Diary*, 107, 151; and NYP, 12 May 1937.
8. Arnd Krüger, *Die Olympischen Spiele 1936 und die Weltmeinung: Ihre aussenpolitische Bedeutung unter besonderer Berücksichtigung der USA* (Berlin: Bartels & Wernitz, 1972), 116–20.
9. Ibid., 125.
10. Richard D. Mandell, *The Nazi Olympics* (New York: Macmillan, 1971), 70–79; and Deborah E. Lipstadt, *Beyond Belief*, 65.
11. Krüger, *Olympische Spiele*, 136–39.
12. Mandell, *The Nazi Olympics*, 70–79.
13. NYT, 5 October 1936; NYWT, 6 October 1936 (Pegler); RLZ, 9 January 1939; and Brundage to Schmitz, 19 August 1939, RG 131/78 (NA).
14. Dedake, "Das Dritte Reich," 171–72; Ladislas Farago, ed., *German Psychological Warfare* (New York: Arno Press, 1972 [1942]), 139–46.
15. Dodd, *Diary*, 149, 246, 333.
16. See Ernst Kris, "German Propaganda Instructions."
17. Dodd, *Diary*, 13.
18. John Higham, ed., *Ethnic Leadership in America* (Baltimore: Johns Hopkins Univ Press, 1978), 70ff.; Gerson, *The Hyphenate*, 101.
19. Bischoff, *Nazi Conquest*, 165; "When I Take Charge of Germany," *Liberty*,

9 June 1932; Niel M. Johnson, *George Sylvester Viereck: German-American Propagandist,* 195, 201; "What Hitler Will Do Next," *Liberty,* 14 May 1938; and Viereck, "Germany Revisited," unpublished manuscript in the Hoover Institution Archives (Ts Germany G 373).

20. *Washington Post,* 3 September 1937.
21. Schonbach, "Native Fascism," 170–71; Rollins, *I Find Treason,* 193; and Klaus Kipphan, *Deutsche Propaganda in den Vereinigten Staaten 1933–1941* (Heidelberg: C., Winter 1971), 120.
22. Hoffmann to Beller, 1 February 1939, NS 42/13 (BA); and E. Kreisel correspondence, NS 42/26 [1939–1940] (BA).
23. NYP, 10 October 1940. Hans Fritzsche, a high-ranking Propaganda Ministry official, knew a lot about Schmitz's activities: see Fritzsche's interrogation of 6 May 1946, IMT, 10–11. See also RG 131/42, 41, 1 (NA).
24. NS 42/20 (BA); Kipphan, *Deutsche Propaganda,* 113 et passim.
25. NAM T-81/27/23870.
26. NS 42/5, 6, 10, and 12 (BA).
27. NS 42/8 and 18 (BA).
28. See the materials on the Amerika-Institut in RG 131/215 (NA).
29. "Bericht über den Film der Vereinigung Carl Schurz 'Germany of Today,' " GCD/312 (LOCMD).
30. NS 42/9, 12, 13, and 14 (BA).
31. Irre to Hoffmann, 13 December 1938, NAM T-81/26/22761; von Gienanth interrogation of May 1946, 17–19. Schumacher/420 (BA) contains excerpts from a letter dated 15 September 1933.
32. Kipphan, *Deutsche Propaganda,* 113, is relevant here.
33. NAM T-81/25/22204; NS 42/13 (BA).
34. Useful material may be consulted in NS 42/Vorlagen 10 and 14 (BA).

CHAPTER TWELVE

1. Sander A. Diamond, *The Nazi Movement in the United States 1924–1941* (Ithaca, N.Y.: Cornell Univ Press, 1974), 140; C. C. Burlingham et al., *The German Reich and Americans of German Origin* (New York: Oxford Univ Press, 1938), 42; and the letter of J. M. Reichler to R. H. Hoffmann, 24 April 1939, NS 42/Vorl. 19 (BA). The State Department possessed an important and rather accurate file on the Bund, and shared it with the White House. See "German-American Bund," PSF State/German-American Bund/drawer 4-1959/box 71 (FDRL).
2. John A. Hawgood, *The Tragedy of German-America: The Germans in the United States of America During the Nineteenth Century—and After,* 295–97; and Andrew M. Greeley and William C. McCready, *Ethnicity in the United States: A Preliminary Reconnaissance* (New York: Wiley, 1974), 114.
3. O'Connor, *German-Americans,* 384–87.

4. Hawgood, *Tragedy of German-America*, 302; and Gerson, *Hyphenate*, 263.
5. Ralph F. Bischoff, *Nazi Conquest Through German Culture* (Cambridge, Mass.: Harvard Univ Press, 1942), 169–72; and Higham, *Ethnic Leadership*, 73–81.
6. See Charles Vece and Mary Bishop, "Organized Life of the Germans in New Haven, Connecticut," CSL, files 928–33.
7. Higham, *Ethnic Leadership*, 66ff.
8. Herbert S. Reichle, "Rückblick und Ausschau für Deutschamerikaner," in *Deutsche Heimat in Amerika* (Berlin: 1937), 55ff.
9. Bischoff, *Nazi Conquest*, 168.
10. Sander A. Diamond, "Zur Typologie der amerikadeutschen NS-Bewegung," VJHfZ, 1975, no. 3: 271ff.; and Lüdecke 293–99.
11. Diamond, *The Nazi Movement*, 115.
12. Ibid., 118.
13. NYP, 15 August 1934; and Diamond, *The Nazi Movement*, 130.
14. Diggins, *Mussolini and Fascism*, makes this point.
15. NYSZ, 27 October 1933; *Siebenbürgisch-Amerikanisches Volksblatt*, 25 October 1934.
16. *Evening Bulletin* (Philadelphia), 24 October 1933; and M. Wagner to S. Schuster, 4 October 1938, NS 20/127/5 (BA).
17. RG 131/1 and 196 (NAS).
18. Leland V. Bell, *In Hitler's Shadow* (Port Washington, N.Y.: Kennikat Press, 1973), 22; Bund Command no. 9, 29 May 1937, RG 131/17 (NAS); Frank C. Hanighen, "Foreign Political Movements in the United States," *Foreign Affairs* 16, no. 1 (October 1937): 11; and Diamond, *The Nazi Movement*, 114. See also Bund Command no. 4, 30 December 1936, RG 131/17 (NAS); (NS 41/Vorl. 15, Fest Folge, [BA]); and audio materials in RG 131/69 (NA).
19. NYWT, 29 March 1934; *Post* (Cincinnati), 8 May 1934; and RG 131/1 (NAS).
20. *Sentinal* (Milwaukee), 2 March 1934; NYT, 22 May 1934; and RG 131/27 (NAS).
21. NYWT, 18 May 1934; *Sentinal* (Milwaukee), 4 October 1935; *Times* (London), 22 April 1938; and NYT, 4 May 1938.
22. T-81/26/23034 (NA); "Germany Today . . . ," RG 131/2 and 101 (NAS); HF, 16 and 24 November 1933.
23. *The Congress Bulletin,* 14 May 1937.
24. Walter Kappe, "Die kulturelle Mission des Bundes Freunde des neuen Deutschland in U.S.A.," RG 131/122 (NAS), and his "Wer wir sind und Was wir wollen" (November 1935), RG 131/101 (NAS); and "Der Amerikadeutsche Volksbund im Kampf um die Einigung des Amerikadeutschtums," R 57/1178/36, and NS 20/127/1 (BA).

25. Sepp Schuster later returned to Germany, where he pursued a career as a Nazi speaker and SA official. In the 1970s, he donated his papers to the German Federal Archives, Koblenz.

26. Donald S. Strong, *Organized Anti-Semitism in America* (Washington, D.C.: American Council on Public Affairs, 1941), 25; Richard Rollins, *I Find Treason* (London: G. G. Harveys, 1941), 92–93; and *The Record* (Norwich, Conn.), 10 May 1942.

27. Diamond, *The Nazi Movement,* 143, 168–69, and "Zur Typologie," 288–91.

28. John R. Carlson, *Under Cover* (New York: E. P. Dutton, 1943), 47; and Rollins, *Treason,* 82–88.

29. RG 131/1/6/101 (NAS).

CHAPTER THIRTEEN

1. Finis Farr, *Fair Enough: The Life of Westbrook Pegler* (New Rochelle, N.Y.: Arlington House, 1975), 130–31.

2. Walter A. Jöhr, *Amerika und der Faschismus* (Bern: P. Haupt, 1937), 34–35. Jöhr predicted that fascism would ultimately fail in the United States, since it lacked real native roots.

3. David F. Schmitz, *The United States and Fascist Italy, 1922–1940,* 82–100.

4. See Child's glowing preface to Benito Mussolini, *My Autobiography* (New York: C. Scribner's Sons, 1928), xviii–xix, J. C. Furnas, *Stormy Weather: Crosslights on the Nineteen Thirties* (New York: G. Putnam's Sons 1977), 210. See also Schmitz, *The United States and Fascist Italy,* 169.

5. As early as 1935, Herman Finer, writing in *Mussolini's Italy* (London: Gollancz, 1935), exposed as hollow fascism's claims to the contrary.

6. Furnas, *Stormy Weather,* 206, 213, 220; Arthur M. Schlesinger, Jr., *The Politics of Upheaval* (Boston: Houghton Mifflin, 1960), 76, 627; and Morris Schonbach, "Native Fascism During the 1930's and 1940's: A Study of Its Roots, Its Growth, and Its Decline" (Ph.D. diss., University of California at Los Angeles, 1958), 109–10.

7. Smith is cited by David H. Bennett in *The Party of Fear: From Nativist Movements to the New Right in American History* (Chapel Hill: Univ. of N. Carolina Press, 1988), 244.

8. MG, 13 October 1933; Robert Bendiner, *Just Around the Corner,* 212; Schlesinger, *Politics of Upheaval,* 79.

9. *Daily Telegraph* (London), 21 November 1934.

10. Strong, *Organized Anti-Semitism,* 83, 97–98.

11. Lipset and Raab, *Politics of Unreason,* 195–96; and Schlesinger, *Politics of Upheaval,* 77. On Long's roots and development, see T. Harry Williams, *Huey Long* (New York: Knopf, 1969).

12. Lipset and Raab, 198–99; PM, 14 September 1937; E. L. Meyer in NYP, 10 March 1937; NYT, 23 August 1937; Drew Pearson in the *New York Mirror,* 15 August 1936; and the *Transcript* (Seattle), 16 October 1936. In his dotage, Smith liked to quote from the *Protocols of the Elders of Zion,* and from similar publications: See *The Cross and the Flag,* xxxiii, 4, 17 and passim. On Smith's anti-Semitism, see Glen Jeansonne, "Combating Anti-Semitism: The Case of Gerald L. K. Smith," in David A. Gerber, ed., *Anti-Semitism in American History* (Urbana, Ill.: Univ of Illinois Press 1986), 155–56.

13. *The New Leader,* 27 February 1937; and A. J. Kahn, "Democracy's Friend," *The New Yorker,* 26 July and 2 August 1947. See also Leo Ribuffo, *The Old Christian Right: The Protestant Far Right From the Great Depression to the Cold War* (Philadelphia: Temple Univ Press, 1983), 123.

14. Robert S. Lynd and Helen Merrell Lynd, *Middletown in Transition* (New York: Harcourt, Brace & Co., 1937), ix–8.

15. Lynd and Lynd, *Middletown in Transition,* 462–63, 497–511.

16. Cited by Lynd and Lynd from Carl Sandburg, *The People, Yes* (New York: Harcourt, Brace, 1936).

17. Willard Range, *Franklin D. Roosevelt's World Order* (Athens, Ga.: Univ of Georgia Press, 1959), 76, looks at Roosevelt's antifascist ideology in the context of his political thought.

18. Michael N. Dobkowski, *The Tarnished Dream: The Basis of American Anti-Semitism* (Westport, Conn.: Greenwood Press, 1979), 121–37, 190–200.

19. Nathan Glazer and Daniel P. Moynihan, *Beyond the Melting Pot* (Cambridge, Mass.: Massachusetts Institute of Technology Press, 1963), 151.

20. Vincent Sheean, *Personal History* (Garden City, N.Y.: Garden City Pub Co. 1936), 14–15.

21. Carey McWilliams, *A Mask for Privilege: Anti-Semitism in America* (Boston: Little, Brown & Co., 1949), 29, 39.

22. "Jews in America," *Fortune* (February 1936); Lipset and Raab, *Politics of Unreason,* 188; and M. M. Tumin, *An Inventory and Appraisal of Research on American Anti-Semitism* (New York: Freeman Books, 1961), 75. On the polls, see G.O. .0068.006 (2/10–15/37) and .0094.006 (8/4–9/37).

23. Irving Kristol, "Liberalism and American Jews," *Commentary* 86, no. 4, makes some interesting comments on the origins of liberalism among American Jews.

24. Furnas, *Stormy Weather,* 561–64.

25. Geoffrey S. Smith, *To Save a Nation: American Countersubversives, the New Deal, and the Coming of World War II* (New York: Basic Books [1973]), 75–76; Strausz-Hupé, *Axis America,* 110–11; and NAM T-81/36/32413-414.

26. *Daily Express,* 17 November 1937; NYHT, 11 and 15 October 1938.

CHAPTER FOURTEEN

1. Sinclair Lewis, *It Can't Happen Here* (New York: Doubleday, Doran & Co., 1935).

2. Lewis was a more cautious interventionist, and less of an Anglophile, than his wife. In fact, he refused to endorse Roosevelt in 1940 until a few days before the election. See Frederick Lewis Allen, *Since Yesterday* (New York: London, Harper & Brothers, 1943), 336; and Mark Schorer, *Sinclair Lewis* (New York: McGraw-Hill, 1961), 600–669.

3. Leo P. Ribuffo, *The Old Christian Right*, 65.

4. Rolf Hoffmann to H. Wagener, NS 42/2 (BA). See also Strong, *Organized Anti-Semitism*, 40–44; Furnas, *Stormy Weather,* 238; and Harold Lavine, *Fifth Column in America* (New York: Doubleday, Doran, 1940), 171.

5. William D. Pelley, "Seven Minutes in Eternity," *The American Magazine* (March 1929): 7ff. Pelley did not adhere to his pledge. Later photographs showing him smoking a rather large cigar.

6. *The Transcript* (Seattle), 19 June 1936; and Schonbach, "Native Fascism," 308.

7. Schlesinger, *Politics of Upheaval*, 80; Rollins, *I Find Treason*, 14.

8. See Pelley as cited by Bennett, *Party of Fear,* 246.

9. NYT, 6 April 1934.

10. Geoffrey S. Smith, *To Save a Nation: American Countersubversives, the New Deal, and the Coming of World War II* (New York: Basic Books [1973]), 140; *The Congress Bulletin*, 19 February 1937; and Strong, *Organized Anti-Semitism*, 155–57. Silver Shirt Pamphlets may be consulted in RG 131/19 (NAS).

11. Smith, *To Save a Nation*, 105; Furnas, *Stormy Wealther,* 239–45; Schlesinger, *Politics of Upheaval*, 81; and Strong, *Organized Anti-Semitism*, 155.

12. *St. Joseph News Press*, 15 July 1938; NYT, 23 July 1938; NYHT, 27 July 1938; and Drew Pearson in the *Washington Herald*, 27 July 1938. See also Strong, *Organized Anti-Semitism*, 71–80, 171; Lipset and Raab, *Politics of Unreason*, 161–62; and Rogge, *The Official German Report*, 190, 214.

13. Gerald B. Winrod, *The United States and Russia in Prophecy and the Red Horse of the Apocalypse* (Wichita, Kans.: Defender Publishers, 1933). Four thousand copies of the pamphlet appeared within three weeks of FDR's first inauguration.

14. These boxes make up the Wilcox Collection at the FDRL, containing material published between 1933 and ca. 1953.

15. NYT, 19 April and 11 May 1938.

16. *News Review* (London), 27 August 1936; and Rollins, *I Find Treason*, 12; and Myron I. Scholnick, "The New Deal and Anti-Semitism in America" (Ph.D. diss. University of Maryland, 1971), 115.

17. Scholnick, *New Deal*, 119.

18. *The New Leader,* 13 March 1937; and Myers, *Bigotry,* 417. See Herman Bernstein, *The History of a Lie: "The Protocols of the Wise Men of Zion"* (New York: J. S. Ogilne Pub. Co., 1921). Disturbed by Henry Ford's dissemination of this lie, Bernstein set out to destroy the *Protocols'* credibility. He proved that the *Protocols* were a Russian forgery, but anti-Semites continue to use them.

19. Strong, *Organized Anti-Semitism,* 83, 97–98.

20. Wyn Craig Wade, *The Fiery Cross: The Ku Klux Klan in America* (New York: Simon & Schuster, 1987), 268.

21. NYT, 27 and 28 May 1936.

22. *Literary Digest,* 16 January 1937; NYT, 18 January 1937; and Wade, *Fiery Cross,* 262.

23. NYT, 3 and 10 March, 4 and 25 April, and 5 and 7 May 1937.

24. *Sunday Referee,* 30 August 1936. See Strong, *Organized Anti-Semitism,* 53–54, 172–75; and Lipset and Raab, *Politics of Unreason,* 167.

CHAPTER FIFTEEN

1. *Christian Free Press,* March 1937, and Geoffrey Smith, *To Save a Nation,* 78.

2. Elizabeth Dilling, *The Roosevelt Red Record and Its Background* (Chicago: by author, 1936).

3. RG 131/39; and *Jewish Chronicle* (London), 18 November 1938.

4. Helmut Heiber, *Goebbels* (New York: Hawthorn Books, 1972).

5. C. P. Oakes to Rolf Hoffmann, 31 October 1933, NS 42/1 (BA); GVDAKV/128 (HI); and Col. Charles L. T. Pichel, quoted by Alton Frye, *Nazi Germany and the American Hemisphere 1933–1941* (New Haven, Yale Univ Press, 1967), 55 (note 12).

6. *Fortune* (February 1936): 79ff.; Strong *Organized Anti-Semitism,* 14; Hanighan, "Foreign Political Movements," 19; Glazer and Moynihan, *Beyond the Melting Pot,* 147–56; Dodd, *Diary,* 145; and NYT, 19 March 1937.

7. Alan Brinkley, *Voices of Protest: Huey Long, Father Coughlin, and the Great Depression* (New York: Knopf, 1982), 199.

8. Ibid., 95, 125.

9. Ibid., 179–87.

10. Furnas, *Stormy Weather,* 227–35; Schlesinger, *Upheaval,* 20–27, 629; Strong, *Organized Anti-Semitism,* 70; Baltzell, *Protestant Establishment,* 231; G. Q. Flynn, *American Catholics and the Roosevelt Presidency 1932–1936* (Lexington, Ky.: Univ of Kentucky Press, 1968), xi, 17–20, 196–98, 234; Charles J. Tull, *Father Coughlin and the New Deal* (Syracuse, N.Y.: Syracuse University Press, 1965), 170; Carlson, *Under Cover,* 238; and Lipset and Raab, *Politics of Unreason,* 182.

11. See the important essay by Seymour M. Lipset, "Three Decades of the Radical Right: Coughlinites, McCarthyites, and Birchers—1962," in

Daniel Bell, ed., *The Radical Right* [*The New American Right*, expanded and updated], (Garden City, N.Y., Doubleday, 1963), 314–26.

12. G.O. .0151.008 (3/10-15/39).

13. RCS .0006.012 (9/38); and Gallup Organization .0121.006 (4/29-54/38).

14. G.O. .0145.008 (1/22-27/39), and .0139.004 (11/24-29/38). The United States took in about 108,000 Jews between 1933 and 1944. The overall annual immigration quota was 153,774. It was never more than fifty-four percent filled. Even the German quota of 25,957 was hardly ever reached. See Richard Breitman and Alan M. Kraut, *American Refugee Policy and European Jewry, 1933–1945* (Bloomington, Ind.: Indiana Univ Press, 1987), 9.

CHAPTER SIXTEEN

1. *Freie Presse* (Cincinnati), 3 January 1936; DW (New York), 19 November 1936; and NYT, 20 March 1938.

2. Bund Command Number 2 (29 October 1936); and Bund Command Number 16 (10 January 1938), RG 131/17. See also Gustavus Myers, *History of Bigotry*, 383–84, 407; Rollins, *Treason*, 61; NYP, 5 March 1937; Hanighan, "Foreign Political Movements," 17; and NYT, 19 July 1937.

3. Bell, *In Hitler's Shadow*, 74–79; Strong, *Organized Anti-Semitism*, 30–31; Diamond, "Zur Typologie," 284; and Bischoff, *Nazi Conquest*, 175–76.

4. The autobiography of W. Schneider of Wiesbaden is useful: See NSDAP Hauptarchiv/531 (HI). A comparison of Bundists with early Nazi Party members reveals some striking similarities. One may refer to Donald M. Douglas, "The Parent Cell: Some Computer Notes on the Composition of the First Nazi Party Group in Munich, 1919–1921," CEH, vol. 10, 55ff.; and Harold J. Gordon, Jr., *Hitler and the Beer Hall Putsch* (Princeton: Princeton Univ Press, 1972), 78–82. See also Diamond, "Zur Typologie," 292–94; Strong, *Organized Anti-Semitism*, 33–34; and Bayor, *Neighbors in Conflict*, 61.

5. Wilhelm Kunze, "Das Blut ist heilig!," RG 131/101 (NAS); quotation from House Report No. 2, Investigation of Un-American Activities and Propaganda, 76th Cong., 1st sess. (Washington, D.C.: 1939), 92.

6. Fritz Kuhn also established Bund Leadership Schools, year-round institutions whose task was to train future cadres. Organizers pressured young people into preparing posters and exhibitions for the German Business League's fairs.

7. Burlingham et al., *The German Reich*, 41; and the *Camp Sutter Pioneer*, no. 6 (March 1940).

8. The Bund's youth magazine, *Junges Volk*, may be consulted in RG 131/104 (NAS).

9. RG 131/145 and 147.

10. NYP, 29 April 1938.

11. A nationalist general had supposedly referred to Franco's "five columns." Four were besieging Madrid, while the putative fifth column was inside the city. At the right moment, it would arise, paralyzing resistance to the nationalist forces.

12. GVDAKV/124 (HI); and NYT, 30 March 1937.

13. *Jewish Post* (Paterson, N.J.), 9 November 1933; *The News* (Chicago), 22 March 1934; Jaeger to Schnuch, 19 January 1935, RG 131/27; NYT, 21 July 1936; NYHT, 21 July 1936; NYT, 15 January 1937; NYT, 24 February 1937; NYWT, 10 March 1937; and *Forward* (New York), 15 August 1937.

14. NYT, 30 August 1937; and RG 131/1 (NAS).

15. NYT, 26 April 1938; NYDN, 26 April 1938. See also Bell, *In Hitler's Shadow*, 22, 68.

16. Burlingham, *German Reich*, 45; and NYT, 26 April and 7 July 1938.

17. *The Nation*, 24 July 1937; and Joseph F. Dinneen, "An American Führer Organizes an Army," *American Magazine*, August 1937.

18. Henry Landau, *The Enemy Within* (New York: G.P. Putnam's Sons, 1937), 300–301.

19. NYT, 8 April, 13 and 30 August, and 7 October 1938; *Jewish News*, 28 May 1937; and Gerson, *Hyphenate*, 114.

20. G.O. .0099.008, 18–23 September 1937 (sample size = 2965).

21. NYT, 15 November 1936, and 27 January, 12 March, 28 and 30 July, 5 August, and 10 September 1937, and 6 January and 3 December 1938; William F. Buckley et al., *The Committee and its Critics* (Chicago: H. Regnery, 1963), 95–99; and August R. Ogden, *The Dies Committee: A Study of the Special House Committee for the Investigation of Un-American Activities, 1938–1944* (Washington, D.C.: The Catholic Univ of America Press, 1945), 33.

22. NYP, 16 August 1934; and Diamond, *Nazi Movement*, 257. The quotation comes from a radio address delivered late in 1937 by Stefan Heym, respected editor of the *Deutsches Volksecho*, on the theme "Nazi Activities in the United States."

23. Leon G. Turrou, *The Nazi Spy Conspiracy in America* (New York: London G. G. Harveys, 1939), 15–19, 33–36, 98–129. See also Trefousse, "Failure," 86–87; and *Look, FBI*, 20.

24. DW, 30 June 1938.

25. RG 131/17 (Bund commands).

CHAPTER SEVENTEEN

1. Count Felix Lückner to Rudolf Hess, 19 September 1933, and Frederick F. Schrader to K. O. Bertling, 21 September 1933, Schmacher/420 (BA).

See also Hans-Adolf Jacobsen, *Nationalsozialistische Aussenpolitik 1933–1938* (Frankfurt am Main: A. Metzner, 1968), 529–30.

2. Jacobsen, *Aussenpolitik*, 532–35; Diamond, *The Nazi Movement*, 131–32, 160, 181 and passim; Luther to Foreign Ministry, 11 February 1934, DGFP, C, vol. 2, 467; and Arthur L. Smith, *The Deutschtum of Nazi Germany and the United States*, 83.

3. NYT, 16 and 31 August and 3 September 1937; Diamond, *The Nazi Movement*, 124 n. 37, 244; and F. Thierfelder, *Die wirtschaftliche Bedeutung des Auslanddeutschtum* (Stuttgart: F. Enke, 1934).

4. Jacobsen, *Aussenpolitik*, 540–41; Leland V. Bell, *In Hitler's Shadow: The Anatomy of American Nazism* (Port Washington, N.Y.: Kennikat Press, 1973) 15, 40; Strong, *Organized Anti-Semitism*, 33; and Diamond, "Zur Typologie," 280–87.

5. AA to Dieckhoff, 30 December 1937, NAM T-120/725/325523-524, and Dieckhoff's memorandum of 7 January 1938, T-120/23/26255-273. The ministry was responding to Dieckhoff's recent complaints.

6. Strong, *Organized Anti-Semitism*, 28; Arthur L. Smith, *The Deutschtum of Nazi Germany and the United States*, 98–99; and affidavit by G. A. Mueller, NG-4365, RG 238 (NA).

7. Jacobsen, *Aussenpolitik*, 545.

8. NYT, 1 March 1938. See also Jacobsen, *Aussenpolitik*, 548–49; Diamond, "Zur Typologie," 286–87, and *Nazi Movement*, 301–3.

9. Smith, *Deutschtum*, 100–101; Fritz Wiedemann interrogation of 10 November 1945, 1435 hrs., and summary of Wiedemann interrogations, 3 October 1945, RG 238 (NA); NAM T-120/725325617-620 (Kuhn-Wiedemann conversation); and Rogge, *Official German Report*, 127.

10. See Jacobsen's comments in Ernst Schulin, ed., *Gedenkschrift für Martin Gohring* (Wiesbaden: F. Steiner, 1968), 363; Burlingham et al., *The German Reich*, 19; Ernst Ritter, *Das deutsche Ausland-Institut in Stuttgart* (Wiesbaden: F. Steiner, 1976), 126; Manfred Funke, ed., *Hitler, Deutschland und die Mächte* (Dusseldorf: Droste, 1977), 145ff.; and Emil Ehrich, *Die Auslands-Organisation der NSDAP* (Berlin, Junker und Dünnhaupt, 1937).

11. Hanighen, "Foreign Political Movements," 10; NYWT, 30 August 1937; and NYP, 2 May 1938.

12. Ehrich, *Auslands-Organisation*, 8–30; and Burlingham et al, *The German Reich*, 27–33.

13. See Bohle's speech of 20 May 1939, in Leipzig, "Das Auslandsdeutschtum in Dienste des Völkerrechts."

14. Facing American interrogators after the war, Bohle lied, and declared, "The United States was absolutely unimportant to me." He lied again when stating, "The Auslandsorganisation had no relations with the Bund organization in the United States. . . ." See Shuster Mission, conversation

with Bohle on 28 July 1945, RG 165 (NA); and IMT interrogation of Bohle, 25 March 1946. See also NAM T-81/8/12388-392.

15. NAM T-81/346/5073590-591; Strölin testimony, IMT, 25 March 1946; Diamond, *Nazi Movement*, 43–45; T-81/352/5081971 and passim; and T-81/370/5105341-345. See also Ritter, *Das Deutsche Ausland-Institut*, 33, 47, 57–61. Csaki was killed in 1943 near Perugia, Italy, in a plane crash.

16. Bohle interrogation, 7 August 1947, 1400–1700 hrs., RG 238 (NA).

17. Smith, *Deutschtum*, 32; Jacobsen, *Aussenpolitik*, 543; Diamond, *Nazi Movement*, 186; Ritter, *Deutsche Ausland-Institut*, 120–25; and NAM T-81/346/5073607.

18. Strölin testimony, IMT, 25 March 1946, 49; and NAM T-81/346/5073587.

19. Smith, *Deutschtum*, 28, 52, 85, 102; and Kipphan, *Deutsche Propaganda*, 51.

20. "Gutachten," in NAM T-81/351/5080109ff.

21. Diamond, *Nazi Movement*, 66–71; Smith, *Deutschtum*, 35; Schonbach, "Native Fascism," 155; and Heinz Kloss, *Brüder vor den Toren des Reiches* (Berlin: P. Hochmuth, 1941), 7.

22. Smith, *Deutschtum*, 38–43; comments by Kloss in NAM T-81/351/5080061; Kipphan, *Deutsche Propaganda*, 51; and Wittke on Kloss, T-81/351/ 5081909-191.

23. See also Strausz-Hupé, *Axis America*, 123.

24. NAM T-81/351/5080043-061.

25. NAM T-81/351/5080177-178; and "Zur Lage in den Vereinigten Staaten," in T-81/351/281-282. See also Arthur L. Smith, *Deutschtum*, 46 n. 62.

26. See also Ritter, *Deutsche Ausland-Institut*, 83; and Rogge, *Official German Report*, 35.

27. Ritter, *Deutsche Ausland-Institut*, 82–89; Diamond, *Nazi Movement*, 196–97; and K. Goetz, *Deutsche Leistung in Amerika* (Berlin: F. Eher Nachf., 1940).

28. Rogge, *Official German Report*, 37–38; Diamond, *Nazi Movement*, 197, 200; and Smith, *Deutschtum*, 46.

29. Diamond, *Nazi Movement*, 49; Jacobsen, *Aussenpolitik*, 222; Rogge, *Official German Report*, 70–71; Burlingham et al., 18 (quoting *Deutsches Volkstum in aller Welt*); Bischoff, *Nazi Conquest*, 4–5; and Hess's Anordnung Nr. 5/39.g. (3 February 1939), NAM T-81/2/12604-606). Hess's former mentor and old friend Professor General (a.D.) Karl Haushofer, was titular head of the league.

30. Poole interrogation of Bohle, NAM T-679/1, 1; T-81/346/5073591; R. E. Murphy et al., *National Socialism* (Washington, D.C.: U.S. Gov't printing office, 1943), 121; Kipphan, *Deutsche Propaganda*, 33–34; and Ritter, *Deutsche Ausland-Institut*, 129.

31. Pichel to Hanfstängl, 15 July 1933, NS 42/2 (BA); and Hoffmann to Colonel Emerson, 13 October 1933, NAM T-81/27/24000. See also the Rolf Hoffmann interrogation summary of 12 July 1945, RG 238; and the War Department summary of the interviews of Hoffmann by Colonel Hale on 20–21 August 1945, RG 338 (NA). Also relevant is Smith, *Deutschtum*, 77.

32. See PWB/SAIC/22 (12 July 1945), RG 238 (NA); and War Department Interrogation Commission, 20–21 August 1945, "Rolf Hoffmann," ibid.

33. F. Peterson to Rolf Hoffmann, 1 June 1938, NS 42/11 (BA).

34. Rogge, *Official German Report*, 187; Schonbach, "Native Fascism," 309; and Hoffmann materials in NS 41/11 (BA).

35. Hoffmann to Edmondson, 30 June 1936, NS 42/5; Hoffmann to Edmondson, 3 February 1939, NS 42/13 (BA); and the testimony of Ulrich von Gienanth, 6 May 1946 [Nürnberg], RG 238 (NA).

36. Grainger to Hitler, 16 September 1931, NS 42/1; Foreign Press Office to Grainger, 22 May 1933, ibid.; Grainger to Hoffmann, 5 June 1933, NS 42/2; Pease to Hoffmann, 26 June 1933, NS 42/1; George Ringrose to Hoffmann, 22 July 1937, NS 22/11. *American Bulletin* to Foreign Press Office, 18 December 1935, NS 42/5; Hoffmann to *American Bulletin*, 2 January 1936; FPO to same, 16 January 1936; Elmhurst materials may be consulted in NS 42/13; and Maude S. DeLand to Hoffmann, 30 October 1936, NS 42/5 (all BA).

37. One correspondent warned Hoffmann against being misled: See G. Guellich to FPO, 12 May 1933, NS 42/1 (BA).

38. Much relevant material appears in NS 42/6 (BA).

39. Major to Hoffmann, 1 June 1936, NS 42/6 (BA).

40. Hoffmann to Snowcroft, 2 August 1938, NS 22/11 (BA).

41. Rogge, *Official German Report*, 109. State Secretary Ernst von Weizsäcker cabled this advice to *chargé d'affaires* Hans Thomsen.

CHAPTER EIGHTEEN

1. Loewenheim, "Diffidence of Power," 28. For a review of recent works dealing with FDR's foreign policy during the previous period, see J. Garry Clifford, "Both Ends of the Telescope: New Perspectives on FDR and American Entry into World War II," DH, vol. 13, no. 2 (Spring 1989), pp. 213–30.

2. See the important reevaluation of Munich by Gerhard Weinberg, "Munich After 50 Years," *Foreign Affairs* 67, no. 1 (Fall 1988): 175–78. Weinberg, however, exaggerates Roosevelt's post-Munich commitment to keeping the U.S. out of the next war.

3. Shirer, *The Collapse of the Third Republic*, 403; and "The Munich Agreement," The House of Commons, 5 October 1938, in Winston S. Chur-

chill, *Blood, Sweat, and Tears* (New York: G. P. Putnam's Sons, 1941), 55–56. See also Maurice Cowling, *The Impact of Hitler: British Politics and British Policy 1933–1940* (London, New York: Cambridge Univ Press 1975), 244.

4. Renner never published the manuscript, which Professor Gerald Stourzh of the University of Vienna called to my attention.

5. Loewenheim, "Diffidence of Power," 35.

6. Brownell and Billings, *So Close*, 225.

7. Dallek, *Franklin D. Roosevelt*, 164–66; James M. Burns, *Roosevelt: The Lion and the Fox* (New York: Harcourt, Brace, 1956), 387; and Wilson dispatches of 14 October (no. 370) and 20 October 1938 (no. 560), PSF/26/27 (Germany, Communications). FDRL; Saint-Quentin to Bonnet, 19 October 1938, DDF, vol. 2, 12, 289–290; and Biddle to Roosevelt, 5 November 1938, second series FDRFA, 2, vol. 12, 21–24.

8. German ambassador in Chile to AA, March 8, 1938, DGFP, D, vol. 5, 821–22; ambassador in Brazil to AA, March 30, 1938, ibid., 824–27; minister in Mexico to AA, 8 April 1938, ibid., 827–29; ambassador in Uruguay to AA, 21 April 1938, ibid., 830–32ff. ambassador in Chile to AA, 7 May 1938, ibid., 834–37; Memorandum of the meeting in Montevideo of the Chiefs of Mission in Argentina, Brazil, Chile, and Uruguay, 28–29 July 1938, ibid., 863–67; ambassador in Brazil to AA, 25 October 1938, ibid., 880–82ff.; minister in Peru to AA, 28 December 1938, ibid., 885–86ff.; NG-189 (RG 238); and John M. Blum, *From the Morgenthau Diaries*, vol. 2 [*Years of Urgency 1938–1941*], 50. See also McKale, *The Swastika Outside Germany* (Kent, O.: Kent State Univ. Press, 1977), 146–47, and Macdonald, *Hitler*, 96–98, 118; Strausz-Hupé, *Axis America*, 174–75. Weinberg, *The Foreign Policy of Hitler's Germany*, 255–60. The Venezuelan government had outlawed the Nazi party in 1936, but it survived underground, with the help of the Germany embassy. See NG-189 (13 June 1939, "Sitzungsbericht"), RG 238 (NA).

9. Macdonald, *Hitler*, 32–57, 118; and Dodd, *Diary*, 362–63.

10. Edward Hallett Carr, *The Twenty Years' Crisis* (New York: Harper & Row, 1964), 235.

11. Mark G. Toulouse, *The Transformation of John Foster Dulles: From Prophet of Realism to Priest of Nationalism* (Macon, Ga.: Mercer University Press, 1985), 98–104 and passim.

12. Nancy Lisagor and Frank Lipsius, *A Law Unto Itself: The Untold Story of the Law Firm of Sullivan & Cromwell* (New York: Morrow, 1988), 119–33.

13. Dodd, *Diary*, 304; Leonard Mosley, *Dulles: A Biography of Eleanor, Allen, and John Foster Dulles and Their Family Network* (New York: Dial Press, 1978), 88–97; and John Foster Dulles, *War, Peace, and Change* (New York: London, Harper & Brothers, 1939), especially ix, 47–52, 71, 83, 133–66.

14. Typical of Landon's political self-image was his oft-repeated campaign phrase "I believe that a man can be a liberal without being a spendthrift."

15. See Herbert Hoover, "America and the World Crisis," a speech delivered on 26 October 1938; "President Roosevelt's New Foreign Policies," delivered on 1 February 1939; "Foreign Policies Today," *Liberty Magazine*, 15 April 1939; and "Shall We Send Our Youth to War?," *American Magazine*, 15 July 1939. All of these pieces were reprinted in Herbert Hoover, *Addresses Upon the American Road 1933–1938* (New York: Charles Scribner's Sons, 1938); *Further Addresses Upon the American Road 1938–1940* (New York: C. Scribner's Sons, 1940); and *Addresses Upon the American Road, 1940–1941* (New York: C. Scribner's Sons, 1941).

16. Roosevelt to Col. and Mrs. Charles A. Lindbergh, 16 December 1933, PPF/1080 (FDRL).

17. Charles A. Lindbergh, Jr., *The Wartime Journals of Charles A. Lindbergh* (New York: Harcourt Brace Jovanovich, 1970), 10–11, 25, 68–75, 115, 155, 156.

18. Leonard Mosley, *Lindbergh* (Garden City, N.Y.: Doubleday, 1976), pp. 14–15, 99, 243, and 250; Furnas, *Stormy Weather,* pp. 266–271; Adler, *The Isolationist Impulse*, p. 305; and Lindbergh, *Wartime Journals*, 103, 446.

19. Lindbergh, *Wartime Journals*, 115, 131, 135; Mosley, *Lindbergh*, 252.

20. FDR to Chief of Staff and Chief of Operations, 10 February 1938, PSF/Navy (originally in OF 92), FDRL. See also David Kahn, "U.S. Views of Germany and Japan," in Ernest R. May, ed., *Knowing One's Enemies: Intelligence Assessment Before the Two World Wars* (Princeton: Princeton University Press, 1984), 491.

21. Lindbergh, *Wartime Journals*, 329, 478–81, 513; NYT, 30 May 1941; FDR to Lindbergh, 16 December 1933, PPF/1080 (FDRL); Adler, *Isolationist Impulse*, 304; MG, 19 December 1938; and Mosley, *Lindbergh*, 283. See also Harold L. Ickes, *The Secret Diary of Harold L. Ickes*, 3 vols. (New York: Simon & Schuster, 1953–1954), vol. 11–12.

22. Mosley, *Lindbergh*, 289; Lindbergh, *Wartime Journals*, 400.

23. Ian Colvin, *The Chamberlain Cabinet* (New York: Taplinger Pub. Co., 1971), 155.

24. Address by Samuel Flagg Bemis to the Foreign Policy Association, 18 March 1939, Borah Papers, "Neutrality Act Revision"/1939 (LOCMD); and Bemis to Senator William E. Borah, 18 April 1939 (LOCMD).

CHAPTER NINETEEN

1. Statement by Roosevelt, 15 November 1938, FDRFA, second series, vol. 12, 83.

2. London *Times*, 16 November 1938.

3. Lindsay to Halifax, 18 November 1938, DBFP, vol. 3, 279.

4. Bonnet to Saint-Quentin, 27 November 1938, DDF, vol. 2, 12, 813–15. Bonnet and Saint-Quentin cited American attitudes as justifications for Munich, as well as for the recently concluded Franco-German consultation agreement. In a dispatch to Bonnet dated 10 December 1938, Saint-Quentin, the ambassador to Washington, observed that Americans accepted the right of Europeans to act as they pleased, but reserved to themselves the right to praise or criticize these actions (or inactions). See DDF, II, 13, doc. 86.

5. G.O., .0139.002 (11/24-29/38).

6. John Harvey, ed., *The Diplomatic Diaries of Oliver Harvey,* 219 (entry of 15 November 1938). Supporters of appeasement, such as British ambassador to Berlin Nevile Henderson, believed that pro-Jewish overreaction to the recent pogroms was undermining Chamberlain's foreign policy.

7. John Cudahy to Roosevelt, 21 January 1939, FDRFA, second series, vol. 13, 167–68.

8. G.O., .0139.003 (11/24-29/38).

9. Bailey, *Man in the Street,* 25; Dodd, *Diary,* 5, 88–89, 131; Weinberg, vol. 1, *The Foreign Policy of Hitler's Germany* 149 n. 75; PPF/19 of the FDRL contains correspondence relevant to the Jewish homeland issue; see also Roosevelt, *Public Papers, 1937 Volume,* 66–67.

10. Biddle to Roosevelt, 10 November 1938, FDRFA, second series, vol. 12, 41–43.

11. PSF/Confidential/Germany/39/Box 44 (FDRL). Herschel Johnson's memorandum was passed on to Sumner Welles, who forwarded it to Roosevelt. Ironically, the British report attributed much of Nazi sadism to homosexuality in German culture.

12. OF 198-a (Misc.) (FDRL); Welles to FDR, 14 February 1939, PSF/ Germany/Welles (FDRL). Hooker, *Moffat Papers,* 223; See Wilbur J. Carr to State, 1 February 1939, and George F. Kennan to State, 17 February 1939 in George F. Kennan, *From Prague After Munich: Diplomatic Papers 1938–1940* (Princeton: Princeton Univ. Press, 1968), 39–46. See also Arthur D. Morse, *While Six Million Died* (New York: Random House, 1968), 256; and Robert E. Herzstein, "USA: Bystander to Genocide," *Jewish Currents,* March, 1969.

13. VB, 20 August and 31 December 1938, 6 and 8 January 1939; FZ, 20 August 1938; *Rheinische Landeszeitung,* 18 November 1938, and 6 January and 2 February 1939; "German Reply . . ." (31 December 1938), RG 131/215 (NAS); Hans Trefousse, *Germany and American Neutrality 1939– 1941* (New York: Bookman Associates, 1951), 28; *Frankfurter Tageszeitung,* 24 December 1938; Strausz-Hupé, *Axis America,* 79, 82, 113; and *Westdeutscher Beobachter,* 2 February 1939.

14. David S. Wyman, *The Abandonment of the Jews: America and the Holocaust,*

1941–1945 (New York: Pantheon Books, 1984), 8. On American anti-Semitism at this time, see Deborah E. Lipstadt, *Beyond Belief,* 122–28; and Sheldon Neuringer, "Franklin D. Roosevelt and Refuge for Victims of Nazism, 1933–1941," in Rosenbaum and Bartelme, 85ff.

15. Biddle 1937–1941, and Germany 1933–1938 in PSF/34/44 (FDRL); FDR to Welles, PPF/19 (FDRL); and NG-1414, RG 238 (NA). David Wyman has written, "Franklin Roosevelt's indifference to so momentous an historical event as the systematic annihilation of European Jewry emerges as the worst failure of his presidency." (*Abandonment of the Jews,* xv).

16. FDR to Hull, October 21, 1938, with the enclosure of Biddle's message of October 6, in PSF/44 (FDRL).

17. Roosevelt, *Public Papers, 1938,* 563–65; and Dallek, *Franklin D. Roosevelt,* 173.

18. A. C. Paz and G. Ferrari, *Argentina's Foreign Policy, 1930–1962* (Notre Dame: Univ of Notre Dame Press, 1966), 44–59; and Blum, *Morgenthau Diaries,* vol. 2, 51.

19. Blum, *Morgenthau Diaries,* vol. 2, 54–55.

20. Harvey, *Diplomatic Diaries,* 233 (25 December 1938).

21. Biddle to Roosevelt, 12 January 1939, in FDRFA, second series, vol. 13, 250–51; and Biddle to Roosevelt, 10 January 1939, ibid., 252–54.

22. Freeman to McIntyre, 28 December 1938, FDRFA, second series, vol. 12, 360.

23. Laski to Roosevelt, 5 January 1939, FDRFA, 2, vol. 13, 41.

24. On 10 December, for example, the Germans informed Great Britain that they intended to achieve parity in "submarine tonnage." This notification was necessary under Article 2(f) of the 1935 Anglo-German Naval Treaty. See Halifax to Phipps, 28 December 1938, DBFP, 3, vol. 3, 452.

25. Message to Congress, 4 January 1939, ibid., 1ff.

26. Harvey, *Diplomatic Diaries,* 236 (4 January 1939). Many Americans mistrusted Roosevelt's aggressive anti-Nazism. Hugh J. Gaffney wrote to the White House, "wondering why he [Roosevelt] is so busy attacking the Germans." See Gaffney to Grace F. Tully, 16 January 1939, FDRFA, second series, vol. 13, 119, and Tully to Gaffney, 20 January 1939, ibid., 164.

27. See Hugh G. Gallagher, *FDR's Splendid Deception* (New York: Dodd, Mead, 1985); and James A. Bishop, *FDR's Last Year, April 1944–April 1945* (New York: W. Morrow, 1974).

28. Schulzinger, *Wise Men,* 59.

29. Foreign diplomats sometimes understood that Roosevelt's political caution did not necessarily imply a lack of boldness in foreign policy. This point

has sometimes eluded Mr. Roosevelt's biographers and critics. See Mallet to Halifax, 27 January 1939, DBFP, 3, vol. 4, 27–29.

30. FDRPC, 13:63; William W. Kaufmann, "Two American Ambassadors," in Gordon A. Craig and Felix Gilbert, *The Diplomats, 1919–1939* (Princeton: Princeton Univ Press, 1953), 649ff.; and James M. Burns, *Roosevelt: The Lion and the Fox* (New York: Harcourt, Brace, 1956), 389.

CHAPTER TWENTY

1. Potocki to Warsaw, 21 November 1938, *Polnische Dokumente zur Vorgeschichte des Krieges* (Berlin: Zentral verlag der NSDAP. F. Eher Nachf., 1940), 8.
2. Potocki to Warsaw, ibid., 17–18.
3. Lukasiewicz to Warsaw, n.d., ibid., 23–24. The cable was probably dispatched during the first week of February 1939. See Waclaw Jedrzejewicz, ed. *Diplomat in Paris 1936–1939: Papers and Memoirs of Juliusz Lukasiewicz, Ambassador of Poland* (New York: Columbia University Press, 1970), 168–70.
4. Saint-Quentin to Bonnet, 12 January 1939, DDF, II, 13, Document 347; *Rheinische Landeszeitung*, 6 January 1939, and VB, 8 January 1939.
5. Conference with the Senate Military Affairs Committee, Executive Offices of the White House, 31 January 1939, 12:45 P.M., in FDRFA, 2, vol. 13, 197–204.
6. Halifax to Mallet, 24 January 1939, DBFP, vol. 4, 4–6. "It would," Halifax noted, "of course be a great help . . . if the President had any further suggestion to make." See also Colvin, *The Chamberlain Cabinet*, 182.
7. Halifax to Henderson, 22 February, 1939, DBFP, vol. 4, 138–39. Mussolini paid more attention to the United States after FDR began to call for rearmament. See Phillips to Roosevelt, 10 February 1939, FDRFA, second series, vol. 13, 286.
8. Roosevelt, *Public Papers, 1938 volume*, 613–20; FDRPC, 13: 115, 138–43, 317, 324; and Roosevelt, *Public Papers, 1939 Volume*, 104–4.
9. Bullitt, *For the President*, 307–17; Jedrzejewicz, *Diplomat in Paris*, 168–70; and Harvey, *Diplomatic Diaries*, 249 (6 February 1939); and Roosevelt to Roger B. Merriman, 15 February 1939, FDRFA, second series, vol. 13, 324.
10. Kennedy to Roosevelt, 3 March 1939, FDRFA, second series, vol. 14, 4–25; Halifax to Lindsay, 17 March 1939, DBFP, vol. 4, 364–65, and 24 March, 1939, ibid., 499. See also Kaufmann, "Two American Ambassadors," in Craig and Gilbert, *The Diplomats*, vol. 2, 658–67. Michael R. Beschloss, *Kennedy and Roosevelt: The Uneasy Alliance* (New York: Norton 1980), 182–94, is particularly useful.

11. George F. Kennan, Report of 29 March 1939, in *From Prague*, 94, and personal letter of 30 March 1939, ibid., 104.

12. See Pell to Roosevelt, 15 March 1939, FDRFA, second series, vol. 14, 88–89; Bullitt to Hull, 17 March 1939, FRUS, 1939, vol. 1, 48–49; and Bullitt to Roosevelt, 23 March 1939, in *For the President*, 332–34; Hooker, *Moffat Papers*, 232–33; Lukasiewicz to Foreign Ministry, 29 March 1939, in *Diplomat in Paris*, 180–83; and Kennedy to Hull, 31 March 1939, FRUS, 1939, vol. 1, 105–6. On 15 March 1939, Herbert C. Pell, minister to Portugal, encouraged FDR by informing him of "[t]he efficacy of the recent American activity [which is] best proven by the hostile clamor it has aroused."

13. Dallek, *Franklin D. Roosevelt*, 23, 89, 152; and Roosevelt, *Public Papers, 1939 Volume*, 192.

14. Kennedy to Hull, 5 April 1939, FRUS, 1939, vol. 1, 112–13; Bullitt to Hull, 7 April 1939, ibid., 117–18; 9 April 1939 ibid., 120–21; and 12 April 1939, ibid., 128. Early in April, Bullitt conferred with Polish Foreign Minister Colonel Josef Beck. It was clear to the American that Beck, who was hostile to his French ally, hoped to mollify Hitler. Ambassadors Biddle and Bullitt thereafter redoubled their efforts to strengthen the Franco-Polish alliance.

15. Geist to Hull, 6 April 1939, FRUS, 1939, vol. 1, 115–16.

16. Geist to Hull, ibid.

17. Roosevelt and the State Department continued to receive disturbing reports from Berlin, predicting further German expansion. See, for example, Geist to Hull, 3 April 1939, FRUS, 1939, vol. 1, 108–9.

18. Biddle to Hull, April 24, 1939, FRUS, 1939, vol. 1, 173–74.

19. Bullitt to Hull, 10 April 1939, FRUS, 1939, vol. 1, 123.

20. Text of a communiqué issued to the press in the names of the prime minister and Lord Halifax, 15 April 1939, DBFP, vol. 5, 218. See Harvey, *Diplomatic Diaries*, 280 (16 April 1939); and Kennedy to Hull, 22 April 1939, FRUS, 1939, vol. 1, 172–73. Relevant here is John C. Walter, "Franklin D. Roosevelt and Naval Rearmament, 1932–1938," in Herbert D. Rosenbaum and Elizabeth Bartelme, *Franklin D. Roosevelt: The Man, the Myth, the Era, 1882–1945*, 203–18.

21. FDRPC, 13:284-323; Phipps to Halifax, 20 April 1939, DBFP, 3, vol. 5, 251, and Sir G. Ogilvie-Forbes to Halifax, 23 April 1939, ibid, 286–87. One has to marvel at Roosevelt's nerve. The leader of a nation with a tiny army wanted the British Empire to introduce conscription!

22. David L. Porter, *The Seventy-Sixth Congress and World War II 1939–1940* (Columbia, Mo.: Univ of Missouri Press, 1979), 19–21.

23. Gary D. Best, *Herbert Hoover: The Postpresidential Years 1933–1964* [Vol. 1, *1933–1945*], (Stanford, Cal.: Hoover Institution Press, 1983), 126.

24. Phipps to Halifax, 5 May 1939, DBFP, vol. 5, 438.
25. Biddle to Hull, 28 April 1939, FRUS, 1939, vol. 1, 176–77.
26. Thomsen to AA, 17 May 1939, DGFP, D, vol. 6, 526ff.

CHAPTER TWENTY-ONE

1. Cited by McWilliams, *Mask for Privilege*, 45. A ditty was soon making the rounds among Jews on New York's Lower East Side:
Holy Moses, King of Jews
Wipes his ass with the *Daily News* . . .
See also Frederick L. Allen, *Since Yesterday: The Nineteen-Thirties in America, September 3, 1929–September 3, 1939* (New York: London, Harper & Brothers), 329. *Catholic Herald* (U.K.), 9 December 1938; Strong, *Organized Anti-Semitism*, 144–46; and the Pelley file, YIVO Archives.
2. Charles H. Stember et al., *Jews in the Mind of America* (New York: Basic Books [1966]), 121–31.
3. Ibid., 54–69.
4. RG 131/139 (NA); and Rogge, *Official German Report*, 45.
5. After 1970, antiliberals were more circumspect, and the main object of their hostility was a new medium, television. Attacks on the media by the far right now contained the code word "liberal elitist media," but it means the "Jewish-controlled" media, particularly television.
6. Bob Thomas, *Winchell* (Garden City, N.Y.: Doubleday, 1971), 98–103, 164–75; Herman Klurfeld, *Winchell: His Life and Times* (New York: Praeger 1976), 74; and Brinkley, *Washington Goes to War,* 221–22.
7. For some valuable film clips on Coughlin, see ETV "The Radio Priest," aired in 1988.
8. Lipstadt, *Beyond Belief,* 127.
9. Wiedemann to Weizsäcker, 27 March 1939, DGFP, D, vol. 6, 140–42; and Lipski to Beck, 19 November 1938, in Waclaw Jedrzejewicz, *Diplomat in Berlin: Papers and Memoirs of Jozef Lipski, Ambassador of Poland* (New York: Columbia University Press, 1968), 465–66.
10. Tull, *Father Coughlin*, 207, 224–28; SJ, 26 May 1941; and Lavine, *Fifth Column*, 97–99.
11. RG 131/84 (NA).
12. RG 131/139 (NA); Rollins, *I Find Treason*, 140; Smythe to Hoffmann, 1 August 1939, NS 42/19 (BA).
13. UP dispatch of 30 September 1938 (WA125).
14. *The Indianapolis News*, 29 December 1938.
15. *Look*, 28 March 1939.
16. *Philadelphia Record*, 29 March 1939.
17. *Daily Worker,* 9 January 1939.
18. Moseley to Blake, 30 March 1939 (Moseley/10/Papers, LOCMD). See

also Robert E. Herzstein, "U.S. Inaction in Refugee Crisis," *Jewish Currents*, July–August 1970.

19. Borah Papers/Subject Files/Frankfurter Nomination (LOCMD).

20. NYHT, 14 May 1938; DW, 8 January 1939; NYP, 5 June 1939; Martin Dies, *Martin Dies' Story* (New York: Bookmailer, 1963), 274; Rogge, *Official German Report*, 287; HUAC, 76th Cong., 1st sess., 3473; Myers, *Bigotry*, 416; WB, 4 August 1938; *6 Uhr Abendblatt* (Wien), 15 December 1938; WB, 16 December 1938; and *Kleine Zeitung* (Graz), 30 March 1939.

21. *New York Times*, 1 June 1939.

22. Moseley to *New York World-Telegram*, 7 June 1939 (Moseley Papers/5/ Letter 1916–1940, LOCMD). Lindbergh's tragic experience may have frightened Moseley. There is a second explanation for the general's obsession with kidnapping: Lindbergh was now emerging as a powerful and respected analyst of European affairs.

23. Moseley to International News Service, 13 June 1939, ibid.

24. *Atlanta Constitution*, 11 June 1939.

25. Moseley to Hoover, 18 December 1942, and Hoover to Moseley, 20 December, 1942 (Moseley Papers/10/Scrapbook, 230–34, LOCMD).

26. Moseley to Baruch, 23 August 1942 (Moseley Papers/10/Scrapbook, 21–22, LOCMD).

CHAPTER TWENTY-TWO

1. In the printed version of these remarks, "Rosenfeld" became Roosevelt.

2. Greenbaum was fined twenty-five dollars. He justified his act by accusing Kuhn of incitement to murder. For Thompson's scathing but somewhat verbose account of the rally, see "On the Record," NYHT, 23 February 1939.

3. NYT, 6 January 1938.

4. Luebke in Higham, *Ethnic Leadership*, 84–85 and passim; Feiler, *America Seen Through German Eyes*, 229; and NYT, 22 February 1939.

5. O'Connor, *German-Americans*, 450; NYT, 26 February 1939; Thomsen to AA, 26 May 1939; and Hoffmann to Chandler, 26 May 1939, NAM T-81/25/22437.

6. Diamond, *Nazi Movement*, 352; RLZ, 22 February 1939; *Rheinisch-Westfälische Zeitung*, 4 January 1939; A. Smith, *Deutschtum*, 107–31; R 57neu/1178 (BA); and *Aussendeutscher Wochenspiegel*, 7 July 1940, R 57neu/5a (BA).

7. RG 131/156 (NA); NYT, 1 May 1939.

8. Diamond, *The Nazi Movement*, 233; RG 131/73 (4 reels containing recordings of a Bund rally).

9. Rollins, *I Find Treason*, 141–44; and Wade, *The Fiery Cross*, 271–72.

10. Vosniatsky later conspired to give American military secrets to the Axis

powers. On his political activities, see Erwin Oberländer, "The All-Russian Fascist Party," in Walter Laqueur and George L. Mosse, eds., *International Fascism 1920–1945* (New York: Harper & Row, 1966), 162–64.

11. RG 131/139 (NA).

12. Bell, *In Hitler's Shadow*, 85; *Daily Express*, 22 February 1939; Carlson, *Under Cover*, 27; NYDN, 20–23 February 1939; NYT, 20–23 February 1939; RG 131/71 (NA, tapes of Bund rallies); "Free America! Six Addresses . . ." (New York: 1939), in RG 131/38 (NA); O'Connor, *German-Americans*, 441; ND no. 2-4/39, in RG 131/104 (NA); G. Smith, *To Save a Nation*, 97; and Klurfeld, *Winchell*, 70.

13. RG 131/137 (NA); Diamond, *Nazi Movement*, 334; NYT, 30 May 1938 and 26 November 1939; and RG 131/194 (NA).

14. Leon G. Turrou, *The Nazi Spy Conspiracy in America*, 56, 191; and *The Hour*, no. 10 (9 September 1939).

15. Edward G. Robinson to Hal Wallis, 20 October 1938, cited by Rudy Behlmer, ed., *Inside Warner Brothers 1935–1951* [New York: Viking Press, 1985], 82.

16. Bernard F. Dick, *The Star-Spangled Screen: The American World War II Film* (Lexington, Ky.: Univ Press of Kentucky, 1985), 52–61; J. Morella et al., *The Films of World War II* (Secaucus, N.J.: Citadel Press, 1973), 27–28; Roger Manvell, *The Films and the Second World War* (South Brunswick, N.J., A. S. Barnes, 1974), 31; and the *Motion Picture Herald*, 29 April 1939.

17. HUAC, 76th Congress, 6, 3705ff., 7, "German-American Bund," and 10, 6043ff. See also NYT, 26 September 1939.

18. NYT, 19 August 1939.

19. RG 131/137 (NA); Diamond, *Nazi Movement*, 334; NYT, 26 November 1939, 30 May 1938, and 5 October 1940; and RG 131/194 (NA).

20. NYT, 6 May and 3 December 1938; NYT, 28 March 21, April and 6 July 1939. New Jersey Supreme Court, *State of N.J. vs. A. Kapprott et al.*, R.S. 2:1578-5,6 (Brief for plaintiffs in error, p. 53); see the legal files in RG 131/25 (NA).

21. On Dewey's prosecutorial techniques, see Richard N. Smith, *Thomas E. Dewey and His Times* (New York: Simon & Schuster, 1984), 242–316.

22. G. Smith, *To Save a Nation*, 153; O'Connor, *German-Americans*, 452; NYT, 28 May 1939; Bund Command Number 22 (1 June 1939), in RG 131/17; NYT, 30 November 1939 and 7 April 1940; Diamond, *Nazi Movement*, 314, 333; and Lavine, *Fifth Column*, 161.

CHAPTER TWENTY-THREE

1. Geist to Hull, 3 May 1939, FRUS, 1939, vol. 1, 178–79.
2. Phillips to Hull, 12 May 1939, FRUS, 1939, vol. 1, 168.

3. Philip V. Cannistraro et al., eds., *Poland and the Coming of the Second World War: The Diplomatic Papers of A. J. Biddle, Jr. United States Ambassador to Poland 1937–1939* (Columbus, Ohio: Ohio State University, 1983). This work contains an account of Biddle's mission, his own recollections, and some relevant documentation.

4. In May, Biddle had informed Roosevelt of Britain's attachment to the discredited appeasement policy; this had ominous implications for the future of the antiaggressor front. See Biddle to FDR, 20 May 1939. On 6 June 1939, FDR wrote a "Dear Tony" note (1667), in which he expressed alarm about imminent German aggression.

5. Berle, *Navigating the Rapids*, 225–26 (6 June 1939).

6. Bullitt to Hull, 10 May 1939, FRUS, 1939, vol. 1, 184–85.

7. FDRPC 13: 284ff.; and Roosevelt, *Public Papers, 1939 vol.*, 366ff. (West Point address, 12 June 1939).

8. John W. Wheeler-Bennett, *King George VI: His Life and Reign* (New York: St. Martin's Press, 1958), 371ff.

9. Ibid., 386–95.

10. Benjamin D. Rhodes, "The British Royal Visit of 1939 and the 'Psychological Approach' to the United States," DH 2, no. 2:197ff; Bendiner, *Just Around the Corner*, 219, Allen, *Since Yesterday*, 342; and Wheeler-Bennett, *King George VI*, 390–95.

11. Helen S. Hitchcock to Roosevelt, 7 July 1939, FDRFA, second series, XVI, 61.

12. Wilson to Hull, 24 June 1939, FRUS, 1939, vol. 1, 193–94.

13. Biddle to Hull, 12 July 1939, FRUS, 1939, vol. 1, 197–98.

14. Dallek, *Franklin D. Roosevelt*, 184, 191; Bullitt, *For the President*, 318; John M. Haight, Jr., *American Aid to France 1938–1940* (New York: Atheneum 1970), 126–29; and Robert Sherwood, *Roosevelt and Hopkins* (New York: Harper & Brothers, 1948), 133. On the Senate and revision of the 1937 Neutrality Act, see Thomas N. Guinsburg, *The Pursuit of Isolationism in the United States Senate From Versailles to Pearl Harbor* (New York: Garland 1982), 197–215. On the political and ethnic considerations motivating congressmen, see David L. Porter, *The Seventy-Sixth Congress and World War II*, chap. 3.

15. Patrick J. Hearden, *Roosevelt Confronts Hitler: America's Entry Into World War II* (DeKalb, Ill.: Northern Illinois Univ Press, 1987), 133; and Hull, *Memoirs*, vol. 1, 656. On FDR's calculations regarding Soviet foreign policy, see Edward M. Bennett, *Franklin D. Roosevelt and the Search for Security: American-Soviet Relations 1933–1939* (Wilmington, Del.: Scholarly Resources 1985), 159ff.

16. Biddle to Hull, 3 April 1939, FRUS, 1939, vol. 1, 106–7; Phipps to Halifax, 6 June 1939, DBFP, vol. 5, 775–76; and Davies's urgent message

to Roosevelt, 8 June 1939, FDRFA, second series, vol. 15, 237–38. Sir Nevile Henderson, an appeaser to the end, believed that Hitler "wishes to come out for peace." This was Chamberlain's view as well. See Henderson to Halifax, 10 August 1939, DBFP, vol. 6, 657.

17. Bullitt to Hull, 3 August 1939, FRUS, 1939, vol. 1, 202–3; and Memorandum of Conversation by Welles, 9 August 1939, ibid., 206–8.
18. See the *Daily Express*, 1 August 1939.
19. Biddle to Hull, 3 August 1939, FRUS, 1939, vol. 1, 331–32, and 15 August 1939, ibid., 215; and Bullitt to Hull, 15 August 1939, ibid., 215–16.
20. Minute by Mr. Troutbeck, 12 August 1939, DBFP, 3, vol. 6, 678–79.
21. Campbell to Halifax, 19 August 1939, DBFP, vol. 7, 78–79.
22. Bullitt to Hull, 18 August 1939, FRUS, vol. 1, 225–26; 19 August 1939, ibid., 226–27; and 19 August 1939, ibid., 227–28; and Johnson to Hull, 21 August 1939, ibid., 230–32.
23. Hitler's delivered his speech before the Reichstag on 28 April 1939. See Max Domarus, *Hitler Reden und Proklamationen 1932–1945: Kommentiert von einem deutschen Zeitgenossen*, vol. 2, i, 1164ff.
24. Small Collections/Masonic Activities (FDRL).
25. "Der Traum von Washington," FT, 22 April 1939. In a speech delivered on 30 January 1939, Hitler had threatened the Jews with destruction if international Jewry unleashed another war among the "Aryan peoples." See also Bräuer to AA, 16 April 1939, GFMM Serial 57, frame 38921ff. (Bonn); and DDPK, Nr. 73, p. 1ff. (16 April 1939).
26. Dieckhoff memorandum of 29 July 1940, DGFP, D, vol. 10, 350ff.
27. Thomsen to Foreign Ministry, DGFP, D, vol. 6, 130, 272. See also Martha Dodd, *My Years in Germany* (London: V. Gollancz, 1939), 216–18; William E. Dodd, *Diary*, 101–2, 157, 204, 386–87; and Arnold A. Offner, *American Appeasement: United States Foreign Policy and Germany, 1933–1938* (Cambridge, Mass.: Belknap Press of Harvard Univ Press, 1969), 235.
28. M. Dodd, *My Years*, 60–62; and Thomsen to AA, 27 March 1939, DGFP, D, vol. 6, 129–34.
29. Lipski to Beck, 7 February 1939, in Jedrzejewicz, *Diplomat in Berlin 1933–1939*, 487–94.
30. IMT, Ribbentrop interrogation, 30 August 1945 (P.M.), 2; and Joachim von Ribbentrop, *Zwischen London und Moskau* (Leoni am Starnberger See: Druffel-Verlag 1953), 251. See also Erich H. Boehm, "Policy-Making of the Nazi Government: A Study in the Determination of Decisions of State" (Ph.D. diss., Yale University, 1952), 415; Telford Taylor, *The Breaking Wave* (New York: Simon & Schuster, 1967), 30; UPI dispatch from Bonn, West Germany, 23 November 1978.
31. Schuster Mission, Ribbentrop interrogation, 10–16, RG 238 (NA); and IMT, Ribbentrop interrogation, 31 August 1945 (P.M.), 24.

32. Lipski to Beck, in Jedrzejewicz, *Diplomat in Berlin*, 540–43 (June 28, 1939); and Weizsäcker to Thomsen, 4 July 1939, NG-2024, RG 238 (NA).

33. Dieckhoff memorandum of 29 July 1940, DGFP, D, vol. 10, 350–62.

34. Henderson to Halifax, 22 August 1939, DBFP, vol. 7, 118, and Halifax to Campbell, citing Chamberlain, 23 August 1939, ibid., 148. The hope that Hitler could be satisfied short of war continued to inspire Chamberlain. See Halifax to Sir P. Loraine, 26 August 1939, ibid., 267. On 23 August, Kennedy had informed Hull of British knowledge of a provision "providing for the fourth division of Poland." See Kennedy to Hull, 23 August 1939, FRUS, 1939, vol. 1, 339–42; Kennedy to Hull, 23 August 1939, FRUS, 1939, vol. 1, 355–56; and Bullitt to Hull, 23 August 1939, FRUS, 1939, vol. 1, 357–58. For a good overview of British and American policy toward Germany, see C. A. MacDonald, *The United States, Britain and Appeasement, 1936–1939* (New York: St. Martin's Press, 1981), chaps. 11–12.

35. Relevant here are Phipps to Halifax, 24 August 1939, DBFP, vol. 7, 202–3; and Phipps to Halifax, 25 August 1939, DBFP, vol. 7, 245.

36. Kirk to Hull, 24 August 1939, FRUS, 1939, vol. 1, 358–60.

37. Bullitt to Roosevelt, 25 August 1939, in ibid., 324.

38. Hull, *Memoirs*, vol. 1, 662.

39. Hooker, *Moffat Papers*, 253; Roosevelt to Hitler, 24 August 1939, in FDRFA, second series, vol. 16, 281–82; and Roosevelt to Hitler, 25 August 1939, in ibid., 320–21. Ambassador Kennedy reported that the British wanted the Americans to put pressure on the Poles. After their betrayal of the Czechs, they could scarcely do so themselves, at least not overtly.

40. Bullitt to Roosevelt, August 26, 1939, in ibid., 344.

41. Brownell and Billings, *So Close*, 250.

42. Lindsay to Halifax, 26 August 1939 (nos. 317 and 318), DBFP, vol. 7, 262.

43. Kennedy to Hull, 30 August 1939, FRUS, 1939, vol. 1, 386–87; Kennedy to Hull, 30 August 1939, ibid., 390–92; and Biddle to Hull, 30 August 1939, ibid., 388.

44. Lothian to Halifax, 31 August 1939, DBFP, vol. 7, 428–29.

45. Lothian to Halifax, 31 August 1939, DBFP, vol. 7.

46. Rep. John W. Boehme, Jr., to Roosevelt, 30 August 1939, FDRFA, second series, vol. 16, 392.

47. Bullitt to Hull, 31 August 1939, FRUS, 1939, vol. 1, 398–99.

48. Bullitt to Hull, 2 September 1939, FRUS, 1939, vol. 1, 408–10.

49. PSF/43 (FDRL); and Roosevelt, *Public Papers, 1939 Volume*, 449–50.

50. PSF Confidential/France/Box 25. No other documents in this series are bound so carefully together, as if to withstand the wear and tear of constant reference to them.

CHAPTER TWENTY-FOUR

1. Kennedy to Hull, 15 September 1939, FRUS, 1939, vol. 1, 426–427.
2. Bullitt to Roosevelt, 8 September 1939, in Bullitt, *For the President*, 369; 16 September 1939, ibid., 372–73.
3. Hull to Kennedy, 11 September 1939, FRUS, 1939, vol. 1, 424.
4. Domarus, *Hitler,* vol. 2, 3, 1377ff.
5. J. M. Burns, *Roosevelt: The Lion and the Fox*, 396.
6. Walter Johnson, *William Allen White's America* (New York: H. Holt, 1947), 515.
7. Johnson, *William Allen White's America*, 518.
8. FDRPC 14:130–34. See also Bullitt, *For the President*, 369ff.; Dallek, *Franklin D. Roosevelt*, 207–11; Bailey, *Man in the Street*, 119, 172.
9. NYDN, 31 August, 2 and 5 September 1939.
10. Graeme Howard, "America's Foreign Policy . . . ," in the *German-American Commerce Bulletin*, June 1939, 3ff.
11. Lindbergh, *Wartime Journals*, 217–18, 277, 360; Furnas, *Stormy Weather,* 275; Mosley, *Lindbergh*, 251.
12. Anne Morrow Lindbergh, *War Within*, 65; and Diary of Harold Ickes, 3757 (23 September 1939), LOCMD.
13. Hull himself had come up with name of William Allen White.
14. Walter Johnson, *The Battle Against Isolation* (Chicago: Univ of Chicago Press, 1944), 42–49; and NYT, 27 January 1980 (Eichelberger obituary).
15. Diary of Harold Ickes, 26 August 1939, 3664–65 (LOCMD).
16. W. A. White to Rep. Joseph W. Martin, 23 October 1939, in Walter Johnson, ed., *Selected Letters of William Allen White 1899–1943* (New York: H. Holt & Co., 1947), 399.
17. Roosevelt to White, 14 December 1939, White Papers, MS 59-41/C-320 (General Correspondence), LOCMD.
18. Charles Chatfield, *For Peace and Justice: Pacifism in America 1914–1941* (Knoxville, Tenn.: Univ of Tenn Press 1971), 319–20.
19. Alan Schaffer, *Vito Marcantonio, Radical in Congress* (Syracuse, N.Y.: Syracuse Univ Press, 1966), 85–97.
20. See the DW editorials on 5, 7, 20, and 22 September, 7, 11, 23, and 25 October, and 3 and 10 November 1939.
21. NYDN, 9 October 1939 and 18 August 1940; and Dalton Trumbo, *Johnny Got His Gun*, Secaucus, NJ: L Stuart, [1970].
22. Boehm, "Policy-Making," 360; Hans L. Trefousse, *Germany and American Neutrality 1939–1941*, 38–39; Erich Kordt, *Wahn und Wirklichkeit* (Stuttgart: Union Deutsche Verlagsgesellschaft 1948), 142; and Andreas Hillgruber, *Hitler's Strategie*, 195–96.
23. NG-1422 (12 September 1939), 1; Tippelskirch and Halder, Ms. nos.

B-809, and Keitel A-912, RG 338 (NA). See also Friedländer, *Prelude to Downfall*, 80, 236.

24. ZD 1606 (12 January 1940); RLZ, 28 November 1939; and Ribbentrop interrogation of 31 August 1945 (P.M.), IMT, RG 238 (NA). One may consult a good example of this moderation in the *Kölnische Zeitung*, 19 August 1940. Many German publications depicted the British Empire as the natural enemy of American interests, for example, Giselher Wirsing, *Der Krieg in Karten 1939–1940* (München: Knorr & Hirth, 1940), 38. See also Strausz-Hupé, *Axis America*, 100; and Trefousse, *Germany*, 29–31, 46, 5.

25. Paul Scheffer et al., *USA 1940* (Berlin: Im Deutschenverlag, 1940), 5–40; *Deutsche Allgemeine Zeitung*, 22 June 1941.

26. Hans-Günther Seraphim, ed., *Das Politische Tagebuch Alfred Rosenberg 1934–35, 1939–40* (Munich: 1964), 101 (entry for 5 October 1939).

27. Annex to the Report of the Commander in Chief, Navy, to the Fuehrer on 10 November 1939, in Navy Department, Office of Naval Intelligence, *Fuehrer Conferences on Matters Dealing With the German Navy* (Washington, D.C.: U.S. Navy Dept 1947; reprinted by University Publications of America).

28. Report of the Commander in Chief, Navy, to the Fuehrer on December 30 1939, in *Fuehrer Conferences* (1939, Annex 1).

29. Trefousse, 39; *Fuehrer Conferences on Matters Dealing With German Navy 1939–1941*, for 23 October and 10 November 1939, and 26 January 1940.

30. Johnson, *William Allen White*, 518.

31. Johnson, *William Allen White*, 518.

32. Leigh, *Mobilizing Consent*, 44.

33. Hearden, *Roosevelt Confronts Hitler*, 143.

34. Haight, *American Aid to France*, 205 and passim. Albert Einstein's letter to FDR in 1939 warned the president that a terrible new weapon was becoming possible. This letter stimulated the president's interest, but it did not lead to the inauguration of a government-funded project. That occurred only on 12 June 1940, when Vannevar Bush of M.I.T. got FDR's approval of a four-paragraph memo mandating the establishment of a coordinating group reporting to the president. See McGeorge Bundy, *Danger and Survival: Choices About the Bomb in the First Fifty Years* (New York: Random House, 1988), 33–39.

35. Mintz, *Revisionism*, 85.

CHAPTER TWENTY-FIVE

1. Dallek, *Franklin D. Roosevelt*, 215; Ernst von Weizsäcker, *Memoirs* (London: 1951), 223; Sumner Welles, *The Time for Decision* (New York: London,

Harper & Brothers, 1944), 73ff.; and Roosevelt, *Public Papers, 1940 Volume,* 111.

2. For Welles's reports on his mission, see the Hull Papers/55/Welles Trip to Europe 1940 (LOCMD).

3. FDRPC 15:213; and Bullitt to FDR, 4 April 1940, PSF/43 (FDRL). See also Bullitt, *For the President,* 408; and Dallek, *Franklin D. Roosevelt,* 220.

4. Statement in the House of Commons, in Churchill, *Blood, Sweat, and Tears,* 276; Richard Hough, *The Greatest Crusade: Roosevelt, Churchill, and the Naval Wars* (New York: Morrow, 1986), 165–66.

5. Shirer, *Collapse of the Third Republic,* 680.

6. Statement in Commons, 4 June 1940, in Churchill, *Blood, Sweat, and Tears,* 297.

7. Winston Churchill, *The Second World War,* vol. 2 (*Their Finest Hour*), 400 (statement to the House of Commons, 4 June 1940).

8. Bullitt, *For the President,* 416–29; and Dallek, *Franklin D. Roosevelt,* 222.

9. Roosevelt to Churchill, 14 June 1940, in Francis Loewenheim et al., *Roosevelt and Churchill: Their Secret Wartime Correspondence* (New York: Saturday Review Press 1975), 103; and Shirer, *Collapse of the Third Republic,* 801. The best authorities on Churchill's dealings with Roosevelt during the summer and autumn of 1940 are Llewellyn Woodward, *British Foreign Policy in the Second World War* (London: Her Majesty's Stationery Office, 1970), vol. 1, chaps. 11–12; and Martin Gilbert, *Winston S. Churchill,* volume 6 (*Finest Hour 1939–1941*) (London: Heinemann, 1983), pt. 3.

10. Churchill, *Their Finest Hour,* 398 (cable to Roosevelt, 11 June 1940); and statement in Commons, 18 June 1940, in Churchill, *Blood, Sweat, and Tears,* 314.

11. Stetson Conn and Byron Fairchild, *The Framework of Hemisphere Defense* [*United States Army in World War II*] (Washington, D.C.: Office of the Chief of Military History, Dept. of the Army, 1960), 34.

12. Warren F. Kimball and Bruce Bartlett, "Roosevelt and Prewar Commitments to Churchill: The Tyler Kent Affair," DH, 5, no. 4:291ff. Kent received seven years in jail for, among other offenses, violation of the British Official Secrets Act.

13. Hermann Rauschning, *The Voice of Destruction* (New York: Putnam, 1940), pp. 61–67. Some scholars believe that Rauschning fabricated these "conversations." What is relevant here, however, is not the accuracy of Rauschning's recollections, but their impact upon the reading public in 1940. For a balanced view of the Rauschning controversy, see Martin Broszat, "Enthüllung? Die Rauschning-Kontroverse," in Hermann Graml and Klaus-Dietmar Henke, *Nach Hitler. Der schwierige Umgang mit unserer Geschichte: Beiträge von Martin Broszat* (München: Oldenbourg, 1986), pp. 249–51.

14. A. M. Sperber, *Murrow: His Life and Times* (New York: Freundlich Books, 1986), 169.
15. Shirer, *Collapse of the Third Republic*, 906–7.
16. W. A. White to Robert Sherwood, 26 July 1940, in Johnson, *Selected Letters*, 409.
17. Johnson, *William Allen White*, 525.
18. Michael W. Miles, *The Odyssey of the American Right* (New York: Oxford Univ Press, 1980), 62–63.
19. Burns, *The Lion and the Fox*, 419; Dallek, *Franklin D. Roosevelt*, 223; Shirer, *Collapse of the Third Republic*, 857. On the patrols, see Captain S. W. Roskill, *The War at Sea 1939–1945*, vol. 1 (*The Defensive*) (London: Her Majesty's Stationery Office, 1954), 343.
20. John Mason Brown, *The Ordeal of a Playwright: Robert E. Sherwood and the Challenge of War* (New York: Harper & Row, 1970).
21. Johnson, *William Allen White*, 542.

CHAPTER TWENTY-SIX

1. See David G. Haglund, *Latin America and the Transformation of U.S. Strategic Thought, 1836–1940* (Albuquerque: U. of N. Mexico Press, 1984), chs. 3–5.
2. Howell M. Henry, "The Nazi Threat to the Western Hemisphere," *The South Atlantic Quarterly* 39, no. 4 (October 1940); Dallek, *Franklin D. Roosevelt*, 233–35; and Heinz Pohle, *Der Rundfunk als Instrument der Politik* (Hamburg: Verlag Hans Bredow Institut, 1955), 451–53; Ribbentrop interrogation of 31 August 1945, IMT, RG 238 (NA).
3. Embassy to–AA, 3, 7, and 11 June, Serial 19/12192-193, Serial 19/12217-218; Serial 19/12254; Serial 57/38822-823 (Bonn); Thomsen to AA, 23 September and 22 October 1940, DGFP, D, vol. 11, 157ff., and 362ff.; Embassy to AA, 27 October 1940, Weizsäcker to German consulate Manila, n.d., NG-4433. See also Strausz-Hupé, *Axis America*, 220. See Vanderbilt to White, 23 July 1940, and Stevenson to White, 15 August 1940, in the White Papers (Committee), LOCMD. See Ickes Diary, 4405 (26 May 1940), and 4590 (19 July 1940), LOCMD.
4. Art. II, sect. 1, last par. of the Constitution of the United States.
5. Elting E. Morison, *Turmoil and Tradition: A Study of the Life and Times of Henry L. Stimson* (Boston: Houghton Mifflin, 1960), 475–96.
6. Johnson, *The Battle*, 69; Sherwood, *Roosevelt and Hopkins*, 167; and Walter Isaacson and Evan Thomas, *The Wise Men: Six Friends and the World They Made* (New York: Simon & Schuster, 1986), 182–86.
7. Johnson, *William Allen White*, 529.
8. William L. Langer and S. Everett Gleason, *The Challenge to Isolation: The*

World Crisis of 1937–1940 and American Foreign Policy (New York: Harper Torchbook, 1964), vol. 2, 695–99.

9. Best, *Herbert Hoover*, vol. 1, 169.

10. Schulzinger, *Wise Men*, 71.

11. Miles, *Odyssey*, 61.

12. Roosevelt, *Public Papers and Addresses 1940 Volume* (New York: Macmillan Co., 1941), 293–303.

13. See Thomsen's comments of 27 March 1940, in NG-1419 (NA RG238); Louis De Jong, *The German Fifth Column in the Second World War* (Chicago: Univ of Chicago Press 1956), 214–15. Reports on the problem of subversion may be consulted in Serial 19 of the AA files, especially frs. 12109ff. Thomsen expressed his views with particular vehemence in *Berichte* nos. 1035 and 1038, dated 29 May and 30 May.

14. On "Bergmann," the *Abwehr*, and sabotage, see NG-1642, NG-1632 (NA, RG 238). See also Karl H. Abshagen, *Canaris* (London: Hutchinson, 1956), 186–87.

15. Bürckner interrogation, RG 165 (NA).

16. *Abwehr* reported on 28 December 1940 that the United Aircraft Company was hiring four thousand more workers in Hartford and Stratford, Connecticut. The information reached Bremen even before Roosevelt had revealed his lend-lease plan to the American people.

17. Thomsen to AA, 19 August 1940, Serial 57, fr. 38852 (Bonn); and Thomsen to von Weizsäcker, 30 September 1940, NAM T-120/20/22923.

18. See, for example, Hoover to Watson, 6 December 1939, wherein the director speaks of German propaganda aimed at undermining the British blockade.

19. NYT, 28 August 1940. The article was written by Russell B. Porter.

20. OF 10, Department of Justice, boxes 6 and 14 (FDRL) contains a good deal of material provided to the White House by the eager Hoover. For the unsubstantiated allegations against Nye, see dossier 904; and for allegations regarding the Nazi threat to Latin America, see dossier 877.

21. Hoover to Watson, 23 February 1940, OF 10b, box 11 (FDRL).

22. Staff Evidence Analysis, 3941-PS, of Colin Ross's 1940 memorandum.

23. See, for example, FDRPC 15:483–99, and 16:367.

24. *Western Jewish Advocate* (Denver), March 1940; *The Bulletin* (Providence, R.I.), 23 April 1940; *The Times-Star* (Bridgeport, Conn.), 4 May 1940; NYHT, 19 May and 6 July 1940; NYT, 23 May 1940; and NYWT, 7 June 1940; and Rupert Hughes, "When Pacifists Are Traitors," *Liberty*, 12 October 1940. See also William L. Shirer, *Berlin Diary* (New York: A. A. Knopf, 1941); 591ff. and "Spawn of the Trojan Horse," *The Oregonian*, 18 May 1940.

25. On *The March of Time* and *The Ramparts We Watch*, see Raymond Fielding,

The March of Time 1935–1951 (New York: Oxford Univ Press, 1978), chaps. 8 and 11.

26. Archer Winston in the NYP, 20 September 1940.

27. Otis Ferguson, "At Your Own Risk," *The New Republic,* 5 August 1940, 189.

28. William Boehnel in NYWT, 20 September 1940.

29. Charles A. Beard, "Time and Archibald MacLeish," Museum of Modern Art Film Division (microfilm file on *Ramparts,* source not legible).

30. NYP, 22 and 29 August 1940; *Variety,* 4 September 1940; and NYT, 19 and 20 September and 2 October 1940.

CHAPTER TWENTY-SEVEN

1. Sperber, *Murrow,* 162–69.

2. On Murrow, see the valuable work by Alexander Kendrick, *Prime Time: The Life of Edward R. Murrow* (Boston: Little, Brown, 1969).

3. Sperber, *Murrow,* 204.

4. *Motion Picture Herald,* 20 July 1940.

5. Roger Manvell, *Films and the Second World War,* 35–36; and T. Perlmutter, *War Movies* (London: Hamlyn, 1974), 20.

6. Roskill, *The War at Sea,* vol. 1, 348. See also Hull, *Memoirs,* vol. 1, 831–43. Churchill was careful not to link the granting of bases to the gift of the destroyers.

7. Waldo Heinrichs, *Threshold of War: Franklin D. Roosevelt and American Entry into World War II* (New York: Oxford Univ Press, 1988), 10. This is a particularly perceptive work.

8. Langer and Gleason, *Challenge to Isolation,* 670.

9. See Leigh, *Mobilizing Consent,* 48.

10. German intelligence learned in late May about Churchill's request for the destroyers and indications of FDR's willingness to go ahead with the proposal. FNC, 21 October 1940, 43ff. See also Norman Rich, *Hitler's War Aims,* 2 vols. (New York: Norton 1974), vol. 2, 416–17.

11. Taylor, *Breaking Wave,* 31; FNC, 6 September 1940, 19; and Bötticher to AA, 14 September 1940, DGFP, D, vol. 11, 78. See also Hillgruber, *Hitler's Strategie,* 200–201.

12. Bötticher telegrams of 28 September and 2 and 9 October 1940, DGFP, D, vol. 11, 209–11, 234–36, 273–75; Bötticher to OKH and Air Ministry, 4 and 11 October 1940, ML-307 (NA).

13. FNC, 11 July 1940; See also Hillgruber, *Hitler's Strategie,* 199; and Ribbentrop, *Zwischen,* 241.

14. Leila A. Sussmann, *Dear FDR: A Study of Political Letter-Writing* (Totowa, N.J.: Bedminster Press, 1963), 111–12.

15. *New York Journal American,* 3 and 9 October, 1 November, and 11 Decem-

ber 1940. See also R. Carlisle, "The Foreign Policy Views of an Isolationist Press Lord," JCH, 9, no. 3.

16. For an interesting description of the campaign, written by a seasoned political reporter, see Warren Moscow, *Roosevelt and Willkie* (Englewood Cliffs, N.J.: Prentice-Hall 1968). For a good account of Willkie's campaign, see Steve Neal, *Dark Horse: A Biography of Wendell Willkie* (Garden City, N.Y.: Doubleday, 1984), chap. 12. On the conscription issue, see J. Garry Clifford and Samuel R. Spencer, Jr., *The First Peacetime Draft* (Lawrence, Kansas: U. Press of Kansas, 1986).

17. Stimson Diaries, 42 and 47 (18 December 1940), 3, and (19 December 1940), 4, LOCMD.

18. Henry L. Stimson and McGeorge Bundy, *On Active Service in Peace and War* (New York: Harper, 1947), 336; and Harold Nicolson, *The War Years 1939–1945* (vol. 2 of *Diaries and Letters*, ed. Nigel Nicolson) (New York: Atheneum 1967), 125–26 (entry for 6 November 1940). See also Heinrichs, *Threshold*, 18.

19. Leigh, *Mobilizing Consent*, 33. The State Department published its *Peace and War: United States Foreign Policy, 1931–1941* in 1943.

20. Conn and Fairchild, *Framework*, 94 (Roosevelt to F.B. Sayre, 31 December 1940).

21. Hearden, *Roosevelt Confronts Hitler,* 179.

22. Churchill, *Their Finest Hour,* 552–69. See also Blum, *Morgenthau*, vol. 2, 214–17.

23. Churchill, *Their Finest Hour,* 573.

24. Blum, *Morgenthau*, vol. 2, 214–17.

25. Stimson Diaries, 170 (16 September 1940), 2 (LOCMD). See also John W. Jeffries, *Testing the Roosevelt Coalition: Connecticut Society and Politics in the Era of World War II* (Knoxville, Tenn.: Univ of Tennessee Press, 1979), 91–94; and Alan Clive, *State of War: Michigan in World War II* (Ann Arbor, Mich.: Univ of Michigan Press 1979), 10, 20–25.

26. Roskill, *The War at Sea*, vol. 1, 354. See also Stimson and Bundy, *On Active Service*, 366 (based on Stimson's diary notation of 16 December 1940).

27. Domarus, *Hitler,* vol. 2, 4, 1661; and FNC, 27 December 1940, 68–70.

28. Henry R. Luce, *The American Century* (New York: Farrar & Rinehart, 1941). The book contains responses by Dorothy Thompson, John Chamberlain, Quincy Howe, Robert G. Spivack, and Robert E. Sherwood.

29. David Halberstam, *The Powers That Be* (New York: Knopf, 1979), 45–63; and Hoover to Watson, 7 January 1941, and Watson to Roosevelt, 18 January 1941, OF 106/561-599 folder (FDRL).

30. One of the reasons for Stimson's appointment of John J. McCloy as special assistant was his knowledge about "subversive German agents." See Stimson Diaries, 171 (16 September 1940), 3, (LOCMD).

31. Johnson, *William Allen White*, 543–52.
32. W. A. White to Hugo T. Wedell, 7 February 1941, in Johnson, *Selected Letters*, 427–28; and W. A. White to Clark Eichelberger, 29 July 1941, in Johnson, *Selected Letters*, 430.
33. Dean Acheson, *Present at the Creation: My Years in the State Department* (New York: Norton, 1969), 3–22.
34. Heinrichs, *Threshold*, 22.

CHAPTER TWENTY-EIGHT

1. W. A. White to J. Edgar Hoover, 28 November 1940, in White, *Letters*, 413–14. On Hoover's role in this area, see Richard G. Powers, *Secrecy and Power: The Life of J. Edgar Hoover* (New York: Free Press, 1986), 228–39.
2. Robert Giroux, "The Poet in the Asylum," *The Atlantic Monthly* (August 1988): 44.
3. RG 131/143 (NA); *Junges Volk* (September 1940); and FA, 11 November 1940 (GVDAKV/128). See also in Walter Laqueur and George L. Mosse, *International Fascism*, 1920–1945, 162–67.
4. GVDAKV/128 (clippings of 15 and 19 August and 31 October 1940); "Vortrag," 11 March 1940, RG 131/149 (NA); *Heimatblatt* (Chicago), 18 September 1941; and F. F. Schrader, *Enemy Within*, in RG 131/121.
5. NYT, 26 September 1939; and Edmund Taylor, *The Strategy of Terror* (Boston: Houghton Mifflin Co. 1940), 269; and Roper for *Fortune* (.0018.008 (6/40). Luce helped Roosevelt by popularizing Taylor's theory of fifth column subversion.
6. RG 131/198 (NA); Draeger interrogation of 21 August 1947, p. 5, no. 1778, RG 238 (NA); RG 131/22/20 (NA); *B'nai B'rith Messenger* (Los Angeles), 23 August 1940; Heinz Soffner in NYP, 10 May 1941; and RG 131/138 (NA).
7. Roper for *Fortune* (.0018.008); FDRPC 15:483–99, 16:367; Dallek, *Franklin D. Roosevelt*, 225; Charles J. Tull, *Father Coughlin and the New Deal* (Syracuse: Syracuse U. Press, 1965), 192–201, 226; *Star* (St. Louis), 30 January 1939; *Tablet*, 29 July 1939; SJ, 24 April 1939; and Ickes, *Lowering Clouds*, 20–28. See also Sayers and Kahn, *Sabotage*, 155; and Bayor, *Neighbors in Conflict*, 28 and passim.
8. Rollins, *I Find Treason*, 124–29; Strong, *Organized Anti-Semitism*, 67, gives the arrest date as 13 January, whereas elsewhere it appears as 14 January. See also Tull, *Father Coughlin*, 223.
9. Given Coughlin's favorable press in Germany, it was easy for the administration to imply that Nazi admiration was proof of German funding. See GVDAKV/123VB, 6 December 1938; RLZ, 28 November 1938; Rogge, *Official German Report*, 306; Ickes, *Lowering Clouds*, 382. See also Strong, *Organized Anti-Semitism*, 61.

10. See the file on Winchell, 5547, with a summary of his letter filed on 15 September 1939 (FDRL), and cross-filed "Christian Mobilizers' Meeting."

11. Ribbentrop to *Geschäftsträger*, 19 July 1941, NG-4542 (NA). See also the Dieckhoff interrogation, 11, NAM T-679/1.

12. NYP, 4 and 8 June 1940; PM, 24 June 1940; NYT, 7 July 1940; *Wisconsin Jewish Chronicle*, 2 August 1940; *New Leader*, 21 September 1940; NYT, 21 September 1940; and NYHT, 26 September 1940. See also Furnas, *Stormy Weather*, 240; Carlson, *Under Cover*, 251; Lavine, *Fifth Column*, 93; Rollins, *I Find Treason*, 130–35; Bayor, *Neighbors in Conflict*, 101, 113; Ickes, *Lowering Clouds* 20; and Myers, *Bigotry*, 470–71.

13. Stember, *Jews*, 134.

CHAPTER TWENTY-NINE

1. See the interrogation of Osami Nagano, International Military Tribunal for the Far East, cited by Hans-Adolf Jacobsen and Arthur L. Smith, Jr., *World War II: Policy and Strategy, Selected Documents With Commentary* (Santa Barbara, Calif.: Clio Books, 1979), 165–66.

2. For an account of reaction to the Stimson Doctrine among American elites and the media, see Justus D. Doenecke, *When the Wicked Rise: American Opinion-Makers and the Manchurian Crisis of 1931–1933* (Lewisburg, Pa.: Bucknell Univ Press, 1983). See also Norman A. Graebner, "Japan: Unanswered Challenge," in Margaret F. Morris and Sandra L. Myres, eds., *Essays on American Foreign Policy* (Austin, Tex.: Published for the Univ of Texas at Arlington by the Univ of Texas Press, 1974), 117–30; and Shoichi Saeki, "Images of the United States as a Hypothetical Enemy," in Akira Iriye, ed., *Mutual Images: Essays in American-Japanese Relations* (Cambridge, Mass.: Harvard Univ Press, 1975).

3. William Roger Louis, *British Strategy in the Far East 1919–1939* (Oxford: Clarendon Press, 1971), 244–67; Christopher Thorne, *Allies of a Kind* (New York: Oxford Univ Press, 1978), 30–34, 61, 78, 107–8; Graebner, "Japan," 136; Berle, *Navigating the Rapids*, 230 (June 27, 1939), and 233 (August 4, 1939).

4. Kimitada Miwa, "Japanese Images of War With the United States," in Iriye, *Mutual Images*, 115.

5. Leigh, *Mobilizing Consent*, 45. The poll was taken in February 1940. See also John W. Dower, *War Without Mercy: Race and Power in the Pacific War* (New York: Pantheon Books, 1986), 156–60.

6. Prange, *At Dawn We Slept*, 81.

7. Ian Nish, *Japanese Foreign Policy 1869–1942: Kasumigaseki to Miryakezaka* (London & Boston: Routledge & K. Paul, 1977), 235–36.

8. Graebner, "Japan," 138–39.

9. Hosoya Chihiro, "The Tripartite Pact 1939–1940," in James W. Morley, ed., *Deterrent Diplomacy: Japan, Germany, and the USSR 1935–1940* (New York: Columbia Univ Press, 1976), 204–15.

10. Chihiro, "Tripartite Pact," 227–57, plus Appendix 5.

11. E. Roosevelt, *As He Saw It*, 12.

12. Hull, memorandum of conversation with the British and Australian ambassadors, 15 February 1941, FRUS, 1941, vol. 4 (*The Far East*), 39–41.

13. Gordon W. Prange, *At Dawn We Slept: The Untold Story of Pearl Harbor* (New York: McGraw-Hill, 1981), 31.

14. Ibid., 45.

15. Ibid., 93–95.

16. Heinrichs, *Threshold*, 35.

17. Grew to Hull, 5 March 1941, FRUS, vol. 4, 58–60. See also Nish, *Japanese Foreign Policy*, 238.

18. Heinrichs, *Threshold*, 32.

19. See Miwa, "Japanese Images," in Iriye, *Mutual Images*, 122.

20. See James M. Drought to Hull, 9 April 1941, and Memorandum Prepared for the Secretary of State, 10 April 1941, FRUS, vol. 4, 132–39.

CHAPTER THIRTY

1. Foreign Affairs Committee of the House of Representatives, 77th Cong., 1st sess., hearings on H.R. 1776, 23 January 1941.

2. Lindbergh, *Wartime Journals*, 217–18, 277, 360; Furnas, *Stormy Weather,* 275; and Mosley, *Lindbergh*, 251.

3. Anne Morrow Lindbergh, *War Within and Without: Diaries and Letters of Anne Morrow Lindbergh 1939–1944* (New York: Harcourt Brace Jovanovich, 1980), 65.

4. A. M. Lindbergh, *War Within*, 109 (entry of 16 June 1940).

5. Bötticher to AA, 20 July 1940, DGFP, D, vol. 10, 254–56; 6 August 1940, ibid., 413–15; and Thomsen to AA, 1 September 1940, NAM T-120/22786-787.

6. Thomsen to AA, 18 September 1940, ibid., frs. 22869-870; Bötticher to AA, 28 September 1940, DGFP, D, vol. 11, 209–11; 16 October 1940, ibid., 307–9; and to OKH, 3 January 1941, NAM T-120/81/62308-309.

7. Justus D. Doenecke, "The Isolationism of General Robert E. Wood," in John N. Schacht, ed., *Three Faces of Midwestern Isolationism* (Iowa City, Iowa: Center for the study of the recent history of the United States, 1981), 11–17.

8. Lisagor and Lipsius, *A Law Unto Itself,* 137.

9. Ronald Radosh, *Prophets on the Right: Profiles of Conservative Critics of American Globalism* (New York: Simon & Schuster, 1975), 212–15; on

disillusionment at the *New Republic*, see David W. Noble, "The New Republic and the Idea of Progress, 1914–1920," MVHR, vol. 38, no. 3.

10. *Vital Speeches* (15 April 1938). See also Cole, *America First*, 84; Mark L. Chadwin, *The Hawks of World War II* (Chapel Hill, N.C.: UNC Press 1968), 9; and Justus D. Doenecke, "Non-interventionism of the Left," JCH 12, no. 2:221ff; and Wittner, *Rebels Against War*, 28.

11. Furnas, *Stormy Weather*, 276–77; Michael Sayers and Albert E. Kahn, *Sabotage! The Secret War Against America* (New York: Harper & Brothers 1942), 199–201; Wayne S. Cole, *Senator Gerald P. Nye and American Foreign Relations*, 178, and *America First: The Battle Against Intervention 1940–1941;* Radosh, *Prophets*, 217; and Miles, *Odyssey*, 66.

12. Thomas C. Kennedy, *Charles A. Beard and American Foreign Policy* (Gainesville, Fla.: Univ Press of Fla., 1975), 88.

13. Lindbergh came to his anti-interventionist position by way of conservative elitism, Beard by way of progressive reform. America First was held together mainly by its hatred for Roosevelt's foreign policy. It is hard to see how such disparate persons and forces could have welded the committee into a serious third party, as some hoped to do.

14. Richard Hofstadter, *The Progressive Historians* (New York: Knopf, 1968), 286–87, and 319–20; Warner I. Cohen, *The American Revisionists: The Lessons of Intervention in World War I* (Chicago: U. of Chicago Press, 1967), 212–29; OF/2039 (Beard) (FDRL); Dodd, *Diary*, xiv–xv; Guinsburg, *The Pursuit of Isolationism*, 245; and J. C. Donovan, "Congressional Isolationists and the Roosevelt Foreign Policy," in L.E. Gelfand, *Essays on the History of American Foreign Relations* (New York: Holt, Rinehart, and Winston, 1972), 350.

15. Charles C. Tansill, "Impressions of Germany," RG 131/143 (NAS). The manuscript is not dated.

16. No such referendum would be necessary if a foreign power invaded the United States.

17. Editorial in the *Emporia Weekly Gazette*, 17 October 1940.

18. Johnson, *William Allen White*, 535.

19. See the confidential report on America First, December 1940, White Papers ("Committee"), LOCMD.

20. *Scribner's Commentator* 11, no. 2 (December 1940); and Lindbergh, *Wartime Journals*, 351, 363, 389, 416, 452.

21. A. M. Lindbergh, *War Within*, 79 (entry of 16 April 1940).

22. Ibid., 81.

23. *Scribner's Commentator* (December 1940); and Furnas, *Stormy Weather*, 279.

24. A. M. Lindbergh, *War Within*, 4–5 (entry of 29 April 1939).

25. PPF/1080 (FDRL).

26. A. M. Lindbergh, *War Within*, 96, 150–51 (entries of 31 May and 12

November 1940). Lindbergh himself rejected pacifism, clearly and consistently.

27. 3760-PS, 28–29 (NA RG238); Thomsen, Vermerk in NAM T-120/330/244052; NG-4659. See also Lindbergh, *Wartime Journals*, 445; Sayers and Kahn, *Sabotage*, 235–37; and Rogge, *Official German Report*, 302–3.

28. Thomsen to AA, 3 July 1940, DGFP, D, vol. 10, 101–2; 18 July 1940, ibid., 243; and 19 July 1940, ibid., 250–51; and Sayers and Kahn, *Sabotage!*, 211–12.

29. At a press conference, a jovial Roosevelt had this to say when questioned about McCormick's testimony: "I want to ask you one question back. Did he speak as an expert? (Laughter)."

30. Stimson Diaries, 59 (3 August 1940), 1, (LOCMD).

31. A. M. Lindbergh, *War Within*, 152–53 (entry of 12 November 1940).

32. See Beschloss, *Kennedy and Roosevelt*, 234ff.; and Hough, *Greatest Crusade*, 167.

33. Kennedy made a gracious statement, indicating that whatever form aid-to-Britain legislation might take, he would support it and the president once the Congress had its say. On the context of his testimony, see William L. Langer and S. Everett Gleason, *The Undeclared War 1940–1941* (Gloucester, Mass.: Peter Smith, 1968), 268.

34. Hoover to Watson, 28 February 1941, OF 10b, box 13, item 666 (FDRL).

35. Radosh, *Prophets*, "Robert A. Taft: A Noninterventionist Faces War"; and Miles, *Odyssey*, 65.

36. On the lend-lease bill and its opponents, see Langer and Gleason, *Undeclared War,* 258ff.

37. NAM 179A, RG 242 (NA); ML 306/5; and ML 299/7/pt. 2.

38. Robert E. Herzstein, *When Nazi Dreams Come True* (London: Sphere 1982).

39. Charles Tansill, "Impressions of Germany," n.d., RG 131/143 (NA).

40. Bertling to F. Wiedemann, 23 June 1938, GCD/313 (LOCMD).

41. Stimson Diary, 47 (19 December 1940), 4, and 140 (14 November 1940), 3 (LOCMD), where Stimson had described Lindbergh as believing in the likelihood of a German victory over Britain.

42. See OF 92/box 1/Lindbergh (FDRL).

43. "Wo Steht der Amerika-Deutsche und wo soll er Stehen?," RG 131/101.

CONCLUSION

1. Hoover to Watson, 4 February 1941, OF 10b/box 12/folder 600-635 (FDRL).

2. Robert Rhodes James, "The Politician," in Churchill Revised: *A Critical Assessment* (New York: Dial Press, 1969), 118.

3. Thomas Mann to Hermann Hesse, 8 February 1947, in Anni Carlsson and

Volker Michels, eds., *The Hesse/Mann Letters: The Correspondence of Hermann Hesse and Thomas Mann 1910–1955* (London: P. Owen, 1976), 107.

4. Kenneth Adelman, "Seeing Too Much" (an interview with Jan Karski), *The Washingtonian*, July 1988, 61ff.

5. Lindbergh, *Wartime Journals*, p. 437 (7 January 1941).

SOURCES

The following collections have been particularly useful. Specific references to, and citations of, documents and printed sources, including memoirs, diaries, and secondary works, occur in the endnotes.

I. Archival collections

Archiv der ehemaligen Reichsstudentenführung und des NSD-Studentenbundes, Bayrische Julius-Maximilians-Universität (Würzburg)

Siegfried Arndt (I*90 phi 600)

Bericht des Theo Clausen (I*ol g 42)

Deutscher Akademischer Austauschdienst (I*30 g 176)

Archives du centre de documentation juive contemporaine, CXLVI

Auswärtiges Amt (Bonn)

Politische Abteilung IX (USA), Po 2 (Steuben Society)

Bundesarchiv (Koblenz)

Allgemeine Sammlung (Auslanddeutschtum materials)

Auslandsorganisation der NSDAP (NS 9)

Vereinigung Carl Schurz e.V.

Nachrichten- und Pressedienste (Zsg. 116), as well as Presseausschnitte der Reichspropagandaleitung der NSDAP

Goerdeler Nachlass, Nr. 16 (Karl Goerdeler NL 113)

Karl Haushofer (NL 122)

NS 20/127, nos. 1–8 (Bund-related material)

NS 42/23 (shortwave broadcasts)

Erich Kraske (NL 139)

Kleine Erwerbungen der NSDAP (NS 20)

Material für Propagandazwecke, including Ausstellung "Amerikadeutschtum im Kampf," 1939 (NS 41)

Reichspressechef der NSDAP (NS 42, Verbreitung von Informations material in USA)

Nachlasssplitter, Kleine Erwerbungen: Karl Megerle (498), Karl Scharping (494)
Sachthematische Bildersammlung (on NS-Gruppen in USA)
Sammlung Brammer Zsg. 101
Sammlung Nadler (Zsg. 115), notes on the weekly Wirtschaftskonferenz, including material from the Reichspresseamt Berlin
Sammlung Oberheitmann (Reicshpresseamt Hesse-Nassau)
Sammlung Sanger Zsg. 102
Sammlung Schumacher, especially Ordner 369, 420, and 481
Hans Steinacher (NL 184)

Connecticut State Library (Hartford, Connecticut) Papers of Thomas J. Dodd
The Hoover Institution on War, Revolution, and Peace (Stanford University)
  The Hoover Library Collection on Germany Deutsche Informationsstelle
  Gesamtverband Deutscher Anti-kommunistischer Vereinigungen *Der Angriff; Der Stürmer; Deutsche Allgemeine Zeitung*; and *Jüdische Rundschau*
  The Hoover Institution Archives
  Papers and private correspondence of Wilfried Bade
  "Germany Speaks," unpublished articles, 1934
  Carl Friedrich Goerdeler, "Reiseberichte"
  Reichskanzlei, Verzeichnis der Neuerwerbungen der Bücherei
  Terramare Office, Berlin

Library of Congress, Manuscript Division
  Papers of William E. Borah
  Papers of Norman H. Davis
  Papers of Cordell Hull (microfilm)
  Papers of Harold Ickes (microfilm)
  Papers of George Van Horn Moseley
  Papers of Henry L. Stimson (microfilm)
  Papers of William Allen White
  Papers of Woodrow Wilson (microfilm)

National Archives
  A. Records of the Office of Alien Property (RG 131), including still pictures, sound recordings, and other documents. Of particular importance are the Records Pertaining to the German-American Bund and Related Organizations, numbers 315-320, which include General Records, Legal Records, and Propaganda Materials. In addition, of some significance are the Records Relating to Deutsches Haus and Related Organizations, particularly numbers 332A through 332C
  B. Collection of Foreign Records Seized, 1941– (RG 242), including

T-81, Records of the National Socialist German Workers Party, and T-120, Records of the German Foreign Ministry

C. DeWitt C. Poole Mission Interrogation Reports (M-679), especially the interrogations of Ernst Wilhelm Bohle, Hans Borchers, Hans Heinrich Dieckhoff, Karl Haushofer, Walter Funk, and Joachim von Ribbentrop

D. Schuster Mission Interrogation Reports (RG 165), especially the interrogations of Ernst Wilhelm Bohle, Leopole Bürckner, Rolf Hoffmann, Wilhelm Keitel, and Joachim von Ribbentrop

E. Microfilm (ML) reproduced by Office of Naval Intelligence, Bremen, Germany, from the Records of the Abwehr Nebenstelle Bremen, between 5 September 1945 and 17 April 1946. Rolls consulted concern the period 1 September 1939 to 1 April 1941

F. The Franklin D. Roosevelt Library (Hyde Park, New York).

Adolf A. Berle, Papers 1938–1944

    Frank Freidel, Transcripts of Interviews

    Franklin D. Roosevelt, Papers as Assistant Secretary of the Navy, 1913–1920

    Papers as President, Alphabetical File

    Papers as President, Official File

    Papers as President, President's Personal File (PPF)

    Papers as President, President's Secretary's File (PSF)

    Papers of Samuel I. Rosenman

    Samuel I. Rosenman, Interview Transcript

Österreichisches Staatsarchiv, Abt. Haus-, Hof-, und Staatsarchiv (Vienna, Austria)

    Neues Politisches Archiv, Gesandtschaftsarchiv Washington, Karton 102, 103, 281, and 471

Staatsarchiv der Freien und Hansestadt Hamburg

Staatliche Pressestelle I, II–IV, and relevant Akten

The Staatsarchiv Nürnberg (Federal Republic of Germany)

    B-128 (Hans Borchers)

    D-66 (Friedhelm Dräger)

    M-119 (Gustav Müller)

Seeley G. Mudd Manuscript Library (Princeton University)

    Typescripts of shortwave radio broadcasts, 1939, maintained by the Princeton Listening Center

II. U.S. Government Publications

U.S. House of Representatives

    Special Committee on Un-American Activities. *Hearings, Investigation of*

Nazi Progaganda Activities and Investigation of Certain Other Propaganda Activities. (73d Cong., 2d sess., 1934); *Hearings, Investigations of Un-American Propaganda Activities in the United States* (76th Cong., 3d sess., 1940); and *Preliminary Digest and Report on the Un-American Activities of Various Nazi Organizations and Individuals in the U.S., Including Diplomatic Consular Agents of the German Government* (76th Cong., 3d sess., 1940)

U.S. Senate, Subcommittee of the Committee on Judiciary.
Hearings on the National German-American Alliance (65th Cong., 2d sess., 1918)

III. Major journals, magazines, newspapers, and miscellaneous or irregularly published material. Other such publications are cited in the endnotes.

The American Magazine
Der Amerikadeutsche
Der Angriff
Atlanta Constitution
Atlantic Monthly 166–168
Der Auslanddeutsche: Halbmonatschrift für Auslanddeutschtum und Auslandkunde (from 1 March 1938 *Deutschtum im Ausland*)
Auslanddeutsche Volksforschung
Aussendeutscher Wochensspiegel
Auswärtige Politik
Die Bewegung
The Blackshirt
B'nai B'rith Messenger
The Bulletin (Providence, R.I.)
Catholic Herald (U.K.)
Chicago Tribune
Christian Science Monitor
The Cincinnati Post
Collier's Magazine 104–108
United States, Department of Commerce, "Circulars" and "Special Circulars" concerning "German Trade with the United States," 1936–1938
The Congress Bulletin
The Cross and the Flag
Daily Express
Daily Telegraph (London)
Daily Worker (New York)

Deutsche Allgemeine Zeitung
Deutsche Arbeit
Deutsche Diplomatisch-Politische Korrespondenz
Deutsche Zeitung
Deutscher Weckruf und Beobachter
Deutsches Volksecho
Deutsches Wollen: Zeitschrift der Auslandsorganisation
The Emporia Weekly Gazette
The Evening Bulletin (Philadelphia)
Foreign Affairs
Fortune
Frankfurter Tageszeitung
Frankfurter Zeitung
Fränkische Tageszeitung
The Free American
Freie Press (Cincinnati)
German-American Commerce Bulletin
The Guardian (Manchester)
Hamburger Fremdenblatt
Hamburger Monatshefte für Auswärtige Politik
Hanseatische Rechts- und Gerichtszeitschrift (Abhandlungen)
Harper's Magazine, 179–180
Heimatblatt (Chicago)
Hessische Landeszeitung
Jewish Chronicle (London)
Jewish Examiner
Jewish Post (Paterson, N.J.)
Junge Garde
Junges Volk
Kansas City Star
Kleine Zeitung
Kölnische Zeitung
Liberation
Liberty
Life
Literary Digest
Look
The Milwaukee Sentinal
Mitteilungen über die Judenfrage
Mitteilungsblatt der Auslandsorganisation der NSDAP
Motion Picture Herald

Nachrichten-Dienst (*Amerikadeutsches Volksbund*)
The Nation
Nationalsozialistische Korrespondenz
The New Leader
The New Republic
The News (Chicago)
The News Review (London)
New York Daily News
The New Yorker
New Yorker Staats-Zeitung
New York Herald Tribune
New York Mirror
New York Post
New York Times
New York World-Telegram
Partiepresse-Sonderdienst (Berlin)
Pforzheimer Anzeiger
Philadelphia Record
PM
Reader's Digest 33–39
Studenten-Pressedienst
(*Reichsstudentenführer*)
The Revealer
Rheinische Landeszeitung
Rheinisch-Westfälische Zeitung
St. Joseph News Press
Scribner's Commentator
Siebenbürgisch-Amerikanisches Volksblatt
6 Uhr Abendblatt
Social Justice
Der Stürmer
Stuttgarter NS-Kurier
Sunday Referee
The Tablet (Brooklyn, N.Y.)
Time
The Times (London)
Times-Herald (Washington)
The Times-Star (Bridgeport)
The Transcript (Seattle)
Variety
Völkischer Beobachter (Munich edition)

Volksparole
Washington Post
Washington Times-Herald
Westdeutscher Beobachter
Western Jewish Advocate
Wille und Macht
Wisconsin Jewish Chronicle
Zeitschriften-Dienst

INDEX

A

483

ABOUT THE AUTHOR

Robert Edwin Herzstein is the author of several highly regarded books on Nazi Germany, including *Waldheim: The Missing Years, The War That Hitler Won* (both reprinted by Paragon House), and *The Nazis* (Time-Life World War II Series). His research on President Kurt Waldheim's hidden past won him worldwide fame. Dr. Herzstein has been a consultant for the U.S. Department of Justice, the World Jewish Congress, the *New York Times*, and ABC News. His most important book to date, *Roosevelt and Hitler: Prelude to War* comes to grips with controversial issues that molded the world in which we live: the Hitler challenge, anti-Semitism in the United States, and Roosevelt's triumph by means fair and foul.

Dr. Herzstein is a professor of history at the University of South Carolina.